T0311256

THE URBAN WHALE

The Urban Whale

*North Atlantic Right Whales
at the Crossroads*

EDITED BY

Scott D. Kraus
and Rosalind M. Rolland

HARVARD UNIVERSITY PRESS

*Cambridge, Massachusetts
London, England*

Printed in the United States of America

First Harvard University Press paperback edition, 2009

Library of Congress Cataloging-in-Publication Data

The urban whale : North Atlantic right whales at the crossroads / edited by
Scott D. Kraus and Rosalind M. Rolland
    p. cm.
  Includes bibliographic references (p.) and index.
  ISBN 978-0-674-02327-7 (cloth: alk. paper)
  ISBN 978-0-674-03475-4 (pbk.)
  1. Right whales—North Atlantic Ocean.   I. Kraus, Scott D.
II. Rolland, Rosalind
QL737.C423U73   2006
599.5′273—dc22   2006043681

To those who laid the foundation of North Atlantic right whale research: David E. Gaskin, John H. Prescott, William E. Schevill, William A. Watkins, and Howard E. Winn

Contents

Color illustrations follow p. 218

Preface

The impetus for producing this book was the twenty-fifth anniversary of the New England Aquarium's right whale research project. Started in 1980, it is one of the longest continuously running whale research programs in the world. However, this book is not just about the Aquarium's program; instead, it represents the cumulative efforts of a large number of researchers at many institutions working in a variety of disciplines.

North Atlantic right whale research efforts are unique in several important ways. First, studies on this species have encompassed most of its known migratory range, covering both calving and feeding grounds. Second, the work described here represents an extraordinary diversity of expertise and multidisciplinary approaches. Third, there has been a remarkable level of cooperation among researchers working on this species, demonstrated by the number of institutions represented in the multiauthor chapters. Finally, there seems to be a unity of purpose among the research community working on right whales: everyone understands that the survival of this species is at stake and that reality supersedes many of the ego, turf, and public relations issues that can plague multi-institutional cooperative efforts. Perhaps the best example of this is the cooperation between U.S. and Canadian scientists and managers. Most researchers in this book are particularly indebted to Jerry Conway of the Canadian Department of Fisheries and Oceans, who facilitated extraordinary progress in conservation research on this species.

The North Atlantic right whale research program was built on the work of legends in the field. Roger Payne and Peter Best's long-running research programs on southern right whales, Steve Katona's 30-year supervision of the *North*

Atlantic Humpback Whale Catalog, and Richard Sear's 25-year program on blue whales in the Gulf of St. Lawrence all stand as examples of the power of long-term studies of this type. Whale research teams are all familiar with the troubles of weather, funding, equipment failures, shifts in animal distribution, and the extraordinary difficulties of trying to answer just one scientific question about whales. In the studies mentioned above, our colleagues have dealt with all of this for decades, providing insights into the biology of large whales that could never be obtained any other way.

For North Atlantic right whales, the success of this research has resulted in large part from the long-term consistent support of several foundations, individuals, and corporations, whose commitment to finding solutions to the right whale's problems is exemplary. The Island Foundation, Sarah Haney and the Canadian Whale Institute, the International Fund for Animal Welfare, the World Wildlife Fund-U.S. and Canada, and the Irving Oil Company deserve mention as champions of a difficult cause. In the United States, funding was provided by the National Marine Fisheries Service for most of these studies, and it was congressional support that made it possible. Senator Judd Gregg of New Hampshire, Senator John Kerry of Massachusetts, former Representative Gerry Studds of Massachusetts, Senator Olympia Snowe of Maine, and former Representative John Baldacci of Maine (now governor) all had the vision and commitment to keep right whales from slipping away. Their support for the right whale research program has made the difference between a chance of survival and certain extinction for this species.

This book is written for those who are concerned about the future of the oceans. There are technical pieces to the text that are appropriate for students and professionals, but it is also written in a style that is more accessible for general readers of science, in the hope that more people will find the plight of this species instructive and interesting. It is the belief of the editors that there are many lessons that right whales have to teach us.

List of Marine Species

Latin names	Common names

Cetaceans

Delphinapterus leucas	Beluga whale
Balaenoptera musculus	Blue whale
Tursiops truncatus	Bottlenose dolphin
Balaena mysticetus	Bowhead whale
Balaenoptera edeni	Bryde's whale
Balaenoptera physalus	Fin whale
Phocoena phocoena	Harbor porpoise
Megaptera novaeangliae	Humpback whale
Sousa chinensis	Indo-Pacific humpbacked dolphin
Orcinus orca	Killer whale
Balaenoptera acutorostrata	Minke whale
Eubalaena glacialis	North Atlantic right whale
Eschrichtius robustus	North Pacific gray whale
Eubalaena japonica	North Pacific right whale
Hyperodoon ampullatus	Northern bottle-nosed whale
Globicephala melaena	Pilot whale (Long finned)
Balaenoptera borealis	Sei whale
Eubalaena australis	Southern right whale
Physeter macrocephalus	Sperm whale
Lagenorhynchus acutus	White-sided dolphin

Latin names	Common names

Mustelids, Otariids, Phocids, and Sirenians

Erignathus barbatus	Bearded seal
Zalophus californianus	California sea lion
Dugong dugong	Dugong
Trichechus manatus latirostris	Florida manatee
Halichoerus grypus	Gray seal
Phoca vitulina	Harbor seal
Phoca groenlandica	Harp seal
Mirounga angustirostris	Northern elephant seal
Phoca hispida	Ringed seal
Enhydra lutris	Sea otter
Enhydra lutris nereis	Southern sea otter
Trichechus manatus	West Indian manatee

Fish, sharks, and invertebrates

Anguilla rostrata	American eel
Homarus americanus	American lobster
Hippoglossoides platessoides	American plaice
Euphausia superba	Antarctic krill
Gadus morhua	Atlantic cod
Micropogonias undulatus	Atlantic croaker
Hippoglossus hippoglossus	Atlantic halibut
Scomber scombrus	Atlantic mackerel
Cetorhinus maximus	Basking shark
Centropristis striata	Black sea bass
Carcharhinus limbatus	Blacktip shark
Chaceon fenneri	Golden crab
Melanogrammus aeglefinus	Haddock
Myxine glutinosa	Hagfish or slime eel
Clupea harengus	Herring
Lophius americanus	Monkfish or goosefish
Engraulis mordax	Northern anchovy
Meganyctiphanes norvegica	Northern krill
Macrozoarces americanus	Ocean pout

Latin names	Common names
Merluccius albidus	Offshore hake
Oncorhynchus spp.	Pacific salmon
Pollachius virens	Pollock
Strombus gigas	Queen conch
Chaceon quinquedeus	Red crab
Urophycis chuss	Red hake
Sciaenops ocellatus	Redfish or red drum
Cancer irroratus	Rock crab
Merluccius bilinearis	Silver hake/whiting
Mustelus canis	Smooth dogfish
Squalus acanthius	Spiny dogfish
Urophycis tenuis	White hake
Scopthalmus aquosus	Windowpane flounder
Pseudopleuronectes americanus	Winter flounder
Glyptocephalus cynoglussus	Witch flounder
Limanda ferruginea	Yellowtail flounder

Abbreviations

ADCP	acoustic doppler current profiler
ASP	amnesic shellfish poisoning
BOF	Bay of Fundy, Canada
C5	stage 5 copepodite of *Calanus finmarchicus*
CCB	Cape Cod Bay
CeTAP	Cetacean and Turtle Assessment Program
CFP	ciguatera fish poisoning
CITES	Convention on International Trade in Endangered Species
CMFY	calves per mature female per year
CTD	conductivity, temperature, depth instrument
DAM	dynamic area management
dB	decibel
DIGITS	digital image gathering and information tracking system
DSP	diarrhetic shellfish poisoning
DTAG	digital acoustic recording tag
EEZ	exclusive economic zone
Eg	*Eubalaena glacialis* (North Atlantic right whale)
ENSO	El Niño–Southern Oscillation
EWS	Early Warning System (aerial surveys)
Fundy	right whale cows that bring their calves to the Bay of Fundy
GIS	geographic information systems
GPS	global positioning system
GSC	Great South Channel (east of Cape Cod)
GSI	Gulf Stream Index
Hz	hertz
IPCC	Intergovernmental Panel on Climate Change

IWC	International Whaling Commission
kHz	kilohertz
MHC	major histocompatibility complex
mPa	micro-pascals
MSR	Mandatory Ship Reporting System
NAO	North Atlantic Oscillation
NARR	North American Regional Reanalysis
NARWC	North Atlantic Right Whale Consortium
NAST	National Assessment Synthesis Team
NAVTEX	narrow-band direct printing telegraph equipment for the reception of navigational and meteorological warnings and urgent information to ships
NCEP	National Center for Environmental Prediction
NEAq	New England Aquarium
NMFS	U.S. National Marine Fisheries Service (also known as NOAA Fisheries)
NOAA	National Oceanographic and Atmospheric Administration
NODC	National Oceanographic Data Center
Non-Fundy	right whale cows that do not bring their calves to the Bay of Fundy
NSP	neurotoxic shellfish poisoning
OPC	optical plankton counter
PCCS	Provincetown Center for Coastal Studies (Provincetown, Massachusetts)
POI	probability of identity
PbTx	brevetoxin
PSP	paralytic shellfish poisoning
RB	Roseway Basin (Nova Scotian Shelf)
SAG	surface-active group (courtship group)
SEUS	Southeast United States
SLR	single-lens reflex (camera)
SOI	Southern Oscillation Index
SONAR	sound navigation and ranging
SPUE	sightings per unit of effort
SST	sea surface temperature
STX	saxitoxin
UNCLOS	United Nations Law of the Sea Convention of 1982
VHF	very high frequency
VPR	video plankton recorder
WHOI	Woods Hole Oceanographic Institution

THE URBAN WHALE

1

Right Whales in the Urban Ocean

SCOTT D. KRAUS AND ROSALIND M. ROLLAND

24 March 1935
St. Augustine, Florida

It was a nice day in the right whale calving ground off St. Augustine, Florida, with light winds and moderate temperatures. A right whale mother, later identified and cataloged as right whale Eg #1045, was preparing for the long journey northward, swimming more each day to get her calf stronger and nursing frequently to help him grow. Suddenly chaos erupted around her. A sport fishing boat, out to harpoon large tuna, had spied the mother and calf lying at the surface. Seized by the thrill of the chase and the human notion that all animals are prey, the fishermen decided to pursue the calf. Using high-powered rifles, the men shot more than a hundred rounds into Eg #1045 in an attempt to drive her off. But she would not leave her calf. More shots were fired into the calf, and it was repeatedly harpooned as it tried to get away. The shallow near-shore waters of the area kept the mother and calf from diving, so the men in the boat had no trouble staying within range.

A New York Herald Tribune *reporter on board took many photographs and reported in detail on the struggle over the course of the day (Fig. 1.1). After an onslaught of bullets and harpoons lasting over six hours, the calf finally expired and was tied alongside the boat. It was only then that the mother right whale left the scene, with hundreds of wounds. The boat returned triumphantly to port, creating quite a commotion as the heroes*

Figure 1.1. Photographs of the last right whale intentionally killed in the United States, the calf of Eg #1045, from the 31 March 1935 *New York Herald Tribune.*

brought their catch to the dock. The calf was lifted out of the water by crane; it measured 5.5 m and weighed over 900 kg. It was the last right whale intentionally killed in the United States.

The mother was not seen again for many years, at least by anyone who had a camera. Then in 1959 Bill Schevill and Bill Watkins from the Woods Hole Oceanographic Institution, beginning a study of whales in Massachusetts Bay, photographed a lone right whale nearby. Later Amy Knowlton at the New England Aquarium would discover that this sighting matched photos of Eg #1045 published in the 1935 Herald Tribune *article. The whale's next encounter with humans was again with Schevill and Watkins, when she was observed "gyrating" off southern Cape Cod on 14 April 1980. She was photographed only a few more times before her last sighting, but never again with a calf. In August 1995 Eg #1045 was photographed by Brian Chmielecki from a National Marine Fisheries Service research vessel on Georges Bank. She had a large propeller wound cutting deeply into the side of her head, undoubtedly the result of an unfortunate encounter with a ship. She has never been seen again.*

The life of right whale Eg #1045 remarkably encapsulates the full sweep of history for this species within one animal's lifetime. After she lost a calf to whaling, she probably learned to avoid humans at all costs. But the bullets she received during that traumatic encounter may have damaged her irrevocably, since she was never again seen with a calf. Her life was apparently ended when she was struck by a ship's propeller, but death was not quick, and infection and pain were probably constant in her last months. If Eg #1045's experiences with humans became known among her kind, right whales would surely avoid us all.

Scott D. Kraus

The North Atlantic right whale, whose population currently numbers about 350 animals, is one of the most endangered large whales (Clapham et al. 1999). Historically this species was hunted to near extinction, and, despite being under protection for seventy years, the right whale population remains at very low numbers. In the past five years alone, at least nine right whales were killed by ships, and four have been killed by fishing gear entanglements in the western North Atlantic.

These deaths were in addition to the natural mortality for the same period, and they have put this population at a crossroads. Human decisions over the next few decades will determine the survival or extinction of this species. Right whales also experienced a significant and unexplained decline in reproduction during the 1990s. Many of the theories about the causes of this reproductive failure have to do with the proximity of right whales to the industrialized east coast of North America. Indeed, between shipping, fishing, ocean noise, pollution (including sewage effluent and agricultural and industrial runoff), the coastal zone of eastern North America is one of the most urbanized pieces of ocean in the world. And right whales, many of which live within that zone for most of their lives, are thus a new phenomenon in the marine world—a truly urban whale.

Recent studies show that the right whale population is declining in size (Caswell et al. 1999; Fujiwara and Caswell 2001). Fujiwara and Caswell claim that, if current trends are not reversed, the North Atlantic right whale will become extinct in approximately two centuries.

Against this sobering background there are two pieces of good news. First, those same models suggest that saving just two females per year could reverse this trend, and most of the actions that would need to be taken are already known. Second, a large number of scientists, government managers, industry representatives, and conservationists have dedicated their efforts to preventing the extinction of this species. This book summarizes the cumulative work of many of them, and it is a testament to their conviction that the extinction of the right whale is not inevitable.

This chapter provides an overview of right whale biology and natural history, referring the reader to detailed discussions of each topic within the book.

North Atlantic Right Whales and Humans: From Whaling to Conservation

Right whales got their name from being the "right" whale to kill, because of their high yields of oil and baleen and the fact that this slow-moving species floats after death. Right whale hunting was started by the Basques over a thousand years ago as a shore-based fishery off northern Spain and western France. By the early 1500s the Basques had expanded their operations to the coasts of Newfoundland and Labrador, and for nearly a century they hunted bowhead whales and a few right whales near the Strait of Belle Isle every summer and autumn. In New England, right whale hunting started from colonial shore-based stations during the late 1600s, peaked in the early 1700s, and persisted at low levels until the early 1900s. Other coastal and pelagic whalers killed right whales at several locations around the North Atlantic until nearly 1900. Chapter 2 describes this decimation of the North Atlantic right whale population and lessons learned about the historic range of these whales from whaling ship logbooks.

Whaling for right whales continued until 1935, when international protection was given to the species by the League of Nations. Subsequently right whales were protected from hunting by the International Whaling Commission (IWC) and, decades later, from commercial trading by the Convention on Trade in Endangered Species. Although there were violations of the hunting ban (most notably by the Soviet fleet in the 1960s, when over 3,300 right whales were killed in the Southern Hemisphere and about 200 were killed in the North Pacific; Tormosov et al. 1998), these intentional kills did not occur in the North Atlantic.

The number of western North Atlantic right whales that survived through the historical periods of hunting is unknown. One model suggests that the population may have reached very low numbers, perhaps only a few dozen, by the mid-1700s (Reeves 2001). Subsequent hunting of other species gave right whales a brief respite until the latter half of the nineteenth century, when right whaling resumed at low but consistent levels until about 1912. Hunting mostly ceased until World War II, when right whales may have been inadvertent targets of antisubmarine patrols along the U.S. east coast (especially in the near-shore calving ground). This model of historical population dynamics—in which right whales were nearly extirpated, recovered slightly, were reduced by more hunting, recovered slightly, were inadvertently killed by warfare, and then recovered slightly—matches the historical record well, although it is not statistically robust.

An alternative model, based on detailed genetic analyses, suggests that North Atlantic right whales were reduced at their lowest level to about 85 breeding individuals (Waldick et al. 2002). This genetic analysis also indicates that the reduction in population size probably occurred sometime before the whaling period. The genetic data, combined with downward revisions of the original estimates of North Atlantic right whale abundance (Rastogi et al. 2004), suggest that the recovery of this species from severe hunting may be inherently limited by intrinsic biological factors. Resolving the differences between these two models will require the integration of the historical and genetic data.

History of Right Whale Research

Whale researchers in the 1950s were mostly in agreement that the North Atlantic right whale was either extinct or very nearly so. But in the 1960s Bill

Schevill and Bill Watkins from the Woods Hole Oceanographic Institution (WHOI), during the course of acoustic studies on other whale species, noticed a few right whales in the vicinity of Cape Cod. Over the following twenty years, whenever the opportunity presented itself, these two researchers made observations on the biology and behavior of right whales. The lessons were clear—right whales in the North Atlantic were not yet extinct, there were periods of time when they remained near the coasts, and they had unique biological characteristics worthy of further study.

Based on the work of Schevill and Watkins, environmental impact assessments for oil exploration activities along the east coast of the United States were required to consider the status of right whales (as well as other endangered large whale species) in and around potential oil drilling lease sites. In 1979 the U.S. Minerals Management Service contracted with Howard Winn at the University of Rhode Island to conduct surveys for marine mammals and sea turtles between Cape Hatteras and Nova Scotia out to the edge of the continental shelf. The Cetacean and Turtle Assessment Program (CeTAP) was the first comprehensive survey of marine mammals and turtles in the western North Atlantic, and it discovered areas where multiple species aggregated seasonally in large assemblages. Some of these areas (Cape Cod Bay, the continental shelf edge near Cape Hatteras) were known from old whaling records, and some (the Great South Channel southeast of Cape Cod) were new discoveries. One of this program's most important findings was that right whales had survived, and that there were more than had previously been thought—perhaps even more than 200 whales!

In 1980 the U.S. National Marine Fisheries Service (NMFS) contracted with the New England Aquarium (NEAq) to assess marine mammal distribution and abundance in the Bay of Fundy (Canada), just above the northern limit of the CeTAP coverage in the Gulf of Maine. The NMFS was concerned about the potential impacts on local marine life of a proposed oil refinery in eastern Maine. Aerial surveys were conducted from early June through the end of October, revealing that within the bay there were finback whales, minke whales, humpback whales, harbor porpoise, white-sided dolphins, pilot whales, and, to everyone's surprise, at least twenty-five right whales, including four mothers with calves. Some writers likened finding right whales in the Bay of Fundy to discovering a brontosaurus in the backyard, but the truth is that fishermen had been seeing the whales for years and simply did not understand the significance of these sightings. NMFS managers immediately grasped their importance, and they provided additional support for several years of studies.

The oil refinery proposal eventually submerged beneath the weight of economic woes and environmental concerns.

The first few years of the NEAq Bay of Fundy studies yielded a wealth of information on the abundance, reproduction, and behavior of right whales. They also allowed the development of photo-identification tools to compare photographs of individual right whales taken by a variety of research groups. The CeTAP studies ended in 1982, but the University of Rhode Island researchers continued aerial surveys for right whales over the Great South Channel through most of the following decade. In 1981 Dr. Charles "Stormy" Mayo of the Provincetown Center for Coastal Studies initiated studies on the feeding behavior of right whales that were almost in his backyard, just outside (and sometimes inside) Provincetown Harbor. In 1984 aerial surveys off the southeastern United States, initiated by David Mattingly, NEAq, and a group of volunteer Delta Airlines pilots, led to the rediscovery of the calving ground off the coasts of Florida and Georgia, a location that had been well known to nineteenth-century whalers. In the next few years additional shipboard surveys conducted by NEAq researchers off the southern tip of Nova Scotia revealed yet another summer feeding ground for right whales, Roseway Basin. The Roseway Basin surveys followed in the footsteps of commercial whaling captains from the 1960s and 1970s, who, in the course of hunting finbacks and humpbacks, had recorded right whales in the region.

By 1985 the major coastal right whale habitats had been identified if not well defined. It became clear that more resources and a better-coordinated research plan would be needed if researchers were to really understand the biology of this species. In 1986, under the leadership of John Prescott and Howard Winn, the NEAq, the University of Rhode Island, WHOI, the Provincetown Center for Coastal Studies, and Marineland of Florida formed the North Atlantic Right Whale Consortium (NARWC). The goals of the consortium were to coordinate research efforts among institutions, bring attention to the plight of the right whale, educate government agencies, and elicit the support of the U.S. Congress for directed right whale research and management efforts.

The NARWC thrived for about five years before the federal money available for independent research dried up. Individual consortium researchers continued their efforts with the support of foundations, corporations, and generous individuals, often going into the field with limited funding and the help of volunteers, just to ensure the continuity of data collection on this species. There were some losses, notably gaps in surveys of the offshore areas in the Great South Channel and on the Nova Scotian Shelf; both have had significant consequences for subsequent population assessments. The outlook, for both right whales and the research community that studied them, was grim during this period.

In 1990 research was published that demonstrated that the leading causes of death in right whales were collisions with ships and entanglements in fishing gear (Kraus 1990). More and more researchers started to take pictures of right whales and submit them to the *Right Whale Catalog* and Database (see the section "The *Right Whale Catalog* and Database" in this chapter). Genetics studies initiated in the late 1980s started bearing fruit, providing gender data, information on habitat use patterns, and evidence that the remaining North Atlantic right whales had descended from just a few females (Brown et al. 1991; Schaeff et al. 1993). By the mid-1990s marine biologists were widely aware that right whales were potentially the next spotted owl—an animal that could very well be brought to extinction by humans if they continued to conduct business as usual.

The North Atlantic Right Whale Consortium was reestablished in 1996, with many of its original goals but with an open membership, a commitment to the open exchange of information, and a mandate to ensure the survival of right whales in the western North Atlantic. The consortium hosted an annual meeting and organized itself as if it were a corporation, with a board, chairperson, secretary, committees, and a review process for scientists wishing to gain access to member data on right whales. The remarkable thing was that the NARWC did not formally exist—all positions were voluntary, and any member could resign at any time. Submission of sightings and photographic data followed strict protocols, and all this information was accessible through the review process to those conducting legitimate scientific endeavors. Data submission was voluntary, yet everyone in the research community contributed. A more democratic community effort in support of research on and conservation of a single species has yet to be seen.

Starting in 1999 lobbying efforts in Washington, D.C., and support from a few key senators and congressional representatives led to increases in funding for right whale research and conservation, including surveys, cataloging, reproduction and habitat studies, and, most importantly, research on ways to reduce the number of right whales killed by ships and fishing gear. In 2002 Fisheries and Oceans Canada initiated research efforts on right whales in Canadian waters. By 2005 the U.S. agencies actively involved in right whale conservation included the NMFS, the Navy, the Office of Naval Research, the Marine Mammal Commission, the U.S. Coast Guard, the Army Corps of Engineers, and the states of Florida, Georgia, Maine, Massachusetts, Rhode

Island, and South Carolina. In Canada, Fisheries and Oceans Canada, Transport Canada, and the Coast Guard are all actively working on right whale conservation.

Worldwide Right Whale Taxonomy, Distribution, and Abundance

Along with dolphins, porpoises, and other whales, right whales belong to the order Cetacea. They feed using fringed baleen plates to filter their food from the water, a characteristic that places them in the suborder Mysticeti, the Latin term for "mustached whale." (The other suborder of cetaceans is the "toothed whales" or odontocetes.) Along with the closely related bowhead whales, right whales belong to a family of whales referred to collectively as balaenidae or "balaenids."

The taxonomic status of right whales has been the subject of mild controversy for over thirty years. A review by Rice (1998) joined right whales and bowheads together under the genus *Balaena* based on morphological characteristics and combined all right whale species into *Balaena glacialis*. Subsequently Rosenbaum et al. (2000a) published a worldwide review of the genetic data, concluding that right whales (*Eubalaena*) should be separate from bowhead whales (*Balaena*) and identifying three right whale species: *E. glacialis* in the North Atlantic, *E. australis* for all Southern Hemisphere right whales, and *E. japonica* in the North Pacific. In 2000 the IWC Scientific Committee considered the genetic and morphological data, decided to retain the generic name *Eubalaena* for right whales, and recognized the three species as proposed.

All three species of right whale are effectively isolated from one another (Fig. 1.2). The two in the Northern Hemisphere are kept apart by the Americas and the Arctic ice, and both northern species are isolated from the southern right whales by equatorial ocean temperatures and seasonal movements. Right whales are too well insulated to spend much time in warm waters without overheating, so crossing the waters of the equator is probably physiologically impossible for them. In the North Atlantic, it is extremely rare to find right whales in water temperatures above 21°C, and most animals are observed in a temperature range of 8–12°C (Chapter 16). Water temperatures in the equatorial zone can range from 26 to 35°C, in an area that can be as wide as 1,000 km around the equator. Furthermore, when western North Atlantic right whales travel south for winter calving off Florida and Georgia, the southern right whales are also traveling south, to the summer feeding grounds off Antarctica. This combination of high tropical temperatures and seasonal separations of more than 16,000 km serves as an effective barrier to any wandering right

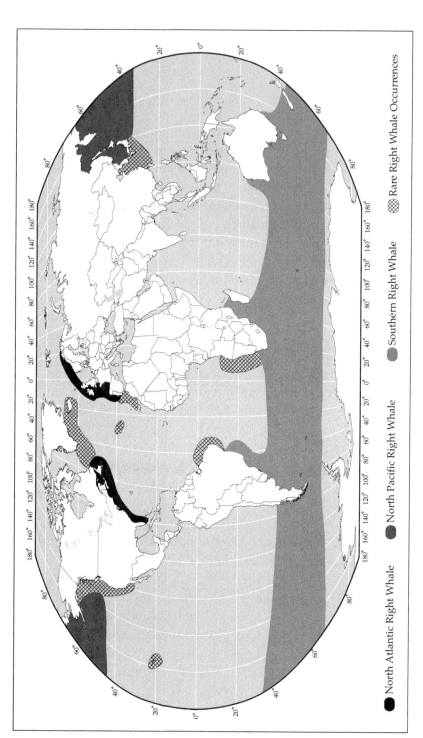

Figure 1.2. Known historical ranges of right whales worldwide. Kerry Lagueux / New England Aquarium.

● North Atlantic Right Whale ● North Pacific Right Whale ● Southern Right Whale ▨ Rare Right Whale Occurrences

whale, and it has a significant meaning to the extremely small populations in the north. There will be no help from the right whales to the south; northern right whale populations are completely isolated and will have to survive on their own.

Southern Right Whales

The most abundant of the right whale species is *E. australis,* which is circumpolar in distribution and currently probably numbers over 8,000 animals (IWC 2001a; see Table 1.1). Southern Hemisphere right whales have healthy subpopulations wintering and calving around South Africa, off the coast of Argentina and Brazil, along the southern coasts of Tasmania and Australia, and in the Auckland Islands south of New Zealand. All of these subpopulations are believed to spend summers feeding in the highly productive waters around the Antarctic, before migrating to their respective winter calving grounds in the high latitudes. Based on genetic (Rosenbaum et al. 2000a) and photo-identification (Rowntree et al. 2001) studies, it is likely that intermixing of these southern subpopulations occurs, in contrast to the two northern right whale species, which inhabit separate ocean basins.

North Pacific Right Whales

In the North Pacific, *E. japonica* is poorly studied, and population estimates are highly uncertain. Recent studies by the NMFS have identified small numbers in the Gulf of Alaska south of the Aleutians, but most North Pacific right whales are believed to occur in the coastal waters of Russia, Korea, and Japan. An estimate from the Sea of Okhotsk of 922 whales (95 percent confidence interval 404–2,108; IWC 2001a) is considered high, and the entire North Pacific stock of right whales probably numbers in the low hundreds.

North Atlantic Right Whales

Historically large (but unknown) numbers of right whales occurred on both the western and eastern sides of the North Atlantic, and both groups were classified as the same species, *E. glacialis.* At present, the eastern North Atlantic population (if there is a discrete group that can be labeled this way) probably numbers in the low tens of whales, and its future is considered highly questionable (IWC 2001a).

The population of *E. glacialis* in the western North Atlantic currently numbers about 350 animals, ranging from the Gulf of Mexico to Iceland. These right whales are the subject of this book. As used here, the term "North Atlantic right whale" or "right whale" refers to the western North Atlantic right whale unless otherwise specified.

Comparisons between Species

In comparing right whales from around the world, several features stand out. All right whale populations were historically hunted to very low levels, but southern right whale subpopulations all appear to be growing at rates of 5–7 percent per year (IWC 2001a, Table 1), an extraordinary rate of recovery for depleted large whale populations (Table 1.1). Limited data and sightings make any evaluation of right whale recovery in the North Pacific impossible at this time. In the western North Atlantic, detailed studies have shown wide variability in population growth rates, which appeared to be about 3.5 percent in the early 1980s (Knowlton et al. 1994) but sank to –2 percent in the late 1990s (IWC 2001b). The contrast between northern and southern right whale population growth is puzzling.

One clue to the different recovery rates of southern and northern right whales may lie in the varying extent of human impacts on these ocean basins. The North Atlantic is perhaps the world's most heavily industrialized ocean, with widespread shipping, fishing, and mineral exploration and extraction. Its coastal zone receives some of the highest levels of agricultural and industrial runoff in the world. (A few regions in the coastal waters of the western North Pacific, the Mediterranean, and the Baltic Sea may be considered equally industrialized and comparably affected by human development.) In the North Atlantic, most right whales breed, migrate, and feed within 80 km of shore. In the Southern Hemisphere, calving frequently occurs in shallow bays and coastal waters, areas that are only marginally industrialized, and southern right whales spend most of their lives feeding in relatively pristine offshore waters around the margins of the Antarctic.

Right Whale Appearance

To the uninitiated, the right whale can be odd and confusing in appearance (Fig. 1.3). It is a large, relatively rotund whale, with a square chin and a large

Table 1.1. Estimated Abundance and Growth Rates of Right Whales Worldwide

Breeding group	Estimated population size (as of 1997)	Annual growth rate
E. australis		
Australia	1,197[a]	0.0825
New Zealand	330[a]	—
South Africa	3,104[a]	0.072
Argentina	2,577[a]	0.071
Tristan de Cunha	226[a]	—
Brazil	137[a]	—
E. japonica		
North Pacific	922[b]	—
E. glacialis		
North Atlantic	300 ± 30[c]	−0.02[d]

a. Total population size and growth rates from IWC (2001a, Table 4). Population size is based on model-derived estimates with a baseline of 1997 (IWC 2001a).
b. IWC (2001a).
c. IWC (2001b).
d. Fujiwara and Caswell (2001).

head that accounts for 25 percent of the total body length in adults. A strongly arched and narrow rostrum (upper jaw) and a bowed lower jaw are characteristic of the species, giving the impression that this whale is "upside down." The large head and bowed jaw house long baleen plates, made of keratin, that are used in feeding. These baleen plates are usually black, number from 205 to 270 on each side of the upper jaw, average 2–2.8 m in length, and are relatively narrow (up to 18 cm) with fine hairlike fringes facing the interior of the mouth.

Right whales are generally black and sometimes have white patches on the belly and chin. Gray or black thickened skin patches called callosities are found on the rostrum, behind the blowholes, over the eyes, on the corners of the chin, and variably along the lower lip and the margins of the jaw. Callosities are composed of spikes of columnar epithelial tissue and from a distance appear similar to barnacles, but no barnacles have ever been found on North Atlantic right whales. These callosity patterns appear light yellow or cream-colored owing to infestations of cyamid crustaceans (whale lice), which densely populate their surfaces. The arrangement of callosities is unique to each right whale and is used to recognize individuals (color plate 3).

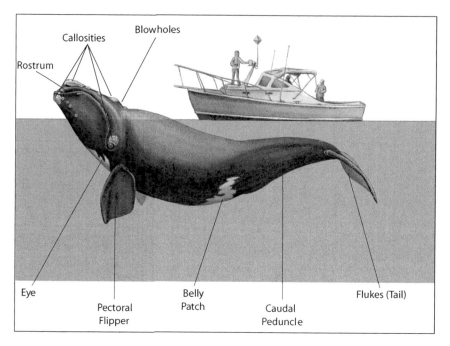

Figure 1.3. Arpeggio (Eg #2753) drawn to scale next to the R/V *Nereid*, showing body features. Scott Landry / Provincetown Center for Coastal Studies.

Adult right whales average about 14 m in length, and adult females are about 1 m longer than adult males (Allen 1908; Andrews 1908). Right whales weigh approximately 36,000–72,000 kg, making them among the largest of all whales. They have a blubber layer up to 20 cm thick that serves for both insulation and energy storage.

Several features make right whales easily identifiable in the field. Except for bowheads (which live in the Arctic) and arguably gray whales, they are the only whales without dorsal fins. The presence of callosities readily distinguishes them from bowheads, and of course there is little or no geographic overlap between the species. Right whales have two blowholes on the top of their heads, and, when seen along the axis of the animal, the blow is characteristically V-shaped and can reach 7 m in height (Fig. 1.4). They have a distinctive, graceful tail that is broad (up to 6 m tip to tip) and all black (color plate 4), and there are no grooves along the throat, as in the balaenopterid whales (e.g., humpback and finback whales).

The *Right Whale Catalog* and Database

Many of the studies described in this book depend on the ability of researchers to tell whales apart using distinctive natural markings. The foundation of most work on this species is a unified *North Atlantic Right Whale Catalog* and Database, which includes all photographed North Atlantic right whale sightings and associated data collected since 1935 (Chapter 3). The photographic identification and cataloging methods were developed early in the 1980s based on pioneering work by Roger Payne on South Atlantic right whales (Payne et al. 1983; Kraus et al. 1986). Photographs and associated sighting data have been contributed by researchers working all over the North Atlantic, and they are matched with archived photographs of individual right whales in the *North Atlantic Right Whale Catalog* (Crone and Kraus 1990; Hamilton and Martin 1999). In this book, individual right whales are referred to by their *Catalog* numbers (Eg# xxxx) or, in some cases, their names. Right whales are occasionally named for distinctive identifying features, and those names are also used here (Chapter 3).

As of the end of 2004, the *Catalog* contained 459 individually identified right whales from the entire North Atlantic Ocean, although many were no longer alive. This included over 250,000 images taken of whales between 1935 and 2004. The sightings database has provided information on the age and sex of individuals, movements and habitat use patterns, reproduction, mortality, and the impacts of human activities on the population. Gender identification was made possible by both visual assessments during photographic surveys and genetic studies. Access to *Catalog* data is managed through a peer review process overseen by the board of the North Atlantic Right Whale Consortium.

Since 1979 North Atlantic right whales have been studied with standardized surveys and photographed from boats, ships, airplanes, and occasionally blimps to assess distribution, abundance, ecology, and behavior. Shipboard and aerial surveys have been conducted annually in most of their known habitats, although offshore areas, including the Great South Channel and the Nova Scotian Shelf, were sampled irregularly during the 1990s (Chapter 4).

Where Do Right Whales Live?

In the western North Atlantic, individual right whales are wide ranging and have been observed from Florida to the Gulf of St. Lawrence, Newfoundland, and southern Greenland. One known male ("Porter," Eg #1133) traveled from

Figure 1.4. The distinguishing features of right whales, including V-shaped blow (a), callosities (b), paddle-shaped flippers (c), and smooth-edged, all-black tail (d). Regina Campbell-Malone / Woods Hole Oceanographic Institution (a), Monica Zani / New England Aquarium (b, c), Yan Guilbault / New England Aquarium (d).

Figure 1.4. (*continued*)

Cape Cod to Norway in less than six months and returned to U.S. waters the following spring (Jacobsen et al. 2004). Right whales photographed in Iceland and Norway have been matched to animals seen in the western North Atlantic, and preliminary genetic data indicate that separation between eastern and western North Atlantic right whales is unlikely (Rosenbaum et al. 2000b).

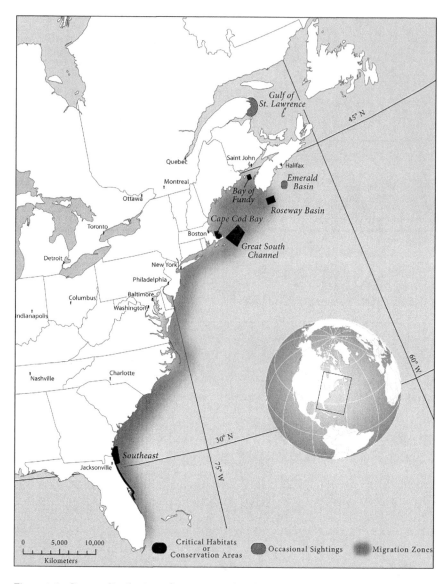

Figure 1.5. Current distribution of western North Atlantic right whales, including critical habitats or conservation areas, coastal migration zones, and areas of occasional sightings. Kerry Lagueux/New England Aquarium.

Over two-thirds of the western North Atlantic right whales aggregate seasonally in one of five known habitats, all in U.S. or Canadian coastal waters (Fig. 1.5). The remaining whales may go to areas still undiscovered, or they may be scattered throughout several areas along the east coast of North America. The only known calving ground is in the coastal waters of the southeastern United States during the winter months. In the spring, aggregations of right whales are present in the Great South Channel and in Cape Cod and Massachusetts Bays. In the summer and fall, right whales are observed in the Bay of Fundy, between Maine and Nova Scotia, and in an area 50 km south of Nova Scotia called Roseway Basin (see color plate 1).

However, right whales do not demonstrate strong fidelity to these identified habitats. Photo-identification and some limited satellite tagging data show that seasonal movements into, out of, and around the so-called critical habitats are frequent and extensive (Baumgartner and Mate 2005). Furthermore, right whales do not engage in a "migration," at least in the way most people imagine this. Right whales do not form "pods" (like dolphins), and they do not move about the ocean in large groups. In fact most right whales are solitary travelers, although a few long-lasting pairs (together up to three months) have been reported. There is no broad populationwide movement to the south in the winter and then north in the summer. Pregnant females migrate to the coastal waters of the southeastern United States with a few juveniles and noncalving females, but most of the right whale population, including most males, is absent from the calving grounds during the winter. The location of the wintering ground for noncalving whales is unknown, but it seems likely that right whales are motivated by the search for food and mates, and that cold water temperature is of minimal importance in determining where a well-insulated whale chooses to spend the winter. This is a critical gap in right whale biology, as current evidence points to midwinter conception. Thus the wintering ground is probably the right whales' mating ground, and identification and protection of this area may well be critical to their survival.

The Suburban Cousins: Non-Fundy Right Whales

Although nearly all right whale cows in the western North Atlantic give birth off the southeastern United States, there is significant substructuring within the population. Schaeff et al. (1993) inferred from genetic and photo-identification data that one group of cows (representing about one-third of the population) does not bring its calves to the Bay of Fundy nursery area. These are referred to in this book as "non-Fundy" whales, and they represent the suburban or perhaps rural cousins of the urban whale. Later work showed that cows bringing six-month-old calves to the Bay of Fundy in the summer had first been brought there by their own mothers when they were calves. In other words, the genetic substructuring by habitat suggests strong maternally directed site fidelity in right whales (Malik et al. 1999), with offspring returning to the mother's summer habitat.

These findings have deep implications; they mean that another summer and fall nursery area must exist, although its location is unknown. Furthermore, since most of the coastal zone of eastern North America has been surveyed in the past twenty-five years, this unknown location is probably offshore and therefore may not be subject to the same negative influences as the urban ocean of the eastern North American coast. This group of whales is likely to be underrepresented in the *Right Whale Catalog* (since near-shore surveys do not photograph non-Fundy whales as often), and this omission could alter population estimates. An offshore right whale may also be expected to encounter different conditions and hazards, which might be reflected in different rates of reproduction and mortality. However, because encounter rates with such whales are low, researchers do not know much about them.

The report by Knowlton et al. (1992) of a cow and calf off Greenland in 1992, historical whaling records, and genetic data on paternity all suggest that, remarkably, there is much more to learn about the wanderings and habitats of this species.

How and What Do Right Whales Eat?

North Atlantic right whales feed primarily on calanoid copepods (zooplankton the size of rice) by swimming continuously with their mouths open at the surface (a strategy sometimes called skim-feeding) or at depths down to 200 m, filtering out zooplankton that collects on the insides of their baleen plates (Chapter 5). Observations of right whales feeding at the surface have led to reports of sea monsters, as these whales skim with their mouths wide open, narrow, callosity-covered rostrums raised in the air and baleen plates partially exposed above the water.

Copepods are not homogeneously distributed; instead they usually form dense aggregations both vertically and horizontally where oceanographic features or fronts concentrate organisms. Concentration may be further enhanced as the zooplankton seek preferred intensities of light or other physical factors during diurnal vertical migration. The right whale is probably unable to take advantage of larger, more mobile prey (e.g., krill or fish) because it swims too slowly (Chapter 5).

Right whales are highly dependent on a narrow range of prey sizes (dictated by the filtering capacity of their baleen), which occur in variable and spatially unpredictable patches in the Atlantic ecosystem. The four northern feeding habitats identified in the western North Atlantic probably have hydrographic and oceanographic conditions that are conducive to the creation of highly concentrated patches of copepods. However, there is substantial variability in copepod production in each of these areas from year to year (Brown et al. 2001; Kenney 2001; Chapter 5). Right whales have adapted to this unpredictability with a large caloric buffer, in the form of blubber, and the ability to travel long distances without feeding between aggregations of food.

Reproduction and Demography

Female right whales give birth to a single calf in the coastal waters of the southeastern United States (Kraus et al. 1986) between December and March, with a peak in calving in January and February. At least two females have had calves over a period of 31 years, suggesting that the reproductive lifespan of North Atlantic right whales is at least that long. Mothers and calves migrate north for spring feeding in the Great South Channel and Cape Cod Bay, then move on to summer feeding areas in the Bay of Fundy and Roseway Basin. While the location of additional summer feeding grounds remains unknown, both Fundy and non-Fundy whales can be found feeding in the Great South Channel in the spring and on the Nova Scotian Shelf during the summer and early fall.

The documented sex ratio of the right whale population is 50:50 (Brown et al. 1994). Work by Hamilton et al. (1998) on demographic structure suggests that 26–31 percent of the population is composed of juveniles, significantly lower than the percentage observed in other baleen whales, and also much lower than expected in a theoretical population experiencing growth.

Behavior assumed to be courtship (referred to as surface-active groups or SAGs) has been described by Kraus and Hatch (2001) and may include as many as forty or more whales. Females at the center of these groups make underwater calls, which apparently attract multiple males from kilometers away. Males compete with one another for repeated mating opportunities with the focal female in an SAG, and these groups can last for several hours. Courtship activities have been reported year round; this is puzzling, because calving occurs in the winter and gestation is estimated to last 12–13 months (Best 1994). Alternative SAG functions have been proposed and are summarized in Chapter 6.

Right whale reproduction declined throughout the 1990s, with evidence for a slight rebound in the years following 2001 (Chapter 6). The potential reasons for this decline include food limitation, disease and/or marine biotoxins, pollutants, genetic factors, and climatic variation. Details on these hypotheses can be found in Chapters 5, 7, 8, 9, and 15 and in the report of the workshop on right whale reproduction (Reeves et al. 2001).

Longevity

Because there are currently no reliable methods to age right whales, their maximum life expectancy is unknown. Toothed whales have been aged using growth rings in their teeth, and some baleen whales (e.g., fin and humpback whales) have been aged by counting annual layers in earplugs from the ear canal. A technique that measures rates of racemization of aspartic acid in the eye lens has been used on bowhead whales to detect age-related changes in the eye (George et al. 1999). However, none of these methods is effective or proven in right whales at this time.

As the narrative that opens this chapter illustrates, a fortuitous photograph of a female right whale in an old newspaper article has provided evidence that this could be a very long-lived species. If the calf killed in 1935 was Eg #1045's first calf, and if she gave birth at age 10 (the mean age of first calving for North Atlantic right whales), then Eg #1045 would have been 70 years old when last seen, making her the oldest whale of known age in the population (Hamilton et al. 1998). This would be considered her minimum age, leaving open the possibility that right whales are very long lived, as is the case with bowhead whales, which may live well over a hundred years (George et al. 1999).

Mortality

Analyses of stranding, entanglement, and photographic data have provided estimates of mortality for North Atlantic right whales, as discussed in Chapter 12 (Kraus 1990; Kenney and Kraus 1993; Knowlton and Kraus 2001). Calf and juvenile mortality ranges from 24 percent in year one down to 5 percent in year three based on estimated deaths (Kraus 2002). Natural mortality rates between the ages of 3 and 10 are lower, estimated to be between 1 percent and

3 percent annually (Kraus 2002). However, Fujiwara and Caswell (2001) suggested that adult female mortality rates are much higher and are the major contributor to the currently declining population.

Data from fifty reliably documented right whale deaths between 1986 and 2005 show that 19/50 (38 percent) were due to collisions with ships and 6/50 (12 percent) were due to entanglements in fishing gear (Kraus et al. 2005). The remaining 25 deaths were attributed to unknown causes or neonatal mortality, which is considered natural mortality. The causes of death among the unknown mortalities are not known, either because the carcass was not retrieved or because it was too decomposed to identify a causal factor or because no obvious factor was found despite a detailed necropsy.

Nevertheless, 50 percent of all confirmed right whale deaths are due to clearly identified anthropogenic sources. In the case of shipping collisions, most right whale habitats are also home to major shipping lanes serving the ports of eastern North America (Knowlton and Kraus 2001; Chapter 14). In the case of fishing, 75 percent of all right whales display scars indicative of entanglements at some time in their lives (Knowlton et al. 2005). Because right whales are coastal whales, they are likely to encounter fishing gear throughout their range, from Florida to Canada (Chapter 13).

Other Conservation Issues

Measuring the responses of populations or of individual whales to the impacts of habitat loss, pollutants, acoustic disturbance, or climate change is difficult, partly because baseline data for comparison with the contemporary situation are lacking and partly because it is difficult to tease apart the multiple potential effects of several variables. Neither the NMFS nor Fisheries and Oceans Canada have yet articulated a management approach to unknown impacts of this type, although there have been regional efforts to minimize the effects of ocean urbanization.

Habitat Loss and/or Degradation

Reeves et al. (1978) hypothesized that intensive industrial use of some coastal areas (e.g., Delaware Bay) by humans since the 1800s may have preempted their use by right whales (because of noise or ship traffic), thereby reducing the potential recovery of the population. Not enough is known about precolonial use of the coastal areas north of Cape Hatteras by right whales to evaluate this idea. Still, there is concern about habitat loss for right whales. Beyond food requirements, and some vague notion about a preference for relatively undisturbed areas with warmer water temperatures for calving, researchers still do not understand the basic habitat needs of this species. Kenney et al. (2001) suggested that this species is occupying only the southern portion of its potential range and that additional habitats suitable for both feeding and courtship may be available north of Nova Scotia. The missing summering group of right whales strengthens this suggestion, since they seem to be surviving in some areas unknown to scientists.

Habitat degradation occurs along a continuum from few or no effects to complete habitat loss. The difficulty for managers and researchers alike is related to the lack of knowledge of how resilient or tolerant a right whale may be to human effects in the coastal zone. How loud does human-generated noise have to be to drive a right whale away from an area? At what levels do pollutants, marine biotoxins, warming waters, or boat traffic start to reduce population viability, by either damaging reproduction or decreasing survival?

For example, the effects of pollutants on right whales (or any other whale species) are unknown, even though they have been found in measurable amounts in every marine mammal. However, direct causal links between various chemicals and measurable changes in health and reproduction have only been identified in pinnipeds (Reijnders 1986; DeSwart et al. 1994; Ross et al. 1995). High contaminant levels have been associated with tumors and reproductive dysfunction in the St. Lawrence beluga population (DeGuise et al. 1995) and with reproductive problems in Northwest killer whales (Ross 2000), but a cause-and-effect relationship has not been proven. Likewise, immune suppression resulting from high tissue levels of contaminants has been suggested as a precipitating factor in widespread die-offs of dolphins in the western North Atlantic and seals in the North Sea from infectious diseases (Geraci 1989; Hall et al. 1992), but conclusive proof of the connection is lacking.

To date, all hypotheses on links between habitat degradation or loss and the lack of population recovery are speculative. As the scale of urbanization increases in coastal zones, these multiple factors could become even more troublesome.

Ocean Noise, Whale Watching, and Research

It has been suggested that the constant din of shipping noise in the North Atlantic may have habituated right whales to ship sounds, making them less likely to avoid oncoming vessels. It is also possible that the higher levels of ambient noise in the ocean have reduced the ability of right whales to hear mating calls over large distances, perhaps reducing mating opportunities (see Chapter 10). High noise levels from seismic operations and shipping activities have been shown to displace other whale species from normal movements (Richardson et al. 1995).

Whale watching has evoked concern, and watching of right whales in the United States has been banned since the mid-1990s. However, since the practice began only in the 1970s in New England and in Canada, whale watching is probably not a significant factor in the slow recovery of the North Atlantic right whale population. Although whale watching could potentially have some effect on the whales by distracting or stressing them, it is difficult to imagine this is a significant problem compared to the fatal threats posed by large ships and fixed fishing gear. It might also be argued that whale watching builds a constituency of humans who care about these ungainly creatures—something that is sorely needed if right whales are to survive.

Research on right whales is heavily regulated in the United States; permits are required just to approach within 0.5 km of any whale by boat or aircraft. Although there has been a large increase in funding for, and therefore research on, right whales over the past ten years, most of this work has been applied to conservation efforts on behalf of the species. It is likely that the benefits of most research activities far exceed the costs, although with species as endangered as this one, this question must be asked for every new method and every change in level of effort.

Climate Change

There is no doubt that the earth's atmosphere is gradually warming. Insofar as this warming trend is largely due to production of "greenhouse gases" (carbon dioxide, methane, and nitrous oxide) from human industrialization and transportation, it might be viewed as controllable or reversible. Although there are many unknowns, most scientists believe that the coming changes, including rises in sea level and oceanic warming, will be catastrophic in some areas. The potential consequences of climate change for right whales are discussed in Chapter 15.

The Evolution of Research Methods

The earliest scientific work on right whales occurred during fortuitous aerial and shipboard encounters, starting with those of Watkins and Schevill in the late 1950s. Survey methods, aimed at assessing population size, were developed during the late 1970s for the CeTAP program (CeTAP 1982), and they have continued to advance with analytical methods that account for variability in platform, sighting conditions, and species behavior (Chapter 4). Right whale studies dramatically changed with the development of photographic methods for identifying individuals in the early 1980s. Tracking individual whales using the photographic records of their activities led to remarkable insights about right whale biology (Chapter 3). Advances in genetics in the late 1980s led to sampling methods for collecting small skin and blubber samples from known individuals (Brown et al. 1991). The DNA extracted from these samples has been used to obtain information on the sex of individuals, compare genetic information with observed patterns of migration and habitat use, evaluate inbreeding, assess paternity, and construct a family tree for the entire population (Chapter 7).

Yet researchers wanted to know more about these whales during the times they could not be followed. Satellite telemetry was used to investigate right whale movements among different areas. Tags inserted directly into the blubber layer on whales' backs provided regular date, time, and location information (Mate et al. 1997; Slay and Kraus 1999; Baumgartner and Mate 2005). However, no satellite tags were successful in transmitting data for longer than about six months, apparently because right whale behavior involves a large amount of body contact and the tags do not survive this physical trauma. Swelling around tagging sites on some individual whales raised questions among veterinarians about the safety of this approach. Successful tagging will probably require improvements in satellite tag durability and ways to minimize physiological impacts. Tagging technology is an excellent example of a research method for which the potential payoff is high—it *could* find unknown critical habitats—but the risk to individual whales is unknown. In this extremely endangered population, biologists and managers are currently approaching the tagging of right whales very carefully, in hopes of answering critical conservation questions while minimizing health risks.

More recently, researchers have been seeking the causes of reduced reproductive rates in North Atlantic right whales. A breakthrough in the ability to determine some physiological parameters in whales (where blood sampling is impossible) is summarized in Chapter 8, which describes research on steroid hormone metabolites measured in fecal samples. These metabolites have been used to identify gender, assess reproductive maturity, identify pregnancy and lactation, and evaluate levels of stress hormones (Rolland et al. 2005). Fecal sampling has also provided insights into the potential roles of marine biotoxins and disease in compromising the reproductive health of right whales.

Concern over right whale reproduction led researchers to try new ways of measuring the potential effects of prey availability and ecosystem changes on right whale health. In the late 1990s, adaptations of ultrasound methods were used to measure the blubber thickness of free-swimming whales to assess fat storage as a proxy for body condition (Moore et al. 2001; Chapter 9). Changes in blubber thickness correlated closely with the female reproductive cycle and may prove to be useful in monitoring right whale health. Detailed photo-analysis was also used to assess health and body condition in right whales (Pettis et al. 2004). Not only does right whale body shape visibly change as conditions change, but occasional skin lesions and other visible indicators appear to reflect poor health (Chapter 9).

Researchers also became curious about what right whales did underwater, as underwater behavior could have significant impacts on the dangers they face from shipping and fishing gear. These led to questions about communication between these whales. How do they find one another when there are so few of them? Studies that helped define the acoustic characteristics of right whales and their hearing are described in Chapter 10, along with a discussion of the potential impacts of noise from human activities. Work using suction cup tags with acoustic receivers and recorders, as well as movement and depth recorders, has yielded insights into right whale behavior underwater (Nowacek et al. 2001), including responses to ships, other whales, and potential alarm calls (Nowacek et al. 2004). Acoustic techniques have also been directly applied to management problems. One large study is deploying passive listening, recording, and transmitting devices at depth to locate right whales within areas if surveys cannot be conducted because of bad weather or poor visibility (Chapter 11). Active sonar systems to detect whales from ships have been tested on other species and are being explored for right whales (Chapter 11).

Finally, in the search for a better understanding of right whale biology and management options, researchers have turned to mathematical models that describe trends in population growth, identify demographic features of populations, and help monitor progress in reducing human sources of mortality (Chapter 16). These models have critical applications for right whales, whose population is so small that normal statistical methods are ineffective. Chapter 16 also summarizes the development of spatial models in geographic information systems to identify oceanographic variables associated with right whale distribution. Remote sensing data have been used to evaluate the oceanographic features in the areas where right whales are found, in the hope that their habitat characteristics can be identified with enough accuracy to allow predictions about their occurrence in locations with a high risk of conflict with human activities. This technique would provide managers with a tool for managing human activities, and it would also help identify the habitat features required by right whales.

The Challenges of Studying Right Whales

Researchers face two problems in studying the biology of right whales. The first is that posed by numbers far smaller than those considered statistically meaningful. Most biometricians would consider thirty cases a minimum sample size for statistical analysis. In this population, hypotheses about biology might require subdivision by sex, habitat use pattern (Fundy and non-Fundy), and age (juvenile and adult). While some of these subgroups (i.e., adult males that go to the Bay of Fundy) might be larger than thirty whales, most are far smaller and therefore difficult to characterize in a robust statistical fashion. The second problem is that right whales live a very long time. It takes about ten years for a female first observed as a calf to reach sexual maturity. Its mother may have a reproductive lifespan longer than a researcher's professional career; barring catastrophe, most of these whales will outlive the scientists studying them. Thus a researcher may expect to see only a portion of a right whale's life, and this circumstance can limit the scope of scientific studies and their conclusions.

There are three strategies to deal with these problems. The first is to recognize that these whales can be really understood only through long-term studies to collect and analyze parameters of interest over multiple years. In some cases, a second approach might be to take advantage of existing data (if appropriate or accurate measurements are even available) and analyze them retrospectively. The third method is to develop mathematical models that take existing data into account and iteratively adjust the model with the addition of new data to narrow in on the best fit to contemporary observations. Given that life is short and funding is unpredictable, this last approach is the strategy with the greatest probability of success.

There is an important corollary to the conundrum of small sample size. Some individual whales are well known to the researchers, and they have high encounter rates. These are the whales that are frequently included in assessments of various parameters, and, unless appropriate precautions are taken, their patterns can dominate the data. Researchers can be lulled into thinking that this self-selected group of animals represents the norm. On the other hand, there are at least two advantages of having a well-known group of whales: the ability to detect individual variations around the "norm," and the possibility that observations that deviate from the expected can teach researchers something new. In this book, each chapter starts with a narrative of events that taught scientists something new about right whales—or at least dramatically illuminated their ignorance.

As for the problem of studying long-lived animals, long-term studies are difficult, requiring sustained fundraising and dedicated fieldwork commitments, under sometimes uncomfortable conditions. The rewards are tremendous, but they are slow to arrive, making such studies somewhat unpopular with both funding agencies and impatient scientists. Given that these large whales will outlive the scientists who study them, the best hope for the security of the species and the continuity of research and management efforts may lie in communal ownership of the data. The NARWC may provide this, and it may also inspire future generations of biologists to take on some of the research made possible by such a long-term dataset.

Contemporary Protection and Management

Under the U.S. Endangered Species Act and the Marine Mammal Protection Act, right whales in U.S. waters benefit from some of the strongest legislative protection measures ever enacted on behalf of rare wildlife. However, North Atlantic right whales also frequently travel offshore in international waters, and they spend a significant portion of their lives in Canadian coastal waters. In Canada, the Committee on the Status of Endangered Wildlife in Canada has monitored endangered species for over twenty-five years, but no regulatory measures have been enacted to support its recommendations for protection until recently. Within the United States, the NMFS is the agency responsible for the management of right whales; in Canada, Fisheries and Oceans Canada is in charge of right whale protection.

The NMFS has designated three critical habitats in the United States: Cape Cod Bay, the Great South Channel, and the coastal waters of the southeastern United States between Jacksonville, Florida, and Brunswick, Georgia, out to 24 km. In Canada, Fisheries and Oceans Canada has designated two conservation zones, one in the Bay of Fundy and one on the Nova Scotian Shelf (Roseway Basin). Although all these habitats have been officially designated and appear on nautical charts, there are few restrictions on human activities within them.

The NMFS has issued an updated recovery plan for right whales (NMFS 2005), which will serve as a blueprint for the agency to follow under the Endangered Species Act and the Marine Mammal Protection Act. Under the recovery plan, implementation teams are responsible for coordinating management actions to ensure the survival of the species. These teams are made up of representatives from the relevant and affected agencies at the federal and state levels. The teams have advisory boards consisting of scientists, conservationists, and industry representatives. The NMFS has also created take reduction teams, one of which is focused on reducing kills of large whales by fishing gear.

Canada has also issued a recovery plan (Anonymous 2000) with recommendations comparable to those in the U.S. plan, and it recently passed the Species at Risk Act, which may provide the legislative authority and mandate to implement many of the features of Canada's plan. The right whale was listed as endangered under the Species at Risk Act in early 2005.

Under the Endangered Species Act and the Marine Mammal Protection Act, the NMFS issues annual stock assessments, which include the allowable "potential biological removal" from that stock that will not measurably impact its prospects for survival. The current potential biological removal for right whales allows for zero whale deaths per year. Reviewing recent events provides a barometer for the effectiveness of current management strategies. Between January 2004 and June 2005, three right whales were killed by ships, one died from fishing entanglements, one neonate died from natural causes, and there were three deaths for which the cause could not be determined. Six of these eight whales were adult females, of which three were carrying near-term fetuses (Kraus et al. 2005). In light of this level of mortality, the future survival of right whales probably depends on the speed with which the recommendations of the recovery plan can be carried out in the United States and the degree to which the recommendations in Canada's recovery plan can be implemented.

An effective conservation program for right whales will require cooperation among and action by many federal and state agencies, scientists, industry, and nongovernmental conservation groups. International cooperation is essential, as this population ranges across national boundaries. Collisions with ships are the greatest documented source of human-induced mortality for this species, claiming at least one or two right whales annually along the east coast of North

America. The fact that right whales migrate across and frequently feed in basins that are also home to shipping lanes does not make managing this issue easy. There have been success stories, notably in the Bay of Fundy, where shipping lanes were moved to reduce the risk of collisions between right whales and ships (Chapter 14). Such stories inspire both the shipping industry and conservationists alike, although this approach will not work everywhere.

The incidence of right whale entanglements in fishing gear is high. Photographic methods for assessing and monitoring right whale encounters with fishing gear have been developed to evaluate the efficacy of management strategies. These analyses show that many whales have been able to escape from entanglements on their own, although it is not known whether injuries sustained during those entanglements compromise long-term fecundity or survival. Fixed fishing gear is distributed broadly all along the coast of North America. Records of entanglements from Newfoundland to Florida show no clear pattern that might inform a management strategy, other than seasonal closures of known whale habitats to risky fishing gear. Nevertheless, with industry cooperation, progress is being made on "whale-safe" fishing gear, some of which is being tested as this book is being written (Chapter 13).

Travels of the Urban Whale

The following is a hypothetical accounting of the first year in the life of a right whale calf named Arpeggio based on her known life history, which illustrates the types of anthropogenic influences that may affect North Atlantic right whales starting shortly after birth.

> *Arpeggio (Eg #2753) was born near the border of Georgia and Florida, probably within 32 km of shore in early January 1997. Her first breath was downwind of two paper mills on shore that provide paper bags and boxes for grocery stores all over the country. Her mother, named Limpet (Eg #1153), spent several hours in this first week shepherding her newborn out of the way of three container ships, a Trident submarine, a navy frigate, a tug and barge, a dredge en route to an offshore dump site, numerous recreational fishing vessels, an oil tanker, and several shrimp boats. Over the first month, Arpeggio would learn that the noises associated with vessel traffic in her underwater world were both loud and constant.*
>
> *At the end of February, Limpet started north to the feeding grounds, with Arpeggio tucked in beside her—it was the calf's first big swim. Their*

destination was Cape Cod Bay, a rich springtime feeding ground for right whales. Mother right whales do not feed in the calving grounds, and since they have been metabolically converting their blubber into milk for the insatiable youngsters over several months, they need to replenish their fat stores. But the journey north was challenging, crossing shipping channels at Savannah, Wilmington, Charleston, and Norfolk; the entrances to Chesapeake and Delaware Bays; and then the entrances to the ports of Newark and New York, Providence and Boston. In addition, as the pair rounded Cape Hatteras, they started to encounter fishing gear in the water column: crab traps, lobster pots, and gillnets, all in increasing densities as they traveled farther into northern waters.

All this time, Limpet and Arpeggio were downwind of the smells of civilization, including power plants, traffic jams, manufacturing facilities, and fast-food restaurants. They also swam through a near-shore mix of outflows from hog farms in the Carolinas, secondary treatment sewage effluent from big cities, and rainwater runoff from storm drains that collect dripped oil from road surfaces. The pair passed across river mouths draining fertilizer and pesticide residues from the agricultural areas of the heartland, some of which eventually dump into the Atlantic. They swam through water containing plasticizers from the toy and bottle industries, pharmaceuticals that pass unused through humans, chemicals from bottom paint on ships, and hormones from birth control pills excreted in sewage.

In late March both whales reached Cape Cod Bay, and Limpet started feeding, straining mouthfuls of copepods from just under the surface of the water, frequently within sight of land. Arpeggio began to learn how to mimic her mother, opening her mouth and trying to find food herself. Although she would not be weaned for another six or seven months, she was beginning to learn the skills she would need to survive on her own. But feeding brings another set of challenges, and the urban ocean does not end at Cape Cod Bay.

In the following months both right whales would ingest small bits of plastic, including a piece of tape, a remnant of monofilament fishing line, a rubber band, and a shredded piece of plastic bag. While feeding, both right whales would also be exposed to marine biotoxins from a red tide outbreak in the Bay of Fundy, protozoa from unknown sources, and pesticide residues from forestry spraying runoff in Maine and New Brunswick. Arpeggio would learn about courtship, that most important feature of a right whale's life, and about the sounds that other right whales make and what those sounds mean. Sometimes ship noise would make it difficult to hear other whales, but these masking events were temporary. Arpeggio got herself briefly entangled in some fishing gear, which is much more densely packed in the Gulf of Maine than anywhere else, but she escaped without serious harm. She encountered whale watching boats, research boats, oil tankers, and ferries.

Aside from the risks of catastrophic death from an encounter with a ship or a piece of rope, what does it mean for a right whale to live in an urbanized ocean?

The basic facts of this journey are not in doubt—a large body of scientific literature and government reports demonstrates that this is the nature of the coastal waters off the east coast of North America. Humans have collectively created an urban ocean zone into which the byproducts of our civilization have been imported. It has all the smells, tastes, and sounds of a busy city street, and for the naïve animal or person traveling in such a place, it poses some risks as well (Chapter 17). This book is about those risks, about whether right whales can adapt to an urban ocean, and about whether changing the ways in which humans live near and on the ocean can minimize conflicts with wildlife. The exploration of these questions has lessons to teach us about our impacts on the marine world. Perhaps, by learning these lessons, humans can help both right whales and themselves.

Allen, J. A. 1908. The North Atlantic right whale and its near allies. *Bulletin of the American Museum of Natural History* 24:227–329.

Andrews, R. C. 1908. Notes upon the external and internal anatomy of *Balaena glacialis*. *Bulletin of the American Museum of Natural History* 24:171–182.

Anonymous. 2000. Canadian Right Whale Recovery Plan. A Canadian Recovery Plan for the North Atlantic Right Whale. World Wildlife Fund Toronto, Ontario, and Department of Fisheries and Oceans, Dartmouth, Nova Scotia, Canada.

Baumgartner, M. F., and B. R. Mate. 2005. Summer and fall habitat of North Atlantic right whales (*Eubalaena glacialis*) inferred from satellite telemetry. *Canadian Journal of Fisheries and Aquatic Sciences* 62:527–543.

Best, P. B. 1994. Seasonality of reproduction and length of gestation in southern right whales, *Eubalaena australis*. *Journal of Zoology (London)* 232:175–189.

Brown, M. W., S. D. Kraus, and D. E. Gaskin. 1991. Skin biopsy sampling of right whales (*Eubalaena glacialis*) for genetic and pesticide analysis. *Report of the International Whaling Commission* 13:81–89.

Brown, M. W., S. D. Kraus, D. E. Gaskin, and B. N. White. 1994. Sexual composition and analysis of reproductive females in the North Atlantic right whale, *Eubalaena glacialis*, population. *Marine Mammal Science* 10:253–265.

Brown, M. W., S. Brault, P. K. Hamilton, R. D. Kenney, A. R. Knowlton, M. K. Marx, C. A. Mayo, C. K. Clay, and S. D. Kraus. 2001. Sighting heterogeneity of right whales in the western North Atlantic, 1980–1992. *Journal of Cetacean Research and Management* Special Issue 2:245–250.

Caswell, H., M. Fujiwara, and S. Brault. 1999. Declining survival probability threatens the North Atlantic right whale. *Proceedings of the National Academy of Sciences* 96:3308–3313.

CeTAP. 1982. A characterization of marine mammals and turtles in the mid- and North Atlantic areas of the U.S. outer continental shelf. Report to the U.S. Bureau of Land Management, Washington, DC, contract no. AA551-CT8-48. 586 pp.

Clapham, P. J., S. B. Young, and R. L. Brownell, Jr. 1999. Baleen whales: conservation issues and the status of the most endangered populations. *Mammal Review* 29:35–60.

Crone, M. J., and S. D. Kraus. 1990. *Right Whales (Eubalaena glacialis) in the Western North Atlantic: A Catalog of Identified Individuals.* New England Aquarium, Boston.

DeGuise, S. D., D. Martineau, P. Béland, and M. Fournier. 1995. Possible mechanisms of action of environmental contaminants on St. Lawrence beluga whales (*Delphinapterus leucas*). *Environmental Health Perspectives* 103:73–77.

DeSwart, R. L., P. S. Ross, L. J. Vedder, H. H. Timmerman, S. H. Heisterkamp, H. Van Loveren, J. G. Vos, P. J. H. Reijnders, and A. D. M. E. Osterhaus. 1994. Impairment of immune function in harbour seals (*Phoca vitulina*) feeding on fish from polluted waters. *Ambio* 23:155–159.

Fujiwara, M., and H. Caswell. 2001. Demography of the endangered North Atlantic right whale. *Nature* 414:537–541.

George, J. C., J. Bada, J. Zeh, L. Scott, S. E. Brown, T. O'Hara, and R. Suydam. 1999. Age and growth estimates of bowhead whales (*Balaena mysticetus*) using aspartic acid racemization. *Canadian Journal of Zoology* 77:571–580.

Geraci, J. R. 1989. Clinical investigation of the 1987–88 mass mortality of bottlenose dolphins along the U.S. central and South Atlantic coast. Final Report to the National Marine Fisheries Service, U.S. Navy (Office of Naval Research), and Marine Mammal Commission. 63 pp.

Hall, A. J., R. J. Law, D. E. Wells, J. Harwood, H. M. K. S. Ross, C. R. Allchin, L. A. Campbell, and P. P. Pomeroy. 1992. Organochlorine levels in common seals (*Phoca vitulina*) which were victims and survivors of the 1988 phocine distemper epizootic. *Science of the Total Environment* 115:145–162.

Hamilton, P. K., and S. M. Martin. 1999. *A Catalog of Identified Right Whales from the North Atlantic: 1935–1997.* New England Aquarium, Boston.

Hamilton, P. K., A. R. Knowlton, M. K. Marx, and S. D. Kraus. 1998. Age structure and longevity in North Atlantic right whales (*Eubalaena glacialis*) and their relation to reproduction. *Marine Ecology Progress Series* 171:285–292.

IWC. 2001a. Report on the workshop on the comprehensive assessment of right whales. Pages 1–60 *in* P. B. Best, J. L. Bannister, R. L. Brownell, and G. P. Donovan, eds. *Right Whales: Worldwide Status.* International Whaling Commission, Cambridge, UK.

IWC. 2001b. Report on the workshop on status and trends of western North Atlantic right whales. Pages 61–87 *in* P. B. Best, J. L. Bannister, R. L. Brownell, and G. P. Donovan, eds. *Right Whales: Worldwide Status.* International Whaling Commission, Cambridge, UK.

Jacobsen, K.-O., M. Marx, and N. Øien. 2004. Two-way trans-Atlantic migration of a North Atlantic right whale (*Eubalaena glacialis*). *Marine Mammal Science* 20:161–166.

Kenney, R. D. 2001. Anomalous 1992 spring and summer right whale (*Eubalaena glacialis*) distribution in the Gulf of Maine. *Journal of Cetacean Research and Management* Special Issue 2:209–223.

Kenney, R. D., and S. D. Kraus. 1993. Right whale mortality—a correction and an update. *Marine Mammal Science* 9:445–446.

Kenney, R. D., C. A. Mayo, and H. E. Winn. 2001. Migration and foraging strategies at varying spatial scales in western North Atlantic right whales. *Journal of Cetacean Research and Management* Special Issue 2:251–260.

Knowlton, A. R., and S. D. Kraus. 2001. Mortality and serious injury of northern right whales (*Eubalaena glacialis*) in the western North Atlantic Ocean. *Journal of Cetacean Research and Management* Special Issue 2:193–208.

Knowlton, A. R., J. Sigurjónsson, J. N. Ciano, and S. D. Kraus. 1992. Long-distance movements of North Atlantic right whales (*Eubalaena glacialis*). *Marine Mammal Science* 8:397–405.

Knowlton, A. R., S. D. Kraus, and R. D. Kenney. 1994. Reproduction in North Atlantic right whales (*Eubalaena glacialis*). *Canadian Journal of Zoology* 72:1297–1305.

Knowlton, A. R., M. K. Marx, H. M. Pettis, P. K. Hamilton, and S. D. Kraus. 2005. Analysis of scarring on North Atlantic right whales (*Eubalaena glacialis*): Monitoring rates of entanglement interaction: 1980–2002. Final Report to the National Marine Fisheries Service. 20 pp.

Kraus, S. D. 1990. Rates and potential causes of mortality in the North Atlantic right whale (*Eubalaena glacialis*). *Marine Mammal Science* 6:278–291.

Kraus, S. D. 2002. Birth, death, and taxis: North Atlantic right whales in the twenty-first century. PhD. Dissertation, University of New Hampshire, 162 pp.

Kraus, S. D., and J. J. Hatch. 2001. Mating strategies in the North Atlantic right whale (*Eubalaena glacialis*). *Journal of Cetacean Research and Management* Special Issue 2:237–244.

Kraus, S. D., K. E. Moore, C. E. Price, M. J. Crone, W. A. Watkins, H. E. Winn, and J. H. Prescott. 1986. The use of photographs to identify individual North Atlantic right whales (*Eubalaena glacialis*). Pages 145–151 *in* R. L. Brownell, Jr., P. B. Best, and J. H. Prescott, eds. *Right Whales: Past and Present Status.* International Whaling Commission, Cambridge, UK.

Kraus, S. D., M. W. Brown, H. Caswell, C. W. Clark, M. Fujiwara, P. K. Hamilton, R. D. Kenney, A. R. Knowlton, S. Landry, C. A. Mayo, W. A. McLellan, M. J. Moore, D. P. Nowacek, D. A. Pabst, A. J. Read, and R. M. Rolland. 2005. North Atlantic right whales in crisis. *Science* 309:561–562.

Malik, S., M. W. Brown, S. D. Kraus, A. R. Knowlton, P. K. Hamilton, and B. N. White. 1999. Assessment of mitochondrial DNA structuring and nursery use in the North Atlantic right whale (*Eubalaena glacialis*). *Canadian Journal of Zoology* 77:1–6.

Mate, B. R., S. L. Nieukirk, and S. D. Kraus. 1997. Satellite-monitored movements of the northern right whale. *Journal of Wildlife Management* 61:1393–1405.

Moore, M. J., C. A. Miller, M. S. Morss, R. Arthur, W. A. Lange, K. G. Prada, M. K. Marx, and E. A. Frey. 2001. Ultrasonic measurement of blubber thickness in right whales. *Journal of Cetacean Research and Management* Special Issue 2:301–309.

NMFS. 2005. Recovery Plan for the North Atlantic Right Whale (*Eubalaena glacialis*). National Marine Fisheries Service, Silver Spring, MD.

Nowacek, D. P., M. P. Johnson, P. L. Tyack, K. A. Shorter, W. A. McLellan, and D. A. Pabst. 2001. Buoyant balaenids: the ups and downs of buoyancy in right whales. *Proceedings of the Royal Academy of Sciences Part B* 268:1811–1816.

Nowacek, D. P., M. P. Johnson, and P. L. Tyack. 2004. North Atlantic right whales (*Eubalaena glacialis*) ignore ships but respond to alerting stimuli. *Proceedings of the Royal Society of London Part B* 271:227–231.

Payne, R., O. Brazier, E. M. Dorsey, J. S. Perkins, V. J. Rowntree, and A. Titus. 1983. External features in southern right whales (*Eubalaena australis*) and their use in identifying individuals. Pages 371–445 *in* R. Payne, ed. *Communication and Behavior of Whales.* Westview Press, Boulder, CO.

Pettis, H., R. M. Rolland, P. K. Hamilton, S. Brault, A. R. Knowlton, and S. D. Kraus. 2004. Visual health assessment of North Atlantic right whales (*Eubalaena glacialis*) using photographs. *Canadian Journal of Zoology* 82:8–19.

Rastogi, T., M. W. Brown, B. A. McLeod, T. R. Frasier, R. Grenier, S. L. Cumbaa, J. Nadarajah, and B. N. White. 2004. Genetic analysis of sixteenth-century whale bones prompts a revision of the impact of Basque whaling on right and bowhead whales in the western North Atlantic. *Canadian Journal of Zoology* 82:1647–1654.

Reeves, R. R. 2001. Overview of catch history, historic abundance and distribution of right whales in the western North Atlantic and in Cintra Bay, West Africa. *Journal of Cetacean Research and Management* Special Issue 2:187–192.

Reeves, R. R., J. G. Mead, and S. K. Katona. 1978. The right whale, *Eubalaena glacialis*, in the western North Atlantic. *Report of the International Whaling Commission* 28:303–312.

Reeves, R. R., R. M. Rolland, and P. J. Clapham (eds.). 2001. Causes of reproductive failure in North Atlantic right whales: new avenues of research. Report of a Workshop held 26–28 April 2000, Falmouth, Massachusetts. Northeast Fisheries Science Center Reference Document 01-16, Woods Hole, MA. 46 pp.

Reijnders, P. J. H. 1986. Reproductive failure in common seals feeding on fish from polluted coastal waters. *Nature* 324:456–457.

Rice, D. 1998. *Marine Mammals of the World: Systematics and Distribution.* Special Publication Number 4, Society for Marine Mammalogy, Lawrence, KS.

Richardson, W. J., C. R. Greene, C. I. Malme, and D. H. Thomson (eds.). 1995. *Marine Mammals and Noise.* Academic Press, San Diego, CA.

Rolland, R. M., K. E. Hunt, S. D. Kraus, and S. K. Wasser. 2005. Assessing reproduction in North Atlantic right whales using fecal hormone metabolites. *General and Comparative Endocrinology* 142:308–317.

Rosenbaum, H. C., R. L. Brownell, M. W. Brown, C. Schaeff, V. Portway, B. N. White, S. Malik, L. A. Pastene, N. J. Patenaude, C. S. Baker, M. Goto, P. B. Best, P. J. Clapham, P. Hamilton, M. Moore, R. Payne, V. Rowntree, C. T. Tynan, J. L. Bannister, and R. DeSalle. 2000a. World-wide genetic differentiation of Eubalaena: questioning the number of right whale species. *Molecular Ecology* 9:1793–1802.

Rosenbaum, H. C., M. G. Egan, P. J. Clapham, R. L. Brownell Jr., S. Malik, M. W. Brown, B. N. White, P. Walsh, and R. Desalle. 2000b. Utility of North Atlantic right whale museum specimens for assessing changes in genetic diversity. *Conservation Biology* 14:1837–1842.

Ross, P. S. 2000. Marine mammals as sentinels in ecological risk assessment. *Human and Ecological Risk Assessment* 6:29–46.

Ross, P. S., R. L. De Swart, P. J. H. Reijnders, H. V. Loveren, J. G. Vos, and A. D. M. E. Osterhaus. 1995. Contaminant related suppression of delayed-type hypersensitivity and antibody responses in harbour seals fed herring from the Baltic Sea. *Environmental Health Perspectives* 103:162–167.

Rowntree, V. J., R. S. Payne, and D. M. Schell. 2001. Changing patterns of habitat use by southern right whales (*Eubalanea australis*) on their nursery ground at Peninsula Valdés, Argentina, and in their long-range movements. *Journal of Cetacean Research and Management* Special Issue 2:133–143.

Schaeff, C. M., S. D. Kraus, M. W. Brown, and B. N. White. 1993. Assessment of the population structure of western North Atlantic right whales (*Eubalaena glacialis*) based on sighting and mtDNA data. *Canadian Journal of Zoology* 71:339–345.

Slay, C. S., and S. D. Kraus. 1999. Right whale tagging in the North Atlantic. *Marine Technology Society Journal* 32:102–103.

Tormosov, D. D., Y. A. Mikhalev, P. B. Best, V. A. Zemsky, K. Seguchi, and R. L. Brownell, Jr. 1998. Soviet catches of southern right whales, *Eubalaena australis,* 1951–1971. Biological data and conservation implications. *Biological Conservation* 86:185–197.

Waldick, R. C., S. D. Kraus, M. W. Brown, and B. N. White. 2002. Evaluating the effects of historic bottleneck events: an assessment of microsatellite variability in the endangered, North Atlantic right whale. *Molecular Ecology* 11:2241–2249.

2

Near-Annihilation of a Species:
Right Whaling in the North Atlantic

RANDALL R. REEVES, TIM D. SMITH,
AND ELIZABETH A. JOSEPHSON

On 17 April 1877, the Daniel Webster, *a sailing bark, left New Bedford on a three-and-a-half-year whaling voyage. The first lowering of the boats for whales was on the Cape Farewell Ground, as described in the following logbook entry for Sunday 17 June 1877:*

At 9 a.m. saw Right Whale cow & calf—lowered three boats . . . Larb. boat struck the calf & Waist boat struck and killed the cow but lost her by the line parting and she went off to windward spouting up blood. After much trouble killed the calf and took him alongside. . . . As the cow & calf kept together, the calf by first one side of the cow and then the other and then on top of her the lines got in an awful fix, and bothered the officers much in working on the whales. We chased the cow off with ship and boats but could not get up with her. . . . In the p.m. cut the calf in (judging he will make 20 bbls) then made sail and stood up in the direction the cow had taken in hopes of falling in with her either alive or dead. The cow was a large 100 bbl whale. At sunset overcast, nothing in sight. Lat 59°42′[N], Long 33°30′[W].

The next spring, after a year spent hunting sperm whales in the North Atlantic and southern right whales in the South Atlantic off Patagonia, the

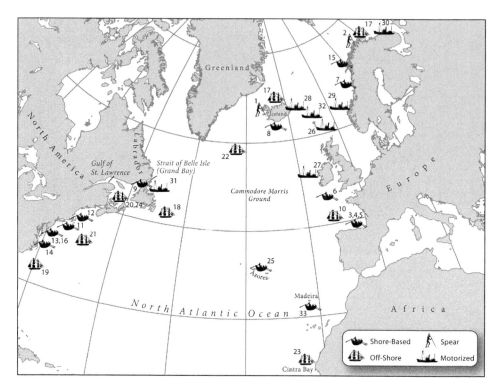

Figure 2.1. General locations of the whale fisheries and subfisheries that took right whales in the North Atlantic, showing the nature of their technologies and techniques. The numbers associated with each icon refer to the subfisheries identified in Table 2.1. Kerry Lagueux / New England Aquarium.

Webster *returned north for more sperm whaling on the Commodore Morris Ground (see Fig. 2.1 for location). There, on Wednesday 8 May 1878, another encounter with right whales was recorded in the logbook:*

> At 10 a.m. raised Right Whales—3 . . . lowered three boats and soon Larb. Boat, Mr. Pope struck and then Mr. Williams and Mr. Wyman struck. All the whales kept together and gave us much trouble as the weather was very rough for boats. Mr. Wymans Iron drew, and after a great deal of hard fighting Mr. Williams line parted, Mr. Popes whale ran to the windward and Mr. Pope went off all alone as none of the boats could make any progress pulling to the windward, but he killed his whale and made an attempt to tow but was obliged to abandon his whale as the ship was nearly out of sight to the leeward. He arrived only about 5 p.m. Ship worked up until night in search of the whale, call

her (a cow the others being, Bulls) 100 bbls. At night took in sails with the view of making short tacks through the night. Larb. & Waist Boats got quite badly stove. Lat. 49°23′N Long. 23°17′W.
    Logbook of the *Daniel Webster*

The Webster *returned to New Bedford on 23 October 1880 carrying a cargo of 1,150 barrels of sperm oil, 550 barrels of whale oil, and 1,088 kg of "bone" (baleen).*

The efforts by the crew of the *Daniel Webster,* described in this logbook extract, were but two skirmishes in a global assault on right whales that probably began in the first millennium AD. Whaling started in the North Atlantic, targeting *Eubalaena glacialis,* then spread into the South Atlantic and Indo-South Pacific, targeting *E. australis,* and finally (by the 1830s) into the North Pacific, targeting *E. japonica* (which had already been hunted for centuries by Asian shore-based whalers). In retrospect, it was one of the most extensive, prolonged, and thorough campaigns of wildlife exploitation in all of human history. In the North Atlantic, the focus of this chapter, the assault proceeded on several fronts for more than a thousand years. Basque whalers conducted whaling campaigns principally in three "theaters" (Aguilar 1986): the Bay of Biscay, the northeastern North Atlantic, and the Strait of Belle Isle between Newfoundland and Labrador (although recent findings suggest that few right whales were taken in the last of these theaters). Vessels from Great Britain, the Netherlands, France, Denmark, and the German seaports eventually joined the attack in the northeastern North Atlantic, and the British opened another theater along the shores of their American colonies. Initially shore-based, the British colonial operations in America had evolved by the middle of the eighteenth century into a broad-scale offshore campaign. As the American offshore whaling industry expanded, new theaters of attack on right whales opened in remote portions of the North Atlantic, the final redoubts of *E. glacialis.* These included a calving area off northwestern Africa (Cintra Bay) and an offshore area south and east of the southern tip of Greenland (Cape Farewell Ground).

Thus the campaign against North Atlantic right whales continued through the nineteenth and early twentieth centuries, drawing to a close only after the declining economic value of its spoils (oil and baleen) and the scarcity of its targets (right whales) had conspired to make further operations no longer worthwhile. Although it is impossible to describe the earlier phases in any detail, data for "mopping-up" operations from about 1850 onward are fairly clear

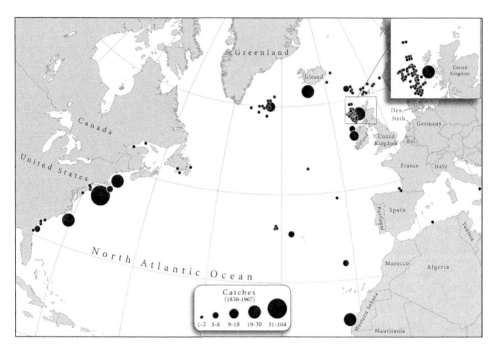

Figure 2.2. Locations of right whales taken or struck and lost in the "mopping up" operation between 1850 and 1967. Specific positions are shown when these were noted, and groups of whales are shown when specific positions were not noted. Kerry Lagueux / New England Aquarium.

(Fig. 2.2). The small remaining alongshore pockets of whales on both sides of the North Atlantic were wiped out by open-boat whalers, and it was left to modern catcher boats operating from shore stations to pick off most of the stragglers that had somehow survived into the twentieth century.

Although it may never be possible to know how many right whales remained when the mopping-up ended and right whales gained legal protection, there must have been very few, possibly only tens (Kenney et al. 1995; Schaeff et al. 1997; Reeves 2001). Given the scale, intensity, and duration of the hunting, it is indeed remarkable that right whales have survived at all in the North Atlantic.

Lessons from History Thus Far

Previous studies have reviewed the history of right whaling in different regions of the North Atlantic using a variety of archival and published sources. Early

Basque whaling was reviewed by Aguilar (1986), and modern whaling in the eastern North Atlantic summarized by Brown (1986). Whaling on right whales in the western North Atlantic from the mid-seventeenth century to the early 1900s was reviewed by Reeves (2001). Historical studies have helped direct survey efforts for right whales in the calving grounds off the southeastern United States, in Cintra Bay, and on the summer Cape Farewell Ground, and historical data have provided the impetus for ongoing archaeological and biological work on Basque whaling in Labrador. Although historical research has provided a general perspective on past right whale distribution, population (or "stock") structure, and numbers, understanding of just how abundant these animals were when whaling began in the North Atlantic has remained vague.

Mitchell (1973) dismissed as greatly exaggerated the "quasitechnical" tabulation of Mowat (1972), who inferred an initial global population of 200,000 right whales. Mitchell himself, without providing details, calculated that a combined total of no more than 300,000 right whales and bowhead whales had been taken globally since the inception of whaling and suggested that the initial (preexploitation) global population of right whales was probably less than 100,000. Importantly, Mitchell (1973, 18) noted that "significant production of whales occurred over this entire period of exploitation, and young as well as adults produced during this time were taken in the catch." In other words, he sensibly assumed that right whale populations had been able to compensate for some of the removals from their ranks by a density-dependent response to reduced abundance.

The U.S. Department of Commerce's now-obsolete recovery plan for right whales (NMFS 1991, 9) acknowledged that "no accurate information on preexploitation numbers exists" but nevertheless asserted that the western North Atlantic population originally had numbered at least 10,000. That assertion was roughly consistent with Gaskin's (1991) crude estimate of 12,000–15,000 right whales in eastern Canadian waters, which assumed that about half the whales killed in these waters by Basques over a 70-year period (1530–1600) were right whales. The figure of 10,000 has continued to be used as a baseline for discussions of carrying capacity and extent of recovery (e.g., Kenney et al. 2001), although several studies have suggested a much smaller preexploitation population size. Reeves et al. (1992) reasoned that there must have been at least 1,000–2,000 right whales present in the mid-1600s to produce the documented oil and baleen exports from the American colonies. Reeves et al. (1999) concluded, using similar logic, that right whales were at least several times more abundant in the western North Atlantic in the mid- to late seventeenth century than they are today. The Canadian recovery plan (Anonymous 2000) referred to 1,200 right whales as an interim recovery goal, noting, based on the analyses by Reeves et al. (1992, 1999), that the population was "considerably larger" in the past than it is today.

Recently Rastogi et al. (2004) used DNA from whale bones collected along the Labrador coast to transform our understanding of the large-scale Basque whale fishery in the Strait of Belle Isle. Contrary to earlier studies (e.g., Tuck and Grenier 1981; Cumbaa 1986), they concluded that the vast majority of the whales taken by Basques in that area during the sixteenth and early seventeenth centuries were bowheads, not right whales, and that North Atlantic right whales had already gone through a population "bottleneck" by the time Basque whaling began in the New World (Chapter 7). Their results raised questions about the magnitude of earlier catches and about historical levels of abundance.

Inferring Population History from Written Sources

This chapter provides an enhanced scientific account of right whale population history. Written sources were used to develop a right whale catch (removal) series that incorporated available records and also included interpolations and extrapolations to estimate whaling removals encompassing areas and periods for which catch records were lacking. It was expected that such a catch series would provide the basis for back-calculations similar to those attempted for western Arctic bowhead whales (Breiwick et al. 1984), eastern North Pacific gray whales (IWC 1993), southern right whales (IWC 2001), and North Atlantic humpback whales (IWC 2002, 2003). To develop the catch series, all whale "fisheries" and "subfisheries" that included right whales as either principal or supplemental target species, or in which right whales were taken opportunistically, were identified.

Fisheries and Subfisheries

Twelve fisheries for large whales were defined that definitely or probably took right whales, and regional subfisheries were defined for several of these (Table 2.1). These fisheries extended around the rim of the North Atlantic (Fig. 2.1). Cultural, economic, technological, and historical similarities link the subfisheries within a fishery to varying degrees. The fisheries and subfisheries are summarized in roughly chronological order.

Nordic Shore Spear-Drift

Spear-drift whaling was practiced in the northeastern Atlantic as early as the twelfth century and lasted in relict form in Iceland until the late nineteenth century (Lindquist 1993). Although the literature includes frequent reference to Norse whaling as early as the late ninth century (e.g., the story of Ohthere, as told to King Alfred of England), the evidence for such an early beginning is equivocal according to Lindquist (1993).

The basic method involved a hunter in an open boat closely approaching a whale and throwing a barbed spear to pierce and wound the animal, with the expectation that it would beach with the marked spearhead lodged in its carcass. The hunter who owned the spear could then claim the "shooter's share." This drift or salvage technique, which presumably involved very high hunting loss, was distinct from "Basque-type" harpoon-line-drogue or tow whaling.

A description of the fishery has emerged from Lindquist's (1993) study of sagas and ancient legal documents. Lindquist provided convincing evidence that rorquals (the groove-throated baleen whales with dorsal fins), including the largest species (blue whales and fin whales), were desirable targets and were among those killed. He also inferred (Lindquist 2000) that Icelandic peasant fishermen took gray whales by spearing and lancing in shallow waters and on sandbars. Although none of the evidence unequivocally identifies right whales as targets, most analyses of this early, relatively primitive whaling reasonably assume that right whales were taken as well (e.g., Guldberg 1884). Two subfisheries are proposed here, one in Norway and one in Iceland.

Basque Local Shore

Basque local shore whaling involved shore-based spotting of whales, pursuit in open boats, and hand harpooning. Cow–calf pairs were selectively targeted. The existence of regulations on whale products from the market of Bayonne in the year 1059 indicates that whaling was already a well-established activity in the area. Right whale catches are recorded from that date up to 1893, although with substantial variation in their frequency per year (Aguilar 1986).

Three subfisheries are defined here, following Aguilar (1986). The French Basque Country subfishery peaked in the thirteenth century and declined after the mid-sixteenth century, with some right whales killed as late as 1688 (Du Pasquier 1986). The Spanish Basque Country subfishery peaked in the second half of the sixteenth century and was in decline by the end of that century

Table 2.1. Fisheries and Subfisheries Known or Suspected to Have Taken Right Whales

Fishery/subfishery[a]	Known period of operation	Technology/methods	Relative species importance	Comments
1. Nordic shore spear-drift/ Iceland	1100s or earlier to late 1800s	Spear thrown to pierce and wound whale with expectation it would beach	Rorqual (e.g., blue and fin whale) calves supposedly preferred	Very high loss rate (i.e., failure to recover struck whales)
2. Nordic shore spear-drift/ Norway	1100s or earlier to perhaps 1700s	Spear thrown to pierce and wound whale with expectation it would beach	Rorqual (e.g., blue and fin whale) calves supposedly preferred	Very high loss rate
3. Basque local shore/ French Basque country	1050s or earlier to ca. 1688; peak in thirteenth century	Shore-based spotting, open boats, hand harpoons	Right whale predominant	Possibly declined after mid-sixteenth century
4. Basque local shore/ Spanish Basque country	Peak in 1550–1600, declining by late sixteenth century	Shore-based spotting, open boats, hand harpoons	Right whale predominant	Only 4 right whales taken in nineteenth century
5. Basque local shore/ Spanish Biscayan coast	Expanding in early seventeenth century; declining by late seventeenth century; finished by 1720s	Shore-based spotting, open boats, hand harpoons	Right whale predominant	Includes Santander, Asturias, and Galicia coasts
6. Basque distant shore/ S Ireland and English Channel	1300s or earlier, to 1500s	Open boats supported by galleons (some with onboard tryworks?), hand harpoons	Right whale (and gray whale?) predominant	
7. Basque distant shore/ Norway	Late 1500s to 1600s	Open boats supported by galleons (some with onboard tryworks?), hand harpoons	Right whale (Nördkaper) predominant	

Fishery/region	Dates	Methods	Species	Notes
8. Basque distant shore/ Iceland	1604–ca. 1750	Open boats supported by galleons (some with onboard tryworks?), hand harpoons	Right whale predominant	In 1670s right whales were hunted on return voyages from the Arctic (Greenland) when ships had failed to fill up from bowheads
9. Basque distant shore/ Newfoundland	Late 1530s to 1632 (some French effort continued to mid-1700s)	Open boats (shallops) launched from shore stations, supported by galleons; hand harpoons	Bowhead whale predominant, right whale supplemental (?)	Includes Gulf of St. Lawrence, Strait of Belle Isle, and Labrador
10. Basque offshore	Early 1600s to mid-1700s	Open boats launched from mother ships (small galleons or caravels), hand harpoons	Right whale predominant (although bowhead important in high latitudes)	Bay of Biscay, Iceland
11. American (British Colonial) shore/ New York	1650–1924, peak ca. 1690–1730	Open boats, hand harpoons	Right whale predominant	Centered on south shore of Long Island
12. American (British Colonial) shore/ New England	1630s to early 1900s, peak ca. 1690–1730	Open boats, hand harpoons	Right whale predominant	Connecticut (1690s–1840s), Rhode Island (1680–1830), Nantucket (1680s–1880s), Cape Cod (1630s–1910)
13. American (British Colonial) shore/New Jersey and Delaware Bay	1660s or earlier to mid- or late 1800s, peak 1675–1725	Open boats, hand harpoons	Right whale predominant (also gray whales in early times?)	Includes Pennsylvania
14. American (British Colonial) shore/ Carolinas	1660s to early 1900s	Open boats, hand harpoons	Right whale predominant	Includes Maryland, Virginia, Outer Banks, and Southeast U.S. Coast Ground

(continued)

Table 2.1. (continued)

Fishery/subfishery[a]	Known period of operation	Technology/methods	Relative species importance	Comments
15. European distant shore/ Old World	1500s	Open boats, hand harpoons	Right whale involved, probably important	Finnmark
16. European (Dutch) distant shore/New World	1630s–1660s	Open boats, hand harpoons	Right whale (or gray whale?) predominant	Delaware Bay, New Jersey, New York
17. Northern European offshore	1600s	Open boats launched from mother ships, hand harpoons	Bowhead whale, right whale (Nördkaper) both important	Northern Norway, Iceland
18. American offshore/ east of Grand Banks	1730s to at least 1760s	Open boats launched from mother ships, hand harpoons	Right and sperm whales	
19. American offshore/ Carolinas	Began 1660; episodes of intensity in 1720s–1750s, 1870s–1880s	Open boats launched from mother ships, hand harpoons	Right whale	Fewer than 20 vessel-seasons, 1875–1880s; southeast U.S. Coast Ground
20. American offshore/ Gulf of St. Lawrence	1730s–1770s	Open boats launched from mother ships, hand harpoons	Balaenids, probably both species	Including Strait of Canso, Strait of Belle Isle, and coast of Labrador
21. American offshore/ coast of Long Island	1760s–1780s, 1820s, 1850s–1890s	Open boats launched from mother ships, hand harpoons	Right whale probably predominant, with sperm and humpback also taken	
22. American offshore/Cape Farewell ("Greenland")	Possibly 1730s–1750s, 1850s–1890s	Open boats launched from mother ships, hand harpoons	Right whale	At least 22 vessel-seasons, 1865–1897
23. American offshore/ Cintra Bay	1855–1866, 1880s	Open boats launched from mother ships, hand harpoons	Right whale	At least 38 vessel-seasons, 1855–1858

#	Fishery	Years	Method	Species	Notes
24.	Canadian (Gaspé) offshore	1804–1893	Open boats launched from schooners, hand harpoons (bomb lances in later years)	Humpback whale and other balaenopterids predominant, right whale supplemental	Gulf of St. Lawrence, Strait of Belle Isle, Labrador
25.	Azores shore	1832–1982	Open boats, hand harpoons	Sperm whale	7 right whales, 1873–1888
26.	Modern shore/British Isles	1903–1914, 1920–1929, 1950–1951	Powered catcher boats, explosive harpoons	Balaenopterids predominant, right whale supplemental	Ca. 100 right whales, 1906–1923
27.	Modern shore/Ireland	1908–1922 (sporadically)	Powered catcher boats, explosive harpoons	Balaenopterids predominant, right whale supplemental	18 right whales, 1908–1910
28.	Modern shore/Iceland	1883–1915, 1935–1939, 1948–1982	Powered catcher boats, explosive harpoons	Balaenopterids predominant, right whale supplemental	More than 13,000 unspecified whales taken 1884–1912, at least 27 right whales
29.	Modern shore/west Norway	1912–1969 (except war years)	Powered catcher boats, explosive harpoons	Balaenopterids predominant, right whale opportunistic	1 right whale, 1926
30.	Modern shore/north Norway	1864–1904, 1918–1920, 1948–1971	Powered catcher boats, explosive harpoons	Balaenopterids predominant, right whale opportunistic (if at all)	More than 5,500 unspecified whales taken 1874–1895
31.	Modern shore/eastern Canada	1898–1971 (except a few years)	Powered catcher boats, explosive harpoons	Balaenopterids predominant, right whale opportunistic	Includes Newfoundland, Nova Scotia, Gulf of St. Lawrence; more than 1,500 unspecified whales taken 1898–1918; 2 right whales, 1937 and 1951
32.	Modern shore/Faeroes	1894–1981 (except war years)	Powered catcher boats, explosive harpoons	Balaenopterids predominant, right whale opportunistic	More than 5,800 unspecified whales taken 1894–1916; 7–9 right whales 1903–1924
33.	Madeira shore	1941–1981	Open boats, hand harpoons	Sperm whale	3 right whales, 1959, 1967

a. The numbers of the fisheries and subfisheries correspond to those on the map in Fig. 2.1.

(Aguilar 1986). The Spanish Biscayan Coast subfishery (Santander, Asturias, and Galicia) started in the thirteenth century, peaked in the early seventeenth century, was in decline by the late 1600s, and was finished by the 1720s.

Aguilar (1986) stressed the windfall value of a single right whale to an early Basque settlement. He believed that a catch of one whale every year or two in each port would have been sufficient to keep the fishery viable, and he cautiously suggested annual total catches of "some dozens" and perhaps close to a hundred, apparently referring to the peak years. A total of forty-seven different whaling ports have been identified, although these were not all active at the same time. Fragmentary data for the Spanish Basque Country subfishery (Zarauz, Lequeitio, and Guetaria from the sixteenth to eighteenth centuries) led Aguilar to conclude that a given port might have taken only one right whale every three years, but there were single-year catches as high as four to ten whales. This subfishery declined to relict status by 1800; only four whales are known to have been taken during the entire nineteenth century.

Basque Distant Shore

Basque distant shore whaling involved Basque technology and expertise applied in foreign settings to the north and west of Basque country (e.g., Norway, Iceland, and Labrador). The fishery was active from the fourteenth century to the middle of the eighteenth century. However, aspects of the technology and practices are uncertain, especially whether the Basques used onboard tryworks (furnaces for boiling blubber into oil). Some of the whaling classified here as Basque distant shore whaling may be more properly assigned to Basque offshore whaling.

Four subfisheries were defined, following Aguilar (1986). The best known is the subfishery centered in Newfoundland, Labrador, and the Strait of Belle Isle (all subsumed, for simplicity, under the term "Newfoundland subfishery"). The Newfoundland subfishery involved both Spanish and French Basques; it was in full-scale operation by the 1530s and had peaked by 1620 (possibly even before 1601). Barkham (1984) estimated that during its peak the station at Red Bay alone (on the north shore of the Strait of Belle Isle) sent 6,000–9,000 barrels of oil to Europe annually; an additional 8,000–9,000 barrels were sent from other harbors, including St. Modeste and Chateau Bay. This subfishery continued until 1697, with twelve galleons still involved as late as 1681. Some effort may have shifted farther west into the Gulf of St. Lawrence after 1697. As discussed later in this chapter, the Newfoundland subfishery may have targeted mainly bowhead whales, which would make it less relevant to the catch history of right whales than previously supposed.

The other subfisheries—Southern Ireland and English Channel, Norway, and Iceland (a Greenland subfishery might also be worthy of inclusion)—lack detailed information on catch, product, effort, and period of operation. To some extent, information from the Norway and Iceland subfisheries is ambiguous concerning the proportion of right whales that would have been included in any tally of kills. According to Aguilar (1986), Basque whalers were active off southern Ireland and in the English Channel from the fourteenth century to the sixteenth century, began whaling in Iceland in 1604, and were present in Norway in the late 1500s. Basque whaling for right whales in Ireland may have commenced as early as the mid-eleventh century (Lindquist 1993). Whaling by "peasant fishermen" off Finnmark during the 1660s and again in 1816–1818, as described by Lindquist (1993), involved right whales taken in the Basque manner and towed to shore. Similarly, right whales were taken by both Basques and Icelandic peasants off western and northwestern Iceland in the 1600s (Lindquist 1993).

Basque Offshore

Aguilar (1986) indicated that small galleons whaled offshore in the Bay of Biscay, and Basque vessels rendered blubber at sea in the northeastern Atlantic as early as the 1630s or 1640s. Martens (1675) referred to the dangers of fire associated with this practice and noted that only the "French-men" (Basques) were willing to take the risk. No attempt is made here to resolve the extent to which the Basques (and others) developed the technology of onboard tryworks that would prove crucial to the rapid growth and geographic expansion of the American offshore whale fishery (see below) starting in about 1760. It is assumed that the Basques did render ("try out") right whale blubber at sea to some extent, although this practice may have been more common in their Arctic fishery for bowheads.

In the absence of details, no subfisheries could be defined. Aguilar (1986) guessed that Basque offshore vessels were capable of killing and processing about seven right whales per voyage and that no more than thirty to forty Spanish vessels were involved in the fishery during the first half of the eighteenth century. As many as thirty-seven ships were active annually in the French component of the Basque Offshore fishery from 1613 to 1700, and about thirty-five per year from 1725 to 1730 (Du Pasquier 1986, 2000). Bowheads (known

Figure 2.3. *Harper's Young People's Weekly* cover illustration.

as *sardako baleak* or *Grand baie baleak*) and right whales (known as *sardes*) were the main targets. Although most voyages were bound to the waters between Spitsbergen and Greenland and therefore were chiefly in pursuit of bowheads, the whalers sometimes (perhaps often, according to Alex Aguilar, pers. comm., 1 August 2005) hunted right whales around Iceland on the return leg of their voyage. For example, in one expedition in 1682, no whales were taken in the northern grounds but eight right whales were secured off Iceland (Du Pasquier 1984). The term "Iceland" may have encompassed the Cape Farewell Ground between Iceland and Greenland—the site of a subfishery of the American offshore fishery.

American (British Colonial) Shore

Shore whaling along the east coast of what is now the United States began in the 1630s and peaked in most areas between the 1690s and about 1730, by which time right whales had become relatively rare in coastal waters. Although marked by spatial and temporal discontinuities, this fishery spanned almost three centuries, obviously becoming "noncolonial" after the American War of Independence, 1775–1783. The fishery extended regionally from the Gulf of Maine south to the Carolinas. Four subfisheries were defined (Table 2.1), primarily on the basis of geographic and market discontinuities but also, in part, because the principal data sources treat the regions separately.

Determining exactly when whaling began along various parts of the American coast is made difficult by the fact that court, church, and town records refer extensively to rules for, or conflicts over, the disposition of "drift" whales (Little and Andrews 1982). It is often a matter of interpretation as to whether active whaling, rather than natural stranding, was responsible for a carcass "drove or cast on shore" (Braginton-Smith and Oliver 2004, 78). The earliest of the subfisheries were those in New England and New York, which began by the mid-1600s and continued well into the twentieth century (Fig. 2.3). The New Jersey and Delaware Bay subfishery probably began somewhat later and ended earlier (Lipton 1975; Reeves et al. 1999). The Carolinas subfishery was established by the 1720s (possibly earlier in Virginia) and continued into the early 1900s (Simpson and Simpson 1988). Whaling on the Outer Banks involved boats launched from shore as well as boats launched from larger vessels that were part of the Carolina subfishery of the American offshore fishery. It is not always possible to determine whether a given record of whaling activity involved true shore whaling or instead "bay whaling," in which a schooner or other large vessel was anchored near shore and the whaleboats were deployed from there.

European Distant Shore

This fishery is not well documented. The two subfisheries defined here are geographically disjunct—one in the Old World involving various North Sea whaling nations (Finnmark, Norway, Svalbard) and one in the New World (Dutch settlements in New York, New Jersey, and Delaware Bay). Whenever they were encountered, right whales were almost certainly taken by this fishery, although Mead and Mitchell (1984) considered the gray whale (now extinct in the North Atlantic) an important target in the New World subfishery centered in Delaware Bay. Whaling in Finnmark was conducted by Basque, English, Dutch, Dano-Norwegian, French (mostly Basque), and German whalers (Klaus Barthelmess, pers. comm., 12 July 2005).

Northern European Offshore

This fishery was essentially an Arctic enterprise focused on hunting bowheads. Typically, the whalemen flensed whales alongside the ship, stowed the blubber, and took it home for rendering into oil. Although right whales (*Nördkapers*) were taken, the numbers were "so small that it is not worthwhile to deduct their estimated blubber and oil from the total figures" (De Jong 1983, 91). Thus De Jong's tables of data for Netherlands ship returns between 1661 and 1826 can be assumed to include occasional right whales, at least some of them taken off North Cape, Norway. De Jong's lists of German (mainly Hamburg, 1669–1801) and British (1772–1833) vessels probably also include at least occasional catches of right whales. Indeed, in 1667, for example, one Hamburg vessel (accompanied by Dutch, Flemish, and Lübeck vessels) left the Svalbard (Spitsbergen) bowhead whaling ground during midsummer for a brief period to hunt right whales off northern Norway, in what could be characterized as "bay whaling" centered in Lopphavet, the Loppa Sea (Barthelmess 2003). This North Cape right whaling may have begun before 1667 and continued for some time because in the early 1690s, a Rotterdam whaling vessel visited northern Norway after the Svalbard season and met several other Arctic whaleships there (K. Barthelmess, pers. comm., 12 July 2005).

American Offshore

This fishery initially involved sloops that ventured a short distance from the New England coast (Little 1988). These sloops (of which Nantucket had twenty-five by 1730) carried two whaleboats and stayed at sea for months. The sloops, and later larger and faster vessels (mostly brigs, schooners, and barks), progressively extended their range over much of the North Atlantic, exploiting right (and sperm, bowhead, and humpback) whales in particular areas (see color plate 2). This fishery was subdivided into six subfisheries, in part because of the existence of distinct "grounds" where whalemen expected to find right whales, and in part as an artifact of recordkeeping. None of the subfisheries lasted long. All exhibited a pattern of discovery, depletion by intensive whaling, and abandonment. Some of them were abandoned and then resumed for brief periods (e.g., the coast of the Carolinas was first exploited in the 1720s to 1760s and then again in the 1870s–1880s), whereas others seem to have undergone only a single pulse of activity (e.g., Cintra Bay in the 1850s to 1860s).

Reeves and Mitchell (1986b) described this fishery and compiled data on effort and kills from written sources, including voyage logbooks (also see Reeves et al. 2002a for additional data on the Cintra Bay subfishery; Reeves and Mitchell 1988 for the Southeast U.S. Coast subfishery; and Table 2.2, for the Cape Farewell subfishery). Some of the encounters with right whales recorded in nineteenth-century American whaling logbooks were incidental or opportunistic; that is, they occurred while whalers were searching primarily for sperm whales (e.g., note the May 1878 event described in the *Webster* logbook extract at the beginning of this chapter). Therefore, not all kills in the fishery fit within one of the six geographically defined subfisheries, and they have been tallied separately.

Little (1988) indicated that the Nantucket whalers had begun whaling near the Strait of Canso and off Newfoundland by the mid-1730s. Whaling near Canso, on the "Cape Breton banks," and around Sable Island (Crèvecoeur 1782) would have been in or near the present-day summer range of right whales. Starbuck (1878, 169) referred to a whale (presumably a right whale) taken in the Bay of Fundy and brought into Boston in August 1733. Another hint that right whales were hunted in the Bay of Fundy was given in a court deposition from 1797. A longtime resident referred to a Nantucket voyage "made up" in the Quoddy/Head Harbor region, including the capture locally of one 70-barrel whale (Reeves and Barto 1985). New England whalers hunted humpbacks, sperm whales, and balaenids around Newfoundland and east of the Grand Banks during the 1750s and 1760s (Reeves and Mitchell 1986b). Given the timing (July–August) and latitude (45°–49°N) of this whaling, the balaenids taken would most likely have been right whales rather than bowheads. A considerable number of Massachusetts vessels were engaged in "the St. Lawrence fishery" during the 1760s and early 1770s, presumably targeting balaenids (Starbuck 1878, 45, 172–173).

Table 2.2. Whaling for Right Whales on the Cape Farewell Ground (Previously Unpublished Data)

Vessel	Position N	Position W	Date	No. seen	No. struck	No. killed	Comments
Adeline Gibbs	59,50	33,33	27 July 1878	Some			"... raised right whales just at dusk"
Ansel Gibbs	59,58	35,02	5 June 1872	Some			Goin' quick
	59,54	33,47	10 June 1872			1	
	59,40	34,30	12 June 1872	Some			Too rough to lower, by 23–25 June they were sailing away to west for Hudson Bay
Astoria			26 June 1878				Reported in log of Adeline Gibbs
A. Houghton	59,10	30,25	21 June 1876			2	Cruised briefly; no sightings
Andrews	60,32	33,22	24 June 1867				Saw finback
	58,20	40,35	28 June 1867				
A. R. Tucker			29 June 1897				Saw "something Small turn flukes, thought it was a right whale calf."
			4 July 1897			1	"Small," 20 bbl; location not given but W of Azores
Mattapoisett			24 June 1878				Reported in log of Adeline Gibbs
Orray Taft			June 1866				Brief visit to CFG, saw whale feed but no whales

Pacific	59,39	39,33	25 June 1866	2	Too foggy to chase
			26 June 1866	2	Chased
			27 June 1866	1	One killed and sank
			28 June 1866	1	
	60,09	36,55	4 July 1866	1	One killed and sank
	60,37	34,05	9 July 1866	1	
Petrel	55,12	33,33	12 June 1891		Steering NNE
			16 June 1891	1	ID uncertain
	60,40	35,50	17 June 1891		
	59,55	35,25	23 June 1891	1	
	60,26	32,50	13 July 1891	1	
	61	33	21 July 1891	1	
	61,00	33,52	22 July 1891	1	Chased
	61	34	23 July 1891	3	Sank
			24 July 1891	2	
			25 July 1891	1	
Mermaid	60,45	34,37	29 July 1891		
	61,00	33,52	22 July 1891	1	Vicinity of Petrel (reported in Petrel log)

Reeves and Mitchell (1986b, Table 2) documented twelve vessel-seasons on the Cape Farewell Ground; supplemental work (see Table 2.2) now suggests that at least twenty-two seasonal visits to this ground were made by American whaleships between 1865 and 1897, accounting for at least twenty-four killed right whales. Altogether, at least 150 right whales were killed in the American offshore fishery between the 1850s and 1890s, the majority of them in the regional subfisheries centered at Cintra Bay, the Cape Farewell Ground, and along the southeastern U.S. coast.

Canadian (Gaspé) Offshore

The Gaspé schooner fishery in the Gulf of St. Lawrence began in the early 1800s and ended in the 1890s (Mitchell and Reeves 1983). Although the Gaspé fishery was primarily a humpback fishery by the mid-1800s, balaenids (some of them probably right whales) were taken at least opportunistically. Two were taken at St. Thomas, Quebec, in 1850 and another in the St. Lawrence estuary above Manicouagan in 1912 (Mitchell and Reeves 1983). Although the Gaspé whalers hunted throughout the Strait of Belle Isle and along the Atlantic coast of southern Labrador, there is no evidence to suggest that balaenids were their principal targets.

Azores Shore

The Azorean open-boat shore whaling industry, which targeted sperm whales, spanned 150 years, from 1832 to 1982. Seven right whales reportedly were taken between 1873 and 1888 (Clarke 1981), and another was struck and lost in 1914 (Brown 1986). Confusion and uncertainty exist concerning whether right whales regularly occurred (or occur) in far-offshore waters of the central North Atlantic. As reported by Reeves and Mitchell (1986b), two were seen from a whaleship in late May 1897 at about 46°30'N, 43°W. This sighting, together with sporadic catches in the Azores (mostly between January and April; Clarke 1981), demonstrates that right whales occur in midocean at least occasionally. However, as shown by Reeves et al. (2004), the midocean right whale ground mapped by Maury (1852, 1853) is likely apocryphal.

Modern Shore

Modern shore whaling began with the Norwegian invention of steam-powered catcher boats in combination with deck-mounted harpoon cannons. Beginning in the 1870s, shore stations proliferated along the rim of the North Atlantic, financed largely by Norwegian capital and manned by Norwegian

Figure 2.4. Skull of one of the last right whales taken in the North Atlantic, killed in 1967 by whalers at the Caniçal whaling station (active 1941–1981), part of the Madeira shore fishery. Dieter Kuesgen, ca. 1982, courtesy of the Barthelmess Whaling Collection, Cologne, Germany.

whalemen. Given this Norwegian involvement and the fact that common methods and equipment were used, a number of operations were combined into a single fishery, with seven subfisheries (Table 2.1). Together, these subfisheries accounted for 140–150 right whale kills between 1889 and 1951. Some additional right whales must have been taken by this fishery in the late 1870s and 1880s. As well, a few of the whales unspecified to species taken in Newfoundland, Iceland, the Faroes, and Finnmark from the late nineteenth century until about 1930 were probably right whales.

Madeira Shore

Madeiran shore whaling was an offshoot of Azorean whaling (Clarke 1954; Brown 1986) and was active only from 1941 to 1981. During this time, right whales were taken on only two occasions: one whale in 1959 (Brown 1986) and two in 1967 (Maul and Sergeant 1977; Fig. 2.4).

Other Fisheries in Which Right Whales Might Have Been Supplemental or Opportunistic Targets

The few kills of right whales inside the Mediterranean Sea (e.g., Allen 1908, 299; Turner 1913) do not appear to have been associated with specific fisheries. Also, discrete events—such as the killing of a right whale in the Thames estuary in 1658 (Faust et al. 2002), a mother and calf in Peterhead Bay, Scotland, about 1806 (Southwell 1884), and a 12-m individual off Orio, Spanish Basque country, in 1901 (dispatched with dynamite; Nores and Perez 1983)—are difficult to assign to a fishery because they appear to have been essentially opportunistic.

Some killing was accomplished with remarkably ad hoc methods on the U.S. coast during the open-boat whaling era. For example, a 12-m right whale that entered Charleston Harbor, South Carolina, in January 1880 was initially chased by a crew from a tugboat employed in a government jetty construction project. Later in the day, it was pursued by four steam tugs, fifty to sixty rowboats, and a few sailing vessels. After the whale had been harpooned from one of the tugs, "the expedient resorted to was for the tugs to ram the whale with their bows whenever the opportunity offered. The animal was thus worried for some time and also received several lance thrusts from the small boats. It bled considerably and was so much weakened by the various blows and wounds that after an exciting chase of several hours it finally succumbed to its tormentors" (Manigault 1885, 99).

There is no certain evidence that right whales were subjected to shore whaling in Bermudan waters. The Bermudan whale fishery, which involved hand-powered open boats and hand-thrown harpoons (essentially Basque or American style), began in the 1600s and lasted until the early twentieth century. Humpbacks were clearly the predominant targets, and sperm whales were taken occasionally (Mitchell and Reeves 1983). One nineteenth-century source mistakenly claimed that right whales were the mainstay of this fishery. Although right whales may have been available to the shore whalers at Bermuda from time to time (see True 1904, 27–30; Reeves 2001), taking a right whale almost certainly would have been an unusual event.

Was There Precolonial Aboriginal Whaling?

Readers may wonder why precolonial North American aboriginal whaling was not included in this study. References to such whaling are frequent in the literature, but the evidence is inconclusive (Reeves and Mitchell 1986a). Little

(1981) reasoned, after a critical evaluation of ethnographic and historical information, that there was "no evidence that prehistoric Indians of New England hunted whales at sea" (p. 59), but also that Indians "were so central to colonial American whaling that historians could describe colonial whaling as Indian whaling" (p. 60). According to Little, the Nantucket Indians, already superb mariners and "drift" (salvage) whalers before the arrival of Europeans (Little and Andrews 1982), quickly learned Basque-type whaling techniques from the colonists and came to play visibly dominant roles as crewmen on the colonist-owned whaleboats.

In spite of Little's expert view, two early references to Indian whaling are disquieting. One is a description of Indians engaged in "off-Nantucket-shore whaling in fragile canoes" in 1642 (Braginton-Smith and Oliver 2004, 163), some thirty years before the Nantucket colonists began organized whaling. The other is Waymouth's oft-quoted 1605 account of Indian whaling in New England (here quoted from True 1904, 20–21): "their manner of killing the whale . . . they go in company of their king with a multitude of their boats, and strike him with a bone made in fashion of a harping iron fastened to a rope . . . then all their boats come about him, and as he riseth above water, with their arrows they shoot him to death."

Farther north, the Inuit had an ancient whale-hunting tradition centered on the bowhead whale. Although it is possible that some of the balaenids killed by Inuit along the Labrador coast (Taylor 1988) were right whales, the seasonal timing of the hunt and the size (length) of the baleen that was traded to Europeans suggest that most of the whales taken were bowheads.

How Many Right Whales Were Killed in the Western North Atlantic?

For practical reasons, the catch series was developed only for the western North Atlantic, defined here as waters to the west of the southern tip of Greenland (i.e., west of 45°W longitude). This partitioning of the catch data is consistent with two of three hypotheses for population structure formulated by Reeves and Mitchell (1986b) and with the concept of a "western North Atlantic stock," as recognized by the Scientific Committee of the International Whaling Commission (IWC 2001, 5).

Interpretation of the catch data in historical sources requires attention to three particular issues: the need to account for whales killed but not landed, any selection for sex or size, and species identification. These issues are discussed here first, followed by estimation of numbers killed.

Adjustments for Hunting Loss

The problem of adjusting, or "correcting," catch data to account for hunting loss—right whales struck or killed but not recovered—has been discussed extensively (see Best and Ross 1986; Reeves and Mitchell 1986a, 1986b; Scarff 2001). Here the existing "average mortality factors" for premodern whaling were adopted: 1.2 for bay (and shore) whaling and 1.5 for open-sea (offshore or pelagic) whaling (IWC 1986, 31). No correction factors were applied to the catches from modern whaling operations.

Although the assumption that right whales float after being killed is largely correct, some carcasses sank and were lost. Those "killed in deep water, if they sink, never rise again" (Douglass 1760, as quoted in Allen 1908, 316). Moreover, right whales were difficult to kill and secure in the exposed and often rough conditions prevalent on the northern feeding grounds (see the logbook entries at the beginning of this chapter; also Kugler 1984, 153). Eschricht and Reinhardt (1866, 39–41) noted that, compared to bowheads, right whales were "much more active, . . . much quicker, and more violent in [their] movements, and accordingly both more difficult and more dangerous to catch."

Age and Sex Selectivity

In general, commercial offshore whalers in the North Atlantic were unselective in hunting right whales; particularly in later years, when the chance of encountering a right whale of any size or of a particular sex was remote, the whalers took whatever they could get. Basque shore whalers hunted selectively for calves, at least in local waters, as they were easier to chase and tow. Once a calf was secured, the mother would stay close to the boats or follow them into sheltered waters where she could be killed more easily. When a female–calf pair was taken, the harpooner who struck the calf received a higher share in the proceeds than the one who struck the mother (Aguilar 1986). Dudley (1725, 261–262) referred to the hazards of attacking female–calf pairs:

> they are chased or wounded, yet as long as they have Sense, and perceive Life in their Young, they will never leave them, nor will they then strike with their Tail, and if, in their running, the young one loses his Hold and drops off [from the mother's tail region], the Dame comes about, and passing underneath, takes it on again. And therefore Care is taken by those who kill these Mate Fish (as they are called) only to fasten the Calf, but not to kill her, till they have first secured the Cow.

For so soon as ever the Calf is dead, the Cow perceives it, and grows so violent, that there is no managing her.

Confusion in Catch Records with Other Species

Catch estimates, particularly for years before the middle of the nineteenth century, are influenced to an unknown extent by the inclusion of other species in the statistics, whether reported as individual whales or as whale products (oil, baleen). Before 1800, some of the whales taken near shore and in bays could have been gray whales (extinct in the North Atlantic for at least the past 200 years; Mead and Mitchell 1984; Lindquist 2000). Also, humpbacks were targeted by American (and other) whalers from the 1750s or earlier (Allen 1916, 306; Reeves et al. 2002b). Although most sources indicate that the large quantities of oil obtained along the north shore of the Gulf of St. Lawrence and in the Strait of Belle Isle by pre-nineteenth century whalers came from balaenids, caution is warranted there as well. For example, a French whaleman's journal indicated that his crew took eleven whales in 1735, of which one was a *ballenne de grand Baye* (Grand Bay whale, presumably a bowhead), one a *cachalot* (sperm whale), and the rest *gibarts* (presumably balaenopterids; see Reeves 1985; Reeves and Smith 2002, 231–232).

Right whale catch estimates derived separately from the amounts of whale oil and baleen exported to London from the American colonies were fairly consistent from 1697 to 1700 for both New York and New England, suggesting that the oil was all from right whales (and not other species whose baleen was considered of little value). This consistency continued up to 1734 for New York, but for New England, the number of right whale kills estimated from the oil exports exceeds the number derived from the baleen records (Reeves et al. 1999, Table 14). This suggests that the exported oil increasingly included oil from humpback whales, whose baleen was far inferior to that from right whales and hence would not have been exported. Here estimates from baleen rather than oil were used to avoid this problem.

A Lower Bound on Total Right Whale Removals

The numbers of right whales reported as having been killed in the western North Atlantic from 1634 to 1951 were compiled from published sources. This included individual whales as well as totals or average numbers mentioned for certain fisheries and subfisheries or numbers killed over periods of

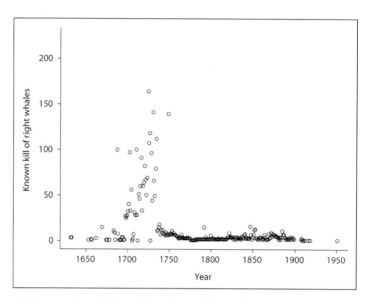

Figure 2.5. Raw numbers of right whales taken in the North Atlantic, based on published records—the foundational data.

years. Some numbers were estimated from records of products exported from the colonies to England, and these could be assigned only in a general manner to the American shore and offshore fisheries, combined. The foundational data (i.e., without interpolation or extrapolation) are far from complete, given the sporadic and scattered nature of the sources. When the data from all sources are combined, approximately 3,100 right whales were reported as having been taken (Fig. 2.5).

These foundational numbers were supplemented in three ways. First, for the American offshore fishery, the annual catch from 1751 to 1790 was estimated at roughly six whales per year. This value was obtained by multiplying the average reported number of right whales taken per voyage in a sample of whaling logbooks (= 0.12, i.e., three whales in twenty-five complete logbooks; Reeves and Mitchell 1986b, Table 1) by the estimated number of whaling voyages (2,089) in the fishery over that period. This latter number was obtained by combining Lund's (2001) list for the years 1776–1791 with the results of an exponential model fitted to the numbers of voyages mentioned by Starbuck (1878, 168–177) for the period 1751–1775.

Second, for periods with missing or grossly underreported catches, numbers were estimated by interpolating or extrapolating the information on levels of whaling activity (e.g., number of crews, boats, or camps engaged in whaling in a particular area at a given time) in preceding or succeeding years. For years before 1751, catches were estimated using exponential curves fitted by eye assuming that the fisheries developed in a continuous manner over three time periods. The first period up to 1696 was the initial expansion phase, for which data are grossly incomplete. The second period, a phase of accelerated growth to the peak catches in 1726, was followed by a third period of rapid decline to 1751. For the years from 1751 to 1825, catches for missing years were interpolated by assuming the mean of the foundational data for each subfishery for all years in the period, and for years after 1825, it was assumed that the foundational data were complete and accurate.

Finally, corrections to account for animals struck and lost were made by multiplying the catch by the mortality correction factors given above for shore-based or offshore fisheries.

These analyses generated lower bounds on the numbers of right whales killed by whalers in the western North Atlantic between 1634 and 1951, totaling roughly 5,500 animals (Fig. 2.6). Although these estimates are improvements over the foundational data, they almost certainly still underrepresent the numbers of whales actually killed. One key uncertainty resides in the numbers from before 1696, where the interpolated line fails to incorporate catches from several subfisheries and does not account, for example, for the 100 or so right whales reported as having been taken in a single year (1687) in the New York subfishery of the American Shore fishery (Reeves and Mitchell 1986a). The estimated catches between 1697 and 1734 were based on baleen exports to England, assuming, in the face of a lack of knowledge to the contrary, that the baleen from all right whales taken was exported. This line interpolates over some years where no export data were available. The line from 1734 to 1751 assumes that catches declined smoothly and not as precipitously as suggested by the foundational data shown in Fig. 2.5.

Nature and Limitations of Sources

In studying the catch history of North Atlantic right whales, the inadequacy of source materials has always been a problem. For example, even though Allen's (1916) historical record of right whale catches in New England was "painstakingly compiled" (Schevill et al. 1986, 79), Reeves et al. (1999, 32) characterized it as "little more than a collection of random hints at what occurred in colonial and early postcolonial times." Indeed, the *Nantucket Inquirer*,

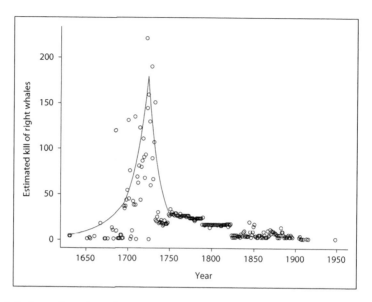

Figure 2.6. Lower bounds on the numbers of right whales killed by whalers in the western North Atlantic up to 1951, showing the reported data adjusted for struck and lost and interpolated or extrapolated to account for some gaps in the published record. The smooth curve from 1634 to 1750, the peak period of right whale removals, was considered to represent the actual removal levels more accurately than the data points. Also, for years between 1751 and 1825, catches for missing years were interpolated by assuming the mean of the foundational data for each subfishery for all years in the period. For years after 1825, it was assumed that reported catch data were complete and accurate, and no interpolations or extrapolations were made.

one of Allen's most important sources of data, did not begin printing until 1822, nearly a century after right whaling in New England had peaked and begun to decline. The availability of newspapers, logbooks, trade records, and other written documents unfortunately becomes more fragmentary the further one delves back in time. In addition, because right whales were the earliest targets of commercial whaling, their history is particularly shrouded by the paucity of written evidence. Nor is the North Atlantic right whale the only species whose written historical record of exploitation is so sparse. The gray whale became extinct in the North Atlantic without leaving any clear signal in the written record (Mead and Mitchell 1984), so one can only speculate on the cause of its demise: Was it the result of excessive whaling? The answer probably will never be known.

For a document to be useful in historical studies, three things must have occurred. First, someone needs to have written something. It can be as rudimentary as a personal diary or account book or as elaborate as a whaleman's book of reminiscences. Between those extremes are newspaper articles, lists of trade goods, and scientific reports. Second, the item needs to have survived in a readable, accessible form. Unfortunately, most personal ledgers, journals, and diaries from colonial times are gone, as are some of the earliest newspapers. Many whaling voyage logbooks have been lost, damaged, or rendered useless because of illegibility. Thus the extant written record constitutes an unknown, and perhaps not very large, fraction of the total information that was originally recorded. Finally, documents need to be identified, located, and obtained. Some items, such as privately held logbooks, are unavailable to researchers, but many are simply difficult to find. Gaining access often requires a sophisticated knowledge of search tools, a great deal of time, and considerable financial resources. Recognizing these difficulties, this chapter is based on intensive, but admittedly nonexhaustive, searches. Unquestionably more source material is to be found on the whale fisheries by deeper investigation of town records, family histories, and collections of old newspapers.

Need for Interdisciplinary Research

Calls for more interdisciplinary research often fail to specify why such an approach is needed. In the present instance, the need seems clear and specific. The "body count" data have been taken as far as possible based on what is readily available, and the fragments of actual data have been linked and extended to produce a plausible time series of catches. Nevertheless, this work has repeatedly been stymied by the limits of knowledge about historical context, and it would have benefited significantly from the insights and perspectives of social and economic historians (here the term "interdisciplinary" is meant to include reference to multiple topic areas within the discipline of history).

A truly interdisciplinary investigation of the first century of whaling in British North America (ca. 1650–1750) would provide a much better basis for assessing the scale of catches. The sharp spike in the catch trajectory between 1697 and 1734, for example, may be largely an artifact of written source availability. It should be possible to determine whether customs records for baleen and whale oil are available for years before 1697, but this would require a better understanding of the British colonial trade and its documentation. Given the relative importance of removals during the earlier period (pre-1697), any ability to extend the records further back in time would have a major effect on estimates of total removals.

It may be impossible to know with certainty what proportion of the baleen and oil exported to England between 1697 and 1734 came from right whales killed by whalers, as opposed to animals that had died of natural causes. How much of the baleen and oil came from other species, such as bowhead, gray, humpback, or pilot whales may also be difficult to determine. It should be possible, however, to understand how representative the customs data are of actual production. For example, what proportion of the oil and baleen recovered from killed whales between Newfoundland and the Carolinas would have been exported to England rather than consumed domestically? Were street lamps in east-coast colonial towns lit with whale oil? Did clothiers, farmers, and tradesmen in the colonies use baleen in their fabrications? Knowledge about the uses of whale products within the New World communities, and the prevailing demographic and economic parameters affecting such uses, would significantly improve early catch estimates. Thus there is a clear need for cultural historians to become involved in the investigatory process. Further, tax avoidance was, at times, a strategic factor affecting both marketing patterns and the written records of the colonial trade in oil and baleen (Reeves et al. 1999). Once again, limited understanding of this aspect of local and regional history makes it difficult to evaluate or quantify the resulting bias in data sources that could dramatically affect catch estimates.

Conclusion

Given the inherent limitations of the historical sources, especially before 1750, it is difficult to reconstruct the past and imagine how many North Atlantic right whales there once were, where they congregated, and what role they might have played in a pristine ecosystem. However, it is clear beyond doubt that the species was conspicuously present during historic times in areas from which it is now almost entirely absent. These areas include Cintra Bay and environs off northwestern Africa, the Bay of Biscay, and northwestern European waters to as far north as Norway and westward to Iceland. It is also clear that, in the early seventeenth century, when European colonists began establishing settlements along the east coast of North America, right whales were much more abundant than they are today.

In view of all the caveats about the catch data, the analysis presented here indicates that considerably more than the lower bound of 5,500 right whales, and possibly twice that number, were killed in the western North Atlantic between 1634 and 1950. During the early years of the American shore and offshore fisheries, for example, it seems reasonable to assume that there was at least a small market for baleen and right whale oil within North America. This would suggest that catch estimates derived only from the amounts of these products exported to England are negatively biased. Because the majority of killed whales in Fig. 2.5 were inferred from the 1697–1734 customs data, additional information on the domestic markets for baleen and oil could have a large effect on the catch estimates. Similarly, additional trade records from earlier years (pre-1697) could have a substantial positive effect on the catch estimates. In contrast, additional information on whaling activity and catches since 1751, and especially since 1825, would probably have proportionately less significance for the estimates.

The results presented here are not inconsistent with the suggestion of Rastogi et al. (2004) that the preexploitation abundance of right whales in the western North Atlantic was less than has been supposed (cf. Gaskin 1991; NMFS 1991; Kenney et al. 2001). However, the catch history supports the view that there were at least a few thousand whales present in the mid-1600s. Because of the extreme depletion of the population by 1900, historical abundance is unlikely to have been greater than the sum of historical catches. Moreover, assuming that births would have offset some of the effects of removals by whaling, actual abundance was probably smaller than the total number of catches. With the historical removal data now summarized and organized by fishery and subfishery, and this first attempt at evidence-based interpolations and extrapolations, the stage is set for additional studies to better elucidate the numbers of right whales killed and, in turn, for modeling to estimate initial abundance. More historical studies, ideally with an interdisciplinary emphasis and including further analyses of the Basque fishery in the Strait of Belle Isle, are needed to develop, test, and refine hypotheses concerning population history and to establish benchmarks for recovery of the western North Atlantic right whale population.

Aguilar, A. 1986. A review of old Basque whaling and its effect on the right whales (*Eubalaena glacialis*) of the North Atlantic. *Report of the International Whaling Commission* Special Issue 10:191–199.

Allen, G. M. 1916. The whalebone whales of New England. *Memoirs of the Boston Society of Natural History* 8(2): 107–322.

Allen, J. A. 1908. The North Atlantic right whale and its near allies. *American Museum of Natural History Bulletin* 24:277–329.

Anonymous. 2000. Canadian Right Whale Recovery Plan. A Canadian Recovery Plan for the North Atlantic Right Whale. World Wildlife Fund Canada, Toronto, ON and Department of Fisheries and Oceans, Dartmouth, NS, Canada, 89 pp.

Barkham, S. 1984. The Basque whaling establishments in Labrador 1536–1632— a summary. *Arctic* 37:515–519.

Barthelmess, K. 2003. *Das erste gedruckte deutsche Walfangjournal. Christian Bullens "Tag-Register" einer Hamburger Fangreise nach Spitzbergen und Northnorwegen im Jahre 1667.* De Bataafsche Leeuw, Amsterdam.

Best, P. B., and G. J. B. Ross. 1986. Catches of right whales from shore-based establishments in southern Africa, 1792–1975. *Report of the International Whaling Commission* Special Issue 10:275–289.

Braginton-Smith, J., and D. Oliver. 2004. *Cape Cod Shore Whaling.* Historical Society of Old Yarmouth, Yarmouth Port, MA.

Breiwick, J. M., L. L. Eberhardt, and H. W. Braham. 1984. Population dynamics of Western Arctic bowhead whales (*Balaena mysticetus*). *Canadian Journal of Fisheries and Aquatic Sciences* 41:484–496.

Brown, S. G. 1986. Twentieth-century records of right whales (*Eubalaena glacialis*) in the northeast Atlantic Ocean. *Report of the International Whaling Commission* Special Issue 10:121–127.

Clarke, R. 1954. Open boat whaling in the Azores: the history and present methods of a relic industry. *Discovery Reports* 26:281–354.

Clarke, R. 1981. Whales and dolphins of the Azores and their exploitation. *Report of the International Whaling Commission* 31:607–615.

Crèvecoeur, J. H. St. John de. 1782. *Letters from an American Farmer.* London. [Reprinted 1971 by Everyman's Library, Dutton, New York.]

Cumbaa, S. L. 1986. Archaeological evidence of the sixteenth century Basque right whale fishery in Labrador. *Report of the International Whaling Commission* Special Issue 10:187–190.

De Jong, C. 1983. The hunt of the Greenland whale: a short history and statistical sources. *Report of the International Whaling Commission* Special Issue 5:83–106.

Dudley, P. 1725. An essay upon the natural history of whales, with a particular account of the ambergris found in the *sperma ceti* whale. *Philosophical Transactions* 33:256–269.

Du Pasquier, Th. 1984. The whalers of Honfleur in the seventeenth century. *Arctic* 37:533–538.

Du Pasquier, Th. 1986. Catch history of French right whaling mainly in the South Atlantic. *Report of the International Whaling Commission* Special Issue 10:269–274.

Du Pasquier, Th. 2000. *Les Baleiniers Basques.* S.P.M., Paris.

Eschricht, D. F., and J. Reinhardt. 1866. On the Greenland right-whale (*Balaena mysticetus,* Linn.), with special reference to its geographic distribution and migrations in times past and present, and to its external and internal characteristics. Pages 1–150 *in* W. H. Flower, ed. *Recent Memoirs on the Cetacea.* Ray Society, London.

Faust, I., K. Barthelmess, and K. Stopp. 2002. *Zoologische Einblattdrucke und Flugschriften vor 1800.* Vol. 4: *Wale, Sirenen, Elefanten.* Hiersemann, Stuttgart, Germany.

Gaskin, D. E. 1991. An update on the status of the right whale, *Eubalaena glacialis,* in Canada. *Canadian Field-Naturalist* 105:198–205.

Guldberg, G. A. 1884. The North Cape whale. *Nature* 30:148–149.

IWC. 1986. Report of the workshop on the status of right whales. *Report of the International Whaling Commission* Special Issue 10:1–33.

IWC. 1993. Report of the special meeting of the Scientific Committee on the assessment of gray whales. *Report of the International Whaling Commission* 43:241–259.

IWC. 2001. Report of the workshop on the comprehensive assessment of right whales: a worldwide comparison. *Journal of Cetacean Research and Management* Special Issue 2:1–60.

IWC. 2002. Annex H. Report of the Sub-committee on the Comprehensive Assessment of North Atlantic Humpback Whales. *Journal of Cetacean Research and Management* 4 (Suppl.):230–260.

IWC. 2003. Annex H. Report of the Sub-committee on the Comprehensive Assessment of Humpback Whales. *Journal of Cetacean Research and Management* 5 (Suppl.):293–323.

Kenney, R. D., H. E. Winn, and M. C. Macaulay. 1995. Cetaceans in the Great South Channel, 1979–1989: right whale (*Eubalaena glacialis*). *Continental Shelf Research* 15:385–414.

Kenney, R. D., C. A. Mayo, and H. E. Winn. 2001. Migration and foraging strategies at varying spatial scales in western North Atlantic right whales: a review of hypotheses. *Journal of Cetacean Research and Management* Special Issue 2: 251–260.

Kugler, R. C. 1984. Historical survey of foreign whaling: North America. Pages 149–157 *in* H. K. s'Jacob, K. Snoeijing, and R. Vaughan, eds. *Arctic Whaling: Proceedings of the International Symposium, Arctic Whaling, February 1983.* Arctic Centre, University of Groningen, Netherlands.

Lindquist, O. 1993. Whaling by peasant fishermen in Norway, Orkney, Shetland, Faeroe Islands, Iceland and Norse Greenland: medieval and early modern whaling methods and inshore legal regimes. Pages 17–54 *in* B. L. Basberg, J. E. Ringstad, and E. Wexelsen, eds. *Whaling and History.* Kommandør Chr. Christensens Hvalfangstmuseum, Sandefjord, Norway.

Lindquist, O. 2000. The North Atlantic gray whale (*Eschrichtius robustus*): an historical outline based on Icelandic, Danish-Icelandic, English and Swedish sources dating from ca. 1000 A.D. to 1792. Centre for Environmental History and Policy, Universities of St. Andrews and Stirling, Scotland, Occasional Papers 1:1–53.

Lipton, B. 1975. Whaling days in New Jersey. *Newark Museum Quarterly* 26(2–3): 1–72.

Little, E. A. 1981. The Indian contribution to along-shore whaling at Nantucket. *Nantucket Algonquian Studies* 8:1–85.

Little, E. A. 1988. Nantucket whaling in the early 18th century. Pages 111–129 *in* W. Cowan, ed. *Papers of the Nineteenth Algonquian Conference*. Carleton University, Ottawa.

Little, E. A., and J. C. Andrews. 1982. Drift whales at Nantucket: the kindness of Moshup. *Man in the Northeast* 23:17–38.

Lund, J. N. 2001. *Whaling Masters and Whaling Voyages Sailing from American Ports: a Compilation of Sources*. New Bedford Whaling Museum, New Bedford, MA.

Manigault, G. E. 1885. The black whale captured in Charleston Harbor January, 1880. *Proceedings of the Elliott Society* September: 98–104.

Martens, F. 1675. *Spitzbergische oder Groenlandische Reise-Beschreibung gethan im Jahr 1671*. Hamburg, Germany.

Maul, G. E., and D. E. Sergeant. 1977. New cetacean records from Madeira. *Bocagiana* 43:1–8.

Maury, M. F. 1852 et seq. *Whale Chart of the World (The wind and current charts)*, Series F. Washington, D.C.

Maury, M. F. 1853. *A Chart Showing the Favourite Resort of the Sperm and Right Whale*. Bureau of Ordnance and Hydrography, Washington, D.C.

Mead, J. G., and E. D. Mitchell. 1984. Atlantic gray whales. Pages 33–53 *in* M. L. Jones, S. L. Swartz, and S. Leatherwood, eds. *The Gray Whale* Eschrichtius robustus. Academic Press, Orlando, FL.

Mitchell, E. D. 1973. The status of the world's whales. *Nature Canada* 2(4):9–25.

Mitchell, E., and R. R. Reeves. 1983. Catch history, abundance, and present status of northwest Atlantic humpback whales. *Report of the International Whaling Commission* Special Issue 5:153–212.

Mowat, F. 1972. *A Whale for the Killing*. McClelland and Stewart Ltd., Toronto, Canada.

NMFS. 1991. Final recovery plan for the northern right whale *Eubalaena glacialis*. U.S. Department of Commerce, National Oceanic and Atmospheric Administration, National Marine Fisheries Service, Office of Protected Resources, Silver Spring, Maryland. 86 pp.

Nores, C., and M. C. Perez. 1983. Mamíferos marinos de la costa asturiana: I. Relaciones de observaciones, capturas y embarrancamientos hasta 1982. *Bol. Cien. Nat. I. D. E. A.* 31:17–48.

Rastogi, T., M. W. Brown, B. A. McLeod, T. R. Frasier, R. Grenier, S. L. Cumbaa, J. Nadarajah, and B. N. White. 2004. Genetic analysis of sixteenth century whale bones prompts a revision of the impact of Basque whaling on right and bowhead whales in the western North Atlantic. *Canadian Journal of Zoology* 82:1647–1654.

Reeves, R. R. 1985. Whaling in the St. Lawrence. *The Collection Horizon Canada* 76:1808–1813.

Reeves, R. R. 2001. Overview of catch history, historic abundance and distribution of right whales in the western North Atlantic and in Cintra Bay, West Africa. *Journal of Cetacean Research and Management* Special Issue 2:187–192.

Reeves, R. R., and M. F. Barto. 1985. Whaling in the Bay of Fundy. *Whalewatcher* 19(4):14–18.

Reeves, R. R., and E. Mitchell. 1986a. The Long Island, New York, right whale fishery: 1650–1924. *Report of the International Whaling Commission* Special Issue 10: 201–220.

Reeves, R. R., and E. Mitchell. 1986b. American pelagic whaling for right whales in the North Atlantic. *Report of the International Whaling Commission* Special Issue 10:221–254.

Reeves, R. R., and E. Mitchell. 1988. History of whaling in and near North Carolina. NOAA Technical Report NMFS 65:1–28.

Reeves, R. R., and T. D. Smith. 2002. Historical catches of humpback whales in the North Atlantic Ocean: an overview of sources. *Journal of Cetacean Research and Management* 4:219–234.

Reeves, R. R., J. M. Breiwick, and E. Mitchell. 1992. Pre-exploitation abundance of right whales off the eastern United States. Pages 5–7 *in* J. Hain, ed. The right whale in the western North Atlantic: a science and management workshop, 14–15 April 1992, Silver Spring, Maryland. Northeast Fisheries Science Center Reference Document 92-05.

Reeves, R. R., J. M. Breiwick, and E. D. Mitchell. 1999. History of whaling and estimated kill of right whales, *Balaena glacialis,* in the northeastern United States, 1620–1924. *Marine Fisheries Review* 61(3):1–36.

Reeves, R. R., P. J. Clapham, and S. E. Wetmore. 2002a. Humpback whale (*Megaptera novaeangliae*) occurrence near the Cape Verde Islands, based on American nineteenth century whaling records. *Journal of Cetacean Research and Management* 4:235–253.

Reeves, R. R., T. D. Smith, R. L. Webb, J. Robbins, and P. J. Clapham. 2002b. Humpback and fin whaling in the Gulf of Maine from 1800 to 1918. *Marine Fisheries Review* 64(1):1–12.

Reeves, R. R., E. Josephson, and T. D. Smith. 2004. Putative historical occurrence of North Atlantic right whales in mid-latitude offshore waters: "Maury's Smear" is likely apocryphal. *Marine Ecology Progress Series* 282:295–305.

Scarff, J. E. 2001. Preliminary estimates of whaling-induced mortality in the nine-teenth century North Pacific right whale (*Eubalaena japonicus*) fishery, adjusting for struck-but-lost whales and non-American whaling. *Journal of Cetacean Research and Management* Special Issue 2:261–268.

Schaeff, C. M., S. D. Kraus, M. W. Brown, J. S. Perkins, R. Payne, and B. N. White. 1997. Comparison of genetic variability of North and South Atlantic right whale (*Eubalaena*), using DNA fingerprinting. *Canadian Journal of Zoology* 75:1073–1080.

Schevill, W. E., W. A. Watkins, and S. E. Moore. 1986. Status of *Eubalaena glacialis* off Cape Cod. *Report of the International Whaling Commission* Special Issue 10: 79–82.

Simpson, M. B., Jr., and S. W. Simpson. 1988. The pursuit of leviathan: a history of whaling on the North Carolina coast. *North Carolina Historical Review* 65(1): 1–51.

Southwell, T. 1884. On the occurrence of the Atlantic right whale, *Balaena biscayen-sis* (Eschricht), on the east coast of Scotland. *Proceedings of the Natural History Society of Glasgow* 5:66–69.

Starbuck, A. 1878. History of the American whale fishery from its earliest inception to the year 1876. Pages 1–768 *in Report of the U.S. Commissioner of Fish and Fisheries,* Part 4, 1875–76. U.S. Government Printing Office, Washington, D.C.

Taylor, J. G. 1988. Labrador Inuit whale use during the early contact period. *Arctic Anthropology* 25(1):120–130.

True, F. W. 1904. The whalebone whales of the western North Atlantic compared with those occurring in European waters with some observations on the species of the North Pacific. *Smithsonian Contributions to Knowledge* 33:1–332.

Tuck, J. A., and R. Grenier. 1981. A sixteenth-century Basque whaling station in Labrador. *Scientific American* 245(5):180–190.

Turner, W. 1913. The right whale of the North Atlantic, *Balaena biscayensis:* its skele-ton described and compared with that of the Greenland right whale, *Balaena mysticetus. Transactions of the Royal Society of Edinburgh* 48:889–922.

Acknowledgments

The authors are grateful to Michael Dyer, librarian of the New Bedford Whaling Museum, for sharing his unpublished manuscript on onboard tryworks and his correspondence on that subject with whaling experts Klaus Barthelmess and Michael Barkham. The authors are also indebted to the editors, Klaus Barthelmess, Alex Aguilar, and Fred Serchuk for careful reviews of the manuscript and to Barthelmess for permitting use of his photograph from Madeira.

3

Right Whales Tell Their Own Stories: The Photo-Identification *Catalog*

PHILIP K. HAMILTON, AMY R. KNOWLTON,
AND MARILYN K. MARX

8 December 1994
Delaware River, Philadelphia

It was dark when we got the call. The right whale was now stuck along a pier at the Hess Oil Company in New Jersey. It seemed that the ordeal had just gotten more bizarre.

I was one of a tired group of people struggling to assist a confused young right whale who had swum up the Delaware River several days earlier, dodging heavy shipping traffic along the way. He had been swimming with his head angled out of the water as if he might have something weighing down his flukes. Perhaps he was entangled in fishing gear, and now that gear had caught on some part of the pier. That was our working hypothesis as we drove to New Jersey from the Philadelphia Coast Guard station.

When we arrived at the pier, it took a moment to comprehend the incongruous scene—the enormous 27,000-kg sea creature utterly dwarfed by a massive oil tanker looming over it. The whale's head was pressed up against some pilings supporting the pier, and, although there was plenty of room for him to turn around and swim out of the area, the whale refused to do so. To determine whether he was entangled and snagged on the pier, we passed a line under him. The line passed freely indicating that nothing was physically holding him there. We then used lines and poles to reorient the young whale's head and point him out to sea, but he just pivoted back so that his head pointed into the pilings.

That night, with stubborn persistence, the whale worked its way under the pier and then into a shallow area encircled with oil booms and laced with a maze of walkways and oil pipes. Here, in this urban wasteland, the creature eventually beached itself. Although we were nearly 160 km from the ocean, the tide still affected the water level in the river, and we quickly realized that the tide was going out. A chaotic scene ensued, with all of us banging pipes and throwing rocks near the whale to urge it into deeper water. Large river tugboats were instructed to speed by to create a wake that we hoped would rock the animal out of the increasingly shallow water. The fire department even prepared to use high-powered hoses to urge it out of the shoals. Suddenly, aided by the wake of the tugs, the whale pushed itself off with several powerful thrusts of its tail, and with the help of people using boat hooks to direct its head through the maze of pilings, the whale finally swam free.

This whale spent a week up the Delaware River with many sightings around Philadelphia, which quickly adopted it as their own. One evening near the end of the week as he swam downstream toward the ocean, he was hit by a tugboat. The captain could not see what damage he had done but was able to catch a glimpse of the whale swimming before it was swallowed up by darkness. Although we were unsure if it would ultimately survive its ordeal, we decided to name this whale "Shackleton" after the famed Antarctic explorer, Sir Ernest Shackleton, a legendary expedition leader who, after his ship was crushed by ice, safely led all of his twenty-eight men out of Antarctica against all odds.

That could have been the end of the story for Shackleton the whale: just a confused little right whale in a very odd place, its fate forever unknown. Why had it swum up the river in the first place? Did it survive? Thanks to the Right Whale Catalog, *however, we know both the beginning and the end of this whale's brush with civilization. As it turns out, the errant young whale was identified as the male calf of Eg #1140, "Wart"; he was her fourth known calf and had been born sometime before 23 January 1994 off the coast of Georgia. In February, he and his mother had traveled down to Florida before reversing course and heading up the coast, likely passing just outside the mouth of Delaware Bay, and ending up in Cape Cod Bay in March. After a month in Massachusetts waters, where Wart spent most of her time feeding, mother and calf continued north and east into the cold waters of the Bay of Fundy where they had remained for July and August. Because calves are typically weaned near the end of their first year, the 11- to 12-month-old Shackleton probably had just been separated from his mother when he swam up the Delaware River in December.*

We had to wait a year and a half before learning that Shackleton had indeed survived his collision with the tug. He was next sighted in August 1996 in the Bay of Fundy with a very distinctive series of white propeller scars on his left side. Not surprisingly, the field notes clearly stated that he showed strong avoidance to the research boat during our first two approaches. Like many right whales, he showed a variety of other scars on his head and chin. Usually we assume that these scars come from rubbing on the bottom of the ocean or from rough contact with other male whales while vying for females. In Shackleton's case, however, we knew the story was quite different and that the scars had resulted from contact with the pilings of an oil refinery pier. Shackleton's story, unique though it may seem, makes one wonder: perhaps many right whales have their own unusual stories to tell.

Philip K. Hamilton

The ability to identify North Atlantic right whales by their natural markings has opened up a world of knowledge that would otherwise be unavailable to scientists. With such a small population of subjects, the opportunity to learn from carcasses is not only relatively rare but also limited by the rapid decomposition of whales after death (Chapter 12). Studying living whales is notoriously difficult; researchers are able to gain just a glimpse of their lives during those fleeting moments when the whale is at the water's surface and researchers happen to be there to witness it. The ability to identify the individual whale in those moments allows scientists to capture only a small piece of a very large puzzle. Yet as more sightings of a known whale are collected over days, months, years, and across the whale's entire migratory range, whole stories begin to emerge. These stories start at the individual level, as Shackleton's did, and, when combined, develop into a population-wide epic narrative.

These stories are the cornerstones for much of the work presented in this book. Through them, scientists have learned that most calving females off the southeastern United States migrate with their calves up the coast to feeding areas off Massachusetts and in the Bay of Fundy, whereas other whales travel greater distances to areas near Greenland and Norway (Knowlton et al. 1992; Jacobsen et al. 2004). Researchers have found that reproductive females generally wean their calves within a year, that they calve every three to five years on average, and that their interbirth intervals increased in the late 1990s (Chapter 6). The *Catalog* records have revealed which individuals use important habitats such as the southeast United States, Cape Cod Bay, Great South Channel, Jeffreys Ledge, Roseway Basin, and the Bay of Fundy. Many of the whales have been classified by sex and age (Brown et al. 1994; Hamilton et al. 1998), and that information has been used to determine that adult females are seen relatively infrequently when pregnant or resting (Brown et al. 2001). Scientists have learned that certain classes of animals are more vulnerable to human-caused injury and mortality (Knowlton and Kraus 2001) and that eliminating the deaths of just two reproductive females each year could reverse the trend toward extinction (Caswell et al. 1999; Fujiwara and Caswell 2001). Genetics data combined with biographies based on photo-identification have revealed population substructure, maternally directed site fidelity, paternities, and familial relationships (Chapter 7) and have shown that ventral skin markings are probably not inherited in this population (Schaeff and Hamilton 1999). The roles of particular individuals in surface-active groups (SAGs) have been described (Kraus and Hatch 2001), including the fact that adult males commonly produce gunshot-like sounds both during these groups and while alone (Parks et al. 2005; Chapter 10) and that females become less social once they reach sexual maturity (Hamilton 2002). All of these studies were either dependent on or enhanced by information from photo-identified individuals.

These stories are captured in an extremely thorough photo-identification database that is the result of a massive, combined effort. Scientists who work with North Atlantic right whales are blessed with an unusually strong ethic of collaboration, which led to the formation of the North Atlantic Right Whale Consortium and to the development of the *North Atlantic Right Whale Catalog*. Under the Consortium, data from all participants have been consolidated into two centralized databases. The survey effort and sightings data are maintained at the University of Rhode Island, and the photo-identification data, known as the *North Atlantic Right Whale Catalog* (hereafter referred to as the *Catalog*), are curated by the New England Aquarium (NEAq).

By the end of 2004, this *Catalog* contained over 33,000 records of 459 individuals photographed from 1935 to the present (Hamilton and Martin 1999), a result of contributions from over 200 organizations and individuals. The data within it are the basis for research and conservation projects conducted by multiple institutions and for management and recovery plans initiated by the National Marine Fisheries Service (NMFS) in the United States (NMFS 2005) and Fisheries and Oceans Canada (DFO; Anonymous 2000). Virtually all of the conservation issues that have been identified were discovered because of the data compiled within this extraordinary resource. New research efforts that are utilizing these data include reproductive and stress hormone studies, marine biotoxin research, parasite studies, blubber thickness measurements using ultrasound, acoustic research, and visual health assessment of individual whales (Chapters 8–10). The ability to monitor this population's vital rates, overall health, and the effectiveness of management efforts is entirely dependent on maintaining this database of identified whales. In fact, the International Whaling Commission (IWC) has recommended that the continuation of right whale photo-identification studies and the processing of the data be given "high priority" (IWC 2001). In short, this database has a fundamental role that influences a broad community with multidisciplinary ocean biology interests. In this chapter, readers will be immersed in the world of photo-identification, learn precisely how it is done, and gain a better understanding of how stories such as Shackleton's continue to inform right whale research.

Telling Right Whales Apart

Right whales have large patches of raised epithelial tissue on their heads termed callosities (Fig. 3.1a). The callosity is cornified skin (like a callus) that is dark in color and forms in many of the same places as hair does on men (along the jaw and above the eyes and lips). However, because they are infested with light-colored amphipods called cyamids, or "whale lice" (family Cyamidae), the callosities appear whitish or cream-colored (Fig. 3.1b). Tens of thousands of these cyamids live on the whale's head and can obscure the underlying callosity. Because they are light in color, cyamids provide contrast against the black skin and serve to define the outline of the callosity. The callosity itself begins to emerge shortly after birth, but the pattern is not well established until 7–10 months later. Although the height of the callosity can change throughout a whale's life (i.e., growing upward and breaking off repeatedly), the placement of the callosity on the whale's head typically remains stable. In rare cases, some callosity tissue on adult whales develops in new places or disappears.

The placement and pattern of the callosity are unique to each individual and enable researchers to distinguish right whales from one another (Payne et al. 1983; Kraus et al. 1986). In addition to the callosity on the top of the

Figure 3.1. (a) Head and right mandible of a right whale showing callosity tissue infested with cream-colored cyamids. Sascha Glinka / New England Aquarium. (b) Close-up of cyamids or "whale lice" on the skin of a right whale. Scott Kraus / New England Aquarium.

rostrum, researchers use white pigmentation patterns on the belly and chin of some animals as well as ridges along the upper edges of the lower lip. Additional callosities used for identification occur on the upper margins of the lower lip (referred to as "lip" callosities), behind the blowholes (typically two patches, but there can be one to four, referred to as postblowhole callosities), on the chin, and along the lower jaw or mandible. Besides these inherited characteristics, right whales collect various marks throughout their lives, such as scars from entanglements in fishing gear, ship strikes, skin lesions, bite marks from attacks by small toothed whales, and other unknown causes. All of these markings, both small and large, have proven useful for individual whale identification (color plate 5).

Determining Sex

The sex of right whales can be determined in three ways. Whales that are seen in close association with a calf at least three times in the course of a season or year are assumed to be female. If a skin biopsy sample is collected, the sex can be determined genetically (Brown et al. 1994). Finally, if the whale rolls over and the genital area is photographed, the relationship of the genital slit to the umbilicus and anus provides a clear indication of sex. In males, the anterior part of the genital slit ends near the umbilicus and the posterior part stops short of the anus and forms a Y. Females have a much shorter genital slit that starts well back from the umbilicus and ends at the anus. Females also have mammary slits that are parallel to the genital slit, which are easy to see with good- to medium-quality photographs (Fig. 3.2).

Photo-Identification Methods

The callosity pattern on the head or rostrum can be either "continuous" (i.e., one uninterrupted patch from the blowholes to the tip of the upper jaw or rostrum) or "broken" (Fig. 3.3). However, because cyamids obscure the pattern and can move, the callosity pattern of some whales may appear to change from broken to continuous. Roughly 40 percent of the cataloged whales are continuous, and 60 percent are broken. Broken and continuous callosity patterns are further subcategorized by the number and placement of islands and peninsulas. Islands are patches of callosity that are not connected to the coaming or bonnet (Fig. 3.3a), and peninsulas are bulges along the outline of a continuous callosity that interrupt a straight line.

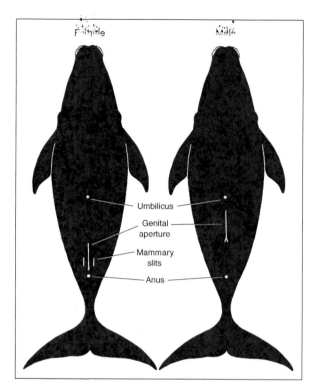

Figure 3.2. Drawings comparing the configuration and placement of the genital slit on male and female right whales. Scott Landry / Provincetown Center for Coastal Studies.

For each cataloged whale, the locations of all callosity tissue and other marks are summarized on a composite drawing (Fig. 3.3b). This drawing distills into a single image almost all of the identifying features of an individual whale that have been captured by many photographs over multiple sightings. These drawings are updated annually to account for new scars and any apparent changes in the callosity pattern (most often as a result of cyamid movement). With the advent of digital matching, the composite drawings have been moved from paper into digital files.

Reviewing the composites is the first step in matching photographs from a sighting of a whale. If sightings are well photographed, comparison to the *Catalog* can be rapid. Callosity patterns are broken down into twenty-four categories with an average of twenty-five whales in each. However, callosity patterns can be difficult to classify for various reasons, and many of the whales have multiple classifications. If the classification is unambiguous, the researcher

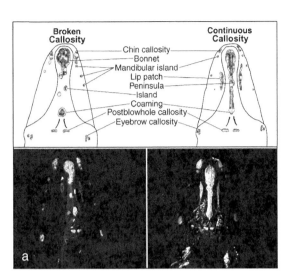
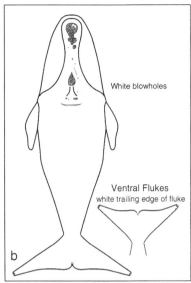

Figure 3.3. (a) Example of photograph and composite drawing of the head for Eg #1233 with a broken callosity pattern and Eg #1027 with a continuous callosity pattern. Cathy LeBlanc / New England Aquarium. (b) Full-body composite drawing of Eg #3250 including scars on the head and flukes. Philip Hamilton / New England Aquarium.

needs only to review drawings of twenty-five or so whales and then look at images for just a few of those twenty-five whose drawings appear similar to the sighting in question. However, if only one side of the head is photographed, or the images are of poor quality, matching an individual from a single sighting can take days.

Aerial versus Shipboard Photographs

Right whale photographs are collected from both shipboard and aerial platforms, and the ratio of shipboard sightings to aerials in the *Catalog* is approximately two to one. Each platform type has its strengths and limitations. Aerial photographs often capture both sides of the head and provide the composite view (overhead) of the callosity. However, they are often more distant and more likely to be poorly focused, making it difficult to identify the whale, detect scars, and assess health parameters (Chapter 9). Aerial photographs are also more expensive and more dangerous to collect than shipboard photographs.

Shipboard photographs tend to be closer and of higher quality but often capture fewer identifying features of the whale. For example, if only one side of a whale's head and body is photographed during a sighting, a researcher has only half the information needed to make the match. Shipboard photographs are necessary to assess scars and health parameters such as body and skin condition accurately, whereas aerial surveys are the only feasible survey option in some offshore habitats that are inaccessible by boat or in areas where right whales are widely dispersed. Because aerial and shipboard images show such different perspectives, comparing them for matching purposes can prove challenging. However, the large amount of identification information available on a right whale (especially the scars) allows for matches to occur between the two types of photographs.

The Digital Age

Initially all right whale photographs were in the form of color slides or black-and-white prints, and all matching was done over light tables using jeweler's loupes to help the viewer focus on small details. With the advent of digital photography, the system for matching and maintaining the photo-identification database has evolved substantially. In 2005 specialized software was developed to process and track digital images and the associated data for individual identification studies. This software, called DIGITS (Digital Image Gathering and Information Tracking System), provides a detailed and easy-to-use format to interact with all aspects of the data, including the capability to search for sightings of whales with similar attributes and compare them side by side on a computer screen.

Although other research organizations have developed semiautomated matching systems where image recognition software reads the image itself (e.g., Kreho et al. 1999), such automated systems are currently not appropriate for the *Right Whale Catalog* because (1) they are difficult to apply to right whale identification features and (2) the population is small enough that the benefit in efficiency does not offset the cost. Most automated matching systems use two-dimensional data from a flat surface, such as dorsal fins and tail flukes, and are not appropriate for the three-dimensional callosity patterns on the lips and heads of right whales. A semiautomated matching program that does incorporate three dimensions was developed for seals (Hiby and Lovell 1990) and has been modified for matching southern right whales (Hiby and Lovell 2001), but the system requires aerial photographs of whales in water clear enough to see the eyebrow callosities. In the *North Atlantic Right Whale Catalog,* only about one-third of the contributed photographs are from aerial platforms, and most of those do not show the eyebrow callosity of the whale because of the poor clarity of northern waters. Without the eyebrows visible, the three reference points that are required to fit a three-dimensional shape into a two-dimensional pattern are absent. Also, aerial and shipboard images provide very different perspectives from each other, and it would be extremely difficult for image recognition software to accommodate both perspectives. Because contributors to the *Right Whale Catalog* will continue to collect photographs from both ship and aerial platforms into the foreseeable future, the DIGITS software was developed to accommodate both types of images and to rely on a detailed coding system, rather than an automated interpretation of the image, to allow for whale-matching searches.

Not only has DIGITS moved the matching process firmly into the electronic realm; it has also moved it into the virtual realm. The software was designed to be server-based and is accessible through a private network on the Internet. This allows data and images to be processed and integrated from field stations. It also provides the framework to allow greater public access to images of this enigmatic species. To take advantage of this Internet-based system, a web site was developed to introduce the public to right whale photo-identification and provide them with enough detail to try to identify individual right whales themselves. The site has background information, matching instructions, a matching game, and a link to search for cataloged whales (www.neaq.org/rwcatalog).

Adding Whales to the *Catalog*

Sightings that are matched to a whale already in the *Catalog* are confirmed by one or two other researchers, and the identity is entered into the sighting record. This record also contains the date, time, latitude, and longitude of the sighting, a code for the observer, and any observed behaviors. However, some sightings do not match existing cataloged whales. These whales are added to the *Catalog* and assigned numbers (and occasionally names) when there is enough photographic information for any given whale to (1) confirm beyond doubt that it does not match any whale in the existing *Catalog* and (2) be certain that average quality photographs of future sightings can be matched to that whale as well. For example, if there are several sightings of a whale that is distinctive enough to recognize as an uncataloged whale, but the photographs are either blurry or only show one side of the head, assignment of a *Catalog* number is delayed until better photographs have been obtained. This conservative approach ensures that data analyses for the population are based on robust identifications with a high probability of reidentification if a whale is photographed in the future. However, this approach also causes problems for some population analyses. For example, survival may be overestimated if whales that were photographed only once with marginal photographs have died. Those deaths would be undetected in *Catalog*-dependent population models because they were never assigned a *Catalog* number and were therefore never considered part of the population.

Cataloging calves poses unique challenges. Because the callosity pattern does not become well established until the late spring and summer months (when the calf is seven to ten months old), any calf that is seen only in the southeastern calving grounds during the winter with its mother will not be photoidentified in its birth year. Many of these calves will be photographed and identified as new juveniles in subsequent years, but their connection with their mother and thus their lineage and age will not be known.

Even for those calves that are photographed in the second half of their birth year, reidentification can be difficult. Young whales generally have few scars if any, and the callosity tissue continues to develop throughout the first year of life, sometimes altering its pattern. Reidentifying these animals in subsequent years generally depends on the distinctiveness of their lip ridges and callosity pattern and on how well photographed they were as calves. For this reason, only 64 percent of the right whales born between 1980 and 2003 (198 out of 288) were photo-identified as calves. An apparent decrease in calf identifications in the late 1990s and early 2000s (Fig. 3.4) was caused primarily by an increased aerial survey effort on the calving ground, increasing the detection of calves whose mothers do not go to the Bay of Fundy (where there is extensive survey effort). In the future, it may be possible to identify some of these calves through a combination of genetic and photographic information (see section on genetics below).

The number of whales that are added to the *Catalog* each year shows a clear discovery curve (Fig. 3.5). Forty-seven and fifty-one whales were added in 1980 and 1981, respectively, and most of those were adults. Since 1982, the numbers have hovered between ten and twenty new whales added annually, and many of those are calves, suggesting that many of the adults were discovered quickly. However, 33 percent of all new whales added to the *Catalog* between

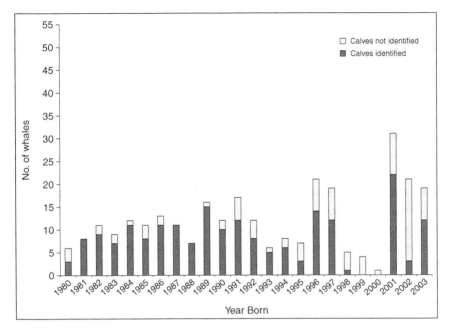

Figure 3.4. Percentage of calves identified in their birth year from 1980 to 2003.

1990 and 2003 were noncalves. Although many of these new whales were juveniles that were likely unidentified calves from previous years, some were whales that were first sighted with a calf in the southeast, indicating that they grew to maturity without being sighted previously. These particularly intriguing and mysterious animals are discussed later in this chapter under the section on irregular whales.

Numbering Whales

Once two or three matchers are confident that photographs of a whale meet the criteria discussed above, the whale is given a *Catalog* number. In most cases, the first two digits of the number reflect the decade and year it was first sighted. The first number reflects the decade (1 for 1980s, 2 for 1990s, 3 for 2000s), and the second number references the year within that decade (e.g., Eg #1701 was first sighted in 1987, Eg #2301 was first sighted in 1993, Eg #3030 was first seen in 2000). The last two digits are taken from the last

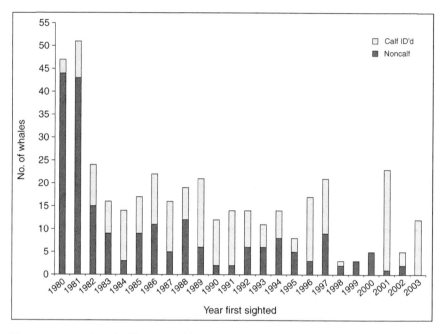

Figure 3.5. Number of calf and noncalf whales added to the *Catalog* each year from 1980 to 2003.

two numbers of the *Catalog* number of the mother, if known. For example, Eg #1901 is the 1989 calf of Eg #1001 "Fermata." If the mother is not known, they are given an order of 10 and will have a 0 as the fourth digit (for example, Eg # 2220 is a male that was first seen in 1992).

Naming Whales

Whales receive names when their callosity pattern or scars resemble something that provides researchers with a mnemonic device to remember the whale. For example, one whale, Eg # 1509 "Rat," has a very distinctive scar on the left insertion of her flukes that resembles a rat chasing a ball (Fig. 3.6a). Another, Eg #1133 "Snowball," has a distinctive mark on the left head that resembles a snowball (Fig. 3.6b). Whales have also been named for their deeds, as was Shackleton, and occasionally "in memoriam," such as "Prescott," who was named for the late director of the New England Aquarium, John Prescott.

Figure 3.6. Photographs showing distinctive marks for which whales have been named. (a) "Rat" was named for the scar that resembles a rat chasing a ball. Jeff Goodyear / Provincetown Center for Coastal Studies. (b) "Snowball" was named for a scar on the left head that looks like a snowball. Mason Weinrich / Whale Center of New England.

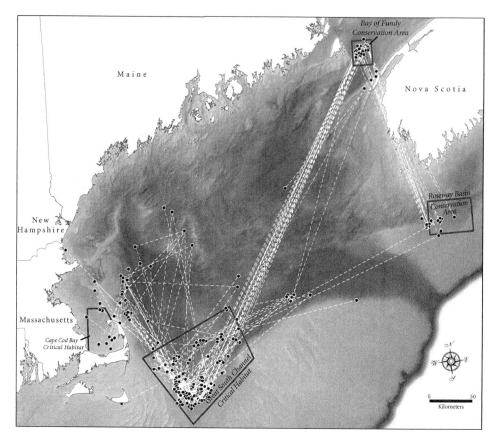

Figure 3.7. Example of right whale movements throughout the Gulf of Maine February through
September 2002. White lines connect sightings of the same individual across areas and give a crude
indication of potential whale movements. Kerry Lagueux / New England Aquarium.

Individual Movements and Habitat Preferences

The *Catalog* has taught us a great deal about individual whale movements
and habitat use patterns. Survey efforts have been focused on the five known
primary right whale habitats: the southeast United States (SEUS), Cape Cod
Bay (CCB), Great South Channel east of Cape Cod (GSC), the Bay of Fundy
west of Nova Scotia (BOF), and Roseway Basin south of Nova Scotia (RB).
Because the survey effort is focused in these five areas, individual movements
between and among these habitats are the best understood (Fig. 3.7).

Although whales of both sexes and all age classes are found in all habitats, some areas are skewed toward particular population segments. For example, primarily reproductive females, calves, and some juveniles inhabit the winter calving ground in the southeast United States, whereas during the summer and fall in Roseway Basin, adult males dominate, and sightings of mother–calf pairs are extremely rare. However, many of the generalizations about these areas have been violated. For example, occasionally large groups of adult males move into the southeast United States and form SAGs. Table 3.1 summarizes the number of males and females identified by area annually to give the reader a sense of the distributions and how they change from year to year. Lack of identifications in a given year generally result from an interruption in survey effort, although the decline in numbers in Roseway Basin and Great South Channel in the early 1990s represents a real distribution shift away from those habitats. Notice the concurrent increase in whales in the Bay of Fundy starting in 1993, an increase that occurred through an influx of whales, not as an artifact of changes in survey effort.

Sighting Frequencies

The photo-identification effort seems to document some whales quite successfully, but the habits of others are poorly understood. This variability in success reflects a combination of when and where the survey effort takes place, when and where an individual whale goes, and what behaviors the whale exhibits that make it easier or harder to photograph (i.e., long feeding dives versus obvious surface-active behavior). A mismatch of any of these three parameters leads to a whale being photographed less frequently, if at all. Those individuals that seem to be well represented by the survey effort are seen frequently (many times per year and during many different years) or regularly (such as some calving females with regular and predictable gaps in their sightings between calving events).

Because of this consistency in most whales' sighting histories, a whale is classified as "presumed dead" if it is not resighted after 6 years (Knowlton et al. 1994). Most mortalities are undetected because carcasses sink at sea (Chapter 12), and this categorization gives us the best guess at how many of the cataloged whales are still alive. This crude assessment makes mistakes (39 of the 459 [8.5 percent] of whales cataloged between 1986 and 2003 were "resurrected" when they were subsequently resighted after a sighting gap of six or

Table 3.1. Whales Identified Annually by Habitat and Sex[a]

Year	SEUS			CCB			GSC			RB			BOF			Total for year
	F	M	Total[b]	F	M	Total[b]	F	M	Total[b]	F	M	Total[b]	F	M	Total[b]	
1980	2			2		2	7	7	19	6	5	14	8	12	24	**64**
1981			**2**	2		2	18	32	61	7	20	31	20	32	56	**102**
1982	3	2	**5**	5	1	7	5	11	20	7	16	26	22	27	52	**100**
1983	1	1	**3**	12	12	28	3	5	9	8	16	26	13	11	26	**76**
1984	12	2	**15**	11	12	23	8	12	22	8	1	29	24	27	54	**115**
1985	4	1	**6**	15	14	32	9	20	32	22	50	11	14	16	31	**104**
1986	16	5	**23**	22	19	44	11	13	27	12	53	81	17	22	42	**152**
1987	13	1	**14**	18	7	25	17	19	42	25	82	82	19	12	31	**152**
1988	8		**9**	11	11	25	30	54	96	18	84	118	23	19	44	**198**
1989	35	6	**41**	11	3	14	16	21	39	7	37	116	43	28	74	**207**
1990	24	6	**33**	20	3	26				19	67	47	36	31	69	**149**
1991	19	1	**21**	19	10	32	1	9	10	5	12	91	27	24	52	**161**
1992	17	10	**28**	23	16	42						17	24	46	72	**131**
1993	30	20	**54**	17	18	37	1		1				51	90	148	**178**
1994	18	6	**26**	11	13	25	2	1	2				73	108	72	**209**
1995	21	4	**26**	33	25	61	2	1	3	1	4	7	74	105	188	**220**
1996	63	36	**102**	34	37	75	3	3	6				68	95	173	**223**
1997	36	11	**50**	22	21	45	3	6	9	1	3	4	85	116	215	**248**
1998	17	16	**33**	42	42	89	10	10	25	1	1	4	50	78	133	**219**
1999	12	1	**14**	33	42	80	46	50	107	6	8	14	68	96	174	**224**
2000	32	18	**53**	36	49	89	29	49	84	3	2	6	62	89	158	**237**
2001	59	23	**89**	28	47	77	68	106	196				64	71	143	**266**
2002	55	7	**71**	14	5	20	58	90	169	12	20	42	52	64	127	**275**
2003	36	21	**69**	9	18	29	49	79	150	2	5	10	39	44	96	**235**

a. The same whale is counted twice if seen in different habitats in the same year. Total for year counts each whale once for that year. SEUS = southeast United States, CCB = Cape Cod Bay, GSC = Great South Channel, RB = Roseway Basin, and BOF = Bay of Fundy.

b. Totals include unique animals of unknown sex.

Table 3.2. Summary of Sighting Gaps from 1980–2003 for 332 Whales
That Were Seen More Than Once, and Believed to Be Alive in 2003[a]

Gap in years	Count of gaps	Percentage of all gaps
1	2,669	79.8
2	388	11.6
3	141	4.2
4	68	2.0
5	30	0.9
6	15	0.4
7	6	0.2
8	8	0.2
9	5	0.1
10	4	0.1
11	3	0.1
12	2	0.1
13	3	0.1
17	1	0.0
	3,343	

a. A one-year gap means the whale was seen in consecutive years.

more years), but it is certainly more accurate than assuming that all whales ever cataloged remain alive to this day. For the analyses that follow in this chapter, only the whales believed to be alive in 2003 under this criterion are used.

The six-year criterion is supported by an analysis of all the sighting gaps (a gap is the span in years between sightings of an individual) for each whale in the *Catalog* (Table 3.2). There were 3,343 sighting gaps from 1980 to 2003 for 332 cataloged whales that had been sighted more than once and were believed to be alive in 2003 (ten whales thought to be alive were removed because they had one sighting only). Eighty percent of those were one-year gaps (i.e., sightings in consecutive years), indicating that many whales are sighted annually. Six years was kept as the cutoff for presumed mortality because 99 percent of all sighting gaps of whales presumed to be alive are six years or less.

Another way to view the gaps in sightings is to determine what percentage of the years each whale was sighted from its first sighting to its last. Figure 3.8 distills this information for the sighting histories of 342 whales into a standard box plot. It shows that whales with sighting histories spanning thirteen years or less ($n = 135$) are generally seen in 90 to 100 percent of the available years, and whales with longer sighting histories are seen less frequently. Because the majority of whales added to the *Catalog* in the past thirteen years were

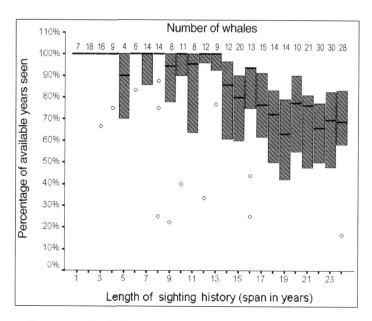

Figure 3.8. Percentage of available years that each whale was sighted, 1980–2003 (342 whales presumed to be alive in 2003 included in the analysis). A whale was considered available from its first sighting year until its last sighting year ("Length of sighting history"). Each box shows the median and the interquartile range, which represents 50 percent of all the values for the group of whales with that sighting length. The open circles represent outliers and extreme values that are more than 1.5 times the interquartile range; see section on "Irregular" whales.

calves at the time (Fig. 3.5), many of these 135 whales represent younger animals, and, therefore, the data suggest that this change in sighting frequency may be age-related and occur around the age of sexual maturity. This apparent decrease in sighting frequency after sexual maturity may be driven in part by the reproductive females, which are known to be seen less frequently in their resting and pregnancy years (Brown et al. 2001). Although they are seen less than the younger whales, Fig. 3.8 shows that older whales are still sighted 70 percent of their available years, even those whales whose sightings span twenty to twenty-four years.

Irregular Whales

Figure 3.8 also shows a class of whales that behave differently than the majority of the cataloged population. These individuals show up as the outliers in the figure, with annual sighting frequencies far below the median for the rest of the population. These whales constitute an interesting segment of the population that is harder to monitor using the photo-identification *Catalog*. Some of these whales, such as Eg #1334, are females that are seen almost solely on the calving ground during calving years. Eg #1334 is seen consistently in the waters off the southeast United States, giving birth every three to four years (even when other whales shifted to five- to six-year calving intervals), but has been seen only three times outside the calving ground during her twenty-year sighting history. One of those three sightings occurred south of Greenland in the Labrador Basin in 1989 with her calf of that year. Perhaps she has taken some or all of her five other calves to this area. Unfortunately, it is too far from land to survey regularly, so this possibility remains only conjecture.

Some of these irregular whales use inshore habitats, but rarely. Eg #1412 is an interesting example. Until recently, she had just four sightings in the *Catalog*. In October 1984, she was seen twice with a calf on Jeffreys Ledge, an area north of Massachusetts Bay. Thirteen years later (1997), she was resighted, again in October with a calf on Jeffreys Ledge (Weinrich et al. 2000). Given the extraordinarily thorough survey effort on the calving ground in 1997, it is noteworthy that this distinctively scarred whale and her calf were missed. Does she use a different part of the calving ground? Or a different calving ground altogether? One of this whale's mysteries was revealed when Marilyn Marx went to Iceland for a right whale survey in 2003 and discovered that Icelandic whale watch captains and scientists had collected right whale photographs and video from several sightings. What individual should appear in those images but the mysterious Eg #1412, once in July 1995 on the Cape Farewell Ground (between Iceland and Greenland) and twice in June 2003 just west of Iceland.

These irregular whales illustrate an important point. Even though there are five areas that are well defined as important habitats, clearly other right whale habitats exist. Many of the whales using these other areas are calving females such as Eg #1334 and Eg #1412, and these mothers pass on knowledge of these habitats to their offspring. Malik et al. (1999) showed that mothers take their calves to specific nursery areas, and those calves tend to return to those areas when they mature and give birth to their own calves. Thus the use of these habitats is culturally perpetuated across generations. Some of these habitats are known. For example, Jeffreys Ledge appears to be an important area for some whales, such as Eg #1412, that are rarely seen elsewhere. Similarly, the Gulf of St. Lawrence is frequented by several mothers that do not take their calves to the Bay of Fundy. These areas, along with the waters around Iceland and the Cape Farewell Ground, may be important habitats for a few whales that rarely visit the well-studied right whale areas. There has been little or no survey effort in most of these regions, and because the majority of sightings have come from opportunistic effort, accurate assessment of right whale frequency in and use of these areas is difficult.

The Difficulty of Whale Classification by Sighting History

Because the habitat use patterns of these irregular whales do not coincide with the timing and distribution of the survey effort, most aspects of their biology are poorly monitored. There is little opportunity to collect skin samples from them because they are rarely sighted during focused shipboard surveys equipped with biopsy equipment, so their genetic profiles are underrepresented. Although most calving events are documented in the southeast, the calves of these whales are rarely photo-identified because of lack of shipboard photos from whatever feeding ground they use later in the year. This lack of shipboard photos also means that health assessments are not available for these individuals. The mortality of these irregular whales is probably underestimated because their carcasses are likely further offshore, and their presumed mortality is probably overestimated because their visitation patterns to the study sites are so unpredictable that they may not be seen for years at a time.

Because of these gaps in the irregular whale data, these whales require their own classification so they can be treated differently for reproduction and survivorship analyses. However, developing consistent criteria to classify them based on their sighting histories remains difficult. Should irregular whales be defined solely by their low sighting frequencies? Or should they be defined in part by where they are sighted? In this book and elsewhere, researchers have used such terms as "offshore whales" and "non-Fundy" in an attempt to categorize some of these irregular whales, but these terms have been poorly defined and inconsistently used. The sighting history of "Rat," Eg #1509, provides a good example. During her twenty-four-year sighting history, Rat has had six calves and over 200 sightings. She has been sighted in the Bay of Fundy only ten times, and those sightings were all in the course of one month in 1997 when she was with her fourth calf. Should this apparently singular event change her classification as a non-Fundy mother?

The example of Rat illustrates how the ability to apply any consistent and meaningful categorization by a whale's habitat use is hampered by the plasticity of right whale movements. Right whales can easily travel hundreds, if not thousands, of kilometers in a matter of months, and, because of this, they are capable of changing their pattern of habitat use overnight. One good example is "Porter," Eg #1133. This adult male was seen regularly in and around the Gulf of Maine from 1981 to 2003. However, in 1999, he made the longest documented journey of any right whale, traveling from Cape Cod in May to northern Norway in September and then back to the Cape the following year (Jacobsen et al. 2004). Clearly this voyage was not expected given his relatively stable coastal sighting history. Another example is Eg #2010, a ten-year-old male that made three whirlwind trips along the eastern seaboard during the winter of 2000. He swam from Florida to Cape Cod Bay in eleven days, then to Georgia in less than twenty-four days, and then, after two weeks in Georgia and Florida, returned to Cape Cod Bay in less than twenty-four days again! Finally, there is "Wart," Eg #1140, the satellite-tagged mother who took her calf from the Bay of Fundy down to Cape Cod and along the Jersey shore before returning to the Bay of Fundy in less than six weeks (Mate et al. 1997). Without the satellite tag data it would have been assumed that Wart and her calf were in the Bay during that entire six-week period, just on the edge of the right whale distribution and thus missed by our photo-identification efforts. These examples of right whale movements and plasticity in habitat use underscore the difficulty of applying standardized classifications based on habitat use patterns.

Estimating Population Size

Two of the big questions in dealing with any endangered species are how many animals are there, and is that number changing? With a small population and a relatively thorough photo-identification effort, using actual counts may be the most reliable means of determining population estimates. As of June 2005, there were 459 cataloged whales, 23 of which were known to be dead and another 116 of which were presumed to be dead. If the known dead and presumed dead animals for each year are removed, the count of whales believed to be alive each year shows a leveling off between 305 and 335 in the mid- to late 1990s (Fig. 3.9). The count of whales presumed to be alive is the number often used when referring to the population size.

The slope of the curve (Fig. 3.9) from 1980 to 1994 is probably a "discovery curve" whereby increasing effort throughout all right whale habitats during this decade led to the discovery and photography of animals that had not yet been identified. However, the leveling off of the curve after 1994 may not reflect the asymptote of discovery but may be the result of an increase in

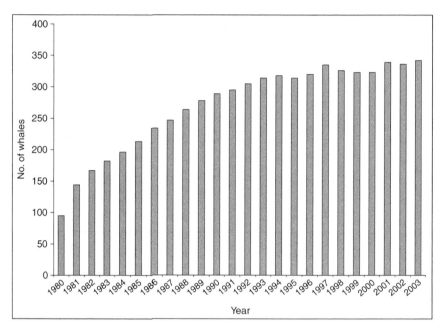

Figure 3.9. Cataloged whales presumed to be alive, 1980–2003.

mortality. Note how the peaks in new whales added to the *Catalog* in 1996, 1997, and 2001 (Fig. 3.5) do not register in Fig. 3.9. This suggests that the new whales added during those years were offset by known or presumed mortality. The curve from 1980 to 1994 may also represent an increase in the population rather than discovery, but there is no reliable way to tease apart these two factors. It should be noted that the numbers for 2001 to 2003 are artificially low, as many of the unidentified calves born in those years are likely alive and will be added to the *Catalog* in future years as juveniles.

Most population estimates incorporate a range of possible numbers (minimum and maximum) with an estimate of the error, and there are a number of different ways to calculate these values. The absolute minimum alive in a given year could be those photographed alive that year, or it could be those photographed that year plus those that were photographed in both a previous year and a subsequent year (clearly those animals were alive in the interim years), or, as shown in Fig. 3.9, it could be the number of cataloged whales that have been seen alive within the past six years. For a maximum value, one could use all the whales in the *Catalog* minus those whose carcasses have been identified, resulting in a maximum of 436 whales in 2003. In addition, one could add all the calves that have been born but not photo-identified in their calf year (though many of these were later added to the *Catalog* as unknown age animals and would therefore be double-counted using this method).

These methods all use actual numbers from the photo-identification effort and therefore do not incorporate any estimate of those whales that have not been photographed (likely more "irregular" whales). A number of new, non-calf animals are added to the *Catalog* each year, indicating that some are missed in the *Catalog*. The estimated maximum value could include an extrapolation from this "new whale discovery rate" to include the number of whales in the population that are alive but have never been photographed. This clearly gets into murky territory. The photo-identification database can tell us little about those animals that have been photographed only occasionally, if at all. Therefore, the maximum number of right whales remains difficult to estimate.

Another way to estimate population size is to apply mathematical models to the database. A standard technique is to use mark-recapture models in which a sample of the population is used to infer the total population size. However, these models depend on a number of assumptions such as random distribution of both animals and survey effort, and the right whale data violate most of these assumptions. In recent years there have been advances in modeling to accommodate more heterogeneity in the data, and although the new approaches provide estimates of vital population rates, they are unable to estimate absolute numbers from the right whale dataset.

The Power of Genetics and Photo-Identification

The increasing power and resolution of the information that can be gleaned from genetic studies hold tremendous promise for furthering our understanding of right whales (Chapter 7). Genetic studies of this population also have important implications for the photo-identification *Catalog*. For example, genetic analyses have already been used to help link a mortality event to a whale's sighting history. Occasionally dead whales are so decomposed on discovery that they cannot be reliably photo-identified based on their markings. This was the case when an adult male named "Delta," Eg #1333 (named after a large scar on his fluke tip shaped like an airplane), washed up on the shores of North Carolina in October 1998. All of the skin and callosity tissue were gone, but the remnants of a scar on his back remained. Matchers were focused on different whales with similar back scars as possible candidates, but none could be confirmed. While the matchers were scratching their heads, Tim Frasier at McMaster University called to say that he had matched it genetically to a known whale. He had Delta's genotype from a previous skin sample on file in the lab, and he was able to match that to the dead whale's genotype. The first genetic match to a *Catalog* whale had been made!

Genetic matching will continue to play an important role in the future. For example, many of those calves that are not photo-identified because they are seen only on the calving grounds can be genetically identified, or genotyped, if a skin sample can be collected from them on the calving ground. When these whales are photographed and biopsied in subsequent years, they can be linked back to their sightings as calves, and thus their identity, age, and maternal lineage will be known. Genetics may also help with the classification of the irregular whales if they contain a unique genetic signature. Such a classification could then be applied to models that utilize the photo-identification database to correct for heterogeneity in population estimates from sightings data. Last, genetic sampling can provide an excellent independent check on the error rate in the *Catalog*. With over 170 whales genetically sampled more than once, researchers will be able to compare genotype identities to photographic identities and thus verify both databases. Given the comprehensiveness of both datasets, this is a powerful validation procedure.

The Evolution of the *Catalog*

Because of this relatively new ability to genotype whales from skin (and fecal) samples, the photo-identification *Catalog* is evolving into a right whale identification database that will include all information related to an individual. No longer is a photograph of a whale necessary to insert a sighting record in the database. Now, any record of a cataloged whale that has been genotyped can be entered in the database based on photographs, skin samples without photographs, and/or feces collected (perhaps with no whale in sight). Also, the locations of whales with implanted satellite tags can now be included in the *Catalog* because these data hold important information on the movements of known individuals.

The process of maintaining the *Catalog* will also likely continue to evolve as technology advances. With the creation of DIGITS, researchers are now able to manage the *Catalog* from any place in the world through the Internet, thus enabling seamless data management even from field stations. The *Catalog* has been and will continue to become more visible to the general public as well, with an increasing web presence and educational curriculum to help train future cetologists.

Researchers will continue to use the *Catalog* as the primary monitoring tool for important demographic variables such as calving rate, interbirth interval, mortality, and population status. More critically, recently developed methods for annually assessing health and human influences from the photographic data can monitor the effectiveness of management actions designed to reduce anthropogenic injuries and mortality. All of these approaches should provide for comprehensive and accurate annual assessments of the status of the population. It is our hope that the strong ethic of collaboration among different research groups that exists today will continue, and more sophisticated, multivariate analyses will be applied across multiple linked databases including genetic, sighting, and oceanographic data. In addition, there will be new uses for *Catalog* data, such as comparing the major histocompatability complex profiles of individual whales to their reproductive history and physical health.

Conclusion

This is a population of whales in which nearly every individual is known. It is comparable to some of the great long-term studies on mountain gorillas, chimpanzees, and elephants. However, unlike the terrestrial animals, right whales are mostly hidden from view, and the views afforded researchers are brief indeed. The *Right Whale Catalog* has developed through an oceanwide collaborative group of researchers, an unusual feature of this long-term study. The right whale photo-identification effort, which uses patterns of callosity tissue and scars to distinguish each right whale, has resulted in a *Catalog* of over 33,000 photographed sightings from 1935 to 2005. This *Catalog* represents 459 numbered (and sometimes named) right whales observed during large numbers of aerial and shipboard surveys over twenty-five years in the North Atlantic.

Although most whales in the *Catalog* are seen frequently in known habitats and are well represented in the data, other "irregular" whales seem to use different areas, and most aspects of their biology are poorly understood. For population assessments and modeling, developing a consistent terminology and classification system for these whales remains challenging. Genetic profiling provides an additional tool to assist in the cataloging of individuals and potentially to estimate population size. Most right whale studies depend on the photo-identification *Catalog,* and it is imperative that this powerful, collaborative database be maintained.

Twenty-five years ago researchers were wondering whether the females in the waters off the southeastern United States were the same whales that appeared in the Bay of Fundy. Today they know the answer to that question and to many others critical to the conservation of this species. Yet it is still not known where many of the right whales spend the winter months, where some of the mothers take their calves after they leave the calving grounds, and when and where conception actually takes place. It is exciting to imagine what new stories will have unfolded twenty-five years from now. Those stories will likely have answered some of the current questions and uncovered new, and perhaps more complex, questions. And eighty years from now? All of today's researchers will certainly be gone, but with luck, some of the right whales alive today may still be plying the North Atlantic Ocean.

Anonymous. 2000. *Canadian Right Whale Recovery Plan. A Canadian Recovery Plan for the North Atlantic Right Whale.* World Wildlife Fund Toronto and Fisheries and Oceans Canada, Dartmouth, Nova Scotia, Canada.

Brown, M. W., S. D. Kraus, D. E. Gaskin, and B. N. White. 1994. Sexual composition and analysis of reproductive females in the North Atlantic right whale, *Eubalaena glacialis,* population. *Marine Mammal Science* 10:253–265.

Brown, M. W., S. Brault, P. K. Hamilton, R. D. Kenney, A. R. Knowlton, M. K. Marx, C. A. Mayo, C. K. Slay, and S. D. Kraus. 2001. Sighting heterogeneity of right whales in the western North Atlantic: 1980–1992. *Journal of Cetacean Research and Management* Special Issue 2:245–250.

Caswell, H., M. Fujiwara, and S. Brault. 1999. Declining survival probability threatens the North Atlantic right whale. *Proceedings of the National Academy of Sciences* 96:3308–3313.

Fujiwara, M., and H. Caswell. 2001. Demography of the endangered North Atlantic right whale. *Nature* 414:537–541.

Hamilton, P. K. 2002. Associations among North Atlantic right whales. MS Thesis. University of Massachusetts, Boston.

Hamilton, P. K., and S. M. Martin. 1999. *A Catalog of Identified Right Whales from the North Atlantic: 1935–1997.* New England Aquarium, Boston.

Hamilton, P. K., A. R. Knowlton, M. K. Marx, and S. D. Kraus. 1998. Age structure and longevity in North Atlantic right whales (*Eubalaena glacialis*) and their relation to reproduction. *Marine Ecology Progress Series* 171:285–292.

Hiby, L., and P. Lovell. 1990. Computer aided matching of natural markings: a prototype system for grey seals. *Report of the International Whaling Commission* Special Issue 12:57–62.

Hiby, L., and P. Lovell. 2001. A note on an automated system for matching the callosity patterns on aerial photographs of southern right whales. *Journal of Cetacean Research and Management* Special Issue 2:291–296.

IWC. 2001. Report of the workshop on the comprehensive assessment of right whales: a worldwide comparison. *Journal of Cetacean Research and Management* Special Issue 2:1–60.

Jacobsen K.-O., M. Marx, and N. Øien. 2004. Two-way trans-Atlantic migration of a North Atlantic right whale (*Eubalaena glacialis*). *Marine Mammal Science* 200: 161–166.

Knowlton, A. R., and S. D. Kraus. 2001. Mortality and serious injury on northern right whales (*Eubalaena glacialis*) in the western North Atlantic Ocean. *Journal of Cetacean Research and Management* Special Issue 2:193–208.

Knowlton, A. R., J. Sigurjónsson, J. N. Ciano, and S. D. Kraus. 1992. Long-distance movements of North Atlantic right whales (*Eubalaena glacialis*). *Marine Mammal Science* 8:397–405.

Knowlton, A. R., S. D. Kraus, and R. D. Kenney. 1994. Reproduction in North Atlantic right whales (*Eubalaena glacialis*). *Canadian Journal of Zoology* 72: 1297–1305.

Kraus, S. D., and J. J. Hatch. 2001. Mating strategies in the North Atlantic right whale (*Eubalaena glacialis*). *Journal of Cetacean Research and Management* Special Issue 2:237–244.

Kraus, S. D., K. E. Moore, C. E. Price, M. J. Crone, W. A. Watkins, H. E. Winn, and J. H. Prescott. 1986. The use of photographs to identify individual North Atlantic right whales (*Eubalaena glacialis*). *Report of the International Whaling Commission* Special Issue 10:145–151.

Kreho, A., N. Kehtarnavaz, B. Araabi, G. Hillman, B. Wursig, and D. Weller. 1999. Assisting manual dolphin identification by computer extraction of dorsal ratio. *Annals of Biomedical Engineering* 27:830–838.

Malik, S., M. W. Brown, S. D. Kraus, A. R. Knowlton, P. K. Hamilton, and B. N. White. 1999. Assessment of mitochondrial DNA structuring and nursery use in the North Atlantic right whale (*Eubalaena glacialis*). *Canadian Journal of Zoology* 77:1–6.

Mate, B. R., S. L. Nieukirk, and S. D. Kraus. 1997. Satellite-monitored movements of the northern right whale. *Journal of Wildlife Management* 61:1393–1405.

NMFS. 2005. *Recovery Plan for the North Atlantic Right Whale (*Eubalaena glacialis*).* National Marine Fisheries Service. Silver Spring, MD.

Parks, S. E., P. K. Hamilton, S. D. Kraus, and P. L. Tyack. 2005. The gunshot sound produced by male North Atlantic right whales (*Eubalaena glacialis*) and its potential function in reproductive advertisement. *Marine Mammal Science* 21:458–475.

Payne R., O. Brazier, E. M. Dorsey, J. S. Perkins, V. J. Rowntree, and A. Titus. 1983. External features in southern right whales (*Eubalaena australis*) and their use in identifying individuals. Pages 371–445 *in* R. Payne, ed. *Communication and Behavior of Whales,* Westview Press, Boulder, CO.

Schaeff, C. M., and P. K. Hamilton. 1999. Genetic basis and evolutionary significance of ventral skin color markings in North Atlantic right whales (*Eubalaena glacialis*). *Marine Mammal Science* 15:701–711.

Weinrich, M., R. Kenney, and P. Hamilton. 2000. Right whales (*Eubalaena glacialis*) on Jeffreys Ledge: a habitat of unrecognized importance? *Marine Mammal Science* 16:326–337.

Acknowledgments

The maintenance of the *Right Whale Catalog* is supported annually by grants from the National Marine Fisheries Service. The development of DIGITS and the public web site was supported by the National Science Foundation under Grant no. DBI-0317297. Any opinions, findings, and conclusions or recommendations expressed in this material are those of the authors and do not necessarily reflect the views of the National Science Foundation.

4

Surveying for Discovery, Science, and Management

MOIRA W. BROWN, SCOTT D. KRAUS, CHRISTOPHER K. SLAY, AND LANCE P. GARRISON

14 July 2003
North Atlantic Ocean, Southwest of Iceland

The crew is on watch on the Cape Farewell Grounds, following in the century-old wake of whalers from New Bedford, Massachusetts who plied these waters for the rich bounty to be had from right whales. We are pressed between a leaden sky and smooth mercury-like sea, a stark contrast to the feather-white, wind-tossed ocean we had been staring at for the past week. Calm gray days like this are best for spotting the two-meter-tall white blow that betokens the breath of a surfacing whale. Did the whalers favor these flat, gray days too?

Bundled against the July cold, Marilyn Marx and I search the sea surface from atop the wheelhouse of the S/V Sedna IV. *Scanning from the vessel's edge out to the horizon and back, our eyes are constantly in motion, trying to capture any disruption on the water surface. We are far from our usual survey areas along the eastern seaboard of Canada and the United States, drawn to the southern margins of the Irminger Sea, halfway between Greenland and Iceland, to see if right whales, hunted in these waters in the 1860s, still made this parcel of ocean their summer home.*

Mysteriously, a large eddy appears to port, then another. In an instant we both think of the typical surface signature, or fluke print, of a right whale

swimming just below the surface. Our first utterances are cut short by the realization that these eddies could only be caused by a right whale. We shout in unison "stop the boat" and stomp our feet on the wheelhouse roof to get the attention of the helmsman. A right whale surfaces within meters of the vessel, exhales in a V-shaped plume, rolls, and dives. Richard Sears bursts out of the wheelhouse to join in our chorus of "right whale!"

Remarkably, we have found our quarry just as the whalers had. A smaller boat is lowered, and we give chase, but rather than harpoon and kill the whale, we plan to capture it on film. Photographs of the unique markings on the whale's head will form the basis for its inclusion in the Right Whale Catalog. *The sea, which had appeared calm from the ship, was rolling with a 2-m swell. How did the whalers catch these whales from rowboats? With bow and arrow in hand, I take aim and get a small sample of skin on the second try. DNA will reveal the genetic relationship of this whale to the others. We track this lone right whale for 16 km; it appears to ignore our presence and swims steadily east. Then, as if all had been an apparition, the whale disappears, lost among the steep swells. We return to the S/V* Sedna IV *with identification photos and skin sample closely guarded. This is the only right whale we will see during our three weeks of survey.*

Named "Hidalgo" (Eg #3410) for the white mustang-shaped marking on the tip of its rostrum, it was a new right whale to the photographic archive (Fig. 4.1). Molecular studies revealed her sex and her relations among the right whale population but not her age. Somehow this whale, who crossed our path so briefly, had been born, thrived, perhaps given birth herself, yet had managed to elude our extensive survey efforts in the typical haunts of right whales along the east coast of North America.

Questions about what this sighting meant to efforts to study this species rang around the dinner table that night and still linger in our minds. Just how many other right whales are we missing? How can we survey to find more right whale habitats? Right whales were mostly forgotten after the cessation of whaling in 1935. Then, starting in the 1950s, decades of surveys and the work of many scientists would lead the North Atlantic right whale to become one of the best-studied marine mammals in the wild. And yet, here was Hidalgo, a mysterious whale, outside of our neat package of right whale knowledge, raising more questions than answers.

Moira Brown

Figure 4.1. Hidalgo (Eg #3410) in the Irminger Sea, southwest of Iceland. Moira Brown / New England Aquarium.

The modern search for western North Atlantic right whales began in Cape Cod Bay, Massachusetts, in the 1950s, after a chance aerial photograph of two right whales came to the attention of Bill Watkins and Bill Schevill, researchers from the Woods Hole Oceanographic Institution. During springtime cruises for years afterwards, Watkins and Schevill searched Cape Cod Bay until right whales were found and then stayed with them to record behavioral observations and collect acoustic recordings (Watkins and Schevill 1982). Thus the species most researchers had concluded was nearly extinct was, in fact, present for several months of the year in Cape Cod Bay. Where else did they persist?

Then in August 1971 six right whales, including a calf, were observed by researchers from the University of Guelph while they studied harbor porpoises in the mouth of Passamaquoddy Bay on the New Brunswick side of the lower Bay of Fundy (Arnold and Gaskin 1972). These sightings added credibility to an August 1966 sighting of fifteen right whales seen in the mouth of the Bay of Fundy from the M/V *Bluenose* (a car passenger ferry) on a crossing between Bar Harbor, Maine, and Yarmouth, Nova Scotia (Neave and Wright 1968; Schevill 1968).

In the late 1970s, Edward Mitchell and Randall Reeves began examining the logbooks from whaling vessels, records of maritime commerce, and coastal newspaper accounts for reports of this species (Reeves et al. 1978; Reeves and Mitchell 1986a, 1986b). From these detailed literature surveys, modern researchers learned of the historical range of right whales and gleaned indications of the number of whales that had been taken by whalers.

Just as the demand for whale oil fueled the hunt and subsequent demise of the right whale, the demand for offshore oil and gas exploration led to systematic environmental assessments and censuses of marine mammals in the western North Atlantic. The first such survey (in 1979) was the Cetacean and Turtle Assessment Program (CeTAP 1982). Howard Winn from the University of Rhode Island was funded for three years by the Minerals Management Service to carry out large-scale aerial and shipboard surveys to census all marine mammals and turtles in the waters between Cape Hatteras and Nova Scotia. The second survey was for a proposed oil refinery near Eastport, Maine, and it was the impetus behind a U.S. National Marine Fisheries Service (NMFS) contract with the New England Aquarium (NEAq) for systematic surveys in the lower Bay of Fundy area in 1980. The Bay of Fundy and the CeTAP surveys demonstrated that right whales still existed and that at least some were reproductively successful. By 1982, the four northern habitats (Bay of Fundy, Roseway Basin, Cape Cod Bay, and the Great South Channel) had been identified as important to right whales in the spring, summer, and autumn for feeding, socializing, and rearing their young.

But where did right whales go in the winter months after they left the northern habitat areas, and where were the calves born? Whaling logbooks yielded records of twenty-five to thirty right whales taken between 1876 and 1882 by whalers based out of Brunswick, Georgia (Reeves et al. 1978). In more recent times there had been sightings of right whales off the coast of Florida between Daytona and Flagler Beaches (Moore 1953), and near Sarasota (Moore and Clark 1963). David and Melba Caldwell (Marineland of Florida) had seen a few right whales stranded dead along the Florida coastline, and Cathy Sakas, Hans Neuhauser, and Charles Cowan (Georgia Department of Natural Resources) found stranded calves on Georgia beaches in the winter of 1981/1982.

This trail of evidence led researchers from the NEAq and Delta Airlines pilot David Mattingly to organize a volunteer group of professional airline colleagues with private aircraft to carry out surveys along the coastline of Georgia and Florida to search for right whales. Despite early skepticism in the public and press, the "Delta Surveys" in February 1984 yielded sightings of thirteen right whales, including three mothers with newborn calves: a fifth habitat area had been confirmed. There have been annual surveys in the calving ground since 1984, and the coastal waters along the southeast United States are still the only known calving ground for this species.

The early observations of right whales by Schevill, Watkins, and Gaskin, the painstaking examination of the whaling records by Reeves and Mitchell, and the environmental assessment surveys led by Winn and Kraus all combined to identify areas where right whales still gathered seasonally. These efforts were the foundation for modern right whale surveys and sparked a scientific curiosity about the biology of right whales and the nature of their movements.

Development of Survey Methods

Whalers were the first professional observers of whales. Commercial whaling for right whales started at least as early as the eleventh century in the Bay of Biscay (Aguilar 1986), but it is unknown how hunters first learned their whaling skills or how searching for right whales evolved. There are records of shore-based whalers from the seventeenth to the early twentieth century maintaining lookouts on high-elevation points on the shoreline to watch for right whales along the U.S. coast. Vessel-based whalers had lookouts posted at the masthead or in the crow's nest who spread the word to the crew on sighting a right whale.

The rediscovery of right whales in the North Atlantic in the latter part of the 1900s made them intriguing to biologists, but the science of studying whales at sea was still new. By the 1960s, scientists working with the International Whaling Commission had watched species after species of large whale fall victim to poor estimations of abundance and consequent mismanagement, which brought many large whales to dangerously low population levels. Although right whales were protected from whaling, the problems of assessing distribution and abundance of any whale species are similar. After the disastrous early efforts to manage whaling, the methods for assessing whale populations have evolved rapidly over the past forty years and now include sophisticated models that account for factors such as the animals' behavior, observer errors, weather, ship or airplane characteristics, and a variety of other variables, all of which can introduce errors in estimation procedures. Still, it is a big ocean, and researchers can never afford to look at very much of it. In making observations of whales at sea and subsequent extrapolations to models of whale biology, it is important to realize the limitations of survey methods. Researchers' exposure to right whales is variable by habitat area and whale behavior, but at best they get a glimpse of what is really going on about 20 percent of the time when they are actually beside a whale at sea on a clear day.

Estimating Whale Abundance and Distribution

In general, surveys designed to determine abundance and spatial distribution of whales are conducted along line transects. Transects (also called tracklines) can be generally described as parallel lines set apart with equal spacing over a survey area (Fig. 4.2). These surveys are designed to collect sightings or random samples of the population across the area of interest. They are most appropriately designed to sample across environmental gradients and be representative of the potential habitats of the species under study (Buckland et al. 1999). Line transect surveys that are intended explicitly for abundance estimation have additional design constraints. These "rules" for conducting rigorous surveys ensure the validity of statistical assumptions that are used to convert encounter rates (i.e., whale sightings per kilometer of trackline) into actual densities of whales (i.e., numbers of whales per unit area). The critical step in developing abundance estimates from line transect surveys is the estimation of the probability of sighting whales within the strip of area covered by the survey. At least some whales within the region around the trackline will not be detected by the observers either because they were unavailable to be seen (e.g., under water) or were simply not seen as a result of observer error, weather conditions, or other factors (Marsh and Sinclair 1989). To improve abundance estimation, it is possible to include sighting probabilities into spatial models of whale density (Hedley et al. 1999; Forney 2000; Buckland et al. 2004).

However, most surveys for right whales are for management purposes and do not conform to the operational constraints of line transect surveys for abundance estimation. Therefore, habitat models using data from these surveys are more appropriately descriptions of the relative abundance of whales within the study area. The critical assumption for these analyses is that sighting probabilities are constant across the surveyed area. To meet this assumption, it is necessary to standardize survey effort used in the analysis to a restricted set of conditions (e.g., weather conditions, sea state, survey altitude, aircraft type) where it is reasonable to assume similar sighting probabilities. When survey effort is not evenly distributed in space, it is further necessary to directly account for the amount of survey effort within a particular spatial location.

These corrections, called sightings per unit of effort (SPUE), are the only way to understand whale distribution fully because surveys are not equally distributed and can be affected by weather, mission, and funding. To illustrate, suppose that researcher A flew 100 km through a coastal area one year and saw 100 whales, or one whale per kilometer. Researcher B, surveying a different

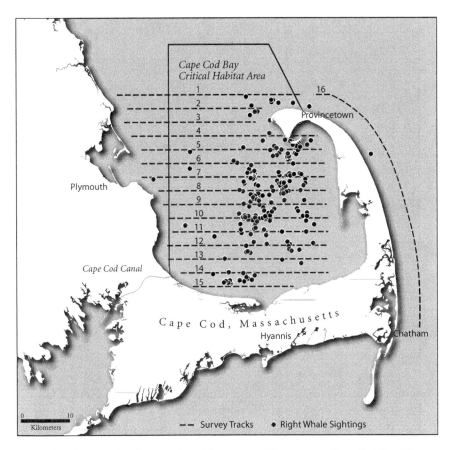

Figure 4.2. An example of systematic aerial survey tracklines set over Cape Cod Bay, Massachusetts, at 2.7-km intervals. Kerry Lagueux / New England Aquarium.

area of the same size, flew for 1,000 km and saw 200 whales, or one whale every 5 km. Comparing absolute whale numbers, one might be tempted to say that Researcher B had twice as many whales in that area. But by correcting for the number of survey kilometers (effort), it is apparent that Researcher A had a SPUE of 1, and Researcher B had a SPUE of 0.2. Assuming equivalent aircraft, conditions, and observers, it is therefore likely that the area surveyed by Researcher A had five times the density of whales as the area of Researcher B. SPUE analyses such as these are critical to focus management efforts, but they do not provide absolute numbers of abundance. Effort correction is also valuable because it allows for the use of data from multiple sources to determine how much scientists have actually looked at any ocean area.

Figure 4.3. Right whales are unique among large whales in that they can be individually identified using photographs taken by observers on both boats and airplanes (see also Fig. 4.7). (a) Researchers photographing right whales in the Bay of Fundy from the New England Aquarium's research vessel *Nereid*. Scott Kraus / New England Aquarium. (b) Eg #1310 alone. Timothy Frasier / New England Aquarium.

Features of All Right Whale Surveys

Systematic surveys, regardless of the platform used, require that a continuous log be kept of time and location (latitude and longitude), visibility, sea state (Beaufort scale), and cloud cover from the start of the survey until the end, with time collected on a regular basis during the survey. This information is critical to assess whale distribution and abundance because it allows researchers to evaluate their own effort and correct estimates for areas that were surveyed differently, or where environmental conditions were different.

Photographic identifications require some alterations in standard survey methodology. On sighting whales while conducting systematic survey transects, survey boats, ships, or light aircraft will break off the trackline to photograph them (Fig. 4.3 and color plate 31). In addition to photographs, researchers in boats sometimes collect skin and blubber biopsies and fecal samples from identified individuals (Chapters 7 and 8). Once the photographic and sample data are recorded, the aircraft or vessel returns to the trackline to continue the survey.

Vessels and aircraft usually record all sightings of marine animals except birds (including cetaceans, sea turtles, sharks, rays, pelagic fish) along with other vessel activity and fishing gear type and location. At the end of each survey day, trackline and sightings data from the daily logs are entered into a program designed for the North Atlantic Right Whale Consortium database and archived at the University of Rhode Island. In 2001 a computerized data logging system, linked to a global positioning system (GPS), replaced the handwritten logs on many surveys (color plate 32).

Right Whale Vessel Survey Methods

A number of research vessels dedicated to studying right whales have been used to survey areas along the eastern seaboard of Canada and the United States. These have varied in size from a 9-m-long inboard diesel boat to 54-m oceanographic ships such as the NOAA R/V *Delaware II,* although the researchers on the larger ships carry out close approaches to whales using rigid-hull inflatables.

The primary goal has usually been to locate and collect photographs and biopsy samples of individual right whales, although these missions have sometimes been combined with oceanographic studies on right whale habitat or acoustic research. Most surveys have been standardized across platforms to have two observers positioned on the highest accessible point with a clear view

Figure 4.4. Researchers using high-powered binoculars to search for right whales from the observation deck on a large oceanographic vessel. Misty Niemeyer / NOAA Fisheries.

forward of the vessel. The two observers scan with the naked eye out to 90° abeam of the vessel and forward to the bow, crossing slightly over each other's forward view field. Optimal survey conditions for right whales exist when visibility is greater than 3.6 km and when the Beaufort sea state is 4 or less. Tracklines for systematic surveys are usually spaced 5.4–9 km apart, depending on the eye height of the observer. On larger oceanographic vessels, there are often three observers searching for right whales with binoculars (up to 25 power) and the naked eye (Fig. 4.4).

In most cases, when a right whale is observed, the vessel breaks track at right angles when abeam of the whale and steams over to the last location. Once the right whale(s) surfaces, the boat moves slowly alongside the animal at a distance of 7–15 m, and observers take high-quality photographs of the whale's callosity pattern, back, scars, and dorsal and ventral sides of the flukes.

From 1980 through 2002, photographs were obtained using 35-mm single-lens reflex (SLR) cameras equipped with telephoto lenses, using color transparency films with ASA ratings between 64 and 400. Some investigators used black-and-white film, usually 100 to 400 ASA. Since 2003 digital SLR cameras have been used extensively to obtain digital images in JPEG format about 1.5 megabytes in size.

Right Whale Aerial Survey Methods

Aerial surveys have been conducted with multiple objectives in mind. Some surveys were designed to assess distribution and abundance, some were designed to manage human activities near right whales, and some have been exploratory. As a rule, most surveys incorporate efforts to find, photograph, and subsequently identify individual right whales. Sightings data have been used to estimate the absolute abundance of right whales (CeTAP 1982), to provide right whale location data to the marine industry to facilitate ship-strike avoidance, and to seek other right whale habitats.

Tracklines for systematic aerial surveys are usually flown at regular intervals and oriented perpendicular to the shoreline and near-shore bathymetry at regular intervals. An east–west flight pattern is often employed to reduce glare, a significant factor in the sightability of marine mammals. For both absolute and relative abundance estimates, analyses are based on data from "on-track" kilometers (i.e., survey tracklines flown with appropriate data collection protocols and adequate observer coverage). These analyses exclude all kilometers flown between tracklines, any circling time over right whales, and transits to or from the airport.

A wide variety of aircraft have been used for surveys (Cessna 170, 172, 182, 185, and 206; Grumman Widgeon and Goose; Lake Buccaneer; Maule; Twin Otter; AT11), but the most commonly used aircraft between 1980 and the present has been the Cessna 337 Skymaster, an in-line twin-engine high-wing aircraft (Fig. 4.5). The O2A model of the 337 Skymaster, developed for low-altitude reconnaissance during the Vietnam conflict, was designed to be tough, maneuverable, and exceptionally stable at low airspeeds, allowing for visual surveillance and photography. Both the military O2 and civilian models have been used in offshore aerial surveys.

All survey aircraft are now equipped with GPS navigation systems, full instrument flight rules instrumentation, marine radios, a life raft, survival suits, signal flares, and emergency position information and rescue beacons. Surveys have been conducted at altitudes of 230–305 m and at a ground speed of approximately 185 km/h, with visibility greater than 3.6 km and winds of less than 33 km/h. This approximately follows methodology developed during the CeTAP study (CeTAP 1982; Scott and Gilbert 1982) and is modified for

Figure 4.5. Cessna 337 Skymaster in flight. Yan Guilbault / New England Aquarium.

each survey area depending on the goals of the research program. Aerial survey teams usually consist of a pilot, a data recorder, and observers positioned on each side of the aircraft. Observers scan the water surface from the forward limit of visibility to directly abeam of the aircraft and from the downward limit of visibility out to at least 3.6 km (Fig. 4.6). The distance of each right whale sighting from the flight track is calculated by measuring the perpendicular distance from the trackline to the GPS position of the whale.

For sightings identified as right whales, survey aircraft leave the trackline to fly directly over the whale(s) to obtain photographs for individual identifications. High-quality photographs are obtained of as many individual right whales within a given aggregation as possible (Fig. 4.7). For each right whale, behavior and interaction with any nearby vessels or presence of other human activity (e.g., dredging, fishing) are noted. At the conclusion of the photographic work on each sighting, the aircraft returns to the transect line at the point of departure and continues the survey.

Aerial survey protocols and observer training were modified in 2003 following the loss of a survey team in a plane crash. Enhanced safety features on federally funded surveys include the use of two pilots, aircraft-ditching training for all pilots and observers, flight suits with thermal protection, flotation for all occupants, and certification of the survey aircraft in compliance with the Federal Aviation Administration Regulation Part 135 (Anonymous 2004).

Surveying for Science: Quantifying 25 Years of Survey Efforts

Systematic surveys for right whales started in the Great South Channel in 1979, the Bay of Fundy in 1980, Roseway Basin in 1982, in the southeastern United

Figure 4.6. Moira Brown (left) and Yan Guilbault scanning the surface of the water from a Skymaster aircraft during a right whale survey. Lisa Conger/New England Aquarium.

States in 1984, and in Massachusetts and Cape Cod Bays in 1985. Although annual survey effort in each of the habitat areas has been inconsistent (mostly as a result of variable funding), the scientific design of the surveys has been standardized across survey areas and platforms. Right whale surveys have identified seasonal aggregations of portions of the right whale population occurring in five geographic locations. Contemporary surveys have identified seasonal movements of whales between or among these consistently visited habitat areas along the east coast of North America (Kraus et al. 1986; Winn et al. 1986). Data collected from surveys within these areas have been used to analyze patterns of habitat use, reproduction, scarring, mortality, growth, health, and life history parameters of right whales.

One example illustrates the proven worth of systematic surveys for right whale conservation. Vessel-based surveys in the Bay of Fundy have continued uninterrupted since 1980. In addition to providing scientists with a wealth of data for the photographic *Catalog* and for monitoring reproduction, they have also provided a platform for a suite of other studies on contaminants, repro-

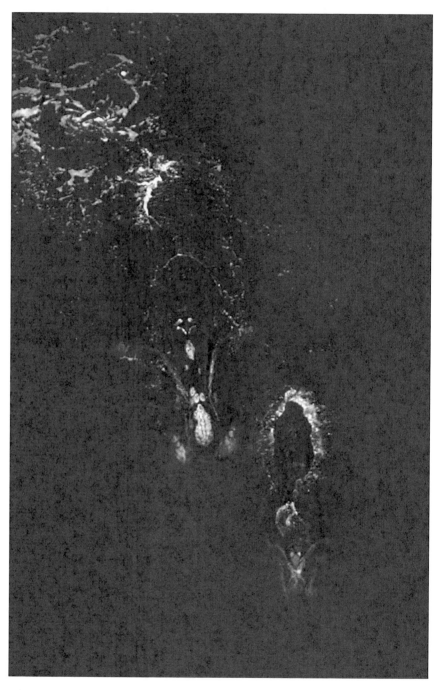

Figure 4.7. Eg #1310 with her calf. Brenna Kraus / New England Aquarium

ductive and stress hormones, genetics, scarring and skin lesions, visual health assessment, and acoustics. One of the more powerful uses of the sighting data was demonstrated in 2003 with the amendment to the Bay of Fundy shipping lanes. The survey data collected in the Bay between 1987 and 2002 clearly demonstrated the overlap between right whales and large vessels transiting the outbound shipping lane from Saint John, New Brunswick, and when combined with the whale mortality data, provided the justification for the Canadian Government to take action. Whale sightings and vessel transit data were used to calculate the relative probability of vessel-whale strikes in the shipping lanes and to identify alternative lanes where the probability of a vessel-whale interaction would be reduced (Chapter 14). Transport Canada implemented the lane change in July 2003 with success. In the following two years, a much lower percentage of right whale sightings occurred in the amended shipping lanes. Moving shipping lanes to protect endangered species was unprecedented and showed that governments, corporations, and whale biologists are capable of working together to find practical, science-based solutions to problems facing right whales.

Exploratory forays searching for right whales over large areas have proven effective at locating right whale habitat areas. CeTAP surveys discovered the Great South Channel spring habitat area, and the Delta surveys located the calving ground in the waters off the southeastern United States. Exploratory surveys have also been used to search for migratory corridors along the mid-Atlantic coastline and other potential summering areas such as the waters south of the Gaspé Peninsula in Quebec, and to evaluate current usage of historical whaling grounds, such as the Cape Farewell Grounds. These latter two surveys were successful in locating whales far beyond the known critical habitats, but time and funding limit the researchers' ability to return to these distant areas annually, and it is unknown if they are as important to right whales as the identified five critical habitat areas.

Beyond the area-specific and exploratory surveys, there have been a number of broad-scale efforts such as the CeTAP surveys and a multiyear aerial survey program over the Gulf of Maine being undertaken by the NMFS Northeast Fisheries Science Center. The extent of systematic survey effort over the past twenty-five years is represented in Table 4.1 and Fig. 4.8. The understanding of right whale biology and life history has come a long way since the first observations in Cape Cod Bay in the 1950s. Surveys have yielded information on almost every aspect of the right whale's life, and, because right whales are so highly endangered, these data are essential for developing management strategies that will assist in the recovery of the species.

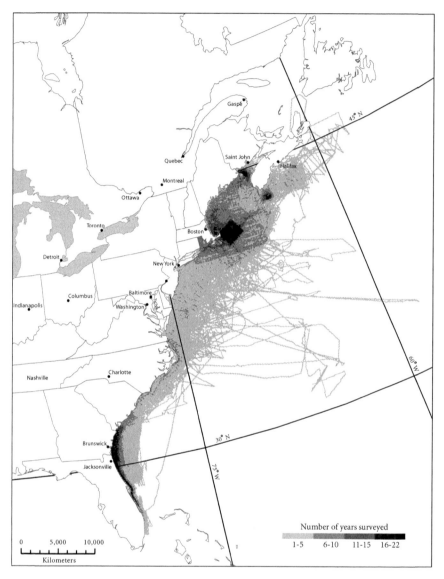

Figure 4.8. Geographic distribution of systematic survey effort along the eastern seaboard of the United States and Canada. Kerry Lagueux / New England Aquarium.

Opportunistic Sighting Data

Sightings collected opportunistically, that is, without quantifiable survey effort, have not been recognized as an important source of right whale data. The exceptions were reports and photographs of right whales collected by naturalists on whale watching boats that often operated outside of areas and seasons routinely surveyed by researchers. These opportunistic photographed sightings are no longer available since whale watching on right whales within 457 m of the animal was banned in the United States in 1990. This resulted in a loss of information because the out-of-season or out-of-habitat sightings were sometimes the "irregular" whales identified in Chapter 3. Such whales do not conform to most common habitat use patterns and are less likely to be seen in traditional survey areas; thus, their presence in population estimates is often underestimated. Further, opportunistic sightings have often led to surveys of areas not previously known to be important to right whales. For example, a whale watching group located on the Gaspé Peninsula in Quebec, Canada, photographed a few right whales every year after 1995, and these sightings led to a dedicated survey in that area. Whale watchers in the Gulf of Maine reported right whales in the autumn in an area off southern Maine and New Hampshire (Jeffreys Ledge) that is now being surveyed to assess its importance to right whales.

A second example of an opportunistic right whale sighting program is the shore-based volunteer sighting network in the southeast U.S. calving ground. This network, founded on a history of opportunistic observations by Forest Wood and David and Melba Caldwell, began in the 1950s. Organized by Jim Hain (Associated Scientists at Woods Hole), Joy Hamp (Marineland of Florida), and Julie Albert (Marine Resources Council), this volunteer sighting network is supplementing the conventional aerial survey programs, particularly on poor weather days when the survey planes cannot fly. It is also adding sighting data south of the primary calving ground for North Atlantic right whales. This program has contributed to right whale science as well as to citizen outreach, education, and stewardship for the marine environment.

Surveys for Management

Some surveys perform multiple functions in an ambitious approach both to learn about right whale biology and protect the whales from the principal human activities threatening their survival: ship strikes and entanglements in

Table 4.1. Principal Investigators Responsible for the Systematic Survey Effort for North Atlantic Right Whales since 1978 and Their Institutional Affiliations

Systematic survey areas	Institution	Principal investigators	Years
Cetacean and Turtle Assessment Program, Cape Hatteras to Scotian Shelf	University of Rhode Island	Howard Winn, Richard Edel, Martin Hyman, James Hain, Randall Reeves, Connie Knapp, Marlene Tyrrell	1978–1982
Bay of Fundy	New England Aquarium	Scott Kraus, Greg Stone, Amy Knowlton, Philip Hamilton, Lisa Conger, Porter Turnbull	1980–2005
	East Coast Ecosystems	Moira Brown, Deborah Tobin	1997–1999
	University of Rhode Island	Howard Winn, Robert Kenney	1992
Roseway Basin	New England Aquarium	Scott Kraus, Greg Stone, Kathy Hazard	1981, 1983–1985, 1986–1991, 2004–2005
	East Coast Ecosystems	Moira Brown	1985, 1992–1996
Roseway Basin and eastern Scotian Shelf	East Coast Ecosystems	Moira Brown, Deborah Tobin	1997–1998
	University of Rhode Island	Howard Winn, Robert Kenney	1987, 1992
Jeffreys Ledge/Stellwagen Bank	Whale Center of New England	Mason Weinrich	2003–2005
Cape Cod Bay	Provincetown Center for Coastal Studies	Charles Mayo	1985–2005
	New England Aquarium	Scott Kraus	1997
	Center for Coastal Studies/Division of Marine Fisheries	Moira Brown, Charles Mayo, Daniel Mckiernan, Edward Lyman, Owen Nichols, Natalie Jacquet	1998–2005

Survey area	Institution	Investigators	Years
Great South Channel	University of Rhode Island	Howard Winn, Robert Kenney	1984–1989, 1991–1993
South Channel Ocean Productivity Experiment	University of Rhode Island	Howard Winn, Robert Kenney	1988–1989
Sighting Advisory System	NMFS Northeast Regional Office	Patricia Gerrior	1998–2002
Offshore Surveys	New England Aquarium	Scott Kraus, Moira Brown	2004–2005
South of Long Island	Riverhead Foundation/State of New York	Robert DiGiovanni	2004–2005
Mid-Atlantic (New Jersey, Delaware, Virginia, North Carolina, South Carolina)	New England Aquarium	Scott Kraus	1992
	University of North Carolina Wilmington	William McClellan, Ann Pabst	2001–2002
	South Carolina Department of Natural Resources and Wildlife Trust	James Powell, Allison Glass	2005
Southeast U.S. calving ground[a]	New England Aquarium	Scott Kraus, Amy Knowlton, Christopher Slay, Lisa Conger, Monica Zani	1984–2005
	Florida Fish and Wildlife Commission	James Valade, William Brooks, Cyndi Taylor Thomas, Jamison Smith, Alicia Windham-Reid	1990–2005
	Georgia Department of Natural Resources	Michael Harris, Barbara Zoodsma, Lisa Conger, Clay George	1993–2005
	Georgia Department of Natural Resources and Wildlife Trust	James Powell, Emily Argo, Cyndi Taylor, Patricia Naessig	2001–2005
Gulf of Maine	NMFS Northeast Fisheries Science Center	Richard Merrick, Timothy Cole	1998–2005
Denmark Strait	New England Aquarium	Scott Kraus	2003

a. The surveys in the southeast U.S. calving ground have had extensive collaborations with the NMFS Southeast Regional Office, U.S. Navy, U.S. Army Corps of Engineers, and the U.S. Coast Guard; Charles Orvitz, Colleen Coogan, Ben Blaylock, Kathy Wang, Steven Swartz, Lance Garrison, Vicky Cornish, Barbara Zoodsma, and Donald Lewis from NMFS; Captain Robert Parlette and Kenneth Connolly from the U.S. Navy; Rudy Nyc of the U.S. Army Corps of Engineers; and Michael Lieberum from the U.S. Coast Guard.

Table 4.2. Location and Dates of Aerial Surveys Supporting State and Federal Management Actions for Right Whales

Activity	Location	Dates effective	Responsible agency
Dredging mitigation	Southeast United States	1988–2005	U.S. Army Corps of Engineers
Early Warning System	Southeast United States	1994–2005	U.S. Army Corps of Engineers, U.S. Coast Guard, U.S. Navy, National Marine Fisheries Service
Sighting Advisory System	Gulf of Maine	1997–2005	NMFS Northeast Regional Office and Northeast Fisheries Science Center
Massachusetts Right Whale Conservation Plan	Cape Cod Bay	1998–2005	Massachusetts Division of Marine Fisheries
Dynamic Area Management	Gulf of Maine	2001–2005	NMFS Northeast Fisheries Science Center

commercial fishing gear. Undoubtedly the most extensive program of this type is the aerial survey on the calving ground, with the primary goal of preventing ships from colliding with right whales. In addition, two other multipurpose programs have been conducted on the northeast feeding grounds. All three survey programs are discussed in detail as case studies (Table 4.2).

Case Study 1: Southeast U.S. Early Warning System

Researchers from the NEAq flew the Delta Surveys from 1984 to 1987 and learned that the coastal zone of Georgia and Florida was the primary calving ground for right whales in the western North Atlantic. By 1988 researchers realized the need to warn mariners (in particular vessels engaged in dredge operations) of the presence of right whales in the area because studies had indicated that one of the main sources of right whale mortality was from collisions with ships (Chapter 14).

During the Carter administration, the home base for the Atlantic Nuclear Submarine Fleet was moved to Kings Bay, Georgia, the shallowest stretch of coastline in the United States. To make this location usable for Trident submarines, dredges created a channel 36 km long, from the inland base to the mouth of the St. Mary's River, and stretching seaward approximately 22 km. From 1987 to 1990, as many as four 75- to 125-m ships were dredging the submarine channel and transiting every few hours to an offshore disposal site 18 km away, twenty-four hours per day. In 1988, researchers were just identifying this region as the heart of the right whale calving ground.

Starting in 1988, aerial surveys were flown as a U.S. Army Corps of Engineers contract requirement for dredging projects at Kings Bay Naval Submarine Channel (St. Mary's River entrance) and the Brunswick Harbor Entrance Channel, less than 40 km to the north, to keep the dredges from hitting and killing right whales. These surveys were flown daily, weather permitting, whenever dredging occurred during the months of December through March, using east-west transects at 5.4-km intervals out to approximately 32 km from shore. All right whale sightings within 27 km of dredging activities were reported to the captains of the dredges. The vessels (capable of speeds up to 26 km/h) were required to operate at 9 km/h or less during the night following a right whale sighting within the area or during periods of limited visibility (e.g., fog or severe weather) for twenty-four hours after a sighting. By 1992 all hopper dredging in the southeast was shifted to the winter months to avoid sea turtle mortality associated with dredging during the warmer months. This led to an increase in dredging traffic at all port entrances in the right whale calving grounds that were being maintained, or even deepened, to facilitate commercial shipping.

During the winter of 1993, the NEAq right whale team flew surveys simultaneously for dredging projects at Kings Bay and Brunswick. Because a sighting buffer of 27 km was required for dredges around the channels and the offshore disposal sites, these surveys extended along the coast from 24 km north of Brunswick, Georgia, to the mouth of the St. Johns River, which is the entrance to the Mayport Naval Base and the Port of Jacksonville, Florida. The survey data showed an extensive overlap between the right whale distribution and the commercial shipping traffic using these ports. It was obvious that providing right whale sightings to all of the dredge traffic in the calving ground was a significant conservation measure, but the majority of the other ship traffic in the region was unaware of the danger facing right whales. This was receiving little attention, and the commercial vessel traffic in this area was increasing (Knowlton 1997).

In 1993 NEAq researchers approached NMFS with a proposal to add a few tracklines at the southern end of the area to provide sighting coverage for all the shipping channels in the calving ground. They also proposed to alert the harbor pilots at all three ports to right whale sightings so that the pilots could relay that information to all commercial shipping traffic. Aerial surveillance for the entire calving season, December through March, would create a large blanket of protection for right whales in their calving grounds. It was unclear how to fund this effort. At the time, the U.S. Navy and the U.S. Army Corps of Engineers were already paying for dredge-related surveys. Then, in January of that year, a U.S. Coast Guard cutter inadvertently ran over and killed a right whale calf off the coast of northern Florida. As a result, the U.S. Coast Guard became a dedicated partner in right whale conservation. They offered to split the cost of aerial surveys three ways among the U.S. Navy, the U.S. Army Corps of Engineers, and the U.S. Coast Guard. Thus the first systematic, daily, large-scale marine mammal management surveys started in the winter of 1994, and they were dubbed the Early Warning System (EWS) Surveys.

Every winter since 1994, calving right whales have been afforded some measure of protection in the area between Brunswick, Georgia, and St. Augustine, Florida, and offshore to about 36 km. The three major entrance channels covered by these surveys serve three commercial shipping ports and two military bases. The EWS has steadily improved, the survey effort has been expanded, and the means of disseminating right whale sighting information to mariners is vastly more efficient. Today, three teams of researchers fly surveys every good weather day from 1 December through 30 March. In recent years, survey coverage has expanded to the north, south, and farther offshore to almost 72 km.

The system for notifying large vessel operators about right whale sightings has also evolved significantly. During the first two seasons, sightings were transmitted from the aircraft to Navy harbor controllers and commercial harbor pilots, who relayed the information to any vessels transiting near a recent right whale sighting. Ships and hopper dredges under way in the vicinity of whales were contacted directly from the aircraft. In 1996 these procedures were augmented by faxing details of each right whale sighting to the U.S. Coast Guard Office of Aids to Navigation in Miami, Florida, which transmitted text notices to mariners with information pertinent to navigation, including right whale sightings. In 1997, sightings were relayed from EWS aircraft directly to the U.S. Navy's Fleet Area Control and Surveillance Facility in Jacksonville. This facility sent the right whale information, almost instantaneously, to all military surface and air traffic in the southeastern North Atlantic. The following year, a pager system designed by Bill Brooks of the Florida Wildlife Research Institute and funded by the Jacksonville Ports Authority and the Institute eliminated the need for survey teams to phone and fax user groups with whale sighting information. In near real time, all groups and agencies now receive sightings information directly from Fleet Control shortly after it has been received from a survey team. Serving as the primary point of contact for all whale sightings in the calving ground, the U.S. Navy's Fleet Control has transformed the EWS system.

In addition to the EWS, the National Marine Fisheries Service implemented a seasonal Mandatory Ship Reporting system in the southeast United States (in 1999) for ships greater than 300 gross registered tons entering the right whale calving ground. The ships are required to report to a shore-based station and in return receive a message about right whales, their vulnerability to ship strikes, precautionary measures the ship can take to avoid hitting right whales, and recent sightings from the EWS system (Silber et al. 2002). Although it is valuable as both an educational and a conservation tool, it is difficult to evaluate whether this program has prevented any ship strikes of right whales.

From all of these efforts, the vast majority of ships traversing the right whale calving ground now know where whales have been sighted within the past twenty-four hours. However, this surveillance effort is only as good as the actions that ship operators make in response to the sighting information. During the passage of vessels in shipping channels, there is anecdotal information suggesting that local harbor pilots often operate at lower than normal speeds when whales have been sighted nearby. There are also many dramatic instances where aerial observers have directly contacted ships via VHF radio and steered them around whales. Hopper dredges are contractually bound to change their operating speeds, and military vessels have protocols for maneuvering in the vicinity of reported right whales. Still, if right whales are near a port entrance, there are no regulations for the large commercial vessels that make up most shipping traffic in the region.

Further, poor weather compromises about 50 percent of all survey trackline miles in a season. Telemetry data (Slay and Kraus 1998) and replicate survey data (C. Taylor and W. Brooks, pers. comm.) indicate that the EWS surveys may locate only 50 percent of the right whales in the area when conditions are favorable. If weather allows only half of the surveys to be completed, and only half of the whales in the area are detected, then as few as 25 percent of right whale occurrence in the EWS survey area may be reported. Therefore, this aerial survey system, as good as it is, provides no protection to a significant portion of the right whales during the winter season, and it is not capable of eliminating ship strikes in the calving ground. A more effective solution would be a management strategy that provided protective measures that are not linked to specific sightings data but simply to the presence or absence of right whales in the calving ground.

Case Study 2: Cape Cod Bay

The Provincetown Center for Coastal Studies has an ideal location for right whale research: Right whales grace the waters of Cape Cod Bay at their back door each winter and spring, and have a history of doing so since the 1600s (Allen 1916). The Center has conducted shipboard surveys for right whales concurrently with oceanographic surveys from the mid-1980s to the present (Hamilton and Mayo 1990). In 1997, the focus of this research effort expanded to assess right whale distribution, the planktonic food supply, and oceanographic features in Cape Cod Bay to determine how best to reduce conflicts between right whales and fishing activities. In March 1997 the NEAq conducted experimental surveys over Cape Cod Bay to compare aerial sightings with those from vessel surveillance. Based on the results of the Aquarium's pilot study, state fishery managers opted to use aerial-based surveillance as the primary tool for monitoring right whale distribution. In 1998, the Massachusetts

Division of Marine Fisheries contracted with the Provincetown Center to fly aerial surveys over Cape Cod Bay and adjacent waters from January through 15 May to monitor the whale's seasonal use and distribution in Cape Cod Bay. The oceanographic sampling was continued, and the combined program continues to this day.

Since 1999 the quality and distribution of the zooplankton resource in Cape Cod Bay have been assessed weekly. Because this work has shown a close correlation between counts of whales from aerial surveys and mean zooplankton density, it appears possible to predict the aggregation of right whales in this habitat, providing a promising new tool for managing the principal causes of mortality in the species. Using the oceanographic and aerial datasets, state managers have tuned their regulatory measures for fisheries accordingly and have published seasonal right whale shipping alerts to reflect these resource-based assessments. Although the direct effect on the operations of ships in the Bay has not been studied, the level of mariner awareness has increased. For example, there have been several instances in which the Army Corps of Engineers have temporarily closed the Cape Cod Canal to large vessels when right whales were detected within or near the eastern entrance.

In addition, the infrastructure of this program has provided a valuable field laboratory for testing alternative right whale monitoring methods. For example, the use of data from the aerial and oceanographic surveys is being correlated with sounds recorded passively on bottom-mounted hydrophones to determine if the presence or absence of right whales can be accurately detected acoustically (Chapter 11).

Case Study 3: Gulf of Maine Sighting Advisory System

Ship Strike Reduction

In 1996, an organization called Green World sued the Massachusetts Division of Marine Fisheries, NMFS, and the U.S. Coast Guard regarding right whale deaths from human activities. The court ordered the creation of a Massachusetts Endangered Whale Working Group and charged them with developing a conservation plan for right whales in Massachusetts's waters, primarily the Cape Cod Bay Critical Habitat. Following this group's recommendations, a right whale surveillance program called the North Atlantic Early Warning System was implemented in 1997 to search for right whales in the near-shore waters of Massachusetts and the Great South Channel in the winter and spring. The U.S. Coast Guard provided a helicopter (HH 60J Jayhawk) for surveillance flights, and the Northeast Fisheries Science Center and the Division of Marine Fisheries provided the observers. The surveys were flown along the shipping lanes between Boston and New York, east of Cape Cod, and in Cape Cod Bay, but observers had limited visibility from that type of aircraft. All sightings were reported to the Northeast Regional Office of NMFS in Woods Hole and disseminated to the marine industry by e-mail, fax, and a website.

Between 1998 and 2002, using conventional survey aircraft, these surveys were expanded to include Cape Cod Bay in the winter and spring and the entire Great South Channel Critical Habitat following tracklines laid out for an earlier study (Kenney et al. 1995). In 2002 the Northeast Fisheries Science Center changed the scope of their surveys from the Great South Channel to include the entire Gulf of Maine. Questions regarding the extent of right whale distribution in the Gulf of Maine had been raised, and the Science Center developed a multiyear program of broadscale surveys from the northeast coast to the Hague Line, southeast to Georges Bank, and south to the waters east of Long Island, New York.

Despite valiant efforts, the North Atlantic Early Warning System program was constrained by poor spring weather conditions and the large size of the survey area. In recognition that it was not feasible to provide real-time information about right whale locations in the Gulf of Maine, NMFS changed the name to the Sighting Advisory System. Nevertheless, information about the locations of sightings probably did reduce the risk to right whales to some degree, and the Sighting Advisory System continues to provide data on right whales to the commercial shipping industry and other marine traffic. Sightings data come from aerial and vessel surveys conducted by several agencies (NMFS, Massachusetts Division of Marine Fisheries, and U.S. Coast Guard) and organizations (Provincetown Center for Coastal Studies, Woods Hole Oceanographic Institution, International Wildlife Coalition, and Whale Center of New England), several whale watch companies, a high-speed ferry company, and from verified opportunistic sightings. An automated fax system transmits all sighting data at the end of each day to pilots, port authorities, ship traffic, NAVTEX, and to the U.S. Army Corps of Engineers traffic controllers, who oversee traffic in the Cape Cod Canal. The sightings data are also posted on web pages and broadcast with a buffer zone of 15 km around the whales for twenty-four hours on the Notice to Mariners and NOAA weather radio.

These management surveys in the Gulf of Maine are fundamentally different from the southeast U.S. surveys. They are less frequent because of poor weather;

sightings are reported at the completion of the survey rather than immediately through a pager system; and the sightability of whales is reduced by long feeding dives in these habitats. However, these surveys have identified persistent feeding aggregations around the Gulf of Maine, in addition to known critical habitat areas, that have a relatively high risk of encounters with human activities, including Jordan Basin, Jeffreys Ledge, Platts Bank, Cashes Ledge, and Wilkinson Basin. Further, there has been a benefit to the whales from the increased awareness among mariners. There are some instances, particularly in the Great South Channel shipping lanes and Cape Cod Bay, where aerial observers have contacted ships operating in the vicinity of right whales and helped them steer around the whales.

In 1999 the NMFS implemented the Mandatory Ship Reporting system off the northeastern United States as described above for the Southeast. The reduction of right whales kills as a result of the system cannot be accurately estimated. However, the level and preferred routes of shipping traffic crossing through right whale habitats are now much better understood, and these data can be used to implement regulations to improve protection for right whales (Chapter 14).

Fishery Entanglement Reduction

The extensive surveys in the Gulf of Maine led to the suggestion that fisheries might be dynamically managed, and high-risk fishing gear could be removed from an area if right whales were sighted within it. In 2001 NMFS developed a Dynamic Area Management (DAM) zone that would be triggered when three or more whales sighted north of 40°00′N were aggregated at a density greater than one whale per 44 km^2 (Clapham and Pace 2001). Once a DAM zone was triggered, a notice would be published in the Federal Register requiring fishermen to remove their gear from the water in the DAM zone or requiring fishermen to abide by additional gear modifications for a fifteen-day period. NMFS could determine whether to impose restrictions on fishing gear in the zone based on a number of factors, including but not limited to weather conditions as they relate to the safety of fishermen at sea. NMFS could also extend the DAM zone for an additional fifteen days based on additional sightings. The DAM program was a component of a suite of protection programs implemented by NMFS designed to protect aggregations of right whales that appeared in areas not typically frequented by right whales. Although an attractive management idea, the time delay between right whale sightings and publication of the notice in the *Federal Register* (a record ten days to three weeks), the difficulty of enforcement, and the reality of weather constraints on both aerial surveys and fishermen have raised questions about the effectiveness of the DAMs. However, the scientific data collected on right whale distribution in the Gulf of Maine during the broadscale surveys may result in refinements to this system.

Benefits of the extensive aerial coverage in right whale habitats include the detection of entangled whales, and a determination of the nature and extent of the entangling lines. The aerial perspective permits a view of the whale in the water that is far better than that afforded from most small boats. Typically the airplane will locate an entangled whale, obtain photographs to document the condition of the whale and severity of the entanglement, and stand by while rescuers are deployed by boat. Once the rescue operation is under way, aerial observers have been used to guide rescuers near the whale during disentanglement efforts, relaying whale behavior over marine radio. However, just as aerial surveys are limited in their ability to reduce the incidence of ship strikes, disentanglement operations are a band-aid solution to a larger management problem, the need to prevent entanglements from occurring in the first place (Chapter 13).

Future of Aerial and Vessel Surveys

After several seasons flying long hours in airplanes or at watch on the bow of a boat searching for right whales over many kilometers of ocean surface, the report of another entangled or ship-struck whale causes many researchers to wonder if there isn't a more effective way to protect these animals from human insults. Nothing can replace the individual photographic identification program for scientific monitoring of the population or the excitement of new discoveries about right whale biology. But visual aerial surveys for management are not the best solution for reducing conflicts with human activities. Not all whales in a survey area are seen, the cost of the aerial surveys is high, and there are safety concerns of flying at low altitudes long distances offshore. Still, the strengths and weaknesses of aerial management surveys are now much better known and in many cases appear to be the only option at this time. The challenge is to recognize the limitations of existing survey methods while researchers work with the shipping and fishing industries to refine protection strategies. Do management-oriented aerial surveys really reduce the impact of shipping and fisheries on right whales?

In the Southeast, the EWS is arguably the most thorough attempt at this sort of management, and yet, whales still get hit by ships, albeit infrequently.

The data suggest that only 25 percent of the whales that are present are detected on a given day, so it could be expected that the EWS is not wholly effective at protecting right whales from ships. Still, it is the best approach currently available until managers can successfully reroute or slow ships in the area or until better right whale detection and monitoring technologies are found. As this book goes to press, the NMFS has proposed vessel management rules to protect right whales, but implementation may be years away.

In the Northeast, the Cape Cod Bay surveys were successful at managing the conflicts with fisheries, in part because they simply relied on the presence or absence of the whales. Now the DMF has implemented permanent year-round modifications to fishing gear, so the aerial surveys in Cape Cod Bay are no longer used for management of fisheries. However, the Massachusetts survey program continues to provide valuable information about right whales and has been continued beyond its original management mission.

The broadscale NMFS surveys that result in the triggering of DAMs in the Gulf of Maine are unpredictable in frequency because of weather and therefore might miss whale aggregations that could be at risk from fishing. The continued high rates of entanglements of right whales in fishing gear indicate that this strategy is not very effective, but the data collected from these surveys may prove useful for modifying protection measures. Are there alternative technologies that are more effective at detecting whales and more cost effective than visual surveys?

A long-term solution is needed whereby protective measures are triggered by the presence of right whales in a particular habitat area. It may be that new technology will emerge that can detect right whales using methods other than visual sightings. Satellite tracking, infrared sensors, radar, sonar, and lidar have been proposed for use in remote detection of right whales, but few have been tested to date. There is hope for the use of passive acoustic detection of whales (Chapter 11). In the interim, visual-based surveys are necessary and will be essential to provide a standard to evaluate the effectiveness of alternative technologies; therefore, it is unlikely that the need for management surveys will be reduced in the near future.

Conclusion

In the earliest days of whaling, the success of a ship depended on the ability of the captain to find the right sort of areas in the ocean where whales might be abundant, and then on the ability of the lookouts to detect the whales they sought. No doubt these voyages were hampered by wind, fog, and waves as well as by the limitations of the ship, the skills of its crew, the costs of keeping it at sea, and the size of its larder. Contemporary surveys face many of the same challenges, but in the case of right whales, the success of the surveys now may mean the success of conservation efforts for the species.

Although visual surveys for management of human activities provide limited protection to right whales, the scientific data obtained during all shipboard and aerial efforts have proven their value repeatedly over the years. The surveys in the southeastern United States provide annual calf counts, and surveys throughout the Gulf of Maine provide photographic identification data for monitoring the population's status. Surveys have discovered new habitats, entangled whales have been detected and responded to by rescuers, and floating carcasses have been found and recovered for necropsy to determine the cause of death. Some vessel–right whale collisions have been avoided by direct communication between aerial observers and the crew of a vessel. These are all good reasons to continue the visual survey programs.

Beyond this, there is the remaining mystery of the missing "offshore" or "irregular" right whales, the unknown location of the winter mating ground, and other summering areas. The nature of human curiosity and the desire for exploration and understanding will take researchers past the neat, yet incomplete, package of present right whale knowledge and drive efforts to continue the search. The ocean remains large and poorly studied; there are many undiscovered places where right whales must go, and there are compelling conservation reasons to find them. Surveys, whether in the form of rigorous expeditions or wild-blue-yonder jaunts, will be needed for decades hence, and major discoveries are doubtless still to come.

Aguilar, A. 1986. A review of old Basque whaling and its effect on the right whales (*Eubalaena glacialis*) of the North Atlantic. *Report of the International Whaling Commission* Special Issue 10:191–199.

Allen, G. M. 1916. The whalebone whales of New England. *Memoirs of the Boston Society of Natural History* 8:107–322.

Anonymous. 2004. *Federal Aviation Regulations, Aeronautical Information Manual—2005.* ASA, Inc. Newcastle, WA.

Arnold P. W., and D. E. Gaskin. 1972. Sight records of right whales (*Eubalaena glacialis*) and finback whales (*Balaenoptera physalus*) from the lower Bay of Fundy. *Journal of the Fisheries Research Board Canada* 29:1477–1478.

Buckland, S. T., D. R. Anderson, K. P. Burnham, and J. L. Laake. 1999. *Distance Sampling: Estimating Abundance of Biological Populations.* Chapman and Hall, London.

Buckland, S. T., D. R. Anderson, K. P. Burnham, J. T. Laake, D. L. Borchers, and L. Thomas. 2004. *Advanced Distance Sampling.* Oxford University Press, Oxford, England.

CeTAP. 1982. A characterization of marine mammals and turtles in the mid- and north Atlantic areas of the US outer continental shelf. Final report, contract AA51-CT8-48. Bureau of Land Management, U.S. Department of Interior, Washington, D.C. 586 pp.

Clapham, P. J., and R. M. Pace III. 2001. Defining trigger for temporary closures to protect right whales from entanglements: issues and options. Northeast Fisheries Science Center Reference Document 01-06. 28 pp.

Forney, K. 2000. Environmental models of cetacean abundance: reducing uncertainty in abundance trends. *Conservation Biology* 14:1271–1286.

Hamilton, P. K., and C. A. Mayo. 1990. Population characteristics of right whales (*Eubalaena glacialis*) observed in Cape Cod and Massachusetts Bays, 1978–1986. *Report of the International Whaling Commission* Special Issue 12:203–208.

Hedley, S. L., S. T. Buckland, and D. L. Borchers. 1999. Spatial modeling from line transect data. *Journal of Cetacean Research and Management* 1:255–264.

Kenney, R. D., H. E. Winn, and M. C. Macaulay. 1995. Cetaceans in the Great South Channel, 1979–1989: right whale (*Eubalaena glacialis*). *Continental Shelf Research* 15:385–414.

Knowlton, A. R. 1997. Comparison of right whale mortalities to ship channels and ship traffic levels. Pages 52–69 *in* Shipping/Right Whale Workshop Report 97-3. New England Aquarium Aquatic Forum Series, New England Aquarium, Boston.

Kraus, S. D., J. H. Prescott, A. R. Knowlton, and G. S. Stone. 1986. Migration and calving of right whales (*Eubalaena glacialis*) in the western North Atlantic. *Report of the International Whaling Commission* Special Issue 10:139–151.

Marsh, H., and D. F. Sinclair. 1989. Correcting for visibility bias in strip transect aerial survey of aquatic fauna. *Journal of Wildlife Management* 53:1017–1024.

Moore, J. C. 1953. Distribution of marine mammals to Florida waters. *American Midland Naturalist* 49:117–158.

Moore, J. C., and E. Clark. 1963. Discovery of right whales in the Gulf of Mexico. *Science* 141:269.

Neave, D. J., and B. S. Wright. 1968. Seasonal migration of the harbor porpoise (*Phocoena phocoena*) and other Cetacea in the Bay of Fundy. *Journal of Mammalogy* 49:259–264.

Reeves, R. R., and E. Mitchell. 1986a. The Long Island, New York, right whale fishery: 1650–1924. *Report of the International Whaling Commission* Special Issue 10: 201–220.

Reeves, R. R., and E. Mitchell. 1986b. American pelagic whaling for right whales in the North Atlantic. *Report of the International Whaling Commission* Special Issue 10:221–254.

Reeves, R. R., J. G. Mead, and S. K. Katona. 1978. The right whale, *Eubalaena glacialis,* in the western North Atlantic. *Report of the International Whaling Commission* 28:303–312.

Schevill, W. E. 1968. Sight records of *Phocoena phocoena* and of cetaceans in general. *Journal of Mammalogy* 49:794–796.

Scott, G. P., and J. R. Gilbert. 1982. Problems and progress in the U.S. BLM-sponsored CETAP surveys. *Report of the International Whaling Commission* 32:587–600.

Silber, G. K., L. I. Ward, R. Clarke, K. L. Schumacher, and A. J. Smith. 2002. Ship traffic patterns in right whale critical habitat: year one of the mandatory ship reporting system. NOAA Technical Memorandum, NMFS-OPR-20. 25 pp.

Slay, C. S., and S. D. Kraus. 1998. Right whale tagging in the North Atlantic. *Marine Technology Society Journal* 32:102–103.

Watkins, W. A., and W. E. Schevill. 1982. Observations of right whales, *Eubalaena glacialis,* in Cape Cod waters. *Fishery Bulletin U.S.* 80:875–880.

Winn, H. E., C. A. Price, and P. W. Sorensen. 1986. The distributional biology of the right whale (*Eubalaena glacialis*) in the western North Atlantic. *Report of the International Whaling Commission* Special Issue 10:129–138.

Acknowledgments

This chapter is dedicated to our four colleagues—Emily Argo, Jacquelyn Ciano, Michael Newcomer, and pilot Thomas Hinds—who tragically lost their lives during an aerial survey in 2003 while engaged in the pursuit of right whale conservation. Their legacy will be realized only when the survey data have been used to develop and implement conservation measures throughout the right whale's international range, ensuring their survival.

More than twenty-five principal investigators, working with at least a dozen different institutions from the mid-1950s to the present day, have conducted aerial and shipboard surveys of right whales. It is not possible in the authorship of this chapter to represent all the researchers who have spent days, weeks, and indeed entire careers planning surveys and raising the funds required to carry them out. A list of the principal investigators involved and the cumulative survey effort resulting from their devoted and painstaking work over the years is presented in Table 4.1 and Fig. 4.8, respectively.

In addition to the principal investigators, systematic survey data were collected by a great number of dedicated and passionate research assistants (more than two hundred individuals) who spent long hours at sea in boats and small aircraft searching for right whales. Aerial surveys could not have been conducted without the skilled services of the following pilots: David Mattingly, George Terwilliger, Jon Hansen, Taylor Spangler, Timothy and Barbara Flynn, Hugh Rawls, Robert Murphy, John Ambroult, and Edward Koffman.

Survey work over the past twenty-five years has been funded by the National Marine Fisheries Service, Fisheries and Oceans Canada, the U.S. Army Corps of Engineers, the U.S. Coast Guard, the U.S. Navy, the U.S. Minerals Management Service, Irving Oil Corporation, Island Foundation, World Wildlife Fund U.S., Massachusetts Division of Marine Fisheries, Georgia Department of Natural Resources, Florida Wildlife Research Institute, British Broadcasting Corporation, and National Film Board of Canada. Permits issued to the principal investigators running these surveys are listed in Appendix A of this book.

5

Enormous Carnivores, Microscopic Food, and a Restaurant That's Hard to Find

MARK F. BAUMGARTNER, CHARLES A. MAYO, AND ROBERT D. KENNEY

April 1986
Cape Cod Bay

We'd known for a long time that there were places east of Cape Cod where powerful tidal impulses meet the sluggish southward-moving coastal current, places where right whales lined up along the rips where plankton concentrate. On a windless day in early April 1986, we decided to see if right whales had found such an area. The winter season, when right whales come to Cape Cod, had been a hard one, and calm days like this were few, so we could at last get to the more distant convergence and, as local fishermen do, see what we could catch.

It was gloomy and nearly dark when we left the port. For those of us who study whales, expectations are usually tempered by reality; we were looking for one of the rarest of all mammals in the shroud of the ocean. Today, however, spirits were high as the daybreak was filled with springtime promise. Along the great outer beach of the Cape, so close to shore that we could smell the land nearby, the first right whale was spotted working along one of those current rips. And as the sun climbed out of the haze, the whale rose and opened that great and odd mouth and skimmed the surface in a silence broken only by the sizzle of water passing through its huge filtering

138

apparatus. Our earlier optimism was warranted, and for several hours we drifted just clear of the linear rip that the whale was working, recording the complex pattern of its movements.

This whale, one well known to those of us studying right whales, was a young female identified as Eg #1223, but given the nickname "Delilah." As the hours passed, Delilah's movements became more convoluted as the current convergence, seen as wavelets on the glassy surface, seemed to be shrinking and moving toward the land. Our work involved collecting samples of the food on which Delilah was feeding with intense focus. Marilyn Marx, in charge of documentation, recorded what appeared to be a declining concentration of the orange plankton that drifted in the rips nearly unseen and that we, like Delilah, could filter from the water with a fine-mesh net. Back and forth along the current edge, Delilah skimmed the surface. It was a magical time, as always when right whales are about and performing.

As the day wore on to afternoon, Delilah's feeding path shifted slowly toward the beach until we could see clamshells on the bottom and hear the chatter of the gathering crowd of beach walkers! Then things began to change, perhaps as the currents driven by the tides changed, and we were soon surrounded by the shrinking rip that marked the conditions causing the food to concentrate. In some incomprehensible way Delilah knew that things were changing in her murky, liquid-green world. Her patterns of movement matched exactly the rip along the surface into which we, perhaps a large piece of flotsam to her, had drifted. She skimmed ever closer. For the very first time that day, Delilah closed her mouth, turned toward us and dove, a lumbering black ghost. She passed below the boat, then stopped suddenly and hung just beneath us. Only a moment passed until, rising against our starboard side, Delilah rolled and firmly struck the side of our vessel with her flipper. With point made (whatever it was, we could not know), she slid silently away, only to rise, mouth opened again, to continue her surface feeding for several more hours.

What was in the mind of Delilah? Certainly this whale was processing information with senses that must have been finely tuned to feeding on an unimaginably different kind of food resource in a sea of uncertainty. And what message was Delilah sending when she momentarily stopped her feeding, came to us, and delivered a firm slap to the boat? We came to understand only the rudiments of right whale foraging that day as Delilah displayed the basic components of a behavior built from millennia of learning and adaptation. Sadly, we will gain no more knowledge from our old and

one-time cantankerous friend, as she was struck and killed by a ship six
years after our encounter in the coastal rip.

Charles (Stormy) Mayo

Right whales are among the Earth's largest animals, but they feed on creatures
that are the size of fleas. In regard to the ratio of a right whale's mass to that
of its prey (50,000 kg to 1 mg, or 50 billion to one), right whale feeding is
equivalent to humans feeding on bacteria. Perhaps as strange, right whales are
carnivores that feed without manipulating their prey or their environment in
any way. Unlike chimpanzees that use their hands to gather food, spiders that
build webs to trap insects, ants that farm fungi, lions that ambush and run
down their prey, or dolphins that herd fish into tight balls to more easily capture them, right whales simply open their mouths, swim forward, and feed on
whatever happens to fall in. They rely utterly on the environment to organize
their prey into mouth-sized aggregations of millions to billions of organisms.

Right whale feeding is often likened to grazing by cows (an image bolstered
by their shared evolutionary roots), which is essentially correct if the cow is
in the desert, looking for a small, continuously moving oasis of grass, blind-
folded. So instead of considering right whales to be lazy or dumb, bear in
mind that the challenge of finding prey aggregations in the ocean is enormous;
with all of our modern technology, researchers cannot find the kinds of super-
abundant aggregations that the whales can. For example, the largest concentrations of their primary prey ever recorded have come from zooplankton
samples collected near right whales (Wishner et al. 1995; Beardsley et al. 1996).
This chapter explores what right whales eat, how they feed, and how they
might go about finding food, but first it examines their unusual feeding apparatus and its implications for how they make a living in the sea.

Why Baleen?

The mouth of a mysticete, or baleen whale, is an extraordinary morphological
adaptation to life in the sea. Gone are the calcified teeth that most mammals
use to capture, kill, and chew food, and in their place are 160–400 baleen
plates, each with hundreds to thousands of filaments that together act as a sieve
(Nemoto 1959) (Fig. 5.1a). These filaments are made of keratin, the same
protein that fingernails and hair are made of, and the size and number of the

filaments determine the filtering efficiency of the baleen. Right, bowhead, and sei whales have the finest and most numerous baleen filaments of all the mysticetes (Fig. 5.1b), which allow them to capture zooplankton, the tiny weak-swimming animals of the sea. Like a sieve, baleen filters only those organisms that are larger than a certain minimum size. Mayo et al. (2001) estimated that the filtering efficiency of right whale baleen is similar to that of the 0.333-mm net commonly used by marine ecologists to sample zooplankton. Organisms smaller than 0.333 mm (just over 1/100 of an inch) are too small to be efficiently retained on the baleen, and most simply pass through it.

Right whales typically swim slowly (ca. 1.5 m/s) while feeding for sustained periods, likely because the work required to push their baleen through the water increases exponentially with their swimming speed. Moreover, optimal flow characteristics through the mouth and baleen are probably maintained at slower speeds (Hamner et al. 1988; Werth 2004). Consequently, the right whale's diet is restricted by the swimming speed of their prey. Small fish such as herring and mackerel are far too fast to be captured by slow-moving right whales, and even some adult euphausiids (krill) may be able to avoid capture by detecting the oncoming whale and swimming to safety. The restrictions on the minimum and maximum size of prey that are imposed by the filtering efficiency of baleen and the right whale's slow swimming speed, respectively, severely limit the number and type of prey species available for capture. For these reasons, right whales feed primarily on a few species of large zooplankton.

To understand why right whales would evolve to focus on such a limited range of prey species, one must consider the way energy is transferred through the food web. Trophic efficiency in marine ecosystems has been estimated at roughly 10 percent (e.g., Ryther 1969; Pauly and Christensen 1995), meaning it takes 1,000 kg of phytoplankton to produce 100 kg of herbivores (e.g., herbivorous zooplankton), 10 kg of zooplantivores (e.g., herring, right whales), and 1 kg of piscivores (e.g., silver hake, humpback whales). The amount of biomass in the ocean can be thought of as a pyramid, with phytoplankton at the wide bottom, and top predators at the narrow apex. Predators evolved to feed at a particular level of the pyramid, and there is considerably more food available to a predator that feeds lower on the pyramid than higher on the pyramid (e.g., there is more biomass available to be eaten when feeding on phytoplankton than on seals). Most marine mammals feed on fish or squid that are relatively high on the pyramid, but right whales take advantage of the increased biomass available at lower levels of the pyramid by feeding on large zooplankton.

Figure 5.1. (a) Head of Eg #1004 with left lower lip and mandible removed to reveal the very large tongue and baleen (note the tip of the tongue has been removed). Michael Moore / Woods Hole Oceanographic Institution. (b) Baleen of Eg #1014 in near-pristine state. Regina Campbell-Malone / Woods Hole Oceanographic Institution.

However, zooplankton concentrations vary widely from location to location and from year to year because of changes in zooplankton production and the processes that aggregate zooplankton. Right whales, therefore, rely on a sometimes unreliable food resource, and because their behavior and morphology are so rigidly adapted to capturing zooplankton, they cannot switch to another prey resource, such as small fish, during times of low zooplankton availability. With such a small population size, the right whale's restrictive filtering apparatus makes it particularly vulnerable to fluctuations in prey abundance caused by environmental variability. Although it is efficient during times of zooplankton plenty, the right whale's remarkable feeding adaptations might doom the species should the zooplankton resources decline.

Right Whale Food

Numerous studies have demonstrated that a single species of zooplankton, the 2- to 3-mm-long calanoid copepod *Calanus finmarchicus* (color plate 6), is the primary prey of North Atlantic right whales in each of the major feeding habitats: Cape Cod Bay (Mayo and Marx 1990), Great South Channel (Wishner et al. 1988, 1995), lower Bay of Fundy (Murison and Gaskin 1989), Roseway Basin (Baumgartner et al. 2003a), and Jeffreys Ledge (M. Weinrich and M. Bessinger, pers. comm.). Most of these same studies indicate that right whales focus on the later juvenile stages (copepodites) and adults of *C. finmarchicus,* particularly stage 5 copepodites (hereafter referred to as *C. finmarchicus* C5) (Fig. 5.2). Payne et al. (1990) and Kenney (2001) documented anomalies in right whale occurrence in Massachusetts Bay and in the Great South Channel, respectively, that were strongly associated with changes in the occurrence of *C. finmarchicus.* There is even evidence to suggest that changes in the annual abundance of *C. finmarchicus* may influence right whale calving rates (Chapter 15).

The life history of *C. finmarchicus* in the North Atlantic is distinguished by a period just before adulthood when copepods cease development and enter a prolonged dormant phase called diapause (Fig. 5.2). A similar resting phase is common in insects and is somewhat analogous to hibernation in mammals. In the open ocean, *C. finmarchicus* emerge from diapause deep in the water column during the late winter and molt into adults (Marshall and Orr 1955). Males emerge first, followed later by females, and these adults mate as they migrate to the surface. Females feed in the surface waters during the early phase of the spring phytoplankton bloom and begin producing eggs at rates

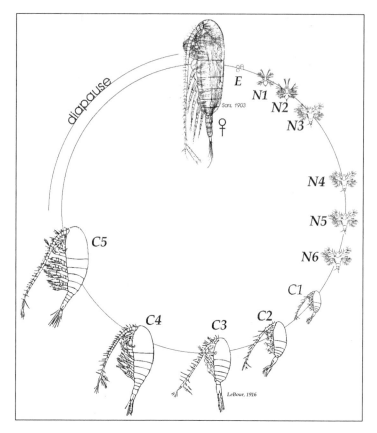

Figure 5.2. Life cycle of *Calanus finmarchicus* depicting the six naupliar stages, five cope-podite stages, and the adult stage. The distance between stages represents the relative time between molts. Drawings adapted from Sars (1903) and LeBour (1916).

of up to 50–70 eggs per female per day (Campbell et al. 2001). After hatching, the early naupliar stages (N1–2) do not feed. The later naupliar stages (N3–6), all copepodite stages (C1–5), and adults feed primarily on phytoplankton. During the copepodite stages, *C. finmarchicus* develops an oil sac filled with wax esters, and by stage C5, this oil sac has reached its maximum size, com-prising up to 50 percent of body volume (Miller et al. 2000) (color plate 6c). By this time, the phytoplankton bloom is nearly, if not already, over, and the longer and warmer days of late spring and early summer have begun to warm the surface waters of the North Atlantic. With no food left to eat, tempera-tures rising, and a significant risk of predation by visual hunters (e.g., fish) in the well-lit surface waters, *C. finmarchicus* migrates to depths greater than 200 m in oceanic waters or near the bottom over the continental shelf and enters diapause (Miller et al. 1991). *C. finmarchicus* does not actively feed during diapause but instead meets all of its nutritional needs during the summer, fall, and early winter by metabolizing the considerable energy stored in its oil sac.

In the Gulf of Maine and Nova Scotian Shelf, phytoplankton production is prolonged relative to oceanic production because of vertical mixing and stratification processes that are unique to the continental shelf (e.g., tidal mixing, fresh water influx from river runoff). This longer period of production allows *C. finmarchicus* to produce more than one generation in a single year. When each generation of copepodites reaches stage C5, it appears that some remain in the surface waters and molt into adults to continue production while others migrate to depth and enter diapause. The highest *C. finmarchicus* production appears to occur in association with the spring bloom, and most of the *C. finmarchicus* population can be found in diapause at depth in the summer and fall (Durbin et al. 2000; Baumgartner et al. 2003b).

When one considers this remarkable life history, particularly the development of an energy-rich oil sac, it is easier to understand why right whales prefer *C. finmarchicus*. *C. finmarchicus* is the dominant copepod in the North Atlantic and is therefore quite abundant. When compared to other copepods, *C. finmarchicus* has a much larger biomass and a higher caloric content. For example, *C. finmarchicus* females (for which there are published data) have a biomass that is nine times larger, a caloric content per unit weight that is 27 percent higher, and a caloric content per individual that is eleven times higher than *Pseudocalanus* spp. females. Hence, right whales would need to consume over an order of magnitude more *Pseudocalanus* than *C. finmarchicus* to obtain the same energy. Clearly, by focusing their foraging efforts on late-stage *C. finmarchicus*, right whales can maximize their energy intake.

Right whales do not feed exclusively on *C. finmarchicus*, however. In Cape Cod Bay, Mayo and Marx (1990) examined zooplankton abundance and community composition in proximity to surface skim-feeding right whales by towing zooplankton nets within 5 m of a whale's feeding path. *C. finmarchicus* dominated in most of the net samples; however, a few of the samples were dominated by *Pseudocalanus, Centropages typicus,* or barnacle larvae (in order of importance). Observers noted that feeding on barnacle larvae was quickly terminated, perhaps indicating that this prey was not suitable (Kenney et al. 2001). Watkins and Schevill (1976) also observed right whales surface skim-feeding on patches of juvenile euphausiids (krill) in Cape Cod Bay, and Collett

(1909) reported that right whales fed on euphausiids in the Hebrides and off Iceland in the northeastern Atlantic.

Reports of North Atlantic right whales feeding on euphausiids are very interesting because adult euphausiids are relatively large and may be capable of evading capture by these slow-moving whales. Estimating the contribution of euphausiids to the right whale diet is difficult for the same reason: adult euphausiids are adept at evading zooplankton nets (Brodie et al. 1978; Wiebe et al. 2004). Collett (1909) reported that right whales likely fed on *Thysanoessa inermis* in the northeastern Atlantic, a euphausiid that is ten times the size of *C. finmarchicus*. Although right whales may be able to capture juvenile euphausiids while slowly and continuously filter feeding, catching adult euphausiids may require a different strategy. Hamner et al. (1988) described a southern right whale surface skim-feeding on the very large and very mobile Antarctic krill during fifteen- to twenty-second feeding bouts at swimming speeds of 4–4.5 m/s. "During these powerful filter-feeding runs," wrote Hamner et al. (1988, 144), "enormous amounts of water were displaced, cascading beside and behind the right whale and producing a large wake." This feeding behavior is strikingly different from the continuous surface feeding observed for North Atlantic right whales characterized as four- to six-minute feeding bouts at swimming speeds of 1.5 m/s (Watkins and Schevill 1976; Mayo and Marx 1990), during which little or no bow wave is produced. The behavior of the southern right whale observed by Hamner et al. (1988) is undoubtedly a response to the size and mobility of *E. superba*. Adults of this euphausiid species can reach lengths of 6.5 cm (twenty-two times the size of *C. finmarchicus*). It is conceivable that North Atlantic right whales might also employ a similar, short-duration, high-speed feeding behavior to capture large and abundant euphausiids (e.g., the northern krill); however, this behavior has not yet been documented.

Studying Right Whale Food

Investigating Diet

Traditional field diet studies often involve some kind of manipulation of the subject animal, ranging from forced regurgitation to killing the animal, extracting the stomach, and examining the contents. For endangered animals, of course, this kind of manipulation is exceedingly undesirable. Before the international ban on harvesting right whales in the 1930s, stomach contents were available for examination, but published reports are anecdotal and lacking in taxonomic detail. Collett (1909, 97), for example, describes the diet of right whales harvested in the northeast Atlantic as "exclusively pelagic crustaceans (the "krill" of Norwegian whalers), a euphausiid about half an inch long, probably *Boreophausia inermis* [i.e., *Thysanoessa inermis*]." Collett's taxonomic identification sounds somewhat speculative, suggesting that perhaps he did not examine stomach contents himself but extrapolated from whalers' observations.

Current diet studies of endangered animals often rely on direct visual observations of feeding. Visual observation of right whale feeding is possible in habitats where surface skim-feeding occurs (e.g., Cape Cod Bay, the Great South Channel). Accounts from whaling days often mention right whales skim-feeding in patches of orange or red water similar to the modern accounts of right whales feeding on surface aggregations of *C. finmarchicus* (e.g., Beardsley et al. 1996). This coloring of the water is produced by the small areas of red pigment (notably at the posterior end of the oil sac) in the otherwise transparent *C. finmarchicus* (color plate 6). More recent and detailed accounts of skim-feeding have been published by Watkins and Schevill (1976, 1979), Wishner et al. (1988, 1995), Mayo and Marx (1990), Kenney et al. (1995), and Beardsley et al. (1996), and most of these reports include net sampling of zooplankton community composition.

Surface observations of feeding are clearly useful for identifying prey species, but most right whale feeding occurs below the surface well out of view. How, then, can researchers use observations to determine diet? Ingenious, animal-mounted video technology has facilitated underwater observations and identification of prey for other marine mammals, but in the turbid coastal environments in which right whales feed, it is impossible to use a back-mounted camera to see what is flowing into the whale's mouth several meters away. Moreover, it is impossible to identify zooplankton prey species that are likely smaller than the resolution of the camera. Instead of using this animal-mounted technology, right whale researchers have relied on both net- and instrument-based zooplankton sampling in proximity to whales to infer diet and prey concentrations during subsurface feeding. This technique is probably accurate for prey identification when sampling is conducted within tens to a few hundreds of meters of a foraging whale.

Qualitative diet analysis using fecal material has been used widely in terrestrial and pinniped research. Whale scat is difficult to collect, but recent advances in genetic and fecal hormone analyses have illustrated the value of fecal material for determining individual identification and reproductive status without any disturbance to the whale (Chapter 8). Microscopic examination of right whale fecal material in the lower Bay of Fundy (Kraus and Prescott 1982; Murison 1986) and in Roseway Basin (Stone et al. 1988) revealed the presence of many *C. finmarchicus* mandibles; body parts from other zooplankton taxa, such as chaetognaths and euphausiids, were found infrequently. These observations underscore the importance of *C. finmarchicus* in the diet of North Atlantic right whales. Sorting fecal material for undigested bits of crustaceans is tedious and may not reveal all of the prey present in the diet, particularly those that are more readily digested. Genetic analysis of prey DNA may represent a more reliable technique for determining diet composition from fecal material than microscopy. This promising method has been used to identify digested prey in stomach contents (Rosel and Kocher 2002) and in fecal material of other species (Jarman et al. 2002, 2004) but has yet to be applied to right whales.

Net Sampling

The most widely used method to sample zooplankton is the net tow. The size of the net's opening can vary from a few tens of centimeters to several meters wide and is chosen based on the size and motility of the zooplankton one intends to catch. Likewise, the net's mesh size is also chosen based on the size of the zooplankton. Net openings of less than 1 m^2 and mesh sizes of 0.150–0.333 mm are adequate for sampling zooplankton in the right whale's diet (although some larger and more mobile euphausiids may require larger net openings). To estimate zooplankton abundance, the net is outfitted with a flowmeter to measure how much seawater is filtered. Zooplankton are enumerated by identifying and counting organisms in an aliquot of the sample (i.e., in a subsample) using a dissecting stereomicroscope, and abundance is expressed as the number of individuals per cubic meter of filtered seawater.

Nets are typically deployed in two modes: vertical hauls and oblique tows. Vertical hauls consist of lowering the net to a particular depth and then slowly raising the net back to the surface. Oblique tows involve towing the net behind a moving vessel while paying out the tow cable until the net reaches the desired depth and then pulling the tow cable back in slowly to bring the net back to the surface (Fig. 5.3a). When lowered to the bottom, both vertical hauls and oblique tows of single nets provide estimates of average water column abundance. To estimate abundance in discrete strata, a depth-stratified sampler is re-

Figure 5.3. (a) Side-by-side 0.29-m² bongo nets being towed at the surface. (b) A 0.25-m² multiple opening and closing net and environmental sensing system that can accommodate up to nine nets. (c) A lowered instrument package consisting of an optical plankton counter (OPC), acoustic Doppler current profiler (ADCP), video plankton recorder (VPR), and a conductivity-temperature-depth (CTD) instrument. Mark Baumgartner / Woods Hole Oceanographic Institution.

quired, such as the multiple-opening-closing net and environmental sensing system (Wiebe et al. 1976, 1985) or the Bedford Institute of Oceanography net and environmental sensing system (Sameoto et al. 1980) (Fig. 5.3b). These sampling systems carry many nets that open sequentially on command from the ship and are typically used for characterizing the vertical distribution of zooplankton.

Net sampling remains the best method for identifying zooplankton species composition, but deployment and sample processing are time-consuming and require taxonomic expertise. Moreover, the spatial scales over which towed nets sample can be quite large compared to the spatial scales at which right whales forage. For example, a depth-stratified sampler that is towed over a kilometer while sampling several 30-m-thick depth strata from the bottom to the surface is not ideally suited for characterizing copepod abundance in patches that are only a few hundred meters wide and a few meters thick.

Instrument-Based Sampling

To observe fine-scale patches of zooplankton, some researchers have turned to instrument-based zooplankton samplers. For each of these instruments, precise taxonomic identification is sacrificed for sampling at smaller spatial scales and reducing deployment and processing time. Prudent use of these instrument-based samplers requires some knowledge of the zooplankton community in which they will be deployed; therefore, net sampling must remain an integral component of their use until the zooplankton community composition in the region of interest is sufficiently understood.

Two instruments, the optical plankton counter and the video plankton recorder, estimate zooplankton abundance in a small volume of water and must be towed or lowered through the water column. The optical plankton counter (Herman 1988, 1992) counts and estimates the size of particles as they pass through the middle of a sampling tunnel (Fig. 5.3c). A light source on one wall of the tunnel produces a beam of light directed across the middle of the tunnel and onto a photodetector on the opposite wall. A particle passing through the beam blocks this light and casts a shadow on the photodetector. The magnitude of the shadow is roughly proportional to the size of the particle in the beam. The optical plankton counter has no intrinsic ability to identify particles, but late-stage *C. finmarchicus* are readily detectable because there are no other abundant organisms in the North Atlantic that are similarly sized. The video plankton recorder (Davis et al. 1992) can be thought of simply as an underwater microscope consisting of a camera focused on a small volume of water illuminated by a strobe light (Fig. 5.3c). The camera records images of the organisms within this volume of water at a rate of thirty frames per second. Unlike the optical plankton counter, the video plankton recorder allows taxonomic discrimination because the organisms captured in the images can be examined and identified.

Acoustic instruments can obtain abundance estimates at distances of meters to hundreds of meters away by emitting a short pulse of sound that travels away from the instrument, echoes off particles or organisms in the water column, and then returns to the instrument. The intensity of the received echo is related to the size and the physical properties of the organism. Many acoustic systems exist (Chu and Wiebe 2003), and the processing and interpretation of the echo data require considerable expertise. Although acoustic methods have no intrinsic ability to identify zooplankton, they are capable of rapidly measuring echo intensity (also called acoustic backscatter) at high vertical and horizontal spatial resolutions over large areas. In regions where the zooplankton community is dominated by a single species (as is the case in many right whale habitats), acoustics offers a means to rapidly map the horizontal and vertical distribution of the dominant species at high resolution.

The Physics of Food Capture

The head and mouth morphology of the balaenids (right and bowhead whales) differs significantly from the rorqual whales (e.g., blue, fin, and humpback whales), and these differences are related to the foraging ecology of these two families. The rorquals feed primarily by engulfing enormous quantities of seawater and food in a single mouthful, and then sieving this seawater through their coarse baleen to trap prey inside the mouth. Pivorunas (1979) estimated that blue whales could engulf at least 60 m^3 (70 tons) of water in one mouthful. Rorquals have loose joints in their lower jaws that facilitate opening the mouth wide, ventral grooves that allow expansion of a unique interior space called the cavum ventrale to accommodate immense volumes of seawater, and a flaccid tongue that turns inside-out to line the cavum ventrale during engulfment (Lambertsen 1983; Orton and Brodie 1987). This feeding method, called lunge feeding, is likely a behavioral adaptation that serves to capture mobile schooling prey, such as euphausiids and small fish.

In contrast to the rorquals, balaenids feed by a method known as ram filter feeding, where the whale simply opens its mouth and swims forward. Right whales have been observed ram filter feeding for several hours without interruption; prey capture and filtering are continuous. To accommodate ram filter-feeding, right whales have very large heads (up to one-third of the body length), arching jaws, long (up to 2.7 m) and narrow baleen plates, and a very large muscular tongue (Fig. 5.1a). The baleen is organized in two racks on either side of the mouth, separated by a space at the front of the mouth called the subrostral gap (Fig. 5.4). This gap is unique to the balaenids, and it allows seawater to continuously enter the mouth as the whale swims forward. Right whale baleen fringes (the hairlike bristles that line the interior surface of the baleen) are finer and denser than rorqual baleen and can, therefore, retain much smaller particles (Nemoto 1959).

Despite the functional similarities, ram filtration by balaenids is not exactly equivalent to towing a plankton net through the water. By moving forward, both balaenids and plankton nets produce hydraulic forces that push zooplankton into the sieve. However, balaenid oral morphology is far more complex

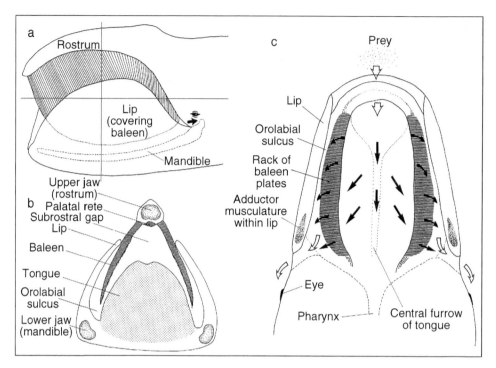

Figure 5.4. (a) Side view of a balaenid head. Arrow indicates where water exits the mouth at the rear end of the orolabial sulcus. Vertical and horizontal lines indicate the planes of sections shown in (b) and (c), respectively. (b) Front view of balaenid mouth depicting the positions of the tongue, baleen, lip, and orolabial sulcus. The subrostral gap is the space between the baleen racks. (c) Top view of balaenid mouth depicting the flow of water through the subrostral gap, through the baleen, and into the orolabial sulcus, exiting just in front of the eye. Drawings adapted from Werth (2004).

than a plankton net, and this complexity promotes hydrodynamic forces that improve filtration efficiency. When a right whale opens its mouth to feed, the lips of the lower jaw move downward away from the upper jaw (rostrum) and laterally away from the baleen (color plate 7). The lower jaw acts as a gigantic scoop, directing water into the mouth between the baleen racks (via the subrostral gap) and also along the outside of the baleen in the space between the baleen and the lips called the orolabial sulcus (Fig. 5.4c). Water entering the mouth through the subrostral gap passes over the tongue, through the baleen, and into the orolabial sulcus and then exits the mouth just in front of the eye. The water that enters the orolabial sulcus at the front and flows along the exterior margin of the baleen is not filtered, but it serves a critical function in the filtration process. The orolabial sulcus narrows from front to back, which accelerates flow along the outside of the baleen relative to the flow inside the mouth (via the Bernoulli effect; Werth 2004). Additionally, the front part of the baleen rack bulges outward toward the lower lip to create a hydrofoil that further accelerates water in the orolabial sulcus (Lambertsen et al. 2005). This acceleration creates a difference in pressure between the interior of the mouth and the orolabial sulcus (i.e., on either side of the baleen) that actually pulls water through the baleen (via the Venturi effect). Thus, filtration is not accomplished by hydraulic forcing alone (as in a plankton net) but is aided by this pressure differential and the associated through-baleen flow.

When a ship moves forward, it pushes water in front of it and produces a compressive bow wave (much to the delight of many dolphins). Although considerably more porous than a ship's bow, plankton nets can also push water. The resulting increase in pressure just in front of the net can alert zooplankton and elicit an escape reaction (Barkley 1964). Avoidance of nets and in situ instrumentation by zooplankton that are especially alert or mobile is a well-known problem in zooplankton sampling (Wiebe et al. 1982) and is presumably a challenge faced by right and bowhead whales as well. However, flow acceleration through the mouth may reduce or eliminate the pressure wave in front of the whale and significantly improve prey capture (Werth 2004; Lambertsen et al. 2005). Werth (2004) built an anatomically accurate, one-fifteenth-scale model of an adult bowhead whale head to examine the hydrodynamics of ram filter feeding. Both flow tank tests with the scale model and mathematical modeling suggested that flow into the mouth was laminar and that no compressive bow wave was formed. In fact, by seeding the water with particles, Werth (2004) was able to observe particles being "pulled" into the model's mouth. This evidence suggests that not only is there no compressive bow wave to alert zooplankton of the oncoming whale but that some mild suction is produced just forward of the mouth. When finally alerted to the presence of the whale, zooplankton are likely within the zone of accelerating water very near the whale's mouth, and escape may be nearly impossible.

Foraging Behavior

Right whale foraging behavior has traditionally been classified into two modes, surface skim-feeding and subsurface feeding, but it appears that the only real difference between the two is the vertical distribution of prey, not the whale's actual foraging behavior. Surface skim-feeding occurs when prey are within

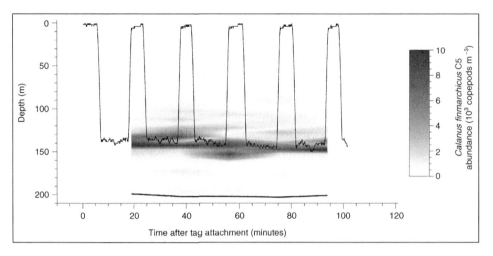

Figure 5.5. Foraging behavior of a right whale tagged with a time-depth recorder in the lower Bay of Fundy. Dive profiles (solid line) are shown over a contour plot depicting the vertical distribution of *Calanus finmarchicus* C5. The sea floor (ca. 200 m) is shown as a thick solid line. Adapted from Baumgartner and Mate (2003).

several tens of centimeters of the sea surface. The whale swims with the front portion of its upper jaw elevated above the sea surface and the rest of its body submerged (color plate 7). Right whales likely control the elevation of the upper jaw above the water based on the vertical distribution of prey. The subrostral gap is triangular in shape (Fig. 5.4b), so positioning the mouth such that the widest space between the baleen racks (i.e., near the floor of the mouth) coincides with the depth of the highest concentration of prey will maximize prey intake. In addition to finely adjusting their vertical position, right whales turn often in response to changing horizontal gradients in prey abundance to remain within the highest concentrations of zooplankton available (Mayo and Marx 1990). Watkins and Schevill (1979) observed sei and right whales feeding on zooplankton in proximity to one another, but the sei whales apparently lacked the right whales' ability to remain in the highest prey concentrations within the zooplankton aggregations. Instead, the sei whales moved completely outside of the aggregations before turning back into them. These differences in foraging efficiency highlight the right whale's extraordinary specialization for feeding on zooplankton.

Studying subsurface foraging behavior is challenging because visual observations are not possible; instead, researchers rely on instrumentation. In the

Great South Channel, Winn et al. (1995) monitored movements and surfacing and diving durations by attaching radio transmitters to right whales and also measured dive depths for some of the tagged whales using acoustic transmitters. Two whales equipped with acoustic transmitters spent the vast majority of their time (97 percent) within 20 m of the surface. In contrast, Goodyear (1993) and Baumgartner and Mate (2003) used acoustic transmitters and time-depth recorders, respectively, to observe right whales foraging well below 100 m and, in some cases, at the sea floor (ca. 200 m) in the Bay of Fundy (color plate 8). Right whales tagged in the Bay of Fundy spent most of their time foraging on discrete layers of diapausing *C. finmarchicus* C5 just above a turbulent bottom mixed layer (Fig. 5.5) (Baumgartner and Mate 2003).

Foraging Behavior and *Calanus* Life History

The habitats where surface feeding is most often observed, Cape Cod Bay and the Great South Channel, are late winter and spring habitats. Although subsurface feeding predominates in all habitats, it is most characteristic of the summer habitats in the lower Bay of Fundy and Roseway Basin. These seasonal differences in diving behavior may be directly related to the life history of *C. finmarchicus*. The year's first generation of *C. finmarchicus* spawned in December–January do not grow to late-stage copepodites until March–April (Durbin et al. 1997, 2000). Right whales cannot efficiently filter eggs, nauplii, or early copepodite stages of *C. finmarchicus,* so the first generation of *C. finmarchicus* is unavailable to right whales until late winter or early spring. Observations of right whales feeding on other copepods in Cape Cod Bay (Mayo and Marx 1990) occur primarily during this period of *C. finmarchicus* unavailability (Fig. 5.6).

When *C. finmarchicus* reaches the later copepodite stages in late winter and early spring, these copepodites remain in the upper water column to feed on phytoplankton that are restricted to well-lit surface waters. Right whales likely feed at or near the sea surface during this time because of the availability of late-stage *C. finmarchicus* in the upper water column. As the surface waters warm, and phytoplankton abundance decreases after the spring bloom in late spring, most late-stage *C. finmarchicus* copepodites (predominantly stage C5) begin to migrate downward to initiate diapause. By summer, the majority of *C. finmarchicus* can be found deep in the water column, and right whales engage in long subsurface dives to forage on these diapausing copepodites (Fig. 5.6). The transition period between *C. finmarchicus* occurrence in surface

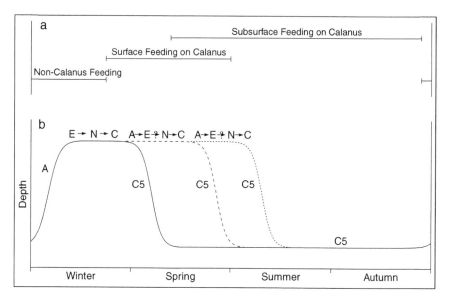

Figure 5.6. Conceptual relationship between right whale feeding and the life history of *Calanus finmarchicus*. (a) Timeline indicating periods when right whales feed on zooplankton other than *C. finmarchicus*, on *C. finmarchicus* near the surface, and on *C. finmarchicus* at depth. (b) Idealized depth distribution of *C. finmarchicus* indicating emergence from diapause, migration to the surface by adults (A), and progression of three generations (solid, dashed, and dotted lines) from eggs (E) to nauplii (N) to copepodites (C). After reaching stage 5 (C5), copepods either remain at the surface to molt into adults and spawn the next generation or they migrate downward and initiate diapause. By late summer and autumn, the entire population of *C. finmarchicus* is at stage C5 and is in diapause deep in the water column.

waters and deep waters spans the time when right whales visit the Great South Channel during April–June. Both surface and subsurface feeding have been observed in the Great South Channel, likely in response to the availability of active *C. finmarchicus* in the upper water column and diapausing *C. finmarchicus* deep in the water column.

Behavioral Implications of Prey Aggregation

At first glance, right whale foraging behavior appears to be profoundly boring when compared to that of the charismatic humpback whale. The humpback has a vast array of behaviors on which it can draw, including bubble-net, flick, lobtail, and cooperative feeding (Hain et al. 1982). Humpback whales use this repertoire primarily for the difficult task of organizing highly mobile prey into mouth-sized aggregations. In contrast, the right whale simply opens its mouth and swims forward, and there is no evidence to suggest that they actively organize zooplankton into exploitable aggregations. Instead, right whales rely wholly on the environment to organize their prey into aggregations suitable for feeding.

To appreciate these differences in feeding behavior, consider a humpback whale that encounters 200 1-kg fish distributed evenly throughout the water column. The humpback can employ a bubble net to corral these fish, push them to the surface, and engulf all of them. If a right whale encounters 200 million 1-mg copepods (200 kg of copepods) distributed evenly throughout the water column, it has no means to aggregate these prey and cannot consume them. The right whale must move on to another location where the environment has organized copepods into a vertically compressed, highly concentrated aggregation. When and where the environment produces these aggregations, they are likely to be pancake-shaped layers that are hundreds of meters wide but only tens of centimeters to a few meters thick. Right whales have no need for elaborate feeding behaviors that are designed to aggregate prey; an "open your mouth and drive" approach is sufficient for feeding on these compact zooplankton layers. This lack of exciting feeding behaviors, however, leads to much more intriguing questions. How does oceanography organize copepods into exploitable aggregations? And how do right whales find them?

Zooplankton Aggregation

Zooplankton are ubiquitous, yet zooplankton concentrations throughout most of the ocean are far too low for right whales to feed profitably. In particular areas, however, a variety of oceanographic processes operating at different spatial and temporal scales can lead to the formation of highly concentrated zooplankton patches. The right whales' survival depends on these oceanographic processes; therefore, it is vital to understand how these processes work.

Many studies have implicated ocean fronts in aggregating prey for top predators. Just as a weather front marks the location where two air masses abut in the atmosphere, ocean fronts demarcate the location where two water masses meet in the ocean. Prey can aggregate at these fronts through interactions between the organisms' vertical swimming behavior and the circulation at the front (Franks 1992). Although fronts provide a plausible mechanism for aggregating zooplankton, the extent to which right whales rely on them for feeding is unclear. Wishner et al. (1995) reported that late-stage *C. finmarchicus* aggregations in the Great South Channel were associated with a fresh water river-runoff plume and suggested that the front separating the river runoff water from the more salty oceanic water may have been responsible for aggregating *C. finmarchicus*. Epstein and Beardsley (2001) studied the structure of this same front and concluded that *C. finmarchicus* likely accumulated there because the copepods, in an effort to maintain a preferred depth, swam upward against the currents moving downward and away from the front. However, Beardsley et al. (1996) sampled intensively near a feeding right whale tagged with a radio transmitter in this area and found no evidence to suggest that a convergent ocean front was responsible for aggregating the copepods on which the whale fed. Right whales do not generally feed in areas with fronts in the Bay of Fundy, yet there is evidence to suggest that right whale occurrence in Roseway Basin on the southwestern Scotian Shelf may be related to the presence of fronts (Baumgartner et al. 2003a).

Aside from ocean fronts, few hypotheses exist to explain the formation of zooplankton aggregations. Yet there must be other mechanisms involved because right whales appear to also feed in areas devoid of fronts. Much work remains to be done to improve the presently poor understanding of the small-scale biological-physical interactions that form and maintain zooplankton aggregations.

Finding Food

Scientists' understanding of the conditions that aggregate zooplankton is exceedingly poor, but right whales must have a very good sense for when and where these aggregations form. But how do they do it? Because experimentation on right whales is not feasible, researchers are left largely with speculation and hypotheses that are difficult to test. Kenney et al. (2001) reviewed many hypotheses about how right whales locate prey over various spatial scales, and the following discussion draws heavily from their work.

At the largest spatial scales (thousands of kilometers), many hypotheses exist to explain right whale navigation during migration or extended excursions. It is likely that most long-distance movements are undertaken to find prey, with the exception of pregnant females migrating to the calving grounds. However, after birth, nursing cows are probably anxious to return to the feeding grounds after fasting during the winter calving season. Much longer trans-Atlantic excursions from the U.S. and Canadian continental shelves to the Labrador Basin, Iceland, and Norway have also been documented (Knowlton et al. 1992; Jacobsen et al. 2004). To navigate over large distances to find either feeding or calving grounds, right whales may rely on their memory, which is informed by topographic landmarks, bathymetric contours, or acoustic sources such as surf or seismic activity. Water masses or ocean currents may similarly act as environmental landmarks for navigation or may directly assist movements. Navigation by the sun has been observed in other taxa, so it is conceivable that right whales use the sun as a compass. A geomagnetic compass may also be available to right whales, as there is evidence of navigation by geomagnetic orientation in a variety of other marine taxa, including sea turtles (Lohmann and Lohmann 1996), and cetaceans (Walker et al. 1992).

At regional spatial scales (tens to hundreds of kilometers), right whales likely rely on learning and memory to locate and choose specific feeding habitats. Right whales preferentially visit habitats frequented by their mothers (Malik et al. 1999; Brown et al. 2001), which suggests that mothers teach calves where to find the best foraging conditions or areas. Mate et al. (1997) documented extensive movements of a tagged female and her accompanying calf throughout the Gulf of Maine and New England shelf and speculated that this mother was showing her calf potential feeding areas. Downstream physical and chemical cues might help right whales locate feeding grounds much the way American eels or Pacific salmon use organic compounds to find river inlets. For example, when returning from the calving grounds off the southeastern United States, right whales may locate the Gulf of Maine by tasting the fresh water plume spilling through the Great South Channel and onto the New England Shelf.

Once right whales locate and occupy a habitat at the regional spatial scale, they are unlikely to remain there long if prey resources are insufficient. Right whales tagged with satellite-monitored transmitters in the lower Bay of Fundy during the summer and early fall left the Bay and ranged widely throughout the Gulf of Maine, western and central Scotian Shelf, New England Shelf, and over the continental slope (Baumgartner and Mate 2005). Of the whales that left the Bay, several returned a few days or weeks later. These observations suggest that right whales are highly mobile and capable of adapting to variability in the regional-scale distribution of prey by visiting many potential feeding areas over a short period of time.

Over spatial scales of several kilometers, right whales probably rely less on long-range navigation abilities and more on their memory and immediate senses. A right whale's goal at this scale is to find super-abundant aggregations of zooplankton. It is difficult to imagine right whales randomly prospecting; instead, they likely have an intimate knowledge of the oceanographic conditions that form and maintain these aggregations. To improve their chances of finding exploitable patches of zooplankton, right whales may first locate the oceanographic features that are responsible for forming the patches, and then search within or near these features. For example, right whales may locate the leading edge of the fresh water plume present in the Great South Channel in the spring by tasting a strong change in salinity. Once the front is located, the whale can prospect back and forth across the front to find copepods that may be aggregated there.

Another possible method to detect prey patches at spatial scales of a few kilometers is cooperation among whales. Right whales are often highly aggregated on their feeding grounds, and in such a small population, it is quite unlikely that this occurs by chance. It is possible that right whales acoustically advertise the presence of abundant food resources (Lowry 1993; Winn et al. 1995), perhaps in an effort to attract other whales and, in particular, a potential mate. However, no evidence of this behavior in right whales has yet been reported.

At very small spatial scales (centimeters to tens of meters), right whales have a number of senses that may help them locate and remain within the highest zooplankton concentrations in an aggregation. Vision may play a significant role for whales that are feeding near the surface during the daytime. Despite having enhanced night vision (as in the bowhead whale; Zhu et al. 2001), vision is probably much less useful for subsurface and nighttime feeding. In the lower Bay of Fundy (a turbid coastal environment), Goodyear (1993) and Baumgartner and Mate (2003) observed whales diving to depths of up to 200 m where very little light penetrates. Kenney et al. (2001) suggested that perhaps the presence of bioluminescent zooplankton within prey aggregations might aid visual detection in the absence of ambient light. Chemical detection of prey might also be possible, but the persistence of this cue might be quite variable because of turbulence and diffusion. At point-blank range, the most reliable sense for directly measuring zooplankton abundance is probably tactile (Kenney et al. 2001). Cetaceans have sensory hairs or vibrissae that are richly enervated and are thus sensitive to deformation (Ling 1977). When zooplankton strike these vibrissae, the resulting bend in the hair may be sensed by the whale. Vibrissae in right whales are located around the mouth (Payne

1976), so they could be used to make fine-scale adjustments to the prey concentration immediately in front of the whale.

It is important to repeat that these hypotheses about sensory modalities are conjectural. Researchers simply do not know how right whales pull off the extraordinary trick of finding food in a vast ocean where most of the environment is unsuitable for feeding. Zooplankton prey resources can vary from year to year and from location to location, so a sophisticated suite of senses and an intimate knowledge of the environment are likely required to survive.

Making a Living on Zooplankton

Right whales need to consume an extraordinary amount of zooplankton virtually every day to survive, but females need even more food to support pregnancy and lactation. If the right whale population is failing to recover, perhaps there just isn't enough food in the ocean anymore to allow for successful reproduction. To determine if food resources are sufficient to sustain right whale population growth, researchers need to answer two seemingly simple questions: (1) how much do right whales need to eat, and (2) how much do right whales actually eat?

How Much Do Right Whales Need to Eat?

Look at the nutrition label printed on the back of just about any food container, and you'll find how much food (or, more accurately, energy) humans need to consume: roughly 2,000 calories per day. Kenney et al. (1986) used estimates for the filtering rate (based on mouth area and swimming speed), filtering efficiency, assimilation efficiency (i.e., how much ingested food is actually used by the body), time spent feeding per day, time spent feeding per year (to account for potential winter fasting), and metabolic rate based on body mass to calculate how much energy right whales need to consume: between 407,000 and 4,140,000 calories per day, which is equivalent to feeding on 0.25–2.6 billion *C. finmarchicus* C5 per day. This feeding rate is between 0.6 and 6.4 percent of right whale body weight per day, which brackets the 1.5–2.0 percent and 4 percent of body weight per day for other cetaceans estimated by Lockyer (1981) and Sergeant (1969), respectively. These calculations neglected the substantial energetic costs of pregnancy and lactation, so the resulting estimates should be considered as requirements for survival only, not reproduction.

The wide range of estimates by Kenney et al. (1986) reflects considerable uncertainties in most of the factors included in their calculations. Perhaps the greatest uncertainty is in the metabolic rate of right whales, which can be accurately measured only in whales that can be physically manipulated using respirometry or isotopic-labeling methods (Costa and Williams 1999). Adult baleen whales cannot be restrained, so direct measurements of metabolic rate are impossible to obtain. Although Kenney et al. (1986) argued that drag from a right whale's baleen might make ram filter feeding very costly in terms of metabolic rate, recent investigations of balaenid filter feeding suggest that a right whale's mouth morphology may reduce this drag (Werth 2004). Another uncertainty in these calculations is the time spent feeding per year. Right whales that visit the calving grounds in the winter do not feed for several months. Females killed in the Long Island fishery, presumably on their northward migration from a fasting period on the calving grounds, were not well nourished and were referred to as "dry skins" by the whalers because of their low oil content (Reeves and Mitchell 1986). However, the distribution, feeding behavior, and energetic needs of the rest of the population during winter are unknown.

How Much Do Right Whales Actually Eat?

Until recently, zooplankton sampling near whales has not matched the fine vertical and horizontal scales at which the whales forage. Prey concentrations exceeding those required by right whales have rarely been observed because typical zooplankton net sampling averages zooplankton abundance over the whole water column (i.e., it averages a dense copepod aggregation contained in a small volume of water with a much larger, empty volume of water). To improve on this sampling problem, Baumgartner and Mate (2003) used an optical plankton counter to measure the abundance of *C. finmarchicus* C5 over fine vertical spatial scales near right whales. They estimated that right whales encountered *C. finmarchicus* C5 concentrations of up to 15,000 copepods per cubic meter and ingested *C. finmarchicus* C5 at a rate of up to 66 million copepods per hour (1.6 billion copepods per day). If this feeding rate were sustainable, right whales could meet their daily metabolic needs in as little as three hours. A bucket sample taken in the Great South Channel near a feeding right whale yielded a late-stage *C. finmarchicus* abundance of 331,000 copepods per cubic meter, from which Beardsley et al. (1996) estimated that the whale was ingesting *C. finmarchicus* at a rate of 1.4 billion copepods per hour! At that rate, it could meet its daily metabolic energy requirement in less than 10 minutes.

Some right whales clearly encounter zooplankton aggregations that allow feeding rates that are sufficient to meet daily metabolic needs if feeding on those aggregations is sustained. However, the persistence of the aggregations (particularly in the face of intense right whale predation) and the frequency with which they are encountered are unknown, so it is unclear if right whales can keep feeding at these rates. Therefore, the instantaneous feeding rates estimated from short-term observations may not accurately estimate daily feeding rates. Over time scales as short as hours or days, right whales probably feed on an irregular boom-and-bust cycle by taking advantage of extremely high concentrations of copepods when they are encountered and then traveling through areas of suboptimal feeding conditions in search of more aggregations.

Is There Enough Food in the Ocean to Sustain Right Whales?

This turns out to be an extraordinarily difficult question because of the spatial scales at which zooplankton aggregate and right whales forage. Imagine assessing how much food is available to people in Florida by randomly sampling locations in the state. Unless you happened to sample a restaurant or a supermarket where most of the food is concentrated, you would grossly underestimate the amount of food available to people. If you followed people around, you would eventually find a restaurant and thereby know that they exist, but you wouldn't know how many restaurants are in the state. Right whale research is at exactly this stage. Long-term monitoring programs rarely detect the high concentrations of zooplankton required by right whales, yet when researchers find whales, they find superabundant zooplankton aggregations. This is almost certainly because the aggregations on which right whales feed are on the order of only a few hundreds of meters to a few kilometers in size.

It is critical to understand the processes that aggregate *C. finmarchicus* if large-scale prey abundance estimates (or proxies such as the North Atlantic Oscillation index; Chapter 15) are to be used to explain variability in right whale population growth. A frequent assumption in studies of right whale population dynamics is that annual *C. finmarchicus* abundance averaged over the Gulf of Maine and Scotian Shelf is proportional to the amount of food available to right whales and that variability in annual right whale birth rates can be directly compared with those large-scale *C. finmarchicus* abundance estimates. Yet, if aggregation mechanisms vary from year to year, then the food available to right whales will not be a function solely of the large-scale average *C. finmarchicus* abundance. A year in which *C. finmarchicus* average abundance is high may turn out to be a poor feeding year for right whales if the physical processes that aggregate *C. finmarchicus* are weak. Conversely, a poor year for *C. finmarchicus* production may mean a good year for right whale feeding if aggregation mechanisms can strongly concentrate the few *C. finmarchicus* available.

For example, both a large-scale *C. finmarchicus* abundance index for the Gulf of Maine and western Scotian Shelf (Greene and Pershing 2004) and in situ net and optical plankton counter sampling over the entire water column in the lower Bay of Fundy (Baumgartner et al. 2003a) suggested that *C. finmarchicus* was more abundant in 2001 than in 2000. However, *C. finmarchicus* sampled in the discrete layers within which right whales were feeding in the lower Bay of Fundy were nearly twice as abundant in 2000 as in 2001 (Baumgartner and Mate 2003). The concentration index (the ratio of peak water column abundance to the average water column abundance) measured near right whales was significantly higher in 2000 than in 2001, indicating that aggregation mechanisms were stronger in 2000 than in 2001. In this case, both the large-scale abundance index and the average water-column abundance of *C. finmarchicus* did not accurately reflect the concentration of prey available to right whales. Caution, therefore, is warranted in attempting to explain trends in right whale reproduction with prey abundances averaged over large spatial and temporal scales.

Feeding and Conservation Efforts

There is considerable interest in developing predictive models of right whale distribution in the conservation and management community (Chapter 16). Imagine a system that could describe where right whales are located at this very moment, or even where right whales will be in a few days or weeks hence. With such a capability, certain areas could be monitored closely, and regulation of human activities within those areas could be more proactive than is currently possible. Because the distribution of right whales throughout most of the year is governed primarily by feeding conditions, predictive models will need to incorporate our growing understanding of the factors that aggregate zooplankton and the whales' feeding response to those aggregations to achieve the accuracies required to effectively manage shipping or fishing activities (kilometers to tens of kilometers).

Fishing gear entanglements pose a serious risk of injury or mortality for right whales (Chapter 13). However, solving this problem has been hindered by a lack of information about where right whales spend their time in the water column and how their diving behavior may interact with fishing gear. Some evidence suggests that copepods in Cape Cod Bay, Bay of Fundy, and Great South Channel can aggregate very close to the sea floor at the same depths where ground lines (ropes connecting traps along the bottom) occur (C. Mayo, S. Kraus, and M. Baumgartner, pers. comm.). If right whales exploit these near-bottom resources, they may be at particular risk of entanglement. A better understanding of right whale diving and foraging behavior, and the environmental conditions that promote the formation of near-bottom copepod aggregations will inform conservation efforts.

Food and feeding also play a role in assessing the outcome of management actions. Without a better understanding of right whale feeding ecology and its relationship to reproduction (Chapter 15), it will be difficult to distinguish between fluctuations in population size that are caused by natural and anthropogenic factors. For example, a decline in calving rates might be the result of human-caused mortalities of reproductively active females or by depressed birth rates resulting from reduced food availability. In assessing the efficacy of management actions to reduce human-caused mortalities, a decline in calving rates might be interpreted as evidence that conservation efforts have failed, when, in fact, the decline is attributable to reduced food resources. In years when environmental conditions favor successful reproduction, management actions could be wrongly credited with increasing calving rates. The outcome of conservation efforts must therefore be evaluated within the context of environmentally induced changes in the population.

Conclusion

Although many other organisms filter feed exclusively on zooplankton in the ocean, only the right and bowhead whales do so to sustain an enormous body mass and a high mammalian metabolic rate. The challenges of eating roughly one billion flea-sized copepods per day are immense, and right whales possess two critical adaptations to meet these challenges: baleen and an extraordinary skill for finding zooplankton aggregations. Zooplankton are weak swimmers and therefore aggregate only where oceanographic conditions allow. Right whales probably use instinct, maternal teaching, memory, environmental cues, their immediate senses, and perhaps even help from conspecifics to find these aggregations from as far as thousands of kilometers to as close as tens of centimeters away. Elaborate feeding behaviors are not required to feed on zooplankton (right whales simply open their mouths and swim forward), but an elaborate feeding apparatus is essential. Right whales have evolved a large head, long baleen plates, fine baleen fringes, and an unusual mouth morphology to maximize both prey intake and filtering efficiency. These remarkable specializations are highly effective in times of zooplankton plenty, but when zooplankton populations decline, right whales are incapable of switching to an alternative food resource. Thus, boom-and-bust cycles in zooplankton abundance will likely affect right whale population dynamics and may ultimately govern the long-term survival of this endangered species.

Barkley, R. A. 1964. The theoretical effectiveness of towed-net samplers as related to sampler size and to swimming speed of organisms. *Journal du Conseil Permanent International pour l'Exploration de la Mer* 29:146–157.

Baumgartner, M. F., and B. R. Mate. 2003. Summertime foraging ecology of North Atlantic right whales. *Marine Ecology Progress Series* 264:123–135.

Baumgartner, M. F., and B. R. Mate. 2005. Summer and fall habitat of North Atlantic right whales (*Eubalaena glacialis*) inferred from satellite telemetry. *Canadian Journal of Fisheries and Aquatic Sciences* 62:527–543.

Baumgartner, M. F., T. V. N. Cole, P. J. Clapham, and B. R. Mate. 2003a. North Atlantic right whale habitat in the lower Bay of Fundy and on the SW Scotian Shelf during 1999–2001. *Marine Ecology Progress Series* 264:137–154.

Baumgartner, M. F., T. V. N. Cole, R. G. Campbell, G. J. Teegarden, and E. G. Durbin. 2003b. Associations between North Atlantic right whales and their prey, *Calanus finmarchicus*, over diel and tidal time scales. *Marine Ecology Progress Series* 264:155–166.

Beardsley, R. C., A. W. Epstein, C. Chen, K. F. Wishner, M. C. Macaulay, and R. D. Kenney. 1996. Spatial variability in zooplankton abundance near feeding right whales in the Great South Channel. *Deep Sea Research II* 43:1601–1625.

Brodie, P. F., D. D. Sameoto, and R. W. Sheldon. 1978. Population densities of euphausiids off Nova Scotia as indicated by net samples, whale stomach contents, and sonar. *Limnology and Oceanography* 23:1264–1267.

Brown, M. W., S. Brault, P. K. Hamilton, R. D. Kenney, A. R. Knowlton, M. K. Marx, C. A. Mayo, C. K. Slay, and S. D. Kraus. 2001. Sighting heterogeneity of right whales in the western North Atlantic: 1980–1992. *Journal of Cetacean Research and Management* Special Issue 2:245–250.

Campbell, R. G., M. M. Wagner, G. J. Teegarden, C. A. Boudreau, and E. G. Durbin. 2001. Growth and development rates of the copepod *Calanus finmarchicus* reared in the laboratory. *Marine Ecology Progress Series* 221:161–183.

Chu, D., and P. H. Wiebe. 2003. Application of sonar techniques to oceanographic-biological surveys. *Current Topics in Acoustical Research* 3:1–25.

Collett, R. 1909. A few notes on the whale *Balaena glacialis* and its capture in recent years in the North Atlantic by Norwegian whalers. *Proceedings of the Zoological Society of London* 7:91–98.

Costa, D. P., and T. M. Williams. 1999. Marine mammal energetics. Pages 176–217 in J. E. Reynolds III and S. A. Rommel, eds. *Biology of Marine Mammals*. Smithsonian Institution Press, Washington, D.C.

Davis, C. S., S. M. Gallager, M. S. Berman, L. R. Haury, and J. R. Strickler. 1992. The video plankton recorder (VPR): design and initial results. *Archiv für Hydrobiologie, Beiheft: Ergebnisse der Limnologie* 36:67–81.

Durbin, E. G., J. A. Runge, R. G. Campbell, P. R. Garrahan, M. C. Casas, and S. Plourde. 1997. Late fall-early winter recruitment of *Calanus finmarchicus* on Georges Bank. *Marine Ecology Progress Series* 151:103–114.

Durbin, E. G., P. R. Garrahan, and M. C. Casas. 2000. Abundance and distribution of *Calanus finmarchicus* on the Georges Bank during 1995 and 1996. *ICES Journal of Marine Science* 57:1664–1685.

Epstein, A. W., and R. C. Beardsley. 2001. Flow-induced aggregation of plankton at a front: a 2-D Eulerian model study. *Deep-Sea Research II* 48:395–418.

Franks, P. J. S. 1992. Sink or swim: Accumulation of biomass at fronts. *Marine Ecology Progress Series* 82:1–12.

Goodyear, J. D. 1993. A sonic/radio tag for monitoring dive depths and underwater movements of whales. *Journal of Wildlife Management* 57:503–513.

Greene, C. H., and A. J. Pershing. 2004. Climate and the conservation biology of North Atlantic right whales: the right whale at the wrong time? *Frontiers in Ecology and the Environment* 2:29–34.

Hain, J. H. W., G. R. Carter, S. D. Kraus, C. A. Mayo, and H. E. Winn. 1982. Feeding behavior of the humpback whale, *Megaptera novaeangliae,* in the western North Atlantic. *Fishery Bulletin* 80:259–268.

Hamner, W. M., G. S. Stone, and B. S. Obst. 1988. Behavior of southern right whales, *Eubalaena australis,* feeding on the Antarctic krill, *Euphausia superba. Fishery Bulletin* 86:143–150.

Herman, A. W. 1988. Simultaneous measurement of zooplankton and light attenuance with a new optical plankton counter. *Continental Shelf Research* 8:205–221.

Herman, A. W. 1992. Design and calibration of a new optical plankton counter capable of sizing small zooplankton. *Deep Sea Research* 39:395–415.

Jacobsen, K-O., M. Marx, and N. Oeien. 2004. Two-way trans-Atlantic migration of a North Atlantic right whale (*Eubalaena glacialis*). *Marine Mammal Science* 20: 161–166.

Jarman, S. N., N. J. Gales, M. Tierney, P. C. Gill, and N. G. Elliott. 2002. A DNA-based method for identification of krill species and its application to analysing the diet of marine vertebrate predators. *Molecular Ecology* 11:2679–2690.

Jarman, S. N., B. E. Deagle, and N. J. Gales. 2004. Group-specific polymerase chain reaction for DNA-based analysis of species diversity and identity in dietary samples. *Molecular Ecology* 13:1313–1322.

Kenney, R. D. 2001. Anomalous 1992 spring and summer right whale (*Eubalaena glacialis*) distributions in the Gulf of Maine. *Journal Cetacean Research Management* Special Issue 2:209–223.

Kenney, R. D., M. A. M. Hyman, R. E. Owen, G. P. Scott, and H. E. Winn. 1986. Estimation of prey densities required by western North Atlantic right whales. *Marine Mammal Science* 2:1–13.

Kenney, R. D., H. E. Winn, and M. C. Macaulay. 1995. Cetaceans in the Great South Channel, 1979–1989: right whale (*Eubalaena glacialis*). *Continental Shelf Research* 15:385–414.

Kenney, R. D., C. A. Mayo, and H. E. Winn. 2001. Migration and foraging strategies at varying spatial scales in western North Atlantic right whales: a review of hypotheses. *Journal of Cetacean Research and Management* Special Issue 2:251–260.

Knowlton, A. R., J. Sigurjósson, J. N. Ciano, and S. D. Kraus. 1992. Long-distance movements of North Atlantic right whales (*Eubalaena glacialis*). *Marine Mammal Science* 8:397–405.

Kraus, S. D., and J. H. Prescott. 1982. The North Atlantic right whale (*Eubalaena glacialis*) in the Bay of Fundy, 1981, with notes on distribution, abundance, biology and behavior. Annual report, contract number NA-81-FA-C-00030, National Marine Fisheries Service, Northeast Fisheries Science Center, Woods Hole, MA.

Lambertsen, R. H. 1983. Internal mechanism of rorqual feeding. *Journal of Mammalogy* 64:76–88.

Lambertsen, R. H., K. J. Rasmussen, W. C. Lancaster, and R. J. Hintz. 2005. Functional morphology of the mouth of the bowhead whale and its implications for conservation. *Journal of Mammalogy* 86:342–352.

LeBour, M. V. 1916. Stages in the life history of *Calanus finmarchicus* (Gunnerus), experimentally reared by Mr. L. R. Crawshay in the Plymouth Laboratory. *Journal of the Marine Biological Association of the United Kingdom* 11:1–17.

Ling, J. K. 1977. Vibrissae of marine mammals. Pages 387–415 *in* R. J. Harrison, ed. *Functional Anatomy of Marine Mammals*, Vol. 3. Academic Press, London, U.K.

Lockyer, C. 1981. Growth and energy budgets of large baleen whales from the Southern Hemisphere. Pages 379–487 *in* Anonymous, ed. *FAO Advisory Committee on Marine Resource Research, Mammals in the Sea,* Vol. III, *General papers and large cetaceans.* FAO, Rome, Italy.

Lohmann, K. J., and C. M. F. Lohmann. 1996. Orientation and open-sea navigation in sea turtles. *Journal of Experimental Biology* 199:73–81.

Lowry, L. F. 1993. Foods and feeding ecology. Pages 201–238 *in* J. J. Burns, J. J. Montague, and C. J. Cowles, eds. *The Bowhead Whale.* Society for Marine Mammalogy, Lawrence, KS.

Malik, S., M. W. Brown, S. D. Kraus, A. R. Knowlton, P. K. Hamilton, and B. N. White. 1999. Assessment of mitochondrial DNA structuring and nursery use in the North Atlantic right whale (*Eubalaena glacialis*). *Canadian Journal of Zoology* 77:1217–1222.

Marshall, S. M., and A. P. Orr. 1955. *The Biology of a Marine Copepod* Calanus finmarchicus (*Gunnerus*). Oliver and Boyd, Edinburgh, U.K.

Mate, B. R., S. L. Nieukirk, and S. D. Kraus. 1997. Satellite-monitored movements of the northern right whale. *Journal of Wildlife Management* 61:1393–1405.

Mayo, C. A., and M. K. Marx. 1990. Surface foraging behavior of the North Atlantic right whale, *Eubalaena glacialis,* and associated zooplankton characteristics. *Canadian Journal of Zoology* 68:2214–2220.

Mayo, C. A., B. H. Letcher, and S. Scott. 2001. Zooplankton filtering efficiency of the baleen of a North Atlantic right whale, *Eubalaena glacialis. Journal of Cetacean Research and Management* Special Issue 2:225–229.

Miller, C. B., T. J. Cowles, P. H. Wiebe, N. C. Copley, and H. Grigg. 1991. Phenology in *Calanus finmarchicus:* hypotheses about control mechanisms. *Marine Ecology Progress Series* 72:79–91.

Miller, C. B., J. A. Crain, and C. A. Morgan. 2000. Oil storage variability in *Calanus finmarchicus. ICES Journal of Marine Science* 57:1786–1799.

Murison, L. D. 1986. Zooplankton distributions and feeding ecology of right whales (*Eubalaena glacialis glacialis*) in the outer Bay of Fundy, Canada. M.S. Thesis. University of Guelph, Guelph, Ontario, Canada.

Murison, L. D., and D. E. Gaskin. 1989. The distribution of right whales and zooplankton in the Bay of Fundy, Canada. *Canadian Journal of Zoology* 67:1411–1420.

Nemoto, T. 1959. Food of baleen whales with reference to whale movements. *Scientific Reports of the Whales Research Institute* 14:149–291.

Orton, L. S., and P. F. Brodie. 1987. Engulfing mechanics of fin whales. *Canadian Journal of Zoology* 65:2898–2907.

Pauly, D., and V. Christensen. 1995. Primary production required to sustain global fisheries. *Nature* 374:255–257.

Payne, P. M., D. N. Wiley, S. B. Young, S. Pittman, P. J. Clapham, and J. W. Jossi. 1990. Recent fluctuations in the abundance of baleen whales in the southern Gulf of Maine in relation to changes in selected prey. *Fishery Bulletin* 88:687–696.

Payne, R. 1976. At home with right whales. *National Geographic* 140:322–339.

Pivorunas, A. 1979. The feeding mechanisms of baleen whales. *American Scientist* 67:432–440.

Reeves, R. R., and E. Mitchell. 1986. The Long Island, New York, right whale fishery: 1650–1924. *Report of the International Whaling Commission* Special Issue 10: 201–220.

Rosel, P. E., and T. D. Kocher. 2002. DNA-based identification of larval cod in stomach contents of predatory fishes. *Journal of Experimental Marine Biology and Ecology* 267:75–88.

Ryther, J. H. 1969. Photosynthesis and fish production in the sea. *Science* 166:72–76.

Sameoto, D. D., L. O. Jaroszynski, and W. B. Fraser. 1980. BIONESS, a new design in multiple net zooplankton samplers. *Canadian Journal of Fisheries and Aquatic Sciences* 37:693–702.

Sars, G. O. 1903. *An Account of the Crustacea of Norway.* Bergen Museum, Bergen, Norway.

Sergeant, D. E. 1969. Feeding rates of cetacea. *Fiskeridirektoratets Skrifter, Serie Havundersøkeleser* 15:246–258.

Stone, G. S., S. D. Kraus, J. H. Prescott, and K. W. Hazard. 1988. Significant aggregations of the endangered right whale, *Eubalaena glacialis,* on the continental shelf of Nova Scotia. *Canadian Field Naturalist* 102:471–474.

Walker, M. M., J. L. Kirschvink, G. Ahmed, and A. E. Dizon. 1992. Evidence that fin whales respond to the geomagnetic field during migration. *Journal of Experimental Biology* 171:67–78.

Watkins, W. A., and W. E. Schevill. 1976. Right whale feeding and baleen rattle. *Journal of Mammalogy* 57:58–66.

Watkins, W. A., and W. E. Schevill. 1979. Aerial observations of feeding behavior in four baleen whales: *Eubalaena glacialis, Balaenoptera borealis, Megaptera novaeangliae,* and *Balaenoptera physalus. Journal of Mammalogy* 60:155–163.

Werth, A. J. 2004. Models of hydrodynamic flow in the bowhead whale filter feeding apparatus. *Journal of Experimental Biology* 207:3569–3580.

Wiebe, P. H., K. H. Burt, S. H. Boyd, and A. W. Morton. 1976. A multiple opening/closing net and environmental sensing system for sampling zooplankton. *Journal of Marine Research* 34:313–326.

Wiebe, P. H., S. H. Boyd, B. M. Davis, and J. L. Cox. 1982. Avoidance of towed nets by the euphausiid *Nematoscelis megalops. Fishery Bulletin* 80:75–91.

Wiebe, P. H., A. W. Morton, A. M. Bradley, R. H. Backus, J. E. Craddock, V. Barber, T. J. Cowles, and G. R. Flierl. 1985. New developments in the MOCNESS, an apparatus for sampling zooplankton and micronekton. *Marine Biology* 87: 313–323.

Wiebe, P. H., C. J. Ashjian, S. M. Gallager, C. S. Davis, G. L. Lawson, and N. J. Copley. 2004. Using a high-powered strobe light to increase the catch of Antarctic krill. *Marine Biology* 144:493–502.

Winn, H. E., J. D. Goodyear, R. D. Kenney, and R. O. Petricig. 1995. Dive patterns of tagged right whales in the Great South Channel. *Continental Shelf Research* 15:593–611.

Wishner, K. F., E. Durbin, A. Durbin, M. Macaulay, H. Winn, and R. Kenney. 1988. Copepod patches and right whales in the Great South Channel off New England. *Bulletin of Marine Science* 43:825–844.

Wishner, K. F, J. R. Schoenherr, R. Beardsley, and C. Chen. 1995. Abundance, distribution and population structure of the copepod *Calanus finmarchicus* in a springtime right whale feeding area in the southwestern Gulf of Maine. *Continental Shelf Research* 15:475–507.

Zhu, Q., D. J. Hillmann, and W. G. Henk. 2001. Morphology of the eye and surrounding structures of the bowhead whale, *Balaena mysticetus. Marine Mammal Science* 17:729–750.

Acknowledgments

We are grateful to Regina Campbell-Malone, Marilyn Marx, Michael Moore, and Alex Werth for sharing photos and figures. Thanks also to Alex Werth and Michael Moore for fruitful discussions and Nancy Copley for creating the *Calanus finmarchicus* life history figure. Support for research was provided by the National Marine Fisheries Service, National Science Foundation, Office of Naval Research, National Aeronautics and Space Administration, and the Massachusetts Division of Marine Fisheries.

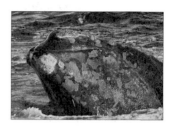

6

High Investment, Low Return: The Strange Case of Reproduction in *Eubalaena Glacialis*

SCOTT D. KRAUS, RICHARD M. PACE III, AND TIMOTHY R. FRASIER

28 August 1987
South of Nova Scotia

We were 65 km off the southern tip of Nova Scotia aboard the M/V Yankee Freedom, attempting to run a whale watching trip like none before it. My colleagues Scott Marion and Scott Mercer had joined me in ganging up on Jerry Hill, owner of the Yankee Fleet out of Gloucester, to convince him that a whale and seabird circumnavigation of the Gulf of Maine would be a really great opportunity. Jerry, adventurous beyond reason, agreed, and we found thirty-five equally foolish, that is, brave souls to join us. We had left Gloucester the previous day in the rain and headed due east to Georges Bank, sighting a few pilot whales and white-sided dolphins along the northern edge of the bank. Birds were scarce, and the weather was marginal, but we overnighted comfortably in the Fundian Channel north of Georges Bank where the food was good, the tall tales flowed freely, and we all enjoyed ourselves. Anticipation was high, as in the morning we were headed to Roseway Basin, an area known to right whale researchers as the "singles bar," where courtship activity among right whales is common.

At daybreak we were confronted with fog, a whale watcher's heartless, implacable, and damp nemesis. As we motored slowly up into the area where right whales are known to congregate, visibility decreased so we could hardly see the bow of the 30.5-m vessel from the bridge. Depression hung in the air, and the only relief was breakfast. Marion, Mercer, and I were being called the Three Scotts of the Apocalypse (these people took their whale watching seriously!). Desperate, I started scanning the radar knowing full well that whales never show up on radar. An odd blotch on the screen caught my attention. It disappeared, then showed up again, larger in the next scan, disappearing in the next, but consistently in a spot about 3 km away. What the heck? I gave Jerry the heading, and we motored slowly in that direction. As we approached the area, the fog lifted slightly so we could see about a kilometer, and sure enough, there was . . . nothing!

Suddenly, the water erupted around us. An adult right whale female surfaced off our stern and immediately rolled onto her back. In front and on both sides of us, male right whales surfaced explosively, rushing to the female. It was like being caught in front of a stampede, only our boat was bigger than the whales, and they were remarkably adept at avoiding us. As we watched (most yelling in either excitement or terror), one of the biggest courtship groups ever observed formed not 90 m from our boat, now silent in the water. Photographs taken over the next few hours revealed over forty right whales in the courtship group. The frenzy lasted for over four hours, and we stayed with the group until a research vessel from the New England Aquarium arrived to document the event properly.

The group would form and reform around one energetic female, and as far as we could tell, the rest of the whales were males. Hydrophones lowered into the water allowed us to listen in on the female's calls, which were constant while the animals were at the surface. She would lie on her back most of the time, with multiple males on both sides of her and sometimes lying across her chin. While upside down, she swam slowly forward and in circles, and males attempted to stay at her sides, while other males would try and displace the males closest to her. About every minute or so, she would roll over for a breath, and at that point several of the closest males would attempt to get underneath her to mate. It was clear that if a male was close, he had the best chance for mating when she breathed. But it was also clear that no male could really keep in the closest position for very long because all of his competitors were trying either to push him out of the way or to sneak up from underneath between him and his intended. Through all of the interactions, this huge group of whales was characterized by rapid head lifts, flippers and tails slashing and throwing water, and loud resonant blows. Whales also continued to approach at high speed from great distances, arriving constantly throughout the period.

The lingering impression after we watched this courtship group is how much energy it takes! And that is the core mystery of right whale mating strategies. These whales are not even courting at the correct time of year: calves are born in winter, and the gestation is about twelve months. So what are they doing mating in the summer? The female is at the focus of this maelstrom of activity for hours, constantly swimming, holding her breath, and calling to make sure the best males are around her. The males are persistent, repeatedly trying to get closer to the female for those mating opportunities that she infrequently offers. Males will come from 10 km away to participate in one of these groups, which can last over six hours. And all of this activity keeps the whales away from their other main activity, feeding. So it costs each participant in terms of time lost feeding and energy lost in the activity.

At the end of the day, all of us were exhilarated and exhausted, as if we ourselves had been participants. Like most whales in the group, we made no contribution to future generations. But we had been privileged to witness over 10 percent of all North Atlantic right whales in one courtship group, and we were left with hope that right whale population recovery will not fail for lack of trying.

Scott Kraus

Three puzzling features of the population biology of the North Atlantic right whale include the variation in calf production from year to year, a consistently low reproductive rate, and a number of adult females who have never been known to give birth. Because healthy reproduction is critical for the recovery of this species, these observations have right whale biologists concerned. At two periods in the 1990s, very low calf production caught the attention of both researchers and managers. Although no obvious cause for low fertility was ever identified, these observations stimulated the development of several hypotheses that are now being tested in field studies. Potential factors that could suddenly reduce reproductive rates include disease events; climatic, oceanographic, or other changes resulting in reduced food availability; and the sublethal effects of toxic contaminants or marine biotoxins. Factors that may be responsible for a consistently lower birth rate could include the genetic features of this very small population; a consistent number of nonreproducing females (for genetic or other reasons); or inherent evolutionary characteristics of this isolated species of right whale, which may never have had the fecundity of the southern right whale.

Here we combine earlier work on right whale reproduction (Kraus et al. 2001) with new analyses and interpretations of data. Photographic identifications provided repeated records of individual whales and their calving events, generating annual records of calf production, calving intervals, age at first parturition, and the number of new mothers. The genetics work has provided information on gender, paternity, matrilineal patterns, and reproductive success.

Caveats

The information presented here represents all of the available data, but it is not necessarily an exact record of all of the births or deaths. Survey coverage has varied from year to year, and consequently, whales were certainly missed in some areas in some years. In particular survey effort on the calving grounds was sporadic from 1984 to 1988 and then limited until 1990. Thus many calves recorded during that period were first observed in the summer feeding grounds around the Gulf of Maine. Because of this, discussions in this chapter sometimes use the period from 1990 onward to evaluate reproduction from a period when survey effort in the calving ground has been relatively consistent.

Calving

Right whales give birth to a single calf in the winter after a twelve- to thirteen-month gestation period (Best 1994). The only known calving grounds are in the coastal waters of the southeastern United States between Savannah, Georgia, and St. Augustine, Florida, and most calves are born from early December through the end of March. The observed number of calves born each year to the North Atlantic right whale population between 1980 and 2005 has varied annually from one to thirty-one (Table 6.1), with an increase over the period (Fig. 6.1). The upward trend in calving results in part from large increases in calf counts in the past five years and may also reflect increases in survey effort during the twenty-five-year period.

Because of survey effort in the area since 1990 (ca. ninety aerial survey days per year), the likelihood of a calf being born and not detected after 1989 is

Table 6.1. North Atlantic Right Whale Reproductive Data, 1980–2005, Including Annual Tabulations of All Births, Calf Mortalities, Identified Cows, New Mothers (Recruits), and Cow Mortalities

Year	Calves (alive)	Calf mortality	Total calves	Cows	Recruits	Cow mortality
1980	6	0	6	16		0
1981	8	0	0	21	5	0
1982	11	2	12	27	7	1
1983	9	0	9	33	6	0
1984	12	0	12	35	5	3
1985	11	0	11	37	2	0
1986	13	0	13	39	6	4
1987	11	1	11	43	5	1
1988	7	1	8	45	2	0
1989	16	2	18	47	3	1
1990	12	1	13	47	2	2
1991	17	0	17	50	4	1
1992	12	0	12	51	3	2
1993	6	2	8	47	2	6
1994	9	0	9	51	4	0
1995	7	0	7	51	2	2
1996	21	3	22	60	11	2
1997	19	1	20	64	7	3
1998	5	1	6	62	0	2
1999	4	0	4	63	1	0
2000	1	0	1	62	0	1
2001	30	4	31	73	11	1
2002	20	1	21	77	4	0
2003	19	0	19	83	6	0
2004	16	1	17	87	4	2
2005	28	1	28	92	5	3

probably very small. In Table 6.1 all calves are tallied, including those identified while traveling as cow–calf pairs, those that remained unidentified because they were seen only in the calving ground (but whose mothers were known), and those that were known to have died in their first year.

Is This Variation in Calving Random?

When investigating variation among counts of right whale calves, researchers are dealing with small numbers. Each birth represents the culmination of a series of events including endocrine cycles of the potential mother, a breeding

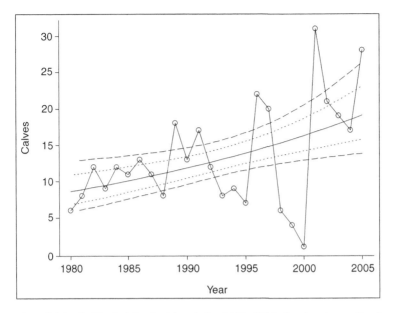

Figure 6.1. Calving in North Atlantic right whales, 1980–2005, showing the predicted exponential increase (smooth solid black line) and observed calf counts (open circles). Upper and lower 95 percent confidence limits (CL) are shown for both a Poisson (dashed lines) and more conservative quasi-Poisson models (long dashed lines). Note that although the fitted values show an increase in the number of calves over the period, the observed calf counts show excessive amounts of variation beyond what is expected for these data.

event, a pregnancy, and successful carrying of a fetus to term. All of these events are subject to interruption by chance occurrences. Consequently each sexually mature female that might breed during a particular year has a less than 100 percent chance of producing a calf. This uncertainty, when summed across all potential mothers, leads to considerable variation in the annual counts of calves. One classical representation of this sort of stochasticity is the Poisson distribution. In the case of right whales, if an average of twelve calves were born in the 1990s (as happened), the model predicts only a 60 percent chance that the number of calves born would be between nine and fifteen!

Many biologists believe that phenomena such as reproduction are more deterministic than games of chance, and given a consistent environment, a series of calf counts would appear less stochastic than a series of random numbers. Surprisingly, North Atlantic right whale calf counts show significantly more variation than would be expected by chance (Fig. 6.1). In particular, calving during two three-year periods, 1993–1995 and 1998–2000, was significantly lower than would have been expected by chance alone. Both periods were followed by significantly more births than would be expected, giving the appearance of a recovery by individual females unable to reproduce during the low years. This significant extra-Poisson variation in the calf production is strong evidence that some population-wide events have affected North Atlantic right whale reproduction.

Female Reproduction

The High Cost of Reproducing

For mammals it takes a lot of energy to have a baby. Right whale calves are born at 4 to 5 m in length and weigh between 700 and 1,000 kg (Fig. 6.2). This is a small amount of baby mass (ca. 1.5 percent) relative to a right whale mother when compared to humans (ca. 8 percent) or African elephants (ca. 2.2 percent), but the whale mother's total investment has just begun at birth. A calf will grow to about 8 m in eight months, and all of this growth is from the mother's milk, which for the first few months is entirely derived from her body stores of fats, proteins, and minerals. Most mammals give birth when food is plentiful, and nursing mothers simply reprocess this food into milk. Right whales have a reproductive cycle that includes fasting by the mother during a critical phase of nursing the young (a behavior shared with most bears, some pinnipeds, and other baleen whales), and they compound this phase with a long-distance migration during the fast. Historical whalers taking mothers and calves in the spring off southern New England and Long Island referred to these lactating mothers as "dry skins" because their blubber yielded so little oil. By the time right whale calves are weaned at about eleven months, they are 9 to 10 m in length and may weigh over 12,000 kg.

This extensive use of maternal body stores by the calf has been suggested as the reason for the interval of three years or more between calves in this species. Female right whales probably need to recover from the drain of nursing their little behemoths and then to rebuild all the body stores needed to reproduce again. Thus a typical cow's sequence is one year of pregnancy, followed by a year of nursing the young, followed by a year of feeding and fattening up for the next calf. If there are events (e.g., disease, malnutrition) that slow the ability of the cow to fatten up, it is likely that calving intervals would become longer. Although it is unknown how reproduction would be delayed, com-

Figure 6.2. Aerial view of right whale mother and calf in the southeastern calving grounds. Gill Braulik / New England Aquarium.

parative work in other mammalian species suggests that food resources, when limited, are a controlling factor (Wade and Schneider 1992).

Calving Intervals

Female right whales need appropriate nutritional and health conditions to recover from the demands of carrying and raising an offspring. Thus the timing between calving events is indicative of extrinsic factors affecting reproduction in this species because intrinsic problems (e.g., consequences of inbreeding) are not likely to vary widely from year to year.

A total of 219 intervals between calving events have been recorded since 1980 (Table 6.2). Knowlton et al. (1994) reported a mean calving interval of 3.67 years for the period between 1987 and 1992. The most frequently observed interval at that time was three years, including fifty-three observations (61.6 percent). Kraus et al. (2001) reported that between 1993 and 1998, mean annual calving intervals increased to over five years. Now, with a longer period to review, it is clear that calving intervals changed from about three and one-half years in 1990 to over five years between 1998 and 2003 and suddenly decreased to just over three years in 2004 and 2005 (Fig. 6.3).

Table 6.2. Calving Intervals of North Atlantic Right Whales

	Calving intervals in years							Mean interval[a]
	2	3	4	5	6	7	8+	
1980	—	1	—	—	—	—	—	—
1981	—	—	1	1	—	—	—	—
1982	—	1	—	1	—	—	—	—
1983	—	2	1	—	—	—	—	3.3
1984	—	7	—	—	—	—	—	3.0
1985	1	6	—	2	—	—	—	3.3
1986	—	5	2	—	—	—	—	3.3
1987	—	4	—	1	—	1	—	4.0
1988	—	2	1	1	1	—	—	4.2
1989	—	7	2	4	—	—	—	3.8
1990	—	7	1	1	1	—	—	3.6
1991	—	4	3	3	2	1	—	4.5
1992	—	7	1	—	1	—	—	3.4
1993	—	—	3	1	—	—	—	4.3
1994	—	—	3	1	—	—	—	4.3
1995	—	1	1	1	1	—	1	4.5
1996	—	—	1	6	2	1	—	5.3
1997	—	2	1	2	3	3	1	5.4
1998	—	—	1	—	3	1	—	5.8
1999	—	—	2	—	—	1	—	5.0
2000	—	—	1	—	—	—	—	—
2001	—	—	1	11	1	2	5	5.3
2002	—	1	2	5	3	2	4	5.2
2003	2	—	2	2	3	2	2	4.9
2004	1	9	—	—	1	—	1	3.2
2005	—	12	8	1	—	—	1	3.5

a. Mean intervals exclude intervals longer than seven years because of inconsistency in the sighting records.

The twenty-six-year dataset of calving intervals was examined using a mixed model approach to account for the repeated measures among mothers (i.e., a single mother may represent several intervals in Table 6.2, and the data may be more similar within a mother than among mothers). Because whales are not seen every year, some cows with longer calving intervals may have had calves during a year in which they were not sighted. Therefore several apparently long birthing intervals from mothers with sparse sighting histories were excluded. As sparse (fewer than ten observations per year) as these data were, calving intervals have varied significantly over time (Fig. 6.3). These data seem to fit well with the annual calf counts because it appears that the inability of

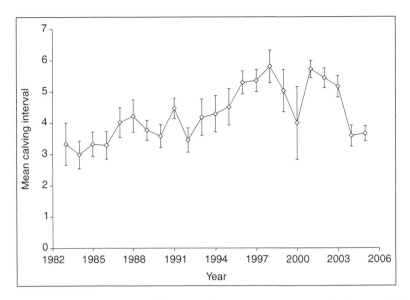

Figure 6.3. Annual average intervals between calves, 1983–2005, estimated using a statistical model that accounts for multiple observations on some mothers. Whiskers indicate one standard error around each estimate.

a significant number of potential mothers to reproduce during the low-calving years in two periods in the 1990s resulted in greater than average mean intervals following those periods.

How Many Females Are Reproducing?

The number of reproductively active females identified during the study has increased slowly to ninety-two in 2005. Because of a "discovery" curve (the rate at which new animals are identified), the number of identified, reproducing females was probably underestimated before 1990. Throughout the study there were additional females old enough to have calves that were never seen accompanied by a calf. This number increased through the 1990s, as calves born in the 1980s became sexually mature but calved later than the mean age of first parturition.

However, there remain a small group of females that, although seen regularly, have never been seen with a calf despite reaching the age of seventeen, at which age 90 percent of all known cows have already given birth. By 2005 there were twelve adult females in this nonparous category, ranging in age from seventeen to well over twenty-five years old. Thus, nearly 12 percent of all adult females have never been sighted with a calf, a number that is both significant and puzzling.

The number of new mothers recruited to the population (by becoming sexually mature and calving) ranged from zero to eleven each year, with no significant increase or decline over the period. In both 1996 and 2001, eleven new cows were added to the reproductive female group, contributing significantly to the variation outside the mean calving rate in both years.

Reproductive Longevity and Lifetime Calving Capacity

By 2005 sixteen right whale cows had produced at least six calves each, and four cows had at least seven calves. Two of these females (Eg #1240, Eg #1246) were sighted in 1974 and in 2005 with calves, indicating a reproductive life-span of at least thirty-one years. If ten years is assumed to be the mean age of first calving, these females were at least forty-one years of age when they calved in 2005.

Not all right whale mothers are equal with regard to calf production. Right whale Eg #1158 has had one calf in twenty-five years. Because she has been seen nearly every year, researchers are reasonably confident that no calves have been missed, and it is possible that she has a condition that prevents her from conceiving or from bringing fetuses to term. Calf production over the twenty-five-year study period by cows that were alive the entire time has ranged from one to seven.

Also, there are two older females that may be experiencing senescence (cessation of reproductive function as a result of aging), although it has never been described in baleen whales. Whale Eg #1005 had a calf in 1976 but has had none since. And one of the right whale research communities' favorite whales, Admiral (Eg #1027), the biggest (and perhaps the oldest) female in the population, has never been observed with a calf.

Age at First Calving

Age at first calving is often thought to reflect the general well-being of any population of whales. Data on right whales have proven to be quite variable, with first births occurring as early as five and as late as twenty-one years (Fig. 6.4). It is difficult to discern any pattern from these data for three reasons. First, the

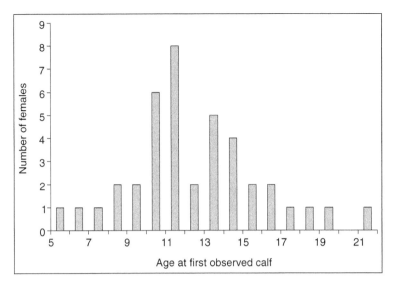

Figure 6.4. Distribution of ages at first calving in North Atlantic right whales.

number of first-birthing mothers in any year is small and highly variable. Second, the "first birth" age assigned to any mother can be biased substantially if that first event was missed, because the observed value would be three or more years too high. Finally, the impact of the longevity of the study on the "first birth" values is significant. For example, it would have been highly unlikely to observe a known twelve-year-old female giving birth for the first time in 1987 because there were many fewer females of known age in the population then as compared to today. Despite these limitations, these data reveal three interesting characteristics: (1) the only females observed to calve at less than eight years old did so in the late 1980s; (2) most females have their first calves at ages ten to eleven, with a second smaller group that calve for the first time at ages thirteen to fourteen; and (3) several females that should have come of age in the 1990s waited for the new millennium to have their first calf.

By 2005 there were thirty-nine females of known age that calved for the first time (i.e., primiparous) during the study period. The mean age of first calving for all primiparous females was 11.4 years, and the median was ten years. However, missed sightings of primiparous cow–calf pairs or early fetal or calf mortality will lead to overestimates of the age of first calving. Several of these first-time calving females had either sighting gaps in their precalving history or had been seen in the southeastern United States without a calf in an earlier year. If the mean age of first calving is recalculated to exclude all females that could have had a calf but were undetected as a result of lack of surveys or sightings, then the mean age of first calving is 10.1 years.

These North Atlantic estimates are comparable with the southern right whales in Argentina, which have an estimated mean age of first calving at 9.1 years (Cooke et al. 2001). It is possible that North Atlantic females mature more slowly than their Southern Hemisphere cousins, or, as Cooke et al. (2001) suggest, the southern right whale estimate may still be low.

Assuming a one-year gestation period, a 10.1-year age of first calving implies that the mean age of sexual maturity is nine years. However, the pattern of first reported parturitions shown in Fig. 6.4 suggests that some percentage of maturing females may lose their first pregnancy. Because baseline calving intervals are about three years in this species, a cow losing a calf in year ten might attempt reproducing again in the next two or three years. The clusters of first calving in years thirteen and fourteen suggest these may be second attempts by those animals that lost fetuses or neonates (therefore undetected by researchers) in years ten and eleven (Fig. 6.4).

Another line of evidence suggesting neonatal and fetal loss in right whales is visitation of the calving grounds by mature cows that do not calve. Because most female right whales go to the waters off the southeastern United States to give birth, and there is no evidence of feeding in the area, why would a non-calving adult female go there in the winter? If calf loss is occurring, any adult female sighting that occurred in the Southeast at least two years before, or three years after another calving could represent a lost calf. There have been sixteen adult females observed in the Southeast that meet these criteria. Although this suggests the occurrence of late-term calf loss or neonatal deaths, such losses are unlikely to be detected by aerial surveys and would be difficult to confirm. Young females may also migrate to the Southeast to learn about calving, but as they approach sexual maturity, it seems more likely that this age class would be found in wintering areas where mating and conception could occur (areas that are still unidentified but certainly do not include the calving grounds off Florida and Georgia). It eventually may be possible to determine the rate of right whale calf loss using fecal hormone analyses (Chapter 8). At the moment, some calf loss certainly occurs without detection, and the uncertainty around this will affect estimates of the age of sexual maturity.

Calves per Mature Female per Year

Another method for evaluating whale reproduction is to adjust observed calf counts by dividing those counts by the number of known reproductive females, providing an annual assessment of calves per mature female per year (CMFY). CMFY statistics suggest one adult female in every four is calving annually, but these analyses are biased by the limited survey effort and the "discovery" of calving females in the early years of the study. Further, whatever caused the increases in calving intervals in the 1990s inevitably caused declines in CMFY. Because the CFMY statistics are sensitive to the age of first calving, and females actually mature over a range of ages, this approach is not particularly reliable as an indicator of calving success.

Male Reproduction

Male right whales do not care for their offspring, cannot monopolize food or territory that might attract a mate, and live in an environment where physical displays that might indicate breeding fitness are invisible. Without any of these enticements, how then does a male find a mate? Primarily he has to listen well because females initiate most courtship activities by calling. However, this means that many males will approach and attempt to mate simultaneously with the calling female, and the resulting mating system is unusual in large whales. Male right whales are "sperm competitors" (Brownell and Ralls 1986), devoting energy to gamete production and delivery rather than physical aggression. Sperm competitors typically have large testes and large or elaborate penises compared to related species that compete for fertilizations in other ways (Parker 1984). Male right whales have the largest testes (up to 980 kg total weight) and among the longest penises (up to 3 m) in the world and are the largest in both categories relative to body weight and length for all baleen whales (Brownell and Ralls 1986).

Except for postmortem histological examination of the testes, no unequivocal criterion for sexual maturity in males is available, although there is the potential for measurement of fecal androgens to shed light on this question (Chapter 8). Males of all ages, including young individuals that cannot possibly be sexually mature, have been seen in surface-active groups indicative of courtship (Kraus and Hatch 2001). Still, it is primarily males over ten years of age that get close enough to a female to have an opportunity for mating.

Figure 6.5. A large and energetic surface-active group (SAG) as viewed from a research vessel (a) and a survey plane (b). Moira Brown / New England Aquarium (a) and Monica Zani / New England Aquarium (b).

Paternity analysis indicates the age of first reproduction for males to be somewhat older (fifteen years plus) (Chapter 7). This may reflect experience in surface-active groups (SAGs) or physical size, weight, and endurance rather than physiological maturity.

Surface-Active Groups

Sexual behavior thought to be indicative of mating has been observed in both the North and the South Atlantic right whale (Kraus and Hatch 2001; Best et al. 2003). Courtship is the most energetic and spectacular behavior displayed by this species (Fig. 6.5). These apparent mating groups, which may include from three to forty animals or more, usually occur when multiple males try to get close enough to the focal female to mate (Kraus and Hatch 2001). Females appear to call males by making groaning sounds resembling the mooing of a cow, which can be heard underwater for several kilometers (Parks 2003a). In response, males can be seen swimming quickly in a beeline for a calling female.

Figure 6.5. (*continued*)

Within SAGs, males appear to compete for the "alpha" positions (those next to the female), which are the best for taking advantage of each mating opportunity when the female breathes (Kraus and Hatch 2001). Males displace one another from these positions on average every fifteen minutes. There is no evidence of either reciprocity among males for access to females or of kin selection between related males.

Females are usually at the center of these SAGs, and they appear to avoid copulation by rolling onto their backs with the genital area out of the water (Fig. 6.5). However, Kraus and Hatch (2001) reported that females roll over to breathe about once a minute, offering males opportunities to mate. Based on the limited data available, it appears that a female may have intromission frequently during a courtship bout with multiple males. Females appear to use SAGs as a means of selecting mates who are agile, strong, and good at breath-holding in the context of courtship, perhaps the only arena in which female right whales can exercise mate choice. The observations of intromission make it clear that this behavior is sexual; however, most observed SAGs probably do not result in fertilizations (see color plate 9).

In the North Atlantic, SAGs are seen year-round and in all known habitat areas, although they are observed much more frequently during the late summer months (Kraus and Hatch 2001). Because all calves are born during the winter, and the gestation period is estimated to be twelve months (Best 1994), then fertilization must also take place during the winter, indicating that the majority of observed SAGs in the North Atlantic are occurring out of season. Because winter is the season when the location of most right whales is unknown, the location of the mating ground(s) is also unknown. Although South Atlantic right whales are observed in SAGs during winter, the majority of females within these SAGs do not give birth the following year, suggesting that the actual mating grounds for the South Atlantic populations are also unknown (Payne 1986; Best et al. 2003).

Further, not all North Atlantic SAGs are reproductive in nature. Juvenile, all-male, and all-female SAGs occur about 20 percent of the time, sometimes lasting for extended periods (Parks 2003b). These observations have led Parks and others to suggest that SAGs fulfill multiple functions for right whales, including socializing, play, practice, and possibly mate selection.

Despite the likelihood of multiple functions, SAGs are considered representative of mating behavior and have been used to evaluate potential mating strategies (Kraus and Hatch 2001). It is likely that SAGs occurring during the spring, summer, and fall represent either sexual practice or social displays and that insemination occurs elsewhere during the winter. Alternatively, gestation could be longer than twelve months, or implantation of the fertilized egg in the uterine wall might be delayed, but there is no evidence for or against either hypothesis in this species. The resolution of these questions will require methods for evaluating pregnancy in right whales, including analyses using fecal hormones (Chapter 8).

This mating system is not fully understood but appears to be a consequence of the prolonged spacing of calves (three- to four-year intervals). Brown et al. (1994) showed that the sex ratio in this population is fifty-fifty, so approximately equal numbers of reproductively active males and females should be expected. Therefore, long calving intervals will create an annual effective adult sex ratio of one female to every three or four males, leading to significant male competition for females. However, a complete understanding of right whale mating will probably depend on the discovery of the wintering mating grounds and observations to determine if all studies to date do truly represent actual mating behavior in this species.

Effects of Differences in Habitat Use on Reproduction

One way to test hypotheses on reproduction in North Atlantic right whales would be to find another group of right whales for comparison. Researchers have compared the North Atlantic right whales with their Southern Hemisphere counterparts, which have provided estimates of reproductive parameters in a closely related species. In the 1980s the North Atlantic right whale population appeared to be growing at a 2.5 percent annual rate (Knowlton et al. 1994), although analyses in the 1990s suggested that the population had gone into a decline (Caswell et al. 1999; Fujiwara and Caswell 2001; Kraus et al. 2005). Reproductive rates of the South Atlantic right whales, whose populations appear to be growing at 6.9–7.1 percent annually (Best et al. 2001; Cooke et al. 2001), may be a good control population, although the two species live in different oceans with different ecological regimes and different recent evolutionary histories.

The non-Fundy North Atlantic right whales might offer another comparison. The non-Fundy cows comprise about a third of the total population of calving females, so analyses on this subset will be compromised by small sample sizes. Nevertheless, if reproductive problems were affecting only the more coastal Fundy whales and not the offshore (non-Fundy) animals, that would be informative about the source of reproductive problems. However, the non-Fundy and Fundy calving rates are highly correlated, suggesting that the two reproductive declines in the 1990s were not related to use of the Bay of Fundy habitat. Using the non-Fundy group of right whales as a comparison for the Fundy group will remain problematic until their summering grounds are found because there is currently no understanding of the nature of that habitat.

What Affects Right Whale Reproduction the Most?

Because variable survey effort and sighting heterogeneity can affect all analyses of reproduction, researchers have adopted fairly conservative approaches to analyzing reproductive parameters in this species. The data indicate higher than normal variability in calving and significant changes in interbirth intervals during the 1990s. However, the reasons for these observations remain unclear.

Calf counts could be low if females were giving birth in areas where the detection of their calves was unlikely, although these calves are usually identified in the northern habitats later in the year of their birth. It is possible there is another calving ground, but since 1990 fewer than five calves have been born outside the winter calving area. Regardless of the northern habitat use pattern (Fundy or non-Fundy), nearly all right whale cows appear to use the southeastern U.S. coastal waters as a calving ground. Reproduction could also be reduced by large numbers of senescent mothers and/or an unstable age structure, although analyses conducted by Hamilton et al. (1998) do not support either hypothesis.

Researchers have long speculated that right whale reproduction is being affected by some combination of genetics, pollutants, food limitations, disease, and loss of critical habitat. If so, then some of these factors may be related to where whales feed and how they use available habitats. A discussion of the potential causes of reproductive variability in this population is given here.

Low Levels of Genetic Variability and Inbreeding

The variable reproductive rates and small size of the North Atlantic right whale population have led to hypotheses that low levels of genetic variability or inbreeding might be retarding its recovery. It appears likely that reproductive rates in this population are lower than those in other species of right whales. But it is unlikely that consistent effects of inbreeding alone could account for the wide annual variation and the 1990s periods of low reproduction. However, reduced genetic diversity in critical areas of the genome that control for immunity (the MHC complex), ontogenesis, or for other areas of reproduction could be contributing to reproductive problems through synergistic effects with disease, contaminants, or temporal and spatial food reductions (Chapter 7).

Potential Effects of Pollutants

Two major pathways of pollutant exposure could affect right whales. First, contaminants including DDT, polychlorinated biphenyls, and polycyclic aromatic hydrocarbons are known to enter whale tissues via their food, including tissues of calves through lactation (Woodley et al. 1991; Weisbrod et al. 2000). The reported levels were considered low relative to those of other marine mammals, perhaps because the low trophic level at which right whales feed minimizes the effects of bioconcentration (O'Shea and Brownell 1994). Second, nonfood items or chemical contaminants might be ingested directly during feeding. Right whales feed in convergence zones and slicks where surface currents concentrate anything that floats, including not only prey items, but also oil, contaminants associated with the surface microlayer, and trash.

Another suite of contaminants has raised new concerns. These include organotin antifouling agents on ship hulls, plasticizers known as phthalates, polybrominated diphenyl ethers used as flame retardants, and alkylphenol ethoxylates used in detergents and pesticides and widely present in sewage effluents. All of these compounds have been proven to disrupt animal reproduction by altering critical endocrine pathways (Colborn and Smolen 1996; Meerts et al. 2001), and they have been identified in a variety of marine animals (Kannan et al. 1997; Lye et al. 1997; DeBoer et al. 1998; Tanabe et al. 1998). None of these compounds has been measured in right whales, although studies to test contaminant effects in vitro are under way with right whale cell cultures at the Wise Lab at the University of Southern Maine.

Food Supply Limitations and Reduced Carrying Capacity

Female right whales require adequate reserves for both reproduction and lactation, and a diminished food supply could cause a reduction in calving (Moore et al. 2001). A possible reduction in the abundance or the concentrating mechanisms of copepods, caused either by competition or oceanographic changes, has been hypothesized as a cause of changes in reproduction. Mitchell (1975) hypothesized that competition from sei whales may have limited the ability of right whale populations to increase after whaling had ceased. Payne et al. (1990) proposed that competition from planktivorous fish such as sand lance, herring, and basking sharks could cause temporary shifts in local right whale distribution. Kenney (2001) suggested that temporary, large-scale hydrographic changes in the Gulf of Maine altered currents and temperatures and prevented the formation of dense patches of copepods in the Great South Channel during 1992, a year when right whales were absent. The importance of very dense patches of plankton prey to North Atlantic right whale feeding patterns has been well established (Chapter 5).

However, data indicating that North Atlantic right whales are food-limited are difficult to evaluate. Although competition or oceanographic changes may alter copepod aggregations, the abundance of planktivorous fish suggests that copepods may be too plentiful to be limiting this population to 350 individuals. Because the Gulf of Maine represents the southern limit of this copepod's distribution, it is possible that local *Calanus* abundance is vulnerable to climatic shifts and that the regional shifts in right whale distribution are related to this (Kenney 2001; Chapter 15). Greene and Pershing (2004) linked right whale calving to *Calanus* abundance and oceanographic changes influenced by the North Atlantic Oscillation (NAO).

It has also been suggested that the current population may represent the approximate carrying capacity for right whales in today's environment, which would result in reduced reproductive rates and low population growth. Although the strict definition of carrying capacity includes population limits imposed by food, space, and environmental conditions, food is frequently assumed to be the controlling factor with regard to right whales. The revised historical records of right whale abundance suggest that a few thousand animals inhabited the western North Atlantic before whaling (Chapter 2), at least an order of magnitude larger than the contemporary population. It is difficult to evaluate changes in the primary right whale habitats over the past 500 years, but there is no evidence of oceanographic changes on a par with the changes in the population size. For this reason, the reduced carrying capacity hypothesis does not appear likely.

Diseases

A number of diseases could be affecting reproduction (including the death of fetuses or neonates) in ways that are consistent with the observed variability in calving and the increase in calving intervals. For example, brucellosis and leptospirosis are known to cause spontaneous abortions and reproductive dysfunction in domestic animals, and both diseases have been found in free-ranging cetaceans (Smith et al. 1974; Miller et al. 1999). Further, a variety of other infectious diseases that could cause neonatal mortality, such as influenza, herpes, and calicivirus, have all been found in cetaceans (Van Bressem et al. 1999), and all are known to affect either reproduction or survivorship in domestic and wild terrestrial mammals. Currently the tools for assessing disease factors in free-swimming large whales do not exist. Further development of analytic methods for antigen detection from skin biopsies, respiratory fluids, or fecal materials may allow the evaluation of disease effects on right whales in the future.

Marine Biotoxins

In the Bay of Fundy both right whale prey, *Calanus finmarchicus,* and fecal samples from right whales contain measurable levels of PSP toxins (paralytic shellfish poisoning, produced by *Alexandrium* spp.). Right whale fecal samples also contain the biotoxin domoic acid (produced by *Pseudo-nitzschia* spp.; Chapter 8). Although the effects of these biotoxins on right whales are unknown, domoic acid toxicosis has been associated with fetal and neonatal deaths in California sea lions (Scholin et al. 2000). Furthermore, PSP and domoic acid have caused mortalities in humpback whales and West Indian manatees, respectively, through their neurotoxic effects (Geraci et al. 1989; Scholin et al. 2000).

Habitat Loss

Reeves et al. (1978) suggested that increased commercial marine use of Delaware and Chesapeake Bays since the 1800s had excluded right whales from those habitats, lowering the potential for population recovery. Low-level pollution, ship traffic, ocean dumping, and dredging have all been invoked in recovery plans as factors that could reduce the habitat available to right whales. Habitat discussions tend to focus on prey resources, although the absence of right whale feeding in the southeastern United States suggests that, at least in that area, other factors are also important. For example if underwater noise makes it impossible for whales to hear one another, it probably eliminates that area from breeding or calving because in both cases whales need to communicate (Chapter 10). Studies on the habitat requirements of this species are needed for better management of conflicts between humans and whales. At the moment, however, all hypotheses on links between habitat quality and reproduction are speculative.

Conclusion: Prospects for Understanding Right Whale Reproduction

In the 1980s, Knowlton et al. (1994) estimated a 2.5 percent annual rate of population growth for North Atlantic right whales, much lower than the growth rates of 6–7 percent per year recorded for southern right whales in Argentina and South Africa (Best et al. 2001). Since that time there have been a continued increase in anthropogenic mortalities (Knowlton and Kraus 2001) and a decline in reproductive rates from 1993 through 2001 (Kraus et al. 2001). Analysis of the current population trends indicates that the North Atlantic right whale population may still be declining in size (Caswell et al. 1999; Fujiwara and Caswell 2001; Kraus et al. 2005).

It is important to separate the intrinsic baseline levels of right whale reproduction from changes that may be caused by extrinsic factors. Although the highest rate (to date) of population growth in North Atlantic right whales is only 2.5 percent, it is not known if this represents the species maximum growth rate. If it is, factors that may be responsible could include genetic characteristics of this very small population (Chapter 7), or it may be an isolated population with different environmental conditions and reproduction patterns than southern right whales. However, the variable survey effort in the 1980s means that the data from that period are incomplete and cannot be used as a baseline for North Atlantic right whale reproduction. Therefore researchers still cannot reasonably estimate this population's potential for calving and population growth after twenty-five years of study.

North Atlantic right whale reproduction declined significantly during two periods in the 1990s, almost certainly because of unidentified extrinsic factors. In addition there was a longer-term slowdown in calving rates between 1993 and 2003. The two short-term declines are correlated with the NAO and calf counts (Greene and Pershing 2004), but they also match the patterns one might expect from a disease event, a series of marine biotoxin blooms, or significant but undetected changes with reproductive effects that happened somewhere in the right whale's range. The decade-long reproductive slump in calving rates could be related to oceanographic changes in primary feeding areas or NAO effects on diminishing prey production, either of which could reduce right whale reproduction by compromising body condition.

It is most likely that some combination of these problems is working against right whales in the North Atlantic. The low genetic diversity in right whales may leave them vulnerable to disease events. Infectious disease and biotoxins could cause reproductive failure directly or might work indirectly to reduce caloric assimilation efficiency or impair behavioral responses in courtship or feeding activities. If some combination of factors is responsible for low reproduction in right whales, it will be difficult to tease out the important ones, but that does not mean the attempt should not be made.

Right whales have a different life history than other baleen whales. Recent work on bowheads by George et al. (1999) has revealed that bowheads live well over 100 years, and some may reach 200 years of age. If right whales are shown to live one hundred years or longer, it might be necessary to rethink the demography of this species. A long-lived right whale scenario would probably include older mean ages of sexual maturity, lower juvenile:adult ratios than most large baleen whales, longer reproductive life spans, and more flexibility in reproductive strategies for both females and males. The age of first parturition has been climbing upward steadily since the first estimates in the early 1990s and now is estimated at ten years. Hamilton et al. (1998) reported lower juvenile:adult ratios for right whales than other baleen whales, which is consistent with a longer-lived life history pattern. In the North Atlantic right whale population, several females have been identified with reproductive life spans over thirty years, also consistent with long-lived life histories.

The development of a long life span allows for the high variability in reproductive success relative to ecological conditions. Right whales live in a patchy environment, and the shifts in distribution within the past twenty years suggest that right whales have been adjusting to spatial and temporal shifts in prey distribution within the study area during that time (Chapter 5). If right whales have a reproductive life span of fifty years or more, the effects of short-term climatic changes, diseases, biotoxins, and food availability on reproduction could be minimized. Such events could contribute to a short-term (ca. ten to twenty years) decline in reproductive success, but the lifetime reproductive success of individuals might not be affected significantly. It is possible that the 1980s were a "good" period for reproductive success in right whales, and the 1990s represent a period of "poor" reproduction. This is consistent with an evolutionary strategy of long-lived animals in patchy and variable environments: survive the lean years and reproduce in the good ones.

The story of North Atlantic right whale reproduction is complex, but it leads to a simple conclusion. Right whales depend on a long life to replace themselves in the population, and ultimately their reproductive success may best be measured over generations. Long-lived mammals are certainly subjected to short-term variation in their environment, which will affect their demography and population growth. This species' life history emphasizes the need to reduce human causes of mortality (especially in females) to nonsignificant levels so that the consequences of natural variation in the environment on reproduction are not compounded by anthropogenic influences.

Nevertheless the elimination of all human-caused mortalities solves only part of the problem for right whales if humans are also responsible for the animals' reproductive failure. Some potential problems may be cumulative (contaminants) or may leave permanent sterility (disease). Right whale researchers and managers must determine whether the current reproductive variations are short-term or long-term ones and whether they are caused by human activities or by normal environmental variation over which humans have no control.

Best, P. B. 1994. Seasonality of reproduction and the length of gestation in southern right whales. *Eubalaena australis. Journal of Zoology* 232:175–189.

Best, P. B., A. Brandão, and D. S. Butterworth. 2001. Demographic parameters of southern right whales off South Africa. *Journal of Cetacean Research and Management* Special Issue 2:161–169.

Best, P. B., C. M. Schaeff, D. Reeb, and P. J. Palsboll. 2003. Composition and possible function of social groupings of southern right whales in South African waters. *Behaviour* 140:1469–1494.

Brown, M. W., S. D. Kraus, D. E. Gaskin, and B. N. White. 1994. Sexual composition and analysis of reproductive females in the North Atlantic right whale, *Eubalaena glacialis,* population. *Marine Mammal Science* 10:253–265.

Brownell, R. L., and K. Ralls. 1986. Potential for sperm competition in baleen whales. Pages 97–112 *in* G. Donovan, ed. *Behavior of Whales in Relation to Management.* International Whaling Commission, Cambridge, U.K.

Caswell, H., M. Fujiwara, and S. Brault. 1999. Declining survival probability threatens the North Atlantic right whale. *Proceedings of the National Academy of Sciences* 96:3308–3313.

Colborn, T., and M. Smolen. 1996. Epidemiological analysis of persistent organochlorine contaminants in cetaceans. *Reviews of Environmental Contamination and Toxicology* 146:91–171.

Cooke, J. G., V. Rowntree, and R. Payne. 2001. Estimates of demographic parameters for the southern right whales (*Eubalaena australis*) observed off Peninsula Valdez, Argentina. *Journal of Cetacean Research and Management* Special Issue 2:125–132.

DeBoer, J., P. G. Wester, H. J. C. Klamer, W. E. Lewis, and J. P. Boon. 1998. Do flame retardants threaten ocean life? *Nature* 394:28–29.

Fujiwara, M., and H. Caswell. 2001. Demography of the endangered North Atlantic right whale. *Nature* 414:537–541.

George, J. C., J. Bada, J. Zeh, L. Scott, S. E. Brown, T. O'Hara, and R. Suydam. 1999. Age and growth estimates of bowhead whales (*Balaena mysticetus*) via aspartic acid racemization. *Canadian Journal of Zoology* 77:571–580.

Geraci, J. R., D. M. Anderson, R. J. Timperi, D. J. St. Aubin, G. A. Early, J. H. Prescott, and C. A. Mayo. 1989. Humpback whales (*Megaptera novaeangliae*) fatally poisoned by dinoflagellate toxin. *Canadian Journal of Fisheries and Aquatic Sciences* 46:1895–1898.

Greene, C. H., and A. J. Pershing. 2004. Climate and the conservation biology of North Atlantic right whales: the right whale at the wrong time? *Frontiers in Ecology and the Environment* 2:29–34.

Hamilton, P. K., A. R. Knowlton, M. K. Marx, and S. D. Kraus. 1998. Age structure and longevity in North Atlantic right whales (*Eubalaena glacialis*) and their relation to reproduction. *Marine Ecology Progress Series* 171:285–292.

Kannan, K., K. Senthilkumar, B. G, Loganathan, S. Takahashi, D. K. Odell, and S. Tanabe. 1997. Elevated accumulation of tributyltin and its breakdown products in bottlenose dolphins (*Tursiops truncatus*) found stranded along the U.S. Atlantic and Gulf coasts. *Environmental Science and Technology* 31:296–301.

Kenney, R. D. 2001. Anomalous 1992 spring and summer right whale (*Eubalaena glacialis*) distribution in the Gulf of Maine. *Journal of Cetacean Research and Management* Special Issue 2:209–223.

Knowlton, A. R., and S. D. Kraus. 2001. Mortality and serious injury of northern right whales (*Eubalaena glacialis*) in the western North Atlantic Ocean. *Journal of Cetacean Research and Management* Special Issue 2:193–208.

Knowlton, A. R., S. D. Kraus, and R. D. Kenney. 1994. Reproduction in North Atlantic right whales (*Eubalaena glacialis*). *Canadian Journal of Zoology* 72:1297–1305.

Kraus, S. D., and J. J. Hatch. 2001. Mating strategies in the North Atlantic right whale (*Eubalaena glacialis*). *Journal of Cetacean Research and Management* Special Issue 2:237–244.

Kraus, S. D., P. K. Hamilton, R. D. Kenney, A. R. Knowlton, and C. K. Slay. 2001. Status and trends in reproduction of the North Atlantic right whale. *Journal of Cetacean Research and Management* Special Issue 2:231–236.

Kraus, S. D., M. W. Brown, H. Caswell, C. W. Clark, M. Fujiwara, P. K. Hamilton, R. D. Kenney, A. R. Knowlton, S. Landry, C. A. Mayo, W. A. McLellan, M. J. Moore, D. P. Nowacek, D. A. Pabst, A. J. Read, and R. M. Rolland. 2005. North Atlantic right whales in crisis. *Science* 309:561–562.

Lye, C. M., C. L. J. Frid, M. E. Gill, and D. McCormick. 1997. Abnormalities in the reproductive health of flounder *Platichthys flesus* exposed to effluent from a sewage treatment works. *Marine Pollution Bulletin* 34:34–41.

Meerts, L. A. T. M., R. J. Letcher, S. Hoving, G. Marsh, A. Bergman, J. G. Lemmen, B. van der Burg, and A. Brouwer. 2001. In vitro estrogenicity of polybrominated diphenyl ethers, hydroxylated PBDEs, and polybrominated bisphenol A compounds. *Environmental Health Perspectives* 109:399–407.

Miller, W. G., L. G. Adams, T. A. Ficht, N. F. Cheville, J. P. Payeur, D. R. Harley, C. House, and S. H. Ridgway. 1999. *Brucella*-induced abortions and infection in bottlenose dolphins (*Tursiops truncatus*). *Journal of Zoo and Wildlife Medicine* 30:100–110.

Mitchell, E. D. 1975. Trophic relationships and competition for food in Northwest Atlantic whales. *Proceedings of the Canadian Society of Zoology Annual Meeting*, pp. 123–133.

Moore, M. J., C. A. Miller, M. S. Morss, R. Arthur, W. A. Lange, K. G. Prada, M. K. Marx, and E. A. Frey. 2001. Ultrasonic measurement of blubber thickness in right whales. *Journal of Cetacean Research and Management* Special Issue 2: 301–309.

O'Shea, T. J., and R. L. Brownell, Jr. 1994. Organochlorine and metal contaminants in baleen whales: a review and evaluation of conservation implications. *Science of the Total Environment* 154:179–200.

Parker, G. A. 1984. Sperm competition and the evolution of animal mating strategies. Pages 1–60 *in* R. L. Smith, ed. *Sperm Competition and the Evolution of Animal Mating Systems.* Academic Press, New York.

Parks, S. E. 2003a. Response of North Atlantic right whales (*Eubalaena glacialis*) to playback of calls recorded from surface active groups in both the North and South Atlantic. *Marine Mammal Science* 19:563–580.

Parks, S. E. 2003b. Acoustic communication in the North Atlantic right whale (*Eubalaena glacialis*). Ph.D. Thesis. MIT-WHOI Joint Program in Oceanography. Woods Hole, MA.

Payne, P. M., D. N. Wiley, S. B. Young, S. Pittman, P. J. Clapham, and J. W. Jossi. 1990. Recent fluctuations in the abundance of baleen whales in the southern Gulf of Maine USA in relation to changes in selected prey. *Fishery Bulletin* 88:687–696.

Payne, R. 1986. Long term behavioral studies of the southern right whale (*Eubalaena australis*). *Report of the International Whaling Commission* Special Issue 10: 161–167.

Reeves, R. R., J. G. Mead, and S. K. Katona. 1978. The right whale, *Eubalaena glacialis,* in the western North Atlantic. *Report of the International Whaling Commission* 28:303–312.

Scholin, C. A., F. Gulland, G. J. Doucette, S. Benson, M. Busman, F. P. Chavez, J. Cordaro, R. DeLong, A. De Vogelaere, J. Harvey, M. Haulena, K. Lefebvre, T. Lipscomb, S. Loscutoff, L. J. Lowenstine, R. Marin, P. E. Miller, W. A. McLellan, P. D. R. Moeller, C. L. Powell, T. Rowles, P. Silvagni, M. Silver, T. Spraker, V. Trainer, and F. M. Van Dolah. 2000. Mortality of sea lions along the central California coast linked to toxic diatom bloom. *Nature* 403:80–84.

Smith, A. W., R. J. Brown, D. E. Skilling, and R. DeLong. 1974. *Leptospira pomona* and reproductive failure in California sea lions. *Journal of the American Veterinary Medical Association* 165:996–998.

Tanabe, S., M. Prudente, T. Mizuno, J. Hasegawa, H. Iwata, and N. Miyazaki. 1998. Butyltin contamination in marine mammals from North Pacific and Asian coastal waters. *Environmental Science and Technology* 32:193–198.

Van Bressem, M.-F., K. Van Waerebeek, and J. A. Raga. 1999. A review of virus infections of cetaceans and the potential impact of morbilliviruses, poxviruses, and papillomaviruses on host population dynamics. *Diseases of Aquatic Organisms* 38:38–65.

Wade, G. N., and J. E. Schneider. 1992. Metabolic fuels and reproduction in mammals. *Neuroscience and Biobehavioral Reviews* 16:235–272.

Weisbrod, A. V., D. Shea, M. J. Moore, and J. J. Stegeman. 2000. Organochlorine exposure and bioaccumulation in the endangered Northwest Atlantic right whale (*Eubalaena glacialis*) population. *Environmental Toxicology and Chemistry* 19: 654–666.

Woodley, T. H., M. W. Brown, S. D. Kraus, and D. E. Gaskin. 1991. Organochlorine levels in North Atlantic right whale (*Eubalaena glacialis*) blubber. *Archives of Environmental Contamination and Toxicology* 21:141–145.

7

Right Whales Past and Present as Revealed by Their Genes

TIMOTHY R. FRASIER, BRENNA A. MCLEOD,
ROXANNE M. GILLETT, MOIRA W. BROWN,
AND BRADLEY N. WHITE

20 August 1995
Bay of Fundy

The New England Aquarium right whale research team is conducting a photo-identification survey of one of the North Atlantic right whales' critical habitat areas, the Bay of Fundy. A whale surfaces to breathe, and from its callosity pattern the crew on the research vessel Nereid *identifies the whale as "Misstip" (Eg #1156). A quick glance through their notes and the team discovers that a sample for genetic analysis has not yet been collected from this whale. They ready themselves; the crossbow is cocked, and a modified arrow designed specifically for collecting small skin samples from whales is readied. The team slowly approaches the whale in the same manner they do to obtain photographs. The darter, although anxious, knows to be patient and wait for the signature "head lift" that precedes the terminal dive, for as the whale is diving, a sample can be obtained from the aft part of the body where the blubber is the thickest and the impact on the whale is minimal. A successful shot is fired, and minutes later, while Misstip is feeding on copepods over 100 m below, the team is prepping the sample to be shipped to the genetics laboratory of Dr. Bradley N. White.*

At the laboratory, DNA is extracted from the skin sample. Because of the toughness of the whale skin, it must be frozen with liquid nitrogen and ground into a fine powder before a variety of chemicals and enzymes are added to break down the cells and make the DNA available for genetic analyses. A section of the mitochondrial DNA (a region that is passed on from mothers to offspring) is then sequenced to identify which matriline Misstip belongs to. Finally, the nuclear DNA is examined, from which, as in a forensic case, analyses of paternity and relatedness can be conducted to determine where Misstip fits in the family tree of the North Atlantic right whale.

Paternity analysis reveals that Misstip is the most successful male yet sampled in this species, fathering four calves between 1980 and 2001. However, although the paternity data provide some answers, they raise even more questions. For example, fertilization is thought to take place during the winter, but Misstip has been seen only during the months of May, June, August, and September. Additionally, he has been seen in only ten of the twenty-two years included in the analysis. So where does Misstip go in the winter to mate, and where did he go during those periods when he was missing for years at a time? The sightings data imply that Misstip frequents habitats currently unknown to researchers including the location of the unknown mating ground(s) for this species. If Misstip is capable of disappearing for a few years, could there be whales that use only these unknown habitats and are therefore never photo-identified or included in estimates of population size and trends?

By using all the samples that have been collected, the family tree for this species is emerging, making it possible to track the DNA of each sampled offspring and determine its parents, even those that have not been identified photographically. If we look closer at Misstip's section of the family tree, even more questions arise. For example Misstip's paternities span thirteen years, and the average interval between them is 4.3 years. Is this expected for a species in which the mating system is thought to be based on sperm competition? Additionally, the genetic profiles of Misstip's offspring indicate that they were conceived only when Misstip mated with females that were particularly genetically dissimilar from himself. Does this mean that right whales are choosing genetically divergent mates or that matings are successful only when they occur between genetically dissimilar individuals? The genetic analyses described in this chapter have been used to address these

questions and gain a better understanding of the factors influencing repro-
duction and right whale recovery.

Tim Frasier

When genetic techniques were first applied to the study of wild populations, they revealed that the interactions of individuals within and between populations were frequently quite different than expected based solely on observational data (Quinn et al. 1987; Gibbs et al. 1990). This has been the case for the majority of populations studied (Hughes 1998). As a result, molecular techniques have become widely integrated with field techniques to study the biology of wildlife populations. Molecular techniques have the potential to be particularly informative in studies of marine mammals, where the majority of behaviors occur underwater or in unknown locations and are therefore not readily observed.

Although the photo-identification of individual North Atlantic right whales has provided the bulk of information leading to the current understanding of this species, many of the questions regarding right whale biology and conservation can be addressed only through comprehensive genetic analyses and the integration of these two research approaches. Methods to collect small skin samples from large free-ranging whales for use in genetic analyses were developed in the late 1980s (Lambertsen 1987) and were soon integrated into field studies of North Atlantic right whales (Brown et al. 1991; Fig. 7.1; color plate 11). As a result of the long-term collaboration between the photo-identification and genetic research teams, skin biopsy samples have now been collected from the majority of identified individuals and have made this one of the most thoroughly sampled species for genetic studies.

In addition to samples collected from living whales, high-quality DNA has also been obtained from historic whale bones, and genetic analyses are being conducted on bones collected from historic whaling sites (Rastogi et al. 2004). Combined, these data provide a powerful opportunity to assess the North Atlantic right whale's past and present based on its DNA and to assess the implications for the recovery and future of this species.

North Atlantic Right Whale Past

Analyses have shown that North Atlantic right whales have low levels of genetic variability at minisatellite (Schaeff et al. 1997), mitochondrial (Malik et al.

Figure 7.1. A crossbow with a modified bolt is used to collect small pieces of skin and blubber from free-ranging whales. Monica Zani / New England Aquarium.

2000), and microsatellite (Waldick et al. 2002) markers (Table 7.1) as well as a long-term reproductive rate that is lower than expected (Chapter 6). These characteristics, along with a 1,000-year history of commercial exploitation and infrequent contemporary sightings within known historical habitats, have led to the widely accepted view that, although once abundant, the North Atlantic

Table 7.1. Comparison of Measures of Genetic Variability in the North Atlantic Right Whale and the Cheetah[a]

Measure	Cheetah (%)	Reference	N.A. right whale (%)	Reference
mtDNA—RFLP data				
Nucleotide diversity	0.182	Menotti-Raymond and O'Brien (1993)	0.08	Schaeff et al. (1991)
Microsatellites				
Allelic diversity	3.4	Menotti-Raymond and O'Brien (1995)	3.2	Waldick et al. (2002)
Heterozygosity	0.39	Menotti-Raymond and O'Brien (1995)	0.31	Waldick et al. (2002)

a. The cheetah is a species typically considered to have low levels of genetic variation. RFLP stands for restriction fragment length polymorphism. Note that although comparable, variability is lower in North Atlantic right whales than in cheetahs in all cases.

right whale was commercially harvested to near extinction. It has been proposed that this extensive history of harvesting has resulted in the current small population size, low genetic variation, and decreased reproductive capacity in this species (Schaeff et al. 1997).

The recent finding of whale bones at historic Basque whaling sites in Labrador, Canada, has provided a rare opportunity to compare early and post-exploitation DNA samples for this species and to test previously held views of whaling in this region (Barkham 1984). To gain further insight into the history of North Atlantic right whales, both historic and extant specimens representing early and postexploitation levels of genetic variability have been genetically assessed. This comparison has resulted in surprising findings that have led to a restructuring in the way both the history and recovery potential of this species are viewed.

Genetic Assessment of Historical Whaling

Called "right" whales because they were considered to be the right whales to kill, the species of this genus (*Eubalaena*), as well as the closely related bowhead whale, were prized by whalers because they traveled slowly, had a thick blubber layer, and often floated after death. Until recently, it was believed that most of the historical exploitation of right whales in the western North Atlantic included Basque whaling in the sixteenth and seventeenth centuries and American whaling from the late seventeenth century through the early 1900s. The general understanding was that Basque whaling caused the most dramatic decline in this population, with American whaling subsequently reducing the population from a few thousand individuals to its current small size.

The presence of Basques along the coasts of Labrador was largely forgotten until the 1970s, when historian Selma Barkham identified nine sixteenth-century whaling ports along the coasts of Quebec and Labrador in the Strait of Belle Isle (Barkham 1977). At Red Bay, Barkham identified a Basque whaling galleon that sank in 1565 (presumably the *San Juan*), and an extensive marine archaeological excavation ensued. Seven years of excavation brought forth a rich assemblage of information on Basque maritime life, navigation, craftsmanship, and numerous whale bones. The majority of these specimens (found in strata both above and below the ship) consisted of limb and caudal bones remaining after flensing of the whale, whereby flukes and flippers were removed for ease of handling and removal of blubber. The location of these bone samples dates them to the time period when extensive Basque whaling was just beginning (the mid-1500s). Therefore, they provide the first opportunity to compare samples representing early exploitation with extant right whale samples and to test hypotheses regarding the impact of exploitation on levels of genetic variability.

From 1530 to 1610, Basque whalers along the coasts of Labrador are estimated to have killed between 25,000 and 40,000 whales (Aguilar 1986). To identify the species represented in the Red Bay marine bone deposit, the osteological characteristics of seventeen historical humeri were examined, and approximately equal proportions of right and bowhead whales (eight and nine, respectively) were identified (Cumbaa 1986). This fifty-fifty species ratio was subsequently combined with the estimated Basque whale oil imports to estimate that the early exploitation population size of the North Atlantic right whale was between 12,000 and 15,000 individuals (Gaskin 1991). This information indicated that right whales were once abundant in the western North Atlantic and has been used to infer what the recovery potential of this species might be (NMFS 1991), although current recovery goals are based on growth rates and trends rather than achievement of a specific population size (NMFS 2005).

Subsequent American whaling removed several thousand whales from 1620 to 1924 (Chapter 2), and it has been suggested that there were likely more than 1,000 right whales in the 1690s to support the level of harvesting that took place in the subsequent three decades (Reeves et al. 1999). Thus, the whaling records suggested that Basque whaling caused the more dramatic decline and was probably responsible for the decreased genetic variability in the western North Atlantic right whale. This view was also supported by recent genetic bottleneck analyses, which suggested that there had not been a significant reduction in genetic diversity since the eighteenth century (Waldick et al. 2002).

Although the importance of Basque whaling in the history of this species has been recognized, information regarding the Labrador fishery was confounded by a shortage of descriptive records and taxonomic uncertainty between bowhead and right whales (Eschricht and Reinhardt 1866; Rice 1998). In particular, the ratio of these species in the Basque harvest has been the subject of dispute. To investigate the impact of Basque whaling on both of these species, scientists from several disciplines recently conducted archaeological and molecular investigations of historic Basque whaling sites.

To study the impact of Basque whaling on the North Atlantic right whale, the bones exhumed during the excavation of the *San Juan* were sampled for genetic analysis. The cold, saline, dark conditions of the water surrounding Labrador allowed for successful retrieval of high-quality DNA (Fig. 7.2). Genetic species identification, using mitochondrial DNA sequence analysis, revealed that of twenty-one humeri (including the original seventeen specimens identified osteologically) only a single bone was from a right whale, and the remaining twenty bones were from bowhead whales (Rastogi et al. 2004). This discrepancy between the osteological and molecular results is likely the result of a lack of reference specimens for osteological comparison and/or sex or age polymorphism in the bowhead specimens.

The finding of only one right whale bone was surprising given previous views that right whales made up either most or roughly 50 percent of the Basque harvest. The genetic data of the same bone specimens used in the osteological analysis indicated that the Basques hunted bowhead whales predominantly, not right whales, in the Strait of Belle Isle. However, these data did not provide conclusive information about the overall species composition of the Basque harvest because of the small number of bones analyzed and the single source location, which might have represented a few seasons that happened to be dominated by bowhead whales. Therefore more extensive sampling was conducted throughout known Basque whaling sites in Quebec and Labrador in 2004, including the two sites that are referred to most frequently in the Basque literature (Red Bay and Chateau Bay). This resulted in the collection and analysis of 188 bones from a range of historic Basque whaling sites (Fig. 7.3). Genetic analyses showed that 183 of these bones came from bowhead whales, one came from a right whale (the original one), one from a blue whale, one from a fin whale, and two from humpback whales. Preliminary DNA profiling has revealed that these bones represent a minimum of ninety-seven individuals.

The species composition of this larger sample set from a wider range of locations supports the hypothesis that the Basques harvested primarily bowhead and not right whales in the western North Atlantic. These results are not consistent with the perspective that Basque whaling was responsible for a dramatic decline in the western North Atlantic right whale. Rather, the population may have been at a relatively small size for the past 500 years, predating commercial exploitation. If small population size is a long-term characteristic of this species, then some of the factors keeping it small have likely been acting for hundreds of years, which is important to consider if efficient and effective conservation strategies are to be developed (Caughley and Gunn 1996).

Historical Mitochondrial DNA

Mitochondrial DNA is nonrecombining, maternally inherited DNA containing highly variable regions (such as the cytochrome b gene and the control region or D-loop). These characteristics make mitochondrial DNA analysis particularly useful for evaluating phylogenetic and demographic history, population structuring, and maternal relationships and lineages. Each individual within the contemporary North Atlantic right whale population contains one of five remaining mitochondrial control region sequences (called "haplotypes"). One of these haplotypes is represented in only four males and will therefore likely be lost soon, as this type of DNA is passed on only from mothers to their offspring (Malik et al. 1999). Assessment of the control region sequence of the single right whale bone from Labrador revealed a sixth haplotype, not found within the estimated 66 percent of the extant population that has been profiled to date. The similarity of this haplotype to those found in the contemporary population indicates that it is not particularly divergent from those found today (Rastogi et al. 2004).

The loss of a mitochondrial haplotype suggests that since the 1500s there has been some loss of genetic variability in this species. This is in contrast to a previous analysis of early twentieth century baleen that did not identify any mitochondrial haplotypes that are not present in the extant population (Rosenbaum et al. 2000). It may seem that the bone sample analyses show conflicting results: It seems clear that the Basques were not responsible for a large decline in the western North Atlantic right whale, but it appears that since this time there has been a loss of genetic diversity within the species. These results can be partially reconciled by interpreting them in the context of the social structure of this species.

North Atlantic right whales show maternally directed site fidelity for summer nursery use, which results in different right whale lineages using different summer nursery areas. This site fidelity is passed from mothers to daughters and has resulted in the substructuring of mitochondrial haplotypes within the population (Malik et al. 1999; see also "Rural Aspects of 'The Urban Whale'").

Figure 7.2. (a) Brenna McLeod (left) and Yan Guilbault drilling into a Basque era whale bone found along the shoreline in Red Bay, Labrador. (b) Rib bone (top right) and skull fragments retrieved from the bottom of Red Bay Harbour in 2004. (c) The base of a bowhead whale skull found on a beach near Middle Bay, Quebec. Moira Brown / New England Aquarium.

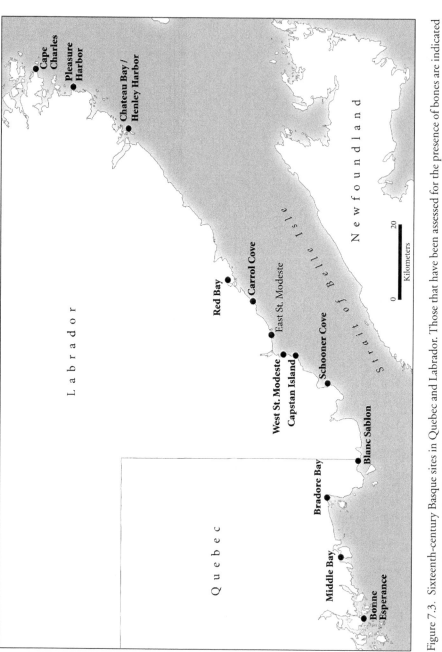

Figure 7.3. Sixteenth-century Basque sites in Quebec and Labrador. Those that have been assessed for the presence of bones are indicated in bold font. Kerry Lagueux / New England Aquarium.

Therefore, it is possible that if a portion of the whales did migrate to the Strait of Belle Isle and were subsequently killed by the Basques, they could have represented unique maternal lineages with unique mitochondrial haplotypes (Rastogi et al. 2004). This loss of a mitochondrial haplotype is significant if it represented the loss of the cultural knowledge that was held within that lineage, such as the location of another summer nursery area (Whitehead 1998; McComb et al. 2001). Such loss of knowledge may be a significant factor in the disappearance of right whales from historically known habitat areas.

Historical Microsatellite DNA

In addition to using the mitochondrial DNA as a molecular marker for population studies, another type of marker, called microsatellite loci, has proven to be useful. Microsatellites are highly variable regions of noncoding DNA that contain short (one- to five-base-pair) segments of DNA repeated multiple times in tandem. Unlike mitochondrial DNA, microsatellites are inherited in the typical Mendelian fashion, with each offspring inheriting one copy from its mother and one from its father. As a result, microsatellites are useful for assessing parentage, relatedness, and gene flow within and among populations. Although each microsatellite region (locus) is a particular segment of the DNA, there is variation in how many times the core sequence is repeated within each locus, and each variant is called an "allele."

Because only one right whale bone has been recovered from the Basque sites, it is difficult to assess preexploitation levels of genetic variability. However, if unlinked nuclear markers are used for analysis, then each allele at each locus is an independent sampling event of the historic right whale gene pool. This effectively increases the sample size and provides information on historic levels of genetic variability. Genotyping one sample at fifteen loci, then, represents thirty independent sampling events from the historic population (two alleles at each of the fifteen loci). To assess the early levels of genetic variability, the right whale bone specimen was profiled at fifteen microsatellite loci, and this profile was evaluated in two ways (Rastogi et al. 2004).

First, the profile was assessed under the assumption that variability within the South Atlantic right whale is representative of historic variability in the North Atlantic right whale. Although the genetic comparison of sister species (or populations) is common in cases where historic specimens are not available, the assumption of similar genetic characters as a result of shared taxonomic history is not always appropriate (Taylor et al. 1997; Bouzat 2001). However,

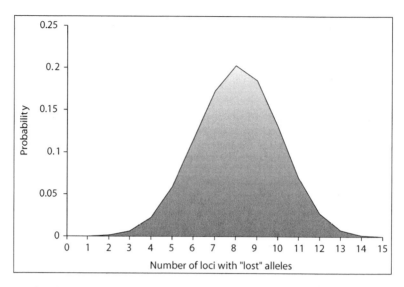

Figure 7.4. The binomial distribution showing the probabilities of observing lost alleles at one to fifteen loci in the historic right whale sample. The two probabilities used to calculate this distribution are $p = 0.54$, and $q = 0.46$ (see Rastogi et al. 2004).

one of the primary questions in right whale biology is why right whale populations in the Southern Hemisphere are growing rapidly while the North Atlantic right whale population is not. Comparative analyses of the demographics of both populations have been used to examine this question, and, therefore, comparative analyses of the genetic variability of these populations were conducted. The South Atlantic right whale, although once reduced by harvesting to around 1,000 individuals, is currently estimated to number about 6,000 (Perry et al. 1999; IWC 2001). Therefore, if the North Atlantic right whale had a historic population size of 10,000–15,000 individuals, historic variability should be comparable (or greater) to that of the extant South Atlantic right whale. Under this conservative assumption, the probability of detecting lost alleles in the historic bone when profiling at fifteen microsatellite loci was calculated, and it was found that lost alleles should have been observed when the historic bone was assessed at seven to nine loci (Rastogi et al. 2004; Fig. 7.4). However, the genotype of the bone specimen did not contain any lost alleles, indicating that preexploitation levels of genetic variability in the North Atlantic right whale were not comparable to those in extant South Atlantic right whales ($p < 0.001$). The two possible explanations are that the

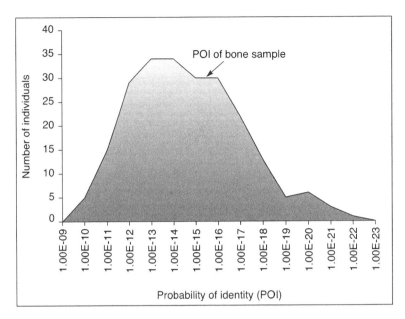

Figure 7.5. The distribution of probability of identity (POI) values for extant North Atlantic right whales. The POI value for the historic bone sample (2.53×10^{-15}) falls within the center of this distribution (arrow).

low levels of variation in the North Atlantic right whale predate exploitation or that the comparison of these two species is not valid.

To examine the genetic characteristics of the bone sample using a method that is not dependent on a cross-species comparison, the probability of identity (POI) statistic of Paetkau and Strobeck (1994) was applied. This statistic measures the probability of two individuals having the same genotype within a population. If exploitation had a significant impact on genetic variability in this species, then the genetic profiles of historic right whale specimens should be unlike those present in the extant population with an increased prevalence of rare or lost alleles. If this is the case, then the POI value of the historic bone specimen should be low using the allele frequencies of the extant population, indicating that it would not be likely to find this genotype in the extant population. However, the POI value of the bone sample falls directly in the middle of the distribution for the extant population, indicating that the genetic characteristics of the population the historic bone came from were very similar to those of the extant population (Fig. 7.5). These data provide strong support for the hypothesis that Basque whaling in Labrador had little effect on the genetic variability in western North Atlantic right whales.

North Atlantic Right Whale Present

To understand the factors influencing the recovery of an endangered species, it is necessary to consider both mortality and reproductive success. Unfortunately the North Atlantic right whale is compromised in both of these respects, with a high rate of mortality caused by anthropogenic factors and a reproductive rate that is lower than its estimated potential. The expected reproductive performance comes from data showing that adult female North Atlantic right whales are capable of giving birth approximately once every three years (Knowlton et al. 1994; Kraus et al. 2001; Chapter 6). Throughout the study period, population size estimates have ranged from about 300 to 350 individuals (IWC 2001; Kraus et al. 2001), and adult females have represented about 30 percent of the total population (Hamilton et al. 1998). This results in an expectation of an average of thirty-three to thirty-nine calving females per year. In the 1980s and 1990s, the observed average for the species was about twelve calves per year, but during the period from 2001 to 2005, calving averaged twenty-three calves per year. In both cases these rates indicate that the reproductive rate is substantially lower than expected. This expected birth rate also seems reasonable based on data from South Atlantic right whales, where population growth rates are consistent with the majority of adult females giving birth once every three years (Best et al. 2001; Cooke et al. 2001).

The primary goals of the ongoing genetic analysis of the contemporary population are to use molecular techniques to obtain a better understanding of reproduction in this species as well as to test hypotheses regarding the role of intrinsic factors (such as low levels of genetic variability and inbreeding) on reproductive success and species recovery. Genetic analyses have also provided important and often unexpected information on other aspects of right whale behavior, habitat use patterns, and status. As a result, the genetic component of the right whale project has become a critical tool for understanding the status of this species and for the long-term monitoring of its recovery.

The integration of over twenty years of individual-based photo-identification data with high-resolution genetic analyses for the majority (66 percent) of all identified North Atlantic right whales has resulted in the rare opportunity to permit construction of the family tree of a whale species (color plate 10). This family tree combines detailed information on reproductive success, parentage, and relatedness for each individual. This level of detail for such a large portion of the species is rare in studies of noncaptive populations and thus provides not only a valuable dataset for understanding the dynamics of the extant North Atlantic right whale population but also for understanding the dynamics of small populations in general.

Genetic Identification of Individuals

With a population existing at such low numbers, the data associated with each individual have a large impact on estimates of population characteristics (Fujiwara and Caswell 2001). One way that genetic data are being used to maximize the information gained from each whale is in the genetic identification of individuals in situations where photo-identification is not possible. This approach is made possible through collaborations with a large number of researchers and has resulted in samples being collected from 66 percent of all North Atlantic right whales alive today. The genetic profiles of these samples provide a database against which all unidentified samples can be compared. This method has been applied to carcasses (having decomposed beyond photo-identification), calving events (identifying mother–offspring pairs that could not be identified photographically), and fecal samples (making identifications in the absence of the whale).

Based on the thirty-five microsatellite loci that are currently being used to profile North Atlantic right whales genetically, the probability that two individuals will share the same genetic profile (Paetkau and Strobeck 1994) is 1.26×10^{12}. This means that two in roughly every 800 billion whales are expected to have the same genetic profile, and therefore these profiles provide adequate resolution to identify individuals in this population of approximately 350.

Individual Identification of Dead Whales

Documenting mortalities in North Atlantic right whales has become a high priority because of the recognition that ship strikes and entanglement in fishing gear represent major threats to species recovery. Moreover, when dead individuals can be identified, this information can be used for population monitoring and helps to identify the age and gender of whales most at risk from anthropogenic mortalities (Knowlton and Kraus 2001; Moore et al. 2005). The majority of right whale carcasses that are recovered exhibit moderate to severe decomposition, which in some cases makes it impossible to identify the individual based on photo-identification techniques (Chapter 12). In such cases DNA is extracted from tissue collected during the necropsy, genetically profiled, and subsequently linked to a known whale in the genetic database. An example of such a case is provided in Chapter 3.

Linking Calves to Mothers

One of the great strengths of the North Atlantic right whale research program is the detailed individual-based life history data available for a large percentage of the population. Although photo-identification techniques have been the primary source of individual-specific data, there is one group of right whales that cannot be assessed in this way: calves that are not seen in known summer feeding or nursery areas.

Calving takes place during the winter, and the majority of births occur in the southeast calving ground, located along the coasts of Florida and Georgia. Although most calves are seen in this region, they do not develop their callosity patterns until the latter half of their first year (Hamilton et al. 1998) and therefore cannot be photo-identified until they are observed in summer feeding or nursery areas. However, different maternal lineages use different summer habitats. This differential nursery use by right whale mothers results in about 60 percent of all calves being taken to the Bay of Fundy in the summer. The remaining 40 percent of calves are taken to another, currently unidentified summer area(s) (Malik et al. 1999). Because many of these "non-Fundy" calves are seen in the southeast calving ground only during their first four months (when callosity patterns are not fully developed), they cannot be photographically identified in their first year. As a result, if these whales are seen later in life, when they are no longer associated with their mother, it is not possible to link them to a calving event or to their mother, and the associated information such as age and familial relationships is lost.

Molecular techniques have been used to link these calves back to their mothers in two ways. The first approach involves maternity analysis of juveniles that have "appeared" in the population but are not linked to known calving events. Although this method has been successfully used to identify the mothers for some of these juveniles, its application is limited because of the difficulty of assessing the age of individuals from photographs and because the resolution of genetic parentage analyses is notoriously low when neither parent is known, particularly in species with low levels of genetic variability (Taylor et al. 1997).

The second approach involves linking the genetic profiles from whales of unknown age to the profiles of calves that were sampled but not photographically identified in the calving ground. This method is simpler than the alternative approach based on maternity analysis and is also more powerful. Comparing complete genetic profiles of samples provides higher resolution than maternity analysis because in parentage analyses (when neither parent is known) less than half of the genetic data can be used to assess inheritance and, therefore, the probability of maternity, whereas the direct comparison of complete profiles is based on all of the genetic information, providing higher resolution. There have not been intensive efforts to sample calves in the calving grounds, however, and of the sixty-four unidentified calves that were born between 1980 and 2001, only one was sampled. Because these unidentified calves represent about 40 percent of all births, an increased emphasis on biopsy sampling in the calving grounds is needed to prevent the loss of these life history data for almost half of the calves of this population.

Identification of Individuals from Fecal Samples

The collection and analysis of fecal samples from terrestrial and marine mammals are providing researchers with a wealth of data ranging from genetic material to hormone and marine biotoxin levels to parasite prevalence (Frantz et al. 2003; Rolland et al. 2005). The utility of right whale fecal analysis is described in Chapter 8; however, one hurdle to overcome is identifying the individual associated with each sample. This is important, as analyses of hormone levels, marine biotoxins, and parasite prevalence are most informative when they can be linked to a specific individual of known age and gender. In some situations (when only one whale is present or when defecation is observed), it is clear where the sample originated. However, for approximately 60 percent of all fecal samples collected, the identity of the whale is unknown. To associate the fecal samples with known individuals in the population, molecular identification is needed. The genetic profiles available for a majority of individuals in this population enable fecal samples of unknown origin to be linked to identified right whales in the *Catalog*.

Two potential sources of right whale DNA are present in the collected fecal samples: baleen that has passed through the whale's digestive tract and epithelial cells that have been sloughed off the intestinal walls during digestion. DNA is extracted from each fecal sample, and a portion of the mitochondrial DNA is sequenced for species identification to confirm that the sample originated from a right whale. Genetic profiles are then obtained by analyzing the samples at a subset of the 35 microsatellite markers. As in a forensic case, each profile is compared to the database to determine which whales can and cannot be excluded as the source of the fecal sample. This information, along with the estimated probability of two samples having the same genetic profile by chance, is used to assign fecal samples to specific whales and provides a method to maximize the information gained from these samples.

Rural Aspects of "The Urban Whale"

One prominent feature of North Atlantic right whale biology is the considerable heterogeneity in the habitat use patterns of different individuals through both space and time (Hamilton and Mayo 1990; Brown et al. 2001; Kenney 2001; Chapter 3). This appears as consistent differences in habitat use patterns between individuals as well as population-wide shifts in patterns of habitat use through time. The levels of individually and temporally based heterogeneity in habitat use observed in North Atlantic right whales are markedly higher than those observed in many other marine mammal species, which compromises many methods for estimating population characteristics (Kraus et al. 2001; Clapham 2002). However, one stable pattern that has emerged is the differential summer nursery use by mothers.

As described above, behavioral and genetic data show that there is significant structuring within this species in relation to Fundy or non-Fundy summer nursery use by mothers. This migration pattern is passed on from mothers to their offspring and results in maternally directed site fidelity to specific summer nursery areas. There is at least one summer nursery or feeding habitat used by this population that is currently unknown to scientists. Additionally, the location of the majority of individuals during the winter months is unknown; indicating that there must also be an unidentified winter habitat(s) that likely includes the mating ground(s).

It is unclear how these differential habitat use patterns are influencing the dynamics within this population. For example, do Fundy and non-Fundy females mate with the same group of males, or do non-Fundy females preferentially mate with males with a high "offshore index"? On the other hand, the female-directed site fidelity for summer nursery areas may not reflect accurately the winter habitat use patterns that would be important for mating, and the population may be structured in a manner completely independent of summer distributions.

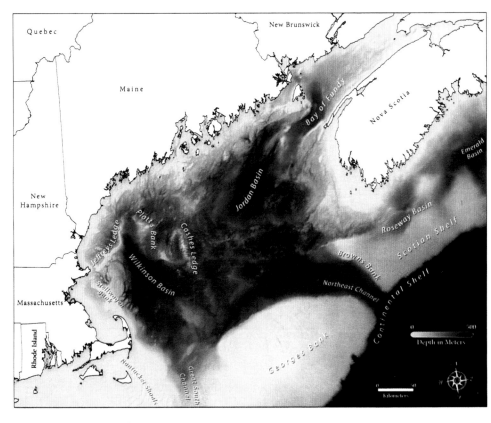

1. Greater Gulf of Maine showing bottom topography and names of significant banks, basins, and deep channels. Kerry Lagueux/New England Aquarium

2. Right whaling as depicted in a watercolor gracing the pages of the nineteenth-century logbook of the ship *Lucy Ann* of Wilmington, Delaware, November 1841–June 1844. This Pacific voyage produced 400 barrels of sperm oil, 1,600 barrels of whale oil, and 12,800 pounds of whalebone (baleen)—not unusual for vessels engaged in the Pacific fishery but far beyond the expectations of a North Atlantic voyage at that time. Embellishments of such high quality are exceptional in these normally prosaic old documents. Courtesy of the Kendall Collection, New Bedford Whaling Museum

3. Right whales can be individually identified by the callosity pattern on their heads, lips, and chins. Examples of callosity patterns from six whales are shown here. Callosity tissue is black or gray cornified skin that appears in these images as ridges or rough surfaces surrounded by tan and orange-colored patches of whale lice. a) Mason Weinrich/Whale Center of New England; b) Yan Guilbault/New England Aquarium; c) Philip K. Hamilton/New England Aquarium; d) Cynthia Browning/New England Aquarium; e) Paula Mackay/New England Aquarium; f) Moira W. Brown/New England Aquarium

4. Right whale tails have broad, black, smooth-margined flukes that are raised whenever the whale engages in a deep dive (a). Both the flukes and the tail stocks are frequently scarred by interactions with ropes (b) and occasionally with ships (c). a) Heather McRae/New England Aquarium; b) Monica Zani/New England Aquarium; c) Amy R. Knowlton/New England Aquarium

5. Scarring from interactions with human activities takes many forms. a) Right whale Shackleton (Eg #2440) shows white scarring on the chin that resulted from his youthful encounters with the pilings of an oil terminal near Philadelphia. b) Right whale Arpeggio (Eg #2753) has propeller scars across her back from an encounter with a small speedboat.

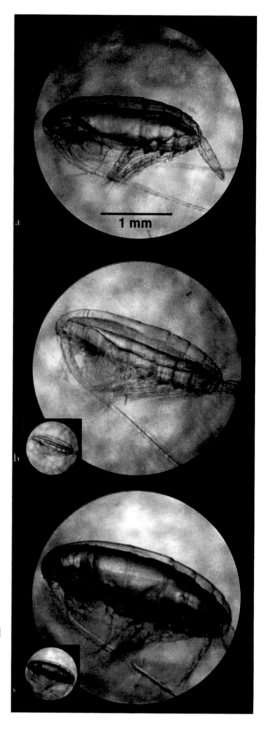

6. a) Stage five copepodite (C5) of *Calanus finmarchicus;* b) *Calanus finmarchicus* C5 with a small oil sac (inset indicates the position of the oil sac in blue); c) *Calanus finmarchicus* C5 with a large oil sac.

Mark Baumgartner/Woods Hole Oceanographic Institution

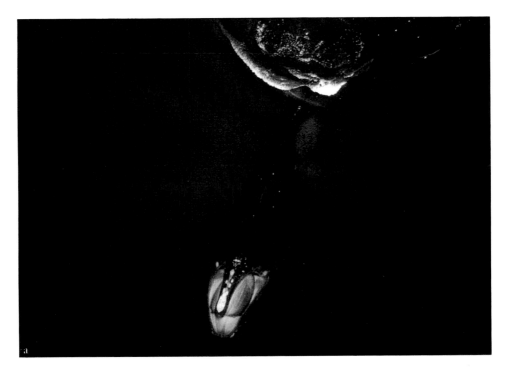

7. a) Aerial view of a female right whale (Eg #1602) feeding just below the sea surface (note calf below her tail). b) Skim feeding right whale with upper jaw elevated above the sea surface. a and b) Provincetown Center for Coastal Studies

8. Right whales are frequently seen with mud on their heads, sometimes in waters over 200m deep, evidence of surprisingly deep dives for this species.

9. Surface-active groups are among the most spectacular and energetic behaviors observed in right whales. Although they are usually associated with courtship, observations of all-male and all-female groups suggest that they may have multiple social functions beyond reproduction. a) Yan Guilbault/New England Aquarium; b) Moira W. Brown/New England Aquarium; c) Scott D. Kraus/New England Aquarium; d) Scott D. Kraus/New England Aquarium

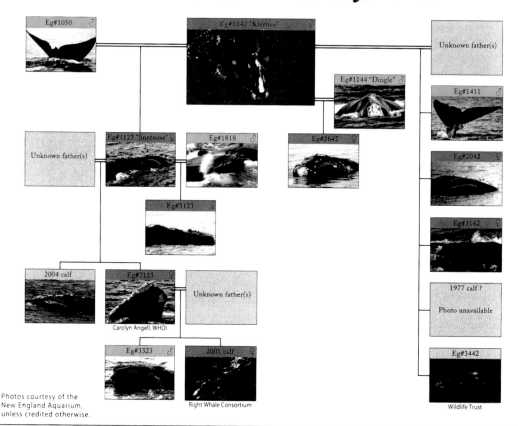

The "Kleenex" Family Tree

Eg#1050 ♂

Eg#1142 "Kleenex" ♀

Unknown father(s)

Eg#1144 "Dingle" ♂

Eg#1411 ♂

Unknown father(s)

Eg#1123 "Snotnose" ♀

Eg#1818 ♂

Eg#2642 ♀

Eg#2042 ♀

Eg#3123 ♀

Eg#3142 ♀

2004 calf

Eg#2123 ♀

Unknown father(s)

1977 calf ?

Photo unavailable

Carolyn Angell, WHOI

Eg#3323 ♂

2001 calf ♀

Eg#3442

Photos courtesy of the
New England Aquarium,
unless credited otherwise.

Right Whale Consortium

Wildlife Trust

10. A portion of the family tree of a female matriarch named "Kleenex" (*Eg* #1142).
By combining genetic profiles with the photo-identification catalog, researchers have
constructed genealogical charts for most of the North Atlantic right whale population.
Graphic courtesy of Woods Hole Oceanographic Institution

11. a) Biopsy darting employs a crossbow and arrows with small biopsy tips (about the diameter of a pencil) to collect skin and blubber samples for genetic, health, and contaminant studies, as well as cell line cultures. b) Biopsy sample processing involves dividing samples for multiple studies. a) Christopher Slay/New England Aquarium; b) Monica Zani/New England Aquarium

12. The use of detection dogs is more than four times as effective as opportunistic methods of collecting right whale fecal samples for hormone, health, and biotoxin analyses. Here Fargo and Dr. Rosalind Rolland narrow in on a sample. Brenna Kraus/New England Aquarium

13. Right whale Arpeggio (Eg #2753) approaches the fishing boat *Rueby*, chartered for a research cruise in Cape Cod Bay. Dr. Rosalind Rolland is shown attempting to collect a sample from the lesion on Arpeggio's back, using a nylon scrubby attached to a pole.

Marilyn Marx/New England Aquarium

14. Dr. Douglas Nowacek and team approach a logging right whale in the Bay of Fundy to attach a suction cup digital acoustic recording tag (DTAG). The DTAG provides data on underwater movements and responses to received sounds of tagged whales.

Cynthia Browning/New England Aquarium

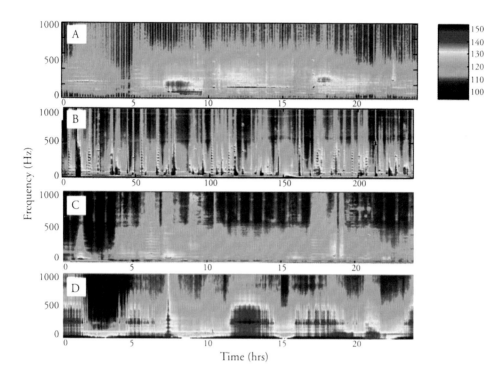

15. Spectrographic examples showing the degree to which acoustic pollution might be interfering with right whale communication: a) ambient noise for one day in Cape Cod Bay, 14 March 2003, b) ambient noise for one week in Cape Cod Bay, 14–20 March 2003, c) ambient noise for one day in Great South Channel, March 2003, and d) ambient noise for one day in the Bay of Fundy, August 2004. In these examples, a color scale is used with yellow to orange to red indicating increasing levels of sound, and green to blue to violet indicating decreasing levels. By this scale, increasing levels of ambient noise are evident as levels of yellow, orange, and red, and the occurrence of a specific, intense acoustic event is shown as a specific burst of these colors. These examples illustrate the spatial and temporal scales of the present-day coastal, acoustic smog that right whales are exposed to in three of the areas where they are known to congregate to feed and socialize.

16. a) This right whale, Stumpy (Eg #1004), was towed ashore by the U.S. Coast Guard at Nags Head on the Outer Banks of North Carolina. The beach crew is contemplating how to haul her up the beach. b) Aerial photograph of Staccato (Eg #1014), hauled up on the beach at Duck Harbor in Wellfleet, Massachusetts. The necropsy has just begun. The front end loader is applying tension to a sheet of blubber. c) A neonate mortality on the beach in Florida. a) Regina Campbell-Malone/© Woods Hole Oceanographic Institution; b) Marilyn Marx/New England Aquarium; c) Yan Guilbault/New England Aquarium

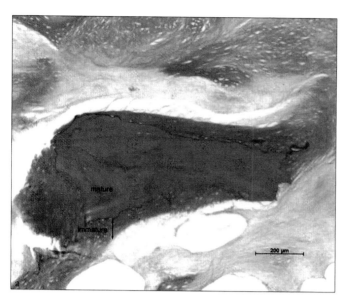

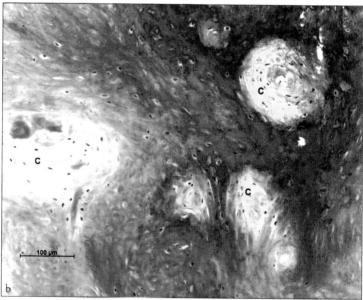

17. Microscopic sections of mandibular bone taken near the surface of a jaw fracture show-ing healing changes. The evidence of tissue repair indicates that this right whale (Eg #2150) survived for some period of time after being struck by a ship. Hematoxylin and eosin stain: a) immature (woven) bone deposited on the surface of a trabecula of normal mature (lamellar) bone; b) islands of cartilaginous tissue; c) amid fibrous tissue; the bluish color of the fibrous matrix in the upper-right corner indicates some mineralization.

Pierre-Yves Daoust/Atlantic Veterinary College

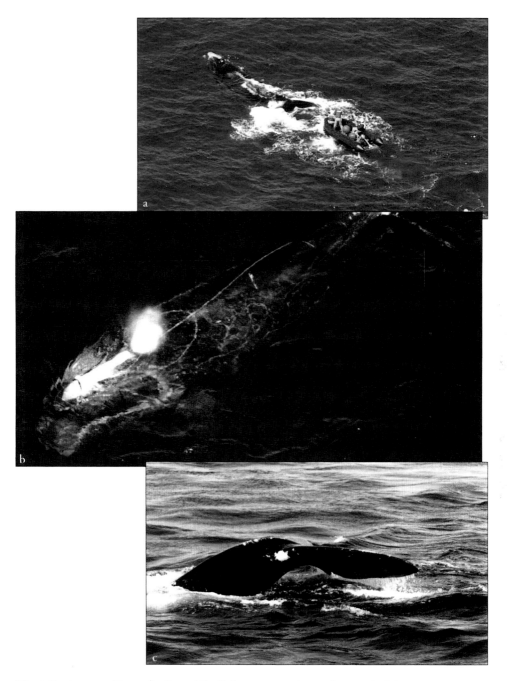

18. a) Provincetown Center for Coastal Studies' crew attempting to disentangle right whale #3346. b) Right whale #1424 photographed from a NOAA Twin Otter, showing the complexity of a fishing rope entanglement. c) Evidence of past entanglements is revealed in photographs of a scarred right whale tail area. a) Katherine A. Jackson/Florida Fish and Wildlife Conservation Commission, under NOAA Fisheries permit #932–1489, under the authority of the U.S. Endangered Species Act; b) Liz Pomfret/NOAA Fisheries; c) New England Aquarium

19. Close encounters between ships and right whales suggest that remarkably, right whales do not perceive approaching large vessels as a danger until too late.

Harriet Corbett/New England Aquarium

20. The consequences of not getting out of the way of a ship are usually fatal for a right whale. This whale was killed off the coast of New Jersey.

William McLellan/University of North Carolina Wilmington

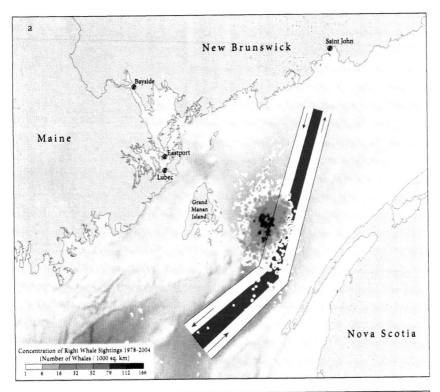

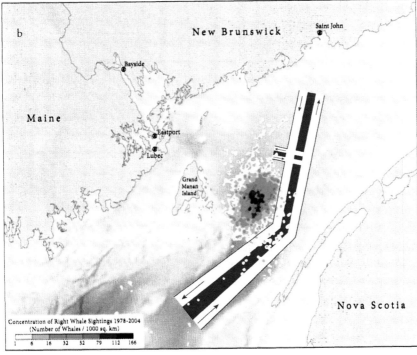

21. Right whale density in the Bay of Fundy in relation to: a) the old shipping lanes and b) the newly designated shipping lanes. Movement of the shipping lanes in July 2003 significantly decreased the probability of a ship's striking a right whale.

Kerry Lagueux/New England Aquarium

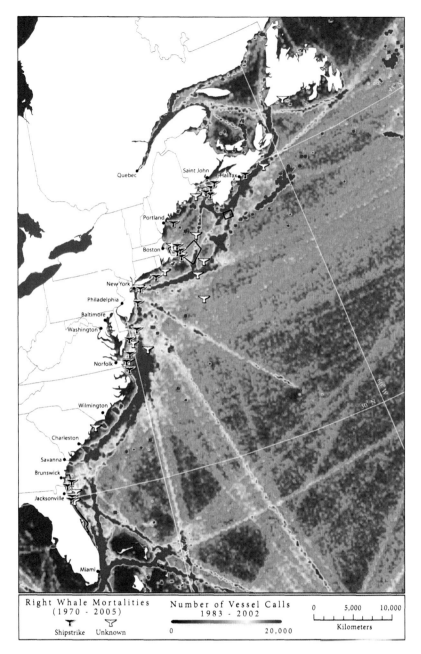

Right Whale Mortalities (1970 - 2005)

Y Shipstrike Y Unknown

Number of Vessel Calls 1983 - 2002

0 — 20,000

0   5,000   10,000
Kilometers

22. Initial location of right whale carcasses, where the cause of death was later determined to be shipstrike or unknown, in relation to ship traffic densities derived from the International Comprehensive Ocean-Atmosphere Data Set (Wang, C., and J. J. Corbett [2005]). "Geographical Characterization of Ship Traffic and Emissions." *Transportation Research Record: Journal of the Transportation Research Board* 1909; Wang, C., J. J. Corbett, J. Firestone. [Wang et al., 2006]. Adapting Bottom-up Methods to Top-down Spatially Resolved Ship Emissions Inventories. Transportation Research Board of the National Academies 85th Annual Meeting, Washington D.C.). Kerry Lagueux/New England Aquarium

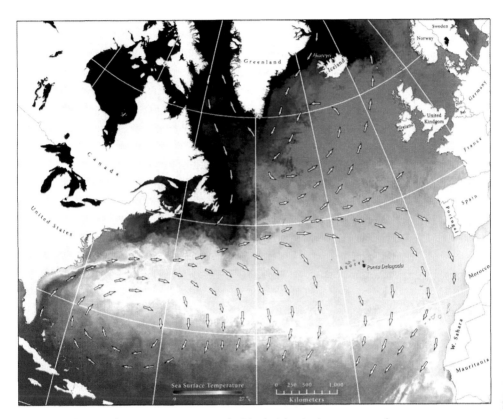

23. Image of the Gulf Stream currents across the North Atlantic. Average sea surface temperatures are shown in false color for May 2004. The arrows show the prevailing currents in the North Atlantic Ocean. The North Atlantic Oscillation (NAO) is measured by the difference in barometric pressure between a semi-permanent low-pressure system near Iceland and a similar high-pressure system near the Azores. When the systems intensify, the pressure difference increases, and the NAO is positive; when the systems weaken, the difference decreases, and the NAO is negative. The Gulf Stream Index (GSI) is measured from the monthly location of the eastward-flowing part of the Gulf Stream. Positive values indicate a more northern position of the current, and negative values, a more southern position. Image source: Feldman, G. C., C. R. McClain, Ocean Color Web, MODIS Sensor Reprocessing 1.1, NASA Goddard Space Flight Center. Eds. Kuring, N., Bailey, S. W. 12/05/2005. http://oceancolor.gsfc.nasa.gov/. Graphic: Kerry Lagueux/New England Aquarium

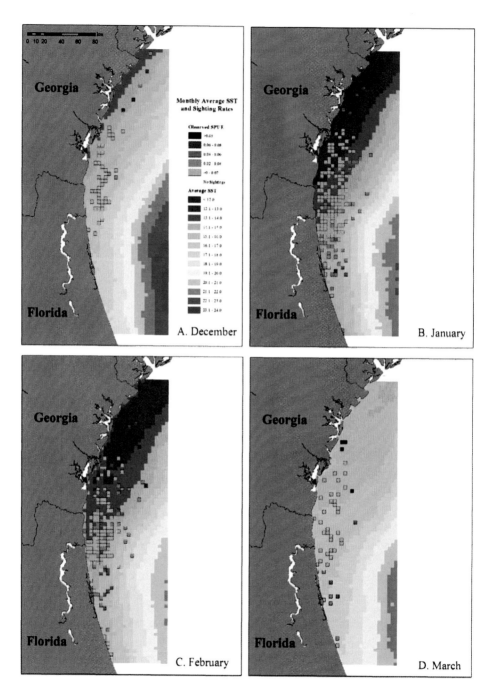

24. Monthly average sea surface temperatures and sighting rates (Sightings Per Unit Effort) for calving female right whales in the southeast U.S. calving grounds. Water temperature and sightings data are averaged across the time series from December 1992 to March 2001.
Lance Garrison/NOAA Fisheries

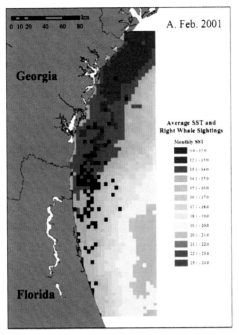

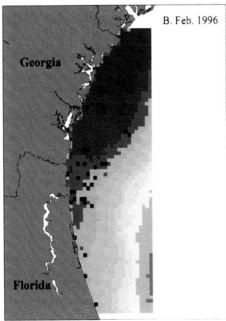

25. Average SST and right whale sightings (black squares) during February 2001 and 1996. During the warmer year (2001), right whale sightings occur further north within the calving habitat. During 1996, when water temperatures were cooler, calving right whales were more concentrated in the southern portion of the region. Lance Garrison/NOAA Fisheries

26. Right whales in close proximity to curious recreational boaters. This activity is forbidden in the United States, and it is dangerous for both the boaters and the whale.

a and b) Jessica Taylor/New England Aquarium

27. Inhabitants of the coastal zone of North America, right whales sometimes get very close to shore throughout their range. a) Christopher Slay/New England Aquarium; b) Provincetown Center for Coastal Studies

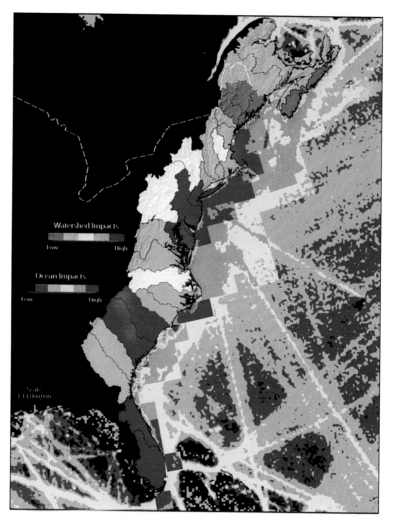

Watershed Impacts
Low   High

Ocean Impacts
Low   High

Scale
1:11,000,000

28. The right whale's urban ocean. This map depicts cumulative relative measures of anthropogenic impacts on the northwest Atlantic Ocean marine environment, as well as cumulative watershed releases that could impact marine areas. Red areas represent extremely urban (a high density of human activities), and blue areas represent relatively untouched oceanic habitats. The marine data are a compilation of dredge disposal sites, shipping intensity, and fishing intensity (averaged by statistical area). The terrestrial watershed overlays include: population density (as an indicator of automobile petroleum products runoff and sewage effluent), the numbers of toxic chemical releases (compiled from the EPA Toxic Release Inventory), and percentage of land in agriculture (as an index of fertilizer and pesticide use). Although each of these watersheds flows into the right whale habitat, runoff impact in the marine environment will be subject to seasonal variation in rainfall, current, and wind conditions at sea, and variable diffusion rates for different compounds. Therefore no effort has been made to incorporate the terrestrial runoff data into the marine environment—this map simply shows potential aquatic impacts adjacent to the coastal zone. Sources include the National Marine Fisheries Service, Environmental Protection Agency, Army Corps of Engineers, data from plate 22, U.S. Geological Society, Environment Canada, and ESRI. Kerry Lagueux/New England Aquarium

29. Right whale behaviors: a) Headlift. b) Posturing. a) Moira W. Brown/New England Aquarium; b) Yan Guilbault/New England Aquarium

30. Right whale behaviors: a) Breaching. b) Lobtailing. a) Lindsay Hall/New England Aquarium; b) Heather McRae/New England Aquarium

31. The New England Aquarium team aboard the research vessel *Nereid* photographs a small surface-active group, obtaining identifications for the North Atlantic Right Whale Catalog. New England Aquarium

32. Researchers record site- and time-specific information on right whale identity, behavior, health, and associations using both computerized logging systems and field data sheets.

a and b) Yan Guilbault/New England Aquarium; c) Christopher Slay/New England Aquarium

33. Many right whales are curious and approach boats. a) A calf (Eg #3350) and the detection dog Fargo meet for the first time. The calf stayed with the motionless dog boat for over half an hour. b) Arpeggio (Eg #2753) approaches fisherman Billy Chaprales for a close look at his boat. She remained with the boat for over 40 minutes. a) Rosalind Rolland/New England Aquarium; b) Scott Kraus/New England Aquarium

34. Mother and calf right whale off the southeastern United States.

Genetic analyses are being used to assess the fine-scale dynamics of gene flow between these different subgroups of individuals. Preliminary analyses, based on nine microsatellite loci, suggested that there may be some reproductive isolation between calves born to Fundy and non-Fundy females (Waldick 1999). However, it is not yet known if this pattern is a result of the Fundy/non-Fundy structuring or if it is indicative of another pattern that is only partially represented by this division. With the samples now being profiled at thirty-five microsatellite loci, the detailed parentage data that are now available, and with the increased number of calves that have been born in the past four years, it will be possible to obtain better resolution in these analyses in the near future. This information will be useful not only in identifying some of the factors influencing fine-scale patterns of gene flow but also in testing hypotheses concerning the influence of particular habitat disturbances or conditions on the reproductive success of individuals.

Genetic Inference of Individuals

Because of the critically endangered status of this species, one important research and conservation goal is to estimate population size and trends. Based on the photo-identification research, the direct count of the number of identified individuals known to be alive is recognized as an accurate estimate of population size (Perry et al. 1999) and is considered one of the most accurate estimates available for any baleen whale (Clapham et al. 1999). This approach is based on the assumption that every right whale is observed in one of the five known habitats at least once every six years. However, the fact that other unidentified summer and winter habitats exist raises the possibility that some whales may never use the well-known habitats. Such whales would never be photo-identified or be included in estimates of population size and trends or be protected by current conservation efforts.

Genetic data have been used to help address this issue and refine estimates of population size through parentage analysis and the resulting genetic inference of individuals. Paternity analysis of all sampled mother–calf pairs from 1980 though 2001 revealed that the fathers for only 45 percent of the calves had been genetically sampled. This result was surprising because genetic profiles were available for 69 percent of all photo-identified males. It indicates that significantly fewer ($p < 0.001$) fathers had been sampled than expected based on the percentage of sampled males identified within the photo-identification *Catalog* (Frasier 2005; Fig. 7.6).

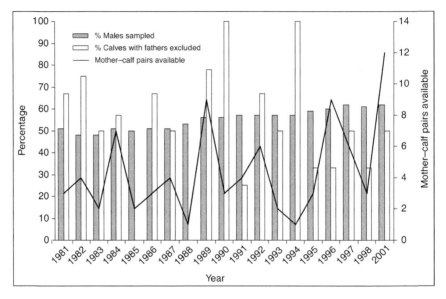

Figure 7.6. Distribution of the percentage of identified males that were sampled and the percentage of calves with all males excluded as fathers, by year. The line represents the number of mother–calf pairs available for paternity analysis in each year. The lack of sampled fathers is not caused by a shortage of sampled males in the early years. No mother–calf pairs were available for analysis in 1980, 1999, or 2000.

There are two possible explanations for this finding. One is that the small percentage (31 percent) of identified but unsampled males was particularly successful and accounts for all the unidentified paternities (55 percent). The other is that the population size is larger than has been estimated, and therefore more unsampled males exist than are currently accounted for in population estimates. The paternal relatedness of calves for which all sampled males were excluded as fathers was assessed to distinguish between these alternatives. Results indicated that the majority of calves must have different fathers, showing that the few identified unsampled males do not account for all the unidentified paternities and that the population must be larger than currently estimated. Although these analyses can only be used to infer males directly, further analyses suggest that there may be a similar number of unidentified females (Frasier 2005). Combined, these findings suggest that the total population size must be larger than is currently estimated to fit the genetic data.

Although studies are currently under way to obtain robust estimates of how much larger the population must be, the take-home message of this result is not the specific number of whales that must be missing but rather that it is necessary to change the general perception of this population. It has previously been assumed that the photo-identification *Catalog* is an accurate representation of the population, whereas now it is clear that there are more whales out there that need to be considered. This type of genetic inference of individuals is a particularly useful research approach for studies of endangered species such as this one, whose estimated status and viability can be dramatically altered by the addition of just a few reproductive females (Fujiwara and Caswell 2001).

Reproduction and Species Recovery

The current understanding of reproduction in right whales is based on information from known mother–calf pairs, and until recently nothing was known about male reproductive success. Because calves stay with their mothers throughout their first year of life, photodocumentation of adult females with calves provides a reliable method to assess female reproductive success. However, right whales are highly promiscuous, and males play no role in raising the offspring, making it impossible to assess male reproductive success using photo-identification techniques. Molecular techniques have been used to fill this gap by identifying fathers and by providing information on the factors influencing male reproductive success.

In small populations with low levels of genetic variability, there is an increased probability that mating pairs will have similar genetic profiles. This can result in a reduction of viable offspring because of genetic incompatibility of the mating pairs. It can also reduce survival and reproductive success of offspring as a result of low levels of variability or the unmasking of deleterious alleles (Charlesworth and Charlesworth 1987; Paterson et al. 1998). The North Atlantic right whale shows several symptoms of a species suffering from these intrinsic problems, such as a high percentage of adult females that have never given birth or have had only one calf and a reduced reproductive performance of those females that have had more than one offspring. The genetic and parentage data are also being used to test hypotheses regarding the role of intrinsic factors on reproductive success and species recovery.

Age of First Fertilization in Males

Based on photo-identification of mother–calf pairs, the average age at which females have their first calf is estimated at about ten years (Chapter 6). Gestation is thought to be about twelve months (Best 1994), indicating that females become sexually mature at an average age of nine years. From the paternity data, only three identified fathers were of known age: two were fifteen and the other was seventeen years old in the year of fertilization. All other identified fathers were of unknown age, with the majority having sighting histories suggesting that they were born before 1980 when field studies began. Based on these data, it appears that males are not obtaining their first paternity until around the age of fifteen or older. In mammals, the energy requirements for males to become sexually mature are often much lower than those for females (Daly and Wilson 1983); therefore, it seems reasonable to assume that male right whales are capable of becoming sexually mature at a similar age as (if not earlier than) females, suggesting that factors such as mate competition are preventing younger males from reproducing.

Mating Behavior

Sexual behavior indicative of mating has been observed in both the North and the South Atlantic right whale (for a full description see Chapter 6). In the North Atlantic, these surface-active groups (SAGs) are seen year-round and in all known habitat areas. However, clustering of calving during winter months suggests seasonality of conception in right whales. With an estimated gestation of one year, it follows that fertilizations must also take place during the winter. However, the winter is the season when the location of most right whales is unknown, and therefore, the location of the mating ground(s) is (are) also unknown. Despite these discrepancies, the observed SAGs have been considered representative of mating behavior and have been used to describe potential mating strategies (Kraus and Hatch 2001).

To gain information on the potential function of the observed SAGs, the relatedness of males relative to focal females was tested. SAGs were used in the analysis only if all individuals involved were identified adults and if there was only one focal female. Additionally, analyses were conducting using all SAGs combined, as well as SAGs that occurred in different habitats separately. The analyses showed that in all cases males were significantly more related to the focal female than was expected (Frasier 2005). This result was surprising, as this pattern is not expected under the current view that the observed SAGs are representative of mating behavior. These data support the suggestion that the observed SAGs serve some social function other than reproduction.

Adoption

Through pedigree analysis of North Atlantic right whales, the first case of adoption in a wild cetacean population has been identified. Analysis of the pedigrees indicated that the genetic profiles of two mother–calf pairs in 1987 were not consistent with parent–offspring relationships as determined by photo-identification techniques and suggested that the calves had been switched between the mothers. Subsequent detailed analyses of both datasets made it possible to rule out all potential sources of error, including errors in sample labeling or tracking, genetic profiling, and photo-identification (Frasier 2005). Therefore, the only plausible explanation was that the calves must have been switched between their mothers.

In this species, each offspring represents a significant metabolic investment for the female and also represents a significant portion of her lifetime reproductive success, suggesting that strong mechanisms for offspring recognition should be in place to minimize the chances of misplaced parental effort. Therefore, the only reasonable scenario is that the females must have given birth in close spatial and temporal proximity, and the calves associated with the wrong mother before mother–offspring recognition cues developed. Such discrepancies in mother–offspring recognition are known to occur in other species (Lorenz 1970; Lunn et al. 2000), although the time frame in which such confusion takes place varies between taxa (Klopfer 1971). This finding raises intriguing questions regarding the mechanisms that right whales use for mother-offspring recognition and the length of time necessary for this recognition system to develop.

Intrinsic Factors and Reproductive Success

One hypothesis to explain, at least in part, the reduced reproduction in right whales is the lack of genetic variability. The first support for this hypothesis came from restriction fragment length polymorphism fingerprinting studies, which found that the level of band sharing between mothers and offspring was significantly lower than expected (Schaeff et al. 1997). This result suggested that matings between genetically similar individuals were unsuccessful and that only those matings that occur between genetically divergent individuals could result in successful fertilizations and pregnancies.

More recent analyses, based on thirty-five microsatellite loci, corroborated this previous finding and provided strong evidence that the lack of genetic variability is influencing reproductive success. Analyses of calves for which both parents had been identified showed that they had significantly higher levels of genetic diversity (measured as internal relatedness; Amos et al. 2001a) than expected under random mating (Frasier 2005). The two possible explanations for this finding are (1) precopulatory mate choice, where whales are choosing to mate with individuals that are particularly genetically dissimilar from themselves; or (2) that the majority of matings are unsuccessful, and successful fertilization and pregnancy result only when individuals that are particularly genetically divergent happen to mate. The genetic relatedness of identified mating pairs was examined to differentiate between these two alternatives. The results showed that the relatedness of identified mating pairs was not significantly higher than expected and, therefore, that precopulatory mate choice for genetically dissimilar mates is not responsible for the observed levels of variation in calves (T. Frasier, unpublished data).

The current hypothesis is that the low level of genetic variability in this species leads to the genetic similarity of the majority of mating pairs, which in turn produces a high incidence of mate incompatibility and unsuccessful fertilizations and pregnancies. Direct analyses of the Major Histocompatibility Complex (MHC) are under way to assess a causal relationship between genetic variability and reproductive success and, further, to assess the influence of genetic characteristics on the potential for species recovery.

The Major Histocompatibility Complex

In addition to using presumably neutral molecular markers for genetic analyses of the North Atlantic right whale (such as the mitochondrial control region and microsatellite loci), other regions of the genome under the influence of selection, such as the MHC, can provide methods to test the influence of genetic variation on right whale reproduction.

The MHC is a family of genes involved in initiating immune responses and in self–nonself recognition. As a result, it is a widely used molecular marker for assessing the influence of genetic traits on individual health and survival in relation to exposure to pathogens (Paterson et al. 1998). Additionally, the MHC is involved in spontaneous abortion, which can result from a breakdown in self–nonself recognition between the mother and fetus when they have similar MHC profiles. Therefore it is also a marker of particular interest for investigating the influence of genetic characteristics on the reproductive success of individuals (Ober et al. 1998).

As discussed, microsatellite data from North Atlantic right whales suggest that matings are successful only between individuals that are genetically dissimilar. The hypothesis is that the low level of genetic variability in this species results in MHC similarity and subsequent spontaneous abortion for the majority of mating pairs. To test this hypothesis directly, the MHC profiles of identified mating pairs and their offspring are currently being compared to test for nonrandom transmission of alleles from fathers to their offspring. If MHC characteristics are influencing reproductive success, then the offspring will inherit paternal alleles that are less similar to the maternal alleles at a higher frequency than expected under the laws of Mendelian inheritance. These analyses may make it possible to estimate the frequency at which fetal loss caused by MHC similarity occurs in this species, thereby providing information on its recovery potential.

Many hypotheses about other factors that may also be influencing reproductive success involve assessing right whale health. To test these hypotheses, several methods have recently been developed to evaluate health and reproduction based on the analysis of fecal samples and visual assessment of photographs (Chapters 8 and 9). The MHC data are also being integrated into these datasets to assess how the genetic characteristics of individuals are interacting with the environment (e.g., parasite prevalence) to result in the observed patterns of right whale health and body condition and neonatal mortality.

Conclusion: North Atlantic Right Whale Future

Genetic information from historical whale bones indicates that sixteenth-century Basque whaling had less of an impact on this species than has previously been thought and that the preexploitation population size was likely smaller than previously estimated. This suggests that this species may not be capable of recovering to the levels expected under the previous view of its history. Small populations are at an increased risk of extinction as a result of environmental and demographic stochasticity and the rapid loss of genetic variation (Lande 1988). However, if this species has been at a relatively small size since before whaling began, then it could be relatively stable at this size and may fare better than expected even if significant signs of recovery are not observed. Supporting this perspective are observations that large whales have several characteristics that may allow them to dampen the effects of environmental and demographic stochasticity to a certain degree, such as large body size, long life span, and the capability of long-range movements (Whitehead 2003).

In addition to these potential reductions to the impact of environmental and demographic stochasticity, recent studies suggest that there are also mechanisms by which some small populations can reduce the loss of genetic variation. Detailed studies of small populations have found that some reproductive patterns that are known to act in large populations (such as mate choice or mate compatibility) can serve to increase the effective population size of small populations and reduce the loss of genetic variation (Amos et al. 2001b).

Combined, these data suggest that the lack of significant signs of recovery in right whales does not necessarily mean that the species is doomed, but rather that the maintenance of the current population size, or slight rates of population growth, may be all that it is capable of under the current conditions. Under this view, conservation actions become more critical than under previous hypotheses because the proposed lower recovery potential of this species means that it may not be able to recover from any perturbations as rapidly as previously suggested.

The genetic data suggest that the low level of genetic variability in this species is influencing reproductive success, with only those matings that occur between genetically divergent individuals being successful. The obvious downside to this finding is that there are not any reasonable conservation actions that could be put into place to minimize this effect. There is, however, also a positive side to this result. Because matings are successful only between individuals that are genetically dissimilar, the offspring of known mating pairs have higher levels of genetic variability than expected from this gene pool. The paternity data indicate that this mechanism may be resulting in a relatively even distribution of paternities per sampled male and low observed variance in male reproductive success. Combined, these data imply that mate incompatibility is decreasing the loss of genetic diversity and increasing the effective population size of the North Atlantic right whale. It is tempting to speculate that this case study is providing a rare glimpse of one mechanism by which some small populations are able to reduce the loss of genetic diversity, increase effective population size, and thereby survive and recover. For the right whale, therefore, although genetic factors may be reducing reproductive success, these factors may also be providing the mechanism that has allowed this species to survive at its small population size for a long time.

Aguilar, A. 1986. A review of old Basque whaling and its effect on the right whales (*Eubalaena glacialis*) of the North Atlantic. *Report of the International Whaling Commission* Special Issue 10:191–199.

Amos, W., J. Worthington Wilmer, K. Fullard, T. M. Burg, J. P. Croxall, D. Bloch, and T. Coulson. 2001a. The influence of parental relatedness on reproductive success. *Proceedings of the Royal Society of London Part B* 268:2021–2027.

Amos, W., J. Worthington Wilmer, and H. Kokko. 2001b. Do female grey seals select genetically diverse mates? *Animal Behaviour* 62:157–164.

Barkham, S. 1977. The Basques: filling a gap in our history between Jacques Cartier and Champlain. *The Canadian Cartographer* 14:1–9.

Barkham, S. 1984. The Basque whaling establishments in Labrador 1536–1632: A summary. *Arctic* 37:515–519.

Best, P. B. 1994. Seasonality of reproduction and the length of gestation in southern right whales *Eubalaena australis*. *Journal of Zoology* 232:175–189.

Best, P. B., A. Brandão, and D. S. Butterworth. 2001. Demographic parameters of southern right whales off South Africa. *Journal of Cetacean Research and Management* Special Issue 2:161–169.

Bouzat, J. L. 2001. The importance of control populations for the identification and management of genetic diversity. *Genetica* 110:109–115.

Brown, M. W., S. D. Kraus, and D. E. Gaskin. 1991. Reaction of North Atlantic right whales (*Eubalaena glacialis*) to skin biopsy sampling for genetic and pollutant analysis. *Report of the International Whaling Commission* Special Issue 13:81–89.

Brown, M. W., S. Brault, P. K. Hamilton, R. D. Kenney, A. R. Knowlton, M. K. Marx, C. A. Mayo, C. K. Slay, and S. D. Kraus. 2001. Sighting heterogeneity of right whales in the western North Atlantic: 1980–1992. *Journal of Cetacean Research and Management* Special Issue 2:245–250.

Caughley, G., and A. Gunn. 1996. *Conservation Biology in Theory and Practice*. Blackwell Science, Inc., Cambridge, MA.

Charlesworth, D., and B. Charlesworth. 1987. Inbreeding depression and its evolutionary consequences. *Annual Review of Ecology and Systematics* 18:237–268.

Clapham, P. J. (ed.). 2002. Report of the working group on survival estimation for North Atlantic right whales. Northeast Fisheries Science Center, Woods Hole, MA, September 27.

Clapham, P. J., S. B. Young, and R. L. Brownell, Jr. 1999. Baleen whales: conservation issues and the status of the most endangered populations. *Mammal Review* 29:35–60.

Cooke, J. G., V. J. Rowntree, and R. S. Payne. 2001. Estimates of demographic parameters for southern right whales (*Eubalaena australis*) observed off Península Valdés, Argentina. *Journal of Cetacean Research and Management* Special Issue 2: 125–132.

Cumbaa, S. L. 1986. Archaeological evidence of the sixteenth century Basque right whale fishery in Labrador. *Report of the International Whaling Commission* Special Issue 10:187–190.

Daly, M., and M. Wilson. 1983. *Sex, Evolution, and Behavior,* second edition. PWS Publishing, Belmont, CA.

Eschricht, D. F., and J. Reinhardt. 1866. On the Greenland right-whale (*Balaena mysticetus,* Linn.), with especial reference to its geographical distribution and migrations in times past and present and to its external and internal characteristics. Pages 1–150 *in* W. H. Flower, ed. *Recent Memoirs on the Cetacea by Professors Eschricht, Reinhardt, and Lilljeborg.* Ray Society, Piccadilly, London, U.K.

Frantz, A. C., L. C. Pope, P. J. Carpenter, T. J. Roper, G. J. Wilson, J. Delahay, and T. Burke. 2003. Reliable microsatellite genotyping of the Eurasian badger (*Meles meles*) using fecal DNA. *Molecular Ecology* 12:1649–1661.

Frasier, T. R. 2005. Integrating genetic and photo-identification data to assess reproductive success in the North Atlantic right whale (*Eubalaena glacialis*). Ph.D. Thesis, McMaster University, Hamilton, Ontario, Canada.

Fujiwara, M., and H. Caswell. 2001. Demography of the endangered North Atlantic right whale. *Nature* 414:537–541.

Gaskin, D. 1991. An update on the status of the right whale, *Eubalaena glacialis,* in Canada. *Canadian Field-Naturalist* 105:198–205.

Gibbs, H. L., P. J. Weatherhead, P. T. Boag, B. N. White, L. M. Tabak, and D. J. Hoysak. 1990. Realized reproductive success of polygynous red-winged blackbirds revealed by DNA markers. *Science* 250:1394–1397.

Hamilton, P. K., and C. A. Mayo. 1990. Population characteristics of right whales (*Eubalaena glacialis*) observed in Cape Cod and Massachusetts Bays, 1978–1986. *Report of the International Whaling Commission* Special Issue 12:203–208.

Hamilton, P. K., A. R. Knowlton, M. K. Marx, and S. D. Kraus. 1998. Age structure and longevity in North Atlantic right whales *Eubalaena glacialis* and their relation to reproduction. *Marine Ecology Progress Series* 171:285–292.

Hughes, C. R. 1998. Integrating molecular techniques with field methods in studies of social behaviour: a revolution results. *Ecology* 79:383–399.

IWC. 2001. Report of the workshop on the comprehensive assessment of right whales: A worldwide comparison. *Journal of Cetacean Research and Management* Special Issue 2:1–60.

Kenney, R. D. 2001. Anomalous 1992 spring and summer right whale (*Eubalaena glacialis*) distributions in the Gulf of Maine. *Journal of Cetacean Research and Management* Special Issue 2:209–223.

Klopfer, P. H. 1971. Mother love: What turns it on? *American Scientist* 59:404–407.

Knowlton, A. R., and S. D. Kraus. 2001. Mortality and serious injury of northern right whales (*Eubalaena glacialis*) in the western North Atlantic Ocean. *Journal of Cetacean Research and Management* Special Issue 2:193–208.

Knowlton, A. R., S. D. Kraus, and R. D. Kenney. 1994. Reproduction in North Atlantic right whales (*Eubalaena glacialis*). *Canadian Journal of Zoology* 72:1297–1305.

Kraus, S. D., and J. J. Hatch. 2001. Mating strategies in the North Atlantic right whale (*Eubalaena glacialis*). *Journal of Cetacean Research and Management* Special Issue 2:237–244.

Kraus, S. D., P. K. Hamilton, R. D. Kenney, A. R. Knowlton, and C. K. Slay. 2001. Reproductive parameters of the North Atlantic right whale. *Journal of Cetacean Research and Management* Special Issue 2:231–236.

Lambertsen, R. H. 1987. Biopsy system for large whales and its use for cytogenetics. *Journal of Mammalogy* 68:443–445.

Lande, R. 1988. Genetics and demography in biological conservation. *Science* 241: 1455–1460.

Lorenz, K. 1970. *Studies in Animal and Human Behaviour,* Vol. I. Harvard University Press, Cambridge, MA.

Lunn, N. J., D. Paetkau, W. Calvert, S. Atkinson, M. Taylor, and C. Strobeck. 2000. Cub adoption by polar bears (*Ursus maritimus*): determining relatedness with microsatellite markers. *Journal of Zoology* 251:23–30.

Malik, S., M. W. Brown, S. D. Kraus, A. R. Knowlton, P. K. Hamilton, and B. N. White. 1999. Assessment of mitochondrial DNA structuring and nursery use in the North Atlantic right whale (*Eubalaena glacialis*). *Canadian Journal of Zoology* 77:1217–1222.

Malik, S., M. W. Brown, S. D. Kraus, and B. N. White. 2000. Analysis of mitochondrial DNA diversity within and between North and South Atlantic right whales. *Marine Mammal Science* 16:545–558.

McComb, K., C. Moss, S. M. Durant, L. Baker, and S. Sayialel. 2001. Matriarchs as repositories of social knowledge in African elephants. *Science* 292:491–494.

Menotti-Raymond, M., and S. J. O'Brien. 1993. Dating the genetic bottleneck of the African cheetah. *Proceedings of the National Academy of Sciences* 90:3172–3176.

Menotti-Raymond, M., and S. J. O'Brien. 1995. Hypervariable genomic variation to reconstruct the natural history of populations: lessons from the big cats. *Electrophoresis* 16:1771–1774.

Moore, M. J., A. R. Knowlton, S. D. Kraus, W. A. McLellan, and R. K. Bonde. 2005. Morphometry, gross morphology and available histopathology in North Atlantic right whale (*Eubalaena glacialis*) mortalities (1970–2002). *Journal of Cetacean Research and Management* 6:199–214.

NMFS. 1991. Recovery Plan for the Northern Right Whale (*Eubalaena glacialis*). Prepared by the Right Whale Recovery Team for the National Marine Fisheries Service, Silver Spring, MD.

NMFS. 2005. Recovery Plan for the North Atlantic Right Whale (*Eubalaena glacialis*). National Marine Fisheries Service, Silver Spring, MD.

Ober, C., T. Hyslop, S. Elias, L. R. Wiekamp, and W. W. Hauck. 1998. Human leuko-
cyte antigen matching and fetal loss: results of a 10-year prospective study. *Human
Reproduction* 13:33–38.

Paetkau, D., and C. Strobeck. 1994. Microsatellite analysis of genetic variation in
black bear populations. *Molecular Ecology* 3:487–495.

Paterson, S., K. Wilson, and J. M. Pemberton. 1998. Major histocompatibility complex variation associated with juvenile survival and parasite resistance in a large
unmanaged ungulate population (*Ovis aries* L.). *Proceedings of the National Academy of Sciences* 95:3714–3719.

Perry, S. L., D. P. DeMaster, and G. K. Silber. 1999. The great whales: history and
status of six species listed as endangered under the U.S. endangered species act
of 1973. *Marine Fisheries Review* 61:1–74.

Quinn, T. W., J. S. Quinn, F. Cooke, and B. N. White. 1987. DNA marker analysis
detects multiple maternity and paternity in single broods of the lesser snow
goose. *Nature* 326:392–394.

Rastogi, T., M. W. Brown, B. A. McLeod, T. R. Frasier, R. Grenier, S. L. Cumbaa,
J. Nadarajah, and B. N. White. 2004. Genetic analysis of sixteenth-century
whale bones prompts a revision of the impact of Basque whaling on right and
bowhead whales in the western North Atlantic. *Canadian Journal of Zoology*
82:1647–1654.

Reeves, R. R., J. M. Breiwick, and E. D. Mitchell. 1999. History of whaling and estimated kill of right whales, *Balaena glacialis,* in the northeastern United States,
1620–1924. *Marine Fisheries Review* 61:1–36.

Rice, D. W. 1998. *Marine Mammals of the World: Systematics and Distribution.* Society for Marine Mammalogy Special Publication Number 4. The Society for
Marine Mammalogy, Lawrence, KS.

Rolland, R. M., K. E. Hunt, S. D. Kraus, and S. K. Wasser. 2005. Assessing reproductive status of right whales (*Eubalaena glacialis*) using fecal hormone metabolites. *General and Comparative Endocrinology* 142:308–317.

Rosenbaum, H. C., M. G. Egan, P. J. Clapham, R. L. Brownell, Jr., S. Malik, M. W.
Brown, B. N. White, P. Walsh, and R. Desalle. 2000. Utility of North Atlantic
right whale museum specimens for assessing changes in genetic diversity. *Conservation Biology* 14:1837–1842.

Schaeff, C., S. Kraus, M. Brown, J. Perkins, R. Payne, D. Gaskin, P. Boag, and
B. White. 1991. Preliminary analysis of mitochondrial DNA variation within
and between right whale species *Eubalaena glacialis* and *Eubalaena australis.* Report of the International Whaling Commission Special Issue 13:217–223.

Schaeff, C. M., S. D. Kraus, M. W. Brown, J. S. Perkins, R. Payne, and B. N. White.
1997. Comparison of genetic variability of North and South Atlantic right whales
(*Eubalaena*), using DNA fingerprinting. *Canadian Journal of Zoology* 75:1073–
1080.

Taylor, A. C., A. Horsup, C. N. Johnson, P. Sunnucks, and B. Sherwin. 1997. Relatedness structure detected by microsatellite analysis and attempted pedigree reconstruction in an endangered marsupial, the northern hairy-nosed wombat *Lasiorhinus krefftii. Molecular Ecology* 6:9–19.

Waldick, R. C. 1999. Assessing the status of the endangered North Atlantic right whale using genetic and demographic data. Ph.D. Thesis. McMaster University, Hamilton, Ontario, Canada.

Waldick, R. C., S. D. Kraus, M. W. Brown, and B. N. White. 2002. Evaluating the effects of historic bottleneck events: an assessment of microsatellite variability in the endangered, North Atlantic right whale. *Molecular Ecology* 11:2241–2249.

Whitehead, H. 1998. Cultural selection and genetic diversity in matrilineal whales. *Science* 282:1708–1711.

Whitehead, H. 2003. *Sperm Whales: Social Evolution in the Ocean.* University of Chicago Press, Chicago.

Acknowledgments

These analyses would not have been possible without the dedication and good aim of the researchers who used bow and arrow to obtain the skin biopsy samples: Christopher Slay, Ree Brennin, Harriet Corbett, Lisa Conger, Beth Pike, Yan Guilbault, Lindsay Hall, Alicia Windham-Reid, Jamison Smith, Mason Weinrich, and Jooke Robbins. Access to the data used throughout this study was kindly provided by the North Atlantic Right Whale Consortium. This work has been supported by The Penzance Foundation through the Woods Hole Oceanographic Institution (WHOI) Ocean Life Institute Right Whale Initiative, the Natural Sciences and Engineering Research Council of Canada, World Wildlife Fund Canada, National Marine Fisheries Service, National Fish and Wildlife Foundation, Department of Fisheries and Oceans Canada, and the Canadian Whale Institute.

8

The Inner Whale: Hormones, Biotoxins, and Parasites

ROSALIND M. ROLLAND, KATHLEEN E. HUNT,
GREGORY J. DOUCETTE, LORA G. RICKARD,
AND SAMUEL K. WASSER

25 July 2000
Bay of Fundy

Even from a distance we knew it was "Admiral" (Eg #1027). As the most massive (and quite possibly the oldest) of all North Atlantic right whales, she was easy to recognize. Earlier in the day, a whale watching boat captain had called on the VHF radio to tell us that a right whale next to his boat was standing on its head with its flukes straight up in the air. Although Southern Hemisphere right whales in Argentina are known to stick their tails up and actually "sail" downwind this way, Admiral is the only northern right whale that has ever been seen doing this. So we knew that she had returned to the Bay of Fundy once again, as she has done most years since she was first photographed here in 1982.

As we approached Admiral to take photographs for the North Atlantic Right Whale Catalog, *a cheer rose up from the boat. Long-term researchers have seen so many right whales killed that sighting Admiral each year gives us hope for the continued survival of all right whales. But even though researchers have been observing her for over two decades, Admiral remains a puzzle. Since 1979 she has been photographed over 180 times in all of the* known right whale habitats, and she frequently has been seen participating in surface-active (courtship) groups. She has the thickest blubber layer of any right whale examined by ultrasound, and she appears to be fat and healthy, yet she has never been seen with a calf. Is Admiral so old that she has stopped cycling? Is she infertile? Or could she be losing her calves during pregnancy or shortly after calving and thus escaping the notice of our surveys?

Unfortunately Admiral is not the only adult female right whale that has never been seen with a calf. At least a dozen mature females in this population have never been photographed with a calf in the southeastern U.S. calving grounds. Many more adult females have had long gaps between calving events. These are disturbing findings for a small, highly endangered population where the reproductive potential of every female is important to the survival of the species. Even within the subset of adult females that have reproduced, the total number of calves produced annually has varied widely (from one to thirty-one), and the overall reproductive rate of the population has been much lower than expected since the 1980s.

As a veterinarian interested in studying the reproductive problem in right whales, my first question for Scott Kraus was "What types of tissue samples can we get from right whales?" He replied that it was possible to get small pieces of skin and blubber using a remote biopsy dart, that it was possible to hold an agar plate over the blowholes during exhalation, and thus get samples of respiratory fluids and cells, and that in the 1980s they had collected fecal samples, which floated on the water surface. Of course I was hoping for blood samples to measure reproductive hormones, do serology for infectious diseases, and look at complete blood counts and serum chemistry. Cultures of the reproductive tracts or fluids as well as histology of gonads of dead whales would be nice too. However, none of this was possible. Then I came up with one of those ideas that led me down an unexpected pathway in life. I had spent the first fifteen years of my veterinary career working with primates and other terrestrial wildlife, and I knew that researchers had recently started to measure reproductive hormones in fecal samples from several species of wildlife. Knowing that the major reproductive hormones are well conserved evolutionarily and therefore have the same molecular structure in creatures as diverse as ring-tailed lemurs and rhinoceros, I thought, why not try to measure fecal hormones in whales?

The next summer, in 1999, I arrived at the New England Aquarium field station in Lubec, Maine, armed with a long-handled, fine-mesh fishing *net to try to collect some right whale fecal samples. More than a few people thought that I had lost my mind! Six years later, what had started as a simple idea of trying to develop a pregnancy test for right whales by measuring metabolites of fecal progesterone (similar in concept to the urine pregnancy test for women) has evolved into an array of collaborative research projects on right whale health and endocrinology. It turns out that there is a lot to be learned through molecular analysis of right whale feces, which can provide us with our first insights into the workings of the inner whale.*

Rosalind M. Rolland

Development of methods to obtain physiological and biomedical information on North Atlantic right whales became an especially pressing issue during the 1990s. The reproductive rate of this small population was substantially lower than that of healthy, growing populations of right whales in the Southern Hemisphere (IWC 2001a), which rebounded following protection from whaling in 1935. The situation appeared to worsen dramatically by the late 1990s, when it became apparent that there was a statistically significant and troubling decline in several reproductive parameters including an increase in female interbirth intervals, an increasing age at first calving, and highly variable yearly calf production (Kraus et al. 2001; Chapter 6). Additionally, starting in the late 1990s (coinciding with a dramatic drop in calving), researchers noted a decline in the physical appearance of many right whales that included an apparent loss of body condition and appearance of epidermal (skin) lesions on many whales (Chapter 9). Recognizing that this evidence of declining health and reproduction represented an important impediment to recovery of this highly endangered species, two International Whaling Commission (IWC) Workshops (IWC 2001a, 2001b) strongly recommended research programs to investigate health and reproductive dysfunction in right whales.

In April 2000 the Northeast Fisheries Science Center (National Marine Fisheries Service) hosted a multidisciplinary workshop to address specifically the issue of low reproductive rates in right whales and to recommend research approaches to investigate this problem (Reeves et al. 2001). At this workshop, five factors were examined that alone or in combination might be affecting right whale reproduction and health adversely: (1) exposure to environmental contaminants, especially endocrine-disrupting chemicals; (2) poor body condition as a result of inadequate food resources; (3) effects related to limited genetic diversity; (4) impacts of undiagnosed infectious disease(s); and (5) exposure to marine biotoxins from harmful algal blooms. The workshop participants concluded that none of these factors could be eliminated as potential contributors to the observed reproductive dysfunction in right whales and that interaction among multiple factors was very likely (for example, reduced immune competence from low genetic diversity enhancing susceptibility to infectious disease).

However, investigating the reasons for compromised reproduction and health in right whales was problematic because of the inability to obtain the necessary biological samples. No nonlethal methods existed to obtain blood or urine samples from free-swimming large whales, which seriously limited our ability to understand right whale physiology or to diagnose and monitor infectious diseases. Therefore, development of diagnostic methods for right whales required a completely new approach.

It turned out that a wealth of biomedical data could be obtained by analyzing fecal samples, providing new insights into right whale health and physiology. This chapter presents a series of investigations based on analyses of fecal (scat) samples, including (1) measurement of reproductive and stress hormone metabolites, (2) assessment of the threat to right whales from exposure to marine biotoxins, and (3) evaluation of the prevalence of protozoan parasites in right whales. The techniques used for collecting fecal samples from free-swimming whales are also described, including the use of scat detection dogs.

Right Whale Feces: Worth Their Weight in Gold

Large wild mammals have always been difficult to study. At the very least, it almost always requires catching the animal to take a blood sample. In the terrestrial environment large mammals are frequently difficult or even dangerous to capture, requiring trap-lines, helicopter chases, rocket netting, anesthetic darting, and the like. These techniques are not only expensive and time-intensive but are highly stressful and can even be dangerous for the animals (and sometimes for the scientists as well). Endangered large mammals pose a special problem because of the potential consequences of stressing or injuring animals during capture.

The North Atlantic right whale carries these problems to an extreme. It is highly endangered, and there is no safe method for capturing a free-swimming large whale. For biologists accustomed to working on other animals, the sheer impossibility of capturing large whales, and the near-complete lack of information on their basic physiology, is astounding. It takes only one day on a research vessel for a researcher to realize, typically with a mounting sense of frustration, that many of the standard tools of wildlife research are useless for studying large whales.

The discovery that right whale feces can be collected has, therefore, been a true breakthrough, opening up the black box of whale physiology. Whale scat contains a wealth of information, including the whale's own DNA, from which its species can be verified and individual identity determined; DNA of prey species and parasites; food items themselves; parasites and microbes; marine biotoxins encountered through the food web; the metabolites of many hormones, including reproductive and stress hormones; environmental contaminants that have been ingested; immune proteins of the gut; and other components. All in all, right whale feces are literally worth their weight in gold to researchers striving to understand the biological mysteries of this endangered cetacean.

How Do You Collect Fecal Samples from Right Whales?

Without exception, this is the first question asked in discussions about these fecal-based studies of right whale health and reproduction. In fact, fecal samples have been successfully collected from several other species of non-captive cetaceans including bottlenose dolphins (Parsons et al. 2003), sperm whales (Smith and Whitehead 2000), blue whales, and humpback whales (Lefebvre et al. 2002). Two important conditions apply to collecting fecal samples from wild cetaceans. First, the animals must be actively feeding (so they are defecating), and second, the scat has to float for at least a little while. Fecal buoyancy may be influenced by season but is probably largely determined by diet (e.g., fat content of prey), as feces from some cetaceans can have a fluid consistency and quickly dissipate following defecation.

In 1999 New England Aquarium researchers started collecting fecal samples from right whales in the Bay of Fundy to determine if it was feasible to measure fecal hormone metabolites in this species. Right whale scat is clumped and buoyant, making it possible to collect samples from the surface of the water using a fine mesh net (Fig. 8.1). Fecal samples can be identified easily by their size, shape, typical brown to orange-red color, characteristic strong odor, and the presence of fine baleen hairs in the samples. Generally there are few other whale species among the aggregations of right whales feeding in the Bay of Fundy, leaving little doubt as to the origin of the samples, and this has re-

Figure 8.1. Collecting right whale scat. Brenna Kraus / New England Aquarium.

cently been confirmed genetically by analysis of fecal DNA (R. Rolland and R. Gillett, unpublished data).

Initially scat was found opportunistically when a whale was observed defecating during shipboard photo-identification surveys or when observers smelled the nearby presence of a sample. Right whales frequently defecate at the surface either during courtship activity when large numbers of whales congregate, while feeding near the water surface, or when fluking up to dive. When defecation was observed, the individual whale could be identified from photographs (Kraus et al. 1986). Sometimes scat was found floating on the water in the area of diving right whales that were not photographed. Molecular methods are now available to determine both the species and individual whale identity from right whale DNA that is extracted from the feces (Chapter 7).

The power of these fecal-based studies is greatly enhanced if the whale can be identified within the *North Atlantic Right Whale Catalog* and database, allowing comparison of results from hormone, parasite, and biotoxin studies with life history information (sex, age, calving history, habitat use, etc.) and genetic characteristics. This *Catalog* is a powerful dataset with which to interpret fecal hormone levels (and other data) on both an individual and population level, as it incorporates the results of over twenty-five years of research on this population (Chapter 3).

Of Dogs and Whales

As the fecal-based research program evolved, it quickly became apparent that analysis of these samples was providing valuable insights into right whale physiology and health. However, this approach was limited by the difficulty of opportunistically locating scat at sea. In 2001 while observing field research in the Bay of Fundy, one of the co-authors (Sam Wasser) suggested using scat detection dogs to increase the number of samples collected. Detection dogs had been successfully used for scat-based population surveys of grizzly and black bears in Canada (Wasser et al. 2004) and kit foxes in California (Smith et al. 2003). Although scat detection dogs had never before worked from a boat, dogs had been used for search and rescue on the water, making it theoretically feasible to use them to find right whale scat.

Training of scat detection dogs follows the techniques used for narcotic, search and rescue, and bomb detection dogs. The dogs are able to detect scent concentrations as low as three parts per million, and they are capable of distinguishing at least eighteen different scents (or species) at distances over 0.5 km (Wasser et al. 2004). Dogs are carefully selected for training based on a strong "play-drive" and willingness to work for a reward (in this case playing with a tennis ball). The dog is introduced to the targeted scat odor through a series of established training techniques and learns to associate finding that specific odor with the reward. When the dog detects the desired scent there is a characteristic change of behavior (e.g., animation, ear-set, tail wagging), motivated by the expectation of the reward. On land, the dog will lead the dog handler to the scat by following the scent cone formed by the sample along an increasing odor gradient to its source.

Fecal surveys with detection dogs on the water involve running transects downwind of aggregations of feeding right whales, perpendicular to the wind direction. A single dog works from the bow of the boat, sampling the air with its nose into the wind. When a right whale defecates at the surface, a scent cone originating from the scat spreads downwind of the sample location. As the dog picks up the scent cone, its change in behavior indicates to the handler that it is "on scent." The handler then interprets the dog's behavior for the boat driver, who steers according to the direction indicated by the dog (Fig. 8.2). If the dog loses the scent, perpendicular transects are resumed until the scent

Figure 8.2. A detection dog ("Fargo") working during a survey for right whale scat in the Bay of Fundy. Yan Guilbault / New England Aquarium.

cone is located again. By following the dog's directional indications into the wind, the handlers usually locate the sample (Fig. 8.3), and the dog is promptly rewarded (color plate 12).

The results of three years using detection dogs (2003–2005) showed that dog sampling efficiency (samples collected per hour) was on average over fourfold higher than opportunistic fecal sample collection during photo-identification surveys (Rolland et al. in press). Dogs detected samples up to 1.93 km away (almost a nautical mile), which was much farther than the human's first detections of odor (maximum of 350 m). From 2003 to 2005 detection dogs found a total of ninety-seven scat samples in the Bay of Fundy, compared to thirty samples collected during photo-identification surveys on the same days (working much longer hours). Thus detection dogs have significantly increased the numbers of fecal samples collected for the studies described in this chapter.

Studying Reproduction in Free-Swimming Whales

Most information on the reproductive physiology of the mysticete (baleen) whales has been derived from examination of the reproductive tracts and gonads

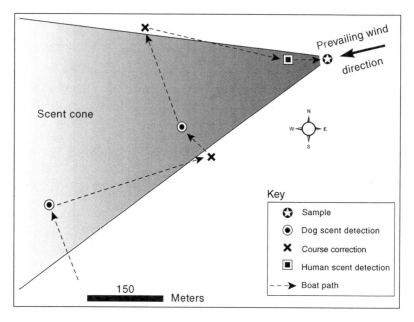

Figure 8.3. Theoretical search pattern followed by the research vessel to locate a right whale scat sample with a detection dog. Shading indicates the scent cone gradient downwind from the sample. When the boat enters the scent cone, the dog detects the odor, and the boat driver steers into the wind. The dog loses the odor when the boat leaves the scent cone, and the boat resumes a transect perpendicular to the wind until the dog has another detection, then turns into the wind again to find the sample. Kerry Lagueux / New England Aquarium.

of either stranded dead whales or those killed during commercial or subsistence whaling operations (Lockyer 1984). Because right whales have been protected for over seventy years, and because the carcasses of stranded right whales are usually too decomposed for analysis of soft tissues, there is not much information on the basic reproductive anatomy or physiology of this species. Therefore, little is known about right whale reproductive physiology, including the basic reproductive cycle of females, pregnancy rates, incidence of abortion or stillbirths, seasonality of reproduction, age of sexual maturation, or the possibility of reproductive senescence.

Studies of terrestrial wildlife have shown that the metabolites of steroid reproductive hormones can be measured by radioimmunoassay (or enzyme immunoassay) in scat, providing insights into reproductive status. Measurements of the metabolites of 17β-estradiol and progesterone in fecal samples have been used to characterize female reproductive status in a variety of captive and free-ranging terrestrial wildlife (reviewed in Schwarzenberger et al. 1996). Similarly assays for fecal testosterone metabolites in males have been applied to study relationships among reproductive state, season, social rank, and behavior in numerous wild mammals (Creel et al. 1997; Barrett et al. 2002; Dloniak et al. 2004). Except for one study of captive sea otters (Larson et al. 2003) and a study of manatees (Larkin et al. 2005), these assays have not been widely used in marine mammals. However, because these techniques had worked in many different animal species, they presented a feasible strategy to measure reproductive hormones in right whales.

Measuring Fecal Steroid Hormones

The steroid hormones (derivatives of cholesterol) are lipophilic or "fat-loving" compounds that share a common pathway for excretion with bile into the gut (and/or in urine), making it possible to measure the hormone metabolites in feces. Included among this class of compounds are the major hormones controlling reproduction: estrogen, progesterone, and testosterone. Glucocorticoids (adrenal "stress" hormones) share this excretion pathway and can also be measured in feces (see "Stress in Right Whales" in this chapter).

Estrogen, progesterone, and testosterone are synthesized primarily by the gonads (and placenta in pregnant females), with a minor contribution from the adrenal glands. These hormones circulate in the bloodstream while acting on their target tissues for variable periods before being metabolized. They are removed from the blood and metabolized in the liver, then excreted in bile and/or urine. Steroid hormones generally survive the passage through the gut in more or less recognizable form because of the small size and stable framework of steroid molecular structure. (This contrasts with protein hormones, which, if they enter the gut at all, appear to be destroyed by intestinal enzymes.) The steroid hormones are not completely unaffected: each hormone is usually altered by the liver, intestinal enzymes, and microflora into several related "fecal metabolite" forms by addition or alteration of various side groups.

Both reproductive and stress hormone metabolites can be extracted from fecal samples and measured by radioimmunoassay using antibodies to the parent hormone (Adlercreutz and Järvenpää 1982; Palme et al. 1996). The radioimmunoassay actually measures a mixture of hormone metabolites that bind to the antibody used in the assay (these metabolites are referred to here as "estrogens," "progestins," and "androgens"). Because hormone metabolism and routes of excretion vary considerably among different species, these assays require validation for every new species studied.

The concentration of fecal hormones reflects the general pattern of serum hormone levels, with a lag time from hours to days that is determined by hormone clearance rates and intestinal transit time for the species (Wasser et al. 1994; Palme et al. 1996). This lag time is not known for reproductive hormones in right whales, but an educated guess might place them somewhere in the vicinity of cows or elephants, basically one or two days. That is, the fecal level of a given hormone represents the serum level of that hormone approximately one or more days before the sample was collected. Although pulsatile and diurnal secretion of hormones into the bloodstream can lead to hourly variation in blood levels, the fecal hormone concentrations are essentially an averaged concentration over time, which simplifies comparison of relative hormone patterns among individuals and groups of animals.

Fecal Endocrinology in Right Whales

As a first step, radioimmunoassays for the fecal metabolites of estrogen, progesterone, and testosterone were validated for right whales (Rolland et al. 2005). These studies showed that hormone metabolites could be measured accurately in right whale scat across a range of concentrations and that there were no interfering substances present in the fecal matrix. This was the first time that this methodology had been validated for any cetacean species, and it confirmed the utility of this method for studying right whale reproductive physiology.

A subset of the scat samples was linked to known right whales through photo-identification, and fecal hormone concentrations were examined relative to the gender, age class (juvenile less than nine years or adult over nine years), and reproductive history for females (resting, lactating, pregnant). Statistical analyses comparing fecal hormone concentrations among known right whales (n = 39) showed that there were significant differences in hormone levels according to age, gender, and reproductive status (Rolland et al. 2005; Table 8.1).

Gender Determination

When levels of fecal reproductive hormones were compared in known whales of different genders, the ratio of fecal androgens to estrogens (AE ratio) proved to be 100 percent accurate in identifying the gender of the sampled whale. Males had a significantly higher AE ratio than nonpregnant females, and the

Table 8.1. Mean (± standard error) Concentrations of Fecal Steroid Hormone Metabolites (ng/g dry weight) in Photo-Identified North Atlantic Right Whales According to Gender, Age, and Reproductive Status[a]

Gender/status (n)	Estrogens (ng/g)	Progestins (ng/g)	Androgens (ng/g)
Females			
Juvenile (6)	35 ± 7.4	116 ± 23.9	1,006 ± 362.0
Resting (4)	57 ± 10.6	295 ± 144.7	1,245 ± 315.8
Pregnant (3)	38,237 ± 7,805	201,240 ± 27,025	8,798 ± 3,777
Lactating (12)	167 ± 16.5	273 ± 45.7	3,011 ± 353.5
Males			
Juvenile (7)	53 ± 7.1	153 ± 23.5	4,422 ± 568.1
Adult (7)	95 ± 20.6	333 ± 42.8	10,203 ± 1,640.7

a. Juveniles are ≤ 9 years old, adults are > 9 years old, and resting females are nonpregnant, non-lactating adults.

Adapted and reprinted from Rolland et al. (2005), with permission from Elsevier.

ratios were widely separated, demonstrating that gender could be determined unambiguously using this hormone ratio (Fig. 8.4). The AE ratio reflected expected differences in the endocrine profile of the two genders in that males would be expected to have higher androgens and females higher estrogens.

Pregnancy

Previously, the only way to diagnose pregnancy in right whales was retrospectively after the whale gave birth and was photographed with a calf. This meant that there was no way to recognize whether females were losing calves during gestation (abortion) or near term (stillbirths). However, fecal progestins of pregnant females were many orders of magnitude higher than those of nonpregnant females, making it easy to identify pregnant right whales (Fig. 8.5a). The estrogen levels also tended to be higher than those in other females. Pregnancy was confirmed by positive identification of the sampled whales with newborn calves during the year following sample collection. If we assume a twelve- to thirteen-month gestation in North Atlantic right whales (Best 1994), pregnant whales were sampled at about seven to nine months of gestation.

Lactation

Because the Bay of Fundy is a nursery area for right whales, fecal samples were obtained from a cohort of lactating females that were actively nursing their calves. When compared to juvenile and resting (i.e., nonpregnant, nonlactating adult) females, lactating whales had a unique hormone profile characterized

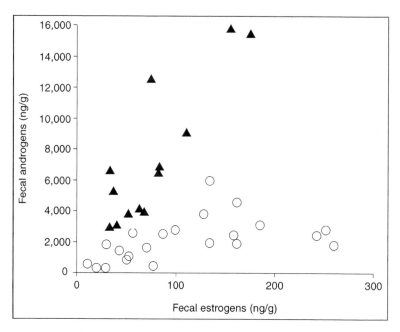

Figure 8.4. Scatterplot showing that the gender of right whales can be determined by the ratio of the fecal androgen to estrogen concentration. Males are indicated by filled triangles (▲), and females by open circles (O). (Data are not log-transformed.) Reprinted from Rolland et al. (2005), with permission from Elsevier.

by significantly elevated estrogens (and androgens), without the extreme elevation in progestins that is characteristic of pregnancy (Fig. 8.5b). This finding is consistent with the hormonal changes accompanying lactation in other mammals (Tucker 1988).

Sexual Maturity in Females

The mean age of first parturition has been used previously to estimate the age of sexual maturation in female right whales. However, the broad range of these ages (five to twenty-one years), the possibility of unrecognized pregnancy loss, and the inability to detect ovulatory activity all make this method inaccurate. Studies of serum hormones in hunted baleen whales have found that sexual maturation is accompanied by significantly increased levels of serum progesterone (Kjeld et al. 1992; Iga et al. 1996). Resting female right whales had almost double the level of fecal progestins found in juveniles (Table 8.1; Fig. 8.5a,b), but such differences were not significant in these studies. This lack of

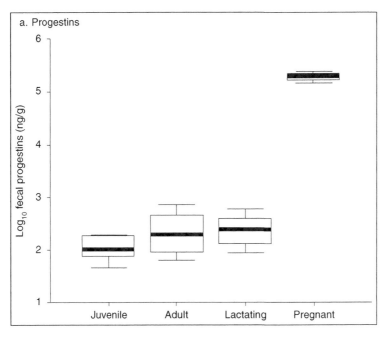

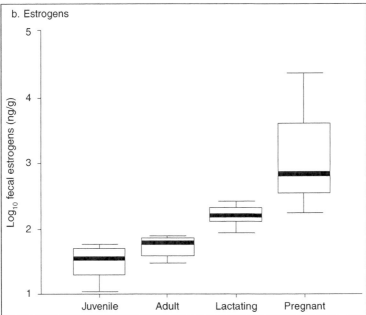

Figure 8.5. Log-transformed fecal progestins and estrogens in female right whales according to age class and reproductive status. For boxplots the line inside the box indicates the median value and the height of the box encompasses the interquartile range (50 percent of values). Reprinted from Rolland et al. (2005), with permission from Elsevier.

significance may be a result of either low statistical power because of small sample sizes or sample collection during anestrus (noncycling) months. Additional samples from known females and during other seasons may clarify this issue, and this technique eventually may determine the range of ages of sexual maturation in females.

Sexual Maturity in Males

Determining age of sexual maturation in male right whales is even more challenging than in females. In right whales, mating behavior is an unreliable indicator of sexual maturity because juveniles of both sexes participate in surface-active (courtship) groups (Chapter 6). Another complication is the seasonality of testicular function in at least some whale species, which involves testicular atrophy and dramatic decreases in serum testosterone levels (Kita et al. 1999; Mogoe et al. 2000). However, results of fecal hormone analyses showed that adult males had over twice the concentration of fecal androgens compared to younger males, with a much wider range of values, most likely indicating enhanced gonadal steroidogenesis following sexual maturation (Table 8.1; Fig. 8.6). This concurs with the results of studies on other whales that found sharp increases in serum testosterone levels accompanying maturation of the male reproductive tract (Desportes et al. 1994; Kita et al. 1999). Through continued sampling of males of known but varied ages, it may be possible to use fecal androgen concentrations to delineate a range of ages for maturation. Seasonality of reproduction in males can also be investigated if fecal samples can be obtained throughout the year.

In summary, analysis of fecal hormone metabolite levels in combination with life history data from photographically identified whales can be used to determine gender, detect pregnancy and lactation, and to assess age at sexual maturity in male right whales. With larger sample sizes from a cross section of the population, future studies should refine hormonal ranges by age class and reproductive state, leading to a better understanding of basic reproductive biology of right whales. Finally comparison of reproductive hormone levels between reproductively successful and unsuccessful whales can help to identify physiological factors underlying the reproductive impairment in this highly endangered whale.

Stress in Right Whales

Chronic stress is another factor in (and indicator of) compromised health and reproduction. Chronically elevated stress increases susceptibility to dis-

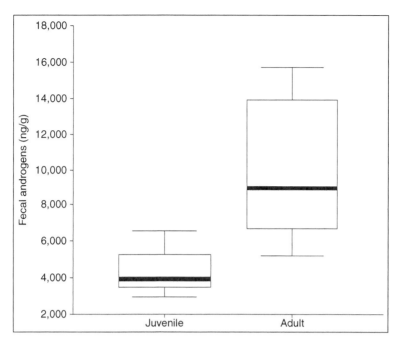

Figure 8.6. Fecal androgens in male right whales according to age class. (Data are not log-transformed.) Reprinted from Rolland et al. (2005), with permission from Elsevier.

ease and directly lowers reproductive hormone levels, causing suppression of reproductive function (Wingfield et al. 1998). North Atlantic right whales are exposed to numerous potential natural stressors (e.g., disease, fasting, courtship activity) and anthropogenic stressors (e.g., shipping traffic, acoustic disturbances, entanglement in fishing gear), but previously there were no quantitative techniques available to evaluate the effects of these factors and their potential impact on health and reproduction.

Stress, Stressors, and the Stress Response

Stress physiologists distinguish between a *stressor,* the environmental event that presents an animal with some problem or challenge, and the *stress response,* the animal's attempt to regain homeostasis in response to the stressor (Balm 1999). Wild animals face many stressors in their lives; however, it is important to note that not all stressors are "bad." For example pregnancy, lactation, competition for mates, and migration are all normal events, but they are still considered stressors because they all require dramatically increased energy expenditure and tend to cause many of the same changes in physiology and behavior that harmful stressors also trigger.

Although the different types of stressors are very diverse, vertebrates have evolved a more or less generalized coping mechanism. The stress response involves dozens of hormones, but a major part of this response is orchestrated by the glucocorticoids, a class of steroid hormones secreted by the cortex of the adrenal gland, including cortisol and corticosterone (loosely referred to as stress hormones, although this oversimplifies matters). A baseline level of circulating glucocorticoids is essential for normal health. However, if an animal experiences, or even just perceives, an environmental stressor, glucocorticoid secretion shoots far above baseline within a few minutes, and a stress response is under way.

Increased levels of glucocorticoids have myriad effects throughout the body, including increases in blood glucose, breakdown and mobilization of fat stores, breakdown of protein and conversion to carbohydrates, increased blood pressure, changes in cognition and memory, and changes in behavior. In addition elevated glucocorticoids cause profound reductions in reproduction, growth, wound healing, and immune function, so that all energy can be diverted temporarily toward dealing with the stressor.

What do stress hormones indicate about right whales? First, an increased level of glucocorticoids can simply indicate that a whale is experiencing some kind of extrinsic challenge: food shortage, water pollution, a disease outbreak, an injury, thermal stress from changing water temperatures, fishing gear entanglement, or stress associated with ship traffic or ship noise. Second, any of these stressors can also indirectly cause problems because the stress response itself, if carried on too long, can adversely affect health and reproduction. A key feature of the stress response is that it functions as a short-term emergency state. If the stressor continues unabated and whales are unable to escape or adapt, they may experience a chronic, long-term elevation of stress hormones.

The adverse consequences of chronic stress often include long-term reductions in fertility and decreases in reproductive behavior; increased rates of miscarriages; increased vulnerability to diseases and parasites; muscle wasting; disruptions in carbohydrate metabolism; circulatory diseases; and permanent cognitive impairment (Balm 1999). Thus over the long term, chronic stress itself can reduce reproduction, negatively affect health, and even kill outright.

Fecal Glucocorticoids in Right Whales

One method for assessing stress in noncaptive whales is measurement of fecal glucocorticoids. Similar to the reproductive hormones, these are steroid hormones that are excreted by the liver, and the metabolites can be measured by radioimmunoassay in feces (Wasser et al. 2000). Fecal glucocorticoid levels have been correlated with known environmental stressors such as drought in African elephant (Foley et al. 2001), distance from roads in northern spotted owls (Wasser et al. 1997), snowmobile traffic in elk and wolves (Creel et al. 2002), and translocation and aggression in spotted hyenas (Goymann et al. 1999).

As a measure of how little scientists know about baleen whales, it is unclear whether the right whale's primary circulating glucocorticoid is corticosterone, cortisol, or a mixture of the two. Small, toothed whales such as belugas and bottlenose dolphins appear to have both cortisol and corticosterone (St. Aubin and Dierauf 2001). In right whales, a corticosterone antibody showed excellent results in fecal validation studies and was used to assess the relationship between fecal hormone levels and the age, gender, reproductive state, and health status of sampled whales (Hunt et al. 2006).

Analysis of fecal glucocorticoid levels (referred to as "cort levels") from 177 right whales revealed that the results fell into three clusters. Most samples (75 percent) were from "low-cort whales" with feces containing less than 50 ng of immunoreactive glucocorticoids per gram of dried feces. These whales were usually reproductively inactive: immature males, immature females, and mature females who were resting (not lactating and not pregnant). The "intermediate-cort" whales had glucocorticoid levels of 50–100 ng/g. These tended to be lactating females and mature males. Samples with fecal glucocorticoids above 100 ng/g ("high-cort whales") were relatively rare, comprising just 9 percent of the samples. When their identity was known, the high-cort whales fell into four groups: (1) pregnant females; (2) some mature males; (3) one whale severely entangled in fishing gear; and (4) young whales, including two calves and one yearling.

Abnormal Elevations of Fecal Glucocorticoids

What does all this mean? Is the fecal corticosterone assay really measuring "stress"? Because captive experiments to prove this link directly are not feasible in baleen whales, fecal glucocorticoid data obtained from two right whales that appeared to be experiencing different levels of stress from fishing gear entanglements were examined. These cases are described below.

Case #1. Churchill (Eg #1102), an adult male, was photographed with a severe fishing gear entanglement in June 2001 and showed marked physical deterioration in the several months before his (presumed) death in September 2001 (see Chapter 9 for details). In the months preceding his death, the fishing line through his baleen became deeply imbedded into his rostrum. A fecal sample was opportunistically collected during a disentanglement effort by the Provincetown Center for Coastal Studies, approximately two months before Churchill disappeared. At this time Churchill was emaciated and showed many indications of debilitated health. His fecal sample contained a glucocorticoid content of 178 ng/g, the highest level yet recorded for a mature male.

Case #2. Piper (Eg #2320), an adult female, was photographed entangled in fishing gear in 2002 and was still entangled in late 2004, when a fecal sample was collected from her. This sample had surprisingly low levels of glucocorticoids (12 ng/g). However Piper appeared to be in remarkably good physical condition for an entangled whale, and, in contrast to Churchill, the lines entangling her were loose. In April 2005 she was photographed free of all visible gear that she presumably had shed herself.

These cases suggest that fecal glucocorticoids may indeed reflect the severity of stress in adult right whales. Whereas the fatally entangled whale had unusually high fecal glucocorticoids, the whale that apparently had habituated to a milder entanglement had low fecal glucocorticoids. Although more data are required, these results provide preliminary evidence that the fecal metabolites that are measured in this assay are indicative of a chronic adrenal stress response in debilitated whales and that fecal glucocorticoids show promise as a noninvasive method to measure stress in right whales.

Normal Elevations of Fecal Glucocorticoids

What about the other groups of whales with elevated glucocorticoids? So far, all known pregnant females have had very high fecal glucocorticoid levels. Pregnancy is itself a physiological stressor, and many mammals show pronounced elevations of glucocorticoids during pregnancy to fuel the metabolic demands of pregnancy and to prepare for lactation.

The calves and yearling with high fecal glucocorticoids present more of a puzzle. It is unknown whether the high glucocorticoid content is normal for young right whales or whether these particular animals were experiencing abnormal amounts of stress. The yearling, for example, may have been experiencing stress associated with its first year of independent foraging after weaning. Likewise, calves are in the process of being weaned in the Bay of Fundy, where their samples were collected. Alternatively it is possible that calves may ingest maternal glucocorticoids via milk (i.e., lactational transfer), and such levels could be elevated if their mothers were experiencing unusually high amounts of stress.

Some of the intermediate-cort whales, those with slightly elevated glucocorticoids, were mature males that also had high fecal androgens. Further analysis revealed that in males (and pregnant females), fecal glucocorticoids were significantly correlated with fecal androgens (Fig. 8.7). The correlation of fecal androgens with fecal glucocorticoids in males was at first difficult to interpret because there was a possibility that the results were falsely inflated by the extremely high androgen content in some fecal extracts. This is because the antibodies used in assays for steroid hormones exhibit slight cross-reactivity to other steroid hormones present in the sample. Subsequent studies of this potential cross-reactivity showed that this issue was minor and was limited to a slight effect in particular whales that had unusually high androgen:glucocorticoid ratios. Therefore it appears that the correlation of fecal androgens and glucocorticoids seen in male right whales is a real biological phenomenon in most cases. It is tempting to speculate that the energetic mating activity exhibited in surface-active groups may be stressful for adult males that are intensely competing for prime spots near the focal female.

In summary, fecal glucocorticoid assays are proving to be an informative technique for studying right whale stress physiology. Because baseline fecal glucocorticoids normally vary with gender, age class, and reproductive state, the levels should be interpreted in light of the individual's life history information. When these factors are known, measurement of stress hormones has great potential as a biomarker of health status as well as a quantifiable measure with which to explore the impact of environmental stressors on right whale health and reproduction.

Marine Biotoxins and Right Whales

In addition to learning about right whale physiology by measuring hormone levels, fecal analyses can shed light on exposure of right whales to substances in their environment such as marine biotoxins. Biotoxins originating from harmful algal blooms are currently an issue of widespread concern, as the frequency, distribution, and diversity of these phenomena have increased to the point where they now pose a threat to virtually all coastal waters from temperate to tropical regions. This includes the right whale habitats along the east coast of North America (Hallegraeff 1993; Anderson 1994), leading to concern that right whales might be at risk from the effects of these toxins. The

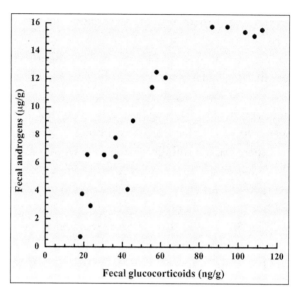

Figure 8.7. The correlation between fecal glucocorticoid and androgen concentrations in male right whales.

approach to investigate this possibility was to (1) see if right whales were being exposed to marine biotoxins, (2) find out which toxins were present, and (3) determine whether the toxin levels might be of concern for right whale health.

Harmful Algal Blooms and Biotoxins

Among the thousands of algal species that comprise the base of marine food webs, only a few dozen are considered harmful or toxic and capable of forming what are termed "harmful algal blooms" (Smayda 1990). These phenomena can be defined as an aggregation of either toxic or nontoxic micro- or macroalgae that cause harm through the production of highly potent biotoxins, the accumulation of high biomass levels, or the physical effects of cells on susceptible organisms. Harmful algal blooms, specifically those caused by microalgal species, have been referred to collectively as "red tides," which is somewhat misleading because they are not always red, and their formation is not related strictly to tides. Nonetheless they can cause discoloration of ocean surface waters as a result of high biomass but may exhibit a variety of colors (e.g., orange, brown, green) depending on the major pigments of the causative organism.

Blooms of toxic microalgal species are responsible for a variety of harmful impacts including massive fish kills, human health effects, marine mammal and bird morbidity and mortality, as well as alterations to marine food webs and the potential to cause changes at the ecosystem level (Van Dolah 2000; Landsberg 2002; Sellner et al. 2003). Exposure of wildlife to algal biotoxins may be direct, by respiratory intake or consuming toxic algal cells, or indirect, via trophic transfer (i.e., ingestion of toxin-laden prey species). Human exposure is generally through consumption of toxin-contaminated seafood, and consequently, the toxins responsible are named for human seafood poisoning syndromes: paralytic shellfish poisoning (PSP, caused by saxitoxins), neurotoxic shellfish poisoning (NSP, caused by brevetoxins), amnesic shellfish poisoning (ASP, caused by domoic acid), diarrhetic shellfish poisoning (DSP, caused by okadaic acid and dinophysistoxins), and ciguatera fish poisoning (CFP, caused by ciguatoxins). These biotoxins represent a diverse group of chemical compounds that vary widely in their potency and the way in which they cause toxicity. Most of these biotoxin groups (comprised of multiple chemical forms or "derivatives") are classified as neurotoxins, and the onset of symptoms in humans usually occurs rapidly (one to three hours) after ingesting contaminated seafood. On a worldwide basis, marine algal toxins are responsible for more than 60,000 human intoxication incidents per year, with an overall mortality rate of 1.5 percent (Ahmed 1991).

Biotoxins and Marine Mammals

The impact of biotoxins on marine mammals is less well understood than that for human populations, yet evidence is mounting that marine algal toxins may have played a significant role in previously unexplained episodic mass mortalities of these animals. In fact, during the period from 1998 to 2003, fully half of the unusual mortality events involving marine mammals were attributed to algal biotoxins as compared to fewer than 10 percent for the preceding six years (T. Rowles, pers. comm.). Although an increased occurrence of harmful algal blooms may partially explain this trend, a greater awareness of these phenomena and their impacts and enhanced toxin detection capabilities have been important contributions to increased recognition of algal biotoxins.

There are several well-documented examples of marine mammal mortality events involving algal biotoxins (reviewed by Van Dolah et al. 2003). For example, Geraci et al. (1989) described the highly unusual mass stranding deaths of fourteen humpback whales in Cape Cod Bay, Massachusetts, between November 1987 and January 1988, apparently as a consequence of consuming Atlantic mackerel contaminated with PSP toxins. The authors suggested that the diving adaptation, which channels blood (and thus the circulating toxin) to the heart and brain and away from organs involved in detoxification (i.e., kidney and liver), rendered the whales more susceptible to PSP toxins. In 1996 the deaths of 149 West Indian manatees in the waters of southwest Florida were linked to exposure to brevetoxins, representing about 5 percent of the entire population of this endangered species (Bossart et al. 1998). The affected animals contained brevetoxins, had edema and hemorrhage in various tissues (e.g., lung, liver), and also exhibited severe trauma to their respiratory system, suggesting inhalation of aerosolized toxin as a primary route of uptake along with oral exposure. A recent report by Scholin et al. (2000) established domoic acid as the likely cause of death for almost sixty California sea lions along the central California coast. The presence of this potent neurotoxin was established unequivocally at each trophic level of the local food web, including the toxin-producing diatom *Pseudo-nitzschia australis,* the planktivorous northern anchovy vector, and the sea lions, with affected animals displaying the behavior and pathology characteristic of the amnesic shellfish poisoning syndrome (Gulland 2000).

Biotoxins and Right Whales

The marine algal biotoxins with the potential to affect North Atlantic right whales can be identified based on the overlap of algal blooms and right whales temporally and geographically (Table 8.2). There are, however, no published data concerning the effects of these biotoxins on right whales in terms of either acute or chronic toxicity or more subtle effects on fetuses and neonatal animals. Nevertheless recent studies have yielded compelling evidence that the PSP toxins represent a risk to right whales by establishing the presence of these biotoxins in their preferred prey species and in the animals themselves. Saxitoxin (STX) and its more than twenty derivatives are a group of neurotoxins, the most potent of which are about 1,000 times more toxic than sodium cyanide. They exert their toxic effect by blocking the opening of voltage-dependent sodium channels, thereby impeding neurotransmission, which results in death by respiratory arrest in humans exposed to as little as 1–4 mg STX equivalents (Evans 1975). It is important to note that, according to

Table 8.2. Marine Algal Toxins under Investigation for Their Potential to Adversely Affect the Health and Reproductive Success of the North Atlantic Right Whale, *Eubalaena glacialis*

Human intoxication syndrome	Toxin class	Source organisms	Mode of action
Paralytic shellfish poisoning (PSP)	Saxitoxin (STX)	*Alexandrium* spp.[a]	Blocks voltage-gated sodium channel (site 1)
Neurotoxic shellfish poisoning (NSP)	Brevetoxin (PbTx)	*Karenia brevis*	Activates voltage-gated sodium channels (site 5)
Amnesic shellfish poisoning (ASP)	Domoic acid (DA)	*Pseudo-nitzschia* spp.	Activates glutamate receptors

a. There are other algal taxa known to produce PSP toxins; however, *Alexandrium* spp. exhibit the closest spatiotemporal overlap with the distribution of *E. glacialis.*

Stoskopf et al. (2001), large mammals generally exhibit a greater sensitivity to the effects of such bioactive compounds.

Dinoflagellates of the genus *Alexandrium* (*A. tamarense* and *A. fundyense*) are the sole PSP toxin producers with a spatial and temporal distribution overlapping that of the right whale in western North Atlantic waters and thus represent the biological source of the toxin. However, the small size of *Alexandrium* cells (ca. 15–45 mm, transdiameter) precludes direct ingestion of these toxic algae by right whales, whose feeding size threshold is dictated by the baleen's efficiency of sieving particles from the water. In fact it has been well established that the diet of the right whale consists predominantly of larger zooplankton grazers, specifically the calanoid copepod *Calanus finmarchicus* and, to a lesser extent, juvenile euphausiids (Chapter 5). Therefore, the most likely route for exposure of right whales to PSP toxins is via trophic transfer through the grazer component of marine food webs.

Transfer of PSP through the Food Web

In piecing together the route of PSP toxin transfer from *Alexandrium* cells to right whales, it is interesting to note that toxicity levels associated with *Alexandrium* generally increase along a gradient extending from southern New England northward into the Bay of Fundy, Canada (Anderson et al. 1994). Peak abundances of this dinoflagellate in the eastern Gulf of Maine–Bay of Fundy region typically occur during the period from July to September (Martin and White 1988), coinciding with the presence of feeding right whales. The right whale's primary food source, *C. finmarchicus,* is known to consume

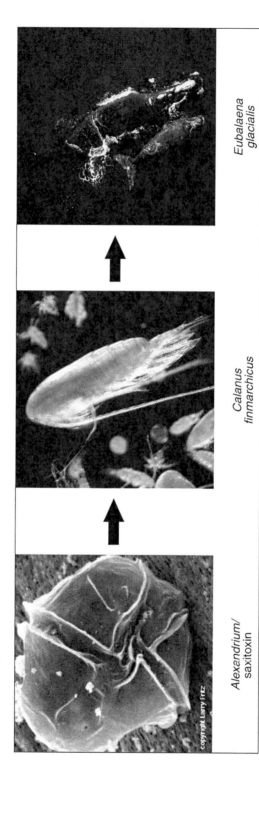

Alexandrium/
saxitoxin

*Calanus
finmarchicus*

*Eubalaena
glacialis*

Figure 8.8. The hypothesized trophic transfer route of PSP toxins from the toxic dinoflagellate *Alexandrium* (Lawrence Fritz / University of New England) to the calanoid copepod *Calanus finmarchicus* (Rebecca Jones / University of New Hampshire) to *Eubalaena glacialis* (Chris Slay / New England Aquarium).

Alexandrium spp. (Turriff et al. 1995), and recent studies have confirmed that PSP toxins do occur in field populations of *C. finmarchicus* (Turner et al. 2000; Doucette et al. 2005) in close proximity to actively feeding right whales (Durbin et al. 2002). The final piece of evidence demonstrating conclusively that these animals are being exposed to PSP toxins has been reported recently and has established the presence of saxitoxin and several of its derivatives in right whale fecal samples (Doucette et al. 2006). Based on the above information, right whales are being exposed to these potent algal neurotoxins primarily through a single zooplankton vector (Fig. 8.8), but what are the potential effects?

Potential Health Effects of PSP in Right Whales

The cumulative toxicity of multiple PSP toxins is commonly expressed in terms of "saxitoxin equivalents." Estimates of right whale ingestion rates for PSP toxins fall in the range of 5–10 mg STX equivalents per kilogram per day (Durbin et al. 2002; Doucette et al. 2006). This rate represents a daily exposure for right whales that is close to the lethal oral dose in humans (ca. 7–16 mg STX equivalents per kilogram) (Evans 1972; Schantz et al. 1975), although a direct extrapolation between humans and whales would be unwise and purely speculative. Additionally, the proposed enhancement of PSP toxicity to humpback whales during a dive (Geraci et al. 1989) may produce similar effects in right whales. Moreover, it has been reported that saxitoxin exhibits specific high-affinity binding to isolated nerve preparations derived from both gray and humpback whales (Trainer and Baden 1999). Thus, the presence of any combination of PSP toxins in right whales would be expected to represent either a direct or indirect risk to these mammals. Direct impacts of toxin exposure could be manifested as physiological or behavioral effects such as alterations in diving patterns or feeding efficiency secondary to respiratory depression. Indirect effects could include enhanced susceptibility to other contaminants or pathogens, or perhaps even an increased potential for ship strikes if whales are spending more time at the surface to breathe. Both pregnant females and young calves in the process of weaning could be exposed to PSP toxins by ingestion of contaminated copepods during spring and summer feeding periods in northern waters. Given the rapid renal clearance rates for the small, water-soluble saxitoxins in humans (i.e., less than twenty-four hours) (Gessner et al. 1997) and the protection of the fetus through its reliance on the mother for renal functions, it seems unlikely (yet unproven) that in utero exposures represent a high risk to unborn animals. However, while young calves are weaning, before their renal system is fully functional, these immature animals could be very susceptible to the effects of biotoxins acquired through their diet (Xi et al. 1997).

Other Biotoxins

The rapidly emerging case for possible adverse impacts of PSP toxins on the right whale population continues to be examined from a growing number of perspectives, but is there any cause for concern with the other algal biotoxins?

The potential for exposure of right whales to brevetoxins (a family of lipid-soluble, sodium channel–activating neurotoxins) does exist, although this appears less likely than for the PSP toxins. Right whales in their calving grounds off Georgia and Florida show a strong preference for water temperatures of 12–15°C (Chapter 16). Because the optimum growth temperature range of the brevetoxin-producing dinoflagellate (*Karenia brevis*) is 22–28°C, the regular overlap of right whales and *K. brevis* blooms seems unlikely. Although contact with low cell numbers may occur, the few high-density *K. brevis* events in this area have been associated with intrusions of warm Gulf Stream waters onto the colder shelf waters, thereby maintaining a temperature-based spatial separation of the whales and dinoflagellates. Because the most likely route of brevetoxin exposure for right whales is via inhalation of aerosolized toxin associated with elevated cell concentrations (no feeding occurs on the calving grounds), this toxin is probably not a threat to these mammals.

On the other hand, domoic acid and diatoms of the genus *Pseudo-nitzschia* that produce this biotoxin are well known to occur in coastal waters of the Gulf of Maine and maritime Canada during the period that right whales are feeding there (Addison and Stewart 1989; Haya et al. 1991; Martin et al. 1993; Fig. 8.9). Domoic acid is a neuroexcitatory amino acid that targets a class of glutamate receptor, causing the death of neuronal cells as well as lesions in areas of the brain rich in these receptors (e.g., regions of the hippocampus). This potent neurotoxin has been associated with several marine mammal mortality events (Van Dolah et al. 2003). The few grazing studies available indicate that copepods, including a species of *Calanus* (i.e., *C. glacialis*), consume both toxic and nontoxic *Pseudo-nitzschia* cells and are capable of retaining toxin following emptying of the gut (Windust 1992; Tester et al. 2001).

The first indication that right whales are being exposed to domoic acid was obtained recently by confirming the presence of this toxin in fecal samples

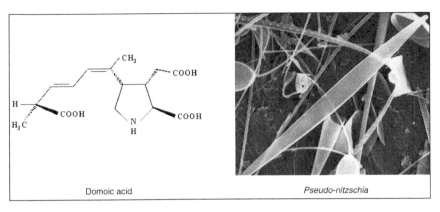

Figure 8.9. Chemical structure of domoic acid and scanning electron micrograph of a *Pseudo-nitzschia* cell. Rita Horner / University of Washington.

(G. Doucette and R. Rolland, unpublished data); however, the primary vector for trophic transfer of this biotoxin to the whales remains to be identified. It is interesting that the potential for direct ingestion of *Pseudo-nitzschia* chains, which can exceed a millimeter in length, does exist. Based on toxicity studies using laboratory animals, it appears that (on a per weight basis) neonates are approximately forty times more sensitive to domoic acid than adults (Xi et al. 1997), likely because of their underdeveloped renal filtration capacity as well as an incomplete development of the blood–brain barrier (Preston and Hynie 1991). As proposed above for the PSP toxins, immature animals in the process of weaning while on the summer feeding grounds could be highly susceptible to the effects of domoic acid exposure. Nonetheless as for PSP toxins, the potential effects of domoic acid on right whales remain unknown.

Future of Biotoxin Research

It is now certain that right whales are being exposed to measurable quantities of both PSP toxins and domoic acid. The route of PSP toxin exposure appears to be via ingestion of the primary prey species, *C. finmarchicus,* now well established to be capable of transferring these toxins from their algal producers. In the case of domoic acid, efforts are under way to identify the primary vector(s) and pathway of toxin trophic transfer within food webs of the northern feeding grounds. It must be realized, however, that any proposed effects of these potent, algal-derived neurotoxins on right whales and their reproductive success are based primarily on laboratory studies of model systems or human symptoms and are speculative. Moreover, no studies have begun to address the issue of the long-term effects of chronic, sublethal exposure. Analysis of fecal material should be expanded to include whales sampled before, during, and after migration into their northern summer feeding grounds to develop a more complete picture of biotoxin exposure in different habitats and over different time scales. And should current efforts to develop right whale cell lines for laboratory-based in vitro toxicity testing prove successful, this may provide a valuable tool for beginning to assess the potential health effects of biotoxins in these highly endangered marine mammals.

Parasites and Right Whales

Negative impacts on fecundity, abundance, and population dynamics from parasitic diseases are well described in many vertebrates (reviewed in Grenfell and Dobson 1995). A variety of parasites have been described in cetaceans (mostly in captive species), some of which are known to have major effects on health (Dailey 2001). However, until recently there were no published studies of parasites in right whales or of their potential for impacts on health and reproduction.

Right whales may be uniquely at risk from morbidity and mortality caused by parasitic diseases for several reasons. Studies have shown that this population has very limited genetic diversity, which is known to increase disease susceptibility in many species (Chapter 7). Furthermore the extensive use of densely populated coastal habitats by North Atlantic right whales may result in exposure to protozoa and other pathogens from sewage outfalls and non-point sources of pollution, such as rainwater runoff from urban, suburban, and agricultural sources. For example in the southern sea otter, a significant cause of mortality has been linked to infection with the protozoan parasite *Toxoplasma gondii* (Cole et al. 2000). The definitive hosts for *Toxoplasma* are cats, and sea otters are exposed to this organism around urbanized coastal areas in waters that are contaminated with domestic cat feces carrying the infective stage of the parasite (Miller et al. 2002). Although it seems unbelievable that contamination of the coastal zone with domestic cat feces is extensive enough that diseases are being transferred to sea otters feeding near heavily populated areas, this research leaves little doubt that this is exactly what is happening.

In 2002, studies were initiated to characterize the types of gastrointestinal parasites found in right whale feces. Samples were analyzed for the presence of helminth parasites (nematodes, trematodes, and flukes) by fecal flotation and sedimentation. Additionally, samples were examined using immunofluorescent methods for the presence of two protozoa, *Giardia* and *Cryptosporidium.* The results showed that 14 percent of whales carried the operculated eggs of an as yet unidentified parasite, but even more surprising, 71 percent of right whale samples were positive for *Giardia,* and 24 percent of the samples were positive for *Cryptosporidium* (Hughes-Hanks et al. 2005). Compared to most other marine mammals, these are exceptionally high infection rates. How are right whales becoming exposed to these protozoa, and are they causing disease?

The Parasites

Giardia and *Cryptosporidium* are microscopic, single-celled organisms found in humans and many animals worldwide (Figs. 8.10 and 8.11). Infection with these protozoa results from ingestion of the infectious cysts *(Giardia)* or oocysts *(Cryptosporidium)* through contaminated food or water. These parasites are one of the most common causes of gastrointestinal disease in humans and terrestrial animals and can cause serious diarrhea, dehydration, weight loss, and even death in severe cases. Both parasites reside in the intestinal tract, damaging the intestinal wall and interfering with digestion, resulting in diarrhea. However, they can also be present without any apparent ill effects. Why some animals and people get very ill when infected with these parasites and others do not is not entirely clear. The species and genotype of the organism, along with host factors such as age, stress, crowding, immune status, and co-occurrence of other diseases, seem to play a role (Thompson 2000; Thompson and Monis 2004; Xiao et al. 2004).

Giardia and *Cryptosporidium* in the Marine Environment

Although *Giardia* and *Cryptosporidium* have been considered primarily contaminants of fresh water, recent evidence confirms that they are present in coastal waters as well. They have been found near sewage outflows, in sediments, and in several species of marine mammals and shellfish (Fayer et al. 2004). These encysted protozoa are able to survive for long periods in the marine environment. But where did they come from? Is it a matter of widespread fecal contamination from land coming into the sea? Or are there organisms specific to certain marine mammals that are naturally cycling within the marine environment?

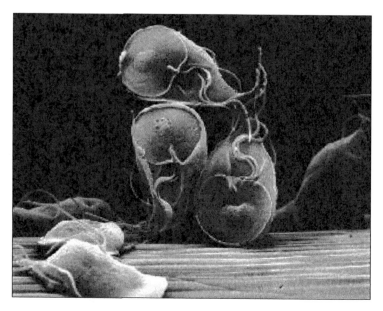

Figure 8.10. Scanning electron microscopic view of *Giardia lamblia* trophozoites. Courtesy of A. González-Robles / CINVESTAV, Mexico.

In all likelihood both terrestrial and marine mammals are contributing to contamination of the marine environment with these protozoa. There is ample evidence that fecal contamination originating on land is entering the sea. It is estimated that as much as 5.45 billion metric tons of livestock manure and 232 million metric tons of human waste are produced worldwide each year, and most of it ends up in rivers, estuaries, and bays, eventually reaching the oceans (Fayer et al. 2004). The presence of particular species of *Giardia* and *Cryptosporidium* in contaminated shellfish and marine waters implicates human waste as well as agricultural runoff as possible sources of marine contamination. However, it is also possible that some marine mammal isolates of *Cryptosporidium* and *Giardia* have distinct host preferences and cycle only among these species. Until genetic typing of isolates obtained from marine mammals is done, it is impossible to determine the source of parasites found in any marine mammal, including right whales.

Giardia and *Cryptosporidium* in Marine Mammals

Information on species of *Giardia* and *Cryptosporidium* in marine mammals is limited, partly because of the inherent difficulty of working with wild pop-

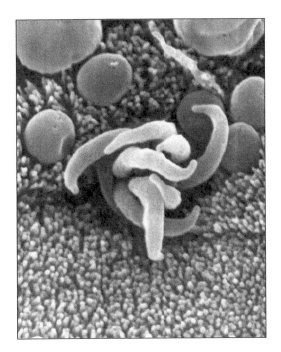

Figure 8.11. Scanning electron micrograph of *Cryptosporidium parvum* from sheep. C. A. Speer / University of Tennessee.

ulations. Nevertheless both *Giardia* and *Cryptosporidium* have been identified in the feces of several different marine mammal species from different geographic regions (Table 8.3). Few isolates of either organism from marine mammals have been characterized genetically, however, and the effect of these infections is unknown. Experimental infections of harp seal pups with *Cryptosporidium* demonstrated that seal pups can show clinical signs of this disease (Olson et al. 2004). The same study also showed that both parasites are capable of using indirect routes of transmission when pups developed infections through fecal contamination of tank salt water.

Giardia and *Cryptosporidium* in Right Whales

The reason for the extremely high prevalences of *Giardia* and *Cryptosporidium* in right whales remains unknown, as do the effects of these infections on right whale health. A close relative of right whales, the bowhead whale, has a much lower prevalence of both parasites (Table 8.3). Could this be because these bowheads live in the western Arctic, an area much less influenced by

Table 8.3. Prevalence of *Giardia* and *Cryptosporidium* in Marine Mammals, Including Right Whales

Host	Parasite	Location	No. positive/No. examined
North Atlantic right whale	*Giardia*	Bay of Fundy, Canada	71% (35/49)
	Cryptosporidium		24% (12/49)
Bowhead whale	*Giardia*	Arctic Alaska	33% (13/39)
	Cryptosporidium		5% (2/39)
Beluga whale	*Giardia*	St. Lawrence estuary	0% (0/11)
		Western Arctic Canada	0% (0/16)
		Arctic Alaska	0% (0/18)
Northern bottle-nosed whale	*Giardia*	Sept-Iles, St. Lawrence estuary	0% (0/1)
Ringed seal	*Giardia*	Arctic Alaska	65% (20/31)
		Ungava Bay, Canada	? (43/[a])
	Cryptosporidium	Arctic Alaska	23% (7/31)
		Ungava Bay, Canada	? (2/[a])
Harp seal	*Giardia*	Gulf of St. Lawrence / Newfoundland	32% (15/47)
Grey seal	*Giardia*	Gulf of St. Lawrence	21% (4/19)
Harbor seal	*Giardia*	St. Lawrence estuary	13% (1/8)
		California, USA	0% (0/13)
	Cryptosporidium	California, USA	0% (0/13)
Bearded seal	*Giardia*	Arctic Alaska	0% (0/22)
	Cryptosporidium	Arctic Alaska	0% (0/22)
California sea lions	*Giardia*	California, USA	0% (1/6)
	Cryptosporidium		50% (3/6)
Northern elephant seals	*Giardia*	California, USA	0% (0/8)
	Cryptosporidium		0% (0/8)
Dugong	*Cryptosporidium*	Hervey Bay, Australia	100% (1/1)

a. Number examined not reported.

Data are from Hill et al. (1997), Olson et al. (1997), Measures and Olson (1999), Deng et al. (2000), Fayer et al. (2004), and Hughes-Hanks et al. (2005).

human population pressures? Alternatively, a different species or genotype of these parasites could be present in bowhead infections. It is also possible that limited genetic diversity in the North Atlantic right whale population allows the parasites to spread more efficiently among whales.

Ongoing studies to genotype the organisms found in right whales should provide answers to some of these questions, such as their origins. Genetic studies of right whales, particularly of the major histocompatibility complex, may shed light on their immune system function and clarify if they have enhanced susceptibility to diseases (Chapter 7). Finally, comparison of the other health indices that have been developed for right whales (e.g., fecal stress hormone levels, visual health assessment scores) with the presence of infection in individual whales may provide insights into the possible health impacts of these protozoa in right whales.

Conclusion

As this chapter illustrates, fecal-based research is providing many new insights into right whale health and reproduction. Analysis of fecal reproductive hormones reliably predicts a whale's gender, reproductive state (pregnancy and lactation), and sexual maturity of males. Comparison of hormone levels to the reproductive history of individual whales (retrospectively and prospectively) can be used to investigate the possibility of pregnancy loss, reproductive senescence, and infertility. Measurement of fecal glucocorticoids provides a quantitative index of relative stress that is useful at both individual and population levels to evaluate health status and the impacts of anthropogenic factors on right whales. Analysis of marine biotoxins in scat has shown that right whales are being exposed to both PSP and domoic acid in the Bay of Fundy, although, as yet, the potential for health impacts remains unknown. Finally, parasitology studies have revealed that right whales have the highest prevalence of infection with *Giardia* and *Cryptosporidium* of any marine mammal yet examined.

To maximize fecal sample collection, the use of scat detection dogs has been indispensable. It is likely that detection dogs could be employed for shipboard surveys of several other marine mammal species, as long as feces were available for prior training. Under the appropriate conditions dogs have the capacity to detect the target species' scat at distances of at least a nautical mile in vast ocean areas.

Without the ability to collect blood from living whales, researchers have until now been in the dark regarding large whale physiology, reproductive cycles, and diseases. The rapidly developing tools for fecal analysis are already shedding light into these areas. The studies described in this chapter form the basis of an individual-based profile of health and reproductive status, improving scientists' ability to understand trends in reproduction, health, and mortality in North Atlantic right whales.

Addison, R. F., and J. E. Stewart. 1989. Domoic acid and the eastern Canadian molluscan shellfish industry. *Aquaculture* 77:263–269.

Adlercreutz, H., and P. Järvenpää. 1982. Assay of estrogens in human feces. *Journal of Steroid Biochemistry* 17:639–645.

Ahmed, F. E. 1991. *Seafood Safety.* National Academy Press, Washington, DC.

Anderson, D. M. 1994. Red tides. *Scientific American* 271:52–58.

Anderson, D. M., D. M. Kulis, G. J. Doucette, J. C. Gallagher, and E. Balech. 1994. Biogeography of toxic dinoflagellates in the genus *Alexandrium* from the northeastern United States and Canada. *Marine Biology* 120:467–478.

Balm, P. H. M. (ed.). 1999. *Stress Physiology in Animals.* CRC Press, Boca Raton, FL.

Barrett, G. M., K. Shimuzu, M. Bardi, S. Asaba, and A. Mori. 2002. Endocrine correlates of rank, reproduction, and female-directed aggression in male Japanese macaques (*Macaca fuscata*). *Hormones and Behavior* 42:85–96.

Best, P. B. 1994. Seasonality of reproduction and the length of gestation in southern right whales *Eubalaena australis. Journal of Zoology (London)* 232:175–189.

Bossart, G. D., D. G. Baden, R. Y. Ewing, B. Roberts, and S. D. Wright. 1998. Brevetoxicosis in manatees (*Trichechus manatus latriostris*) from the 1996 epizootic: gross, histologic, and immunohistochemical features. *Toxicologic Pathology* 26:276–282.

Cole, R. A., D. S. Lindsay, D. K. Howe, C. L. Roderick, N. J. Thomas, and L. A. Baeten. 2000. Biological and molecular characterization of *Toxoplasma gondii* strains obtained from southern sea otters (*Enhydra lutris nereis*). *Journal of Parasitology* 86:526–530.

Creel, S., N. M. Creel, M. G. L. Mills, and S. L. Monfort. 1997. Rank and reproduction in cooperatively breeding African wild dogs: behavioral and endocrine correlates. *Behavioral Ecology* 8:298–306.

Creel, S., J. E. Fox, A. Hardy, J. Sands, B. Garrott, and R. O. Peterson. 2002. Snowmobile activity and glucocorticoid stress responses in wolves and elk. *Conservation Biology* 16:809–814.

Dailey, M. D. 2001. Parasitic diseases. Pages 357–379 *in* L. A. Dierauf and F. M. D. Gulland, eds. *CRC Handbook of Marine Mammal Medicine.* CRC Press, Boca Raton, FL.

Deng, M., R. P. Peterson, and D. O. Cliver. 2000. First findings of *Cryptosporidium* and *Giardia* in California sea lions (*Zalophus californianus*). *Journal of Parasitology* 86:490–494.

Desportes, G., M. Saboureau, and A. Lacroix. 1994. Growth-related changes in testicular mass and plasma testosterone concentrations in long-finned pilot whales, *Globicephala melas. Journal of Reproduction and Fertility* 102:237–244.

Dloniak, S. M., J. A. French, N. J. Place, M. L. Weldele, S. E. Glickman, and K. E. Holekamp. 2004. Non-invasive monitoring of fecal androgens in spotted hyenas (*Crocuta crocuta*). *General and Comparative Endocrinology* 135:51–61.

Doucette, G. J., J. T. Turner, C. L. Powell, B. A. Keafer, and D. M. Anderson. 2005. ECOHAB-Gulf of Maine. Trophic accumulation of PSP toxins in zooplankton during *Alexandrium* blooms in Casco Bay, Gulf of Maine, April–June, 1998. I. Toxin levels in *Alexandrium* and zooplankton size fractions. *Deep-Sea Research* 52:2764–2783.

Doucette, G. J., A. D. Cembella, J. L. Martin, J. Michaud, T. V. N. Cole, and R. M. Rolland. 2006. PSP toxins in North Atlantic right whales (*Eubalaena glacialis*) and their zooplankton prey in the Bay of Fundy, Canada. *Marine Ecology Progress Series* 306:303–313.

Durbin, E., G. Teegarden, R. Campbell, A. Cembella, M. F. Baumgartner, and B. R. Mate. 2002. North Atlantic right whales, *Eubalaena glacialis,* exposed to paralytic shellfish poisoning (PSP) toxins via a zooplankton vector, *Calanus finmarchicus. Harmful Algae* 1:243–251.

Evans, M. H. 1972. Tetrodotoxin, saxitoxin, and related substances: their applications in neurobiology. *International Review of Neurobiology* 15:83–176.

Evans, M. 1975. Saxitoxin and related poisons: their actions on man and other animals. Pages 337–345 *in* V. R. LoCicero, ed. *Toxic Dinoflagellate Blooms.* Massachusetts Science Technology Foundation, Wakefield, MA.

Fayer, R., J. P. Dubey, and D. S. Lindsay. 2004. Zoonotic protozoa: from land to sea. *Trends in Parasitology* 20:531–536.

Foley, C. A. H., S. Papageorge, and S. K. Wasser. 2001. Non-invasive stress and reproductive measures of social and ecological pressures in free-ranging African elephants (*Loxodonta africana*). *Conservation Biology* 15:1134–1142.

Geraci, J. R., D. M. Anderson, R. J. Timperi, D. J. St. Aubin, G. A. Early, J. H. Prescott, and C. A. Mayo. 1989. Humpback whales (*Megaptera novaeangliae*) fatally poisoned by dinoflagellate toxin. *Canadian Journal of Fisheries and Aquatic Sciences* 46:1895–1898.

Gessner, B. D., P. Bell, G. J. Doucette, E. Moczydlowski, M. A. Poli, F. M. Van Dolah, and S. Hall. 1997. Hypertension and identification of toxin in human urine and serum following a cluster of mussel-associated paralytic shellfish poisoning out-breaks. *Toxicon* 35:711–722.

Goymann, W., E. Möstl, T. Van't Hof, M. L. East, and H. Hofer. 1999. Non-invasive fecal monitoring of glucocorticoids in spotted hyaenas, *Crocuta crocuta. General and Comparative Endocrinology* 114:340–348.

Grenfell, B. T., and A. P. Dobson. 1995. *Ecology of Infectious Diseases in Natural Populations.* Cambridge University Press, Cambridge, UK.

Gulland, F. 2000. Domoic acid toxicity in California sea lions (*Zalophus californianus*) stranded along the central California coast, May–October 1998. Report to the National Marine Fisheries Service Working Group on Unusual Marine Mammal Mortality Events. U.S. Department of Commerce, NOAA Technical Memorandum NMFS-OPR-17A, Washington, DC. 45 pp.

Hallegraeff, G. M. 1993. A review of harmful algal blooms and their apparent global increase. *Phycologia* 32:79–99.

Haya, K., J. L. Martin, L. E. Burridge, B. A. Waiwood, and D. J. Wildish. 1991. Domoic acid in shellfish and plankton from the Bay of Fundy, New Brunswick, Canada. *Journal of Shellfish Research* 10:113–118.

Hill, B. D., I. R. Fraser, and H. C. Prior. 1997. *Cryptosporidium* infection in a dugong (*Dugong dugon*). *Australian Veterinary Journal* 75:640–641.

Hughes-Hanks, J. M., L. G. Rickard, C. Panuska, J. R. Saucier, T. M. O'Hara, L. Dehn, and R. M. Rolland. 2005. Prevalence of *Cryptosporidium* spp. and *Giardia* spp. in five marine mammal species. *Journal of Parasitology* 91(5):1225–1228.

Hunt, K. E., R. M. Rolland, S. D. Kraus, and S. K. Wasser. 2006. Analysis of fecal glucocorticoids in the North Atlantic right whale (*Eubalaena glacialis*). *General and Comparative Endocrinology* 148:260–272.

Iga, K., Y. Fukui, and A. Miyamoto. 1996. Endocrinological observations of female minke whales (*Balaenoptera acutorostrata*). *Marine Mammal Science* 12:296–301.

IWC. 2001a. Report of the workshop on status and trends in western North Atlantic right whales. *Journal of Cetacean Research and Management* Special Issue 2:61–87.

IWC. 2001b. Report of the workshop on the comprehensive assessment of right whales: a worldwide comparison. *Journal of Cetacean Research and Management* Special Issue 2:1–60.

Kita, S., M. Yoshioka, and M. Kashiwagi. 1999. Relationship between sexual maturity and serum and testis testosterone concentrations in short-finned pilot whales *Globicephala macrorhynchus. Fisheries Science* 65:878–883.

Kjeld, J. M., J. Sigurjónsson, and A. Árnason. 1992. Sex hormone concentrations in blood serum from the North Atlantic fin whale (*Balaenoptera physalus*). *Journal of Endocrinology* 134:405–413.

Kraus, S. D., K. E. Moore, C. E. Price, M. J. Crone, W. A. Watkins, H. E. Winn, and J. H. Prescott. 1986. The use of photographs to identify individual North

Atlantic right whales (*Eubalaena glacialis*). *Report of the International Whaling Commission* Special Issue 10:145–151.

Kraus, S. D., P. K. Hamilton, R. D. Kenney, A. R. Knowlton, and C. K. Slay. 2001. Reproductive parameters of the North Atlantic right whale. *Journal of Cetacean Research and Management* Special Issue 2:231–236.

Landsberg, J. H. 2002. The effects of harmful algal blooms on aquatic organisms. *Reviews in Fisheries Science* 10:1–113.

Larkin, I. L. V., T. S. Gross, and R. L. Reep. 2005. Use of faecal testosterone concentrations to monitor male Florida manatee (*Trichechus manatus latirostris*) reproductive state. *Aquatic Mammals* 31:52–61.

Larson, S., C. J. Casson, and S. Wasser. 2003. Noninvasive reproductive steroid hormone estimates from fecal samples of captive female sea otters (*Enhydra lutris*). *General and Comparative Endocrinology* 134:18–25.

Lefebvre, K. A., S. Bargu, T. Kieckhefer, and M. W. Silver. 2002. From sanddabs to blue whales: the pervasiveness of domoic acid. *Toxicon* 40:971–977.

Lockyer, C. 1984. Review of baleen whale (Mysticeti) reproduction and implications for management. *Reports of the International Whaling Commission* Special Issue 6:27–50.

Martin, J. L., and A. White. 1988. Distribution and abundance of the toxic dinoflagellate *Gonyaulax excavata* in the Bay of Fundy. *Canadian Journal of Fisheries and Aquatic Sciences* 45:1968–1975.

Martin, J. L., K. Haya, and D. J. Wildish. 1993. Distribution and domoic acid content of *Nitzschia pseudodelicatissima* in the Bay of Fundy. Pages 613–618 *in* T. J. Smayda and Y. Shimizu, eds. *Toxic Phytoplankton Blooms in the Sea.* Elsevier Scientific Publishers B. V., Amsterdam.

Measures, L. M., and M. Olson. 1999. Giardiasis in pinnipeds from Eastern Canada. *Journal of Wildlife Diseases* 35:779–782.

Miller, M. A., I. Gardner, C. Kreuder, D. Paradies, K. Worcester, D. Jessup, E. Dodd, M. Harris, J. Ames, A. Packham, and P. Conrad. 2002. Coastal freshwater runoff is a risk factor for *Toxoplasma gondii* infection of southern sea otters (*Enhydra lutris nereis*). *International Journal of Parasitology* 32:997–1006.

Mogoe, T., T. Suzuki, M. Asada, Y. Fukui, H. Ishikawa, and S. Ohsumi. 2000. Southern minke whale (*Balaenoptera acutorostrata*) testis during the feeding season. *Marine Mammal Science* 16:559–569.

Olson, M. E., P. D. Roach, M. Stabler, and W. Chan. 1997. Giardiasis in ringed seals from the western arctic. *Journal of Wildlife Diseases* 33:646–648.

Olson, M. E., A. Appelbee, and L. Measures. 2004. *Giardia duodenalis* and *Cryptosporidium parvum* infections in pinnipeds. *Veterinary Parasitology* 125:131–132.

Palme, R., P. Fischer, H. Schildorfer, and M. N. Ismail. 1996. Excretion of infused ^{14}C-steroid hormones via faeces and urine in domestic livestock. *Animal Reproduction Science* 43:43–63.

Parsons, K. M., J. W. Durban, and D. E. Claridge. 2003. Comparing two alternative methods for sampling small cetaceans for molecular analysis. *Marine Mammal Science* 19:224–231.

Preston, E., and I. Hynie. 1991. Transfer constants for blood-brain barrier permeation of the neuroexcitatory shellfish toxin, domoic acid. *Canadian Journal of Neurological Sciences* 18:39–44.

Reeves, R. R., R. M. Rolland, and P. J. Clapham (eds.). 2001. Causes of reproductive failure in North Atlantic right whales: New avenues of research. Report of a workshop held 26–28 April 2000, Falmouth, Massachusetts. Northeast Fisheries Science Center Reference Document 01–16, Woods Hole, MA. 46 pp.

Rolland, R. M., K. E. Hunt, S. D. Kraus, and S. K. Wasser. 2005. Assessing reproductive status of right whales (*Eubalaena glacialis*) using fecal hormone metabolites. *General and Comparative Endocrinology* 142:308 317.

Rolland, R. M., P. K. Hamilton, S. D. Kraus, B. Davenport, R. M. Gillett, and S. K. Wasser. In press. Faecal sampling using detection dogs to study health and reproduction in North Atlantic right whales (*Eubalaena glacialis*). *Journal of Cetacean Research and Management*.

St. Aubin, D., and L. A. Dierauf. 2001. Stress and marine mammals. Pages 253–270 *in* L. A. Dierauf and F. M. D. Gulland, eds. *CRC Handbook of Marine Mammal Medicine*. CRC Press, Boca Raton, FL.

Schantz, E. J., V. E. Ghazzarossian, H. K. Schnoes, F. M. Strong, J. P. Stringer, J. O. Pezzanite, and J. Clardy. 1975. Paralytic poisons from marine dinoflagellates. Pages 267–274 *in* V. R. LoCicero, ed. *Toxic Dinoflagellate Blooms*. Massachusetts Science and Technology Foundation, Wakefield, MA.

Scholin, C. A., F. Gulland, G. J. Doucette, S. Benson, M. Busman, F. P. Chavez, J. Cordaro, R. DeLong, A. De Vogelaere, J. Harvey, M. Haulena, K. Lefebvre, T. Lipscomb, S. Loscutoff, L. J. Lowenstine, R. Marin III, P. E. Miller, W. A. McLellan, P. D. R. Moeller, C. L. Powell, T. Rowles, P. Silvagni, M. Silver, T. Spraker, V. Trainer, and F. M. Van Dolah. 2000. Mortality of sea lions along the central California coast linked to a toxic diatom bloom. *Nature* 403:80–84.

Schwarzenberger, F., E. Möstl, R. Palme, and E. Bamberg. 1996. Faecal steroid analysis for noninvasive monitoring of reproductive status in farm, wild and zoo animals. *Animal Reproduction Science* 42:515–526.

Sellner, K. G., G. J. Doucette, and G. Kirkpatrick. 2003. Harmful algal blooms: causes, impacts and detection. *Journal of Industrial Microbiology and Biotechnology* 30:383–406.

Smayda, T. J. 1990. Novel and nuisance phytoplankton blooms in the sea: evidence for a global epidemic. Pages 29–40 *in* E. Granéli, B. Sundström, L. Edler, and D. M. Anderson, eds. *Toxic Marine Phytoplankton*. Elsevier, New York.

Smith, D. A., K. Ralls, A. Hurt, B. Adams, M. Parker, B. Davenport, M. C. Smith, and J. E. Maldonado. 2003. Detection and accuracy rates of dogs trained to find scats of San Joaquin kit foxes (*Vulpes macrotis mutica*). *Animal Conservation* 6:339–346.

Smith, S. C., and H. Whitehead. 2000. The diet of Galapagos sperm whales (*Physeter macrocephalus*) as indicated by fecal sample analysis. *Marine Mammal Science* 16:315–325.

Stoskopf, M. K., S. Willens, and J. F. McBain. 2001. Pharmaceuticals and formularies. Pages 703–727 *in* L. Dierauf and F. M. D. Gulland, eds. *CRC Handbook of Marine Mammal Medicine*. CRC Press, Boca Raton, FL.

Tester, P. A., Y. Pan, and G. J. Doucette. 2001. Accumulation of domoic acid activity in copepods. Pages 418–420 *in* G. M. Hallegraeff, S. I. Blackburn, C. J. Bolch, and R. J. Lewis, eds. *Harmful Algal Blooms 2000*. IOC of UNESCO, Paris, France.

Thompson, R. C. A. 2000. Giardiasis as a re-emerging infectious disease and its zoonotic potential. *International Journal for Parasitology* 30:1259–1267.

Thompson, R. C. A., and P. T. Monis. 2004. Variation in *Giardia:* implications for taxonomy and epidemiology. *Advances in Parasitology* 58:69–137.

Trainer, V. L., and D. G. Baden. 1999. High affinity binding of red tide neurotoxins to marine mammal brain. *Aquatic Toxicology* 46:139–148.

Tucker, H. A. 1988. Lactation and its hormonal control. Pages 1393–2413 *in* E. Knobil and J. D. Neill, eds. *The Physiology of Reproduction*. Raven Press, New York.

Turner, J. T., G. J. Doucette, C. L. Powell, D. M. Kulis, B. A. Keafer, and D. M. Anderson. 2000. Accumulation of red tide toxins in larger size fractions of zooplankton assemblages from Massachusetts Bay, USA. *Marine Ecology Progress Series* 203:95–107.

Turriff, N., J. A. Runge, and A. D. Cembella. 1995. Toxin accumulation and feeding behaviour of the planktonic copepod *Calanus finmarchicus* exposed to the red-tide dinoflagellate *Alexandrium excavatum*. *Marine Biology* 123:55–64.

Van Dolah, F. M. 2000. Marine algal toxins: Origins, health effects, and their increased occurrence. *Environmental Health Perspectives* 108 (Supplement 1):133–141.

Van Dolah, F. M., G. J. Doucette, F. M. D. Gulland, T. L. Rowles, and G. D. Bossart. 2003. Impacts of algal toxins on marine mammals. Pages 247–269 *in* J. G. Vos, G. D. Bossart, M. Fournier, and T. O'Shea, eds. *Toxicology of Marine Mammals*. Taylor and Francis, New York.

Wasser, S. K., S. L. Monfort, J. Southers, and D. E. Wildt. 1994. Excretion rates and metabolites of oestradiol and progesterone in baboon (*Papio cynocephalus*) faeces. *Journal of Reproduction and Fertility* 101:213–220.

Wasser, S. K., K. Bevis, G. King, and E. Hanson. 1997. Noninvasive physiological measures of disturbance in the Northern Spotted Owl. *Conservation Biology* 11:1019–1022.

Wasser, S. K., K. E. Hunt, J. L. Brown, K. Cooper, C. M. Crockett, U. Bechert, J. J. Millspaugh, S. Larson, and S. L. Monfort. 2000. A generalized fecal glucocorticoid assay for use in a diverse array of non-domestic mammalian and avian species. *General and Comparative Endocrinology* 120:260–275.

Wasser, S. K., B. Davenport, E. R. Ramage, K. E. Hunt, M. Parker, C. Clarke, and G. Stenhouse. 2004. Scat detection dogs in wildlife research and management: application to grizzly and black bears in the Yellowhead Ecosystem, Alberta, Canada. *Canadian Journal of Zoology* 82:475–492.

Windust, A. 1992. The responses of bacteria, microalgae and zooplankton to the diatom *Nitzschia pungens* f. *multiseries* and its toxic metabolite domoic acid. M.Sc. thesis, Dalhousie University, Halifax, NS, Canada.

Wingfield, J. C., D. L. Maney, C. W. Breuner, J. D. Jacobs, S. Lynn, S., M. Ramenofsky, and R. D. Richardson. 1998. Ecological bases of hormone-behavior interactions: the "emergency life history stage." *American Zoologist* 38:191–206.

Xi, D., Y. G. Peng, and J. S. Ramsdell. 1997. Domoic acid is a potent neurotoxin to neonatal rats. *Natural Toxins* 5:74–79.

Xiao, L., R. Fayer, U. Ryan, and S. J. Upton. 2004. *Cryptosporidium* taxonomy: recent advances and implications for public health. *Clinical Microbiology Reviews* 17:72–97.

Acknowledgments

Special appreciation goes to Phillip Clapham, who early on understood the value of these studies for right whale conservation. We also thank Patricia Lawson, Richard Merrick, Teri Rowles, Greg Silber, and Janet Whaley for their continuing support for this research. Thanks to Kerry Lagueux for expert assistance with graphics. We are grateful to the members of the New England Aquarium Right Whale Team, the many individuals who have helped collect samples in the Bay of Fundy and elsewhere, and to the members of the North Atlantic Right Whale Consortium for access to the photographic and life history information in the *North Atlantic Right Whale Catalog* and Database. Photographs of right whales in the Bay of Fundy were taken with permission from Fisheries and Oceans Canada. Funding for these projects was from the National Marine Fisheries Service and the Northeast Consortium (to R. Rolland), and operational funds from the National Ocean Service and National Marine Fisheries Service (to G. Doucette).

9

External Perspectives on Right Whale Health

ROSALIND M. ROLLAND, PHILIP K. HAMILTON,
MARILYN K. MARX, HEATHER M. PETTIS,
CAROLYN M. ANGELL, AND MICHAEL J. MOORE

16 September 2001
Offshore east of Cape Cod

Churchill (Eg #1102) is not doing well. The fishing lines entangling his head and mouth are deeply embedded under the skin of his rostrum, and the wound is badly infected. Because the lines are so tightly wrapped around his head, he has been unable to open his cavernous mouth to feed, forcing him to live off his blubber layer for months. His formerly rotund shape and shiny black skin have given way to white blotches and gray peeling skin, protruding bones around the spine and back, deep radiating cracks in the skin around his blowholes, and a heavy covering of orange whale lice: sure signs of decaying health. He is basically skin and bones. His struggles to shake himself free of fishing gear have come to an end. He is offshore, seeking warmer water to reduce the demands of trying to keep warm without his insulating blubber. But there is no life left in him, and after a few final weak blows, he sinks into the abyss, taking his satellite telemetry buoy with him, never to be seen again.

Churchill's ending did not reflect his life. He was a bit of a Don Juan among right whales, with a sighting record in which 45 percent of all observations of him were made while he was engaged in courtship activities. From genetic paternity analysis, we know that he had at least two calves with different females: a male (Eg #2303) in 1993 with Slash (Eg #1303) and a female in 1997 named Silver (Eg #2705) with Yawn (Eg #1405). Clearly, Churchill had been a healthy male. He had adapted to different conditions as well. For the first ten years of our records, Churchill was sighted only in the offshore habitats of the Great South Channel and the Nova Scotian Shelf. However, after 1991, when oceanographic patterns in the Gulf of Maine changed, Churchill was seen only in the coastal waters of Massachusetts and in the Bay of Fundy. His last three months were atypical in this regard, as the sightings while he was entangled ranged from the offshore waters east of Cape Cod up to Nova Scotia and the Gulf of St. Lawrence. A satellite telemetry buoy attached to Churchill showed widespread travels while he was entangled in fishing gear: over one hundred days Churchill traveled almost 9,000 km.

The last time that Churchill was photographed free of fishing gear was in the summer of 1998 in the Bay of Fundy, when Michael Moore and Carolyn Angell obtained a measurement of his blubber thickness by touching him briefly on the back with an ultrasound probe. He wasn't seen again until 8 June 2001, when a National Marine Fisheries Service aerial survey team photographed him in the Great South Channel with a heavy green fishing line wrapped around his rostrum, lodged tightly in his baleen. The next day, the Provincetown Center for Coastal Studies' disentanglement team traveled to Churchill's last location to evaluate his condition and attempt to free him from the gear. Their assessment found that Churchill was in a very poor physical state, that the line was tightly embedded around his rostrum, and that his condition was so serious that extreme measures should be taken to disentangle him. The team was able to attach a VHF/ satellite telemetry buoy to the fishing line trailing 18 m behind Churchill, allowing them to track his movements and relocate the whale for further disentanglement attempts.

Between 8 June and 30 August, five attempts were made by a dedicated group of Canadian and U.S. biologists, veterinarians, technicians, and government personnel to rescue Churchill. Numerous lengthy consultations on Churchill's condition with a group of experts led to the consensus that without intervention, Churchill would surely die. The decision was made to try using a combination of chemical restraint (sedatives) and physical restraint using a newly developed tail harness to slow down the whale and allow the team to get close enough to surgically dissect out the line embedded in his rostrum. This would be the first attempt ever at sedating a free-swimming whale. Fortunately a protocol had already been developed to sedate large whales at a workshop organized by Michael Moore in February 2000. One of the biggest challenges in attempting sedation of a 45,000-kg whale was figuring out how to deliver such a large dose of the drugs. Terrence Hammar, an engineer from Woods Hole Oceanographic Institution, and David Brunson, a veterinary anesthesiologist from the University of Wisconsin, designed a whale-sized, gas-powered syringe to deliver the huge volume of the sedative that was needed. Veterinarians had decided that the drug midazolam should be tried first, and David Brunson made a superconcentrated form of this sedative to keep the volume to a minimum. By the time Churchill got entangled, all of the pieces were in place to attempt to sedate a large whale at sea.

On 26 June the disentanglement team accompanied by veterinarians, technicians, and National Marine Fisheries Service personnel set out to Churchill's last location to try sedation and disentanglement. Two doses of the drug were successfully given using the syringe mounted on a pole, but without apparent effect on the whale, and the disentanglement attempt failed. Churchill's condition appeared to be worsening as well. On 14 July another attempt was made, and Churchill was given a higher dose of the drugs, again with no apparent effect. Attempts at slowing Churchill down with a tail harness were also unsuccessful. At this time Churchill's health had noticeably worsened. A fecal sample collected at this time contained the highest levels of stress hormones that had yet been seen: more evidence that Churchill's health was rapidly deteriorating.

Over the following two months Churchill was continuously tracked as the team looked for a chance to attempt another rescue. Choppy seas and foggy weather over the summer made for few weather windows. Additionally, Churchill's travels took him too far offshore for a rescue as he swam all the way north to the Gulf of St. Lawrence. On 30 August the final rescue attempt was made when he returned to the Great South Channel. This time four doses of sedative were successfully given and had a brief effect on the whale, but it was still not enough to allow him to be freed of the lines. At this time Churchill was in extremely poor condition. An aerial survey team located Churchill for the final time on 10 September and noted that he was lying motionless near the surface with his head submerged, breathing only occasionally. On 16 September, the satellite buoy stopped transmitting, *presumably because Churchill had sunk to the sea bottom, 4.5 km below the surface.*

Rosalind Rolland and Scott Kraus

During the mid- to late 1990s biologists observed that many western North Atlantic right whales appeared thin and that many whales had skin lesions, leading to the overall impression that the health of the population was worsening. These symptoms of failing health led researchers to think about techniques to quantify the physical changes that were being observed. Churchill's deterioration during the months that he was fatally entangled in fishing gear provided a graphic example of the physical changes that signal poor health in right whales, and he became the "poster child" for physical decline in these whales, teaching researchers which visual cues to use to assess right whale health from the outside.

Because right whales spend most of their lives underwater, travel the entire length of the eastern United States and maritime Canada (and beyond) yearly, and have individual sighting variability, it is difficult to monitor health regularly and to assess population trends. A few methods have been developed to evaluate health in other free-swimming cetaceans based on external features and morphology. Length and width measurements of gray whales using vertical aerial photogrammetry reliably detected changes in body condition associated with fasting during winter migration (Perryman and Lynn 2002). Thompson and Hammond (1992) monitored the prevalence of skin lesions on the dorsal fins of bottlenose dolphins using images routinely taken for photo-identification. Wilson et al. (1999) evaluated the relationship of skin lesion occurrence in dolphins relative to both natural and anthropogenic environmental factors.

This chapter presents three techniques that have been used to assess body condition and health in right whales from the outside: the external perspectives on right whale health. The first two methods are based on analyses of images taken for photo-identification of individual whales, which are archived in the *North Atlantic Right Whale Catalog* (Chapter 3). These include an analysis of the prevalence and types of skin lesions seen on right whales and a visual health assessment technique based on a system of scoring physical parameters that can be evaluated from photographs. The final section describes the adaptation of ultrasound methodology to evaluate body condition by measuring the blubber thickness of free-swimming right whales.

Skin Lesions in Right Whales

One of the most obvious visual indicators of health in animals is the appearance of their skin or coat. As noted above, starting in the mid-1990s, researchers began to notice a dramatic increase in skin lesions on right whales, prompting concern for their health status. Sleek black skin (sometimes with white belly patches or chins) is normal for a healthy right whale, but many whales were being seen with a variety of abnormal white or blisterlike epidermal (skin) lesions. These observations led to a thorough investigation of skin lesions in right whales for the period 1980–2002 to (1) describe the types of lesions, (2) look at changes in lesion occurrence over time and across habitats, and (3) investigate whether certain ages or sexes were predisposed to develop skin lesions (Hamilton and Marx 2005).

For this study over 25,000 sightings of 439 right whales were reviewed, including images (photographs, slides, digital images) taken in all known right whale habitats. Lesions were classified into two broad categories based on their morphology: white lesions and "blisterlike" lesions (referred to as blister lesions here). Lesions are marks that generally persist for a matter of weeks or months before they resolve into smaller marks or depressions or disappear completely. The appearance of lesions contrasts with that of scars, which are usually permanent white marks with clearly defined borders, and with skin sloughing, which appears as gray skin patches with patterns that vary daily.

Types of Lesions

White lesions appeared in many different shapes and sizes, but all were light in color (creamy white to translucent gray) with indistinct edges (Fig. 9.1). These lesions were classified into four subcategories by their shape, size, and location: circular, outline, swath, and variable. Circular lesions were the most common subcategory. These lesions were bright white, and they were usually found on the head. Outline lesions were translucent-white and outlined the edges of the callosity tissue, the blowholes, or the margins of the lips. Swath lesions were the rarest lesion type and occurred on the head or just behind the blowholes. These were also the largest lesions (more than 45 cm^2), translucent-white in color, often with gray centers, although they occasionally had yellow and pink hues as well. Variable lesions included any white-colored mark that did not fall into one of the three categories above. These were mostly large, amorphous patches of translucent white skin and were generally found on the back or peduncle.

Figure 9.1. Examples of white lesions on right whales: (a) circular (three white arrows) and outline (black arrow) lesions; (b) circular (circled), outline (white arrow), and variable lesions (boxed); (c) swath lesions; and (d) variable lesions on the peduncle. (a) Scott Kraus / New England Aquarium, (b) Cinda Pitt Scott / New England Aquarium, (c) Greg Grund / New England Aquarium, (d) Chris Slay / New England Aquarium.

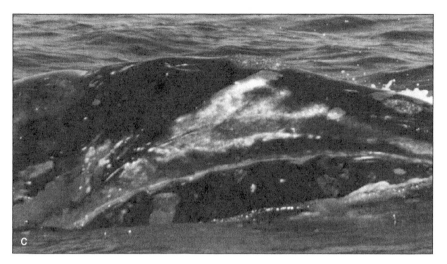

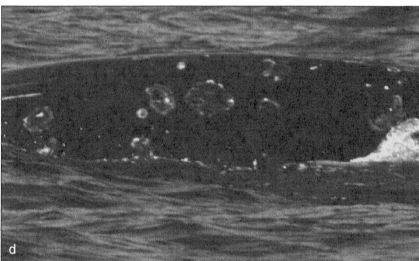

Figure 9.1. (*continued*)

Blister lesions were not as common as white lesions, and they were categorized into only two subcategories: small blisters and craterous eruptions (Fig. 9.2). Small blister lesions were blisterlike vesicles that were multifocal, found primarily on the back, and resolved to small dots. Craterous eruptions referred to single 10- to 15-cm diameter craters in the skin that had raised edges and often had proliferative tissue protruding from the center. In two cases, craterous eruptions resolved over time into cyamid-filled divots.

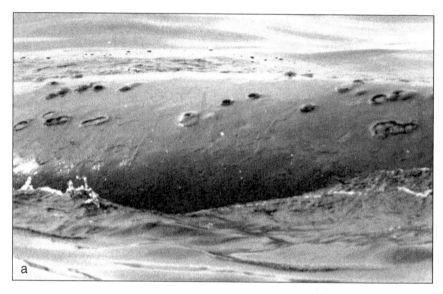

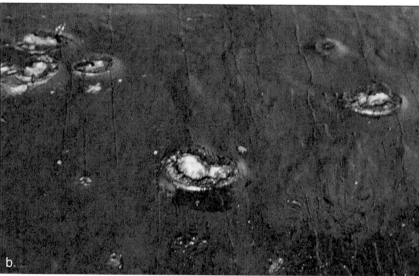

Figure 9.2. Examples of blister lesions on right whales: (a) small blisters; (b) craterous eruptions on a dead whale. (a) Marilyn Marx / Provincetown Center for Coastal Studies, (b) Stephanie Martin / New England Aquarium.

Several miscellaneous lesion types that have not been fully analyzed were also observed. These included tattoolike lesions, spiral or dotted lines that trail from circular white lesions, multicolored splotchy lesions that covered large areas of the back, and raised skin patches that are unlike blisters (Fig. 9.3). Although Hamilton and Marx (2005) did not provide epidemiological data on these lesion types, examples are included here for comparison with the other lesion subcategories.

White Lesion Characteristics

When the data on occurrence of white lesions were analyzed, some interesting patterns emerged. White lesions were found on 52 percent of the 439 whales that were analyzed, and they occurred mostly on whales in the Bay of Fundy. There was a dramatic increase in the prevalence of white lesions in the Bay during the late 1990s, with a peak of 41 percent of the identified whales affected by white lesions in 1999 (Fig. 9.4). Males and females were equally likely to have white lesions, as were adults and juveniles. Through examination of a series of photographs of individuals, it became apparent that, for most whales, these lesions either resolved into white scars or disappeared altogether in a matter of months. However, in a few cases, white lesions remained relatively unchanged for over a year. Sixty-four percent of the whales with white lesions had either a recurrence (after healing) or persistence of the lesions in another habitat and/or season following the initial lesion occurrence (Table 9.1).

The increased prevalence of white lesions in the Bay of Fundy coincided with a dramatic increase in the number of whales using this area in the mid-1990s (Fig. 9.4). A crude measure of whale density (largest count of identified whales over two-week periods) was significantly correlated with lesion occurrence. Because a contagious disease is more likely to spread when whales are aggregated, this finding supported the hypothesis that the lesions were caused by infectious organisms. The picture was not that clear, however, as there was no evidence that affected mothers were passing lesions on to their calves (possibly the result of immunity from passive antibody transfer through milk). Additionally males, which are more social than females (Hamilton 2002) and more likely to have physical contact in surface-active groups, were no more likely than females to have white lesions.

The white lesion subcategory of particular concern was swath lesions. These lesions were relatively rare (only six cases), but five of the six affected whales were either known or believed to have died (i.e., presumed dead) after being

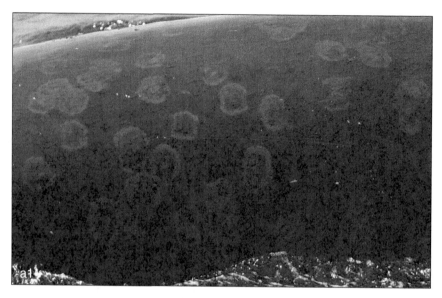

Figure 9.3. Examples of miscellaneous lesions on right whales: (a1 and a2) tattoo-like lesions; (b1) spiral or dotted lines trailing from lesions on the nuchal region; (b2) spiral or dotted lines trailing from lesions on the back; (c) multicolored, splotchy lesions on the back; and (d) rough, nonblister patch on the nuchal region. (a1) Lindsay Hall / New England Aquarium, (a2) Elizabeth Pike / New England Aquarium, (b1) Brenna Kraus / New England Aquarium, (b2) Carolyn Angell / Woods Hole Oceanographic Institution, (c) NOAA, National Marine Fisheries Service (NMFS), obtained under permit no. 775-1600-09, (d) Moira Brown / New England Aquarium.

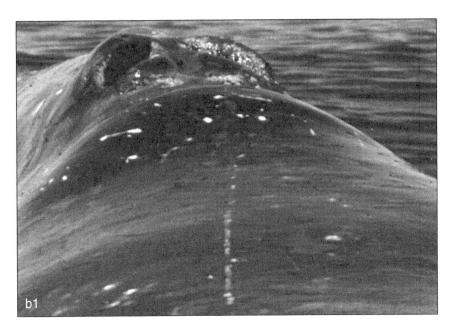

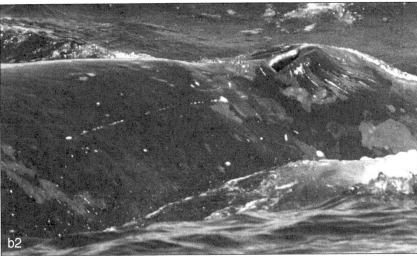

Figure 9.3. (*continued*)

photographed with swath lesions. All of the affected whales had been entangled in fishing gear either before or during the lesion event, and many of them were categorized as "severely thin" when last sighted (see visual health assessment section below). This correlation of swath lesion occurrence with entanglements

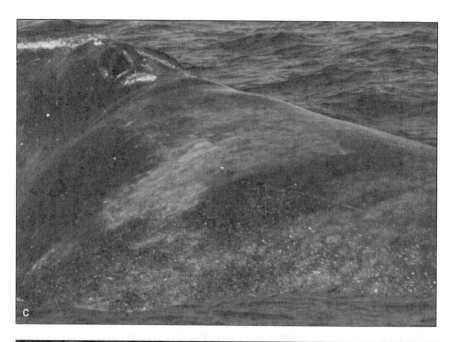

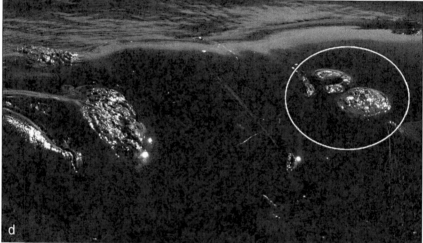

Figure 9.3. (*continued*)

and reduced body condition suggests that the presence of these lesions may be related to physical deterioration and stress. Sublethal effects of entanglements may weaken a whale's immune system and allow secondary infections to occur, resulting in the appearance of swath lesions.

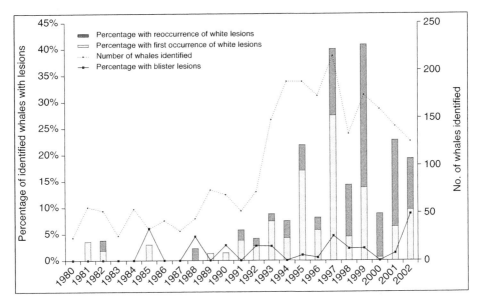

Figure 9.4. The occurrence of lesions on right whales in the Bay of Fundy, 1980 to 2002. The bars represent the percentage of whales with white lesions on the head: light-colored bars for whales with the first lesion occurrence and dark-colored bars for whales with a recurrence of lesions. The solid line represents blister lesions detected anywhere on the body, and the dotted line represents the total number of whales identified in the Bay of Fundy that year. Reproduced with permission from Inter-Research Science Center *Diseases of Aquatic Organisms*.

Table 9.1. Persistence/Recurrence of White Lesions on 227 Whales That Had White Lesions Detected Anywhere on Their Bodies[a]

No. of habitat-years lesions were detected	No. of whales	Percentage of total
1	82	36.1
2	56	24.7
3	32	14.1
4	26	11.5
5	12	5.3
6	10	4.4
7	4	1.8
8	3	1.3
10	1	0.4
17	1	0.4
	227	

a. Each whale is counted once. Whales that were seen with lesions in more than one habitat-year either experienced a recurrence of white lesions or had lesions that persisted across habitats or years.

Blister Lesion Characteristics

Most of the blister lesions were small blisters; craterous eruptions were detected on only three whales. Blister lesions showed no obvious regional or temporal pattern (Fig. 9.4). Overall, fewer whales had blister lesions (17.3 percent) than white lesions, and generally fewer than 5 percent of all identified whales were affected annually. Blister lesions were equally likely to occur in Cape Cod Bay and the Bay of Fundy, the two areas where thorough shipboard photo-identification efforts have been undertaken. Like the white lesions, blister lesions appeared on both sexes and age classes equally.

Detecting lesions requires high-quality photographs, and this is particularly true for blister lesions. Because white lesions often appear on the head, they are generally captured with any photo-identification image. In contrast the back of the whale where most blister lesions occur is a large area that often remains submerged and is, therefore, difficult to photograph consistently. Lesion detection is also influenced by light conditions, whale behavior, and the platform from which the images were taken. For example Cape Cod Bay is one of the more difficult places to photograph right whales because surveys there occur in the winter and early spring, when both weather and light conditions are often poor. Furthermore, whales in this area tend to dive for long periods, and they exhibit unpredictable swimming and diving patterns with single breaths between surfacings, making the collection of a good series of photographs difficult. For these reasons, lesions of all types may be underrepresented in Cape Cod Bay datasets.

Causes of Skin Lesions

Because only one lesion from a dead whale has been sampled from this population (Moore et al. 2005), the causes of these lesions remain speculative. It is clear that they indicate some form of compromised health, and the differences in lesion occurrence and temporal patterns suggest separate etiologies for the two broad lesion categories. The lesion subcategories may represent different disease entities altogether, which should become clear with further studies. Nevertheless the spike in white lesion occurrence in the late 1990s, associated with an increased whale density in the Bay of Fundy, suggests an infectious disease etiology for certain lesion types. In contrast blister lesions appear to be a more chronic condition affecting a smaller number of individuals. White lesions increased during the same period that calving intervals lengthened and whales appeared to be in worse body condition (see visual health assessment section), further indicating that some skin lesions are cause for concern.

Although the etiology of these lesions remains unknown, factors that could cause or exacerbate lesion occurrence or severity include water quality changes (temperature, salinity, contaminants) (Wilson et al. 1999; Weisbrod et al. 2000); ultraviolet radiation exposure (Morison 1989; Wilson et al. 1999); infectious disease (Van Bressem et al. 1999; Gaydos et al. 2004); hormonal fluctuations (Aldhous 1990; Wingfield et al. 2001); and nutritional stresses such as a vitamin A–deficient diet (Beckman et al. 1997). Determining the cause(s) of skin lesions will require increased efforts to collect tissue samples from living and stranded whales for histological studies, electron microscopic analyses, and bacterial, fungal, and viral culture (color plate 13). Maintaining a quality photographic effort, especially from shipboard rather than aerial platforms (because lesions are best assessed from shipboard images), is essential to continue monitoring the types and prevalence of lesions in right whales. Future research may determine whether these skin lesions are indicators of a primary health problem in right whales (e.g., infectious disease) or if they are mainly a reflection of changing environmental factors in right whale habitats. Of the environmental factors, salinity in particular should be investigated further because there was a strong low-salinity anomaly in the Gulf of Maine between 1996 and 2000 that coincided with the peak lesion years (Mountain 2004; Patrician 2005).

Assessing Physical Condition from Photographs

In 2000 New England Aquarium researchers began to explore the potential for using the photographic images in the *North Atlantic Right Whale Catalog* to assess health in right whales. As a result a new technique was developed to evaluate visually both individual whale and populationwide health (Pettis et al. 2004).

"Health" is a relative term, defined as the "state of the organism when it functions optimally without evidence of disease or abnormality" (Stedman 2005, 641). Because it is essentially impossible to look at typical internal indicators of health in right whales, external features indicative of relative health status were identified. Right whales severely and chronically entangled in fishing gear, such as Churchill, provided good models to track such changes. For most entangled whales, pre- and postentanglement photographs were available for comparison, allowing for a detailed evaluation of changes in physical condition. Figure 9.5 illustrates the visible physical changes in Churchill's appearance from a preentanglement image taken in 1991 and a postentanglement image taken in 2001 in the months before he died. Although it was obvious to researchers that Churchill's condition deteriorated drastically when he was entangled, the challenge was to identify the physical parameters that were used to come to that overall conclusion and to develop a scoring system that could be systematically applied to right whale images. Additionally the selected physical parameters had to be visible in photographs routinely taken for photoidentification purposes.

After reviews of numerous images of whales from the *North Atlantic Right Whale Catalog,* four visual health assessment parameters were identified, and scoring criteria were established. The selected physical parameters included (1) body condition, (2) skin condition, (3) rake marks around the blowholes, and (4) cyamids around the blowholes. Parameters were evaluated using a numerical scoring system with lower scores indicating less severe or better health. The criteria for the assessment and scoring of individual parameters are described below.

Body Condition

Body condition is a general measure of a whale's energy reserves. This parameter reflects a subjective assessment of the relative amount of blubber (a highly specialized version of mammalian subcutaneous fat) based on external body contours. In both terrestrial and marine mammals, body condition has been associated with reproductive success and survival (Young 1976; Lockyer 1986, 1993; Guinet et al. 1998; Shulte-Hostedde et al. 2001). In right whales blubber accumulates in the area just behind the blowholes (the nuchal crest or cervical region), and whales with substantial blubber reserves actually have a "fat roll" or "neck roll" in this region. Because this area is usually visible in photographs taken for whale identification, it was used to evaluate body condition. When viewed laterally, right whales in good condition have a flat or slightly rounded dorsal profile between the blowholes and the peduncle. In contrast, whales that are in poor condition have a dip (or concavity) in the postblowhole area that becomes increasingly prominent in thinner whales. Whales in good condition were scored 1, whales with a slight to moderate concavity behind the blowholes were scored 2, and whales with severe concavity were scored 3 (Fig. 9.6).

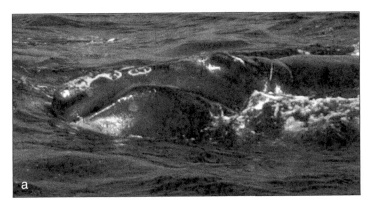

Figure 9.5. (a) Churchill (Eg #1102) before entanglement in 1991 and (b) following entanglement in 2001, showing the deterioration in his physical condition. (a) Kit Curtain / New England Aquarium, (b) Provincetown Center for Coastal Studies, under NOAA Fisheries permit no. 932-1489, under the authority of the U.S. Endangered Species Act.

Skin Condition

To evaluate skin condition, the presence and severity of three factors were evaluated: (1) skin lesions, (2) extensive skin sloughing, and (3) presence of orange cyamids (whale lice). Whales with apparently good skin condition were scored 1, and whales with poor skin condition were scored 2. A two-point scoring system was used for this parameter because it became apparent that classification in an intermediate category was highly subjective (Fig. 9.7).

Rake Marks

Rake marks were defined as two or more parallel lines in the skin just forward of each blowhole. The term "rake mark" used in the visual health assessment should not be confused with tooth rake marks described for cetaceans (George et al. 1994), as these rake marks are not caused by interspecies interactions. The origin of rake marks is not known; however, they often become more prominent in right whales that are in poor health. Rake marks were scored independently for the left and right blowholes, as they are often not symmetrical. Whales with very few to no rake marks were scored 1, whales with several radiating marks were scored 2, and whales with deeply furrowed and/or bright marks were scored a 3 (Fig. 9.8).

Cyamids around the Blowholes

The presence of cyamids in and around the blowholes of whales has been associated with long-term entanglement events and other injuries (Osmond and Kaufman 1998). Whales with no to few cyamids in or around the blowholes were given a score of 1, and whales whose blowholes were largely or entirely covered with cyamids were given a score of 2 (Fig. 9.9).

Application of the Visual Health Assessment Method

Over 200,000 photographs of right whales from 1935 through 2000 taken from both aerial and shipboard platforms were analyzed. All sightings of a particular whale in each habitat were evaluated together, resulting in a score entry for the four health parameters for each habitat and year. Sometimes one

Figure 9.6. Example of body condition scoring criteria. This parameter was scored based on the shape of the whale's back. (a) A score of 1 was assigned to whales with fat rolls or a flat back behind the nuchal crest; the arrow indicates the placement and appearance of a fat roll. (b) Whales that exhibited a slight to moderate dip were assigned a score of 2; the arrow indicates the placement of the dip in back. (c) Those whales with significant dips in their backs or sides and those that exhibited a hump behind the nuchal crest were scored 3; the large arrows indicate the area on the back of the whale that exhibited a dip as well as an indentation in the side of the animal. The smaller arrow points out the "hump" often observed on severely thin whales. (a) Owen Nichols / New England Aquarium, (b) Elizabeth Pike / New England Aquarium, (c) Jennifer Beaudin Ring / New England Aquarium. Adapted from Pettis et al. (2004).

Figure 9.7. Example of skin condition scoring criteria. This parameter was scored based on the absence or presence of skin lesions, blisters, excessive skin sloughing, and coverage of orange cyamids on large areas of the body. (a) Whales with black skin that showed limited sloughing were scored as 1. (b) Whales with significant lesion coverage, swath lesions, blisters, extensive sloughing, and/or a large area of body covered with orange cyamids were scored 2; the arrows point out the body areas with poor skin condition attributes. (a) Heather Pettis / New England Aquarium, (b) Sean Beavor / New England Aquarium. Adapted from Pettis et al. (2004).

or more of the parameters could not be scored for a set of photographs because of image quality, angle, distance, or because only one side of the whale was photographed. Rake marks, body condition, and cyamids around the blowholes were difficult to detect from aerial photographs, and therefore, when only aerial images were available, these parameters were scored only if the parameter area was clearly visible. In contrast, skin condition could be routinely scored from aerial images because skin lesions, skin sloughing, and large patches of cyamids on the body were readily visible.

Body Condition of Reproductive Females

The next step was to test the ability of the technique to detect predictable differences in right whale condition. Body condition fluctuates throughout the various stages of the reproductive cycle in mammalian females because of the high energetic demands of pregnancy and lactation (Young 1976). In whales that have been examined, the blubber is thickest during pregnancy and is depleted throughout lactation (Lockyer 1981). Historical whaling data also indicated that females with calves yielded reduced amounts of oil, reflecting a depletion of blubber fat stores during lactation (Rice and Wolman 1971; Reeves and Mitchell 1986).

Body condition scores of females in different stages of the reproductive cycle (resting, pregnant, lactating) were compared to see if fluctuations in this single parameter could be detected. The majority of reproductive females were scored poorest (appeared to be thinnest) in the year they were supporting a calf (i.e., during lactation) and scored best (appeared to be fattest) in the year prior to giving birth (i.e., pregnant), a conclusion that is supported by the results of quantitative measurements of blubber thickness collected using ultrasound (Angell 2005). These results demonstrated that body condition scores were detecting visual changes in external body contour resulting from fluctuations in blubber reserves experienced by cows during gestation and lactation. It follows that if the health assessment scoring technique can be used to detect these fluctuations in reproductive females, then it may also be useful to detect populationwide changes in body condition caused by factors other than reproduction.

Predicting Survival

Another goal of this health assessment method was to improve the ability to estimate survival of individuals based on their appearance. There are currently no methods to assess right whale mortality accurately, as many whales die at sea

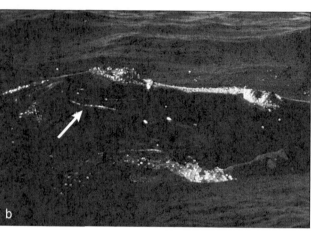

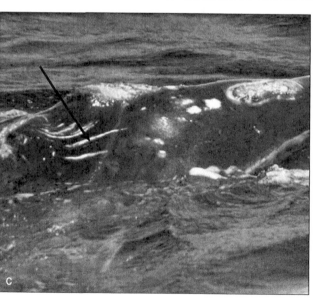

and are never detected (Kraus et al. 2005). The presumed dead classification (described in Chapter 3) provides an estimate of which whales may have died, but it is based solely on gaps in sighting histories longer than six years and is not statistically rigorous (Caswell et al. 1999).

Field observations had suggested that some "presumed dead" whales appeared to be in poor health at their last sighting (i.e., presence of skin lesions, thin body condition, large areas of cyamid infestation). To test this observation, health assessment scores for the individual parameters as well as the overall composite scores were compared for presumed dead and living whales during three time periods: 1981–1985, 1986–1990, and 1991–1995. Because a six-year sighting gap is required for a whale to be classified as presumed dead, the dataset for this analysis included sighting data for 1981–1995 (at the time of this analysis, whales last sighted in 1996–2000 had not yet been classified as presumed dead). Health assessment scores were grouped into five-year periods for analysis to ensure large enough sample sizes for statistical analyses.

Whales that became presumed dead consistently had poorer body condition scores at their last sighting compared to whales that were resighted and known to be living. The other health parameters showed significantly worse scores during some of the time intervals but not others, but all of the health assessment parameters indicated that presumed dead whales were in poorer health during the interval 1991–1995 (Table 9.2). Additionally, of ten whales that have been coded as severely thin, only two have been resighted (Table 9.3). One of these whales was seen six months after being coded in poor condition, but its body condition could not be reassessed at that sighting, and the whale has not been photographed since. These results suggest that this visual health assessment method, used in conjunction with sighting histories, provides better mortality estimates than gaps in sighting history alone. Additionally,

Figure 9.8. Examples of rake mark scoring criteria. Rake marks were defined as two or more parallel lines forward of each blowhole and were scored independently for the right and left sides of the head. Arrows in these photographs illustrate the area inspected for this parameter. (a) Whales with zero to few parallel lines extending from the blowholes forward to the head were scored as 1. (b) Whales with several parallel lines in this area that appeared to radiate around the blowhole but were not significantly deep or long were scored as 2. (c) A score of 3 was assigned to whales with many deep or long lines radiating around the blowhole. (a) Laura Morse / New England Aquarium, (b) Lisa Conger / New England Aquarium, (c) Provincetown Center for Coastal Studies. Adapted from Pettis et al. (2004).

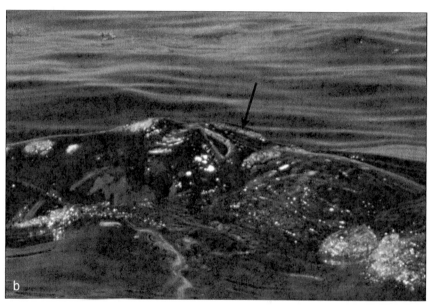

Figure 9.9. Examples of scoring criteria for orange cyamids around the blowholes. (a) Whales with no or few cyamids (individuals or small aggregates) were assigned a score of 1. (b) Whales whose blowholes were significantly covered with orange cyamids were scored as 2. Arrows in these photographs illustrate the area inspected for this parameter. Christopher Slay / New England Aquarium. Adapted from Pettis et al. (2004).

Table 9.2. Comparison of Visual Health Assessment Scores between Presumed Dead and Living Right Whales from 1981 to 1995, Broken into Three Five-Year Intervals[a]

Parameter	1981–1985	1986–1990	1991–1995
Cumulative scores	**7/195**	16/402	11/489
Rake marks left	12/298	27/624	**21/683**
Rake marks right	**13/294**	25/615	**21/679**
Body condition	**15/329**	29/704	24/707
Skin condition	19/429	31/764	31/804
Cyamids around blowholes	10/233	**21/471**	16/557

a. Cell values (*n* presumed dead/living) represent the number of presumed dead whales evaluated in the time frame/the number of living whales evaluated in the time frame. The null hypothesis (H_0) being tested is: scores of presumed dead whales > living whales (indicating worse visual health assessment scores). Bold cells indicate statistical significance at $p < 0.05$. Comparisons were made using Wilcoxon one-tailed test.

Table 9.3. Right Whales with Body Condition Scores of 3 (Severely Thin) between 1935 and 2000 and Their Present Status (as of 2004)

Whale ID#	Sex	Year of birth	Year scored body condition 3	Years since last sighted	Present status	Comments
1163	F	1981	1991	12	Presumed dead	Calving year; previously entangled
1907	F	1989	1991	n/a	Dead in 1991	Entangled
2233	F	1992	1993	11	Presumed dead	Entangled
1135	F	Unknown	1996	8	Presumed dead	Calving year
2557	F	1995	1997	7	Presumed dead	Entangled
1333	M	Unknown	1998	n/a	Dead in 1998	
1617	M	Unknown	1994; 1998	1	Alive	Sighted in 2003
2212	M	1992	1998	6	Presumed dead	Entangled
1014	F	Unknown	1999	n/a	Dead in 1999	Shipstrike
1505	M	1985	1999	5	Unknown	

Note: Right whales are presumed dead following a six-year sighting gap. The status of whales that have not been seen in less than six years is considered unknown.

it appears that the body condition parameter in itself may serve as a useful predictor of mortality in right whales.

The Future of Visual Health Assessment Studies

Much of the health assessment data point to a widespread deterioration of health in North Atlantic right whales during the 1990s. These observations may reflect a populationwide disease or starvation event. This period coincides with the significant reproductive decline previously described (Chapter 6), and studies are currently under way to investigate the role that compromised health may have played in this trend.

The visual health assessment technique will enable researchers to develop a more accurate picture of the role health plays in right whale reproductive success and survival. Individual health assessment scores can be coupled with genetic profiles, stress and reproductive hormone data from fecal analyses, and blubber thickness to investigate the interrelationships between different health indicators and reproductive success. This method has already been used to assess the condition of entangled whales to determine appropriate disentanglement action plans. Finally, a powerful aspect of the visual health assessment technique is its ability to assess archived images, thereby increasing its utility for retrospective analyses related to reproduction and survival.

Acoustic Measurement of Right Whale Blubber Thickness at Sea

In 1995 right whale researchers from Woods Hole Oceanographic Institution started a program to determine whether low calving rates in right whales were related to inadequate food resources. Observers reported that many right whales seemed to be thinner compared to previous years, which, in females, might impact reproduction. To test this hypothesis, researchers wanted to compare the blubber thickness of different whales relative to their reproductive success as recorded in the *North Atlantic Right Whale Catalog* and database.

In livestock farming a simple ultrasound device is placed on the back of the animal to measure subcutaneous fat thickness. Because fat and muscle have different densities, high-frequency sounds will bounce off the interface. The ultrasound device measures the time it takes for sound to echo back from the interface between the skin surface and the base of the fat layer, from which blubber thickness can be calculated. A manufacturer of ultrasound devices for pigs reconfigured one of their instruments to penetrate the 20 cm or so of

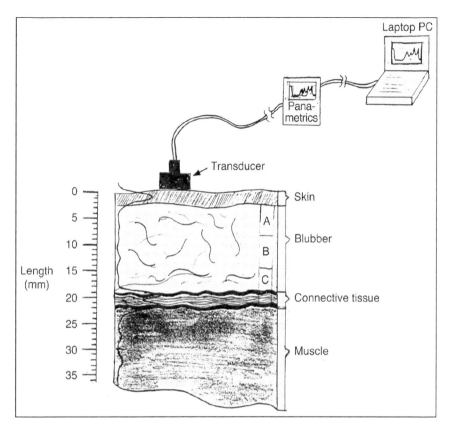

Figure 9.10. A sketch of a slice through right whale blubber with an ultrasound transducer placed on the skin surface. Sound is emitted from the transducer, bounces off the blubber–muscle interface, and is recorded again in the transducer. The time for this to occur is transmitted as voltage to a recording system back in the boat.

blubber that right whales have, in contrast to the usual 2 or 3 cm in a domestic pig. But placing the probe flat on the back of a moving whale at sea was a challenge. Right whales typically surface, blow about four times at twenty- to thirty-second intervals and then submerge for another dive, so the system had to be deployed rapidly.

To accomplish this, a 5.5-m lightweight carbon fiber tube was attached to the bow of the boat with a cable running through it from the ultrasound probe at the tip back to the display unit in the boat (Fig. 9.10). The first successful measurement of right whale blubber thickness was made on a calf in the Bay

Figure 9.11. A surfacing right whale on the left of the picture is gently touched by a hinged ultrasound probe on the tip of a 12-m cantilevered carbon fiber pole balanced on a bowsprit extending from a 7.6-m-long power boat. The upper steering station allows a good view of the surfacing whale. New England Aquarium.

of Fundy in 1996. The thrill of making a noninvasive anatomic measurement on a free-ranging large whale at sea was overwhelming. It had never been done before. Indeed in the international arena, scientific whaling permits were still being justified on the basis that blubber thickness could only be measured with a knife.

The first flush of success was followed by a string of failures. The signal was too weak to penetrate the full depth of an adult right whale's blubber. The whales in Cape Cod Bay surfaced too briefly to be approached. The pole broke. But slowly methods were developed to do what had seemed easy at first but in reality was a very involved process.

Ultimately, a 7.6-m boat with an upper steering platform was used to give a good view of the whale from above (Fig. 9.11). A 12-m carbon fiber pole was assembled from two racing sailboat masts sleeved into one another, and the pole was cantilevered off the bow to give extra reach (Fig. 9.12). A hinged landing plate system housing the ultrasound probe was combined with an instrument

Figure 9.12. A hinged ultrasound transducer embedded in a light plexiglass disk is lowered flat on the back of a right whale to measure its blubber thickness acoustically. Carolyn Angell / Woods Hole Oceanographic Institution.

designed to measure flaws in welded steel and other structures (the Panametric 9100). It took a custom software package using a high-speed interface to a laptop computer to record the echoes off the blubber–muscle interface in sufficiently rapid succession that adequate data quality could be obtained (Fig. 9.13). Further data analysis was required to actually interpret a single measure of blubber thickness from the host of echoes obtained from each whale.

Thus it was not until 1998, four years after the project started, that collection of consistent data began (Moore et al. 2001). The same method was used for the next five years, acoustically sampling right whales for blubber thickness every August in the Bay of Fundy. For comparative studies, blubber measurements were taken of southern right whales off South Africa during two separate field seasons. These whales were accessible only in the southern winter, so they were not sampled at the equivalent time of year to the Bay of Fundy whales, but a physiological time scale was used to normalize measurements between the two locations (Angell 2005). The following is a summary of the results from this research program.

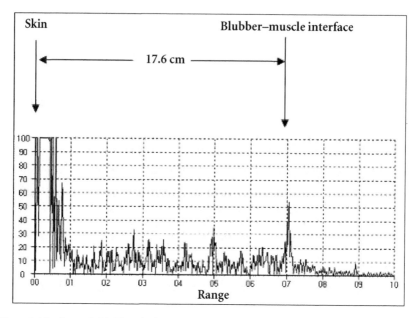

Figure 9.13. Acoustic blubber thickness measurement of an *E. glacialis* adult female in the Bay of Fundy. Left-hand arrow shows where the ultrasound transducer made contact with the skin. Right-hand arrow indicates sound echo from the subdermal connective tissue sheath at the blubber–muscle interface. Blubber thickness is 17.6 cm.

The Skinny on Blubber in Right Whales

Adult female right whales were of primary interest for looking at the relationship between blubber thickness and reproductive success, but usually the identification, gender, and history of each individual were available only after photographs were analyzed back in the lab. Thus blubber thickness was measured on whichever whale allowed the researchers to get close enough for what were referred to as "touches" with the ultrasound probe. As a whale surfaced, the research boat fell behind and to one side, matching the speed and direction the whale was moving. If this maneuvering did not appear to affect the whale's behavior, the probe was placed for about a second on its back as it surfaced. After each touch the boat was stopped to examine the data quality, clean and disinfect the probe, and look for another whale. Some days data were obtained from thirty or more whales, but other days from only one or two. Weather was a factor, as windy, foggy days were not productive. Interestingly, it was on the flat calm days when the whales showed the greatest awareness of the touches. It seemed that when there were ripples or bigger waves in the water, another tickle on the back was of no consequence, whereas when there was no other stimulus during surfacing, the probe touch was more noticeable.

Data were collected from 172 individual right whales in the Bay of Fundy and 116 in South Africa, with multiple data from some individuals over a five-year period (1998–2002). Much effort was expended in developing analysis tools to ensure that an accurate measure of blubber thickness was obtained from each whale. The analyses were restricted to a defined area on the back of the whale, between 30 percent and 50 percent of its length, which does not vary in thickness within an individual, as established by measuring blubber thickness on dead right whales.

Whales were classified as calves (less than a year), juveniles (one to eight years), or adults (nine years or older). Adult females were divided into lactating, near pregnant (three to six months prior to the estimated start of pregnancy), pregnant, resting, and nulliparous (never observed in close association with a calf). These assignations were made in hindsight, on the basis of subsequent observations of the sampled individuals, such as calving and suckling events.

Blubber thickness measurements ranged from 8 to 22 cm in North Atlantic right whales and 5 to 26 cm in South African right whales. Blubber thickness of three North Atlantic right whale calves was measured, and the same individuals were measured again as yearlings. All of them showed a significant decrease in blubber thickness as yearlings. This finding was most likely a result of the major stress calves experience as they wean and learn how to forage efficiently.

Female North Atlantic right whales that were soon to become pregnant had significantly thicker blubber than other adult life stages, whereas the blubber of lactating females was significantly reduced. Four individual females were sampled in multiple years at different stages of the reproductive cycle. In three of these females blubber thickness decreased by several centimeters (2–4.5 cm) over the period from before pregnancy to the end of lactation. The fourth female was only 1 cm thinner as a juvenile than she was near the end of lactation three years later. Furthermore, reproductively active North Atlantic right whale females got fatter with increasing time after weaning their calves. These data taken together suggest that females need to get fat to get pregnant and that lactation is a major energetic drain from which they have to recover by replenishing reserves of body fat before they can breed successfully again.

Blubber thickness estimates from South African right whale mothers sampled in early lactation (September) were significantly thicker than those sampled in midlactation (November), again demonstrating the high energetic cost of lactation. The opposite was seen in their calves, which gained in blubber thickness significantly over the same time period.

Blubber was also significantly thicker overall in southern right whales compared to northern right whales. Blubber thickness was measured acoustically, but it is also evident visually as discussed in the visual health assessment section of this chapter. Southern Hemisphere right whales commonly have a substantial fat roll behind their blowholes that is rarely so prominent and often absent in North Atlantic whales.

Lessons Learned Using Blubber Thickness Measurement

The general patterns of changes in fat reserves have been well documented in the balaenopterid whale species (Lockyer 1981, 1986, 1987) but not in right whales. The combination of long-term life history data from the *North Atlantic Right Whale Catalog* coupled with acoustic blubber thickness measurements provided a unique view of physiological features of the reproductive cycles of right whales. Right whales appear to accumulate blubber thickness during preparation for pregnancy, with a marked off-loading of lipid reserves during lactation. Southern right whales appeared to be in significantly better condition (based on thicker blubber measurements) than North Atlantic right whales. These differences in blubber reserves may be a contributing factor to the poor reproductive success in North Atlantic right whales as compared to those in the Southern Hemisphere. In addition, juvenile right whales appear to depend, in part, on lipid reserves accumulated during suckling for postweaning growth and maintenance.

Two important questions arose from this research. (1) Blubber thickness increases substantially before pregnancy. Is this increase a trigger for successful ovulation, or do females get pregnant soon after weaning but fail to carry fetuses to term until they have sufficient fat reserves? (2) These results, along with those generated by the visual assessment of body condition, demonstrate the ability to detect changes in body fat condition. However, studies in other mammalian species have demonstrated large differences among indices of body fat in their ability to predict total body fat (Prestrud and Pond 2003). How well do blubber thickness measurements or visual assessments of the dorsal body profile predict total body fat of right whales? To understand the significance of these body fat condition indices fully, it is important to define the relationships between each index and total body fat (Stephenson et al. 2002), although this clearly is not feasible in right whales.

To date the focus has been on females, but, in other mammals, male fertility also appears to be affected by body fat condition (Foote 1978; Frisch 1997). Understanding the role of body fat reserves in the fertility of male right whales will involve comparing body fat condition with paternity by individual males. Paternity data are now becoming available for the right whale population, as described in Chapter 7, making this analysis feasible.

These data also have implications for understanding right whale energetics and how food availability may affect body fat condition. Further studies should compare temporal trends in food availability with available body fat condition data.

The labor involved in making acoustic measurements of blubber thickness at sea is intense. Therefore these data are being compared to results from aerial photogrammetric assessment of body width to length and to body condition from visual health assessment using photographs. This analysis will determine if and how these measures of condition relate to one another, to generate a robust, more easily acquired assessment of body condition in this species.

Conclusion: Does Whale Health Reflect Environmental Health?

The three methods described in this chapter have all contributed greatly to researchers' knowledge of right whale health as evaluated from outside the whale. Both the patterns in occurrence of skin lesions and the results from the visual health assessment scoring indicate that something occurred to compromise the health and body condition of right whales during the 1990s. Whether these findings are directly related to the dramatic decrease in calving success and the other changes in reproductive parameters seen in females during the same period remains unknown, but it seems more than coincidental. The acoustic measurement of blubber thickness is the first method to quantitatively assess body condition in living whales and provides a method to cross validate with the body condition scores from the visual health assessment and aerial photogrammetry. Additionally, these results emphasize the importance of adequate blubber reserves to successful reproduction of females.

Factors that may be affecting both individual and populationwide right whale health can be divided broadly into intrinsic and extrinsic factors. Intrinsic factors include the impacts of limited genetic diversity in right whales and the effects of disease or physiological abnormalities on the whales (Chapters 7 and 8). Extrinsic factors embody both anthropogenic effects on habitat quality and naturally variable environmental influences. These include habitat loss or degradation affecting food quality, quantity, or fine-scale distribution (as right whales need very high patch densities to forage efficiently); exposure to environmental contaminants and marine biotoxins; variations in ocean salinity and temperature; and the impacts of global climate change both indirectly through effects on the food web and through direct impacts on the whales themselves (Chapter 15). Distinguishing among the impacts of these various factors will not be an easy task. However, the first step was to develop the health-monitoring tools, which are now in place. These measures of right whale health can be used in tandem with habitat quality data to test hypotheses about the impacts of environmental variables on right whale health and reproduction and to monitor the status of both individual whales and the population as a whole.

Aldhous, P. 1990. Equality of the sexes? *Nature* 347:701.

Angell, C. 2005. Blubber thickness in Atlantic *E. glacialis* and *E. australis*. Ph.D. Thesis. Boston University, Boston.

Beckman, K. B., L. J. Lowenstine, J. Newman, J. Hill, K. Hanni, and J. Gerber. 1997. Clinical and pathological characterization of northern elephant seal skin disease. *Journal of Wildlife Diseases* 33:438–449.

Caswell, H., M. Fujiwara, and S. Brault. 1999. Declining survival probability threatens the North Atlantic right whale. *Proceedings of the National Academy of Sciences* 96:3308–3313.

Foote, R. H. 1978. Factors influencing the quantity and quality of semen harvested from bulls, rams, boars and stallions. *Journal of Animal Science* 47:1–11.

Frisch, R. 1997. Body weight, body fat and ovulation: relation to the natural fertility of populations. Pages 139–166 *in* R. Dorfman, and P. Rogers, eds., *Science with a Human Face: In Honor of Roger Randall Revelle*. Harvard University Press, Cambridge, MA.

Gaydos, J. K., K. C. Balcomb, R. W. Osborne, and L. Dierauf. 2004. Evaluating potential infectious disease threats for southern resident killer whales, *Orcinus orca*: a model for endangered species. *Biological Conservation* 177:253–262.

George, J. C., L. M. Philo, K. Hazard, D. Withrow, G. M. Carroll, and R. Suydam. 1994. Frequency of killer whale (*Orcinus orca*) attacks and ship collisions based on scarring on bowhead whales (*Balaena mysticetus*) of the Bering-Chukchi-Beaufort Seas stock. *Arctic* 47:247–255.

Guinet, C., J. P. Roux, M. Bonnet, and V. Mison. 1998. Effect of body size, body mass, and body condition on reproduction of female South African fur seals (*Arctocephalus pusillus*) in Namibia. *Canadian Journal of Zoology* 76:1418–1424.

Hamilton, P. K. 2002. Associations among North Atlantic right whales. M.Sc. Thesis, University of Massachusetts, Boston.

Hamilton, P. K., and M. K. Marx. 2005. Skin lesions on North Atlantic right whales: categories, prevalence and change in occurrence in the 1990s. *Diseases of Aquatic Organisms* 68:71–82.

Kraus, S. D., M. W. Brown, H. Caswell, C. W. Clark, M. Fujiwara, P. K. Hamilton, R. D. Kenney, A. R. Knowlton, S. Landry, C. A. Mayo, W. A. McLellan, M. J. Moore, D. P. Nowacek, D. A. Pabst, A. J. Read, and R. M. Rolland. 2005. North Atlantic right whales in crisis. *Science* 309:561–562.

Lockyer, C. H. 1981. Growth and energy budgets of large baleen whales from the Southern Hemisphere. *Food and Agriculture Organization of the United Nations, Rome,* Fisheries Series 3:379–487.

Lockyer, C. H. 1986. Body fat condition in Northeast Atlantic fin whales, *Balaenoptera physalus,* and its relationship with reproduction and food resource. *Canadian Journal of Fisheries and Aquatic Sciences* 43:142–147.

Lockyer, C. H. 1987. The relationship between body fat, food resource and reproductive energy costs in North Atlantic fin whale (*Balaenoptera physalus*). *Symposium of the Zoological Society of London* 57:343–361.

Lockyer, C. H. 1993. Seasonal change in body fat condition of Northeast Atlantic pilot whales and their biological significance. *Report of the International Whaling Commission* Special Issue 14:325–350.

Moore, M. J., C. A. Miller, M. S. Morss, R. Arthur, W. Lange, K. G. Prada, M. K. Marx, and E. A. Frey. 2001. Ultrasonic measurement of blubber thickness in right whales. *Journal of Cetacean Research and Management* Special Issue 2:301–309.

Moore, M. J., A. R. Knowlton, S. D. Kraus, W. A. McLellan, and R. K. Bonde. 2005. Morphometry, gross morphology and available histopathology in North Atlantic right whale (*Eubalaena glacialis*) mortalities (1970–2002). *Journal of Cetacean Research and Management* 6:199–214.

Morison, W. L. 1989. Effects of ultraviolet radiation on the immune system in humans. *Photochemistry and Photobiology* 50:515–524.

Mountain, D. B. 2004. Variability of the water properties in NAFO subareas 5 and 6 during the 1990s. *Journal of Northwest Atlantic Fisheries Science* 34:103–112.

Osmond, M. G., and G. D. Kaufman. 1998. A heavily parasitized humpback whale (*Megaptera novaeangliae*). *Marine Mammal Science* 14:146–149.

Patrician, M. R. 2005. An investigation of the factors underlying the abandonment of the Roseway Basin feeding ground by the North Atlantic right whale (*Eubalaena glacialis*): 1993–1999. M.Sc. Thesis, University of Rhode Island, Narragansett.

Perryman, W. L., and M. S. Lynn. 2002. Evaluation of nutritive condition and reproductive status of migrating gray whales (*Eschrichtius robustus*) based on analysis of photogrammetric data. *Journal of Cetacean Research and Management* 4:155–164.

Pettis, H. M., R. M. Rolland, P. K. Hamilton, A. R. Knowlton, S. D. Kraus, and S. Brault. 2004. Visual health assessment of North Atlantic right whales (*Eubalaena glacialis*) using photographs. *Canadian Journal of Zoology* 82:8–19.

Prestrud, P., and C. M. Pond. 2003. Fat indices of arctic foxes *Alopex lagopus* in Svalbard. *Wildlife Biology* 9:193–197.

Reeves, R. R., and E. Mitchell. 1986. The Long Island, New York, right whale fishery: 1650–1924. *Report of the International Whaling Commission* Special Issue 10: 201–220.

Rice, D. W., and A. A. Wolman. 1971. The life history and ecology of the gray whale (*Eschrichtius robustus*). *American Society of Mammalogists* Special Publication 3. 142 pp.

Schulte-Hostedde, A. I., J. S. Millar, and G. J. Hickling. 2001. Evaluating body condition in small mammals. *Canadian Journal of Zoology* 79:1021–1029.

Stedman's Medical Dictionary for the Health Profession and Nursing, 5th ed. 2005. Lippincott Williams & Wilkins, Baltimore, MD.

Stephenson, T. R., V. C. Bleich, B. M. Pierce, and G. P. Mulcahy. 2002. Validation of mule deer body composition using in vivo and post-mortem indices of nutritional condition. *Wildlife Society Bulletin* 30:557–564.

Thompson, P. M., and P. S. Hammond. 1992. The use of photography to monitor dermal disease in wild bottlenose dolphins (*Tursiops truncatus*). *Ambio* 21: 135–137.

Van Bressem, M. F., K. V. Van Waerebeek, and J. A. Raga. 1999. A review of virus infections of cetaceans and the potential impact of morbilliviruses, poxviruses and papillomaviruses on host population dynamics. *Diseases of Aquatic Organisms* 38:53–65.

Weisbrod, A. V., D. Shea, M. J. Moore, and J. J. Stegeman. 2000. Organochlorine exposure and bioaccumulation in the endangered Northwest Atlantic right whale (*Eubalaena glacialis*) population. *Environmental Toxicology and Chemistry* 19: 654–666.

Wilson B., H. Arnold, G. Bearzi, C. M. Fortuna, R. Gaspar, S. Ingram, C. Liret, S. Pribanic, A. J. Read, V. Ridoux, K. Schneider, K. W. Urian, R. S. Wells, C. Wood, P. M. Thompson, and P. S. Hammond. 1999. Epidermal disease in bottlenose dolphins: impacts of natural and anthropogenic factors. *Proceedings of the Royal Society of London Part B* 266:1077–1083.

Wingfield, J. C., S. E. Lynn, and K. K. Soma. 2001. Avoiding the "costs" of testosterone: Ecological bases of hormone–behavior interactions. *Brain Behavior and Evolution* 57:239–251.

Young, R. A. 1976. Fat, energy and mammalian survival. *American Zoologist* 16: 699–710.

Acknowledgments

The lesion analysis would not have been possible without the dedicated efforts of many photographic contributors to the *North Atlantic Right Whale Catalog* and to the many matchers who have helped maintain this valuable database. Particular thanks go to Lisa Conger, Martie Crone, Amy Knowlton, and Beth Pike for their dedicated matching efforts. Special thanks also go to the Provincetown Center for Coastal Studies, whose right whale surveys detected almost half of all blister lesions. Funding to maintain the *North Atlantic Right Whale Catalog* and perform the lesion analysis was provided by the National Marine Fisheries Service. Photographs for the health assessment section were contributed by the following Right Whale Consortium organizations: New England Aquarium, Woods Hole Oceanographic Institution, and the Provincetown Center for Coastal Studies. Funding for the visual health assessment was provided by the National Marine Fisheries Service. Michael Moore and Carolyn Miller Angell gratefully thank all those who assisted with field work, especially Michael Morss and Peter Best. The blubber ultrasound project was made possible with funds provided by Massachusetts Environmental Trust, Office of Naval Research, National Marine Fisheries Service, Northeast Consortium, and the Hussey Foundation.

10

Acoustic Communication: Social Sounds and the Potential Impacts of Noise

SUSAN E. PARKS AND CHRISTOPHER W. CLARK

21 July 1999
Bay of Fundy, Canada

The surface of the water in the Bay of Fundy was glass, the reflection so per-fect that the division between ocean and sky was almost imperceptible. The smell of productivity, of an ocean full of life, surrounded us as we sat there on a small 4.5-m inflatable boat with the engine shut down. It was quiet, with a pair of terns occasionally breaking the silence as they swooped over the water protesting our intrusion into their world. A 68-kg speaker hung suspended under the boat as I prepared for my first playback experiment to North Atlantic right whales; I was a little nervous.

I was new to right whale research, having spent only a few days on the water the previous year getting familiar with their behavior, their sounds, and their researchers. The plan for the day was to play back a recording of scream sounds from a surface-active group (SAG) in the hopes of testing the theory that the sounds are what draw other whales into these groups. So, after some mild teasing from Scott Kraus about the potential consequences of a male right whale mistaking our white-hulled boat for a female whale, we were ready to start.

We began by scanning the area around the boat to get a sense of how many whales were in the area. The answer appeared to be two: one off to

the east at least 2 km away, and another off to the north. They were surfacing at regular intervals and going on long dives, suggesting that they were
feeding or searching for food. After twenty minutes, we were ready to start
the playback. I had a hydrophone in the water, listening for sounds made
by nearby whales and monitoring the sounds that we were about to transmit. I pushed play, and the test began. I slowly increased the volume until
it sounded as though a right whale SAG was right next to the boat. And
then we waited.

We didn't have to wait long before we had our answer as to whether
these sounds could be used by other right whales to find SAGs. When the
playback started, the whale to the north made a decisive heading change
and started swimming toward our vessel. And he kept coming. I had not
been very close to a right whale before, no closer than 50 m away during
photo-identification passes from the Research Vessel Nereid. When he surfaced, breaking through the glassy surface, heading straight for us, full speed
ahead and only 30 m away, I was a bit concerned. The video clips of this
first approaching whale that I occasionally show at talks are always muted.
This is mainly because all you would hear would be me voicing shrill concern about the whale rapidly approaching and then swimming under the
boat, and Scott telling me that everything was perfectly okay, the whale knew
where we were, and we wouldn't have a problem. He was right. The whale
skimmed below our small boat, barely visible in the murky water. He surfaced on the other side and then turned around to come back. The playback
tape had ended by this time, but he hung around, swimming and looking
for what had sounded like such an exciting event.

It was an amazing experience to see a whale clearly react to a sound
that we played and disturbing to know that we interrupted his feeding for
what ended up not being a SAG after all. But the experience was forma-
tive in making me want to know what these whales were "saying," and more
importantly, why? Were there human activities and human sounds that
were equally disruptive, that either repelled the whales or kept them from
hearing a real SAG, resulting in their missing out on an important social
interaction? And how many of these disturbances were there in the daily
life of each right whale? Even if each event was only minimally disruptive,
the cumulative effect could be staggering. Now several years later I am still
wrestling with those questions, but I always think back to the impact that
one whale had on my life. I'm hoping that I can return the favor by help-
ing others to understand what the whales are saying and by determining

what humans can do to allow them to continue to live as they have for mil-
lennia. Otherwise, right whales will have to adapt to their new urban en-
vironment, find new habitats, or become extinct. These are the only options.

Susan E. Parks

Little is known about the acoustic behavior of the North Atlantic right whale despite hundreds of years of interaction with humans, first as the "right" whale to kill and later as the "right" whale to protect from extinction. The major focus of North Atlantic right whale research has been on conservation, as described throughout this book, leaving many basic questions about behavior and sound production unanswered. The large size and inhospitable marine habitat of these creatures make it difficult to conduct research that links particular sounds with specific individuals or specific behaviors.

The sounds made by most baleen whale species have been recorded over the past 40 years, but relatively few studies have attempted to associate sound production with behavioral observations. The humpback whale is one exception, as it has been the focus of several studies on sound production and behavior. Various studies have demonstrated differences in sound production in different behavioral contexts such as the feeding calls in Alaska (D'Vincent et al. 1985) or song and competitive group sounds on the breeding grounds (Payne and McVay 1971; Tyack and Whitehead 1983). Researchers have also found gender differences in sound production: Only male humpback whales sing the elaborate songs (Winn and Winn 1978).

Sound production by the southern right whale has also been well studied (Payne and Payne 1971; Cummings et al. 1972; Saayman and Tayler 1973), including extensive research on its repertoire (Clark 1982, 1983, 1984). This latter work, conducted between 1976 and 1978 off the Patagonian coast of Argentina, linked the production of particular sounds with different behaviors and levels of activity by simultaneously combining visual observations and acoustic recordings. Playback experiments demonstrated the southern right whale's ability to discriminate the sounds of right whales from those of other whale species (Clark and Clark 1980). Surprisingly the acoustic behavior of the North Atlantic right whale, located off the east coast of the United States, remained relatively poorly described. Some of the earliest reports of North Atlantic right whale sound production described low-frequency signals of feeding right whales (Schevill et al. 1962; Schevill and Watkins 1962). These publications gave examples of sounds but provided little information about the behavior accompanying the sound production.

There has been a recent resurgence of interest in describing North Atlantic right whale acoustics. In general North Atlantic right whale vocalizations are similar to those described for the southern right whale population, with a range of sound types being produced. The sounds are generally tonal and low frequency, with most of their energy below 1 kHz. The sounds are divided between stereotyped, simple signals and a collection of highly variable, tonal sounds (Wright 2001; Parks 2003a; Parks and Clark 2005; Parks et al. 2005). A number of different researchers have attempted to characterize the call rate, frequency range, and source level for the North Atlantic right whale (Matthews et al. 2001; Vanderlaan et al. 2003). Information on the acoustic repertoire of the North Atlantic right whale is critical for effective development of passive acoustic localization systems to discriminate right whale sounds from those of other species and to pick them out of the background noise in areas where they are at the greatest risk from human activities (described in Chapter 11).

Information on the sound production of North Atlantic right whales related to particular behaviors is also important to determine if certain sounds can be correlated with times when right whales are particularly vulnerable. For example, are there particular sounds associated with surface behaviors or the presence of calves when right whales could be more vulnerable to collisions with vessels? This chapter describes the current understanding of sound use by right whales, including the sounds they produce related to their behavior, what they can hear, and the potential problems they might experience because of increasing levels of noise pollution in the oceans.

Recording and Analyzing Sounds

A variety of methods have been used to make recordings of right whale sounds over the years. Fundamentally all that is needed is an underwater microphone, or hydrophone, and some method for recording the signals received. Methods have ranged from tape recording sounds from a single hydrophone deployed over the side of a small boat to multihydrophone arrays, which use temporal differences in a sound's arrival at each sensor to locate the position of the sound source (Miller and Tyack 1998; Laurinolli et al. 2003; Parks 2003a). Arrays of synchronized bottom-mounted autonomous recorders, or "Pop-ups," have been used to detect, locate, and track right whales over periods of many months (Clark et al. 2002; Chapter 11). Small digital acoustic recording

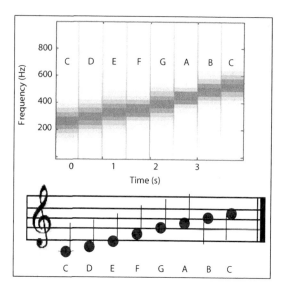

Figure 10.1. An example of a spectrogram of a musical scale, illustrating how spectrograms provide a time–frequency graph of a sound. Frequency changes (e.g., from bass to soprano) are represented by the y axis, duration by the x axis, and intensity changes correspond with the darkness of the plotted sound (light is quiet, dark is loud).

devices attached to whales with suction cups have been used to eavesdrop on the sounds produced and heard by individuals (Johnson and Tyack 2003; Nowacek et al. 2004; Chapter 11). These methods provide information on the sounds that individual right whales make. They also give researchers insights into what sounds whales hear, including those produced by other marine animals, from waves breaking or rain hitting the sea surface, and, frequently, of noise generated by many kinds of motor-driven vessels (e.g., speedboats, fishing boats, and commercial ships).

Sounds are commonly analyzed by measuring their frequency, duration, and intensity. The easiest way to visualize this is by using a graph called a spectrogram that shows a plot of intensity, frequency, and time on a single graph. Figure 10.1 shows an example of a spectrogram of a simple musical scale, with the corresponding musical notes. Differences in the frequency displayed in the spectrogram correspond to differences that can be heard in recordings, making it possible to pick the sounds of interest out of the background noise or the periods of silence. These spectrograms can be inspected visually much more rapidly than by listening to the sounds in real time. They also make it easier to distinguish particular call types visually and to make measurements of descriptive features of the sound to quantify the differences that researchers hear.

Sounds Produced by North Atlantic Right Whales

North Atlantic right whales make a variety of sounds. They do not produce the melodious songs that have been described for humpback whales (Payne and McVay 1971) or the haunting sounds of the bowhead whales in the Arctic (Würsig and Clark 1993). However, their repertoire consists of a similar diversity of sound types. Recordings have been made of North Atlantic right whales in most of their known range. Their sounds can be divided into three main categories: (1) blow sounds; (2) broadband impulsive sounds; and (3) tonal call types (Fig. 10.2). All of these call types have also been described for southern right whales.

Blow Sounds

Blow sounds coinciding with a right whale's exhalation have been recorded. It is not known whether blow sounds are intentional signals that serve a communicative function or are just produced incidentally. In most cases when a right whale breathes, it is not possible to hear it under the water. This could be a function of intensity, as most recordings may not be made close enough to the whale to pick up the exhalation. In SAGs or other social situations, whales will occasionally make more forceful exhalations, and the sounds can be heard clearly both above and below water. These sounds have been recorded from over 500 m away and have different acoustic characteristics than normal exhalations (Clark 1983). These social blow sounds could be detectable by other whales at greater distances than normal exhalations because of their greater amplitude or intensity (Würsig and Clark 1993).

Broadband Sounds

Broadband sounds can be broken down into two categories. The first category consists of nonvocal slaps, generally less than 0.2 seconds in duration, that result from the whale striking the surface of the water with parts of its body. These include sounds from breaches (where the whale jumps out of the water), flipper slapping, and tail slapping or lobtailing (color plate 30). These are not unique to right whales, as many other whale species produce similar

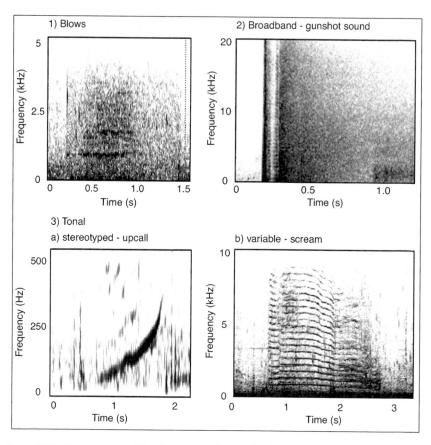

Figure 10.2. Spectrograms of the three major classes of right whale sounds: (1) a blow recorded underwater, (2) a gunshot sound, and (3) examples of the two classes of tonal calls, (a) a stereotyped up-call and (b) an example of a modulated tonal scream call. Note the different frequency and time scales for these different call types.

sounds. Although there are often clear echoes produced by these slaps, there is currently no evidence that right whales use this type of signal as a form of sonar.

The second category of broadband sounds is the "gunshot" sound, a very impressive, loud, cracking sound that a whale produces internally while at or near the surface of the water (Parks et al. 2005). The gunshot sound has been recorded only from the balaenid whales, including bowhead and southern right whales (Würsig and Clark 1993). It is unclear how this sound is produced. Although it is similar to slap sounds, it is much more intense than sounds from flipper or tail slapping and involves no visible external movements by the whale. Its function is unknown, but current data suggest that it may serve a communicative function with other right whales. The gunshot sound appears to be produced primarily by males in the late summer and early fall and could be related to mating or male–male agonistic behavior.

Tonal Calls

Tonal calls are the most diverse group of sounds that right whales produce. These can be divided into simple, low-frequency, stereotyped calls and more complex, frequency-modulated, higher-frequency calls. The classic right whale stereotyped tonal call is referred to as the up-call because it sweeps from low to higher frequency in a short "whoop." The up-call appears to be used in social contact situations: from mothers to their calves when they get separated, between males in SAGs on entering the group, and by whales swimming alone, possibly searching for other members of their species. The other stereotyped tonal calls are a down-call that sweeps from high to low frequency (like a backward up-call) and a constant call with a relatively flat frequency component.

The frequency-modulated call type referred to as the scream call includes a wide array of tonal, harmonically rich, moaning sounds. These sounds are produced primarily by the focal female in SAGs, but there is some evidence that males can produce similar signals as well. These sounds can be flat with no rise or change in frequency, or the frequency can waver up and down. They can be short, less than a second, or last up to four seconds in duration. They can be completely tonal or consist of chaotic sections at any point within the call where the clear harmonic structure of the sound breaks down, and it looks more like the broadband blow sound. Scream calls have not been successfully subdivided into discrete call types, as they appear to be graded along a continuum of variation.

Behavioral Contexts for Right Whale Sounds

Surface-Active Groups and Sounds

Right whales produce their entire known repertoire of sounds while in SAGs (see Chapter 6). This probably occurs because most right whale sounds serve a social communication function, and SAGs are a very commonly observed social interaction in right whales. Careful observational work coupled with recordings from a hydrophone array has demonstrated that different whales produce

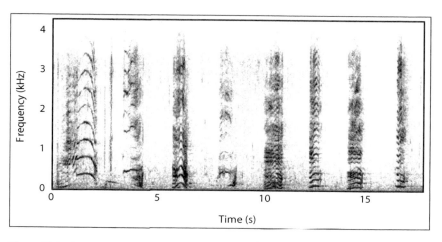

Figure 10.3. A spectrogram representing a sequence of tonal scream calls recorded from a surface-active group.

different call types in these groups (Parks 2003a). It is extremely difficult to determine which whale is vocalizing when there are multiple individuals in close body contact rolling around at the surface. Associating a sound with an individual whale often depends on slight separation of the individual from the group or on a visual cue such as a visible exhalation associated with blow sounds or a head-lift associated with gunshot sound production.

The focal female in the SAG produces the screams that are the predominant sounds recorded from these groups. Sometimes these sounds are produced at very high rates, with a call being emitted from the female every few seconds (Fig. 10.3). Males produce up-calls (the contact call) as they enter the group and when the focal female swims away from the group or dives and disappears. Males will sometimes swim around at the surface at the last position of the departed female, producing up-calls, apparently searching or calling for the female to return. Males also produce gunshot sounds in SAGs, apparently in competitive situations, when males are jostling for position around the female. In SAGs males are competing to get close to the female in the center of the group, presumably for access to mating opportunities (Kraus and Hatch 2001). Use of the gunshot sound by males in SAGs agrees with the previously proposed function of the sound as an agonistic threat (Clark 1983; Würsig and Clark 1993). Both males and females produce loud blow sounds in SAGs, and although unconfirmed at this time, both may produce gunshot sounds and up-calls (Fig. 10.4).

Figure 10.4. A diagram showing an aerial view of a surface-active group in the Bay of Fundy. Whales responsible for making different call types appear in different shades of gray and are marked with letters. The focal female whale (A) produces scream calls, approaching males (B) produce up-calls, female calves (C) produce warble or scream-like calls, and males within the group (D) produce gunshot sounds and noisy blow sounds.

One intriguing observation was that female calves make screamlike calls when in SAGs with their mothers in the Bay of Fundy. These calls are stuttered, slightly higher in frequency than the normal screams, but show every sign of developing into the full female cry. It is unclear at what stage of development a female calf starts participating in SAGs with her mother, but sighting information suggests that calves are not frequently seen in SAGs before six months of age (Parks 2003a). No unusual tonal sounds have been recorded from SAGs containing male calves.

Gunshot Sound Displays

Male gunshot sound displays are a newly described aspect of right whale behavior. Nine observations have been made of single adult male right whales engaged in an elaborate stereotyped behavioral display at the surface (Fig. 10.5). During this display the male produces sequences of dozens of very loud

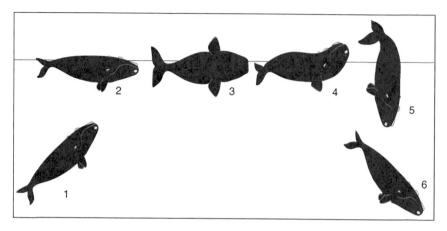

Figure 10.5. A diagram of the typical surfacing pattern of a lone male during a gunshot display. The whale (1) swims to the surface, (2) begins to make gunshot sounds, (3) rolls on its side and makes flipper slaps, (4) makes dramatic head-lifts, often followed by very intense gunshot sounds, and then (5) goes on a very slow dive, often raising the flukes high out the water (6) before starting the cycle again.

gunshot sounds (Parks et al. 2005). They are produced just before surfacing, at the surface, or immediately after diving. The whale will occasionally lift his head out of the water while keeping the rest of his body parallel to the surface, producing an extremely loud gunshot sound after his head is pulled back into the water (color plate 29). Each whale appears to have unique aspects to its gunshot display. Some whales make flipper slaps or tail slaps as part of the display sequence, and other whales will swim in tight circles at the surface. Diving males sometimes produce tonal sounds (up-calls or screamlike sounds), then resurface and repeat the same behavioral and acoustic gunshot display sequence again. Because only adult male right whales have been recorded producing gunshot sounds in the Bay of Fundy, it has been hypothesized that this sound plays a role in reproduction. This could be a male reproductive advertisement display, similar to bird song, but there have been no observations of whales approaching males who are making these displays or observations of these males moving to join other whales after completing the display. Results of genetic paternity analysis have found that none of the males producing gunshot displays are known fathers of any of the calves in the population (T. Frasier, pers. comm.), so it is unclear whether there are any reproductive benefits from these displays.

Gunshot sounds are also produced in SAGs but are produced singly, unlike the series of gunshot sounds produced in the solo whale displays. In SAGs males may be using this vocalization to threaten other males in the group. More work is needed to determine the functional significance of the gunshot sound and the role that these acoustic displays may play in right whale behavior and reproduction.

Mother–Calf Acoustic Contact

Very little is known about acoustic communication between mother right whales and their calves. In the first three or four months of their lives calves are rarely seen separated from their mothers and may be able to stay in contact visually. As a calf gets older it will frequently be observed out of visual range of its mother. In these situations, the whales likely use sounds to find one another. Up-calls have been recorded in the presence of reuniting mothers and calves, and it is likely that this is one sound used to bring back together separated mothers and their calves. It is unclear if the mother produces the up-call or if the calf also calls its mother. Mother–calf pairs could also have other, quieter sounds that they use to stay in contact over short ranges, which have yet to be recorded. Quieter sounds would reduce the risk of other whales or predators eavesdropping on the communication and using it to find the vulnerable calf. More research is needed to determine all the sounds used by mothers and their calves and their functions.

New Approaches to Understanding Right Whale Communication

Playback Experiments

The acoustic playback trial that was described in the narrative at the beginning of this chapter was part of a set of experiments carried out from 1999 to 2001 (Parks 2003b). The purpose was to determine if right whale males were attracted primarily by female scream calls and not by gunshot sounds or other SAG sounds. These studies involved playbacks of female SAG sounds recorded from North Atlantic right whales, female SAG sounds recorded from southern right whales (twenty years earlier), and gunshot sounds recorded from North Atlantic right whales. The southern right whale calls were included to increase the number of examples being played back, as they appeared superficially to be the same as North Atlantic SAG sounds in terms of their frequency and variability.

The playback experiments consisted of three trial periods of twenty minutes each. In the preplayback, playback, and postplayback observation periods, observers scanned around the platform and recorded the position of each surfacing whale to roughly track the orientation or heading of all visible whales and to document any changes in whale position or behavior. Whales that approached closely or were approached by another research vessel in the area were photographed to identify individuals.

Whales approached the transmitting vessel during most of the SAG sound playbacks, including recordings from both the North Atlantic and southern right whales. No whales approached the gunshot playbacks. The biggest surprise came from the identification of the individuals that approached the playbacks. All of the whales of known sex that approached the North Atlantic SAG playbacks were adult males (twenty-eight males, no females). However, the whales approaching the southern right whale SAG playbacks were both males and females, almost a fifty-fifty split (six males, seven females), and the ages ranged from young calves with their mothers to older adults.

There are three possibilities to explain this difference in response. The first is that the North Atlantic right whales did not recognize the "voice" of the individual southern right whale females, and all whales were interested in a potentially new female in the population. The second is that southern and northern right whales have been separated for a long period of time, and it is possible that there have been changes in their acoustic repertoires that are subtle to humans but vastly different to the whales. In this scenario, the whales were simply curious about the right-whale-like sounds that they were hearing. The third possibility is that the Southern Hemisphere recordings were made on the calving grounds in the winter months, whereas the playbacks were conducted in the summer on the North Atlantic right whale feeding grounds (opposite seasons). It is possible that SAGs on the calving ground are socially very different from those on the feeding grounds, and therefore, sounds from these groups would attract different groups of animals.

Right Whale Hearing

It is safe to assume that right whales can hear each other because they respond to playbacks and manage to find each other in the limited visibility of the North Atlantic waters. However, it is unknown how high or how low a frequency they can hear, or their hearing sensitivity at any frequency. There have been no direct measures of hearing in any baleen whale species because the animals are too large for behavioral tests and cannot be restrained for electro-physiological tests such as those used to test the hearing of human infants. Instead all current estimates of baleen whale hearing are from indirect evidence as follows. First, the frequency range of optimal hearing is thought to coincide with the frequency range of the calls produced by the whales (Wartzok and Ketten 1999). Playback experiments with several species have documented behavioral responses to conspecific calls (Clark and Clark 1980; Watkins 1981; Tyack 1983). Playback experiments have also shown responses of gray whales to the calls of killer whale predators (Cummings and Thompson 1971). Additional studies of baleen whale reactions to anthropogenic noise sources have documented responses at higher frequencies, up to at least 15 kHz (Watkins 1986). Playback experiments have demonstrated directional hearing capabilities in baleen whales by showing precise orientation toward and localization of the sound source (Clark and Clark 1980; Tyack 1983).

Although right whale hearing cannot be measured directly, a large body of research has been developed to predict hearing capabilities based on the anatomy of the inner ear for both land and marine mammals (Ketten 1984; Greenwood 1990; Ketten 1992). This technique was used to analyze right whale ear anatomy to predict the right whale hearing range. Preliminary work indicates that right whale hearing is predicted to be between 12 Hz and 22 kHz (Parks 2003a), which is similar to the frequency range of sounds that they produce. This means that right whales may be able to hear both slightly lower and slightly higher frequency sounds than humans (humans can hear approximately 20 Hz–20 kHz at birth). The sensitivity of right whale hearing in any particular frequency range is not known, and it is our hope that future research will address this question. The disturbing feature of the presumed hearing capabilities in right whales is that most noises from human shipping activities completely overlap the predicted frequency range of whale hearing (Fig. 10.6). Therefore, the sounds that human activities generate in the ocean can be heard by right whales and can potentially damage their hearing or limit the range over which they can hear each other (see Chapter 11).

Noise Pollution

The ocean is naturally a very noisy place, with sounds coming from weather-generated waves, earthquakes, and the many marine organisms that use sound

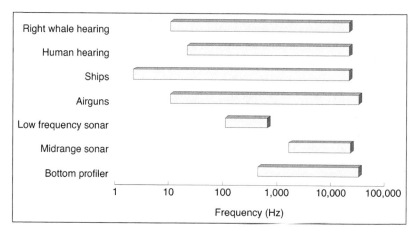

Figure 10.6. A diagram illustrating the overlap in frequency of noise from human activities and the hearing abilities of right whales. Note that the maximum high-frequency cutoff for this figure is 30 kHz, although several sound types have energy at higher frequencies. The intensity and duration of different noise sources vary (noise data from Richardson et al. 1995).

to communicate. Sounds produced by right whales have evolved over millennia to avoid interference from the frequencies of natural ambient noise in the ocean. They produce sounds in the frequency range of relatively low ambient noise to make communication signals easy to hear. Their signals also utilize low fundamental frequencies, which will increase the range of sound transmission (Clark 1983).

Ever since the advent of engine-driven ships over 140 years ago, the world's oceans have experienced ever-increasing levels of noise from human activities, such as noise from shipping, oil exploration, and naval sonar (Richardson et al. 1995; Andrew et al. 2002; NRC 2003). Increasing background noise from human activities is a major component of the urban ocean environment. Indeed, there are some areas along the eastern seaboard of the United States where ambient noise levels are so persistently loud that they surpass noise exposure thresholds established by the Occupational Safety and Health Administration as unacceptable for humans. These ambient noise levels may limit the detection threshold for baleen whales because their vocalizations have most of their energy below 1 kHz, which coincides with the highest average ambient noise levels in today's oceans (Urick 1983). Therefore, understanding the role of acoustic communication in the lives of right whales is important to determine the potential impact of anthropogenic noise on their communication, reproduction, and survival.

Noise has been a topic of concern for humans for several decades, and there is evidence that exposure to loud sounds can cause permanent hearing loss and increase stress levels. The Occupational Safety and Health Administration has instituted restrictions on noise levels for people in the workplace, but no such restrictions exist in the ocean. The problem is made even worse because sound is transmitted much more efficiently in water than in air. Sound waves travel through water and air in the same way. However, the densities of air and water are very different, which leads to differences in sound propagation. For example the speed of sound in the ocean (ca. 1,550 m/s) is 4.5 times faster than that in air (ca. 333 m/s). Previous research on deep ocean temperature trends have made use of this property to transmit sounds underwater literally around the world (Munk et al. 1994).

Even the way in which the loudness of a sound is reported differs between air and water. For both air and water, sound levels are reported in a unit called the decibel (dB), which is measured on a logarithmic scale relative to a reference pressure in micro-Pascals (mPa). The difference in reference pressure for air and water and the differences in density and sound speed for air and water mean that decibels for sounds measured in air are very different from decibels measured in water. A sound that in air would have a pressure value of 0 dB would be closer to 61.5 dB in water (Wartzok and Ketten 1999). The dB level of a vacuum cleaner is 80 dB with respect to 20 mPa at 1 m (the in-air reference pressure), a rock concert is approximately 120 dB, and a jet engine is about 140 dB (Pierce 1981). By comparison, the underwater sound level values for right whale calls and slap sounds cover a wide range from 155 to 200 dB with respect to 1 mPa at 1 m (the in-water reference pressure) (Parks and Tyack 2005), and the levels for naval sonar can be as high as 230 dB (see Richardson et al. 1995 for more details). On learning about such high sound levels, people are immediately concerned about how loud these underwater sounds are. However, most people are unaware that the in-air and in-water decibel sound levels being reported are on different scales, and this difference must be taken into consideration in discussing how loud an underwater sound is.

The issue of ocean noise has come to the forefront of public concern in recent years with reports of mass strandings and deaths of several whale species coincident with the use of military sonar (Dalton 2003). Although there is no clear understanding about the link between military sonar and whale deaths, it has caused heightened public concern and awareness. However, military sonar is only a tiny part of the noise in the ocean that our civilization produces. The major human sources of noise include many activities such as ship traffic, construction in harbors and marinas, dredging, fishing and bottom-mapping depth finders, and seismic oil exploration.

By far the greatest and most ubiquitous anthropogenic contributor to ocean noise today is commercial shipping traffic. Shipping noise is primarily the result of propeller cavitation and the inefficient conversion of engine force into ship motion. Construction activities in the water, such as blasting and pile driving, make very loud, broadband sounds. Dredging (the removal of sediment from a channel to produce sufficient depths for vessel navigation) is the underwater equivalent to plowing on land and generates noise from the movement of rocks and earth. Military sonar can be divided into two categories: active, where sound is actively generated to reflect sound off submarines and surface vessels for detection, and passive, which relies on listening for sounds produced by the objects of interest. For decades the military has had to deal with the noise in the ocean limiting the effectiveness of both types of sonar. Active sonar is useful because it provides a mechanism for detecting a quiet submarine when the background noise level is too high to hear it simply by listening. Other types of active acoustic tools are used because there is no passive acoustic alternative. Examples include fish-finding and bottom-mapping sonar used to look for fish in the water column below the vessel and to map the surface layer of the bottom, respectively. Seismic survey sounds are intentionally designed to reflect off layers below the seafloor, so the sound energy is compressed into a very intense, short-duration pulse, equivalent to small controlled explosions.

These sources of sound vary in both intensity and duration. Sounds such as those from construction and naval sonar are very loud but relatively short-term and uncommon. By comparison noises from shipping and oil exploration are both loud and almost constant in some areas. Different parts of the right whale habitat have more ship traffic than others. In general the closer the whales are to the coast, the greater the occurrences of shipping, fishing, and recreational traffic raising low-frequency background noise levels to what people experience on modern city streets. Even offshore environments are not immune to the increase in noise. Military sonar, seismic exploration, and offshore shipping and fishing activities have all increased around the world in the past fifty years, meaning that anthropogenic noise is now common throughout the world's oceans.

It is not known what effect the increase in ocean noise has had or is having on right whales. Over short distances, noise from a passing ship would make it difficult for a right whale to hear a sound that it could hear perfectly well if the ship were not there. This type of situation is referred to as masking and occurs when a sound of interest is obscured by other interfering sounds, usually of the same or similar frequencies. It is analogous to two people standing next to a road. They can have a normal conversation if there are no cars, but if a car goes by, they either have to talk louder or wait until the noise level is lower to communicate. This masking of acoustic signals is also familiar to anyone who has been in a really loud dance club or sports stadium, where shouting and body language are the only forms of communication.

Right whales may be able to adapt to increased noise in their environment. On a very stormy day with waves breaking, ambient noise levels are naturally very high. Right whales had to cope with those situations before people introduced mechanical noise into the ocean. However, in the past, the storm-generated loud sounds lasted for a few hours or days, not years. There are several ways that right whales could modify their behavior in response to noise. For example, they could call louder, call more often, move to a quieter area, delay communication until it gets quieter, or shift the frequency of their calls away from the frequency band of high noise. In fact there is evidence that right whales shift their calls into a higher frequency band in the presence of increased noise from vessels (Parks 2003a). Unfortunately this strategy has a cost because the higher-frequency calls do not carry as far, so the range over which the whale can be heard is reduced.

Indeed one problem for assessing the impact of noise on right whales lies in uncertainties about the ranges over which right whales want to communicate and what they are communicating. For contact calls it is known that they will countercall over distances of at least 8 km, and that on quiet days under good conditions scientists can hear these calls 24 km away (C. W. Clark, unpublished data). For surface-active group sounds, the data show that whales arrive from at least 8 km away to participate in these intensely social activities (Kraus and Hatch 2001).

As an example of potential impacts, assume that historically right whales expected to communicate over 16 km. If modern underwater noise levels are superimposed on the western North Atlantic coastal environment, the average level of ambient noise will be raised by a factor of ten. In this scenario, the communication area for a right whale in the coastal waters of the United States has shrunk from an average of 813 km^2 to 80 km^2. The chance of two whales hearing each other today has been reduced to 10 percent of what it was a hundred years ago. Given today's population of 350 whales, does this mean that the rise in ambient noise level has significantly reduced the probability of whales finding each other to mate or find food? Is this reduction in communication range another factor that partially explains why the population has not recovered?

Noise can have more chronic impacts on right whales than simply causing short-term masking events or limiting the range of communication. There is evidence from studies with terrestrial animals that elevated levels of noise can induce a chronic stress response (Evans 2003; Otten et al. 2004). This could mean that increasing underwater noise around North Atlantic right whales could contribute to physical and neurological problems resulting from chronic stress. The levels of noise that right whales are exposed to could lead to short-term or even permanent hearing loss, making it difficult for them to hear other whales or ships in the area. Another consideration is the question of whether right whales view a ship as a threat only when it is extremely close, even if they do hear it approaching from a distance. A right whale does not necessarily have any innate reason to avoid a ship unless it has been injured by one in the past. Right whales have very few natural predators, and they may not view a ship as dangerous until it gets very close. Unfortunately there are relatively few encounters between ships and right whales in which the right whale survives to learn this lesson.

More research is needed to understand how and if right whales can cope with an increasingly noisy ocean. The consequences for right whales may be that critical communication sounds related to reproduction, navigation, and survival will be masked by the sounds of the multitude of human endeavors on the ocean. It is possible that such circumstances could contribute to declines in the right whale population, and there is good reason to believe that the cumulative effect of multiple stressors is greater than any one impact alone.

Conclusion

Understanding of right whale acoustic communication, like many aspects of right whale biology, is just beginning. Advances over the past decade have greatly increased understanding of both the sound types and the hearing of right whales. Ongoing research is investigating the use of these sounds in different social settings, differences in sound production related to age and sex, and changes in acoustic behavior resulting from exposure to noise. Future acoustic research will provide a window into the social lives of these animals that is currently often limited to what can be seen at the surface. Given all of the challenges faced by this species, the time available to answer these questions may be limited. In any case, underwater noise in the marine environment is a serious issue that goes far beyond this species. There are no known marine vertebrate species that lack hearing, and the continued increase of noise in the ocean has the potential to affect thousands of species and many marine ecosystems. Right whales, by virtue of living on the brink of extinction, are perhaps just the first species for which these noise issues have become a serious consideration for their continued survival.

Andrew, R. K., B. M. Howe, and J. A. Mercer. 2002. Ocean ambient sound: comparing the 1960s with the 1990s for a receiver off the California coast. *Acoustics Research Letters Online* 3:65–70.

Clark, C. W. 1982. The acoustic repertoire of the southern right whale, a quantitative analysis. *Animal Behavior* 30:1060–1071.

Clark, C. W. 1983. Acoustic communication and behavior of the southern right whale. Pages 163–198 *in* R. S. Payne, ed. *Communication and Behavior of Whales. American Association for the Advancement of Science Selected Symposium 76.* Westview Press, Boulder, CO.

Clark, C. W. 1984. Acoustic communication and behavior of southern right whales, *Eubalaena australis. National Geographic Society Research Reports* 17:897–907.

Clark, C. W., and J. M. Clark. 1980. Sound playback experiments with southern right whales (*Eubalaena australis*). *Science* 207:663–665.

Clark, C. W., J. F. Borsani, and G. Notarbartolo-di-Sciara. 2002. Vocal activity of fin whales, *Balaenoptera physalus,* in the Ligurian Sea. *Marine Mammal Science* 18:281–285.

Cummings, W. C., and P. O. Thompson. 1971. Gray whales, *Eschrichtius robustus,* avoid the underwater sounds of killer whales, *Orcinus orca. Fishery Bulletin* 69:525–530.

Cummings, W. C., J. Fish, and P. Thompson. 1972. Sound production and other behavior of southern right whales, *Eubalaena glacialis. Transactions of the San Diego Society of Natural History* 17:1–14.

Dalton, R. 2003. Scientists split over regulations on sonar use. *Nature* 425:549.

D'Vincent, C. G., R. M. Nilson, and R. E. Hanna. 1985. Vocalization and coordinated feeding behavior of the humpback whale in southeastern Alaska. *Scientific Report of the Whales Research Institute, Tokyo* 36:41–47.

Evans, G. 2003. A multimethodological analysis of cumulative risk and allostatic load. *Developmental Psychology* 39:924–933.

Greenwood, D. G. 1990. A cochlear frequency-position function for several species—29 years later. *Journal of the Acoustical Society of America* 87:2592–2605.

Johnson, M. P., and P. L. Tyack. 2003. A digital acoustic recording tag for measuring the response of wild marine mammals to sound. *IEEE Journal of Oceanic Engineering* 28:3–12.

Ketten, D. 1984. Correlations of morphology with frequency for Odontocete cochlea: Systematics and topology. Ph.D. Thesis, The Johns Hopkins University, Baltimore, MD.

Ketten, D. R. 1992. The marine mammal ear: Specializations for aquatic audition and echolocation. Pages 717–754 *in* D. Webster, R. R. Fay, and A. N. Popper, eds. *The Evolutionary Biology of Hearing.* Springer-Verlag, New York.

Kraus, S. D., and J. J. Hatch. 2001. Mating strategies in the North Atlantic right whale (*Eubalaena glacialis*). *Journal of Cetacean Research and Management* Special Issue 2:237–244.

Laurinolli, M. H., A. E. Hay, F. Desharnais, and C. T. Taggart. 2003. Localization of North Atlantic right whale sounds in the Bay of Fundy using a sonobuoy array. *Marine Mammal Science* 19:708–723.

Matthews, J. N., S. Brown, D. Gillespie, M. Johnson, R. McLanaghan, A. Moscrop, D. Nowacek, R. Leaper, T. Lewis, and P. Tyack. 2001. Vocalisation rates of the North Atlantic right whale (*Eubalaena glacialis*). *Journal of Cetacean Research and Management* 3:271–282.

Miller, P. J., and P. L. Tyack. 1998. A small towed beamforming array to identify vocalizing *resident* killer whales (*Orcinus orca*) concurrent with focal behavioral observations. *Deep-Sea Research* 45:1389–1405.

Munk, W. H., R. C. Spindel, A. Baggeroer, and T. G. Birdsall. 1994. The Heard Island Feasibility Test. *The Journal of the Acoustical Society of America* 96:2330–2342.

Nowacek, D. P., M. P. Johnson, and P. L. Tyack. 2004. North Atlantic right whales (*Eubalaena glacialis*) ignore ships but respond to alerting stimuli. *Proceedings of Biological Sciences, The Royal Society* 271:227–231.

NRC. 2003. *Ocean Noise and Marine Mammals.* National Academy Press, Washington, DC.

Otten, W., E. Kanitz, B. Puppe, M. Tuchscherer, K. P. Brussow, G. Nurnberg, and B. Stabenow. 2004. Acute and long term effects of chronic intermittent noise stress on hypothalamic-pituitary-adrenocortical and sympatho-adrenomedullary axis in pigs. *Animal Science* 78:271–283.

Parks, S. E. 2003a. Acoustic communication in the North Atlantic right whale (*Eubalaena glacialis*). Ph.D. Thesis. MIT-WHOI Joint Program in Oceanography. Woods Hole, MA.

Parks, S. E. 2003b. Response of North Atlantic right whales (*Eubalaena glacialis*) to playback of calls recorded from surface active groups in both the North and South Atlantic. *Marine Mammal Science* 19:563–580.

Parks, S. E., and C. W. Clark. 2005. Variation in acoustic activity of North Atlantic right whales in three critical habitat areas in 2004. *Journal of the Acoustical Society of America* 117:2469.

Parks, S. E., and P. L. Tyack. 2005. Sound production by North Atlantic right whales (*Eubalaena glacialis*) in surface active groups. *Journal of the Acoustical Society of America* 117:3297–3306.

Parks, S. E., P. K. Hamilton, S. D. Kraus, and P. L. Tyack. 2005. The gunshot sound produced by male North Atlantic right whales (*Eubalaena glacialis*) and its potential function in reproductive advertisement. *Marine Mammal Science* 21: 458–475.

Payne, R. S., and S. McVay. 1971. Songs of humpback whales. *Science* 173:585–597.

Payne, R. S., and K. Payne. 1971. Underwater sounds of southern right whales. *Zoologica* 58:159–165.

Pierce, A. D. 1981. *Acoustics. An Introduction to its Physical Principles and Applications.* McGraw-Hill, New York.

Richardson, W. J., C. R. Greene, Jr., C. I. Malme, and D. H. Thomson. 1995. *Marine Mammals and Noise.* Academic Press, San Diego.

Saayman, G. S., and C. K. Tayler. 1973. Some behavior patterns of the southern right whale, *Eubalaena australis. Sonderdruck aus Zeitschrift für Säugetierkunde* 38: 172–183.

Schevill, W. E., and W. A. Watkins. 1962. Whale and porpoise voices: a phonograph record. Woods Hole Oceanographic Institution, Woods Hole, MA. 24 pp.

Schevill, W. E., R. H. Backus, and J. B. Hersey. 1962. Sound production by marine animals. Pages 540–566 *in* M. N. Hill, ed. *Bioacoustics.* Wiley, New York.

Tyack, P. 1983. Differential response of humpback whales, *Megaptera novaeangliae,* to playback of song or social sounds. *Behavioral Ecology and Sociobiology* 13:49–55.

Tyack, P., and H. Whitehead. 1983. Male competition in large groups of wintering humpback whales. *Behaviour* 83:132–154.

Urick, R. J. 1983. *Principles of Underwater Sound.* Peninsula Publishing, Los Altos, CA.

Vanderlaan, A. S. M., A. E. Hay, and C. T. Taggart. 2003. Characterization of North Atlantic right-whale (*Eublaena glacialis*) sounds in the Bay of Fundy. *IEEE Journal of Oceanic Engineering* 28:164–173.

Wartzok, D., and D. R. Ketten. 1999. Marine mammal sensory systems. Pages 117–175 *in* J. E. Reynolds III and S. A. Rommel, eds. *Biology of Marine Mammals.* Smithsonian Institution Press, Washington, DC.

Watkins, W. A. 1981. Activities and underwater sounds of fin whales. *Scientific Report to the Whales Research Institute* 33:83–117.

Watkins, W. A. 1986. Whale reactions to human activities in Cape Cod waters. *Marine Mammal Science* 2:251–262.

Winn, H. E., and L. K. Winn. 1978. The song of the humpback whale *Megaptera novaeangliae* in the West Indies. *Marine Biology* 47:97–114.

Wright, D. R. 2001. Categorization of northern right whale, *Eubalaena glacialis,* sound. M.A. Thesis, Boston University, Boston.

Würsig, B., and C. W. Clark. 1993. Behavior. Pages 157–199 *in* J. J. Burns, J. J. Montague, and C. J. Cowles, eds. *The Bowhead Whale.* Special Publication No. 2, Society for Marine Mammalogy. Lawrence, KS.

Acknowledgments

Many thanks to the numerous researchers and scientists and funding agencies that made this research possible. Much of the acoustic recordings and playback data were collected with extensive assistance from the New England Aquarium and the *Song of the Whale* crew and research team from the International Fund for Animal Welfare. Julie Arruda, Scott Cramer, Jennifer Trehey O'Malley, and especially Darlene Ketten of the Woods Hole Oceanographic Institution were critical to the data collection and modeling for the hearing and anatomy research. This work was funded in large part by grants and contracts from the Commonwealth of Massachusetts Division of Marine Fisheries, Northeast Consortium, National Oceanographic and Atmospheric Administration, National Marine Fisheries Service, National Fish and Wildlife Foundation Whale Conservation Fund, Reinhart Coastal Research Center, and the Packard Foundation. S. Parks's doctoral research was supported in part by a NDSEG fellowship.

11

Listening to Their World: Acoustics for Monitoring and Protecting Right Whales in an Urbanized Ocean

CHRISTOPHER W. CLARK, DOUGLAS GILLESPIE, DOUGLAS P. NOWACEK, AND SUSAN E. PARKS

Summer 1972
Lincoln, Massachusetts

What now appears so obvious was once unknown or so imperceptible to our senses as to be invisible. Civilization is drowning out the sounds of whales and other undersea creatures. If we'd only paid closer attention, would the situation now be better than it is? Are we still missing more of the obvious? Probably so, especially when it comes to these large, ponderous right whales that graze the upper layers of the ocean for sparsely distributed food and only come into view when at the surface to breath. Through our visually dominated senses we label them dimwitted and proclaim them predisposed for extinction. How depressingly true, especially as they are confronted with civilization's insidious expansion into coastal seas, a habitat they once freely roamed without the threat of ship collision, entanglement, toxic waste, and noise pollution. But pause and think again before giving up on them. What messages are before us even now that we are missing altogether or maybe misinterpreting? The point is that we're not listening, or if we are, we're not listening very well.

333

The first time I heard a right whale was in the summer of 1972. After the first of many raucous dinners with Roger and Katy Payne and their four children in their Lincoln, Massachusetts, farmhouse, Roger took me up to the garret, sat me down in front of a pile of black and white photographs, slapped a pair of enormous headphones over my ears, and turned on a tape recorder. Immediately I was awash in the faint, rhythmic swishing of waves on a pebbled shore, followed by a deep, throaty exhalation of a beast I could not see but that seemed about to consume me. Rising out of the hypnotic rhythms of the waves and heavy breathing came a distant call, a sound that seemed to emerge from the depths before reaching a crescendo that held me in a trance. I wanted to hear more. And the whales did not disappoint me. Within a few seconds a massive volume of sound rocked me backwards, a similar upswept call, only this time coming from the invisible heavy breather. It was as if, diving without light, I had just entered a vast underground cavern, with other passageways that I could not see but could sense by subtleties in the reverberations of the voices around me. I was submerged, and all around me the sounds of bodies moving through water, of breathing at the edge of sea and sky, and of calling across some distant bay held me captive, mesmerized, transfixed.

Those first voices became intensely real a few years later when for twenty-two months, thanks to the pioneering work of Roger and Katy, my wife Janie and I spent every waking hour listening to, photographing, following, and counting individually identified southern right whales in the Golfo San José, Argentina. The immediate culmination of our small effort would be summarized in a series of scientific papers describing and quantifying what we heard and saw and what we thought we deduced from measurements and statistics. One interesting result, not immediately obvious to us during those long days of listening and watching, was that the whales would call and countercall with each other across the expanses of the bay. These exchanges would take hours to unfold, and so recognition of such acoustic partnerships was invisible to us at the time. But after some analysis and a flurry of sound playback experiments, that reality came into focus: the familiar upswept whoops were used by the distant whales to initiate and maintain contact throughout the expanse of the gulf. At the time none of our studies appeared to be of much benefit to the whales, but the benefit to me was that I had found my calling: whale acoustic communication.

Now some thirty years later, under the shadow of a desperate struggle for survival by the remnant northern right whale population, what we first

learned from the southern right whales along the windswept shores of Pata-
gonia is being put to good use. The right whale behavior of long-distance
contact calling is becoming the centerpiece for detecting their presence and
estimating their distribution and numbers in the interest of conservation.

Christopher W. Clark

This chapter is about listening to right whales and how, by using modern technology, scientists can do a better job of detecting their presence and esti-mating their distribution to offer them better protection in their increasingly urbanized environment. These techniques hold great promise as a means of monitoring for right whales throughout large portions of their domain over the entire year. A total of nineteen North Atlantic right whales have been killed by ship strikes in the past twenty years (Kraus et al. 2005). Population models show that if only two females can be saved each year from such untimely deaths, the species might not become extinct after all (Caswell et al. 1999). Although great efforts are being made by the shipping industry to avoid collisions with right whales, they are just too hard to spot in anything but the calmest con-ditions, and if a ship captain does see a right whale ahead of his vessel, it will often be too late to change course. In spite of the best efforts of aerial survey teams to find right whales and alert vessels to their presence, three whales have been killed by ships in the past year alone. If twenty-four-hour acoustic mon-itoring can be implemented, ship captains could be told before they leave port where the whales are congregated and plan their routes accordingly.

This chapter is also about the potential threat from man-made ocean noises. As Chapter 1 points out, right whales in the western North Atlantic now live in an urban environment, and nowhere is this urbanization more apparent than in the rising tide of acoustic smog that bathes the coastal waters of North America. A sad irony of this listening story is that while researchers are finally gaining the ability to apply acoustic tools for monitoring this right whale pop-ulation, the amount of noise that humans are pouring into the ocean makes it difficult to detect calling whales. By extension, if the biggest difficulty in de-tecting calling whales is a result of anthropogenic noise, imagine what the whales must be contending with. In essence, human activities are destroying the right whale's acoustic habitat. Near the end of this chapter some acoustic scenes are provided to illustrate this point, and it is proposed that one effect is analogous to habitat fragmentation. From any perspective, biological, regulatory, or political, the acoustic environment in which right whale communication evolved is disappearing fast. Within a whale's lifetime the quiet bays and rich feeding grounds have become acoustic garbage dumps. The north–south migratory path has become a gauntlet through which the whales must travel in partial deafness, their acoustic perception bleached by the incessant din of humanity.

Why is it important to listen to whales and their environment? All existing anatomic, physiological, and behavioral evidence indicates that right whales are especially well adapted for producing and perceiving sound. This is consistent with conclusions from other marine mammal species for which more data are available (e.g., bottlenose dolphin, killer whale), but right whales specialize in low-frequency (<1,000 Hz) sounds (Clark 1983; Ketten 2000; Matthews et al. 2001; Parks and Tyack 2005). It makes evolutionary sense that in the ocean medium, which conducts light so poorly but transmits sound so efficiently, selection would favor the auditory sense. From the standpoint of observing, monitoring, and understanding right whale society, and especially their communication system, sound is arguably the very best way to get the inside story. Scientists can take advantage of the whale's adaptations for producing and perceiving sounds to better understand their behavioral ecology as well as to monitor their distribution and occurrence in critical habitats.

Call Detection

Right whales produce a wide variety of sounds as discussed in Chapter 10. Some of these sounds are distinctive enough to be considered species specific. Here one type of right whale call that can be used to detect and recognize right whales acoustically is described qualitatively and through illustration. The best sound type to rely on for detecting right whales is the contact call, but other calls, as illustrated in Chapter 10, might prove important as well.

The contact call, or up-call as it is sometimes referred to, turns out to be the right whale's most common call and the call type most consistently associated with right whales. This is the sound that William Schevill and William Watkins, two distinguished marine scientists from Woods Hole Oceanographic Institution, first published in their classic 1962 phonograph record, accompanied by a spectrographic image (Schevill and Watkins 1962). It is the same call that Dorothy Spero recorded in the early 1980s in the Bay of Fundy. It was the most common call recorded by International Fund for Animal Welfare scientists aboard the *Song of the Whale* research vessel during their right

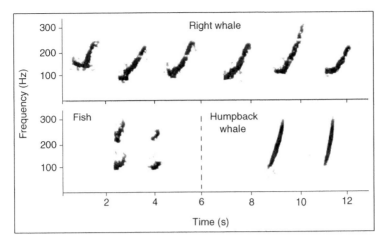

Figure 11.1. Spectrographic examples of six typical right whale contact calls, two fish sounds, and a pair of humpback song notes.

whale research in the late 1990s, and that Dana Wright analyzed and discussed in her masters thesis (Matthews et al. 2001; Wright 2001). It was the first confirmed right whale call recorded using Cornell's autonomous pop-up recorders in the Great South Channel in late spring of 2000 and in Cape Cod Bay during the early spring of 2001.

Up-calls are not produced by right whales in all behavioral contexts. As discussed in Chapter 10, different types of sounds (e.g., screams) are more prominent in surface-active groups (SAGs) of mixed sex (Parks and Tyack 2005). However, SAGs are relatively rare, so relying on SAG sounds to detect whales is a poor strategy. The gunshot sounds, though loud, frequent, and distinctively informative under some contexts (e.g., there are probably males in the area), are too easily confused with other types of knocks and bangs from other sources. Realistically, if one wants to detect the presence of a right whale acoustically, the best bet is to listen for the sound they are most likely to make: a contact call, a distinctive low-frequency glissando that rises from about 50 Hz (approximately an octave above the lowest note on a piano) to about 440 Hz (orchestral A on a piano) and lasts about one to two seconds, as illustrated in Fig. 11.1.

Unfortunately detecting a contact call during most of the year is extremely challenging. Right whales are so rare, and they are distributed over such a huge area, that finding whales really is a needle-in-the-haystack crusade. Even with acoustics, where the detection area is typically one hundred times greater than the visual sighting area, the total area in which to search is so vast that one must be very strategic as to where one listens. As an example, during the late fall and winter months, a small but critical portion of the population migrates from the Gulf of Maine down along the east coast to a Georgia–Florida winter habitat. If it is assumed that the width of this migratory corridor is 50 km and it runs the length of 3,000 km, this amounts to an area of 150,000 km^2. Even if one optimistically assumed that the entire population is distributed uniformly within this area (not an assumption supported by data), the density is about one animal every 500 km^2.

There are many other animals in the ocean that produce sounds that can be confused with right whale up-calls. Various species of fish are one source of confusion, and another is the humpback whale. Both make frequency-modulated sounds in the 50- to 500-Hz frequency band and have characteristics similar to right whale calls. The consequence of these acoustic similarities is that one has to be clever and careful when attempting to detect a right whale. For example, in 2000, 14,000 hours of recordings were collected on the western side of Georges Bank east of Cape Cod, Massachusetts, and automatically analyzed for detections of right whale contact calls. Hundreds of thousands of sounds with energy in the same frequency range and with the same duration as right whale up-calls were detected, but only 227 were right whale calls. The rest were notes from the songs of singing humpbacks (Clark and Clapham 2004) that could be distinguished from right whale sounds only by extracting detailed information on the frequency contour of every sound and using a statistical process (Gillespie 2004).

An important feature that can be used to distinguish reliably between humpbacks and right whales is acoustic context or syntax. That is, humpback song is composed of hierarchically organized notes that are repeated in patterns, whereas right whale contact calls occur one at a time, separated by relatively longer intervals of silence. Thus, a series of regularly spaced up-calls, interspersed regularly with other types of sounds, are from a singing humpback, whereas a single up-call or even a short series of up-calls is in all likelihood a right whale. Presently, such syntactic contextual information is used by expert analysts to distinguish between right whales and humpbacks but is not yet incorporated into automatic detection methods. Figure 11.1 illustrates some fish sounds and humpback song notes that have some characteristics in common with and are sometimes confused with right whale up-calls.

The Acoustic Communication Window

Other than a right whale's predisposition to produce up-calls, there is something else about these sounds that makes them more likely to be detected. The acoustic characteristics of the contact call are beautifully matched to the shallow, coastal environment in which right whales spend most of their lives. In this environment, two factors, transmission loss and ambient noise, strongly influence how far away one whale can hear the call of another, or how far away a human-designed system can detect a right whale. Transmission loss quantifies how much energy a sound loses as it travels farther and farther away from the calling whale. It takes into consideration many components such as the sound's frequency content, water temperature, depth of the calling whale, and the depth of the receiving whale. In other words transmission loss is controlled by the features of the sound, the positions of the two animals in space, and the characteristics of the water mass and ocean floor separating the two (see Jensen et al. 1994, Fig. 1.16).

The second factor, ambient noise, is the measure that describes or quantifies how much sound there is in the environment across a range of frequencies. In layman's terms one can think of the measure of ambient noise as a number that describes how noisy a place is. In regard to how ambient noise affects the task of detecting a whale call, the ambient noise level of greatest interest is that which occupies the same frequency band as the call. In shallow-water (<100–300 m) right whale habitats without the influence of vessel noises, there is typically a window of low ambient noise between about 100 Hz and 300 Hz (Clark 1983, Table 1).

For many animal species, it is not uncommon to find that long-distance contact sounds fall into a frequency range where both transmission loss and ambient noise are low (Marler and Marten 1977; Wiley and Richards 1978). This combination creates an acoustic window, a window of opportunity for long-range acoustic communication in which the call loses less energy per distance than if it were in a different frequency range, and the chance or probability of hearing the call against the background of ambient noise is maximized (Clark and Ellison 2004).

Right whales are no different. When it comes to the frequency content of their contact calls, the calls fall neatly within a frequency range where, in shallow water, both the transmission loss and natural ambient noise are low (Clark 1983). Figure 11.2a illustrates the typical difference between transmission loss

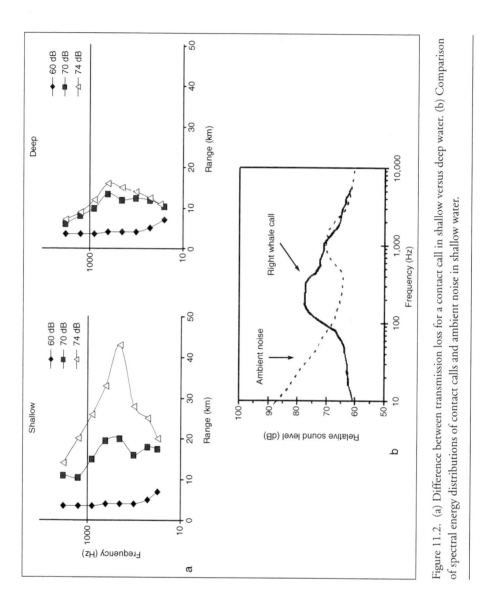

Figure 11.2. (a) Difference between transmission loss for a contact call in shallow versus deep water. (b) Comparison of spectral energy distributions of contact calls and ambient noise in shallow water.

for a contact call in shallow versus deep water, and Fig. 11.2b compares the frequency spectrum level of contact calls with the frequency spectrum level of ambient noise in shallow water. This window of opportunity for communication offers a significant advantage for a right whale producing or listening for a contact call in shallow water. For example, the transmission loss for a typical 100- to 300-Hz contact call at 30 km is half that for a call at either 50–100 Hz or at 800–1,200 Hz, and the presumed ancient ambient noise level in the frequency band for the contact call is a factor of two less than those in these two surrounding frequency bands. Translating these combined benefits into distance means that a right whale producing a typical contact call in shallow water can be detected about four times farther away than a whale producing a call at a lower or higher frequency.

Recent ocean acoustic work has started to apply these same principles to estimate detection and communication ranges for right whales (Desharnais 2004), and these predictions are supported by empirical results. Behavioral research using state-of-the-art suction-cup tags equipped with hydrophones attached to right whales has provided remarkable glimpses into the acoustic behaviors of individual whales and into the acoustic world to which these individuals are exposed (Matthews et al. 2001; Johnson and Tyack 2003; Nowacek et al. 2004). These eavesdropping episodes have allowed scientists for the first time to gain some sense of how often and under what circumstances a whale produces sounds. These tags not only record acoustics but also log the behavior of the whale, using accelerometers that record the movements of the whale in three dimensions, and a magnetometer, or digital compass (color plate 14). Because the tag is attached directly to the whale, researchers know when the tagged whale vocalized because the strength and characteristics of the recorded sounds differ from those of sounds recorded from distant whales. By knowing exactly when a tagged whale produced a sound, combined with data on behavior and environment (water temperature and depth), a great deal can be learned about the circumstances in which whales vocalize and how often they vocalize. These factors are very important for evaluating the effectiveness of detecting whales by their sounds.

The tag recordings, many of which were compiled by Matthews et al. (2001), have provided interesting results, including some very important hints for passive acoustic efforts. Rates of vocalizations produced by tagged whales ranged from zero to seven calls per hour (Matthews et al. 2001), whereas among all calls recorded by the tags, including sounds produced by other whales, calling rates ranged from one to seventy-two calls per hour. In addition, the calls made by individual whales were often produced in clusters. For example, one whale produced a series of four calls about halfway through the tag attachment but made no sounds before or after this cluster. One of the values of the tagging data is that they provide information about a single individual as it engages in its daily activities. If one were able to sample a representative cross section of the population using this method (e.g., males and females, old and young), then probability functions could be constructed that describe the chance that an individual animal in a given situation will produce a call. Such modeling exercises are critical for maximizing the chances of detecting a whale using passive acoustic methods.

As discussed above, sound traveling through the ocean is affected by many factors, one of which is the depth of the water and the depth at which the sound is produced. It was apparent that a subset of the tagged whales produced moans almost exclusively in the top 10 m of water (Matthews et al. 2001). Whale sounds were recorded on the tags when the tagged whale was well below the surface (e.g., 100 m), but these calls were all made by other whales. Here again, the activities of individual whales are important because detecting a sound produced near the surface can be more difficult at long range based on the normal, downward refracting conditions in the ocean. In other words, sounds produced near the surface normally do not travel as well into deeper waters, so if sensors are deep in the water column, whales vocalizing near the surface would be more difficult to detect.

Right Whale Calls in Cape Cod Bay and the Great South Channel

In 1998 on a hot summer day on Cape Cod, over a meal of beer and fresh fish, Moe Brown and Chris Clark were pondering the problem of finding right whales. Moe had finished her first year of aerial surveys in Cape Cod Bay, and Chris had just returned from working in Hawaii on humpback whales. For the Hawaii project Cornell engineers had built an autonomous seafloor recording device, affectionately referred to as a "pop-up" (Clark et al. 2002; Fig. 11.3). A pop-up is a complete sound collection system packaged inside a 43-cm glass sphere protected by a hard plastic casing and is light enough to be deployed and recovered by a single person from a small boat. It is typically anchored on the bottom with sandbags tied to a simple releasing mechanism controlled by internal circuitry. Pop-ups can be preprogrammed to record at a wide range of frequencies and on a fixed schedule. After hearing Chris's explanation of how a pop-up worked, Moe suggested deploying some in Cape

Figure 11.3. Pop-ups on deck of *Song of the Whale.* Doug Gillespie / International Fund for Animal Welfare.

Cod Bay to listen for right whales during the same period when she was conducting visual surveys. With initial support from the International Fund for Animal Welfare, a pilot project in 2000 expanded into a four-year project merging the acoustic detections from pop-ups with Moe Brown's aerial survey and Stormy Mayo's ecological monitoring efforts in Cape Cod Bay. This has now evolved into an ongoing project using moored buoys that automatically detect right whale calls and relay data back to a website server via a cell or satellite phone link. Some of the highlights of these studies are briefly described and synthesized here.

For the pilot study in 2000, Cornell and International Fund for Animal Welfare scientists working aboard the *Song of the Whale* research vessel deployed a set of six pop-ups near the shipping lane to the east of Cape Cod and extending eastward onto Georges Bank. The pop-ups were deployed in two triangular arrays, where units in each array were spaced ca. 1.6 km apart, and the centers of the two arrays were 16 km apart (Clark and Clapham 2004). The units recorded sound in the 10- to 2,000-Hz range continuously for twenty-

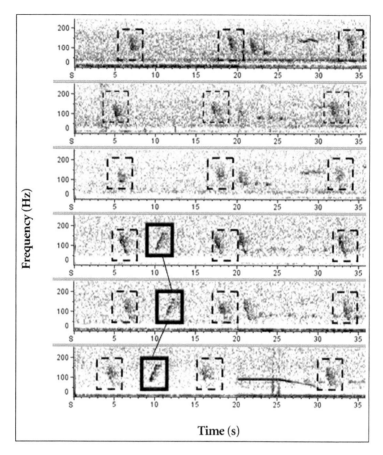

Figure 11.4. Spectrographic example of six-channel pop-up array data with a right whale call on three channels (solid bold boxes) and humpback song notes on six channels (dashed boxes).

five days. After retrieval, all the acoustic data from the units were merged and scrutinized for right whale sounds using specialized software (Fig. 11.4). By use of time-of-arrival location techniques, a whale that was detected on one three-element array could be located out to a range of about 8 km, and a whale detected on both three-element arrays could be located out to about 32 km (Clark et al. 1996; Desharnais 2004). As mentioned earlier, the recordings were full of humpback singers, but only 227 right whale contact calls were detected, and those that were located were coming from whales separated by many kilometers.

Many (n = 96) of the 227 calls occurred in the early hours on 26 May 2000 and were located and attributed to at least two whales. During this day five right whales were seen within 8 km of the pop-ups by the aerial survey team. This observation is consistent with the working hypothesis that the occurrence of contact calls is a good proxy for the presence of right whales. It also underscores an important consideration: the time of day when whales are most communicative is not necessarily the time of day when they are most likely seen by aerial observers. Although the actual number of whales detected acoustically was low during this first application of pop-ups, the data proved invaluable for developing reliable detectors to distinguish between humpback and right whale calls.

Since then, pop-up arrays have been used to monitor and locate right whales in Cape Cod Bay and the Great South Channel for large portions of the year. More recently, pop-up sampling has expanded to include the Bay of Fundy, Jeffreys Ledge, Stellwagen Bank, and the whales' migratory route off Savannah, Georgia to Cape Fear, North Carolina. These efforts allow simultaneous monitoring of several critical areas for long periods of time to gain a large-scale perspective on whale occurrence and acoustic behaviors.

The amount of data collected via such pop-up deployments is staggering. A major effort is being devoted toward developing improved detectors and quantifying the trade-off between identifying every right whale call versus detecting the presence of at least one calling whale. The cost of identifying every right whale call is the time to sort through the huge number of false detections, whereas the cost of detecting at least one calling whale is that some right whales will be missed. This trade-off relationship between false detections and missed calls can be quantified as seen in Fig. 11.5. This result suggests that one detection strategy is to choose a point on the curve where the percentage of calls detected is reasonably high but the number of false detections is quite low. In other words, the priority is to determine if right whales are in the area, not the absolute number of calls they produce. So, for example, based on the curve in Fig. 11.5, the point could be chosen where 60 percent of the calls will be detected and the false alarm rate is fewer than five false detections per day. By this strategy the efficiency of detecting a single call is only 60 percent. However, because right whales tend to produce several calls within a few minutes of each other, the probability of detecting at least some of the calls produced by each whale is higher. Similarly, if more than one call must be detected before it can be inferred that a right whale has been found, the probability of a false alarm is much lower.

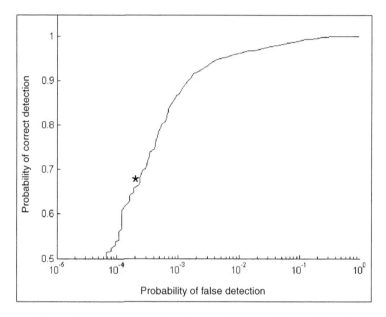

Figure 11.5. Example of receiver-operating characteristics curve showing the trade-off between the probability of false detections (abscissa) and the probability of correct detections (ordinate) using the Gillespie detection algorithm for northern right whale contact calls. The asterisk marks the point on the curve where 70 percent of the contact calls would be detected with only twenty-six false detections.

What Does Listening Tell Us about Right Whales?

After all these years of recording and analyzing many tens of thousands of right whale sounds, one can conclude that right whales have a difficult time staying quiet for very long. However, a long time for a right whale is really, really long for a human. So even if the calling rate (measured, for example, in moans per day) of an individual is relatively low by human standards, technology doesn't have an opinion about a long time and can listen continuously for months and months. Researchers have found that even individuals that are alone and that might remain silent for many hours tend to produce contact calls in bursts (for example, three to five calls in five minutes), a behavior that further increases our likelihood of detecting the animal. Thus, the challenge of listening for right whales comes down to overcoming scientists' short attention span relative to right whale calling behavior. Researchers cannot change right whale calling behavior, but new listening technologies can be applied to eavesdrop on the right whale's world for extremely long periods of time and to listen for whales in many places simultaneously. Because of the whales' penchant for calling, chances are high that if a whale is in range of a sensor for more than a few hours, it will call and be detected.

One of the obvious ways of evaluating the reliability and benefit of acoustic monitoring is by comparing acoustic detection results with visual survey results. For the combined 2001–2004 datasets, there were a total of forty-nine days on which complete aerial surveys were conducted and a pop-up array was operating in Cape Cod Bay. When seasons are compared on a coarse scale, aerial and acoustic results are similar: in years when sighting densities are high, call counts are high, and in years when sighting densities are low, call counts are low. The acoustic method detects whales earlier in the season and is far more likely than aerial surveys to detect a right whale when there are few whales (about six to eight) in the area. For example, in the 2001/2002 season, pop-ups were first deployed on 23 December 2001, the first whale call was detected on 23 December, and whales were heard intermittently throughout the next six weeks before the first whale was seen in an aerial survey on 7 February 2002. The next season pop-ups were deployed earlier, on 21 November 2002, and the first whale call was detected on 23 November 2003, but the first whale wasn't seen until 25 January 2004.

Figure 11.6 provides an example of within-year acoustic variability and shows right whale call detections during the six-month recording season in Cape Cod Bay in 2002/2003. This acoustic record indicates that a few whales intermittently and briefly entered the Bay from mid-November through early January, and there was a period of prolonged but variable occurrence of presumably many whales from mid-January to early May. Thus, during the early months of November through January, when whales are rarely seen on aerial surveys, there are periodic bursts of calling lasting from a few hours to a few days. What appears to be happening is that a few whales, either alone or in small groups, enter and quickly travel through the Bay while calling intermittently. These behaviors suggest that animals are checking the area out for its potential as a food resource.

An example of between-year variability in call detections in Cape Cod Bay for April 2002 and 2003 is shown in Fig. 11.7. April is often the month with the highest numbers of right whales, but if food availability is low, whales will not congregate there to feed.

Right whale calls can often, but not always, be heard over greater ranges than initially anticipated. This became most apparent during the analysis of

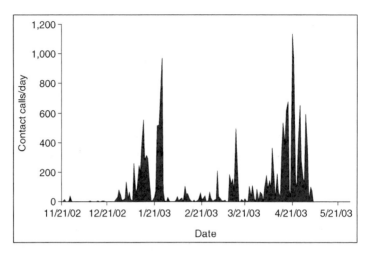

Figure 11.6. Daily contact call detections, Cape Cod Bay, 21 November 2002 through 21 May 2003.

the 2002/2003 data, when on many occasions the same sound could be detected on all six pop-ups. This result indicates that under certain circumstances (for example, when ambient noise is low and a whale's contact call is loud) two whales could communicate over distances of at least 32–48 km. So a whale outside of the Bay could hear the calls of a whale inside the Bay, or a whale to the east of the Cape off Wellfleet could hear a whale in the Great South Channel. The functional significance of contact calling in the context of feeding and scouting for food remains a mystery because the present understanding assumes that whales do not share food resources and that one whale does not require another whale to be able to eat. This raises the intriguing question: if this is primarily a feeding period, why are the whales calling?

Using Acoustics to Protect Right Whales

Acoustic monitoring of right whales can give researchers fascinating insights into how they communicate and how they migrate. However, if the information gathered is not used to reduce the numbers of animals killed every year, then this effort is for naught. The most common cause of anthropogenic mortality in right whales is collisions with ships, and many measures are already in place to try to reduce the number of vessel–whale interactions. Mandatory ship reporting schemes are in operation in two critical right whale habitats

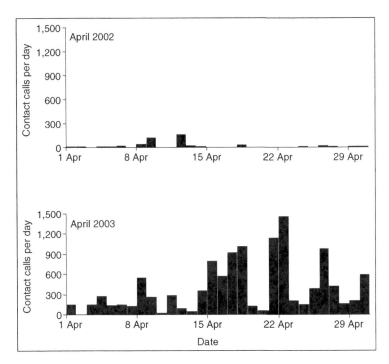

Figure 11.7. Daily contact call detections, Cape Cod Bay, April 2002 and April 2003.

east of Cape Cod and off Florida (see Chapter 14). Vessels entering these regions must report in to the U.S. Coast Guard, who sends them back the latest information on right whale locations. One proposed new measure to protect right whales includes rerouting ships away from the areas most frequently used by right whales. Effective use of this reporting scheme is, however, hampered by a lack of reliable and timely information on where right whales are. This lack of information reflects the limitations of aerial surveys, which can be flown only under favorable weather conditions. Furthermore, surveys are expensive, dangerous, and cannot simultaneously cover large portions of whale habitat. This is where acoustic monitoring is arguably the most promising tool for identifying where whales are and roughly how many there are.

Passive Listening

From 2000 to 2005, pop-up recorders have been deployed off the coast from southern Maine to the Great South Channel in an effort to determine whether or not acoustic monitoring could provide a viable alternative to aerial surveys for detecting right whales. Although all of the analyses are not completed, it is fair to say that this acoustic monitoring effort has demonstrated that acoustic systems are more likely to detect whales under low-density conditions than aerial surveys. Thus, for Cape Cod Bay, of the forty-nine days between 2001 and 2004 with both a complete aerial survey and pop-up acoustic array monitoring, there were eight days (20 percent) when no whales were seen and no whales were heard, there were eighteen days (44 percent) when no whales were seen but whales were heard, and there was one day (2 percent) when whales were seen but no whales were heard. Aerial survey does have its advantages compared to acoustics, especially when it comes to the accuracy of positioning individual animals. During a visual survey one can count the number of animals within a group even if they are only a few meters apart. In contrast, the location accuracy for a calling whale using a pop-up array is on the order of several hundreds of meters, and one cannot determine if there is more than one animal at that location.

Further support for the value of acoustic monitoring comes from more recent work in habitats where visual surveys are less frequent. Beginning in winter 2004, pop-up recorders have been deployed off the mid-Atlantic coast to determine if whales could be detected on their migrations to and from the calving grounds. Although right whale density is expected to be extremely low in this area, and the ambient conditions are poor (mostly because of high levels of shipping traffic), their calls were detected during the northbound migration in 2004, even under extremely challenging conditions. These results strongly suggest that it is now quite possible to search for unknown feeding grounds using widespread listening systems.

These pop-up monitoring results, though encouraging and yielding significant scientific data, are not the solution for mitigating the potential impacts from ship strikes. To take these acoustic discoveries and apply them to the conservation of right whales, information is needed about the presence and distribution of whales in real time so that a ship can change its route or reschedule its passage through an area with right whales.

An exciting new development in this direction is the deployment in 2005 of prototype automatic right whale detection buoys. These buoys look something like a navigation marker with a large float at the surface anchored to the sea floor. In reality though, they are packed with sophisticated electronics, which can do analyses normally carried out back in the lab but that are now performed continuously on the buoy in real time. A cell or satellite telephone communications system is used to transmit information on right whale presence back to shore so that researchers know right whales are in the area within hours of the sensors receiving contact calls. Not only may this be a better way of detecting right whales than aerial surveys, but such systems can reduce the costs of protection measures such as speed and routing restrictions if ship management becomes dynamic in real time.

In the next few years a network of these real-time buoys will be established throughout the critical habitats off the New England coast. One promising option is to work with the U.S. Coast Guard to strategically instrument some of their navigational buoys. This might also be the most effective way of monitoring for right whales along their migration route where they cross the paths of the densest shipping traffic along the east coast. It is very realistic that in the not-too-distant future ship captains, fishermen, regulators, scientists, and students will all be able to access these data via the Internet and receive e-mail messages alerting them that a whale has been detected. Such access will make it possible to make responsible, timely, strategic decisions that will significantly reduce the chances of a right whale being struck or entangled.

Active Acoustics

There are other ways to use acoustics to reduce ship strikes, either by making sound to alert the whales to the potential danger of an approaching ship or to detect the whales so as to avoid hitting them. The first application is referred to as active acoustic deterrence, and the second will be referred to as active acoustic detection (also known as sonar).

Active acoustic deterrence has been used successfully to inhibit dolphins and porpoises from entangling in fishing nets but has never been used successfully with large whales (Kraus et al. 1997). Recently, however, Nowacek et al. (2004) demonstrated that right whales responded strongly to a synthetic acoustic stimulus designed to alert the animals. Suction-cup acoustic recording tags (Johnson and Tyack 2003) were used to measure the whales' response to a sound designed to pique their auditory system and give them information about the sound's location. Conceptually, the sound is like a siren on a police or fire vehicle, which is designed to alert people of the vehicle's presence and location, not to alarm or frighten them. Unlike humans who hear sirens and have learned to get out of the way, nobody has trained right whales how to respond to a siren: they don't know to pull over to the side of the road and stop! Indeed, the researchers were interested in learning two things: (1) would whales show any response to the alerting sound; and (2) what would be the nature of their response if one occurred?

What the researchers found was fascinating. For consistency, all of the whales were tested in the same situation, at the beginning of a foraging dive just as they reached foraging depth. Of the six whales tested, five demonstrated exactly the same response. Some time after the onset of one particular part of the alerting sound (specifically, a sound that started at 4 kHz and swept down to 500 Hz over a period of two seconds), all five whales broke off their foraging activity and started swimming toward the surface. Their ascent pattern, however, differed significantly from their normal ascents. Normally the whales ascend at a vertical angle of ca. 50°–60° relative to the bottom and maintain a relatively consistent fluke stroke rate, often gliding as they near the surface (Nowacek et al. 2001). But during experimental response, they took a much shallower angle toward the surface (ca. 30°) and swam consistently, fluking at a significantly higher rate. Under normal circumstances after a foraging dive, a whale comes to the surface and remains relatively still while taking several breaths, effectively resting at the surface. The whales exposed to this alerting sound, however, only occasionally went all the way to the surface to breathe. Instead they kept swimming just a few meters below the surface, coming only briefly to the surface to grab a breath. Therefore, in the context of ship strikes, this alerting sound would probably not reduce risk. In fact it might actually increase the risk of harm because at only a few meters depth the whales are still very vulnerable to being hit by a ship but would not be seen.

Research into the use of active acoustic detection (sonar) of whales to mitigate human activities is still in the early stages. There are numerous technical challenges in attempting to detect a whale with active acoustics, especially right whales that spend a significant amount of time at or very near the surface. At shallow depths the whale is both at greatest risk of being struck by a ship and is also nearly impossible to detect with active acoustics. Still, there are reasonably good prospects that active acoustic detection will work under certain circumstances. In 2003 Peter Stein of Scientific Solutions, Inc., built a customized sonar system specifically for whales that was tested off southern California during the gray whale migration in January. The system successfully detected gray whales out to distances of at least 900 m, even in water depths of less than 30 m. However, the chance of this technique working on a commercial ship to detect and avoid whales effectively seems remote because current ship speeds would require operators to recognize the sonar target as a whale and take immediate action to avoid it. In addition, sonar effective for right whale detection will be emitting sounds in frequencies that many toothed whales can hear, and there might be consequences associated with widespread implementation of such a system. It is possible that active detection, in combination with autodetection buoys and ship speed protocols, might be useful to increase detections of right whales in busy shipping lanes or near harbors seasonally frequented by the whales, but the technical challenges indicate this may be years away.

Fragmenting Their Acoustic World:
The Urbanization of Critical Habitats

Developing acoustic systems to detect right whales has provided many useful insights into where right whales are and perhaps why they are there. In doing this work researchers have also been confronted by the harsh reality that the rising tide and high variability of ambient noise from human activities is making it difficult to detect calling whales. If researchers are having difficulty listening for right whales through the smog of anthropogenic noise, imagine what it must be like for the whales. Color plate 15 provides four examples to illustrate typical acoustic conditions for three critical areas inhabited by right whales. In these examples, each of the bright orange-red bands of color represents the passage of a vessel. In Cape Cod Bay, for example, some of these events represent the noise of commercial ships moving goods between Boston and ports along the east coast, and other bright orange-red bands are from smaller vessels such as fishing boats. Another way to show this is with a map that shows the ambient noise landscape around Cape Cod (Fig. 11.8). These acoustic scenes are persistent throughout the year and have probably been this way since the advent of modern shipping and the completion of the Cape Cod Canal in 1940.

In one sense the illustrations in Fig. 11.8 and color plate 15 are the acoustic scenes in which right whales must now communicate. From a whale's perspective, its coastal habitats are aglow with the cumulative acoustic noise generated by vessel traffic. If the assumptions presented in Chapter 10 are correct, the communication area for a right whale in the coastal waters of the United States has shrunk to 10 percent of what it was one hundred years ago. Those habitats that less than a century ago undulated with the natural sounds of whales, waves, and tides are now acoustically fragmented, and this acoustic fragmentation is increasing, persistent, and unrelenting.

One can hope that the acoustic trends in the ocean are reversible. Perhaps ships will be rerouted to reduce the noise levels in areas where whales

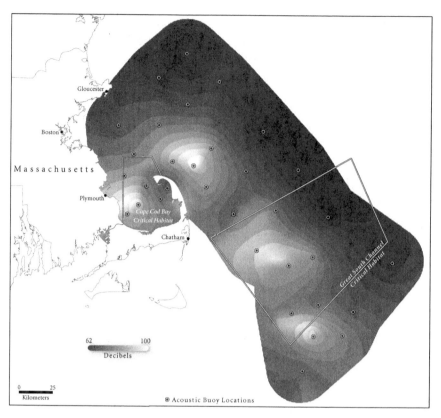

Figure 11.8. Acoustic map of the ambient noise field in and around Cape Cod Bay, Massachusetts. The gray scale provides a measure of the relative noise levels in the 80- to 350-Hz range, the frequency used by right whales for contact calling. The values are a composite from acoustic samples collected on autonomous seafloor recording units on a March day, 2003, and were computed as the average spectrum level from a single fifteen-minute sample.

congregate to mate and feed. It is conceivable that engineers seeking more efficient propulsion systems will develop quieter ships and that, gradually, the worldwide din of shipping will decrease. In the near term, however, there are increasing numbers of ships, fishing boats, and recreational boats, and this trend appears unlikely to change.

Conclusion

The best available evidence indicates that right whales rely heavily on sound for survival. In particular, their contact calls are optimized for long-range communication in the coastal areas where they breed, raise their young, and forage. Recent applications of listening technologies have vastly increased the ability to detect right whales throughout their home range and over long periods of time and provide tangible opportunities for reducing the chances of ship strikes and fishing gear entanglements. Data from these same listening devices are also revealing that the rising tide of ocean ambient noise from human activities is a serious threat to right whale communication. Human noise pollution is not the only threat, and it does not result in bodies on the beach, but its slow, inexorable rise is insidious. It is similar to the pernicious creep of natural habitat loss on land as the result of one more residential development, strip mall, highway, or industrial complex. But in this case the loss of habitat is from the collective acoustic smog generated by civilization. Bit by bit, the right whale's acoustic habitat is being eroded and fragmented. Where once the acoustic habitat provided nearly continuous opportunities for long-range communication, that most vital sense for the whales, there now remain only islands of opportunity that contract and expand with the comings and going of human activities. With each passing season that tide of acoustic smog rises, and another chance to communicate drowns. It is the price the natural world pays, and in this particular case it is the price that right whales pay, for human progress.

Caswell, H., M. Fujiwara, and S. Brault. 1999. Declining survival probability threatens the North Atlantic right whale. *Proceedings of the National Academy of Sciences* 96:3308–3313.

Clark, C. W. 1983. Acoustic communication and behavior of the southern right whale. Pages 163–198 *in* R. S. Payne, ed. *Behavior and Communication of Whales*. Westview Press, Boulder, CO.

Clark, C. W., and P. J. Clapham. 2004. Acoustic monitoring on a humpback whale (*Megaptera novaeangliae*) feeding ground shows continual singing into late spring. *Proceedings of the Royal Society London, Part B* 271:1051–1057.

Clark, C. W., and W. T. Ellison. 2004. Potential use of low-frequency sounds by baleen whales for probing the environment: evidence from models and empirical measurements. Pages 564–582 *in* J. Thomas, C. Moss, and M. Vater, eds. *Echolocation in Bats and Dolphins*. University of Chicago Press, Chicago.

Clark, C. W., R. Charif, S. Mitchell, and J. Colby. 1996. Distribution and behavior of the bowhead whale, *Balaena mysticetus,* based on analysis of acoustic data collected during the 1993 spring migration off Point Barrow, Alaska. *Report of the International Whaling Commission* 46:541–552.

Clark, C. W., J. F. Borsani, and G. Notarbartolo-di-Sciara. 2002. Vocal activity of fin whales, *Balaenoptera physalus,* in the Ligurian Sea. *Marine Mammal Science* 18:281–285.

Desharnais, F. (ed.) 2004. The 2003 workshop on detection and localization of marine mammals using passive acoustics. *Journal of Canadian Acoustics.* 32:1–171.

Gillespie, D. 2004. Detection and classification of right whale calls using an "edge" detector operating on a smoothed spectrogram. *Journal of Canadian Acoustics* 32:39–47.

Jensen, F. B., W. A. Kuperman, M. B. Porter, and H. Schmidt. 1994. *Computational Ocean Acoustics.* American Institute of Physics, New York.

Johnson, M. P., and P. L. Tyack. 2003. A digital acoustic recording tag for measuring the response of wild marine mammals to sound. *IEEE Journal of Oceanic Engineering* 28:3–12.

Ketten, D. R. 2000. Cetacean ears. Pages 45–106 *in* R. R. Fay, A .N. Popper, and W. W. L. Au, eds. *Hearing by Whales and Dolphins.* Springer, New York.

Kraus, S. D., and J. J. Hatch. 2001. Mating strategies in the North Atlantic right whale (*Eubalaena glacialis*). *Journal of Cetacean Research and Management* Special Issue 2:237–244.

Kraus, S. D., A. J. Read, E. Anderson, K. Baldwin, A. Solow, T. Spradlin, and J. Williamson. 1997. Acoustic alarms reduce porpoise mortality. *Nature* 388:525.

Kraus, S. D., M. W. Brown, H. Caswell, C. W. Clark, M. Fujiwara, P. K. Hamilton, R. D. Kenney, A. R. Knowlton, S. Landry, C. A. Mayo, W. A. McLellan, M. J. Moore, D. P. Nowacek, D. A. Pabst, A. J. Read, and R. M. Rolland. 2005. North Atlantic right whales in crisis. *Science* 309:561–562.

Marler, P., and K. Marten. 1977. Sound transmission and its significance for animal vocalization. *Behavioral Ecology and Sociobiology* 2:271–302.

Matthews, J., S. Brown, D. Gillespie, M. Johnson, R. McLanaghan, A. Moscrop, D. Nowacek, R. Leaper, T. Lewis, and P. Tyack. 2001. Vocalisation rates of the North Atlantic right whale (*Eubalaena glacialis*). *Journal of Cetacean Research and Management* 3:271–282.

Nowacek, D. P., M. P. Johnson, P. L. Tyack, K. Shorter, W. A. McLellan, and D. A. Pabst. 2001. Buoyant balaenid whales: the ups and downs of buoyancy in right whales. *Proceedings of the Royal Society of London, Part B* 268:1811–1816.

Nowacek, D. P., M. P. Johnson, and P. L. Tyack. 2004. North Atlantic right whales (*Eubalaena glacialis*) ignore ships but respond to alerting stimuli. *Proceedings of the Royal Society of London, Part B* 271:227–231.

Parks, S. E., and P. L. Tyack. 2005. Sound production by North Atlantic right whales (*Eubalaena glacialis*) in surface active groups. *Journal of the Acoustic Society of America* 117:3297–3306.

Schevill, W. E., and W. A. Watkins. 1962. *Whale and porpoise voices: a phonograph record.* Woods Hole Oceanographic Institution, Woods Hole, MA.

Wiley, R. H., and D. G. Richards. 1978. Physical constraints on acoustic communication in the atmosphere: implications for the evolution of animal vocalizations. *Behavioral Ecology and Sociobiology* 3:69–94.

Wright, D. R. 2001. Categorization of northern right whale, *Eubalaena glacialis,* sounds. M.A. Thesis, Boston University, Boston.

Acknowledgments

Thanks to Moe Brown, Stormy Mayo, and Dan McKiernan for unflagging encouragement, inspiration, and support; the Cornell Bioacoustics team for pop-up development and data analysis; Mark Johnson, Peter Tyack, and the field crew who made the DTAG experiments a reality; and the *Song of the Whale* crew and research team. This work was funded by grants and contracts from International Fund for Animal Welfare (C.W.C.), Northeast Consortium (C.W.C., S.P. via P. Tyack), National Marine Fisheries Service (C.W.C., D.P.N., S.P.), Commonwealth of Massachusetts Division of Marine Fisheries (C.W.C.), and National Fish and Wildlife Foundation Whale Conservation Fund (C.W.C. via D. McKiernan, S.P.).

12

Right Whale Mortality:
A Message from the Dead to the Living

MICHAEL J. MOORE, WILLIAM A. MCLELLAN,
PIERRE-YVES DAOUST, ROBERT K. BONDE,
AND AMY R. KNOWLTON

9 February 2004
Nags Head, North Carolina

*School vacation, skiing with the kids; the cellular "ball and chain" rings:
another dead right whale. I've come to dread such calls, as they invariably
mean canceling commitments and a depressing week of long-distance truck
driving, long hours, and a sad retrieval. Abandoning the kids to friends, I
meet up with colleagues, and we drive to Virginia from New Hampshire
as we get phone updates on the carcasses of a mother and calf found floating off the mouth of Chesapeake Bay. Gaseous decomposition has expelled
a fetus out of the mother's mouth. Observers tied the fetus to the mother at
sea, but weather and mechanical problems precluded retrieval of the dead
whale. Three days later the carcasses had drifted south to Nags Head, North
Carolina, where they were towed ashore. This is the reverse of the migration northward the whales would have taken a few months later en route
to their bountiful northern feeding grounds.*

*As the necropsy team of over twenty individuals prepared for the task
ahead on a cold snowy beach, the mass of the dead mother resisted many
attempts to drag her up the beach. Finally, three excavators and two bull-*

dozers got her up, but not before we lightened the load by separating the head from the remainder of her carcass. From the outset, we knew the whale to be Stumpy (Eg #1004), previously identified from an old wound on her left fluke. Over the next twenty-four hours we carefully dismembered her to establish a cause of death. In the end, she showed clear evidence of external trauma that was blunt and probably was caused by a collision with a large ship. As we cleaned our tools, we reflected back on her life as told by the Right Whale Catalog: *she was first sighted in 1975 18 km NNE of Province-town, Massachusetts, and had been sighted many times since, often frequenting the Bay of Fundy, Massachusetts Bay, waters east of Florida, and occasionally the Great South Channel. She had successfully reared calves in 1980, 1987, 1990, 1993, and 1996. In retrospect it was a great loss, as Stumpy was a reproductively active female with the potential of having calves for many more years. But after being hit by a ship, she had been reduced to just a pile of stinking flesh and bones on a beach in North Carolina.*

Michael Moore

Since 1970 there has been a burgeoning effort to take dead North Atlantic right whales apart to maximize our understanding of their causes of death and to pursue research opportunities. Specific maritime interests, such as defense agencies, shipping companies, and fishermen, are under substantial pressure to mitigate their negative impacts on right whale survival in the western North Atlantic. Scientists who respond to each right whale death and attempt to determine how that animal died owe these industries an objective and complete appraisal of each case to ensure that the diagnoses reached are as accurate and complete as possible, given the many factors that conspire against a complete analysis.

This chapter tells the story of a process whereby useful information can be obtained in an effort to further the conservation of right whales. It discusses the reasons for examining dead right whales, describes how the procedure is done and what results have been found, and then puts the findings of each dead whale in the broader context of the population as a whole.

Why Examine Dead Right Whales?

People have been examining dead whales for at least the past 2,355 years (Aristotle 350 BCE). Aristotle, as translated by D'Arcy Wentworth Thompson in

1918, wrote "the whale with the air-passage in its forehead . . . has hairs in its mouth resembling pigs' bristles . . . breasts . . . supplied with milk . . . sleep with the blow-hole over the surface of the water, and breathe through the blow-hole." Historically, right whales that stranded were probably used for food as well as materials. In the nineteenth century they were also the focus of the curiosity of naturalists (Eschricht and Reinhardt 1866) and regarded as museum sources of morphological and anatomic samples and data. Then in the twentieth-century era of commercial whaling, biologists acquired a variety of biological data from the decks of whaling operations (Thompson 1918; Omura et al. 1969; Tormosov et al. 1998). In the 1970s research scientists realized that strandings represented a window into the health of marine mammals. Over the past thirty years there has been a slow evolution toward a more intensive forensic, histopathologic approach to better understand the natural and human-induced mortality factors at work on many marine mammal species.

So, why still go down to the beach to examine stranded whales when so much is already known? In the case of right whales, research conducted during the 1980s demonstrated that significant numbers of this species were dying from human activities (Kraus 1990). Indeed, researchers know specifically that fixed fishing gear and ships kill right whales more commonly than any other factor (Moore et al. 2005). But that is just the tip of the biological iceberg of information that needs to be gathered on these whales. The need for ongoing assessment has never been greater.

Federal and state management programs are currently making legislative and enforcement changes in attempts to reduce right whale mortality. It is, therefore, critical to continue to investigate the causes of right whale mortalities, which at this time show little evidence of declining. Between February 2004 and April 2005 there were eight known right whale deaths (Kraus et al. 2005); three of those were pregnant females. This continuing high level of anthropogenic mortality requires a forensic approach to whales on the beach; it is necessary to know how these whales died to determine whether management actions have been effective. The most recent series of data on dead right whales form the basis of this chapter.

Dealing with a Dead Right Whale

The management of dead right whales is a formidable, messy, and evolving art. Researchers are still far from extracting all of the available information from

Figure 12.1. Aerial photograph of a dead right whale, Staccato (Eg #1014), floating in Cape Cod Bay with attendant scavenging birds. Marilyn Marx / New England Aquarium.

each case, considering that the organs alone weigh in the tons. Indeed, often the carcass is not even retrieved, leaving, at best, some aerial images that may allow identification of a known individual. Most floating dead right whales are reported by fishermen, U.S. and Canadian Coast Guard personnel, or other mariners (Fig. 12.1). Such reports result in a stream of communication among federal managers, stranding network participants, and scientists as an appropriate response is mobilized, altered, stood down, and remobilized, as weather and other variables affect the plans.

Attempts are made to tow every right whale carcass to shore. These events invariably are hampered and prolonged by poor weather, challenging logistics, and inadequate resources. Successful recoveries have been made with near-shore floaters (carcasses within 32 km of land). Attempts to relocate and tow whales from farther offshore have not been successful to date. The key to success in near-shore events has been a rapid response with good aerial survey support, good communication among vessel, plane, and onshore coordinators, and a rapid identification of where the necropsy will take place. Cues that have led aerial observers to carcasses include oil slicks and flocks of scavenging birds. Drift analyses of the carcass factoring wind, tide, and water movements have assisted both in carcass relocation and in assessment of the most likely place of death. Where vessels have been able to attach radio transmitters to carcasses, relocation efforts have been assisted enormously.

Other carcasses are discovered as they float ashore, and these events are fundamentally easier to deal with than those that are found offshore. The shore property owner is faced with a removal problem and is, therefore, more willing to work with a necropsy crew than is the owner of a property to which one might wish to tow a carcass. Thus necropsy site selection can be a major planning issue. In addition to practical considerations of bringing the carcass ashore, a necropsy site requires proximity to a nearby disposal site and vehicular access. However, in many coastal areas there may be nearby dwellings affected by odors, and habitats for protected and endangered species that should not be disturbed. To complicate things, the disposal of the tons of material generated from a carcass or its parts can represent major environmental and hazardous waste problems and must be carried out in compliance with state and local regulations. These issues have all led to delays in securing suitable sites to conduct a right whale necropsy.

Once on the beach, whales are hauled above the high tide line to ensure full access. Researchers use heavy excavators or front-end loaders for this and a variety of other tasks throughout a necropsy event (color plate 16; Fig. 12.2). Measurements are taken, such as total length, flipper and fluke dimensions, girths, and blubber thickness using a standard necropsy protocol (McLellan et al. 2004), which includes complete details on data recording and sampling protocols. Early efforts are always made to identify the whale involved so that it can be placed in the context of all the sighting and associated data in the *North Atlantic Right Whale Catalog* (Hamilton and Martin 1999). This is done by taking a comprehensive set of photographs of the callosity pattern on top of the head, chin and mandibular callosities, lip and lip ridges, postblowhole callosities, and scars (or lack of scars) along the body and tail regions (Chapter 3). Decomposition frequently hampers identifications, but the callosity patterns on the head and chin can often be seen even if the skin is gone. Genetic identification from either skin or other samples has allowed for the identification of extremely decomposed carcasses, neonates where the mother is unknown, and carcasses floating at sea that could not be retrieved or appropriately photographed (Chapter 7).

Samples are routinely collected for histopathology, parasitology, life history, genetics, and toxicology. Such samples include skin, baleen, blubber, stomach contents, urine, feces, liver, kidney, muscle, bone, eyeballs, ear bones, a routine suite of organs for general histology, and any other tissues of abnormal appearance. The skeleton is ultimately dissected free from the carcass and retained for accession into a museum collection. Particular care is made to

Figure 12.2. Using an excavator to peel the blubber off Eg #1004. Virginia Aquarium Stranding Program.

retain the vestigial pelvic bones, hyoid bones, and any other small fractured parts.

Findings from Dead Right Whales

A major goal in a right whale necropsy is to establish objectively either the presence or absence of human impacts with respect to the cause of death in the context of natural processes. In these forensic investigations the question of physical trauma is the first major issue that gets evaluated. If evidence of trauma is present, researchers attempt to establish if it occurred before, at the time of, or after death. Determining if the heart was beating, and hence circulating blood to the organs, is critical to understand the timing of traumatic events. Evidence for an antemortem event (before death) includes the presence of gross and microscopic hemorrhage (patches of blood cells outside their vessels), edema (an excess of extracellular fluid), and wound reaction and tissue repair. A postmortem event (after death) would not have these tell-tale reactions. A cause-of-death analysis is trickier in some circumstances, partly because some

Table 12.1. Summary of Right Whales That Died in the Northwest Atlantic between 1975 and April 2005 and Were Necropsied (*n* = 39)[a]

Year	ID number(s)	Sex	Age (y)	Quality (1–4)	Presumed cause of death
1975	USNM 504257	M		4	Undetermined
1976	USNM 504343	M	0	3	Possible collision
1979	USNM 504886	M	3		Vessel collision
1981	HNN 893	M	0		Undetermined
1983	Eg #1128	M	2		Vessel collision
1986	MH86142 Eg	F	2		Vessel collision
1988	Jan 17	M	0	4	Undetermined
1989	MH89424 Eg	M	0	2	Live perinatal
1989	Jan 26		0	4	Undetermined
1991	Eg #1907	F	2	3	Vessel collision
1992	Eg #1223	F	min 12	3	Vessel collision
1993	RKB-1424	M	0	2	Vessel collision
1993	RKB-1425	F	0	4	Undetermined
1995	Eg #2366	M	2.5		Entanglement
1995	Eg #2250	M	min 4	4	Probable vessel collision
1996	02 Jan 96 calf	F	0	4	Undetermined
1996	Eg #1623	M	min 12	3	Vessel collision
1996	Eg #2220	M	min 5	4	Vessel collision or septicemia
1996	RKB-1430	F	0	4	Undetermined
1996	GA96II2201	M	0		Undetermined
1997	Eg #2450	F	min 4	3	Vessel collision
1997	RKB-1449	M	0	3	Undetermined
1998	Eg #1333	M	min 21	4	Undetermined
1998	RKB-1451	F	0	3	Undetermined
1999	Eg #1014	F	min 28	3	Vessel collision
1999	Eg #2030	F	min 10	4	Entanglement
2001	Eg #1238	M	min 19	4	Entanglement
2001	RKB-1452	M	0	3	Vessel collision
2001	NY-2680–2001	F	0	3	Vessel collision
2002	VMSM 20021097	F			Undetermined
2002	WAM 577 Eg	F		4	Undetermined
2002	Eg #3107	F	1	3	Entanglement
2003	Eg #2150	F	min 12	3	Vessel collision
2004	Calf	F	0	1	Live stranded
2004	Eg #1004	F	30	3	Vessel collision
2004	Eg #1909	F	min 15	3	Vessel collision
2005	Eg #2143	F	14	3	Past vessel collision
2005	Eg #2301	F	12	3	Entanglement
2005	Eg #2617	F	9	4	Vessel collision

a. Excludes known dead right whales not examined by necropsy (*n* = 28). ID number is NEAq catalog number unless unavailable. Quality: 1, alive; 2, fresh; 3, moderately decomposed; 4, decomposed. Blank cell, no data. Source in part: Moore et al. (2005).

types of damage are more subtle, and partly because postmortem decomposition is always a problem in this species, as the case studies below will attest.

Of the sixty-seven right whales known to have died between 1970 and May 2005, thirty-nine were examined by necropsy of varying detail (Knowlton and Kraus 2001; Kraus et al. 2005; Moore et al. 2005). The primary diagnoses have been classified in three areas: blunt and sharp trauma from vessel collisions (*n* = 19), acute and chronic fishing gear entanglement (*n* = 5), and neonatal or undetermined mortality (*n* = 14) (Table 12.1).

Blunt Trauma

These mortalities often show no obvious evidence on the surface of the whale, although in hindsight there can be subtle and not so subtle surface bruises and swellings that overlie broken bones. The thick blubber coat serves as a shock absorber and load distributor, so that the skin and blubber are not lacerated, but underlying jaws, ribs, skull bones, and vertebrae can be severely fractured. These skeletal fractures usually have associated soft tissue lacerations that can lead to extensive internal bleeding and associated infections. Broken jaws do not necessarily result in immediate death, as there is good evidence of significant healing in three cases, but these fractures may compromise the whale's efficiency in filtering food. Major trauma to the skull, however, has resulted in severe hemorrhage and death (Fig. 12.3). Occasionally, severe internal hemorrhage can occur without fractures following blunt trauma, particularly intrathoracic and pulmonary hemorrhage, because of the flexibility of the rib cage. This can result from a sudden and severe increase in intrathoracic pressure (compounded by the normally closed blowhole) followed very shortly by rapid decompression as the springlike ribs move back to their normal position. In a few right whale necropsies, the final determination of the cause of death has come down to a relatively small fracture of bone or tearing of soft tissue occurring in a disproportionately important region of the body.

A typical case is illustrated by a whale (Eg #2150) examined on 4 October 2003 at Culloden Wharf, Digby, Nova Scotia. This was a female first seen in 1991 as an adult of unknown age that had her first and only calf in 2001. On 2 October 2003 she was seen floating dead near Digby. She was towed by a local fishing boat through the night into the teeth of a gale. At the necropsy site, a swell was running, so the tow line was transferred to a small boat to get the carcass close to the beach. One of the team had to swim the line ashore to a waiting backhoe. Fortunately the beach was a slippery slab of basalt rock, so

Figure 12.3. Eg #2150. Major fracture (arrows) in the skull that penetrated the brain case. Andrea Bogomolni / Woods Hole Oceanographic Institution.

the carcass slid easily up above the high tide line. Over the next two days, the necropsy revealed a broken jaw, a massive fracture across the back of the skull, and clotted blood around the spinal column in the area of the neck and chest that had been stabilized into puttylike consistency by the heat of decomposition (Fig. 12.3).

Sharp Trauma

These cases show obvious propeller cuts, often in patterned, repeated lines, reflecting the relative movement of the ship and whale as the propeller rotated. The cuts can be superficial, in which case whales can survive with healing but leaving major scars, or they can penetrate vital organs such as the brain, lungs, or liver, or sever large segments of tissue in the tailstock, with rapid death from loss of blood. In 2005, a right whale carcass was found floating off the south-

Figure 12.4. Multiple lacerations in a right whale calf induced by a large ship propeller. Case RKB 1424. Robert Bonde/U.S. Geological Survey.

east coast of Georgia and towed in to Jacksonville, Florida. The whale had survived an encounter fourteen years earlier with a large vessel that left it with three deep propeller lacerations that penetrated nearly to the vertebral column. She had survived this event and was thereafter called "Lucky" (Eg #2143). Fourteen years after this initial encounter with a ship, Lucky was pregnant with her first calf. As her abdomen expanded to make room for the growing fetus, one of the old, healed propeller lacerations opened up, allowing a deep pathway for infection that slowly killed her and her near-term fetus.

A more typical case of sharp trauma, previously described by Moore et al. (2005), was a calf, RKB 1424 (Fig. 12.4). (Some calf cases die before they are assigned a number in the *Right Whale Catalog;* thus, they are identified by a field number.) On 15 January 1993 it was hit by a twin-screw 25-m vessel traveling at 28 km/h. Profuse bleeding continued for forty-five minutes before visual contact was lost. A necropsy five days later showed two distinct and separate propeller lacerations, one from the peduncle to the dorsal cranium and the other from the ventral left flank along the ventral throat to the head. There were massive fractures to the skull with associated clotted blood and fractures to some flipper bones and a rib. The diagnosis was severe antemortem sharp trauma.

Fishing Gear Entanglement

This can result in immediate death if the whale is entangled in enough gear to be unable to return to the surface to breathe, as apparently was the case with a right whale that washed ashore in the Magdalen Islands in the Gulf of St. Lawrence in November 2001. More commonly a fishing gear entanglement is not acutely lethal, but instead, the whale is wrapped up in serial loops of rope (and sometimes net) with gear in the mouth or around the flipper, body, and tail stock. If the whale is attached to heavy bottom gear, the degree of injury may depend on how quickly it breaks free and how severely it gets wrapped in the line. If the entangling gear remains anchored to the bottom, or the gear has heavy weights hanging from it or is fixed in more than one place on the body, it will cinch increasingly tighter as the whale flexes and extends to swim. This results in progressive constriction and tissue damage. Such cases have involved multiple wraps around the upper jaw, the flipper, the tail, or in some cases the entire body.

In one case of a younger whale (Eg #2030), the gear was tightly wrapped around both flippers and across the back, essentially cutting the whale in half as it grew in size. Before the whale died, part of the dorsal blubber coat was peeled back by the incising rope. In other cases (e.g., Eg #1247, Eg #2233, Eg #3107), line with trailing gear that has been wrapped around the tail for long periods of time has resulted in line cutting into the leading edge of the flukes and peduncle, eventually severing major arteries. These chronic entanglement cases are the most gruesome deaths imaginable, and although less frequent than the acute ship trauma cases, they represent the worst form of right whale morbidity and mortality in terms of animal welfare.

Another entanglement typical of many recent cases was Eg #2301. This twelve-year-old female was first sighted in 1993 as a calf. She had her first calf in 2003. In September 2004 she was sighted on Roseway Basin, off the southwestern tip of Nova Scotia. She was entangled with two lines that were stretched tightly over her blowholes and around her left flipper. Disentanglement attempts were made repeatedly in rough seas. At one point the rescue team felt that a line could have parted, after a cutting tool was inserted under it, but the entanglement did not appear to release. The whale was sighted again

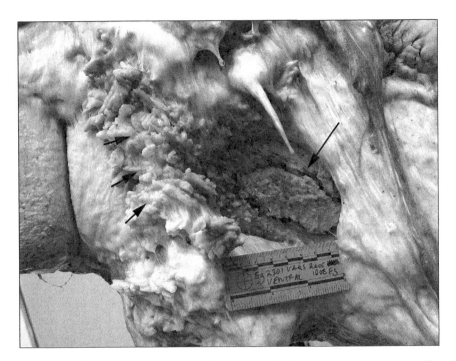

Figure 12.5. The chronic trauma induced by the entangling lines on the humerus bones of the left flipper of Eg #2301. A large amount of ossified reactive repair tissue is evident (short arrows). There is a wedge of infected bone in the radius bone (long arrows). The elbow joint is the vertical space between two bones in the left of the picture. Michael Moore / Woods Hole Oceanographic Institution.

in December 2004, off Nags Head, North Carolina, when it seemed possible that one of the entangling ropes had slackened. On 3 March 2005 her carcass was spotted partially buried in the sand on a barrier beach off the eastern shore of Virginia. A necropsy team examined her as best they could, despite the remote location and lack of any machinery access. Much of the entangling line had been cut free, but there was a severe entanglement of rope wrapped in the left baleen plates, which had exited the mouth on the right side, traveled over and behind the constricted blowhole and was firmly wrapped around the left upper part of the flipper. These lines had cut into the flipper such that there was a 60-cm-wide gash in the leading edge. There was substantial long-term tissue repair attempting to wall off the resulting major laceration (Fig. 12.5).

Neonatal Mortality

Right whales calve in the coastal waters from northern Florida to south-eastern North Carolina during the winter. Perinatal mortalities can exhibit trauma related to complications during delivery (bruising, aspiration of water and other foreign objects into the airways) or of abortion or stillbirth. Two live-stranded calves have been observed with evidence of neonatal complications. Additionally, calves and juveniles are also found dead in a generally poor nutritional state with resulting wasting and emaciation. This is probably a result of a lactation-dependent calf that is separated from its mother. Such starvation can kill a calf directly or reduce the animal's health significantly, which can lead to other secondary causes of death.

Challenges of Postmortem Decomposition

The information that can be obtained from the necropsy of dead whales is significantly limited by their very fast rate of internal decomposition. The thick blubber layer that made right whales desirable to hunt and insulates and maintains body heat in the living whale also limits heat loss by convection in the dead animal. Additional internal postmortem heat is generated by bacterial decomposition initiated by the intestinal flora. This efficient heat retention and the pressure buildup associated with gas production by decomposing bacteria are the equivalent of a pressure cooker within which the temperature can remain at or above normal mammalian temperature for many days. A dead 13-m-long fin whale had a core temperature of 28°C after eight days of being stranded in near-freezing salt water (Brodie and Paasche 1985). For an animal as large as a right whale, twenty-four hours are sufficient to result in extensive decomposition of all internal organs, regardless of the water temperature. Although the appearance of these organs may still be adequate to identify significant macroscopic lesions such as pneumonia or liver abscesses, the usefulness of microscopic examination is often greatly compromised. Further delays in opening the carcass (e.g., retrieving carcasses from offshore) only exacerbates this problem. Moreover, after only a few days, the huge pressure buildup within the thoracic and abdominal cavities can result in extrusion of most internal organs through the mouth, umbilicus (especially in young calves) or, occasionally, the anus. Thus abdominal organs are often found in the thoracic cavity during necropsy of a decomposed whale.

With these considerations, one may question the value of the massive human and financial efforts required to conduct a comprehensive dissection of a decomposed large whale. The results, however, can be surprisingly worthwhile. The skeletal system, for example, resists postmortem decomposition and, therefore, can almost indefinitely hold morphologic evidence of acute and chronic injuries. Acute fractures as a result of ship strikes have been identified all too commonly in right whales. Because of decomposition, free-standing blood at the fracture sites may not always be proof that the fractures occurred before, rather than after, the whale's death. However, superficial bruises may be a good indication of an antemortem process. Moreover, where hemorrhage is associated with obvious edema, it is reasonable to assume antemortem trauma, as it is an indication of a pumping heart, although an attempt should always be made to confirm hemorrhage and edema histologically. New bone formation, either secondary to age-related degenerative changes or to infection, has been described in old skeletons of odontocetes (Kompanje 1995) and in a Bryde's whale (Paterson 1984). New bone formation has also been described in right whales following severe chronic entanglement in fishing gear, with resulting laceration of soft tissues and rope-induced erosion of underlying bone structures (Moore et al. 2005). New bone formation, characterized by growth of a mixture of osseous and cartilaginous tissues, is part of the normal healing process associated with bone fracture and, in smaller mammals, remains as a permanent record of a past traumatic injury. In large whales, however, remodeling activities in fractured bones, which eventually lead to callus formation, may not be as extensive as, or may be slower than, those in smaller mammals (Philo et al. 1990). Some fractures may, therefore, be misinterpreted as acute if examination is confined to a macroscopic evaluation.

Microscopic examination of the fractured surfaces of bones may help to assess the relative age of such fractures because it can reveal the presence of early callus formation characterized by deposition of immature bone and production of cartilaginous tissue, indicating a fracture at least a few days old (color plate 17). Moore et al. (2005) also warn of instances in which gross evidence of ossification of soft tissues overlying sites of chronic bone injury was lost when the bones were cleaned for museum preparation and advise that such lesions should be carefully recorded and sampled.

Death caused by traumatic injury can also be revealed by the presence of an abundant amount of clotted free blood within the thoracic and/or abdominal cavities. Antemortem leakage of blood secondary to vascular tears rapidly results in formation and subsequent polymerization of fibrin, the typical process of blood coagulation. This process leaves more solid masses of blood than is normally found within the confines of large blood vessels, but the intense pressure and heat in the decomposing carcass tend to convert this into crumbly material, which may not be immediately recognized as blood clots. Abundant dark, red-tinged, gelatinous material can sometimes be found between the blubber and underlying muscle mass over large expanses of the body in some decomposed whales. This may be interpreted as evidence of bruising, although autolysis rarely permits confirmation of this interpretation by microscopic examination or other means. Alternatively, this material may represent a postmortem change. This feature is also seen commonly in livestock, particularly sheep, in which the fleece acts as a very good insulator against loss of heat generated by postmortem decomposition (Thomson 1984).

Gravity acts on these large carcasses as well. As fluids are released from the tissues through the relentless action of the pressure cooker, they end up pooling at the lower regions of the carcass and can confound the interpretation of lesions produced by blunt trauma. All of these factors are working against the forensic biologist attempting to determine the cause of death in a large whale.

Now that the process of examination of dead right whales has been described along with the limitations and challenges of interpretation faced by observers, it is possible to discuss the information in the context of the life history of the right whale population.

Causes of Death

At least nineteen of the thirty-four right whales that have been examined by necropsy since 1970 have been killed by ships, and five by fishing gear entanglement (Moore et al. 2005; Kraus et al. 2005; Fig. 12.6). Since 1986, sixty-one whales have been observed to carry fishing gear, of which at least six are confirmed to have died (Kraus et al. 2005). Since 1970 there have been sixty-four dead right whales reported; thus, close to half of the deaths reported have been caused by human activities. Of the remaining entanglement cases, twelve are assumed dead, given subsequent absence from the sighting record and extremely poor health at the time of the last sightings. A further eight whales remain entangled in fishing gear and are of uncertain status as of June 2005. Since 1986 thirty-three whales were either disentangled by rescue teams or shed their gear. Chronically entangled whales sometimes carry fishing gear for years, which compromises both feeding and swimming and causes them

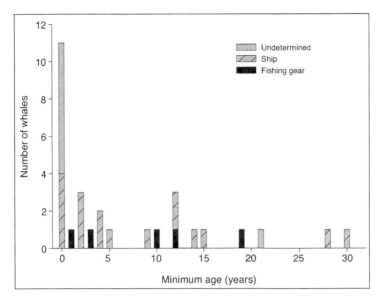

Figure 12.6. Graph showing the number of right whales that died at each year of minimum age. Gray bars show undetermined diagnoses, black bars show fishing gear entanglement, and hatched bars show ship strikes. Note age was unknown for four whales listed in Table 12.1.

to lose weight, so they sink at death, unlike healthy whales that float if killed quickly (e.g., a ship collision). Thus, because the carcasses are often not recovered, right whale mortality from fishing gear is probably underestimated to a greater degree than that from ship kills (Knowlton and Kraus 2001; Moore et al. 2005).

Demographics and Trends of Right Whale Mortality

Measurement data from all known-age right whale mortalities were plotted against age (Fig. 12.7). From this curve, ages can be estimated for right whale mortalities with measurements but without known histories to determine age. From these age determinations, whales were classified as calves (birth to one year), juveniles (one to nine years), and adults (ten years and older). These life stage classifications were combined with data on genders to create a demographic profile of mortalities in North Atlantic right whales.

The number of necropsied whales that died in each year of age, categorized into those hit by ships, entangled in fishing gear, or died from undetermined

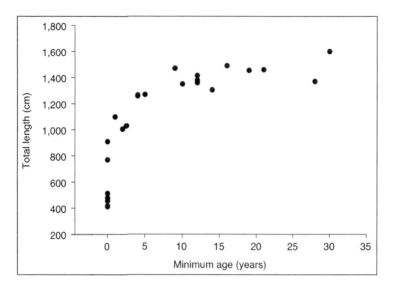

Figure 12.7. Graph comparing minimum age with length of right whales that died and were measured and identified in the *Catalog* as to year of first sighting. Data from Moore et al. (2005).

causes, is shown in Fig. 12.6. These two classes of anthropogenic impacts are the major factors causing mortality following weaning. Ship collision deaths show a bimodal trend, first as young juveniles and then again in the early reproductive, lower teenage years. The distribution of mortalities between the two genders and among calves, juveniles, and adults shows no obvious pattern, although the risk of dying in a given year as a calf or a juvenile is significantly greater than that for an adult.

An analysis of the age at which right whales first seen as calves were estimated to have died (Kraus 1990, 2002) indicated that 26 percent to 31 percent of animals died in their first year, 10 percent in their second, and 5 percent in their third. Rates then ranged from 1 percent to 4 percent for ages 4 through 10. This pattern mimics that found for mortalities examined as shown in Fig. 12.6.

Comparing recent estimates of mortality with the actual observed deaths suggests that the underreporting of mortality may be very large. Demographic models suggest that during the period 1980 to 1998, crude mortality rose to 3–5 percent and was primarily affecting reproductive females (Caswell et al. 1999; Fujiwara and Caswell 2001). In a population of 350 animals, a 4 per-

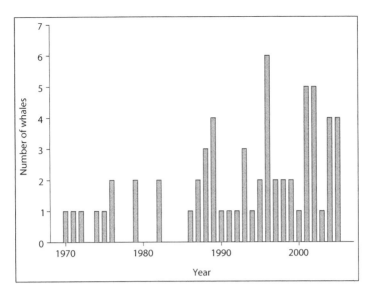

Figure 12.8. Graph showing the number of right whale mortalities recorded each year between 1970 and April 2005.

cent mortality rate predicts that fourteen animals will die annually. In the past twenty years 2.4 mortalities have been reported on average each year (Fig. 12.8). This leads to an estimate that only 17 percent of mortalities have been detected (Kraus et al. 2005).

In the fourteen months between 3 February 2004 and 30 April 2005, eight right whale mortalities were recorded, 2.9 times the average annual rate. This increase in reported deaths may reflect improved sighting effort and reporting awareness, but it is not simply a natural variation in mortality. If only 17 percent of mortalities are being detected, up to forty-seven right whales (8/0.17) could have died in this period (Kraus et al. 2005).

Lessons from Beached Whales

In addition to the conservation urgency of determining the cause of death, a beached right whale also represents a major research opportunity. Limited time and resources, as well as the rapid rate of decomposition, inevitably limit these opportunities to brief windows. In spite of the challenges, significant scientific advances have been made.

Routine morphometric data have been collected, the compilation of which (Moore et al. 2005) has led to the publication of growth curves and allometric graphs that allow estimation of total length from the dimensions of other body parts. Such data support ongoing studies of changes in right whale size and shape with age and life history stage. Samples of right whale baleen have supported analyses of a time-series study of stable isotope ratios (Wetmore 2001). Baleen plates grow at about 4 cm per year, and the nutritional histories of several individuals are being mapped out along the length of the plates.

Imaging and histological studies of right whale ear bones have allowed a careful estimate of the hearing range of right whales (Chapter 10). Skulls and other bones have been routinely submitted to various museums, such that partial or complete specimens have been archived for twenty-four whales as of June 2005. Body parts (specifically baleen, flippers, and flukes) have been transported to laboratories for engineering studies to examine the simulated interaction of fishing gear with these key entanglement points (Cavatorta et al. 2005). Blubber samples are currently being used to look at differences in heat flow from the body after whales have fattened up from a summer of feeding and thinned from a winter of migration and fasting. The larynx has also been collected from a number of whales for anatomic studies. Finally, research on cyamids (the small ectoparasites that give the characteristic color to right whale callosity patches) has been entirely dependent on sampling dead right whales (Rowntree 1996; Kaliszewska et al. 2005).

Conclusion: The Prognosis

About 50 percent of all confirmed mortalities result from accidental kills by ships and entanglements in fishing gear. The recent loss of a number of reproducing right whales in a short period illuminated the importance of bringing human-caused mortality under control. The apparent increasing mortality trend may in part reflect increased offshore sighting effort, but, nonetheless, the current mortality rate far exceeds sustainability, given the population size. Further analyses of the population suggest that the numbers of reported dead whales may represent fewer than one-third of all actual mortalities. Thus understanding and reducing the human causes of right whale deaths remain priorities if right whales are to survive in the North Atlantic. The fact that human sources of mortality are nearly doubling the death rate in this population represents a crisis for this species, but theoretically, and we hope in practice, one that can be managed.

Postscript: The End of the Road for Eg #1909

Eg #1909 was found on the beach at Corolla, North Carolina, on 24 November 2004. She was necropsied by Bill McLellan, Sue Barco, and others. After the necropsy was completed, half of the bones were taken to Massachusetts, and the other half were buried on the beach in Corolla or stored at the Virginia Aquarium. The National Oceanic and Atmospheric Administration granted the New Bedford Whaling Museum permission to display the skeleton. To get the skeleton all in one place and cleaned up, I made a journey down to Corolla with Dave Taylor and Bob Rocha from the museum to retrieve the buried bones. For the bones, it was something of an epic road trip. They were first hauled 10 km down the beach on a trailer by a backhoe. They then spent the next morning in a trailer repair shop acquiring new brakes and springs for the trailer. High winds then denied the bones entry onto the Chesapeake Bay Bridge Tunnel. Undaunted, they had a picturesque trip up the western shore in a gathering snowstorm, ending Thursday night in deepening snow on the New Jersey Turnpike in four-wheel drive. By Friday they were laid to rest in a snow bank in a woodlot by a stream in western Massachusetts under the care of Tom French. In the spring, maggots and weather will prepare them for their new role as an exhibit to educate future generations about twenty-first-century large whale mortality factors.

I am overwhelmed by the efforts being expended by so many people interested in the right whale problem. This was just another day for this right whale biologist and colleagues, but as the bones were laid down in the pure white snow, it just seemed so futile. I lose track of which necropsy was which: it all merges into a blur of wasted potential. A whole community of biologists, conservationists, and managers is working for the same goal: survival of a species in coexistence with important industries. But knowledge is power, and the more we know, the greater the chances of stopping the accidental killing, ensuring that right whales do not just become a series of dusty bones to be forgotten on the shelves of museums on the North American east coast.

Note: This specimen should be articulated and on public display in the New Bedford Whaling Museum, New Bedford, Massachusetts, some time in 2008.

Michael Moore

Aristotle. 350 BCE. *Historia Animalium,* Book 1, Part 5. http://classics.mit.edu/
    Aristotle/history_anim.html.

Brodie, P., and A. Paasche. 1985. Thermoregulation and energetics of fin and sei
    whales based on postmortem, stratified temperature measurements. *Canadian
    Journal of Zoology* 63:2267–2269.

Caswell, H., M. Fujiwara, and S. Brault. 1999. Declining survival probability threatens
    the North Atlantic right whale. *Proceedings of the National Academy of Sciences*
    96:3308–3313.

Cavatorta, D., V. Starczak, K. Prada, and M. Moore. 2005. Friction of different ropes
    in right whale baleen: an entanglement model. *Journal of Cetacean Research
    Management* 7:39–42.

Eschricht, D. F., and J. Reinhardt. 1866. On the Greenland right-whale (*Balaena
    mysticetus*). Pages 1–150 *in* W. H. Flower, ed. *Recent Memoirs on the Cetacea by
    Professors Eschricht, Reinhardt, and Lilljeborg.* Published for the Ray Society, Lon-
    don, 312 pp.

Fujiwara, M., and H. Caswell. 2001. Demography of the endangered North Atlantic
    right whale. *Nature* 414:537–541.

Hamilton, P. K., and S. M. Martin. 1999. *A Catalog of Identified Right Whales from
    the Western North Atlantic: 1935–1997.* New England Aquarium, Boston.

Kaliszewska, Z. A., J. Seger, V. Rowntree, S. Barco, R. Benegas, P. Best, M. Brown,
    R. Brownell, Jr., A. Carribero, R. Harcourt, A. R. Knowlton, K. Marshall-Tilas,
    N. J. Patenaude, M. Rivarola, C. M. Schaeff, M. Sironi, W. A. Smith, and T. K.
    Yamada. 2005. Population histories of right whales (Cetacea: *Eubalaena*) inferred
    from mitochondrial sequence diversities and divergences of their whale lice (Am-
    phipoda: *Cyamus*). *Molecular Ecology* 14:3439–3456.

Knowlton, A. R., and S. D. Kraus. 2001. Mortality and serious injury of northern
    right whales (*Eubalaena glacialis*) in the western North Atlantic Ocean. *Journal
    of Cetacean Research and Management* Special Issue 2:193–208.

Kompanje, E. 1995. Differences between spondylo-osteomyelitis and spondylosis de-
    formans in small odontocetes based on museum material. *Aquatic Mammals* 21:
    199–203.

Kraus, S. D. 1990. Rates and potential causes of mortality in North Atlantic right
    whales (*Eubalaena glacialis*). *Marine Mammal Science* 6:278–291.

Kraus, S. D. 2002. Birth, death and taxis: North Atlantic right whales in the twenty-
    first century. Ph.D. Thesis. University of New Hampshire, Durham.

Kraus, S. D., M. W. Brown, H. Caswell, C. W. Clark, M. Fujiwara, P. K. Hamilton,
    R. D. Kenney, A. R. Knowlton, S. Landry, C. A. Mayo, W. A. McLellan, M. J.
    Moore, D. P. Nowacek, D. A. Pabst, A. J. Read, and R. M. Rolland. 2005. North
    Atlantic right whales in crisis. *Science* 309:561–562.

McLellan, W., S. Rommel, M. Moore, and D. Pabst. 2004. *Right Whale Necropsy
    Protocol.* Final Report to NOAA Fisheries for contract no. 40AANF112525

U.S. Department of Commerce, National Oceanic and Atmospheric Administration, National Marine Fisheries Service, Office of Protected Resources, Silver Spring, MD. 51 pp.

Moore, M., A. Knowlton, S. Kraus, W. McLellan, and R. Bonde. 2005. Morphometry, gross morphology and available histopathology in Northwest Atlantic right whale (*Eubalaena glacialis*) mortalities (1970 to 2002). *Journal of Cetacean Research and Management* 6:199–214.

Omura, H., S. Ohsumi, T. Nemoto, K. Nasu, and T. Kasuya. 1969. Black right whales in the North Pacific. *Scientific Reports of the Whales Research Institute* 21:1–78.

Paterson, R. 1984. Spondylitis deformans in a Bryde's whale (*Balaenoptera edeni* Anderson) stranded on the southern coast of Queensland. *Journal of Wildlife Diseases* 20:250–252.

Philo, L. M., C. Hanns, and J. C. George. 1990. Fractured mandible and associated oral lesions in a subsistence-harvested bowhead whale (*Balaena mysticetus*). *Journal of Wildlife Diseases* 26:125–128.

Rowntree, V. J. 1996. Feeding, distribution, and reproductive behavior of cyamids (Crustacea: Amphipoda) living on humpback and right whales. *Canadian Journal of Zoology* 74:103–109.

Thompson, D. A. W. 1918. On whales landed at the Scottish whaling stations, especially during the years 1908–1914. Part 1. The Nordcaper. *Scottish Naturalist* 82: 197–208.

Thomson, R. 1984. *General Veterinary Pathology*, 2nd edition. W. B. Saunders Company, Toronto, Canada.

Tormosov, D., Y. Mikhaliev, P. Best, V. Zemsky, K. Sekiguchi, and R. L. Brownell. 1998. Soviet catches of southern right whales *Eubalaena australis, 1951–1971;* biological data and conservation implications. *Biological Conservation* 86:185–198.

Wetmore, S. 2001. Stable isotopic investigations into the foraging ecology of North Atlantic right whales. M.Sc. Thesis. University of Massachusetts, Boston.

Acknowledgments

Necropsies were led and undertaken by people too numerous to list here. We thank them all. Necropsies were conducted under NMFS permit to Dr. Teri Rowles or with the support of Canada's Department of Fisheries and Oceans. Funding was provided by the U.S. Geological Survey, National Marine Fisheries Service, NMFS Support Contracts to New England and Virginia Aquaria, Canadian Department of Fisheries and Oceans, the Hussey Family, and the Penzance Foundation.

13

The Entangled Lives of Right Whales and Fishermen: Can They Coexist?

AMANDA J. JOHNSON, SCOTT D. KRAUS,
JOHN F. KENNEY, AND CHARLES A. MAYO

10 May 1999
Cultivator Shoals, offshore Gulf of Maine

How it happened is unknown, even to the whale (Eg #2030) herself. For more than ten years, her sighting records documented her travels around the North Atlantic, doing what all right whale females do while growing up. Through the early 1990s she spent all of her time in the Gulf of Maine, surface feeding in Cape Cod Bay, taking an occasional visit out to the Nova Scotian Shelf, and spending a lot of time in the Bay of Fundy during the summers. In 1996 she visited the calving grounds in the coastal waters of Florida and Georgia, and about the same time, she started engaging in mating behavior, both precursors to learning all the things that mother right whales need to know.

Then, sometime before 10 May 1999, she encountered a rope attached to fishing gear. She may never have seen it, as it could have happened at night or at depth, but when she hit it, she twisted and spun, frantically trying to extricate herself. In the process, she only managed to get herself in deeper trouble, as the rope somehow got itself wrapped around her body behind the blowholes and then around both flippers as well. By the time a

National Marine Fisheries Service (NMFS) survey aircraft spotted her on 10 May, she was truly tied up. But that sighting was too far offshore and too late in the day for a rescue attempt, and it was not until 9 September that she was resighted by a New England Aquarium research team in the Bay of Fundy.

What followed was as valiant an effort as the Provincetown Center for Coastal Studies has ever launched to disentangle a right whale. Over the next ten days, the Provincetown Center for Coastal Studies and New England Aquarium teams worked together to try to disentangle Eg #2030 from her predicament. A satellite telemetry buoy was attached so she could be tracked, and on every good weather day, disentanglement teams were with her, attempting to remove the gear. But ropes around flippers are nearly impossible to reach from the surface, and the tension on the line over her back was so great that it was already deeply embedded in the skin and blubber, and no conventional rescue gear could get under it to cut it free. On 14 September, she left the Bay, leaving her would-be rescuers frustrated, sad, and desperately concerned about her fate.

The satellite tag tells her story from here onward. She traveled southwest toward Portland, Maine, until she was about 80 km offshore. She then turned south and headed through the Great South Channel out to the continental shelf edge east of New York, where she stayed until 21 September. She started westward, but the buoy became detached from her on 24 September, and all hope of finding her for subsequent rescue attempts vanished.

On 20 October 1999, the Marine Mammal Stranding Center in Brigantine, New Jersey, reported a dead entangled right whale offshore. The Coast Guard towed it in for a necropsy, and researchers quickly confirmed that it was Eg #2030. She had been dead for about ten days, but all of the forensic evidence to determine the cause of death was intact. Ropes had cut into the bone of both flippers, and the wrap of rope across the back had cut down to and into the muscle through over 15 cm of blubber. The necropsy report states, "Massive traumatic injury induced by entanglement in fishing gear. Starvation." The end of Eg #2030 was neither swift nor painless.

The death of Eg #2030 was tragic but was not entirely in vain. She taught us a lot about our limitations in dealing with problematic entanglements. Her bones went to the Museum of the Earth at the Paleontological Research Institution in Ithaca, New York, with the hope of inspiring a new generation of children. And samples went to numerous scientists along

the east coast, all contributing in some way to the preservation of this
species. Still, no researcher, fisherman, or fisheries manager ever wants to
repeat this event.

Scott D. Kraus

North Atlantic right whales are vulnerable to entanglements in fishing gear
because they live in and travel along the coastal zone of eastern North America, where many people make their living from the sea. Over 75 percent of all
well-photographed right whales show scars from having been entangled at one
time in their lives. Nearly every year an entangled right whale dies or disappears. So each right whale faces the risk of getting entangled in fishing gear,
and for some, that event is fatal. However, it is a rare day that any one of the
thousands of fishermen along this coast sees a right whale, and even rarer to
see one entangled in his gear. This is the crux of a remarkably challenging
conflict between right whales and humans: how can an entire industry be regulated, at sometimes significant costs, to eliminate an event that an individual fisherman rarely observes? Yet how can it not be regulated, if each event
has significant consequences for a species on the brink of extinction? This
chapter is about the attempts by researchers, managers, and fishermen to resolve this in a way that allows fishermen to continue fishing and right whales
to survive.

Description and Distribution of Fixed Gear

Fixed fishing gear exists throughout the known range of right whales along the
east coast of the United States and Canada. Fixed gear, as the name implies,
is stationary gear that is "set" or lowered to the ocean floor by a fisherman, left
unattended for a period of time (ranging from hours to days), and then hauled
to retrieve the catch. The two most common types of fixed gear utilized in the
northwest Atlantic are pots (also called traps) and gillnets.

Common types of pot fisheries include those that target crustaceans such
as lobsters and crabs, mollusks, and some species of fish (Table 13.1). The
lobster industry uses most of the Gulf of Maine and the continental shelf
south of Nantucket Island, Massachusetts, to Long Island, New York, and the
crab industry has pot fisheries across the shelf from Nova Scotia to Cape Hatteras, North Carolina. Fixed-gear fisheries targeting species managed through

Table 13.1. Common Target Species of Pot and Gillnet Fisheries along the U.S. East Coast

Pot fisheries	Gillnet fisheries	
Crustaceans	Northeast groundfish	Other species
American lobster	(multispecies)	Monkfish
Red crab	Atlantic cod	Spiny dogfish
Rock crab	Witch flounder	Black tip shark
Golden crab	American plaice	Smooth dogfish
Mollusks	Yellowtail flounder	Croaker
Conch	Ocean pout	
Fish	Haddock	
Slime eel (or hagfish)	Pollock	
Black sea bass	Winter flounder	
	Windowpane flounder	
	Redfish	
	White hake	
	Whiting	
	Offshore hake	
	Red hake	
	Atlantic halibut	

fishery management plans, such as conch and black sea bass, occur in these areas as well as emerging fisheries that are not yet regulated through fishery management plans (e.g., hagfish).

Common gillnet fisheries include those in the northeast that target groundfish (multispecies), monkfish, and spiny dogfish; as well as those in the mid-Atlantic and southeast targeting shark species such as black tip, smooth dogfish, and spiny dogfish; croaker; and other species (Table 13.1). Gillnets are also used in a variety of other fisheries from Nova Scotia to Florida.

Fixed gear is used in waters ranging from the beach out to the edge of the continental shelf, although the vast majority is typically fished in less than 366 m of water. From Florida up through the mid-Atlantic, this area extends seaward roughly 37 to 111 km. In the northeast, this area is much more extensive and, in waters of the Gulf of Maine, Georges Bank, Roseway Basin, and the Scotian Shelf, fishing activities extend to more than 278 km from shore in some locations.

From north to south, there are a wide variety of species being targeted by the different gear, and much variation in the ways fishermen use that gear. This combination means that there are no typical gear configurations. The overall amount of effort (e.g., number of vessels, amount of gear, number of days fished) in many of these fisheries is not known and in some cases difficult to

Figure 13.1. Entanglement of right whale Eg #3107, displaying wraps of line around the tail stock. Timothy Frasier / New England Aquarium.

estimate. Fishing effort can fluctuate from one fixed-gear fishery to another by changing seasonally and annually, and effort can move away from fixed-gear fisheries altogether. This occurs because of a variety of factors, such as the availability of target species, market prices, regulations, and seasonal weather conditions. Also, many fishermen maintain permits for more gear than they currently fish, hedging bets against a future of abundant resources. This makes an assessment of the actual numbers of traps or gillnets in the water extremely difficult.

The Nature and Extent of Fishing Gear Entanglements

Because right whales spend much of their lives within 80 km of the coastline of the United States and Canada, it is not very surprising that they become entangled in fixed fishing gear with some regularity. Still, the actual mechanism of entanglement is not well understood. There is no evidence that adult right whales are curious about or attracted to fishing gear, although calves have been

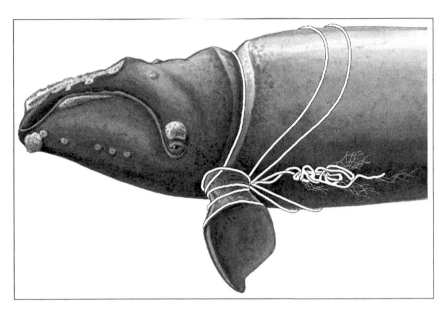

Figure 13.2. Illustration of right whale Eg #2030, displaying wraps of rope around the body. Scott Landry / Provincetown Center for Coastal Studies.

occasionally observed playing with rope, seaweed, and debris. In right whales, entanglements in fishing gear have been observed as wraps of rope around the tail stock (Fig. 13.1), flippers, or body (Fig. 13.2), ropes passing through the mouth and baleen (and sometimes around the rostrum; Fig. 13.3), or gillnet draped or wrapped over the head. The fact that right whales get wrapped up in fishing gear suggests that encounters with gear are surprising to the whale, eliciting an escape response, which may involve rolling and turning. On two occasions where an observer believed entanglements were recent, whales were observed to be swimming rapidly, surfacing frequently, and making erratic turns.

In an analysis of fishing gear involved in entanglements of right and humpback whales, Johnson et al. (2005) examined cases from twenty-nine individual right whales that were reported entangled thirty-one times (one whale was entangled three separate times) between 1993 and 2002, leading to nine known or potential deaths (potential deaths were based largely on a visual health assessment method developed by researchers at the New England Aquarium; Chapter 9). However, these numbers are certainly underestimates of the impact of fishing gear on right whales, as the actual number of right whale entanglements exceeds the number of entanglements that are reported.

Figure 13.3. Photograph of right whale Eg #2320, displaying rope over the rostrum and through the baleen on the right side of the head. Provincetown Center for Coastal Studies.

From 1986 to the present, there were twelve whales that either were never seen again after an entanglement event or whose health condition was poor at the time of their last sighting. These whales are presumed to be dead, either because of a complete disappearance from the *Right Whale Catalog* for six years or more or in some cases because the injuries sustained and the appearance of the whale indicated that survival was unlikely. From 1986 on, the total number (eighteen) of known deaths and presumed deaths (six and twelve, respectively) attributable to encounters with fishing gear is nearly equivalent to the number of right whale kills from shipping (nineteen) (Kraus et al. 2005).

Right whales have been reported entangled all along the east coast of both Canada and the United States, including the area between Nova Scotia and Newfoundland, the Bay of Fundy, coastal Maine and New Hampshire (Jeffreys Ledge), Massachusetts coastal waters (Stellwagen Bank), offshore in the Gulf of Maine, the Great South Channel, Rhode Island through the mid-Atlantic region, and the coastal waters of Georgia and Florida. This is consistent with the fishery information given above: any co-occurrence of whales and fixed gear may lead to encounters between them. It should be noted that an area in which a whale is reported entangled may not necessarily be the place where the entanglement initially occurred. Higher numbers of reported entanglements may occur in areas that are well surveyed, such as the Bay of Fundy and Massachusetts coastal waters, which are both high-use areas for right whales during certain times of year. In addition, entanglements affect males and females approximately equally, with thirteen females, thirteen males, and three of unknown sex documented by Johnson et al. (2005).

Most entanglements are reported in May, July, and September. These months coincide approximately with the timing of right whale movements between areas. From May through July, whales are leaving the Great South Channel, transiting across the Gulf of Maine, and moving into summering habitats, including the Bay of Fundy, the Nova Scotian Shelf, and the Gulf of St. Lawrence. In September, right whales are beginning to leave the summering habitats for areas that are still unknown (Kenney et al. 2001). During these times, right whales may be vulnerable because moving between areas may elevate the chances of encountering fishing gear. However, these months are also when many surveys take place, so researchers are more likely to see and report entanglements. Right whales may also be vulnerable to entanglements while they feed, as Johnson et al. (2005) reported that 77.4 percent of the right whale entanglement events that were analyzed involved the mouth.

Documentation of Gear Types and Analysis Methods

Although the mechanics of how a whale becomes entangled are unknown, understanding the nature of the entangling fishing gear is important in the development of methods aimed at reducing entanglements. Documentation of the type of gear as well as the part of the gear that a whale encounters is necessary to develop alternative fishing gear or techniques that will reduce the chances of entanglements or the risk to the whale should an entanglement occur.

When an entangled whale is sighted, and the event is reported quickly, an established plan to disentangle the whale is put into motion. If disentanglement efforts result in any of the entangling gear being recovered, the gear is typically turned over to the NMFS Gear Research Team for analysis. Efforts are made to learn everything possible about the gear and determine what type of gear it was, what particular fishery it came from, where it was set, and when it was lost. Generally, only in the rare cases where the owner of the gear can be identified and subsequently interviewed will answers to these questions be found. Without the owner, the recovered gear tells less of a story. In these cases,

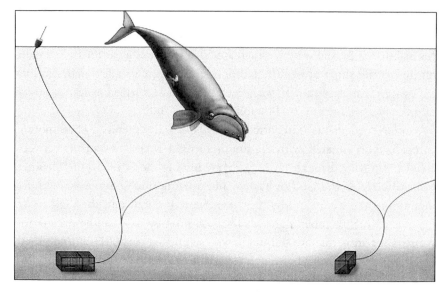

Figure 13.4. Generalized pot gear configuration. Scott Landry / Provincetown Center for Coastal Studies.

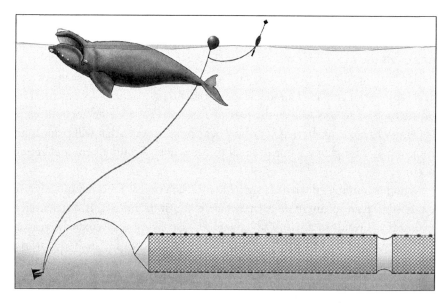

Figure 13.5. Generalized gillnet gear configuration. Scott Landry / Provincetown Center for Coastal Studies.

the experience of the Gear Research Team is critical, but it can be challenging to evaluate what has been recovered. Gear type can usually be determined if a portion of a gillnet or a trap is recovered; however, linking the gear to a specific fishery is not common. Often only less identifiable items are recovered, and they do not result in any gear type determination. In a case when the recovered gear consists only of rope, with no additional identifiable characteristics, it is classified as "unknown gear."

Parts of Gear Involved in Entanglements

Fixed fishing gear can be broken down into a variety of components. These include buoy line (also known as end line), groundline, floatline, and lines associated with the surface system. Buoy line is the vertical rope that connects the gear on the ocean floor to the buoys and/or high flyers at the surface. Surface system line is used to connect buoys and high flyers to each other and to the buoy line. Fishermen use buoys and high flyers to mark the location of their gear as well as to alert other fishermen to the presence of their gear to reduce gear conflicts (e.g., another fisherman setting his gear across someone else's gear).

Groundline is used to connect traps to each other and is also used in gillnet gear to connect a string of net panels to an anchor. Trap gear can be fished in a variety of ways, including as singles, doubles that are connected by one groundline, or trawls, which are strings of traps connected to each other by groundlines. Floating groundline creates arcs of line that float up into the water column (Fig. 13.4). In gillnet gear, floatline is the line that runs across the top of gillnets, holding the net panels upright in the water column (Fig. 13.5).

Summary of Right Whale Entanglement Data

In the Johnson et al. (2005) study, fourteen cases resulted in gear type identification: eight in lobster pot gear, two in gillnets, and one each in pot-related, crab pot, Danish seine, and aquaculture gear. Four mortalities were documented. In the two years following that study, seven right whales were first reported entangled; gear was recovered and identified from one and consisted of a heavy monofilament from an unknown gear type as well as lobster gear (Whittingham et al. 2005).

Johnson et al. (2005) concluded that all parts of fixed fishing gear create entanglement risk, as all have been recovered from entangled right and humpback whales. Buoy line and groundline were recovered and identified more often than floatline and surface system line, but comparing the relative risks associated with each gear part is not possible, partly because of a lack of information regarding the types and amounts of fixed gear being fished. In addition 40 percent of the fishing lines examined from both species could not be identified to a specific part of the gear because many times a whale is entangled in a piece of rope that has no distinguishing characteristics (Johnson et al. 2005).

In some cases the configuration of an entanglement on the whale's body may change as the whale moves, making it difficult to draw conclusions about how the entanglement occurred. Therefore, assessing entanglements is extremely difficult without knowing where the whale first contacted the gear and how the whale reacted on encountering the gear. These factors, among others, contribute to the challenges whale rescuers face when attempting to disentangle right whales.

Right Whale Disentanglement

Many people ask, why not just cut the ropes off the whales? If only it were so easy. Many entangled whales are freely swimming and hard to approach, some are entangled in places that cannot be reached from a vessel, and all entanglements involve animals the size of a bus, which could kill the would-be rescuers, perhaps inadvertently, perhaps purposefully. Nevertheless, since fishermen have gone to sea, they have been removing fishing gear from whales to rescue their gear. Recently the effort to disentangle whales has been motivated by management actions and the concern about the decline of the right whale population.

Beginning in the 1970s, Jon Lien of Memorial University in Newfoundland, Canada, developed one of the first structured whale disentanglement programs. Jon's disentanglement efforts were specifically aimed at assisting fishermen who caught mostly humpback whales in fish traps along the Newfoundland coast. Though the focus of his rescue efforts was on the more common fish-eating whales, Jon once attempted to free a right whale tangled in the heart of an anchored cod trap and memorably described how difficult the whale was to deal with because of its determination to prevent the approach of rescuers.

Experiences with right whales, including those described during whaling voyages, confirm that this species is particularly strong and difficult to control. Modern disentanglement efforts are severely hampered by the right whale's uncooperative nature and require strategies and techniques that are not necessary for other species. Because of their immense strength, right whales entangled in fixed fishing gear routinely break it free from the bottom anchoring system. Then, a free-swimming whale with ropes or nets attached presents the challenge of safely approaching and controlling it during disentanglement efforts (color plate 18a).

Many of the techniques used to deal with free-swimming entangled right whales, as well as other species of endangered cetaceans, have been developed at the Provincetown Center for Coastal Studies on Cape Cod and are used by a network of people along the coast of eastern North America who are trained to various levels to assist with rescue efforts. All stages of a disentanglement effort are supervised by the National Oceanic and Atmospheric Administration or Fisheries and Oceans Canada. These federal agencies provide both the necessary permits to work on marine mammals and access to extensive resources, including vessels and aircraft as well as Canadian or U.S. Coast Guard support ships.

Free-swimming whales present a particularly vexing problem at the outset of any disentanglement effort because their mobility initially makes it difficult for rescue teams to locate them. Essential in the early phases of any effort to free a whale is the initial reporter's willingness to stand by with the whale until a team of network members can get to the scene. The second step involves the attachment of a very-high-frequency (VHF) radio tag and/or a satellite transmitter to the entangling gear. The satellite transmitter buoy can locate the whale anywhere, whereas the VHF tag can be used by a rescue team to track the whale over close-range distances of several kilometers. The combination of both tags carried by a buoy is necessary for long-term tracking that is required in right whale entanglements. Finally, aircraft may be used both for visual tracking of the whale and for locating the VHF signal from attached tag packages. Aircraft support has become common practice to relocate and undertake disentanglement of whales that are highly mobile (color plate 18b).

At the core of the rescue is the effort to bring the whale under control, particularly to prevent diving. Methods to subdue free-swimming whales were initially developed by historic whalers, who applied drag and buoyancy to bring whales to a stop at the surface. Drag was applied by attaching empty kegs, air-filled bladders, or a whale boat to the harpoon in the whale. In the modern variation of the old technique, drag in the form of fishing floats or the inflatable rescue boat is attached by a control line tied into the entangling gear. The addition of sea anchors and drogues may be needed to tire and slow the whale. Occasionally efforts to subdue an entangled whale involve either

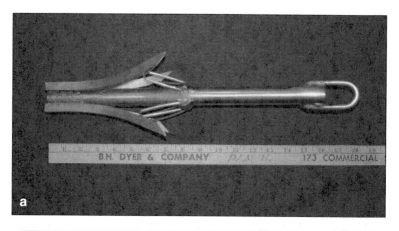

Figure 13.6. (a) Flying jam grapple used to attach a telemetry buoy to the trailing line. Provincetown Center for Coastal Studies. (b) Flying jam cutter designed to pick up and hook onto an entangling line that is wrapped tightly on a whale. Provincetown Center for Coastal Studies.

stealthy boat approaches or rapid high-speed approaches, which may permit some opportunities for cutting gear "on-the-fly." In most cases right whale entanglements are so complicated and severe that efforts to reduce mobility or subdue the whale are required to give the rescue team both the time and the control needed to cut the entangling lines.

The basic procedure is for a small inflatable boat to approach the whale and begin the systematic cutting of the attached ropes and, in some cases, netting.

To aid disentanglement efforts, specialized knives of many shapes and forms have been developed, along with a variety of mechanical cutters (Fig. 13.6a,b), which allow the efficient cutting of the gear while limiting the damage to the whale. Because right whales are more capable of doing damage to the rescue team and equipment than other species are, great caution is needed, and the successful disentanglement of a right whale depends on an experienced crew.

The success of right whale disentanglement using the techniques described is difficult to measure; however, in approximately half of the entanglements initially deemed life-threatening, enough gear has been removed to result in a postdisentanglement assessment that the whale is likely to survive. Furthermore, extensive records on individual right whales demonstrate that many severely entangled whales that were subsequently released are alive and thriving.

The systematic disentanglement of whales might seem to be a solution to entanglements caused by traditionally deployed fixed fishing gear. However, although disentanglement efforts are important, they will be unable to reduce serious injury and mortality enough to assure the recovery of the species. Confronted by the immediate need to mitigate anthropogenic impacts, the disentanglement of right whales does have a place in the overall strategy to aid in the species' recovery. Disentanglement should be seen as an important stopgap measure that offers some hope of slowing the rate of serious injury and mortality until fishing methods that reduce entanglement risk have been implemented.

Documentation of Scarring from Entanglements

Because right whales are studied widely using individual photo-identification, thousands of photographs are taken of this species each year. Beyond the individual whale information in these large photographic datasets, both entanglements and collisions with ships leave scars on right whales that can be evaluated to monitor the levels of such interactions (color plates 5b and 18c).

In a recently completed study of right whale scarring by Knowlton et al. (2005), 608 separate scars from entanglement interactions were documented between 1980 and 2002. Of the photo-identified population, a total of 338 of 447 whales (75.6 percent) were entangled in fishing gear at least once. The number of entanglement events per individual ranged from zero to six (mean = 1.4 events per whale). The number of females and males scarred by entanglement was nearly equal, consistent with the known entanglement data presented above.

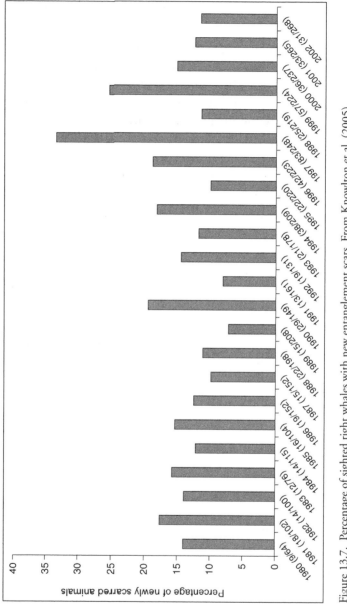

Figure 13.7. Percentage of sighted right whales with new entanglement scars. From Knowlton et al. (2005).

The scarring data suggest that on average, 15 percent of all right whales are newly entangled in fishing gear annually (Fig. 13.7). Since 1994, when the number of adequately photographed whales has been consistently over 200, the percentage of whales entangled annually has ranged from 10 percent to 33 percent. If these percentages are applied to an estimated population of 350, the annual number of entanglement interactions could range from 35 to 116 whales. This suggests that the rate of right whale entanglements is higher than previously believed, but it also shows that many whales escape from entanglements on their own, precluding documentation of the entanglement by methods other than scarring analyses.

The Knowlton et al. (2005) study shows that for all years except one (1988), the percentage of entangled juveniles (expressed as a ratio of entangled juveniles to the total number of entangled whales) exceeded their proportion of the population. Further, at least twenty-five of the fifty-five serious entanglement scarring events (45 percent) involved calves or juveniles (where serious entanglement is defined as any animal seen with line and any animal with a cut deeper than 8 cm), suggesting that this age class is more vulnerable to serious injury from entanglement than adults. This has important implications for efforts to reduce the severity of entanglements. Because juveniles are still growing, any gear that remains on the whale as the result of an entanglement is likely to become embedded and eventually infected. Also, young whales may not have the strength of an adult to break free from ropes.

Continued monitoring is needed to evaluate the effectiveness of management actions designed to reduce entanglements. Annual assessments of scarring events may offer one way to do this. For example, if the amount of rope in the water column is reduced, there should be a concurrent reduction in the number of new entanglement scars detected. Ultimately, many rope-scarred whales migrate, feed, engage in courtship, and have calves. Thus, a large number of entanglements may occur with no long-term effects. However, scarring from entanglements is still occurring at a very high rate, indicating that most entanglements of right whales are undetected, and therefore, some unknown percentage of those entangled whales may die.

Entanglement Risk Reduction Measures

In 1996 NMFS established the Atlantic Large Whale Take Reduction Team (Take Reduction Team) to address interactions between commercial fishing gear and large whales, which include right, humpback, and fin whales. All three of these species are listed as endangered under the Endangered Species Act. Although minke whales are not listed as endangered or threatened, they are protected by the Marine Mammal Protection Act and benefit from actions taken to reduce entanglement of large whales. The Take Reduction Team is composed of a number of stakeholders, including fishermen, conservationists, scientists, and federal and state resource managers from Maine through Florida and is responsible for providing recommendations to NMFS for drafting and developing a take reduction plan. The Atlantic Large Whale Take Reduction Plan (Take Reduction Plan) was created in 1997 to reduce the risk of large whale entanglement from lobster trap or pot and gillnet fisheries. Elements of the Plan include time and area closures, gear modifications, outreach, disentanglement, and research.

Evolution of Gear Modifications

Modifying fishing gear is the most widely supported approach for reducing interactions between whales and fixed fishing gear. The development and implementation of successful "whale safe" gear modifications would protect the whales and still allow the fishing industry to continue plying its trade.

To develop a strategy for gear modifications, NMFS convened a group in the mid- and late 1990s, primarily made up of whale researchers and fishermen, called the Gear Advisory Group. This group was established to (1) gather information from the fishing industry on current fishing gear and practices and (2) identify potential gear modifications or changes to fishing practices that might benefit the whales and still allow industry to continue to fish. This crucial exchange between the whale research community and the fishing industry became the basis for the development of gear modifications. Discussions covered the use of weak links placed at buoys (i.e., a breakable component of gear that will part when subject to a certain tension load), which are designed for entanglements that involve the mouth. If the whale catches the buoy line in its mouth, it then theoretically slides up the line to the weak link, and the link is supposed to part when a certain force is applied. For gillnet gear, weak links incorporated into the floatline are designed to part when a whale encounters the gear, preventing the whale from drowning.

In addition, the group considered bottom-release devices (to eliminate some vertical lines), visual and audible deterrents, biodegradable materials, lipid-soluble materials, and a variety of changes in fishing practices, including the use of sinking groundlines in pot and gillnet fisheries (to prevent arcs of line in the water column). In addition, several gear research needs were identified, including the need to better understand in situ gear configurations and the loads exerted on the gear under commercial conditions.

As one outcome of the Gear Advisory Group discussions, the group noted that the placement and appropriate breaking strength of weak links in various fisheries were unknown. The Gear Advisory Group recognized that few data were available regarding the loads exerted on the gear under normal commercial conditions (i.e., hauling, setting, or fishing). To collect this information, underwater recording load cells, designed and fabricated by NMFS, were used to collect data from a wide variety of pot and gillnet gear from Florida to Nova Scotia. These data have been considered by the Take Reduction Team in discussing recommendations for breaking strengths and placement of weak links and have been incorporated into regulations governing a variety of fisheries.

To promote developing gear modifications, NMFS has solicited input and ideas directly from the fishing industry and a broad range of disciplines and has developed a number of fishing gear research initiatives. These include research carried out by fishermen, engineers, graduate students, the NMFS Gear Research Team, and others. In addition, several states, including Maine, Massachusetts, Georgia, and Florida, participate in activities funded under the Endangered Species Act (Section 6) in cooperation with NMFS managers.

The process of developing gear modifications for whale conservation can seem slow, and it frequently includes failures and disappointments. Partly, this is because such work occurs at the interface of engineering, biology, and fishing, and the integration of conflicting requirements is challenging. There likely will be bumps in the road ahead, but continued efforts to develop gear modifications will likely significantly reduce the interactions between whales and fixed fishing gear.

Testing whether something works for fishermen is vastly easier than testing whether the modifications will really work for an endangered whale. For one thing, any testing of gear modifications by attempting to create an encounter with a large whale is neither feasible nor legal. Even if a gear modification did not involve directly contacting the whale, permits to conduct research on endangered species are difficult to obtain, take years of paperwork, and are not accelerated by the urgency of the problem. This situation frustrates managers and researchers alike, and it remains an obstacle to endangered species recovery. Unfortunately, it means that many gear modifications cannot meet the normal scientific standards of proof, and those interested in developing better gear for right whales are left guessing about what will work. There is some hope for modeling gear–whale interactions, whether using scaled models in tanks or in computer simulations, to better understand entanglement events. However, in the foreseeable future, the lack of testability will challenge gear researchers and biologists.

Potential Long-Term Solutions

Although it is difficult to evaluate the success of management measures, it is clear that they have not been successful at eliminating right whale entanglements, including some that were fatal. Uncertainty about the rate of right whale entanglement indicates that this problem may be worse because many entanglements are not reported or detected. A long-term solution to reducing the risk of entanglement will most likely result from the combination of a suite of management measures, gear modifications, and continued outreach to fishermen.

Currently, the Take Reduction Plan consists of a suite of management efforts aimed at eliminating or reducing interactions between whales and fixed fishing gear, including temporal and spatial measures based on right whale aggregations as well as gear modifications that have been developed and implemented. These gear modifications include requiring weak links at buoys in vertical buoy lines, prohibiting use of floating line as groundlines in pot and gillnet fisheries, and placing weak links in the float line of gillnets. All of these measures have the benefit of being generally workable by fishermen, and they appear to be logically moving in the right direction for whales. However, the continued rates of both scarring and reported entanglements indicate that more needs to be done.

Proposed New Ideas

A number of potential new gear modifications have been identified, and research to develop them is under way. They address the parts of the gear that present entanglement risks and include changes to the surface buoy systems that mark the gear, the vertical lines that connect the surface buoys to the gear on the bottom, and the gear on the bottom. In addition techniques that would eliminate or reduce the number of vertical lines in the water column are being considered. The current status of gear modifications and research can be found at the Atlantic Large Whale Take Reduction Plan web site: http://www.nero.nmfs.gov/whaletrp/. Some examples of proposed gear modifications are described below.

Surface Buoy Systems

A proposed modification to the surface buoy system would remove approximately 18.3 m of horizontal rope near the surface of the water. As right whales often skim feed open-mouthed at the surface, this modification would reduce the amount of line present in the path of feeding whales, thus reducing the entanglement threat of this part of the gear.

Timed-Release Systems

The Time Tension Line Cutter bottom release is an example of a modification to the buoy line. This is a device, located at the bottom of the buoy line, that will release the buoy line from the bottom gear after a predetermined load and time period have been reached. The device cuts the buoy line away from the bottom gear if the load exerted on the buoy line exceeds the time that the device is set to accommodate. For instance, if normal fishing conditions usually require five minutes to haul the gear, the device could be set to trigger the cut after an eight-minute time period. This would allow for normal hauling of the fishing gear; however, if a whale became entangled in the buoy line, it would be released from the bottom gear after pulling on the buoy line for eight minutes.

Vertical Line Reduction

Eliminating the buoy line from the water column until the gear is hauled is also being investigated. This could be accomplished by storing the buoy and buoy line on the ocean floor until released by some type of device. This device could be a simple timing mechanism set to release the buoy and line at the time the fisherman expected to return to haul the gear. Alternatively, an acoustic signal could release the gear. Although the successful development and implementation of this type of system could significantly reduce the numbers of vertical lines associated with fixed fishing gear, not having surface buoys to mark the location of pots or nets would create several problems. Without buoys on the surface, other fishermen would be unaware of the presence of gear below them. This could result in more gear being set on top of it, or mobile gear (gear that is towed across the ocean bottom) being dragged through the unmarked gear, moving or destroying it. Clearly challenges beyond the basic technological hurdles of developing gear modifications can add to an already complex problem.

Alternative Ropes

No truly whale-safe rope currently exists. The history of rope-making is one of making strong, longer-lasting, cheaper, and more pliable ropes. Currently polypropylene (also known as "polypro") is a widely used synthetic rope because it is durable, strong, easy to handle, and inexpensive. However, polypro is dangerous to whales (and sea turtles) because once it is wrapped around a body or appendage, it rarely comes loose, and it takes years to degrade. Advocates of returning to natural fiber ropes, which lack the durability and strength of synthetic ropes, do not have the support of the fishing industry. Fishermen report that the weaker ropes will have to be replaced more frequently, creating a financial burden, and may break easily, possibly leading to more ghost gear (i.e., lost fishing gear).

However, researchers struggling to reduce accidental fishing entanglements of right whales have been pushing the envelope of engineering with a number of innovative approaches. None are currently in use beyond some at-sea testing, and getting permits to test novel fishing gear has proven to be a formidable barrier. Some of these developments are described below.

Illuminated Rope

Some biologists working with right whales believe that vision is the primary mode of sensory detection for prey finding and near-field navigation. Whales have adapted to the wavelength absorption characteristics of the oceans and have developed light-gathering and enhancement methods, retained high levels of resolution acuity, and developed special pupillary and retinal mechanisms to adjust to different light levels and above- and below-water vision requirements. Haldiman and Tarpley (1993) reported that the eye anatomy of closely related bowhead whales is similar to that in all other cetaceans that have been studied. If so, swimming at night and at depths below the photic zone could put right whales at risk in areas where fishing gear occurs. Visual cues could offer an opportunity to give right whales a warning of an impending collision with a net or rope.

Researchers have proposed testing ropes made with fluorescence or light-emitting diodes to determine if right whales would react to lighted ropes by avoiding them, but permits to conduct such tests have been delayed for years. Nevertheless the research continues on the engineering of such ropes. Fluorescence converts light from one wavelength to another, which can increase visual contrast by producing extra bright colors. Fluorescent polypropylene ropes have been constructed that glow for up to forty-eight hours after five minutes of direct light. Other options on the drawing board are miniature lights built into the ropes at regular intervals. Lights or fluorescence must emit the wavelengths that are transmitted well through water (blue-green to green for northern waters).

Stiff Rope

One novel concept for reducing the number of entanglement deaths of cetaceans and sea turtles is to create a rope that becomes stiff in the water column, so that it will not wrap around an animal's body or appendages. If the rope cannot wrap, the whales and/or sea turtles should effectively bounce off the stiffer line, and entanglement will be prevented. However, a rope that is stiff enough to not entangle a cetacean will present problems to fishermen if it does not coil. Therefore a rope that is stiff in the water, but sufficiently pliable to coil on a boat deck is needed. No such rope currently exists.

Researchers have tried mechanical rope designs, ropes with different chemical properties that become stiff in water, and ropes with tensioning cords that can be made rigid after they are set in the water column. At the moment there are some prototypes in the field, and research is ongoing.

Weak Rope

Another alternative suggested by many biologists is the development of ropes that will break before right whales become fatally entangled. Although weaker breaking-strength rope presents several problems for fishermen, development has continued, resulting in normal-diameter fishing ropes with good handling characteristics and substantially lower breaking strengths (approximately 272–499 kg). One use for these weak ropes might be in gillnet fisheries as floatline (the rope that suspends the net panel of a gillnet), effectively functioning as a continuous "weak link." Preliminary tests with a few fishermen suggest that weak floatline may be a viable entanglement reduction strategy for gillnet fisheries. Another potential use would be to use them at one end of a lobster trap string for a marker buoy. It probably could not function as a hauling line, but it would provide a marker to prevent gear conflicts with other fishermen.

Degradable Ropes

Some of the "star wars" notions for solving the entanglement problem have revolved around making ropes that would degrade rapidly after a whale became entangled. One idea that has a lot of appeal is to develop chemical formulations of rope that would be inert in water but rapidly degrade when in contact with lipids, or fats, which are found in high levels in whale blubber. The problem with this approach is that most rope polymers are extremely stable (which is why they are good for long-lasting ropes), and developing compounds with chemical bonds that would dissolve on exposure to lipids is extremely challenging. Another proposal involves embedding a catalyst within all ropes that, on activation, could dissolve standard fishing polypropylene (D. Mattila, pers. comm.). The catalyst could be activated by light (assuming entangled whales reach the surface), a solution fired from a paint ball gun (assuming the whale is encountered by a disentanglement team), or possibly by contact with lipids (a variation on the first idea, with all of its chemical challenges). Neither of these ideas has reached the prototype stage, but in the long term, such ideas may offer hope for a permanent solution to entanglement.

Need for Future Research

When and How Do Right Whales Use the Water Column?

Fishermen have suggested that right whales may not use the entire water column, making the placement of fishing gear in some areas safe. Right whales are capable of diving to great depths (at least 300 m), and in at least one case, a right whale was recorded diving nearly to the bottom on each dive during a transit across the middle of the Gulf of Maine (Mate et al. 1997). Within the different feeding areas, right whales are extremely good at choosing depths where high concentrations of copepods occur (Mayo and Marx 1990; Winn et al. 1995; Baumgartner and Mate 2003).

These studies do not provide hope that there are any patterns of right whale diving behavior that could reduce entanglement risk. Because plankton patches are ephemeral, seasonal, and dependent on a variety of oceanographic conditions, suitable feeding aggregations may occur almost anywhere in the Gulf of Maine and at any depth. In addition, adult *Calanus* copepods are known to overwinter near the ocean floor in the deep ocean basins in the Gulf of Maine (Chapter 5). In this context a likely right whale foraging strategy would be to sample for prey species throughout the water column, even while transiting between areas known to be feeding grounds. Therefore it is probable that fixed fishing gear anywhere in the water column could create a risk of entanglement.

Whale Sensory Abilities That May Help Reduce Entanglements

Because fixed fishing gear is distributed very broadly both near shore and offshore along the coast of North America, strategies to reduce entanglements must be comprehensive and flexible. Records of right whale entanglements from Newfoundland to Florida show no clear pattern that might inform a management strategy around seasonal closures or restrictions on gear type. One option being explored is to determine if there are any ways to prevent the entanglements from ever occurring by taking advantage of the inherent sensory abilities of right whales.

The sensory abilities available to right whales are the standard mammalian ones: touch, temperature, hearing, seeing, taste, and smell. Touch is probably not an option for avoiding entanglement because by the time a whale is touching fishing gear, it is too late. Temperature may be used by whales for broad-scale navigation and perhaps to find prey, but it is difficult to imagine how temperature could be used to initiate avoidance of fishing gear. In fact because thermoclines (thermal depth stratification) may signal aggregations of food, creating an artificial thermal signal around fishing gear might elicit curiosity in whales and make entanglements more likely. There is no information on whether right whales have a sense of smell or taste. Molecules that stimulate both sensory modes in terrestrial environments disperse slowly in the water column and would be at the mercy of currents. Therefore an alerting mechanism dependent on these modes might not be predictable and would probably not provide an immediate warning of danger. Even if the whales did have such abilities, researchers would have to find an aversive smell or taste and then figure out how to get it into fishing gear.

Right whales use sound for communication, and their hearing is believed to be quite comparable to that of humans (Parks 2003), but no evidence of echolocation (biological sonar) has ever been reported in a baleen whale (Beamish 1978). Therefore, enhancing the acoustic target strength of fishing gear is not a viable strategy. Active acoustics, in the form of "pingers" or acoustic deterrents, have been successful in reducing bycatch of dolphins and porpoises (Kraus et al. 1997; Barlow and Cameron 2003). In humpback whales low-frequency (4 kHz) acoustic deterrents were used to try to keep animals out of cod traps in Newfoundland (Lien et al. 1992). Although the number of entanglements was not reduced, the severity of the entanglements was, through mechanisms that remain unknown. When aversive sounds were played back to right whales by researchers seeking methods to move whales away from ships, the whales responded by swimming to the surface (Nowacek et al. 2004). In both of these studies, neither whale response would necessarily reduce entanglements.

Further, concern about the growing noise levels in marine mammal habitats is increasing (Chapter 11). If one imagined pingers on every lobster trap in the Gulf of Maine during the summer, most of the Gulf of Maine would be ensonified at a very high level. Acoustic deterrents carry an inherent paradox. To be effective, they must be within the hearing range of the target animal. But large amounts of sound in that hearing range could interfere with that species' communication. Because animals need to communicate to raise young, find food, and find mates, interfering with the communication of a severely endangered species is not a good idea.

In the light-ropes development, the assumption is that vision is a primary sensory mode for right whales. The optical properties of seawater are affected by the presence of phytoplankton, suspended particles, and dissolved organic matter, resulting in a light field that is dominated by the green portion of the spectrum. Marine mammals that have been examined have lost their short-wavelength cones (Levenson and Dizon 2003) and have peak sensitivity in the green portion of the spectrum. This results in essentially black-and-white vision, where green light is seen as bright against a dark background. The light-rope research premise is that green visual cues may offer an opportunity to give right whales a warning of an impending collision with a net or rope, although no testing has yet been done.

Predicting Right Whale Occurrence for Managing Fisheries Conflicts

The use of satellite ocean imagery, oceanographic data, geographic information systems, and the application of spatial statistical methods might eventually allow the prediction of potential movement and distribution patterns of right whales, assisting managers in identifying and possibly managing areas where there are high levels of conflict with human activities (Chapter 16). However, the development of such predictive capabilities has proven challenging. Although there are areas that support seasonal zooplankton aggregations that are suitable for right whales, many zooplankton patches are ephemeral, occurring in places and times that are not easily explained by contemporary oceanographic understanding. Even well-established habitats can be abandoned for a year or more by right whales, presumably because food resources are inadequate (Kenney et al. 2001). Therefore, predicting right whale movements is probably dependent on a better understanding of marine ecosystems than currently exists. It may also require new satellite sensing technologies, a better integrated ocean-observing system, and advances in whale detection or tracking capabilities. These developments, combined with improved definitions of the habitat requirements of right whales, may lead to predictive models of this species' distribution and movements.

Conclusion: Can Fishermen and Right Whales Coexist?

It is clear that entanglements of right whales in fishing gear pose a problem for this species. Johnson et al. (2005) concluded that any type of fixed fishing gear is capable of entangling a whale, and any part of that gear can be involved. Unlike entanglements of smaller cetaceans, right whale entanglements are more complex for a variety of reasons. It is difficult to infer anything about an entanglement without witnessing the entanglement event. Also, the gear on a whale's body can move over time as a result of the whale's behaviors and movements, and all parts of fixed gear (buoy line, groundline, floatline, and surface system line) can entangle large whales, although it is difficult to know which ones create the most risk. All of these factors make it very difficult to manage fisheries and identify appropriate gear modifications.

Still, many factors are working in our favor that, when combined, will help both right whales and fishermen.

- A variety of gear research ideas are being tested to create more whale-friendly gear modifications that are also safe and workable for fishermen. NMFS and other independent gear researchers are working directly with fishermen to help develop solutions.
- Right whale research continues to play an important role in dealing with the entanglement problem. Aerial and shipboard surveys are being conducted to help determine right whale movements and migrations, and more research is focusing on where and how right whales use the water column.
- Analysis of annual right whale scarring events from photographs taken during surveys allows for monitoring of fishing gear entanglement events and can be used to assess the efficacy of the management strategies employed.
- The large whale disentanglement network is widespread and can respond to reports of entangled whales. At least some of these whales will be disentangled, and every event improves future success. Also, the more gear

that is retrieved from entangled whales, the more that can be learned about entanglement events.
- NMFS is working with the Take Reduction Team to continue to reduce serious injury and mortality to large whales from entanglements in commercial fishing gear.

Although the current fishing gear technology and management strategies are not fully effective for protecting right whales, a large multistakeholder effort to solve this problem is under way. It is moving forward with industry involvement and support, gathering more information about entangling gear, and developing new gear that will be whale safe and also workable for the fishing industry. In light of this effort, it is only a matter of time before fishermen and right whales will be able to coexist successfully.

Barlow, J., and G. A. Cameron. 2003. Field experiments show that acoustic pingers reduce bycatch in the California drift gillnet fishery. *Marine Mammal Science* 19:265–283.

Baumgartner, M. F., and B. R. Mate. 2003. Summertime foraging ecology of North Atlantic right whales. *Marine Ecology Progress Series* 264:123–135.

Beamish, P. 1978. Evidence that a captive humpback whale (*Megaptera novaeangliae*) does not use sonar. *Deep Sea Research* 25:469–472.

Haldiman, J. T., and R. J. Tarpley. 1993. Anatomy and physiology. Pages 71–156 *in* J. J. Burns, J. J. Montague, and C. J. Cowles, eds. *The Bowhead Whale*. Society for Marine Mammalogy, Lawrence, KS.

Johnson, A. J., G. S. Salvador, J. F. Kenney, J. Robbins, S. D. Kraus, S. C. Landry, and P. J. Clapham. 2005. Fishing gear involved in entanglements of right and humpback whales. *Marine Mammal Science* 21:635–645.

Kenney, R. D., C. A. Mayo, and H. E. Winn. 2001. Migration and foraging strategies at varying spatial scales in western North Atlantic right whales: a review of hypotheses. *Journal of Cetacean Research and Management* Special Issue 2: 251–260.

Knowlton, A. R., M. K. Marx, H. M. Pettis, P. K. Hamilton, and S. D. Kraus. 2005. Analysis of scarring on North Atlantic right whales (*Eubalaena glacialis*): Monitoring rates of entanglement interaction: 1980–2002. Final Report to the National Marine Fisheries Service. 20 pp.

Kraus, S. D., A. Read, E. Anderson, K. Baldwin, A. Solow, T. Spradlin, and J. Williamson. 1997. Acoustic alarms reduce porpoise mortality. *Nature* 388:525.

Kraus, S. D., M. W. Brown, H. Caswell, C. W. Clark, M. Fujiwara, P. K. Hamilton, R. D. Kenney, A. R. Knowlton, S. Landry, C. A. Mayo, W. A. McLellan, M. J. Moore, D. P. Nowacek, D. A. Pabst, A. J. Read, and R. M. Rolland. 2005. North Atlantic right whales in crisis. *Science* 309:561–562.

Levenson, D. H., and A. Dizon. 2003. Genetic evidence for the ancestral loss of short-wavelength-sensitive cone pigments in mysticete and odontocete cetaceans. *Proceedings of the Royal Society of London Part B* 270:673–679.

Lien, J., W. Barney, S. K. Todd, R. Seton, and J. Guzzwell. 1992. The effects of adding sounds to codtraps on the probability of collisions by humpback whales. Pages 701–708 *in* J. A. Thomas, R. A. Kastelein, and A. Y. Supin, eds. *Marine Mammal Sensory Systems.* Plenum Press, New York.

Mate, B. R., S. L. Neukirk, and S. D. Kraus. 1997. Satellite-monitored movements of the northern right whale. *Journal of Wildlife Management* 61:1393–1405.

Mayo, C. A., and M. K. Marx. 1990. Surface foraging behavior of the North Atlantic right whale, *Eubalaena glacialis,* and associated zooplankon characteristics. *Canadian Journal of Zoology* 68:2214–2220.

Nowacek, D. P., M. P. Johnson, and P. L. Tyack. 2004. North Atlantic right whales (*Eubalaena glacialis*) ignore ships but respond to alerting stimuli. *Proceedings of the Royal Society of London Part B* 271:227–231.

Parks, S. E. 2003. Acoustic communication in the North Atlantic right whale (*Eubalaena glacialis*). Ph.D. Thesis. MIT-WHOI Joint Program in Oceanography. Woods Hole, MA.

Whittingham, A., M. Garron, J. F. Kenney, and D. Hartley. 2005. *Large Whale Entanglement Report 2003.* National Marine Fisheries Service, Northeast Regional Office. 137 pp.

Winn, H. E., J. D. Goodyear, R. D. Kenney, and R. O. Petricig. 1995. Dive patterns of tagged right whales in the Great South Channel. *Continental Shelf Research* 15:593–611.

Acknowledgments

The authors thank the Provincetown Center for Coastal Studies Disentanglement Team and the Atlantic Large Whale Disentanglement Network for their hard work and dedication. The expertise of the National Marine Fisheries Service Gear Research Team has been invaluable for acquiring information about the gear recovered from entangled large whales and working with the fishing industry to develop gear modifications that will not only reduce entanglements but be workable for industry. A variety of gear researchers and industry members continue to work to develop whale safe gear modifications. Mary Colligan, David Gouveia, Diane Borggaard, Gregg LaMontagne, and Brian Hopper receive special acknowledgment for their efforts in the reduction of right whale entanglements through management. Other individuals who have contributed to or assisted with this work are Dana Hartley and Amy Knowlton.

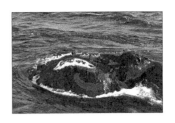

14

Running the Gauntlet: Right Whales and Vessel Strikes

AMY R. KNOWLTON AND MOIRA W. BROWN

7 January 2001
St. Simon's Island, Georgia

Our aerial survey team had a harrowing experience during today's flight. As the plane transited to the offshore area after lunch, a mother and calf right whale pair was sighted. They were recognized as "Mavynne" (Eg #1151) and her calf, reported by the Early Warning System team earlier that day. As we circled, we noticed a large container ship headed straight for them. We flew over to get the name of the ship and hailed it on VHF radio. The mate responded immediately, but it quickly became obvious that his first language was not English and that we had a communication problem. One of our observers tried to explain that the ship had two endangered whales immediately off its bow and advised the mate to alter course in either direction. The ship continued, bearing down on the pair and a collision appeared imminent. Then, momentarily, the message seemed to get through, and observers in the plane could see the ship altering its course to starboard. Immediately the mood in the plane changed as we began to feel relief and even exhilaration that we actually had routed a ship around Mavynne and her calf, most likely saving their lives.

But as the plane banked around again, we felt renewed horror at the sight below. Somehow the ship's mate had decided that he'd turned the wrong way initially and was coming hard back to port. Once again, the mother and calf pair was directly in the ship's path. The ship appeared to maintain its speed throughout the incident. With about one ship's length of distance separating the whales from that huge bulbous bow, the whales disappeared below the surface. Observers in the plane held their breath with cameras poised to document the worst. When the ship was halfway over the point where mom and calf had last been seen, we saw fluke prints upwelling just outside of the ship's wake. The whales were swimming hard, beneath the surface, away from the vessel!

Circling one more time, we were able to confirm that the two whales had survived seemingly unscathed! They surfaced together, swimming at a rapid pace away from the ship, the whale calf closely flanking its mom.

This is the closest encounter that I've ever witnessed between a ship and whales. It was clear that these whales did, at the last minute, display some avoidance behavior. One could only speculate what would have happened had they been just to the starboard side of the bow or if there had been no escape route. Clearly not all right whales demonstrate avoidance, or if they do, much of the time the last minute reaction isn't enough, as too many right whale deaths are caused by ship collisions. On this day Mavynne and her calf had a bit of luck on their side.

Lisa Conger

The eastern seaboard of the United States and Canada is host to one of the highest levels of shipping traffic worldwide (Endreson et al. 2003). The overlap between ship traffic, concentrated near port entrances, and the near-coastal distribution of right whales has been a detrimental combination for this highly endangered species. The encounter described above took place just 13 km from the coast with a vessel bound for Jacksonville, Florida. This may be a common occurrence for right whales along the entire east coast, even though such close encounters have only rarely been witnessed.

Vessel collision is the leading cause of mortality for North Atlantic right whales (Knowlton and Kraus 2001; Kraus et al. 2005; Chapter 12). Since 1970, there have been sixty-seven carcasses reported, at least twenty-four of which have died as the result of ship strike. Why do these strikes happen? Can't the whales hear an approaching ship and move out of the way? Or alternatively, can't the vessel captain see the whale(s) and avoid the collision? These are the questions repeatedly asked by mariners, and the simple answer apparently is "no." Both the problem and potential solutions are complex (color plate 19).

This chapter summarizes what is known (and unknown) about ship strikes of right whales, the tools that have been considered for mitigation efforts, the pros and cons of mitigation strategies, the jurisdictional framework for regulating ship traffic, and both proposed and adopted policy changes.

The Nature and Extent of Collisions between Vessels and Whales

The frequency with which right whales have been struck by ships has resulted in a level of mortality that is not sustainable by this small, endangered population. To begin to solve the problem of ship strikes, information was needed on how and why these strikes were happening and when and where they predominantly occurred.

Many avenues of research have been pursued to try to answer some of these questions. All right whale carcasses have been evaluated carefully (when possible) to ascertain cause of death, approximate location of death, and to describe the physical damage to the whale from human-related interactions (Knowlton and Kraus 2001; Moore et al. 2005; Chapter 12). Laist et al. (2001) and Jensen and Silber (2003) collected anecdotes of ship–whale collisions worldwide to gather insight into the speed and size of vessels involved, the fate of the whale, and what the ship operators saw just before the strike. Laist et al. (2001) also reviewed available stranding data to estimate the levels of ship strike mortality in all large whale species. An analysis of propeller-cut dimensions on living and dead right whales has provided information on the size of the propellers that struck the whale, allowing for an estimate of the size of the vessels involved (James Wood, pers. comm.). A study of the hydrodynamic effects of passing ships on right whales examined which parameters would increase or decrease the risk of collision (Knowlton et al. 1995, 1998). Cavanagh et al. (2004) explored the influence of environmental conditions, surface-image interference, and hull baffling on the transmission of ship noise through the water in advance of merchant ships. Finally, a study using digital acoustic recording tags assessed right whale responses to acoustic playbacks of alarm stimuli as well as ship noise (Nowacek et al. 2004; Chapter 11) and evaluated general diving behavior (Nowacek et al. 2001).

These studies have been conducted to understand why right whales are vulnerable to collisions with vessels, and each has provided some insights that may be helpful in developing mitigation measures to reduce the probability of ship strikes.

Where Have Ship Strikes Occurred?

The exact location of right whale ship strikes is not typically known, except in four witnessed instances. However, plotting carcass locations provides some indication of the proximity to an area with human activities. Color plate 22 shows the initial sighting location of right whale carcasses ($n = 47$), where cause of death was determined to be the result of a ship strike or of unknown cause, in comparison to ship traffic density along the east coast and port entrances. The results indicate that ship-struck carcasses are found close to shipping lanes and in dense ship traffic areas, both in high-use right whale areas and along migratory corridors (Knowlton 1997; Knowlton and Kraus 2001). The average distance to the nearest shipping channel for the ship-struck carcasses was 18.3 km (range 0–48 km), and for carcasses that died of undetermined or natural causes, the average distance to shipping channels was 42.8 km (range 0–159 km).

Ship-Caused Whale Kills

The problem of mortality from ship strikes is not unique to right whales. The review by Laist et al. (2001) showed from the 1970s through the 1990s a minimum of 13 percent to 20 percent of large whale strandings in the United States, Italy, France, and South America were the result of ship strikes. Fin whales were the most frequently killed, followed by right whales and humpbacks, but the relative impact to right whales is greater because the population size is so small. Of the fifty-eight anecdotal records found by Laist et al. (2001), only two were before the 1950s, one in 1885, and another in the 1930s. From the 1950s onward, several ship strikes were documented in each decade with thirty documented in the 1990s. This increase in records may be attributable, in part, to the increase in ship numbers. Registered ships greater than 100 gross tons almost tripled from just over 11,000 in 1890 to nearly 31,000 in 1950, more than doubling again to nearly 74,000 ships in 1980, and up to 87,000 ships by 1998 (Southall 2005).

Before 1991, documented right whale ship strikes were uncommon, with only seven events occurring between 1972 and 1990. During the next fourteen years (1991–2005), a total of seventeen ship-struck carcasses were detected, typically one to two per year. The number of deaths from ship strikes could be considerably higher than documented. Mortalities noted as "unknown cause" included carcasses not retrieved for examination, and some of these whales (especially ones found near a major shipping channel) may have also died as the result of a vessel strike.

Unlike chronically entangled whales that are more likely to sink as they become emaciated, ship-struck whales are usually healthy and fat, so they tend to float for weeks and are more easily detected (Knowlton and Kraus 2001). Improved reporting, active retrieval of floating carcasses, and thorough necropsies have led to an increase in the number of documented ship strikes: five of the seven ship-struck carcasses documented since 2001 were first observed offshore and retrieved for examination. Yet the number of ship-struck carcasses initially found on the beach has not increased over several decades. Carcass detection is low as well, suggesting that many ship kills are not reported (Kraus et al. 2005). Thus it may be that mortalities from ship strikes have been a chronic problem but had simply gone undetected previously.

The Size of Vessels Involved in Whale Strikes

There are only four witnessed accounts of collisions between vessels and right whales: two were fatal, and two were not. On 5 January 1993 the 25-m U.S. Coast Guard cutter *Point Francis* struck and killed a right whale calf off St. Augustine, Florida, while traveling at 26.3 km/h. The crew did not see the whale before it was struck. Of the two sets of propeller cuts found on the carcass, one set was consistent with the size and configuration of the propeller from the Coast Guard vessel. The second set was not, suggesting a postmortem strike (after death) by a larger vessel (J. Wood, pers. comm.).

In November 2004 an adult female (Eg #1909) was struck and killed by the 274-m-long U.S. Navy amphibious assault vessel, *Iwo Jima,* traveling at 39 km/h, approximately 27.8 km east of the entrance to Chesapeake Bay. The lookout saw the whale directly ahead of the ship, but it was too late for avoidance action to be taken. No impact was felt, but the crew saw blood in the water astern and reported the strike. The carcass came ashore one week later with the flukes severed (Fig. 14.1).

In December 1994 a tugboat estimated at 13.7 m in length struck a whale known as "Shackleton" (Eg #2440), a one-year-old male that unwittingly swam up the Delaware River to Philadelphia (Chapter 3). The strike occurred at night and resulted in a series of propeller cuts on the whale's left flank, but

Figure 14.1. Carcass of Eg #1909 showing her tail severed by a ship. Virginia Aquarium Stranding Response Program.

Shackleton survived the collision and has been sighted regularly since the accident (Fig. 14.2).

In March 2005, Eg #2425 sustained apparently nonfatal injuries when struck by a 12.8-m recreational vessel traveling 37 km/h. The captain didn't see the whale and thought he had hit a submerged log until a right whale surfaced thirty seconds later thrashing and bleeding. The propeller mangled approximately 1.2 m of the left fluke tip, but it was still partially attached (Fig. 14.3). The whale was resighted on 2 September 2005 off the coast of Massachusetts and appeared to be in grave condition: the skin was ghostly pale, the body was covered in orange cyamids (an indicator of poor health; Chapter 9), and she looked emaciated. Veterinarians who reviewed her case suspected she would die within weeks of that sighting. Alhough a small number of right whales are still alive despite missing part of their flukes, this case clearly indicates that even strikes by relatively small vessels can lead to fatal injuries.

James Wood analyzed photographs and measurements of propeller cuts on two dead right whale calves and was able to suggest, based on the estimated propeller diameters (ranging from at least 2 m to perhaps greater than 4.6 m),

Figure 14.2. Photo of propeller marks on the back of Shackleton (Eg #2440), resulting from a collision with a tugboat when he wandered up the Delaware River as a young whale. Lisa Conger / New England Aquarium.

Figure 14.3. Propeller cuts and mangled fluke of Eg #2425, which was accidentally struck by a 13-m recreational vessel in Florida. Monica Zani / New England Aquarium.

that the vessels involved in those strikes ranged from 40 m to 152 m. Finally, the review of all large whale strike anecdotes by Laist et al. (2001) revealed that the majority (76 percent) of severe and lethal injuries resulted from collisions with vessels greater than 80 m in length (twenty-nine out of thirty-eight incidents).

Speed of the Vessel and Fate of the Whale

The speed of the vessel, known for three of the four witnessed strikes, ranged from 28 to 39 km/h at the time of the collision with the right whale. In his review of ship strikes worldwide, Laist et al. (2001) reported that 89 percent (twenty-five of twenty-eight) of the lethal and severe injury cases where speed was known involved vessels moving at speeds of 26 km/h or faster, with the remaining three cases involving vessels moving at 18.5–26 km/h. Very few strikes were documented at vessel speeds less than 18.5 km/h (three events), and none of these resulted in a serious injury. Jensen and Silber (2003) documented three additional strikes at less than 18.5 km/h, none of which resulted in death or serious injury. These findings suggest that at vessel speeds less than 26 km/h, most whales may be able to avoid the ship and avoid death or serious injury.

Whale Avoidance by Vessel Operators

A right whale was seen before the ship strike in only one of the four witnessed accounts. In the remaining three cases, one whale had been observed feeding in the area before it turned toward the vessel and was struck, and, in two cases, the whale was seen at some undetermined amount of time before the strike. Laist et al. (2001) found that in forty of the forty-three (93 percent) anecdotal accounts where this information was available, the whale was either seen too late to avoid collision ($n = 23$) or was not seen at all before it was struck ($n = 17$). In Wood's analysis of one of the calves, he noted that when the animal was hit, its body was arched with the head and tail in the down position. This suggests the calf may have been trying to avoid the vessel.

Location on Vessel's Hull Where Strikes Occur

The only direct evidence that is available to assess which part of the vessel's hull strikes the whale is the damage found on carcasses or surviving whales. Propeller cuts or gashes typically result from an interaction with the propeller and/or the keel (color plate 20). Broken bones (i.e., skull and vertebrae) or signs of hemorrhage are usually attributed to blunt trauma from the bow of the vessel. It is not known whether other types of interaction (such as hitting the sides or bottom of the hull) would result in damage to the whale. Of the twenty-four dead right whales determined to have been struck while alive, fifteen had evidence of propeller cuts or gashes, and nine had signs of blunt trauma. In addition, twenty-eight living whales have been sighted with propeller cuts or gashes on their body (it is impossible to see evidence of blunt trauma on a living whale) (Knowlton and Kraus 2001; Moore et al. 2005; NEAq, unpublished data).

Vessel Sounds and a Whale's Ability to Detect Them

The extent of right whale hearing is not completely understood; however, it is assumed that right whales can hear in the same frequency range in which they vocalize (Chapter 10). Based on this premise, the sound generated by ships is within the hearing range of a right whale.

What a right whale hears in advance of an approaching ship appears to vary considerably depending on the type of ship and the type of environment. The sound produced by ships can be heard by right whales from many kilometers away, but their ability to differentiate it from ambient noise and to recognize it as an approaching threat may occur only when a vessel is in close proximity. Cavanagh et al. (2004) determined that a whale at depth (below 2 m from the surface) is likely to be aware of a merchant ship at ranges greater than 1 km. But because of propagation loss near the surface, a right whale within a couple of meters of the surface may be able to detect the ship at ranges of only 400–500 m from the source (the propeller), or approximately 200–300 m off the bow. This is often referred to as the "bow-null" effect. How ship noise is influenced by changes in vessel speed was not explored in their study. All evidence indicates that right whales can probably hear ships; therefore they have either become habituated to ships and do not perceive them as a threat or are simply responding too late to successfully avoid them.

Whale Responses to Approaching Vessels

Nowacek et al. (2004) conducted playbacks to four right whales using a vessel noise stimulus that was collected from a 120-m container ship passing within 100 m of a recording station. The playback was begun two minutes after the whale initiated a dive (estimated to be foraging at a depth of approximately 60–80 m), and the playback device was towed slowly along the assumed path of the underwater whale (Nowacek et al. 2001). They also collected data from right whales equipped with digital tags during three events when ships passed within 1.8 km of the whale. For all the playbacks and opportunistically collected vessel approaches, no response by the whales (i.e., no deviation from normal behavior) was detected. However, in all these cases the minimum distance of the sound from the whale was 160 m, and more likely even farther.

There are very few accounts of whale behavior just before impact or in near-miss situations. In addition to the flight response exhibited by Mavynne and her calf described in the opening narrative, Laist et al. (2001) were able to find behavioral information for only three of the fifty-eight anecdotes collected. In one case, a whale of undetermined species breached in front of a submarine as it was leaving port, landing on its bow; in another case, a humpback whale lunged quickly just before being struck by a whale watch vessel; and in the third case, a pod of gray whales dove when a commercial ship was within 27 m, but the last whale to dive was struck. The humpback whale received a minor injury, and the fate of the other two whales was unknown.

Vessel Hydrodynamics That Influence the Risk of Collision

A ship moving through the water creates hydrodynamic forces that can pose a danger to another ship if they are passing too closely: the ships can be drawn toward one another, resulting in a collision. The influence of these hydrodynamic forces on whales was explored using computer simulations (Knowlton et al. 1995, 1998). These studies showed that a "passive" whale (one that takes no avoidance action) just subsurface (minimum of 4 m) is not in any increased danger from a passing ship if it is not directly in its path. If the whale is just inside the beam width (the widest part) of the approaching vessel, it will tend to get pushed away from the bow by positive sway (lateral) forces before getting drawn in toward the ship by the negative sway forces as it passes. It may end up in the ship's wake after the ship has passed by.

A passive whale that is submerged under the ship is in increasing danger of collision with either the ship or the sea floor as water depth decreases. If a whale "appears" (for example, if ascending from depth) after the initial positive sway force near the bow has passed, it can be drawn into the ship even if it is outside the beam (for certain ships). For example, a whale coming up from a dive and appearing amidships alongside a passing vessel can get drawn in toward the ship's hull and propeller by the negative sway force. The strength of these forces increases with the speed of the vessel as well as with increasing length, width, and draft measurements. If a whale does take avoidance measures, its ability to escape the hydrodynamic forces drawing it toward the ship will be most influenced by the vessel's speed: the higher the speed, the greater the hydrodynamic forces.

Further computer modeling is needed to test the effect of a number of variables on whale–vessel collision risk. The variables include vessel beam and draft dimensions and vessel speed combined with whale behavior and the distance at which the whale initiates a reaction. This modeling will be a useful tool for assessing the relative risk to whales from various vessel types and speeds.

Mitigation Strategies and Their Limitations

Recommendations to reduce the effects of ship strike mortality on right whale recovery were first outlined in the 1991 Right Whale Recovery Plan (NMFS 1991) and have since been reiterated in the Canadian Right Whale Recovery Plan (Anonymous 2000) and the 2005 Right Whale Recovery Plan (NMFS 2005). At this time, information on the few witnessed collisions indicates that speeds of at least 26 km/h, and vessels at least 24.4 m in length cause the majority of mortal injuries to right whales.

The many factors influencing whale–vessel interactions and vessel operations were reviewed between 1997 and 2005 by a group of port authorities, shipping companies, federal agencies, conservation groups, and scientists. In 2000 and 2001 a comprehensive evaluation by these stakeholders of all potential management options led to a report entitled "Recommended Measures to Reduce Ship Strikes of North Atlantic Right Whales" (Russell et al. 2001). This report, submitted to the National Marine Fisheries Service (NMFS) in August 2001, outlined a strategy to reduce the potential for whale–vessel interactions in U.S. waters.

The three main approaches that have been explored to mitigate ship strikes of right whales include (1) educating mariners about when and where right whales are found and identifying precautionary measures that should be taken to avoid collision; (2) developing technological approaches to detect right whales and either alert the mariner or alert the whales to an approaching ship; and (3) altering ship operations via routing and speed restrictions in right whale habitats.

Mariner Education

Over the past five years there has been a coordinated effort to increase the awareness of right whales among professional mariners who sail the east coast of the United States and Canada. Information on right whales has been published in the four volumes of the *U.S. Coast Pilot* that covers the eastern United States and in the three volumes of *Sailing Directions for the Canadian Maritimes*. Critical habitats in the United States and conservation areas for right whales in Canada have been delineated on nautical charts. Other efforts include workshops and the distribution of brochures, flyers, videos (*The Prudent Mariner*), and other information to mariners on the endangered status of the right whale, its distribution and seasonal migrations, and precautionary measures to avoid collisions.

In an effort to improve right whale awareness before a mariner steps on a ship, a merchant mariner educational module was developed for inclusion in maritime academies and U.S. Coast Guard training facilities (Russell et al. 2005). This module provides mariners with training on right whale distribution and recommends avoidance procedures for their voyage-planning process. Although the efforts have been focused on U.S. schools, there is a need to introduce this module to foreign maritime schools because few merchant ships are U.S. flagged or staffed with U.S.-educated crews.

Monitoring right whale distribution and providing real-time information on sightings to mariners have been a dedicated focus of many aerial surveys in the southeast calving ground for over a decade and, more recently, in the northeast habitat areas (Chapter 4). Right whale sighting information is available over the radio broadcast Notice to Mariners, NAVTEX (an automated shipboard communication system), and on the Internet in three right whale habitat areas. In addition the International Maritime Organization adopted, and in 1999, NMFS and the U.S. Coast Guard implemented, two Mandatory Ship Reporting Systems. Designed specifically for right whales, one ship reporting system is in place in the southeast United States calving ground from 1 December to 15 April, and the other encompasses two critical habitats in the northeast, Cape Cod Bay and the Great South Channel, and operates on a year-round basis. Ships are required to send a formatted message with the vessel name, destination, route, and speed to an automated computer system when they enter the reporting area. In return, the vessel receives a message with recent sightings, general information about right whales, and precautionary measures. International Maritime Organization approval of these two Mandatory Ship Reporting Systems was unprecedented, as they had not previously used ship-routing measures to protect a mobile species.

Many mariners have stated, "tell us where the whales are, and we will avoid them." However, the data show it is difficult to detect right whales visually (Chapter 4), and it is unlikely that the person at the helm can take appropriate avoidance action in time. Although educational efforts are probably helpful for reducing ship strikes of right whales, their effectiveness is limited. During bad weather or at night, and even during good weather, whales are often missed. Awareness of right whales is an important first step toward reducing the effects of human activities, but education alone does not reduce the overlap in space and time of ships and right whales.

Technological Solutions

Several technological approaches have been considered that either detect whales more reliably or attempt to move whales out of the path of an oncoming vessel. The first option involves attaching something to the whale, such as a satellite-monitored transmitter or an implantable chip, that a transiting vessel could monitor. In theory this instrumentation would provide near-real-time information to the ship's crew, allowing them to take avoidance action. Practically, efforts thus far have met with limited success. Satellite and radio-monitored transmitters implanted into numerous right whales have had limited longevity, lasting from only a few days to a maximum of 125 days (Baumgartner and Mate 2005).

Others have proposed the use of active sonar detection either with a device on a vessel or placed on channel buoys in high-use right whale areas. Devices on a vessel ideally would detect a whale at a sufficient distance to allow the vessel operator to take avoidance action. Sonar devices placed on buoys would be designed to detect whales either within or approaching a shipping channel and alert vessels coming into the area of the whale's presence. In practice these two options have drawbacks. First, active sonar devices would place additional sound in the water, and noise pollution from shipping is already of concern for marine mammals and other marine species (Southall 2005). It would also be necessary to either equip all vessels or channels with sonar devices and trained personnel and require vessels to transit only in certain corridors. At this time, sonar detection is not considered a viable option (Chapter 11).

Another detection method that is showing promise is the use of passive acoustics. Bottom-deployed units equipped with a hydrophone recording and transmission system have been able to detect right whale vocalizations, using an algorithm to differentiate right whale vocalizations from those of other species (Chapter 11). The advantage of this system is that data could be provided daily, regardless of weather conditions. However, it will be necessary to test this method by comparing right whale presence in the vicinity of the buoys versus received vocalizations to assess how frequently individual right whales vocalize and to determine its feasibility in several right whale habitats or migratory corridors.

Acoustic deterrent devices have been used to alert different toothed whales and dolphins to the presence of fishing gear and divert them away from potentially harmful interactions (Kraus 1999). The feasibility of acoustic deterrent devices to move right whales out of the way of ships was explored by Nowacek et al. (2004) during studies in the Bay of Fundy and is described in Chapter 11. Although the use of acoustic deterrents for right whales is still being studied, it does not presently appear to be a realistic solution for mitigating ship strikes with right whales.

Finally, there are efforts under way to correlate data on biological and physical oceanographic conditions found in areas of right whale aggregation to attempt to predict right whale distribution from remote sensing data (Chapter 16). At a minimum this work will help us to understand what conditions must exist for right whales to move into an area, but its use for reducing interactions between whales and ships is doubtful.

Altering Ship Operations

The third avenue of pursuit that holds the most promise of reducing collision risk is altering ship operations in right whale habitats and migratory corridors. This approach has met with the most resistance from industry, primarily because of the perceived economic impact. Interestingly, however, during the consultation process of the Ship Strike Committee (a committee convened under the direction of the NMFS), the one important piece of advice provided by the shipping industry was that voluntary measures will not work, and any changes to shipping operations must be regulated. After reviews of the management options, it was determined that the only viable solutions for mitigating ship strikes of right whales would be speed reductions and routing changes. The potential impact of regulatory measures on the international shipping industry requires some knowledge of how the system works.

Commercial shipping is broadly categorized into liner service and tramp, or bulk, shipping. Liner service encompasses ships that sail on a regular basis to designated ports at predefined schedules. Schedulers assume that ships will operate at a given speed throughout the transit. Although weather can be a factor, no allowance is made for it because of its unpredictability. Liner service schedules are advertised, and the company's ability to meet the timetables consistently is used to measure its success. Ships engaged in the liner service trade have increased in size and speed since 1945 and now include some of the fastest ships in the world; a modern container ship can cruise at 48 km/h (Kendall and Buckley 1994).

Tramp, or bulk shipping vessels, so named for the vagabond nature of the voyages, have no fixed, repetitive schedules, and voyage destinations are dictated by the availability of cargo. Although most bulk ships tend to be of more moderate size and draft than liner ships, newer vessels have increased in both size and speed (Kendall and Buckley 1994).

Ports represent another facet of the shipping industry that must be considered in developing regulations. Ports compete with one another, and regulations that increase the time to get to a given port could impede their ability to attract business. As the container ship industry has grown, ports have invested a great deal of money into expanding and improving infrastructures to attract the lucrative liner business. Ship operators are under tremendous pressures to meet schedules, and unexpected delays could result in increased costs for that trip. If the delays are frequent at one location, ships may divert to a different port.

Jurisdictional Framework

The United Nations Law of the Sea Convention of 1982 (UNCLOS III) provides a legal framework for vessels at sea. UNCLOS III entered into force in 1994. Although the United States is not a party to this convention, the United States abides by many of the laws to avoid confrontation with other nations. One of the primary purposes of UNCLOS III was to develop a legal order for the oceans to facilitate international communication, especially in regard to the utilization of resources, the conservation of living resources, and the preservation of the marine environment.

The ocean zones defined in UNCLOS III that pertain to right whales are the territorial sea and the exclusive economic zone (EEZ). The territorial sea extends out 19.3 km from the coastline of the coastal state (i.e., coastal country), within which that state has sovereignty. The coastal state can unilaterally adopt regulations within the territorial sea to regulate shipping to protect the marine environment as long as these regulations do not deny innocent passage (continuous and expeditious passage that is not prejudicial to the peace, good order, or security of the coastal state).

The EEZ is adjacent to the territorial sea and extends out to 321.9 km from the coastline of the coastal state (or as otherwise negotiated). Within the EEZ the coastal state has sovereign rights (but not sovereignty) for conserving and managing living resources. Therefore, existing laws and regulations pertaining to the conservation of living resources, such as the Endangered Species Act and Marine Mammal Protection Act, must conform to provisions of UNCLOS III. Within the territorial sea, a coastal country can adopt regulations and make them a condition for the entry of foreign vessels into its ports. Within the EEZ, the coastal country must provide scientific and technical evidence describing the issue and seek approval from the IMO to adopt special mandatory measures within the EEZ.

Some additional regulatory tools for protecting right whales are found in international agreements such as the Safety of Life at Sea Convention, within which the concept of ship's routing measures was introduced, including areas to be avoided, recommended tracks, precautionary areas, and mandatory ship reporting systems (IMO 1994, 1991). Measures such as these have been adopted worldwide for particularly hazardous areas of navigation and areas where particularly sensitive environments warrant extra caution.

The most controversial issue, from a regulatory standpoint, is the use of speed restrictions to protect right whales. Speed restrictions are not a consideration in routing measures. If speed restrictions are to be adopted as a regulatory measure, they could be implemented by the U.S. government within the territorial sea (19.3 km from the coast), but any measure beyond the territorial sea would require approval and adoption by the IMO.

Policy Changes to Alter Ship Operations

Policy changes enacted under the Endangered Species Act and Marine Mammal Protection Act have done little to ameliorate the ship strike problem. Three Critical Habitats were designated under the Endangered Species Act in 1994, but these have provided no protection from vessel–whale interactions. Starting in 1997, NMFS prohibited vessels from approaching within 457 meters (500 yards) of a right whale. However, operators of most vessels typically do not see right whales before they are struck, and there are no measures that require them to change how they operate within right whale habitats. Until vessel operations are managed through national and international regulations to reduce right whale kills, the existing reporting and educational efforts will be inadequate. Some steps moving toward this regulatory framework have been taken or are in development. These include the changes in the shipping lanes in the Bay of Fundy (Canada), a rulemaking process in the United States to consider changes in vessel operations, as well as the possibility of emergency rulemaking in advance of regulations.

The Bay of Fundy Traffic Separation Scheme

The Bay of Fundy is one of five known seasonal right whale habitats and is used in the summer and fall by one-third to one-half of the known right whales annually. Fisheries and Oceans Canada designated an area within the Bay as a right whale conservation area in 1993 (Brown et al. 1995). This conservation area was bisected by mandatory shipping lanes, originally adopted by the IMO to organize the shipping traffic and protect fishing vessels from being hit by large ships. The shipping lanes provide for the separation and organization of traffic greater than 20 m in length between the southeastern entrance of the Bay and the Port of Saint John, New Brunswick, to the north. Large tankers, cargo ships, bulk carriers, and container ships use these lanes where fog and foul weather are common navigational hazards.

Little was known about right whale distribution in the Bay of Fundy in the 1980s, and ship strikes were not recognized as a threat to recovery. However, three right whales were killed by ships in the Bay of Fundy between 1992 and 1997, provoking a series of actions from the research community to reduce the potential for more collisions. In 1993 the authors traveled to Saint John, New Brunswick, to meet with the radio operators at Fundy Traffic (Marine Communications and Traffic Services, Canadian Coast Guard). These operators maintain radio contact with all vessels in the shipping lane and monitor each ship's passage on radar. They agreed to transmit a right whale alert to all traffic moving through the shipping lanes from June through November and distribute educational material through harbor pilots and the local port authority (Brown 1994).

By the late 1990s, analysis of right whale survey data showed a direct overlap between high concentrations of right whales and the outbound traffic lane

Figure 14.4. A close encounter between a ship and a right whale in the Bay of Fundy.
New England Aquarium.

in the summer and autumn months (Fig. 14.4; color plate 21a). At the same
time, population data suggested that ship-related mortalities and injuries to
right whales were significant obstacles to the successful recovery and viability
of the species (Kraus 1990; Anonymous 2000). In 1999 a right whale brief-
ing session was held in Saint John, New Brunswick, and a volunteer vessel–
whale working group of whale biologists and marine professionals was formed.

The primary question asked by the mariners was about right whale distribution: Do right whales stay in the same places within a season and from year
to year? In response, right whale survey data from fourteen years were analyzed to show where the highest right whale concentrations were located, and
Fundy Traffic provided the radar data on vessel movements through the area.
Chris Taggart and Angelia Vanderlaan (Dalhousie University) performed a
probability analysis of where right whales and vessels were most likely to interact and identified a boundary in the bay where vessel traffic could transit with
minimal interaction with right whales, such that the relative probability of a
collision would be reduced by 80 percent (Taggart and Vanderlaan 2003; color
plate 21).

By 2001 the results of these analyses made it clear that the aggregations of
right whales were seasonally consistent and overlapped with the outbound
shipping lane. Because the whales could not be moved, the best way to reduce
the probability of a ship strike was to amend the location of the lanes away

from high concentrations of right whales (Brown 2003). The Canadian Right Whale Recovery Team and the regional and national Canadian Marine Advisory Council (a joint Transport Canada and Coast Guard group that advised mariners on issues of marine safety) agreed that a shift in the location of the shipping lanes was a viable option. In the autumn of 2001 and winter and spring of 2002, the Maritime Office of Transport Canada Maritime Safety held public consultations in Nova Scotia and New Brunswick to consider the implications of the suggested changes for fisheries and other whale populations.

Because the IMO originally mandated the Fundy lanes, any changes had to be approved by them. In April 2002 the Marine Safety Office of Transport Canada submitted a proposal to the Subcommittee on Safety of Navigation to amend the traffic separation scheme in the Bay of Fundy for the purpose of reducing ship strikes of right whales. The proposal was approved at the subcommittee level in July 2002 and forwarded to the Marine Safety Committee, where the action was adopted in December 2002.

The amended lanes were implemented on 1 July 2003 (color plate 21b). This was not a minor undertaking, as the amendment required changes to a total of seven nautical charts by the Canadian Hydrographic Service at the approximate cost of $30,000 per chart. Fundy Traffic operators were instrumental in the smooth implementation of the new lanes. Their direct communication with the ships prevented any problems with the safe navigation of vessels transiting the amended lanes.

This case study proved that biologists, industry, and government could work together to find a solution to a conservation problem. The direct impact on the shipping industry is a longer passage through the Bay of Fundy (9 km for the Saint John traffic and 20 km for the Bayside and Eastport traffic). The shift in shipping lanes affected Nova Scotia fishermen, who now fish in the shipping lanes instead of to the east of them. However, the fishermen agreed to the lane shift during consultation to help protect right whales. Rather than the typical ideological chasm that appears to exist between conservationists and industry, the members of the vessel whale-working group were able to transcend their personal stake in the issue to develop and implement an area-specific compromise solution to promote the coexistence of vessels and right whales in the Bay of Fundy.

Rulemaking Process in the United States

In June 2004, NMFS published an Advanced Notice of Proposed Rulemaking in the *Federal Register* outlining an east coast–wide strategy for reducing the risk of ship strikes with right whales in U.S. waters. On 26 June 2006, NMFS published the Proposed Rule in the *United States Federal Register* (71 FR 36299). The strategy consists of five elements:

> (1) continue ongoing conservation and research activities to reduce the threat of ship strikes; (2) develop and implement additional mariner education and outreach programs; (3) conduct ESA section 7 consultations, as appropriate, with Federal agencies that operate or authorize the use of vessels in waters inhabited by right whales; (4) develop a Right Whale Conservation Agreement with the Government of Canada; and (5) establish new operational measures for commercial and recreational mariners. (71 FR 36299)

Under item 5, certain routing measures and speed restrictions of no greater than 18.5 km/h have been proposed in the areas outlined below. The southeast U.S. calving ground would be managed by routing ships into defined east-west lanes and requiring them to reduce speed west of 80°51.6′N from 15 November through 15 April. In the mid-Atlantic, a migratory corridor would be defined for whales going to and departing from the winter calving grounds off the southeast United States, and a speed restriction would be imposed within 56 km of port entrances between 1 November and 30 April.

In Cape Cod Bay, a winter and springtime feeding habitat, routes would be developed to reduce the risk of collision. Because right whales tend to spend most of their time in the eastern side of Cape Cod Bay, vessels would be requested to transit along the western side of the Bay. Speed restrictions would be imposed throughout the Bay from 1 January to 15 May. An area off Race Point at the tip of Cape Cod is a migratory corridor for whales departing Cape Cod Bay heading to the Great South Channel, and the traffic lanes leading to Boston transit across this corridor. The proposed management measure is a speed restriction within this area from 1 March through 30 April. In a separate proposal to the IMO, NMFS has requested a slight shift in the Boston shipping lanes just to the north of Cape Cod Bay. The northern leg of the lanes would be shifted 12° to the north and narrowed by approximately 1/2 nm to avoid known aggregations of humpback and right whales.

The Great South Channel east of Cape Cod is a major spring feeding habitat for right whales. As the Mandatory Ship Reporting data show, it is also the conduit for ships transiting between ports in the northeast United States and the Canadian Maritimes and for any ship transiting to or from the south (Fig.

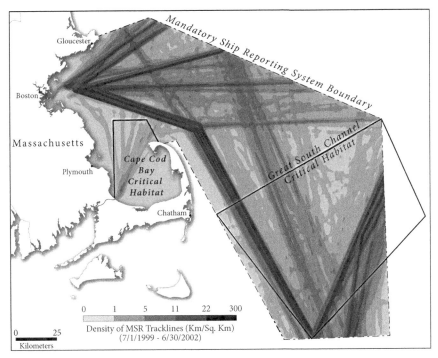

Figure 14.5. Mandatory Ship Reporting data showing ship traffic within the GSC Critical Habitat (Ward-Geiger et al. 2005). Kerry Lagueux / New England Aquarium.

14.5). NMFS proposes to restrict vessel speed within the Great South Channel from 1 April to 31 July. NMFS is also considering creating an "Area to Be Avoided" east of the shipping lanes leading to Boston. This proposal would have to be submitted to the IMO for international approval. Although there are designated shipping lanes leading to Boston that bisect the Great South Channel, ships heading to points farther north and east of Boston are not required to stay in these lanes.

Throughout the entire eastern seaboard, dynamic area management is being considered for situations where whales aggregate in unexpected places. This measure would place a buffer around a group of right whales for a predetermined period of time and require vessels to divert around or reduce speed if transiting through this buffer. This would theoretically protect whales that appear in areas that are not seasonally managed.

Since the publication of the Advanced Notice of Proposed Rulemaking, and in advance of a final rule, efforts to put measures into place both voluntarily and with regulations have been under way on two different fronts.

Emergency Rulemaking

The proposed rule has just been released following public comment, the publication of an Environmental Impact Statement, and a Port Access Route Study to look at the feasibility of routing measures in the northeast and southeast United States (undertaken by the U.S. Coast Guard at the request of Congress). The process for developing a proposed rule has been extremely lengthy, and implementation of a final rule could still be some time away if it actually comes to pass.

Between February 2004 and April 2005, eight right whales died, at least four as the result of collision with vessels. Six of the eight were females, three were carrying a fetus at the time of their death, and two had previously calved (Kraus et al. 2005). The slow-moving rulemaking process and the reluctance of many stakeholders to embrace speed restrictions as a management option prompted the environmental community to petition the federal government in May 2005 requesting them to implement emergency rules to protect right whales within sixty days. NMFS responded in September 2005 and rejected the petition, noting that they were moving forward on rulemaking and that emergency rulemaking could slow down that process. In November 2005, the environmental community filed a lawsuit against NMFS arguing that the decision not to pursue emergency rulemaking was arbitrary and capricious.

Voluntary Speed Restrictions

In May 2005, NMFS requested the U.S. Coast Guard to put out an advisory to ships via Notices to Mariners that included: "language from NOAA recommending speeds of 12 knots or less in areas used by right whales, when consistent with navigational safety." The Coast Guard responded in June 2005 that to include this language would be viewed as an endorsement of speed restrictions and noted that concerns such as national security and other legal aspects needed to be considered as well as the recovery of right whales. As a result of this negative response from the Coast Guard, the environmental community filed suit against them in November 2005.

Economic Impacts to Shipping and Ports

As ship strike mitigation strategy has evolved, the shipping industry has expressed serious concern regarding the potential economic impacts. Some port authorities worry that if it takes ships longer to get to ports, and these delays are unexpected, some companies may unload their cargo in alternative ports. Shipping companies are concerned about incurring extra longshoremen charges if vessels are delayed or even miss an entrance opportunity in some tidally restricted ports. The cruise ship industry is concerned about not being able to meet its obligation to passengers if their ships experience delays. There is a considerable difference between planned delays (those that would be incurred by seasonal management areas) and unplanned delays (incurred if dynamic management is imposed). There will be economic impacts, but a preliminary review suggests the extent of these impacts will not be extensive.

Potential Benefits to Right Whales

If the strategy outlined in the Advanced Notice of Proposed Rulemaking and the changes in the Bay of Fundy shipping lanes had been put in place in 1970, and if these regulations had prevented every ship strike within the proposed management areas, it can be estimated how many of the right whales killed during this period might have survived (dynamic management options were not included). Under these assumptions, sixteen of twenty-four ship-struck whales (67 percent) might have survived. Of the eight whales that would not have been protected, one of them died off the coast of Texas, where sightings are extremely rare, another died off Halifax, Nova Scotia, where there has been no dedicated effort to understand whale distribution in proximity to shipping lanes, and the remainder were killed during times not covered by the recommended measures. Some of these latter whales could hypothetically have been protected under dynamic management. Although these measures clearly would not protect every right whale from a ship strike, they would certainly provide a greatly enhanced level of protection. Because many right whales disappear from this population and their presumed deaths are undetected, the level of protection may be even greater than can be estimated based on known mortalities.

Enforcement

Enforcing the proposed regulations will require a well-defined effort. Options include careful monitoring of the Mandatory Ship Reporting System data to assess vessel movement through restricted areas (although this may be difficult to do on a real-time basis) and utilizing the transmission data from the newly required Automated Identification System. This system broadcasts information on the ship's identity, which is collected using VHF receivers at a few ports but could be acquired by other parties. With these receivers, the location and speed of any large vessel could be determined in real time.

Other possible enforcement options include at-sea monitoring of ship traffic to determine vessel speed and presence in "Areas to Be Avoided," and dockside checking of ships' logs and electronic charting to determine how they transited through a managed area. Compliance with regulations needs to be monitored closely with appropriate fines imposed for violations for these regulations to be effective.

Conclusion

Fatal ship collisions with right whales are occurring throughout their range at a pace that is clearly unsustainable. Increased vessel speeds and bigger ships may be at the root of this chronic problem that has likely plagued right whales for decades. Measures taken to date in the United States have done little to mitigate the risk, and more proactive measures are clearly needed and may be on the horizon. Although solving this problem will not be simple or easy, through the efforts of many stakeholders, a reasonable resolution that would reduce the threat of collision substantially has been developed and could be implemented almost immediately. There could be costs associated with these changes, but, more importantly, they will require a shift in the present paradigm of ship operations. Changes in technology that have allowed for bigger and faster ships have had unintended consequences for large whales, especially right whales. To address these negative consequences, the international shipping community may need to operate their ships in ways never before considered. It will be a challenge to have such changes accepted internationally, yet it would be a disservice to mariners who genuinely care about the health of the oceans to allow this species to go extinct when tangible solutions are at hand.

Anonymous. 2000. *Canadian Recovery Plan for the North Atlantic Right Whale.* World Wildlife Fund Canada, Toronto, Ontario; Department of Fisheries and Oceans, Dartmouth, Nova Scotia, Canada.

Baumgartner, M. F., and B. R. Mate. 2005. Summer and fall habitat of North Atlantic right whales (*Eubalaena glacialis*) inferred from satellite telemetry. *Canadian Journal of Fisheries and Aquatic Sciences* 62:527–543.

Brown, M. W. 1994. Caution mariners: Please avoid collisions with right whales. Prepared for the Minister of Supply and Services, Communications Directorate, Department of Fisheries and Oceans (DFO/4982), Ottawa, Ontario, Canada.

Brown, M. W. 2003. Guide to the implementation of stewardship measures to reduce interactions between vessels and right whales in two right whale conservation areas in the waters of Atlantic Canada. Final project report for the Government of Canada Habitat Stewardship Program for Species at Risk. Canadian Whale Institute, Ingramport, Nova Scotia, Canada. 20 pp.

Brown, M. W., J. M. Allen, and S. D. Kraus. 1995. The designation of seasonal right whale conservation zones in the waters of Atlantic Canada. Pages 90–98 *in* N. Shackell and M. Willison, eds. *Marine Protected Areas and Sustainable Fisheries.* Science and Management of Protected Areas Association, Wolfville, Nova Scotia, Canada.

Cavanagh, R., A. Eller, W. Renner, and D. Spiegelthal. 2004. Final report: Low-frequency sound field in advance of merchant ships. Prepared by Science Applications International Corporation for Florida State University, Contract FSU#1368-902-24/NOAA#NA03NMF4720496. 57 pp.

Endreson, Ø., E. Sørgård, J. K. Sundet, S. B. Dalsøren, I. S. A. Isaksen, T. F. Berglen, and G. Gravir. 2003. Emission from international sea transportation and environmental impact. *Journal of Geophysical Research* 108 (D17): ACH 14–1–22.

International Maritime Organization. 1991. *Ship's Routing.* 6th edition. International Maritime Organization, London.

International Maritime Organization. 1994. Guidelines and Criteria for Ship Reporting Systems. Resolution MSC.43(64), adopted on 9 December 1994.

Jensen, A. S., and G. K. Silber. 2003. Large Whale Ship Strike Database. NOAA Technical Memorandum NMFS-OPR-25.

Kendall, L. C., and J. J. Buckley. 1994. *The Business of Shipping.* Cornell Maritime Press, Centreville, MD.

Knowlton, A. R. 1997. Comparison of right whale mortalities to ship channels and ship traffic levels. Pages 52–69 *in* Shipping/Right Whale Workshop Report 97-3. New England Aquarium Aquatic Forum Series, New England Aquarium, Boston.

Knowlton, A. R., and S. D. Kraus. 2001. Mortality and serious injury of northern right whales (*Eubalaena glacialis*) in the western North Atlantic Ocean. *Journal of Cetacean Research and Management* Special Issue 2:193–208.

Knowlton, A. R., F. T. Korsmeyer, J. E. Kerwin, H. Wu, and B. Hynes. 1995. The hydrodynamic effects of large vessels on right whales. Final report under NMFS Contract no. 40EANFF400534. 31 pp.

Knowlton, A. R., F. T. Korsmeyer, and B. Hynes. 1998. The hydrodynamic effects of large vessels on right whales: Phase two. Final report under NMFS Contract no. 46EANF60004. 13 pp.

Kraus, S. D. 1990. Rates and potential causes of mortality in North Atlantic right whales. *Marine Mammal Science* 6:278–291.

Kraus, S. D. 1999. The once and future ping: Challenges for the use of acoustic deterrents in fisheries. *Marine Technology Society Journal* 33(2):90–93.

Kraus, S. D., M. W. Brown, H. Caswell, C. W. Clark, M. Fujiwara, P. K. Hamilton, R. D. Kenney, A. R. Knowlton, S. Landry, C. A. Mayo, W. A. McLellan, M. J. Moore, D. P. Nowacek, D. A. Pabst, A. J. Read, and R. M. Rolland. 2005. North Atlantic right whales in crisis. *Science* 309:561–562.

Laist, D. W., A. R. Knowlton, J. G. Mead, A. S. Collet, and M. Podesta. 2001. Collisions between ships and whales. *Marine Mammal Science* 17:35–75.

Moore, M. J., A. R. Knowlton, S. D. Kraus, W. A. McLellan, and R. K. Bonde. 2005. Morphometry, gross morphology and available histopathology in North Atlantic right whale (*Eubalaena glacialis*) mortalities (1970–2002). *Journal of Cetacean Research and Management* 63:199–214.

National Marine Fisheries Service. 1991. *Recovery Plan for the North Atlantic Right Whale (Eubalaena glacialis)*. National Marine Fisheries Service, Silver Spring, MD.

National Marine Fisheries Service. 2005. *Recovery Plan for the North Atlantic Right Whale (Eubalaena glacialis)*. National Marine Fisheries Service, Silver Spring, MD.

Nowacek, D. P., M. P. Johnson, P. L. Tyack, K. A. Shorter, W. A. McLellan, and D. A. Pabst. 2001. Buoyant balaenids: the ups and downs of buoyancy in right whales. *Proceedings of the Royal Society of London Part B* 268:1–6.

Nowacek, D. P., M. P. Johnson, and P. L. Tyack. 2004. North Atlantic right whales (*Eubalaena glacialis*) ignore ships but respond to alerting stimuli. *Proceedings of the Royal Society of London Part B* 271:227–231.

Russell, B. A., A. R. Knowlton, and B. Zoodsma. 2001. Recommended measures to reduce ship strikes of North Atlantic right whales. Report to National Marine Fisheries Service. 31 pp.

Russell, B. A., W. T. McWeeny, and A. R. Knowlton. 2005. Voyage planning and marine environmental protection measures to avoid collisions with the North Atlantic right whale. Education modules developed for National Marine Fisheries Service, Order EA 133F-03-SE-0573/0572.

Southall, B. L. 2005. Shipping noise and marine mammals: A forum for science, management, and technology. Symposium held on 18–19 May 2004, Arlington, Virginia, U.S.A., by NOAA Fisheries Acoustics Program. 40 pp.

Taggart, C. T., and A. Vanderlaan. 2003. Regional time/space conflicts in vessel traffic and fishing effort with right whales in the Bay of Fundy. Final Project Report, Habitat Stewardship Program for Species at Risk, Oceanography Department, Dalhousie University, Halifax, Nova Scotia, Canada. 16 pp.

Wang, C., and J. J. Corbett. 2005. Geographical characterization of ship traffic and emissions. *Transportation Research Record: Journal of the Transportation Research Board* 1909:90–99.

Wang, C., J. J. Corbett, and J. Firestone. 2006. Adapting bottom-up methods to top-down spatially resolved ship emissions inventories. Transportation Research Board Annual Meeting, Paper no. 06-1253, Washington, DC.

Ward-Geiger, L. I., G. K. Silber, R. D. Baumstark, and T. L. Pulfer. 2005. Characterization of ship traffic in right whale critical habitat. *Coastal Management* 33:263–278.

Acknowledgments

Thank you to Bruce Russell, Lindy Johnson, Pat Gerrior, Greg Silber, Barb Zoodsma, the members of the Ship Strike Committee, and many others too numerous to list here for the years of dedication to working through the process of developing and, we hope, implementing a U.S. ship strike strategy. In Canada, we would like to thank the members of the vessel whale working group and Canadian Recovery Team as well as representatives from Transport Canada Marine Safety, the Canadian Hydrographic Service, and Fisheries and Oceans Canada. The shipping studies by the authors were funded in the United States by the Oak Foundation, NMFS, and the International Fund for Animal Welfare, and in Canada by World Wildlife Fund U.S., World Wildlife Fund Canada, and the Habitat Stewardship Program of Environment Canada.

15

Right Whales and Climate Change: Facing the Prospect of a Greenhouse Future

ROBERT D. KENNEY

14 March 2004
Gulf of Mexico

Lisa Norman was fishing with her husband in the Gulf of Mexico, about 3 km off Panama City Beach in the "Panhandle" of Florida when they spotted something swimming in the water—something big. It was two whales, and one looked much larger than the other. It was a mother right whale and her calf, but the Normans didn't know that. Lisa took some photos and then didn't think much about it for the next three weeks. On 8 April, Bob Williams took a photograph of the calf about 72 km to the west, between Navarre and Fort Walton Beach. The next day, Good Friday, Chris Cramer took a photo of the bottom of the mother's flukes, back near Panama City. Lisa saw a newspaper story about the April sightings, so she contacted the National Marine Fisheries Service to tell them about her sighting the previous month. Eventually the photos of all three sightings found their way to the right whale research lab at the New England Aquarium. Lisa's photos were clear enough to see that the whales were right whales but not clear enough to identify the individual whales. Bob's and Chris's photos were better but still did not show enough of the whales to match them to known individuals in the Right Whale Catalog. *Maybe we'd never know who the Gulf of Mexico mother and calf were.*

On 31 May, the Aquarium's research crew aboard a chartered fishing boat got a break in a stretch of foggy weather and cruised out to the Great South Channel. They sighted more than thirty right whales that day, including two mother–calf pairs. Their new photos finally enabled them to match those from 8 and 9 April: the Gulf of Mexico mother was Eg #2360. She (and this was the first evidence that she was a she) had given birth to her first known calf that winter.

Eg #2360 was first sighted on 16 December 1993, probably as a juvenile, about 17 km east of Fernandina Beach, Florida. She was not seen again for almost four and a half years. Between 1998 and 2002, Eg #2360 was sighted nine times all around the Gulf of Maine. During the 2003/2004 winter season, she was sighted four times before showing up in the Gulf of Mexico in March: on 29 December, 11 km off Little Cumberland Island, Georgia (alone); on 14 January, 13 km off Ponte Vedra Beach, Florida (alone, and although nobody realized it at the time, very pregnant); on 25 January, just off Indiatlantic, Florida (with a small calf); and on 30 January, 3 km off the entrance to the Miami ship channel.

The sightings in the Gulf of Mexico occurred a month and a half after Eg #2360 and her calf were seen off Miami, but it was only fifty-two days after the last sighting in the Gulf that they were seen in the Great South Channel. About four months later, in late September, they were photographed by the New England Aquarium crew on R/V Nereid in the Bay of Fundy. Their entire journey, from Indiatlantic to Miami to the Florida Panhandle, then back along the Gulf and Atlantic coasts to the Great South Channel and Bay of Fundy, covered nearly 5,600 km (assuming a coastal route but no other side trips). Their unusual excursion into the Gulf of Mexico made up about 2,900 km, more than half of their trip.

This was only the third time that North Atlantic right whales have been documented in the Gulf of Mexico. In March 1963, three Sarasota residents in two boats observed two whales in shallow water off New Pass for over an hour. Maybe they saw a mother–calf pair, or possibly a mother and a yearling. They reported their observations to Eugenie Clark, the renowned shark biologist, who published the sighting report along with the equally renowned mammalogist Joseph Curtis Moore (Moore and Clark 1963). In February 1972, a right whale calf stranded at Surfside Beach near Freeport, Texas (Schmidly et al. 1972).

> *What makes the occasional right whale wander into the Gulf? Are*
> *females with their calves more prone to such peregrinations? Is it related to*
> *climatic factors? We may never know the answers to these questions. Both*
> *1963 and 2004 were years of minimum values in the winter North At-*
> *lantic Oscillation (NAO), but the NAO in 1972 was positive and increas-*
> *ing. We do know that climate does have a relatively clear influence on the*
> *biology of western North Atlantic right whales today and is likely to have*
> *even more impacts as global temperatures continue to increase in the near*
> *future.*
>
> *Robert Kenney*

The short version of the story is that the Earth's climate is changing. Today's rate of change is unprecedented; it is largely a result of human-caused factors, and these changes are going to continue well beyond the lifetimes of anyone alive today. The summary presented here is based on a small subset of the very large and growing volume of information that is available. Information has been selected from U.S. and international sources that are accessible on line to make it easier for interested readers to find the details. The primary sources have been the third assessment report of the Intergovernmental Panel on Climate Change (IPCC 2001), a summary report from the U.S. Global Change Research Program (NAST 2001), a series of reports from the Pew Center on Global Climate Change (Wigley 1999; Neuman et al. 2000; Kennedy et al. 2002; Smith 2004), a report on abrupt changes from the National Academy of Sciences (NAS 2003), and reports focused on climate-change effects on biological systems from the International Geosphere-Biosphere Program (Barange and Harris 2003) and from the Intergovernmental Panel (IPCC 2002). To keep the summary readable, these same sources are not cited repeatedly for every statement of fact or theory. In fact, they all essentially agree on the generalities and on most of the specifics.

Observed Changes to Date

Since the beginning of the Industrial Revolution in the eighteenth century, the concentrations of carbon dioxide (CO_2), methane (CH_4), and nitrous oxide (N_2O) in our atmosphere have increased dramatically, by 31 percent, 151 percent, and 17 percent, respectively (Table 15.1). The dominant sources of these

Table 15.1. Changes in Global Atmospheric and Oceanographic Parameters from before the Industrial Revolution (1000–1750), from the Present (in AD 2000), and Projected for 2100

	Year(s)		
Parameter	1000–1750	2000	2100
Atmospheric CO_2	280 ppm	368 ppm	540–970 ppm
Atmospheric CH_4	700 ppb	1750 ppb	
Atmospheric N_2O	270 ppb	316 ppb	
Global mean temperature		+0.6°C[a]	+1.4–5.8°C[b]
Mean sea level		+10–20 cm[a]	+13–95 cm[b]
Arctic sea ice thickness		−100–200 cm[a]	Continued thinning[b]

Sources: IPCC (2001); NAST (2001).
a. Net change from 1900 to 2100.
b. Projected change from 2000 to 2100.

"greenhouse gases" are anthropogenic, principally combustion of fossil fuels and deforestation. They are called greenhouse gases because incoming short-wave radiation (visible light) from the sun penetrates the atmosphere and reaches the Earth's surface, but outgoing long-wave radiation (infrared or heat) is blocked by these gases, warming the atmosphere. Carbon dioxide is the dominant greenhouse gas.

There are excellent time series of measurements of atmospheric greenhouse gases back to the middle of the nineteenth century. The best data come from sampling stations at the summit of Mauna Loa in Hawaii and at the South Pole, both locations far from industrial sources. Estimates of atmospheric CO_2 stretching back about 150,000 years have been obtained by sampling air bubbles trapped in ice sheets in Greenland and Antarctica. Present CO_2 concentrations, and their rate of increase, are greater than at any time in that 150,000-year record. This interval included two transition periods when the Earth was warming up and coming out of ice ages, once about 10,000 years ago and another about 140,000 years ago.

Have increased concentrations of CO_2 and other greenhouse gases caused temperatures to increase? Widespread instrumental measurements good enough to compute global average temperatures (i.e., lots of people with thermometers in many places all over the world) go back to 1861. A variety of proxy measurements are available that allow us to make estimates of temperatures in the more distant past, extending that record in the Northern Hemisphere, more or less continuously and spatially complete, back to about AD 1000. These proxies include historical data (newspapers, ships' logs, agricultural harvest records, etc.), tree rings, coral reefs, pollen, ice cores, and lake and ocean sediments. Once the interannual variability (i.e., the noise) in the proxy-derived temperature data is smoothed by calculating running means, the global average temperature in 1861 did not differ much from what it had been for the previous 860 years, including the so-called "Medieval Warm Period" (ca. 1100–1300) or "Little Ice Age" (ca. 1350–1900). Global mean temperatures began to increase sharply around 1900, peaked in the early to mid-1940s, declined slightly and leveled off until the mid-1980s, and then began another phase of steep increase that continues today. Global average temperature increased by 0.6°C (±0.2°), or 1.1 ± 0.4°F, during the twentieth century (Table 15.1). In the Northern Hemisphere, the twentieth century increase was the greatest in the past 1,000 years, the 1990s were the warmest decade of the second millennium, and the average temperature now is higher than the maximum values in the 1000–1860 proxy record. Coupled ocean–atmosphere global circulation models clearly demonstrate that the majority of warming can be attributed to greenhouse gases from human sources. Models that also incorporate the cooling effect of shading by clouds, smoke, and industrial aerosols in the atmosphere fit the observed temperature increase pattern extremely well, removing much of the doubt about attributing global warming to greenhouse gases. The number of days with record high temperatures and number of heat waves have also increased in numerous locations.

Have there been any other effects already beyond warming temperatures? Two obvious effects of warmer temperatures are that ice melts and water evaporates faster. Glaciers in both the Northern and Southern Hemispheres are retreating, and the snow-caps on mountains in many areas are disappearing. Large slabs of Antarctic ice shelves have broken off and floated away in recent years. Sea level increased 10–20 cm during the twentieth century (Table 15.1), caused both by ice melting and by thermal expansion as ocean waters warm. In the Arctic, late-summer sea-ice thickness has decreased by about 40 percent, and since the 1950s, the extent of Arctic sea-ice cover has declined by 10–15 percent. Because what goes up must come down, increased evaporation must lead to increased precipitation. Precipitation over the continents had increased by 10–15 percent by 2000. Heavy precipitation events have become more frequent, particularly at middle and high latitudes in the Northern Hemisphere. On the other side of the equation, the frequency of droughts has also increased, especially around the equatorial regions. Although this sounds like a contradiction, it is because weather patterns have shifted, and the frequency of extreme weather events has increased. There have been numerous demonstrated effects of climate change on terrestrial flora and fauna (e.g., changes in average flowering dates, range expansions, altitudinal shifts in mountain species); however, a review of those is beyond the scope of this chapter. Similar changes can be predicted in marine habitats, although they would be expected to take longer because the high heat capacity of water would tend to buffer the changes.

Projections of Future Changes

Predicting the future is uncertain. This is especially true for predictions of climate change because the basic element that drives everything else, the atmospheric concentration of CO_2, is itself uncertain. Will greenhouse gas emissions continue to grow unchecked in the name of economic growth? Will the global political community reach the modest emission-reduction targets that have been set in the Kyoto Protocol, an average reduction of about 5 percent from 1990 levels? Inability to answer those questions with any confidence leads to substantial uncertainty in model projections of future climate trends. The likely range of atmospheric CO_2 levels at the end of the twenty-first century is broad (540–970 ppm) (Table 15.1), and the full possible range is even broader (490–1,250 ppm).

Whatever the level at which greenhouse gas emissions eventually stabilize, whether lower than, the same as, or higher than today, their effects on the atmosphere and the consequences for planetary life will not level off for many years afterward. The time scales vary greatly: atmospheric CO_2 levels will stabilize 100–300 years after emissions level off, and temperatures will stabilize after a few centuries. Sea level will continue to rise for much longer. The effect of thermal expansion on sea level will last for centuries, and the component of increasing sea levels caused by ice melting will continue for several millennia.

However, there are some shorter-term effects that are not uncertain at all. The world *is* going to get warmer: you can take that to the bank! The global average temperature will increase by another 1.4–5.8°C over the twenty-first century (Table 15.1). That projected increase is two to ten times the observed increase in the twentieth century and is completely unprecedented over the past 10,000 years, since the end of the most recent ice age. The more obvious effects of warmer temperatures will certainly increase. Sea levels will keep rising, by another 13–95 cm by 2100. Glaciers and polar ice will continue melting, with one model predicting that year-round ice will completely disappear from the Arctic Ocean within the current century. The hydrological cycle will further intensify, with increased evaporation. Global mean precipitation is projected to increase by another 5–20 percent, with more year-to-year variation, more record temperatures, more floods, and more droughts.

Effects on Marine Ecosystems

The predictability of more specific effects caused by global warming decreases with smaller spatial scales: global effects are very predictable, regional effects are only somewhat predictable, and local effects are essentially not predictable. Average ocean temperatures will increase, although the increase will lag behind changes in the atmosphere, and some regions may see cooling instead. The mean distributions of plankton populations and productivity are likely to shift. It is likely that, over the long term, there will be both positive and negative impacts on marine species and food chains, which are generally not predictable at the level of single species. One thing that is clear is that risk of extinction for species that are already vulnerable will increase because any change in environmental conditions is likely to increase stress on an already stressed population.

Changing temperatures will not be the only impacts on the ocean. Sea level changes are certain, but they are primarily a concern for humans living in low-lying coastal communities and for a few specific marine environments (e.g., coastal marshes, coral reefs) but not for oceanic environments generally. Increases in precipitation (which also increase river runoff into coastal regions) will affect salinity, water chemistry, and nutrient levels, all of which can impact productivity. Warming temperatures and decreasing salinity will enhance stratification, forcing earlier occurrence of the spring phytoplankton bloom and potential cascading effects through the food chain. There is a great concern for potential changes in the occurrence of disease organisms and harmful algal blooms, but with very low predictability.

There is one other prediction with a relatively high certainty level: humans should expect to be surprised by drastic, possibly abrupt, changes. Many models predict that continued increases in greenhouse gases over the twenty-first century could lead to substantial alterations in physical and biological systems over the ensuing decades to millennia. Abrupt and nonlinear changes caused by climate alterations are most likely for ecosystems through effects on their function, biodiversity, and productivity; however, such changes have low predictability.

There is also concern about potential changes in decadal- and longer-scale atmospheric patterns that have strong influences on regional ocean circulation, water mass formation, and weather patterns. Three of these patterns that are potentially relevant to right whales are the North Atlantic Oscillation (NAO), Gulf Stream location, and El Niño–Southern Oscillation (ENSO).

NAO

The North Atlantic Oscillation is the dominant mode of decadal-scale inter-annual variability in climate in the North Atlantic (Hurrell 1995; Mantua et al. 2002). There is a semipermanent low-pressure system near Iceland and a similar high-pressure system near the Azores (color plate 23) that tend to intensify or weaken synchronously. The NAO index is the difference in barometric pressure between the two systems, expressed as the anomaly from the average difference over a base period. When the systems intensify, the pressure difference increases, and the NAO is positive; when the systems weaken, the difference decreases, and the NAO is negative. The effects of NAO variability are most apparent during the winter; therefore, standard practice is to look at the average of the monthly values from December through March (Hurrell 1995). The conditions associated with positive NAO conditions include warm winter weather in Europe and central North America; principal jet stream and wind pattern west to east; and cold temperatures in the northwestern Atlantic and Labrador Sea, enhancing sea-ice freezing and deep-water formation. Negative NAO conditions include cold winter weather in Europe and central North America; major jet stream track with large meanders; increased storminess along the U.S. east coast; and warm temperatures in the northwest Atlantic and Labrador Sea, inhibiting the formation of sea ice and deep water and enhancing the southward transport of cooler, fresher, surface water in the Labrador Current. The NAO has shown a tendency to remain for extended periods in primarily positive (e.g., early 1970s to 1995) or negative (1950s and 1960s) phases (Hurrell 1995). NAO variability has increased significantly since 1995. There is some speculation that continued global warming could affect the NAO, but there is no consensus about the nature or direction of those impacts.

Gulf Stream

The Gulf Stream is a warm western-boundary current that flows north along the southeastern U.S. coast until turning more eastward near Cape Hatteras, North Carolina (color plate 23). The current flows across the basin before splitting into one branch that flows north into the Norwegian Sea and one that flows south along the European coast (Sverdrup et al. 1942). The warm Gulf Stream is responsible for the relatively mild climate in the British Isles, which are actually at the same latitude as Labrador. The Gulf Stream Index (GSI) is a measure of the mean monthly north-south position of the eastward-flowing part of the Gulf Stream (Taylor 1995, 1996), estimated from the first principal component of latitude at the intersections of the northern edge of the current with six different meridians of longitude. Positive values indicate a more northern position of the current, and negative values, a more southern position. About 60 percent of the variability in GSI is correlated with NAO variability (Taylor et al. 1998). Global warming effects on either the NAO or the deep thermohaline circulation would affect the Gulf Stream's intensity and location.

ENSO

El Niño is an unusual, irregularly periodic warming in the eastern tropical Pacific Ocean. The phenomenon occurs most intensely during the Southern Hemisphere summer (Northern Hemisphere winter) and is correlated with a "see-saw" in atmospheric pressure between the eastern and western sides of the South Pacific, known as the Southern Oscillation (Philander 1990). The Southern Oscillation Index (SOI) is the standardized sea-level barometric pressure difference between Tahiti and Australia, very similar to the NAO. Low SOI values correspond to El Niño years. Although ENSO is primarily a phenomenon of the South Pacific, there are recognized long-distance effects in the Northern Hemisphere, including influences on winter temperatures in the Labrador Sea that are similar to those of the NAO: colder during high SOI and warmer during low SOI. In addition, about 10 percent of the variation in the Gulf Stream Index can be attributed to SOI variability (Taylor et al. 1998). Climate models predict an increase in frequency of El Niño years caused by global warming, which is probably already under way. There were strong El Niño events in 1983, 1987, and 1998 and weaker drops in the SOI in 1992–1994 and 2003.

Effects of Climate Change on North Atlantic Right Whales

North Atlantic right whales obviously have adapted to substantial environmental changes since they diverged from southern right whales at least 3 million years ago (Malik et al. 2000). In their more recent history, they survived the Pleistocene glaciations over the past 1.7 million years as well as the Medieval Warm Period and Little Ice Age of the past millennium. Why should researchers be at all concerned about their survival through the current and coming period of global climate change? One reason is that the current rate of change is largely unprecedented; there are few periods in the geological record where the rate of temperature change was the same or greater than what is occurring presently. Approximately half the total warming estimated for the North Atlantic since the end of the last ice age occurred in only a decade (NAS 2003).

In truth the impacts of global climate change on North Atlantic right whales during the twenty-first century and afterwards are largely unpredictable, but researchers can make some logical deductions based on what is known about right whale biology. There are several possible avenues of impact. Warmer temperatures could affect them directly, could have effects on the distribution and occurrence of disease-causing organisms or toxic phytoplankton (e.g., red tides), or could affect right whales via impacts on their food. Scientists already have some interesting observations of such interactions regarding direct effects and effects on food resources, which allow us to make some reasonable speculations about future impacts.

Direct Temperature Effects

There are few or no direct data about thermal tolerances in right whales. Given their thick blubber layers, it is likely that thermoregulation is physiologically less demanding for them in cold water than in warm water (i.e., it is probably easier for a right whale to stay warm than to cool off). A thermal modeling study of the thicker blubber layer in the closely related bowhead whale concluded that bowheads could maintain a 200°C difference across their blubber, enough so they could swim in liquid oxygen (Hokkanen 1990)!

In the North Atlantic Right Whale Consortium database today there are more than 5,000 right whale sightings where sea-surface temperature (SST) was measured nearby. The average is 12.3°C, and the overall range is 0.0–21.8°C. Satellite-tagged whales have been seen to move in days or weeks across the Gulf of Maine, between the Bay of Fundy and mid-Atlantic, or to far offshore beyond the continental shelf (Mate et al. 1997); they probably crossed through a variety of water masses of varying temperature during those movements. Right whales are also known to make repeated foraging dives to near-bottom depths (Goodyear 1993; Nowacek et al. 2001; Baumgartner and Mate 2003), which go between relatively warm surface water and cold water below the thermocline, and back again, in only minutes. Despite such evidence for right whales' tolerances for changing temperatures, it is still possible that they have an upper thermal limit beyond which they suffer from heat stress. If such limits do exist, temperature increases in the Gulf of Maine as large as those that are projected to occur in the next century (up to 5.8°C) have the potential to exclude right whales from some portions of their existing range within the Gulf of Maine system, at least during the warmer seasons.

In their present calving grounds off the coasts of Georgia and northern Florida, right whales seem to select cooler water, with most sightings in waters below 20°C and relatively few in warmer waters only slightly farther south and offshore (Kraus et al. 1993; Ward 1999). The upper end of the temperature range of right whale habitat in the calving ground is very similar to that in the Gulf of Maine feeding grounds, suggestive of an upper thermal limit but not definitive evidence. Kenney (2002) speculated that this cool-water distribution pattern may have evolved as an adaptation for avoiding shark predation on the newborn calves, but it could just as well be a strategy for avoiding heat stress in warm water by the adult while minimizing heat loss in cold water for the calf.

If the apparent right whale preference for calving in cooler water is, in fact, a result of their temperature tolerance, as ocean temperatures continue to rise, the whales would be subject to thermal stress and associated negative impacts. To avoid higher temperatures, they may be forced to use a different area for their winter calving grounds. Researchers might expect to see the calving ground shift northward. Such a shift could represent a reoccupation of historical calving grounds that are currently not used or used very rarely. Reeves et al. (1978, 1999) described how whalers during the early colonial era hunted right whales in Delaware Bay. The peak of their whaling season was in the winter, almost exactly matching the occurrence of right whales off Florida and Georgia today. Roger Payne (1995) has commented on the remarkable geographic similarities between Cape Cod Bay and the southern right whale calving grounds at Península Valdés in Argentina, and Schevill et al. (1986) believed that at least two right whale calves had been born in Cape Cod Bay during their study. It is possible that the historical calving range may have been broader and that Delaware Bay and Cape Cod Bay, and perhaps other areas, were calving grounds for northern substocks of the population that have since been extirpated.

Such an extended calving area along the North American coast would be similar to observations along the Atlantic coast of South America, where right whale calving grounds exist in Argentina (Payne et al. 1990; Rowntree et al. 2001) and Brazil (de Oliveira Santos et al. 2001). The geographic separation of the Península Valdés (latitude 42–43°S) and Brazilian calving grounds

(22–26°S) is similar to that between Cape Cod (41–42°N) and the Georgia–Florida calving ground (27–32°N). A northward shift in the calving grounds caused by warmer temperatures could very well turn out to have no significant effect unless the new calving area has a higher or lower risk of ship strike, fishing gear entanglement, or serious disturbance than the old one.

On the other hand if the right whale preference for particular calving conditions is related solely to avoidance of shark predation, warming could increase numbers of large sharks in the region, increasing the predation risk to the calves.

There have been recent right whale distributional changes in the Gulf of Maine region, which may or may not be related to changes in the temperature regime. Right whales were absent from the Great South Channel in 1992, which corresponded with an influx of unusually cold water, possibly enhanced by regional cooling caused by atmospheric aerosols from the 1991 eruption of Mt. Pinatubo in the Philippines (Kenney 2001). From 1993 through 1999, the summer–fall feeding ground in Roseway Basin was apparently abandoned (Brown et al. 2001; Patrician 2005). It is likely, however, that such distributional changes as these, even where a clear correlation to temperature can be demonstrated, are driven by prey availability and not by temperature directly (Kenney 2001; Patrician 2005).

Effects on Prey Resources and Right Whale Reproduction

North Atlantic right whales feed on zooplankton, especially large calanoid copepods (Chapter 5). Right whales require dense aggregations of these copepods to feed effectively (Kenney et al. 1986), and the formation of adequate patches is dependent on the combined effects of hydrographic factors and copepod behavior (Kenney and Wishner 1995; Chapter 5). Therefore, any climate-induced changes in hydrography in the Gulf of Maine and adjacent waters have the potential to significantly affect right whale prey abundance and quality.

Calanus finmarchicus is more than just the principal prey species of North Atlantic right whales; it is the dominant zooplankton species in much of the subpolar North Atlantic and a key prey species in marine food webs in the region (Bigelow 1926; Marshall and Orr 1972; Wiebe et al. 2002). The Gulf of Maine–Georges Bank area is at the boundary between sub-Arctic and temperate oceanic regimes. The continental shelf in the entire region is dominated by southwestward-flowing currents that extend from Newfoundland to North Carolina. The major water sources into the Gulf of Maine are cooler and fresher surface water coming in across the Scotian Shelf and warmer and saltier slope water coming in at depth from offshore through the Northeast Channel (between Georges Bank and Browns Bank; color plate 1). Temperature increases related to global warming could have the effect of shifting the subpolar–temperate regime boundary farther to the north and outside of the Gulf of Maine. Because *Calanus* is primarily a subpolar species, such a change might be expected to result in a decline in *Calanus* abundance within the Gulf region.

Calanus population abundance in the Gulf depends on repeated "restocking" by animals that come in from the Scotian Shelf and with the slope water influx. Greene et al. (2004) found a rough correspondence among large-scale *Calanus* abundance, an index of temperature in the slope water, and the NAO index, related to the currents bringing new *Calanus* into the Gulf. They were unable to show a simple statistical correlation between NAO and *Calanus*, which they concluded was because of variable time lags and nonlinear relationships in the physical and biological responses involved. Therefore, the availability of the most important prey of right whales within the Gulf of Maine depends on a complex combination of (1) *Calanus* abundance in source regions outside the Gulf; (2) oceanographic conditions responsible for the rate of *Calanus* influx into the Gulf; (3) *Calanus* feeding, growth, and reproductive rates within the Gulf; and (4) the physical mechanisms that cause *Calanus* to aggregate into the dense patches that right whales require. Anything that affects Gulf of Maine oceanography, such as NAO variability or strength of the Labrador Current, can affect Gulf of Maine *Calanus* abundance and, therefore, right whale feeding success. Given the high energetic demands of pregnancy for a female right whale (Chapter 6), anything that influences feeding success may affect reproductive success.

Interannual variability in the numbers of calves born and the average interval between calves for individual females both increased in the 1990s (Chapter 6), and the survival rate of right whales, especially adult females, also declined in the 1990s (Caswell et al. 1999). Those changes corresponded in time with changes in the oceanographic regime on the eastern Scotian Shelf (DFO 2003) and with increasing variability in the NAO. However, there is an even closer correlation between right whale reproductive success and North Atlantic ocean–atmosphere dynamics.

Greene et al. (2003) incorporated the right whale calving data into an analysis with *Calanus*, oceanographic, and NAO data. The initial comparisons showed approximate correspondences without clear statistical correlations. A complicating factor is that whether or not a particular female gives birth depends in part on her recent reproductive history because nearly all females require a minimum of three years between calves (Knowlton et al. 1994). Using a simple reproductive model, where the probabilities of a female transitioning between pregnant, lactating, and resting–recovery phases are functions of *Calanus* abundance (Greene and Pershing 2004), and with a time series of broad-scale mean *Calanus* abundance as input, the model output was a very close fit to the observed calving frequencies.

Updated Correlation Analysis

For this chapter calving rate was correlated against NAO, SOI, and GSI through the 2004 calving season. Calving rates for western North Atlantic right whales were estimated from the total number of different mother–calf pairs seen each year (with a year defined as December–November), plus any dead calves recorded where all known mothers for that year could be excluded. Fundy calves were the mother–calf pairs identified that summer–fall in the Bay of Fundy. Non-Fundy calves were calculated by subtracting Fundy calves and dead calves from the total number of calves born each year. All of the calving data come from the *North Atlantic Right Whale Catalog* at the New England Aquarium, and the available time series spanned the years from 1980 through 2004.

Corresponding time series of monthly NAO, GSI, and SOI values were obtained on line from the NOAA Climate Prediction Center in Camp Springs, Maryland (NAO and SOI) or the Plymouth Marine Laboratory in Plymouth, England (GSI).

Winter mean NAO was calculated as the average of the four monthly values from December of the previous year through March (Hurrell 1995). Annual mean SOI was calculated as the average of the twelve monthly values from October of the previous year through September (Philander 1990). Without a clear precedent for calculating annual mean GSI, the same October–September scheme as with the SOI data was used, particularly because it is a better match to a right whale's annual cycle than is a standard calendar year. Table 15.2 summarizes all six calving and atmospheric index time series, and Fig. 15.1 compares them graphically. The three calving rates (total, Fundy, non-Fundy) were then correlated with the three atmospheric indices at time lags of zero, one, and two years for a total of twenty-seven separate correlation analyses. The correlations were done using nonparametric Spearman rank-order correlation tests.

Given twenty-seven correlation analyses and a 5 percent level of significance, one would expect one or possibly two significant results by chance alone. There were five statistically significant correlations ($p < 0.05$), and four others that

Table 15.2. Calving Success in Western North Atlantic Right Whales, 1980–2004, Compared to the Winter Mean North Atlantic Oscillation Index (NAO: December–March), Mean Annual Gulf Stream Index (GSI: October–September), and Mean Annual Southern Oscillation Index (SOI: October–September)[a]

		Calves				
Year	Total	Fundy	Non-Fundy	NAO	GSI	SOI
1980	6	4	2	−0.60	−0.63	−0.74
1981	8	7	1	−0.29	−0.62	−0.10
1982	12	6	5	−0.45	−1.15	−1.06
1983	9	4	5	0.95	−0.30	−2.94
1984	12	11	1	0.51	0.15	−0.10
1985	11	5	6	−0.46	1.38	0.09
1986	13	6	7	−0.15	0.00	−0.41
1987	11	7	4	−0.43	−0.33	−2.36
1988	8	4	3	−0.49	0.01	0.33
1989	18	11	5	1.77	0.09	1.59
1990	13	9	3	0.85	0.81	−0.58
1991	17	9	8	0.42	1.05	−1.04
1992	12	4	8	1.04	1.06	−2.13
1993	8	4	2	1.17	0.76	−1.93
1994	9	5	4	0.56	1.60	−1.71
1995	7	3	4	0.72	2.05	−0.85
1996	22	19	2	−0.97	0.52	0.53
1997	20	12	7	0.20	−0.47	−1.01
1998	6	0	5	−0.11	−0.70	−1.61
1999	4	0	4	0.04	−0.48	1.20
2000	1	0	1	0.66	0.97	1.16
2001	31	19	8	−1.13	1.95	0.62
2002	21	6	14	−0.22	1.20	−0.75
2003	19	14	5	−0.55	0.43	−1.06
2004	17	9	7	−0.77	−0.91	−0.54

a. Total includes all identified mother–calf pairs plus any dead calves for which all known mothers can be ruled out. Fundy calves are those brought to the Bay of Fundy habitat during that season. Non-Fundy calves are computed by subtracting Fundy and dead calves from the total.

approached significance ($0.05 \leq p < 0.10$) (Table 15.3). The best fits were with Gulf Stream Index. Total calving was significantly correlated with GSI with both one- and two-year lags and was weakly correlated with SOI with a one-year lag. Non-Fundy calving was significantly correlated with NAO with a two-year lag, GSI with a one-year lag, and SOI with a two-year lag; and weakly correlated with GSI with a two-year lag. Fundy calving showed no significant correlations, but weak correlations with NAO (an inverse relationship) and

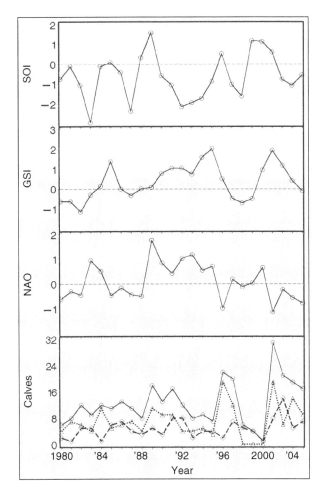

Figure 15.1. Comparisons of total calves (circles and solid line), Fundy calves (triangles and dotted line), and non-Fundy calves (diamonds and dashed line) to winter mean NAO, annual mean GSI, and annual mean SOI.

with GSI with a one-year lag. The results show that all three atmospheric cycles may be correlated with calving in North Atlantic right whales at one- to two-year time lags, primarily in the non-Fundy component of the population. The direct impacts on the whales are probably caused by prey availability, with the atmosphere driving the oceanography, which in turn controls the rate at which *Calanus* comes into the Gulf of Maine, the growth rates of *Calanus*, and the aggregation of *Calanus* into dense patches.

Table 15.3. Spearman Rank-Order Correlations (R), with Associated Significance Probabilities (p), of Total, Fundy, and Non-Fundy Annual Calving Frequencies, 1980–2004, with Winter Mean North Atlantic Oscillation Index (NAO), Mean Annual Gulf Stream Index (GSI), and Mean Annual Southern Oscillation Index (SOI) at Zero-, One-, and Two-Year Time Lags (in Parentheses)

Index	Total		Fundy		Non-Fundy	
	R	p	R	p	R	p
NAO (0)	−0.266	0.198	−0.341	0.095[b]	−0.096	0.647
NAO (1)	−0.039	0.853	0.017	0.936	−0.212	0.310
NAO (2)	0.166	0.428	−0.095	0.653	0.399	0.048[a]
GSI (0)	0.261	0.207	0.095	0.653	0.217	0.297
GSI (1)	0.601	0.002[a]	0.375	0.065[b]	0.408	0.043[a]
GSI (2)	0.416	0.039[a]	0.254	0.220	0.346	0.090[b]
SOI (0)	0.076	0.718	0.181	0.386	−0.213	0.307
SOI (1)	0.378	0.063[b]	0.304	0.140	0.292	0.157
SOI (2)	0.296	0.151	0.209	0.317	0.417	0.038[a]

a. Significant at $p < 0.05$.
b. Significant at $p < 0.10$.

Long-Term Prospects

Can North Atlantic right whales adapt to a warmer world and a warmer ocean? If the rate of change were slow enough, then the answer would certainly be "yes." Right whales have adapted to changing environments over the evolutionary history of their species, probably many times. Unfortunately the rate of global climate change that is currently happening is much greater than at most times in the recent geologic past, perhaps too fast for right whales to adapt and survive, especially given their very small population size and the associated increased risk of extinction.

The western North Atlantic population of right whales today is much smaller than it was at some point in the distant past (Chapter 2). The fact that short-term variability in their calving correlates with atmospheric and oceanographic cycles and with variability in prey resources (Greene et al. 2003; Greene and Pershing 2004) suggests that sometimes right whales in the Gulf of Maine region are existing at close to the carrying capacity of the feeding grounds that they are presently using. Kenney et al. (2001) proposed that the surviving remnant of the western North Atlantic right whale population occupies the southern periphery of their historical range. If the original population was an order of magnitude or more larger, they must have utilized other feeding grounds, which were more likely to the north and east and not to the south.

It is true that researchers still do not know the location of one or more currently used feeding grounds; however, those grounds may not represent the population's original optimal core habitat. The fact that non-Fundy calving correlates strongly with environmental variability indicates that those (still unknown) feeding grounds may not be capable of supporting much larger numbers of right whales. It also supports the hypothesis that there are other historical feeding grounds that the whales have yet to reoccupy to any substantial degree. In their current "marginal" (in both senses of the word: on the geographic edge and with lower than optimal quality) habitats, the whales encounter fluctuations in the availability of their prey caused by natural variations in the atmosphere and ocean. Those fluctuations lead to similar fluctuations in reproductive success: booms when feeding is good and females mature younger and give birth regularly at three-year intervals and busts when feeding is bad and females mature at later ages and take five or six years or longer to recover between calves. This would lead to periods of healthy population growth alternating with periods of slow growth. The addition of human-caused mortality, historically because of continued low-level whaling and now a result of ship strikes and entanglement in fishing gear, means that the net population growth rate (births minus deaths) is modest during the boom periods and zero or negative during the busts, maintaining the population at low numbers with limited or sporadic recovery. The real hope for North Atlantic right whales is to eliminate human-caused mortality and give them a better chance at reoccupying their historical feeding grounds, a luxury that has not been afforded them since the earliest beginnings of North Atlantic whaling. The likelihood of negative impacts from future climate change adds that much more urgency to the need for addressing the mortality component of the population equation.

One hypothesis is that the population has stayed stuck in their marginal habitat and has never reoccupied the other portions of their original range from which whalers or natural disasters had wiped them out because of strong maternally directed site fidelity. A calf learns the geography of its world, including the location of the feeding grounds, by following its mother around for its first year of life. Once the calf learns all there is to know from its mother about the feeding grounds, for the rest of its existence it continues to go back to those same feeding grounds but probably not to others that might exist. So maybe there is a good explanation for why the whales that stray into the Gulf of Mexico tend to be mother-calf pairs: a behavioral tendency for adult females to wander more when they have calves could be a beneficial trait in a species with such a matrilineal system.

Conclusion

Global climate is changing as you read this and will continue to change for the foreseeable future. The state of knowledge about right whales, as good as it is, does not allow researchers to predict how the whales will respond to the certainty of global warming and its attendant impacts on the ocean. Scientists already have evidence that ongoing atmospheric and oceanographic variations are influencing right whale calving through effects on their food supply, and continuing global warming is likely to have further impacts on right whale prey resources. If they cannot adapt, North Atlantic right whales might be the first large whale species to go extinct in modern times at the hand of humans. If that occurs, it will not be at the hands of whalers, although they certainly pushed them toward this point. Instead, we will be able to point fingers only at ourselves; at our insatiable thirst for fossil fuels, foreign imports, and fish; and at our inability to see our own long-term impacts on our increasingly urbanized home planet and its oceans.

On the other hand this species has survived for a very long time, through ice ages, warm periods, and everything in between. Because they live a long time, it may be that right whales can wait out the bad periods and thrive in the good ones. In addition, there are examples of whales that wander to far-off places such as Norway, Greenland, and Iceland, suggesting perhaps that matrilineal fidelity to feeding grounds might be more flexible than is currently believed. Maybe the whales have their own Columbuses, Cabots, and Cartiers: adventurers that are more likely to wander farther than the rules say they ought to. Further, because researchers don't know where the offshore or non-Fundy whales go in the summer, it may be that some of those whales live in habitats that are better than the one that the inshore whales occupy. There are probably other, even better, feeding grounds that have not been used by right whales for generations, and the offshore whales might be more likely to find them in their wanderings: Eg #2360, the 2004 Gulf of Mexico whale, was seen only once in the Bay of Fundy and never in Cape Cod Bay during her twelve-year sighting history. The clearest need is to eliminate human sources of mortality to give the whales a fighting chance. So even though the global climate change picture is not a pretty one, there is hope that the resilience and mysterious travels that enabled North Atlantic right whales to survive the whalers will also serve them well in the face of a warming and changing ocean.

Barange, M., and R. Harris (eds.). 2003. *Marine Ecosystems and Global Change.* IGBP Science no. 5. International Geosphere-Biosphere Program, Stockholm, Sweden. www.igbp.kva.se/uploads/IGBP_5_GLOBEC.pdf.

Baumgartner, M. F., and B. R. Mate. 2003. Summertime foraging ecology of North Atlantic right whales. *Marine Ecology Progress Series* 264:123–135.

Bigelow, H. B. 1926. Plankton of the offshore waters of the Gulf of Maine. *Bulletin of the U.S. Bureau of Fisheries* 40(II):1–507.

Brown, M. W., S. Brault, P. K. Hamilton, R. D. Kenney, A. R. Knowlton, M. K. Marx, C. A. Mayo, C. K. Slay, and S. D. Kraus. 2001. Sighting heterogeneity of right whales in the western North Atlantic: 1980–1992. *Journal of Cetacean Research and Management* Special Issue 2:245–250.

Caswell, H., M. Fujiwara, and S. Brault. 1999. Declining survival probability threatens the North Atlantic right whale. *Proceedings of the National Academy of Sciences* 96:3308–3313.

de Oliveira Santos, M. C., S. Siciliano, S. P. de Souza, and J. L. Altmayer Pizzorno. 2001. Occurrence of southern right whales (*Eubalaena australis*) along southeastern Brazil. *Journal of Cetacean Research and Management* Special Issue 2:153–156.

DFO. 2003. State of the Eastern Scotian Shelf Ecosystem. Maritimes Region Ecosystem Studies Report 2003/04. Scientific Advisory Secretariat, Department of Fisheries and Oceans Canada, Dartmouth, Nova Scotia. http://www.mar.dfo-mpo.gc.ca/science/rap/internet/ESR_2003_004_E.pdf.

Goodyear, J. D. 1993. A sonic/radio tag for monitoring dive depths and underwater movements of whales. *Journal of Wildlife Management* 57:503–515.

Greene, C. H., and A. J. Pershing. 2004. Climate and the conservation biology of North Atlantic right whales: the right whale at the wrong time? *Frontiers in Ecology and the Environment* 2:29–34.

Greene, C. H., A. J. Pershing, R. D. Kenney, and J. W. Jossi. 2003. Impact of climate variability on the recovery of endangered North Atlantic right whales. *Oceanography* 16(4):98–103. http://www.tos.org/oceanography/issues/issue_archive/issue_pdfs/16_4/16.4_Greene.pdf.

Greene, C. H., A. J. Pershing, B. C. Monger, M. C. Benfield, E. G. Durbin, and M. C. Casas. 2004. Supply-side ecology and the response of zooplankton to climate-driven changes in North Atlantic Ocean circulation. *Oceanography* 17(3): 60–71. http://www.tos.org/oceanography/issues/issue_archive/issue_pdfs/17_3/ 17.3_mercina.pdf.

Hokkanen, J. E. I. 1990. Temperature regulation of marine mammals. *Journal of Theoretical Biology* 145:465–485.

Hurrell, J. W. 1995. Decadal trends in the North Atlantic Oscillation: regional temperatures and precipitation. *Science* 269:676–679.

IPCC. 2001. *Climate Change 2001: Synthesis Report. A Contribution of Working Groups I, II, and III to the Third Assessment Report of the Intergovernmental Panel on Climate Change.* Cambridge University Press, Cambridge, UK. http:// www.grida.no/climate/ipcc_tar/.

IPCC. 2002. *Climate Change and Biodiversity.* IPCC Technical Paper V. World Meteorological Organization, Geneva, Switzerland. http://www.ipcc.ch/pub/ tpbiodiv.pdf.

Kennedy, V. S., R. R. Twilley, J. A. Kleypas, J. H. Cowan, and S. K. Hare. 2002. Coastal and Marine Ecosystems and Global Climate Change: Potential Effects on U.S. Resources. Pew Center on Global Climate Change, Arlington, VA. www.pewclimate.org/global-warming-in-depth/all_reports/coastal_and_marine_ ecosystems/index.cfm.

Kenney, R. D. 2001. Anomalous 1992 spring and summer right whale (*Eubalaena glacialis*) distributions in the Gulf of Maine. *Journal of Cetacean Research and Management* Special Issue 2:209–223.

Kenney, R. D. 2002. North Atlantic, North Pacific, and southern right whales (*Eubalaena glacialis, E. japonica,* and *E. australis*). Pages 806–813 *in* W. F. Perrin, B. Würsig, and H. G. M. Thewissen, eds. *Encyclopedia of Marine Mammals.* Academic Press, San Diego, CA.

Kenney, R. D., and K. F. Wishner (eds.). (1995). The South Channel Ocean Productivity EXperiment: SCOPEX. *Continental Shelf Research* Special Issue 15:373–611.

Kenney, R. D., M. A. M. Hyman, R. E. Owen, G. P. Scott, and H. E. Winn. 1986. Estimation of prey densities required by western North Atlantic right whales. *Marine Mammal Science* 2:1–13.

Kenney, R. D., C. A. Mayo, and H. E. Winn. 2001. Migration and foraging strategies at varying spatial scales in western North Atlantic right whales: A review of hypotheses. *Journal of Cetacean Research and Management* Special Issue 2: 251–260.

Knowlton, A. R., S. D. Kraus, and R. D. Kenney. 1994. Reproduction in North Atlantic right whales (*Eubalaena glacialis*). *Canadian Journal of Zoology* 72:1297– 1305.

Kraus, S. D., R. D. Kenney, A. R. Knowlton, and J. N. Ciano. 1993. Endangered right whales of the southwestern North Atlantic. Final Report, Contract no. 14-35-0001-30486. U.S. Department of the Interior, Minerals Management Service, Herndon, VA.

Malik, S., M. W. Brown, S. D. Kraus, and B. N. White. 2000. Analysis of mitochondrial DNA diversity within and between North Atlantic and South Atlantic right whales. *Marine Mammal Science* 16:545–558.

Mantua, N., D. Haidvogel, Y. Kushnir, and N. Bond. 2002. Making the climate connections: bridging scales of space and time in the U.S. GLOBEC program. *Oceanography* 15(2):75–86. http://www.tos.org/oceanography/issues/issue_archive/issue_pdfs/15_2/ 15_2_mantua_et_al.pdf.

Marshall, S. M., and A. P. Orr. 1972. *The Biology of a Marine Copepod.* Springer-Verlag, New York.

Mate, B. R., S. L. Nieukirk, and S. D. Kraus. 1997. Satellite-monitored movements of the northern right whale. *Journal of Wildlife Management* 61:1393–1405.

Moore, J. C., and E. Clark. 1963. Discovery of right whales in the Gulf of Mexico. *Science* 141:269.

NAS. 2003. *Abrupt Climate Change: Inevitable Surprises. Executive Summary.* National Academies Press, Washington, DC.

NAST. 2001. *Climate Change Impacts on the United States: The Potential Consequences of Climate Variability and Change.* U.S. Global Change Research Program, Cambridge University Press, Cambridge, UK. www.usgcrp.gov/usgcrp/Library/nationalassessment/foundation.htm.

Neuman, J. E., G. Yohe, R. Nicholls, and M. Manion. 2000. *Sea-Level Rise & Global Climate Change: A Review of Impacts to the U.S. Coasts.* Pew Center on Global Climate Change, Arlington, VA. www.pewclimate.org/global-warming-in-depth/all_reports/ sea_level_rise/index.cfm.

Nowacek, D. P., M. P. Johnson, P. L. Tyack, K. A. Shorter, W. A. McLellan, and D. A. Pabst. 2001. Buoyant balaenids: the ups and downs of buoyancy in right whales. *Proceedings of the Royal Society of London Part B* 268:1811–1816.

Patrician, M. R. 2005. An investigation of the factors underlying the abandonment of the Roseway Basin feeding ground by the North Atlantic right whale (*Eubalaena glacialis*): 1993–1999. M.S. Thesis, University of Rhode Island Graduate School of Oceanography, Narragansett, RI.

Payne, R. 1995. *Among Whales.* Charles Scribner's Sons, New York.

Payne, R., V. Rowntree, J. S. Perkins, J. G. Cooke, and K. Lankester. 1990. Population size, trends and reproductive parameters of right whales (*Eubalaena australis*) off Peninsula Valdes, Argentina. *Report of the International Whaling Commission* Special Issue 12:271–278.

Philander, S. G. H. 1990. *El Niño, La Niña, and the Southern Oscillation.* Academic Press, New York.

Reeves, R. R., J. G. Mead, and S. Katona. 1978. The right whale, *Eubalaena glacialis,* in the western North Atlantic. *Report of the International Whaling Commission* 28:303–312.

Reeves, R. R., J. M. Breiwick, and E. D. Mitchell. 1999. History of whaling and estimated kill of right whales, *Balaena glacialis,* in the northeastern United States, 1620–1924. *Marine Fisheries Review* 61(3):1–36.

Rowntree, V. J., R. S. Payne, and D. M. Schell. 2001. Changing patterns of habitat use by southern right whales (*Eubalaena australis*) on their nursery ground at Península Valdés, Argentina, and in their long-range movements. *Journal of Cetacean Research and Management* Special Issue 2:133–143.

Schevill, W. E., W. A. Watkins, and K. E. Moore. 1986. Status of *Eubalaena glacialis* off Cape Cod. *Report of the International Whaling Commission* Special Issue 10: 79–82.

Schmidly, D. J., C. O. Martin, and G. F. Collins. 1972. First occurrence of a black right whale (*Balaena glacialis*) along the Texas coast. *Southwestern Naturalist* 17:214–215.

Smith J. B. 2004. *A Synthesis of Potential Climate Change Impacts on the U.S.* Pew Center on Global Climate Change, Arlington, VA. www.pewclimate.org/ global-warming-in-depth/all_reports/synthesisimpacts/index.cfm.

Sverdrup, H. U., M. W. Johnson, and R. H. Fleming. 1942. *The Oceans. Their Physics, Chemistry, and General Biology.* Prentice-Hall, New York.

Taylor, A. H. 1995. North-south shifts of the Gulf Stream and their climatic connection with the abundance of zooplankton in the UK and surrounding seas. *ICES Journal of Marine Science* 52:711–721.

Taylor, A. H. 1996. North-south shifts of the Gulf Stream: ocean–atmosphere interactions in the North Atlantic. *International Journal of Climatology* 16:559–583.

Taylor, A. H., M. B. Jordan, and J. A. Stephens. 1998. Gulf Stream shifts following ENSO events. *Nature* 393:638.

Ward, J. A. 1999. Right whale (*Balaena glacialis*) South Atlantic Bight habitat characterization and prediction using remotely sensed oceanographic data. M.S. Thesis, University of Rhode Island Graduate School of Oceanography, Narragansett, RI.

Wiebe, P., R. Beardsley, D. Mountain, and A. Bucklin. 2002. U.S. GLOBEC northwest Atlantic/Georges Bank program. *Oceanography* 15(2):13–29. http:// www.tos.org/oceanography/issues/issue_archive/issue_pdfs/15_2/15_2_wiebe_ et_al.pdf.

Wigley, T. M. L. 1999. *The Science of Climate Change. Global and U .S. Perspectives.* Pew Center on Global Climate Change, Arlington, VA. http://www.pewclimate. org/global-warming-basics/basic_science/wigley.cfm.

Acknowledgments

Work on this chapter was supported through the URI-NOAA Cooperative Marine Education and Research Program, funded by the NOAA National

Marine Fisheries Service. Many thanks to Hal Walker, U.S. Environmental Protection Agency, and Andy Pershing, Cornell University, for reviewing a draft of this chapter and keeping me from making any serious errors in trying to simplify the climate change and oceanographic information.

16

The Big Picture: Modeling Right Whales in Space and Time

LANCE P. GARRISON

2 January 1996
Off the Coast of Florida

During an aerial survey on this day, a nine-year-old female right whale (Eg #1707) was sighted off the Florida coast entangled in fishing gear. Fishing line was cinched tight around her body near the flippers, and she was trailing over 91 m of rope and some lobster buoys behind her. The line appeared to be cutting into her skin, and it was clear that something needed to be done. When she was next sighted thirteen days later near Jacksonville, Florida, a team of biologists from the Florida Department of Environmental Protection (now the Fish and Wildlife Research Institute) and the New England Aquarium (NEAq) were ready. They launched a boat, found the whale, cut off over 46 m of the fishing line, and attached a buoy with a radio transmitter (designed for use on manatees) to the trailing line. This buoy would allow the disentanglement team from the Provincetown Center for Coastal Studies (PCCS) to relocate the whale and attempt a full disentanglement in the near future. Over the next several weeks she was tracked nearly daily by airplane as she headed south to Daytona, Florida. She then reversed course and traveled steadily north along the coast. The winds remained high and were unfavorable for a disentanglement effort.

Time was running out, and this whale would likely head offshore after rounding Cape Hatteras and would no longer be accessible by small boat.

On 24 January Chris Slay from the NEAq and Stormy Mayo from the PCCS climbed aboard the U.S. Coast Guard cutter Metompkin *out of Charleston, South Carolina, and headed to sea into the teeth of a squall. Because of the very rough seas, they were unable to disentangle the whale, but they did attach a telemetry buoy equipped with both satellite and radio transmitters in hopes of locating her again in calm weather to cut off the lines. In honor of the Coast Guard's extraordinary efforts, the whale was subsequently named for their boat: "Metompkin."*

Over the next several months, as the Argos satellite tracking system reported daily positions to our computers over the Internet, we watched Metompkin's satellite track head northeast and out to sea. The tag went farther and farther offshore, and we became increasingly excited. Could she be heading to one of the missing right whale habitats? Some nineteenth-century whaling records referred to an area in the middle of the Atlantic as a whaling ground, and it had been nicknamed Maury's Smear (from an ill-defined mark on one of Lieutenant Maury's whaling charts). Our excitement rose as the tag made its way slowly and steadily in that direction. But was the tag still attached to its tether? Or was it just drifting with the currents? Right whales average a swimming speed that is not much greater than the 4–6 km/h Gulf Stream, so speed was not a clear determinant. Drift specialists from the University of Miami were consulted, and the track of the tag was compared to oceanographic buoys drifting in the Gulf Stream.

After two months of making steady progress eastward, the tag began to double back on itself. For the next three and one-half months the tag/whale moved erratically around a 160 by 322 km area west of the Azores. By the end of June the tag started moving steadily northeast along the same track that it followed when it entered the area over three months before. On 4 July, the tag stopped broadcasting.

Whether this track resulted from a drifting tag or a meandering whale could never be conclusively determined, but the data were more in support of the former. The oceanographers believed that the buoy had broken free from the whale just days after the tagging and had been drifting almost the entire time. Metompkin showed up in the Bay of Fundy in August later that year completely free of fishing gear. Since this event, a right whale, named "Porter" (Eg #1133), swam from Cape Cod to the northern tip of Norway,

*making Metompkin's potential journey more plausible. Although her true
story is still a mystery, the excitement from the potential discovery of where
she went, and where other right whales may go, remains.*

Philip K. Hamilton

Metompkin's potential wanderings following the disentanglement attempt and
tagging are typical of those right whales that have been followed closely for
any significant length of time. When these opportunities arise, researchers hope
to uncover some of the remaining mysteries about these enigmatic creatures.
However, more often than not, the technology fails, or the wanderings of a
lone whale fail to provide the deep insights that are desired. It is both frus-
trating and fascinating that after two decades of intensive study of this small
population, researchers still do not know the answers to some basic questions
about the life history of the North Atlantic right whale. Where is the wintering ground for noncalving whales? Where do the non-Fundy whales go in the
summer? Is there a winter breeding ground?

In addition to these larger-scale problems, there are other issues that must
be understood to effectively conserve this species and aid in its recovery. Those
who study ecology and biology quickly learn that variability is the rule rather
than the exception. Dealing with biological variation in any management
framework is inherently difficult because it means that regulations must be
adaptable to the underlying variability in the processes driving right whale
spatial distribution and population dynamics. For example in the summer
feeding grounds of the Bay of Fundy and Roseway Basin (on the Nova Scotian Shelf), Baumgartner et al. (2003) observed large changes in the abundance of right whales between 1999 and 2001 that were correlated with local
changes in physical environmental conditions. However, they were also likely
associated with changes in food availability or other environmental factors
throughout the region.

Similarly the numbers of calving females observed in the southeastern
United States calving grounds and their calf production have varied from year
to year (Greene et al. 2003). The interannual variations in abundance, calving success, and spatial distribution may be related to regional temperatures
(Keller et al. 2006; Chapter 15), food availability in feeding habitats (Greene et
al. 2003), overall changes in body condition in the population (Pettis et al.
2004), or more likely some combination of all of these factors. Given what

has occurred during the past decade, the questions remain: Why do things vary so much from year to year? Can scientists predict what is coming next?

Perhaps more fundamentally, researchers are still uncertain as to the overall status and trends of this population. The population's size was reduced by historical whaling, and it has persisted at a low level or recovered slowly throughout the second half of the twentieth century (Chapter 2). It is also apparent that there was decreased reproduction during the 1990s (Chapter 6) and that human-induced mortality as a result of entanglement with fishing gear and vessel strikes has continued (Chapters 13 and 14). However these data alone do not tell us the impacts of the observed mortalities on the long-term productivity of this population. Because of the difficulties in surveying a rare animal over large spatial scales, it is difficult to generate an abundance estimate for the right whale with sufficient accuracy or to evaluate trends associated with either changes in reproductive success or survival of adults. Understanding the trends in the population dynamics of the species is critical for management and conservation.

The dramatic growth in right whale research over the past two decades has provided a wealth of information about the distribution, life history, population genetics, and basic biology of this species. However, the extremely small population size and the infrequent and irregular observations of right whales mean that understanding this species requires the use of analytic tools to deal with missing and limited data. The approach to these difficulties is the development of mathematical models that can assimilate data, represent ecological processes, and provide meaningful assessments of current status and possible future outcomes.

Population Modeling: Basic Concepts

The use of mathematical modeling to assess population dynamics was traditionally considered to be separate from organismal biology that focused more on processes at the level of the individual. During the past few decades, these separations have faded, and mathematical approaches to describing biological processes have become fundamental to the management and conservation of living resources. Originally population modeling focused on mechanistic approaches in which relatively simple scientific laws could be represented mathematically to provide both accurate descriptions and predictions over a large range of scales. These mechanistic models described the intrinsic population growth rate, which reflected a balance between increases in population size (birth and immigration) and decreases in population size (death and emigration). This balance between gains and losses remains fundamental to most models used in population dynamics today.

Animal reproduction and survival rates are affected by the availability of resources such as food and space. Variation in such resources caused by factors external to the population (e.g., climate shifts, habitat destruction) result in variation in birth and death and are "density-independent" processes because they are not a function of population size. Processes internal to the population will also affect vital rates. Competition for resources at large population sizes reduces the amount of food that can be consumed and thereby the amount of energy available for reproduction. Competition may even increase mortality rates because some individuals starve. Thus, a population's growth rate may be related to its size, and this is described as "density-dependent" population regulation.

Building on these basic principles of population dynamics, mathematical models add greater complexity and realism by allowing population vital rates to vary by life-history stages (e.g., individual age or size) and in time and space. This increasing complexity both adds biological realism and greatly increases the demands for data to support the model. Inevitably some important process will be ignored in any model representation of a natural population. This brings to mind the oft-repeated adage that all models are wrong, but some are useful (McCullagh and Nelder 1983).

Developing Mathematical Models of Populations

Mathematical models to study biological systems require clearly defined questions. This crystallizes the major features of the biology that the model must adequately represent and also identifies those that can be safely ignored. The second step of development may be described as "abstraction," in which the researcher distills the major features of the biological system being studied into an understandable conceptual framework. Once the processes that are going to be included in the model are defined, the modeler moves on to "formulation," where the mathematical equations are developed along with the associated parameters that represent the system. In general the formulations follow relatively well-established sets of equations that have been used frequently in mathematical modeling. The next step, "parameterization," either develops values for input parameters that drive the behavior of the model or, alternatively, defines a mechanism whereby parameters can be estimated from existing data.

If model results are to be useful, then the parameters must have a well-defined relationship with reality as represented by available data. Increasing the complexity in the model may be more realistic, but it comes at the cost of increasing the number of parameters that must be estimated. The model must also have a well-defined mechanism for validation. That is, the results and predictions from the model are compared to data to verify that the model adequately represents the system being studied and to judge whether it is effective at answering the questions. Model development and application are frequently iterative. Each application and validation of the model identifies processes to be included or data that must be collected. One of the values of mathematical models is that they can be used to evaluate the understanding of a system and highlight areas where research is needed. However, the most important test of a model's value is its usefulness in addressing critical management questions. Useful models answer well-defined problems and have a clear relationship to data both in parameterization and validation.

Right Whales in Time: Modeling Right Whale Demographics

For the right whale, the critical questions that need to be answered concern the current status and future of this species. The right whale population is small, and despite the cessation of commercial whaling seventy years ago, there are no signs of recovery similar to that of its cousin in the Southern Hemisphere or many of the other large whales (Best et al. 2001). Furthermore, the right whale is still experiencing mortalities every year in the reproductive segments of the population, and there is evidence for periodically reduced reproduction. With all of these challenges, it is clear that the situation is critical for right whales, but the question is how critical? Are right whales in danger of extinction under current conditions, and what conservation efforts will be effective to aid recovery?

Stage-Based Models

To address these questions, researchers at the Woods Hole Oceanographic Institution (Caswell et al. 1999; Fujiwara and Caswell 2001) developed and applied a stage-based population model that recognizes that individuals within the population may have different survival rates and contribute differently to reproduction. For example, juveniles typically have lower survival rates than adults, and larger or older whales are generally most responsible for reproduction. The population structure or demography is defined as the relative abundance of classes of individuals in different reproductive states. Demographic models consider juveniles to be different from reproductive adults, for example, and the vital rates specific to each of these life history stages are represented in the model structure. Particularly for small populations, population growth rates are more sensitive to the survival and numbers of reproductively active individuals than they are to overall population size. Thus, to understand the status of the right whale population, it was necessary to formulate the models to estimate stage-specific vital rates.

In the stage-based model the life history stages reflect discrete changes in the behavior and physiology of the organism. The essential characteristics of the defined stages include (1) that they can be reliably identified and (2) that there is a significant difference in the vital rates (i.e., growth, death, reproduction) between the defined stages (Caswell 2001). Defining the stages in this model is equivalent to the abstraction phase of model development described above, whereby the complex and continuous life history of the right whale is distilled into a fairly small and simple set of definable stages or demographic classes.

Right whale life history has been abstracted into seven discrete stages that describe the demographic structure of the population (Fujiwara and Caswell 2001; Fig. 16.1). This included discrete stages for female and male right whales and included a death stage to represent the probability of mortality in the population. Mature whales were defined as those at least nine years old. The life-cycle graphs shown in Fig. 16.1 represent the stages and show the potential transitions of individuals from one stage to the next with arrows. The time step used in this model is one year, and each arrow represents the probability, denoted p_{ij}, that an observed right whale in a given stage i will be observed in stage j in the following year. For example, between any two years a mature female (stage 3) may either remain in stage 3 (the small circular arrow, p_{33}) or may transition into becoming a mother (i.e., mature female seen with a calf, stage 4, p_{34}). The transition probabilities represented by arrows connecting each stage to stage 5 represent the annual mortality rates for each life-history stage. Right whale birth rates are related to the transition probabilities from stages 2 to 4 and 3 to 4 because these represent the probability that immature (stage 2) and mature (stage 3) females will produce a calf in any year. Thus, the transition probabilities represent the events in right whale life history that drive the dynamics of this population.

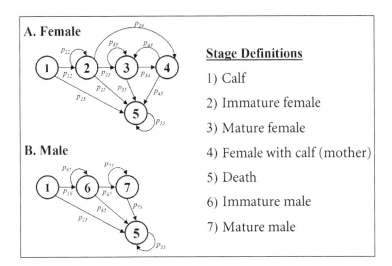

Figure 16.1. Life-cycle graphs depict the structure of the stage-based model of right whale population dynamics (after Fujiwara and Caswell 1999).

The critical parameters to be estimated for this model are the annual transition probabilities. In long-lived, mobile organisms such as right whales, it is not possible to observe mortality or other events on a constant basis directly. Instead, Caswell and Fujiwara took advantage of the long history of photographic data on right whales and the fact that individuals can be identified reliably through time. These data were used as a multistage mark–recapture analysis to estimate survival and transition probabilities. Mark–recapture techniques have been used widely in wildlife studies to estimate population size and survival rates of animal populations (reviewed in Burnham et al. 1987; Lebreton et al. 1992).

Originally, mark–recapture applications involved actively capturing and tagging individuals, then recapturing from the same population and determining the proportion of marked individuals in the recapture event. This proportion estimates the probability of capturing any individual (marked or unmarked) in the population and thus estimates total population size. For right whales, the unique natural markings (Chapter 3) are used to identify individuals over time, and the "capture–recapture" event occurs each time an individual is photographed.

This method for abundance estimation was later expanded to estimate individual survival probability. Mark–recapture methods to estimate survival hinge on a relatively simple concept. Briefly, if a set of animals is observed at one point in time, t_0, and then again at some later time, t_1, there are three possible outcomes for each identified individual: (1) the individual is alive and seen (or captured); (2) the individual is alive but not seen; or (3) the individual is dead and therefore not seen (Lebreton et al. 1992). Repeated observations allow direct calculation of survival probabilities and capture rates. For example if an animal is seen at t_0, not seen at subsequent sampling events t_1 and t_2, but is seen at t_3, then the animal was "alive but unseen" at the previous sampling events. Assuming that all marked animals have the same capture probabilities at any given time step, information on the proportion of animals in each category is used to infer the capture probabilities and survival rates for the entire population. The more individuals that can be observed and the longer the capture history, the greater is the reliability in the estimates of survival rates (Lebreton et al. 1992).

This approach was extended to evaluate the transitions between multiple life history stages by Nichols et al. (1992), and the methodology for estimating parameters was developed and applied to the stage-based model for right whales by Fujiwara (2002). A key point is that the probability of seeing a marked individual in a particular life history stage is a function of both the likelihood that the individual is in that stage and the likelihood of seeing (i.e., capturing) the individual. The methods developed by Nichols and Fujiwara must estimate not only the transition and survival probabilities, represented in Fig. 16.1, but also the stage-specific capture probabilities. The statistical methods used to estimate the large number of parameters from a large amount of data are complex (Fujiwara 2002). The approach assumes that all individuals within a stage have the same capture probabilities; however, these probabilities can vary across time. In their analysis Fujiwara and Caswell (2001) accounted for variation in right whale survey effort in each year so as to better represent stage-specific capture probabilities between 1980 and 1995.

Fujiwara and Caswell (2001) described the results of two model formulations, one in which the transition probabilities did not change with time and a second that included changes in survival rates for each stage across the time series. The results of the static model indicated that, on average, the mortality rates of calves (p_{12} = 0.08) and mothers (p_{15} = 0.17) are the highest of all stages. This is generally consistent with the life history data of long-lived mammal species, where mortality rates are highest for newborns and young animals. Mothers also experience higher mortality rates because of the energetic costs and risks of giving birth and, in the case of right whales, the increased risks associated with the long migration from the summering grounds to the winter calving ground in the southern United States. Under this time-invariant model, the right whale population was predicted to be stable with an annual population increase of approximately 1 percent per year (Fujiwara and Caswell 2001).

However, the best model indicated that the vital rates were not constant in time. Based on this second model, there was a declining trend in population growth rates from 1.03 (i.e., 3 percent annual increase) in 1980 to 0.98 (i.e., 2 percent annual decrease) in 1995. The reduction in population growth rate was largely a result of decreased survival of mothers while the survival rates of other stages were generally stable. The survival rates of mothers declined from 0.94 in 1980 to 0.62 in 1995. This decline resulted in a decreased life expectancy for female right whales from an estimated 51.8 years to 14.5 years and a reduction in lifetime reproductive output from 5.27 to 1.26 calves (Fujiwara and Caswell 2001).

Under the scenario presented at the end of 1995, with a 2 percent decrease in population size each year, and incorporating the probability of random events affecting the survival of individuals, a probability distribution for the likelihood of extinction was generated. The results of these stochastic model projections indicated a 50 percent probability of extinction of the right whale within 208 years, a 5 percent probability of extinction within 130 years, and a 25 percent probability within 165 years (Fujiwara and Caswell 2001).

However, the model results suggested that the picture is not completely negative, and there remains a possibility of the successful recovery of this species. Most notably, small changes in female survival rates may have a significant impact on population growth rates. Model simulations indicated that increasing survivorship by only one mature female annually could improve the population growth rate to nearly one, resulting in stability in population size and increasing the time to extinction. Preventing the deaths of two females per year could return the population to positive growth rates and prevent extinction (Fujiwara and Caswell 2001). This suggests that effective management actions that reduce the risk of human-caused mortalities can have a significant impact on this population.

The forward projections and estimates of the time to extinction presented in Fujiwara and Caswell (2001) make the critical assumption that the survival and other vital rates estimated in 1995 remain constant throughout the time frame of the simulations. However, right whale vital rates are not constant in time, and the model formulation described here does not include potential effects of environmental variability on the reproduction and survival rates of right whales. Notably there is an apparent correlation among large-scale climate variability indicated by the North Atlantic Oscillation (NAO), availability of *C. finmarchicus,* and the observed calving rates of right whales (Chapter 15). The effects of climate variability may have a significant impact on the conclusions of the stage-based model, and these effects have not been accounted for in the predictions given in Fujiwara and Caswell (2001). Climate variability and changes in prey availability may be more significant than impacts of human activities and are less amenable to management. However, reducing human-induced mortality could provide a buffer against unfavorable climatic changes (Greene and Pershing 2004).

The model developed by Fujiwara and Caswell provides critical insights into the status and population dynamics of the right whale. The strength of this approach is that it represents the different life history stages that are important for population dynamics, and it accounts for the effects of demographics that are especially important for small populations. In addition, the model makes efficient use of the large sightings database available for this species and extracts information useful for management and conservation. A significant weakness of the approach to date is that it does not adequately model the underlying processes that could contribute to changes in vital rates and oversimplifies a known source of variability resulting from climatic changes. Thus, the predictions forward from 1995 should be treated with caution. The model formulation is flexible, and it will be interesting to incorporate the additional data collected over the past decade as well as other environmental covariates.

Right Whale Movements: Development and Application of Habitat Models

As right whales move through the ocean, they are exposed to varying degrees of risk from human interactions. The fisheries that result in entanglement of right whales (and other large whales) occur mostly in the northeastern United States (Chapter 13). Vessel strikes, the major known cause of right whale deaths, also vary regionally because of the concentration of large vessels around the major commercial ports of eastern North America (Chapter 14). Within these broad regional patterns, the direct human threats to right whales are localized to intensive fishery grounds and major corridors for commercial shipping. Therefore, understanding the movements of right whales on both regional and local scales can help identify areas where the risk of human interactions is high and may assist in developing effective strategies to reduce those interactions.

In all northern areas, food availability appears to be an important factor determining spatial distribution for this population. The primary limiting resource for right whales is the abundance and density of the copepod *Calanus finmarchicus*. The total biomass of *C. finmarchicus* is highly variable from year to year, and the processes such as upwelling and oceanic fronts that concentrate these copepods are also variable in time and space (Chapter 5). In some cases there are predictable areas where copepod densities are high in relation to persistent frontal zones (e.g., the Great South Channel; Kenny et al. 1995; Wishner et al. 1995). However, in some areas (such as Cape Cod Bay) the availability of the food resource is less predictable (Mayo and Marx 1990). This spatial and temporal variability in prey directly affects both the population dynamics of right whales and their movements on regional scales. Although right whales are certainly adapted to deal with this variability in a given year by seeking more favorable feeding areas, their relatively low population size increases their risk from long-term changes in resources (Greene and Pershing 2004). This short-term variability also complicates management measures that must likewise adapt to unusual or unpredictable movements of whales.

What Constitutes Right Whale Habitat?

Spatially explicit models of right whale movements and habitat are a developing tool for exploring these complex processes. "Habitat" is defined as the suite of physical and biological characteristics necessary for the survival of the population (Harwood 2001). These environmental requirements (e.g., appropriate temperatures, salinities) are typically set by the physiology of the organism. For example, in warm-blooded animals, metabolic processes are most efficient at some intermediate temperature because both low and high temperatures require additional energy for thermoregulation. The distribution of a species along an environmental gradient will thus often be dome-shaped or unimodal. This "species–environment curve" is characterized by an optimum peak and tails that define the tolerance of the species for variability in the environment (Austin 2002). These curves are not necessarily symmetric. For example, right whales are likely to be less sensitive to cold water temperatures than they are to high temperatures because they are adapted to colder environments.

Environmental factors are frequently correlated with one another, and it can be difficult to determine which factors among many actually define the species' habitat. Teasing apart environmental factors requires the application of multivariate direct gradient analyses (e.g., canonical correspondence analysis; ter Braak 1987) or the use of partial regression approaches that independently evaluate the contribution of each variable to explaining the spatial distribution of the organism (Borcard et al. 1992). Accounting for the correlation between environmental variables adds complexity to the analysis and modeling of habitats; however, this also reflects the underlying biological reality. Particularly for large mobile animals such as right whales, the individual is constantly responding to multiple interacting features, changes in physiological condition, and the demands of life history (e.g., mating, calving, socializing) to make the decisions that drive spatial movements.

The Problem of Spatial Autocorrelation

An additional statistical and analytic challenge for modeling species' habitats is spatial autocorrelation in the distribution of both the animal and environmental features. Spatial autocorrelation means that locations close together in space are more likely to be similar to one another than those spaced farther apart (Legendre and Fortin 1989; Lichstein et al. 2002). Fine-scale autocorrelation in animal distribution may result from behaviors or movements that are independent of external environmental features (Legendre 1993). For example, attraction between individuals caused by social or behavioral factors can result in locally higher numbers of animals than would be predicted from environmental factors alone. This type of patchy spatial distribution would have high spatial autocorrelation at small scales that is independent of environmental variables.

The common presence of spatial autocorrelation in species distributions results in analytic challenges for evaluating species–environment relationships and developing habitat models. Traditional statistical methods assume that there is no underlying relationship between separate observations, and therefore, they can be treated as random samples from a probability distribution (Gumpertz et al. 1997; Legendre and Legendre 1998). Because this is not the case in spatially autocorrelated data, this complicates the procedures used to develop models. Ignoring spatial autocorrelation when fitting models will tend to overestimate the strength of the apparent relationship between the habitat variable and the spatial distribution of the animal (Gumpertz et al. 1997; Lichstein et al. 2002). Therefore, it is critical to quantify and account for the spatial structure in the data so as to avoid incorrect interpretation of the importance of different habitat variables.

Animal Distribution

The response variable for habitat models is information on the spatial distribution of the species. These data are typically counts at particular locations within the study area. In the case of marine mammals in general, and right whales in particular, these data are most frequently collected during visual surveys either aboard vessels or from airplanes.

Habitat Variables

In addition to animal counts, it is necessary to measure the suite of habitat variables that may be important to the species being studied. The measurement of habitat variables can be more difficult than observing the target species. It is often impossible to sample habitat variables at the same location where data are collected on species abundance. For example, the collection of zooplankton samples by net or other means is accomplished only at discrete points in space. Therefore, the measurement of this important habitat variable is often accomplished at a lower spatial resolution than that of the response variable (i.e., right whale occurrence). In these cases, it is critically important to understand the potential scale of spatial autocorrelation in the environmental variables and design the sampling scales accordingly (Borcard et al. 1992; Legendre 1993).

Remote Sensing

Applications of habitat models are increasingly focused on the prediction of animal spatial distributions at locations that have not been sampled. To develop these predictive surfaces, it is necessary to know something about the spatial distribution of the environmental variables across a broader area or at a higher spatial resolution than was actually sampled during the study. Habitat studies have therefore come to rely heavily on features that can be measured by remote sensing.

In marine applications the most commonly applied remotely sensed variable is sea surface temperature (SST) measured by satellite imagery. The advanced very high-resolution radiometer deployed aboard polar orbiting satellites provides data on surface water temperatures on a global scale. Other satellite imagery is available that measures ocean color at the surface, which is an indicator of phytoplankton biomass and productivity.

Satellite imagery is not without significant limitations. Direct measurements of SST or ocean color may not be available at the location and time of the study if there is cloud cover, and satellite imagery has limited spatial resolution. On a global scale, the highest resolution for SST data is 4×4 km square spatial cells (National Oceanographic Data Center 2005). However, some regional applications have spatial resolutions of approximately 1.4×1.4 km (NOAA CoastWatch 2005). Finally, because of slight variations in the position of the satellite as it orbits, the position of the imagery can be shifted in space and fail to match the intended location on the earth. Correcting for this is known as georeferencing, and it can be extremely labor intensive.

Geographic Information Systems

Data collection and assimilation pose a significant challenge in the development and application of habitat models. However, in recent years, the availability of geographic information systems (GIS) has grown tremendously, and this has greatly increased the ability to gather and manage the spatial data needed to develop these models. GIS applications are spatially referenced databases where each piece of data explicitly includes information on spatial location. GIS systems provide a common framework in which to manage multiple map projections, accurately calculate distances and areas over the earth's surface, and access numerous other functions. The growth of GIS applications has resulted in the recent development of spatially referenced data warehouses by government, private industry, and academic institutions. Although many of these data are available at different spatial resolutions, in different map projections, and collected by a range of instrumentation, standard formats have been developed and broadly adopted to provide the metadata (i.e., information about data) that allow any researcher to accurately incorporate these diverse data streams into their GIS application. GIS applications have, therefore, made it far simpler to gather and assimilate the spatial data needed to support the development and application of habitat models.

Feeding, Migration, and Calving Habitat Features

The two major critical habitat types for right whales (and other large whales) are those that support feeding and calving (Harwood 2001). The spring–fall feeding grounds in Cape Cod Bay, the Gulf of Maine, and the Bay of Fundy have been intensively studied across multiple scales. The main feature of these areas is high densities of copepods either near the water surface or at accessible depths (Kenney et al. 1986, 2001). Although the requirements for feeding are fairly well known, there has been comparatively little work describing the features of the calving habitat for right whales. This is a critical gap in knowledge because calving females and calves suffer the highest mortality rates in the population. During both migration and residence in the calving area, right whales are exposed to high densities of commercial shipping traffic as they cross all of the major commercial ports along the eastern seaboard of the United States.

A seasonal migration from cold-water feeding habitats to warmer calving grounds is a common feature among large whales. Right whales do not typically feed during the migration or residence period in the calving ground. Therefore, migration imposes a significant energetic cost on individuals. The reasons for these large-scale migrations are likely a complex function of metabolic and social requirements. The most plausible theories focus on increased probability of calf survival in the calving grounds. First, warmer water temperatures are likely necessary for calves that are born without the thick blubber layer of adults. Second, high-latitude regions generally have higher average wind speeds, greater frequency of storms, and greater wave heights than the tropics during winter months. Calves are relatively weak swimmers, and they may easily be separated from their mothers during storm events with high winds and waves. Separation from the mother for even a short time is likely fatal for newborn calves. Finally, predation on calves may be reduced in southern environments, though there are relatively few available data on the latitudinal distribution of predation on the calves of baleen whales (Corkeron and Conner 1999). Within calving habitats, fine scale spatial partitioning may have as much to do with social and behavioral factors as with environmental constraints on mothers and calves (Erstes and Rosenbaum 2003; Elwen and Best 2004a).

Right Whale Calving Habitat Comparisons: Southern and North Atlantic Right Whales

Southern Right Whales

The southern right whale undertakes seasonal migrations between the Antarctic and temperate waters along the South African coast. The latter are primarily calving grounds, and mothers with calves typically have residence times of weeks to months in these habitats (Best 2000). The South African coast is oriented largely along an east–west axis, and the coastline is characterized by a series of coastal embayments and headlands that offer protection from predominant wind and wave directions (Elwen and Best 2004a).

Analyses of a long time series of sightings data across broad regional scales found that mother–calf pairs occurred more frequently in bays that provided greater protection from prevailing wind and swell and over ocean floors with gentle slopes and sandy bottoms. Cow–calf pairs were generally closer to shore than unaccompanied whales and were more strongly associated with protected areas (Elwen and Best 2004a, 2004b).

Elwen and Best hypothesized that selection of protected, shallow water habitats by calving females was related to improved calf survival through both protection from conspecifics and calm wind conditions. However, they found that there was no difference in reproductive success as a function of spatial distribution and associated habitat variables (Elwen and Best 2004c). Instead, spatial patterns indicated that calf mortality was correlated with the presence of noncows independent of environmental variables. These data on calf mortality suggest that social factors including interactions with aggressive conspecifics may outweigh environmental effects in determining the spatial distribution of calving females (Elwen and Best 2004c).

North Atlantic Right Whales

There are some important differences in both the behaviors of the whales and physical features of the calving habitats of the North Atlantic right whale. Most notably, there is no evidence that the primary calving habitat is also the primary breeding ground. The vast majority of the sightings in the southeastern United States during aerial surveys are of either pregnant females or mother–calf pairs. Immature whales and unaccompanied males and females are occasionally seen during these surveys along with infrequent surface-active groups of four to ten whales. At the current population size, it does not appear that the social factors and avoidance of aggressive conspecifics are as important for determining spatial distribution of North Atlantic right whales as it may be for the South Atlantic right whales.

The spatial structure of the habitat features is also quite different from that of the southern right whale along the South African coast. The coastline of the eastern United States is largely oriented in a north–south direction, and therefore there is a significant latitudinal gradient in water temperatures that is not present on the South African coast. Winter sea surface temperatures range from less than 5°C in New England and the Gulf of Maine region to greater than 25°C in waters off the coast of southern Florida. In addition, the presence of the Gulf Stream imparts a strong onshore–offshore gradient in water temperatures, particularly in areas south of Cape Hatteras, North Carolina. Gulf

Stream waters are warmer than 20°C during winter months, and water closer to shore is generally cooler, ranging between 8° and 12°C in the southeastern United States. In southern Florida the warm Gulf Stream waters approach very close to the shoreline. In contrast to the situation in South Africa, the strong gradients in water temperature on the U.S. coast may have an important effect on the distribution of calving right whales.

The bathymetry and shoreline shape of the United States is also quite different from that of the South African coast. The shoreline is generally smooth and does not have the same degree of complexity and small, protected embayments and rocky shorelines. South of Cape Hatteras, water depths less than 50 m extend up to 100 km from shore in South Carolina and Georgia (National Geophysical Data Center 2005).

Developing a Model of the North Atlantic Right Whale Calving Habitat

The North Atlantic right whale calving habitat is found off the coast of northern Florida and Georgia, where pregnant females go to give birth annually between mid-November and the end of March. This region has been studied intensively by aerial surveys during winter months since 1992. Although the surveys occur along line transects, they were not designed to estimate abundance or spatial distribution of right whales, but they are instead a tool to provide immediate information to mariners on the locations of right whales to allow ships to actively avoid collisions. The spatial extent of these surveillance, or early warning system, surveys has varied through time.

The maps presented here summarize sighting rates (i.e., sightings per unit effort or SPUE) and environmental variables by months (December to March) across the time series from 1992 to 2001 (color plate 24 and Fig. 16.4). The discussion here is limited to the broad-scale patterns in correlation between environmental variables and right whale spatial distribution in the calving habitats. The annual average of SPUE in the calving habitat has varied significantly during the past decade, reflecting changes in calving rates in the population. These patterns are known to be correlated to environmental events outside the calving habitat, including food availability during the summer months in the Gulf of Maine (Greene and Pershing 2004) and possibly other factors. In the development of a habitat model for the calving ground, it is therefore important to recognize the influence of environmental factors outside the study area.

Water temperature is an important predictor of right whale spatial distribution in the calving habitat. An intensive study of sightings and survey effort

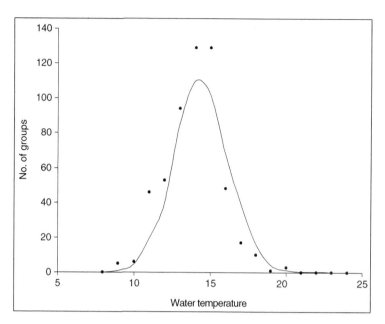

Figure 16.2. The number of right whale groups sighted by 1°C temperature bins during Early Warning System surveys in the southeast United States. The points indicate observed data, and the line represents a smoothing function. These patterns reflect both the distribution of right whales and survey effort in temperature bins.

data (Keller et al. 2006) showed the expected dome-shaped unimodal relationship with sea surface temperature and the likelihood of observing right whales. In Keller's analysis of the survey data, right whales showed a consistent preference for waters between 13° and 16°C. Right whale groups are most commonly seen in water in this temperature range during aerial surveys (Fig. 16.2).

This relatively strong relationship with water temperature is reflected by changes in calving right whale spatial distribution in each month of the survey period. During December, when calving right whales are first arriving in the habitat, sighting rates are higher in the northern portion of the survey range. During January and February the sighting rates increase and become concentrated in the southern portion of the survey range as water temperatures cool. In March the sighting rates decline as whales leave the habitat, and the distribution again shifts farther north (color plate 24).

Changes in spatial distribution associated with water temperature are also reflected in variation between years. During colder years, the spatial distribution

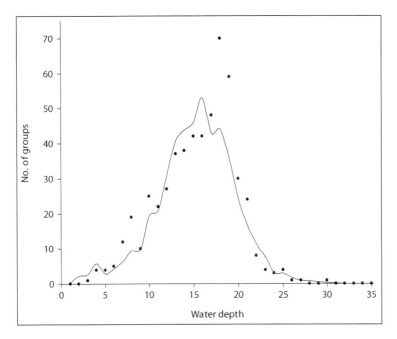

Figure 16.3. The number of right whale groups sighted in 1-m depth intervals during Early Warning System surveys in the southeast United States. The points indicate observed data, and the line represents a smoothing function. These patterns reflect both the distribution of right whales and survey effort.

of the right whales shifts farther south (color plate 25). In warm years, the distribution extends farther north in the habitat. These results indicate a strong fidelity to a relatively narrow temperature range in calving right whales.

Water depth is also a potentially significant factor determining right whale distribution. In the calving grounds, right whales have only very rarely been observed in water depths greater than 20 m, and peak sighting rates occur in depth ranges between 13 and 19 m (Figs. 16.3 and 16.4). However, water depth is strongly correlated with the general onshore–offshore patterns in water temperature. The cooler water temperatures preferred by right whales occur close to shore and over shallower water depths, whereas the warmer waters of the Gulf Stream occur farther away from shore over deeper waters. Also, distance from shore may influence calf survival because near shore, shallow, turbid waters may reduce exposure to predators (e.g., large sharks) or interactions with conspecifics. Areas closer to shore also offer greater protection from wind and wave action by the sheltering action of the shoreline. Given

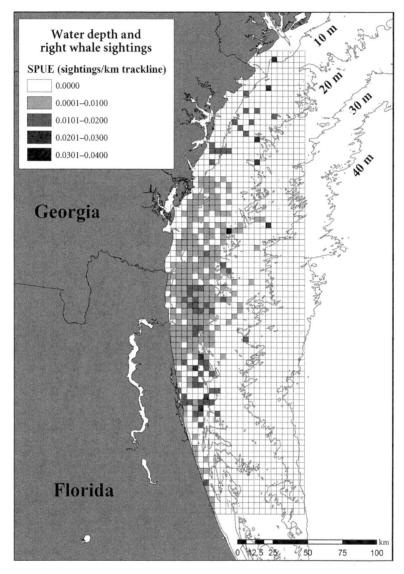

Figure 16.4. Average calving right whale sightings per unit effort (number of sightings per kilometer of survey effort) and bathymetry in the southeast U.S. calving ground. Nearly all sightings of right whales occurred in 10–20 m water depth.

the potential mechanisms for habitat selection in calving right whales, it is likely that water depth per se is not the critical habitat variable, but rather that the correlates with water depth associated with areas closer to shore are important.

Unlike bathymetry and water temperature, there is no readily available high-resolution direct measurement of winds. Therefore, regional wind patterns were examined using output from climate models that describe and predict large-scale weather patterns. The National Center for Environmental Prediction has developed a regional climate model covering North America and the adjacent ocean waters (National Center for Environmental Prediction 2005). The model spatial resolution is 32 × 32 km square cells, and it has been parameterized using weather observations from numerous stations both on land and over water. The model output includes a large suite of weather variables resolved vertically at multiple altitudes and resolved temporally at three-hour intervals.

Model data on predicted winds at 10 m above ground during the period from 1992 to 2002 were used to examine regional wind patterns. These were developed into maps of monthly average wind speeds for December–March (Fig. 16.5). The climate model indicates that the region from Cape Canaveral to Georgia has calmer winds relative to areas farther north, and this latitudinal gradient is strongest during December and January. Higher wind levels are consistently present along the mid-Atlantic coast north of North Carolina. In the calving grounds, areas close to shore are predicted to have generally lower average wind speeds, consistent with sheltering by the shoreline from prevailing westerly winds.

In conclusion, water temperature appears to play an important role in determining the spatial distribution of calving female right whales in the southeastern United States. In addition, right whale distribution is correlated with water depth, which may indicate selection for locations relatively close to shore. The available data also suggest that, at least on a regional scale, the calving area has generally lower wind speeds than regions farther north, particularly north of North Carolina.

Application of Right Whale Habitat Models

There are two major applications of right whale habitat models that operate on different spatial scales. First, habitat models may be used to predict variation in spatial distribution within regional feeding and calving habitats. In the

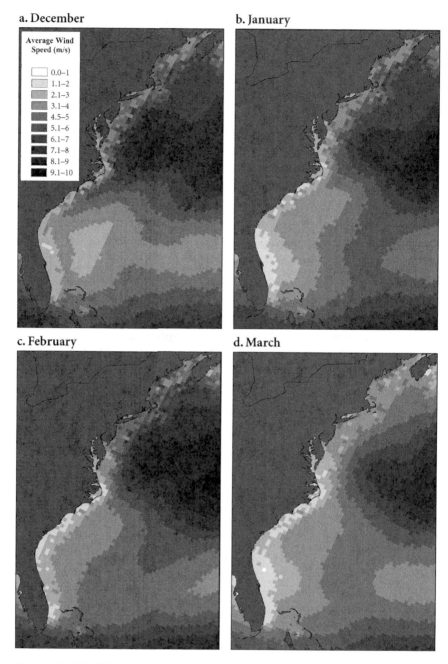

a. December

b. January

Average Wind
Speed (m/s)

0.0–1
1.1–2
2.1–3
3.1–4
4.5–5
5.1–6
6.1–7
7.1–8
8.1–9
9.1–10

c. February

d. March

Figure 16.5. Monthly average wind speeds (m/s) at 10 m above ground based on results from the National Center for Environmental Prediction (2005) North American Regional Reanalysis Model.

example of the calving habitat, the observed relationships between water temperature and right whale distribution support the use of this approach to predict movements inside the calving grounds. Understanding the movements of right whales on these scales can allow managers to predict areas where there is a high risk of interaction between human activities and right whales. For example, there is a relatively high amount of vessel traffic in the southern portion of the calving area associated with the port of Jacksonville, Florida. The predicted concentration of whales in this area during both colder months and in colder years increases their exposure to this high-traffic vessel area.

The second major goal of habitat models is to predict the locations of the unknown right whale habitats. These include migratory pathways along the southeastern U.S. coast, the potential summer habitats of the non-Fundy mothers, the winter breeding grounds, and the wintering areas for large males. Predictions of this type require a leap of faith to extend the model beyond the spatial range of available data. This is inherently risky, as the relationships and patterns observed where data were collected may not apply outside of that area. For example, the surveys and analysis of the calving habitat are restricted to the region off northern Florida and Georgia. However, several recent surveys have indicated that right whales may also use areas farther north through South Carolina and southern North Carolina as a winter calving area (W. McLellan, pers. comm.). If water temperature alone is a critical habitat variable, then this region is an equally suitable habitat for right whales because water temperatures of 12–15°C occur close to shore north of the known calving area. Still, there may be other factors limiting the northern distribution of calving right whales that are not represented in the available data. The relatively higher wind speeds in the northern areas may limit the suitability of these areas in most years. Ultimately, the reliability of a habitat model, or indeed any model, is limited by the extent of the available data. Extrapolations of the predictions of models beyond the limits of the data are best considered testable hypotheses rather than reliable predictions. A remarkably useful outcome of modeling efforts is when they can be used to identify critical areas where research is needed to improve management and conservation.

Conclusion: Models as Tools for Right Whale Conservation

The modeling efforts described here have proven essential to the management and conservation of North Atlantic right whales. The demographic models describe many of the fundamental characteristics of the population, document the impacts of observed mortalities, and assess the potential future direction of the North Atlantic right whale under various scenarios. Habitat models provide much more detailed information on the underlying processes that drive the movements of right whales on both regional and local scales. Understanding these processes is critical for developing management efforts that match the biology of the species and predict and adapt to variability. However, the most critical role of these modeling exercises is that they provide a tool to explore and assimilate the extensive and diverse streams of data that are being collected. The development and application of the models both maximize the use of those data and provide important directions for future research. Models are only as good as the data that support them, and it is important that research on the North Atlantic right whale continues to address specific processes and hypotheses about the ecology and dynamics of this critically endangered species.

Austin, M. P. 2002. Spatial prediction of species distribution: an interface between ecological theory and statistical modeling. *Ecological Modeling* 157:101–118.

Baumgartner, M. F., T. V. N. Cole, P. J. Clapham, and B. R. Mate. 2003. North Atlantic right whale habitat in the lower Bay of Fundy and on the SW Scotian Shelf during 1999–2001. *Marine Ecology Progress Series* 264:137–154.

Best, P. B. 2000. Coastal distribution, movements, and site fidelity of right whales, *Eubalaena australis,* off South Africa, 1969–1998. *South African Journal of Marine Science* 22:43–55.

Best, P. B., J. L. Bannister, R. J. Brownell, Jr., and G. P. Donovan (eds.). 2001. *Right Whales: Worldwide Status.* International Whaling Commission, Cambridge, U.K.

Borcard, D., P. Legendre, and P. Drapeau. 1992. Partialling out the spatial component of ecological variation. *Ecology* 73:1045–1055.

Burnham, K. P., D. R. Anderson, G. C. White, C. Brownie, and K. H. Pollock. 1987. *Design and Analysis Methods for Fish Survival Experiments Based on Release-Recapture.* Monograph 5. American Fisheries Society, Bethesda, MD.

Caswell, H. M. 2001. *Matrix Population Models: Construction, Analysis and Interpretation.* Sinauer Associates, Sunderland, MA.

Caswell, H., M. Fujiwara, and S. Brault. 1999. Declining survival probability threatens the North Atlantic right whale. *Proceedings of the National Academy of Sciences* 96:3308–3313.

Corkeron, P. J., and R. C. Connor. 1999. Why do baleen whales migrate? *Marine Mammal Science* 15:228–1245.

Elwen, S. H., and P. B. Best. 2004a. Environmental factors influencing the distribution of southern right whales (*Eubalaena australis*) on the south coast of South Africa I: Broad scale patterns. *Marine Mammal Science* 20:567–582.

Elwen, S. H., and P. B. Best. 2004b. Environmental factors influencing the distribution of southern right whales (*Eubalaena australis*) on the south coast of South Africa II: Within bay distribution. *Marine Mammal Science* 20:583–601.

Elwen, S. H., and P. B. Best. 2004c. Female southern right whales *Eubalaena australis*: Are there reproductive benefits associated with their coastal distribution off South Africa? *Marine Ecology Progress Series.* 269:289–295.

Erstes, P. J., and H. C. Rosenbaum. 2003. Habitat preference reflects social organization of humpback whales (*Megaptera novaengliae*) on a wintering ground. *Journal of Zoology* 260:337–345.

Fujiwara, M. 2002. Mark-recapture statistics and demographic analysis. Ph.D. Thesis. Woods Hole Oceanographic Institution/Massachusetts Institute of Technology. Woods Hole, MA.

Fujiwara, M., and H. Caswell. 2001. Demography of the endangered North Atlantic right whale. *Nature* 414:537–541.

Greene, C. H., and A. J. Pershing. 2004. Climate and the conservation biology of North Atlantic right whales: the right whale at the wrong time? *Frontiers in Ecology and the Environment* 2:29–34.

Greene, C. H., A. J. Pershing, R. D. Kenney, and J. W. Jossi. 2003. Impact of climate variability on the recovery of endangered North Atlantic right whales. *Oceanography* 16:96–101.

Gumpertz, M. L., J. M. Graham, and J. B. Ristaino. 1997. Autologistic model of spatial pattern of Phtyophthora epidemic in bell pepper: effects of soil variables on disease presence. *Journal of Agricultural, Biological, and Environmental Statistics* 2:131–156.

Harwood, J. 2001. Marine mammals and their environment in the twenty-first century. *Journal of Mammalogy* 82:630–640.

Keller, C. A., L. I. Ward-Geiger, W. B. Brooks, C. K. Slay, C. R. Taylor, and B. J. Zoodsma. 2006. North Atlantic right whale distribution in relation to sea surface temperature in the southeastern United States calving grounds. *Marine Mammal Science* 22(2):426–445.

Kenney, R. D., M. A. M. Hyman, R. E. Owen, G. P. Scott, and H. E. Winn. 1986. Estimation of prey densities required by western North Atlantic right whales. *Marine Mammal Science* 2:1–13.

Kenny, R. D., H. E. Winn, and M. C. Macaulay. 1995. Cetaceans in the Great South Channel, 1979–1989: right whale (*Eubalaena glacialis*). *Continental Shelf Research* 15:385–414.

Kenney, R. D., C. A. Mayo, and H. E. Winn. 2001. Migration and foraging strategies at varying spatial scales in western North Atlantic right whales. *Journal of Cetacean Research and Management* Special Issue 2:251–260.

Lebreton, J. D., K. P. Burnham, J. Clobert, and D. R. Anderson. 1992. Modeling the survival and testing biological hypotheses using marked animals: A unified approach with case studies. *Ecological Monographs* 62:67–118.

Legendre, P. 1993. Spatial autocorrelation: trouble or new paradigm? *Ecology* 74: 1659–1673.

Legendre, P., and M.-J. Fortin. 1989. Spatial pattern and ecological analysis. *Vegetatio* 80:107–138.

Legendre, P., and L. Legendre. 1998. *Numerical Ecology.* Elsevier Science, Amsterdam, Netherlands.

Lichstein, J. W., T. R. Simons, S. A. Shriner, and K. E. Franzreb. 2002. Spatial autocorrelation and autoregressive models in ecology. *Ecological Monographs* 72: 445–463.

Mayo, C. A., and M. K. Marx. 1990. Surface foraging behaviour of the North Atlantic right whale, *Eubalaena glacialis,* and associated zooplankton characteristics. *Canadian Journal of Zoology* 68:2214–2220.

McCullagh, P., and J. A. Nelder. 1983. *Generalized Linear Models.* Chapman and Hall, New York.

National Center for Environmental Prediction. 2005. North American regional reanalysis. Homepage http://wwwt.emc.ncep.noaa.gov/mmb/rreanl/index.html.

National Geophysical Data Center. 2005. Bathymetry, topography, and relief. http://www.ngdc.noaa.gov/mgg/coastal.

NOAA CoastWatch. 2005. CoastWatch Homepage. http://coastwatch.noaa.gov.

National Oceanographic Data Center. 2005. 4 km AVHRR Pathfinder Project. http://www.nodc.noaa.gov/sog/pathfinder4km.

Nichols, J .D., J. R. Sauer, K. H. Pollock, and J. B. Hestbeck. 1992. Estimating transition probabilities for stage-based population projection matrices using capture–recapture data. *Ecology* 73:306–312.

Pettis, H., R. M. Rolland, P. K. Hamilton, S. Brault, A. R. Knowlton, and S. D. Kraus. 2004. Visual health assessment of North Atlantic right whales (*Eubalaena glacialis*) using photographs. *Canadian Journal of Zoology* 82:8–19.

ter Braak, C. J. F. 1987. The analysis of vegetation-environment relationships by canonical correspondence analysis. *Vegetatio* 69:69–77.

Wishner, K. F., J. R. Schoenherr, R. Beardsley, and C. Chen. 1995. Abundance, distribution, and population structure of the copepod *Calanus finmarchicus* in a springtime right whale feeding area in the southwestern Gulf of Maine. *Continental Shelf Research* 15:75–507.

Acknowledgments

Much of the assimilation of GIS data including right whale sightings and SST information was accomplished through a collaborative project with members of the marine mammal research group at the Florida Fish and Wildlife Conservation Commission, Florida Fish and Wildlife Research Institute including Ms. Leslie Ward-Geiger, Dr. Cherie Keller, and Mr. Rene Baumstark. The author gratefully recognizes the foresight and dedication of those who have planned and executed the right whale aerial surveys in the southeastern U.S. calving grounds. Opinions expressed herein are those of the author and do not reflect the official policy of the National Marine Fisheries Service.

17

The Urban Whale Syndrome

SCOTT D. KRAUS AND ROSALIND M. ROLLAND

20 September 1999
North Cape Region, Norway

The e-mail came in on the morning of 20 September 1999. Nils Øien, one of our colleagues in Norway, wrote to report a right whale swimming around in a nearby fiord in the North Cape region. The excitement around the office was palpable. Could it be one of the surviving remnants of the eastern North Atlantic right whales? Nils sent the photographs electronically the next day, and Marilyn Marx made the match nearly immediately. Porter! It was Eg #1133, a male from the North Atlantic Right Whale Catalog *and long known to western North Atlantic right whale researchers (Fig. 17.1). What on earth was he doing in Norway, and specifically North Cape? Ironically, right whales were historically called the "North Cape Whale," or "Nordkaper," a name presumably acquired from Norwegian and Icelandic whalers to describe this species. In fact, Porter went right to a Bay called Lopphavet, which was a right whale whaling ground in the 1600s, but no sightings had been reported from there in hundreds of years.*

It is difficult to imagine what motivates a right whale to travel thousands of kilometers as Porter did. It could have been a normal habitat exploration. In wild mammals, males do wander, and there may be good evolutionary reasons to do so—a successful discovery of new feeding grounds could improve one's condition and potentially increase reproductive success. It could have been a coincidence, but given the precise location in a his-

Figure 17.1. Porter (Eg #1133) in the North Cape region of Norway. Karl-Otto Jacobsen / Polar/Environmental Centre, Tromso, Norway.

torical right whale area, this seems doubtful. On the other hand, how could he know to go to that specific place? Could this trip be maternally directed site fidelity? He had been seen in the Bay of Fundy, but not as a calf. It seems unbelievable that there is a cultural memory of Lopphavet that was passed on to him, and yet, there he was, in a location where his ancestors over thirty generations ago went and were killed by our ancestors.

Regardless of Porter's reasons, he traveled from the Great South Channel in the spring of 1999 to Norway, a distance of over 4,428 kilometers in less than four months. He did not remain in Norway long and returned to Cape Cod Bay in the beginning of March 2000. This whale gives biologists pause: notions of whale population structure are frequently based on north–south migrations and the idea that the vast unproductive regions in the middle of the ocean basins serve as effective barriers to east–west movements. In this case, Porter's travels remind us that these distances may not be that significant for a whale and that migrations are not always what we believe.

Scott D. Kraus

The travels of Porter demonstrate that many puzzles remain in the study of right whales. They also suggest that the capacity of this species to adapt to environmental changes, whether anthropogenic or natural, may be greater than heretofore believed. If Porter can find old whaling grounds thousands of kilometers from his normal range, perhaps other whales can too. Nevertheless, a majority of North Atlantic right whales live most of their lives within 160 km of the heavily populated eastern coast of North America (color plates 26 and 27). The consequences of this habitat use pattern is that these whales are exposed to multiple types of human activities and that they will probably continue to manifest higher mortality and lower reproductive fitness because of this exposure.

The Urban Whale Syndrome

In the medical field a "syndrome" is defined as a group of signs and symptoms that occur together and characterize an abnormal condition. The numerous and diverse afflictions that the right whale population is suffering as a result of human impacts can be characterized as the "Urban Whale Syndrome." The features of this syndrome are as follows:

1. Increased mortality from human activities. In the right whales' case, this includes mortality from collisions with ships (Chapter 14) and fatal entanglement in fishing gear (Chapter 13). It may also include undocumented mortalities from acute toxic chemical spills or exposures or from terrestrial-origin diseases.

2. Decreased reproduction. There are potentially multiple causes of the reproductive problems seen in right whales, some of which result from living in coastal urban or industrial zones and some of which occur naturally (Chapter 6).

3. Poor body condition or skin lesions as signs of compromised health. These observations in right whales are associated with reduced reproductive rates and reduced survival (Chapter 9). The causes remain unknown, but because these conditions have not been reported in southern right whales, they are likely related to something in the western North Atlantic habitat.

4. Habitat loss. This includes exclusion from an area because of high levels of human activity or the loss of normal communication abilities within an area as a result of intense underwater noise (Chapter 11).

What Is the Evidence?

Ship Kills

Since 1986, there have been nineteen documented records of right whales being killed by ships along the east coast of the United States and Canada. An additional five are presumed dead from the injuries sustained and the fact that they were never seen again after the last sighting when they were injured. A review of the right whale mortalities from ship strikes shows that they have occurred in nearly every portion of their range from Florida to Nova Scotia (Chapter 14). Busy shipping ports are present throughout the range of right whales, and at least three of them (Bay of Fundy, Great South Channel, and the southeastern United States) have shipping lanes running through critical right whale habitats.

Fishing Entanglements

Since 1986, at least six right whales were killed by entanglements in fishing gear, and another fifty-five were observed carrying fishing gear (Kraus et al. 2005; Chapter 13). Of those fifty-five, twelve are believed to be dead because of their subsequent disappearance from the sightings record. But this is only a small part of the interactions between right whales and fishing gear. As early as 1990 there was evidence that nearly 60 percent of all right whales had been entangled in fishing gear at some time in their lives (Kraus 1990). This percentage increased to nearly 75 percent in the past ten years, which indicates that at least 300 right whales were entangled at some time in their lives. Many rope-scarred whales migrate, feed, engage in courtship, and have calves. Thus, a large number of entanglements may occur with no apparent long-term effects. However, scarring from entanglements is still occurring at a rate of ten to twenty whales per year, indicating that most entanglements of right whales are undetected. Further, eight animals are still carrying gear, and the consequences to their health and ability to survive are unknown.

Reproduction

Twenty-five years of North Atlantic right whale calf counts show significantly more variation than expected by chance alone (Chapter 6). During two three-year periods, 1993–1995 and 1998–2000, calf numbers were significantly lower than expected, and both periods were followed by significantly more births than would be expected, giving the appearance of a recovery by individual females unable to reproduce during the low-calving years. In addition, mean calving intervals for all right whale cows averaged slightly over three years in the 1980s but increased through the 1990s to over five years between 1996 and 2002. In 2004 and 2005, mean calving intervals decreased to 3.2 and 3.5 years, respectively. The annual calf counts suggest that North Atlantic right whales experienced a dramatic reduction in reproductive rates twice in the 1990s, but the calving interval data suggest a chronic reproductive problem that lasted over a decade. These two types of reproductive dysfunction probably have different sources and are likely related to extrinsic factors in their habitat.

Anthropogenic Factors Potentially Affecting Health and Habitat

Although direct mortality of right whales from fishing and shipping has been discussed in earlier chapters, the urban whale syndrome is also caused by in-direct impacts of human activities on both reproduction and mortality that are more subtle and difficult to quantify. These include the effects of low ge-netic diversity, food limitation, environmental contaminants, petrochemical spills, marine debris, infectious disease, marine biotoxins, underwater noise, and habitat loss. Of these issues, there may be little humans can do with re-gard to genetic problems or oceanwide food limitation (if either of these proves to be a factor). However, the other factors that are either directly or indirectly related to human activities are discussed below.

Contaminants

Two contaminant studies on right whales have measured blubber levels of DDT and its metabolites, PCB congeners, a limited number of other organo-chlorine pesticides, and polycyclic aromatic hydrocarbons (Woodley et al. 1991; Weisbrod et al. 2000). O'Shea and Brownell (1994) suggested (in a review of the concentrations of DDT and PCB congeners) that levels in baleen whales were too low to have any biological impact. On the other hand, some scientists have suggested that declining reproduction in right whales may be linked to these chemicals (Colborn and Smolen 1996) because the fasting-while-lactating behavior of this species exposes newborn calves (through milk) to large loads of lipophilic toxicants that have accumulated in the blubber of the mother. Some of these chemicals may have their greatest effects (at the lowest dose) on endocrine, immune, neurological, and reproductive systems during early calf development, as has been documented for laboratory animals and other species of wildlife (Colborn et al. 1993; Rolland et al. 1995).

Work is only beginning on a suite of chemicals that are known to have caused reproductive and developmental problems in a number of terrestrial and marine species through endocrine disruption and other mechanisms (e.g., organotins, phthalates, brominated and chlorinated flame retardants, and alkylphenols) (DeBoer et al. 1998; Colborn and Smolen 2003). These chemicals are widespread in the marine environment. Given the potential for exposure of right whales to these chemicals (and others), studies are warranted, particularly in light of the mysterious and significant periodic drops in right whale reproduction.

In addition there is growing concern about the increases in mercury contamination at all levels of marine food chains. Mercury is widely distributed in the pelagic environment, is bioaccumulated, and appears to concentrate below thermoclines in the open ocean (Monteiro et al. 1996). Over the past century mercury levels in the upper layers of the ocean have increased between 1.1 percent and 1.9 percent per year, while mercury at deeper layers has increased at 3.5 percent to 4.8 percent per year (Monteiro and Furness 1997). In mammals and humans excess mercury can disrupt nervous, excretory, and reproductive systems (Wolfe et al. 1998).

In sum, there is a growing body of evidence that indicates that the existing levels of contaminants in marine mammals have adversely affected reproduction and the immune systems of mammals inhabiting industrial coastal waters (Ross 2000). Worse, the levels of several proven immunotoxic contaminants in marine mammals suggest that these species may suffer from increased vulnerability to disease (Ross 2002). Although there is no comparable evidence for right whales, and they may be partially protected by eating at lower trophic levels, these whales live much of their lives in heavily contaminated waters, and they are undoubtedly being exposed to these chemicals. Progress in developing right whale cell lines in the Wise Laboratory at the University of Southern Maine may finally yield a method to study effects of contaminants of concern in right whales at the cellular and DNA level.

Emerging Diseases

The sharp periodic declines in right whale reproduction and the pattern of occurrence of some of the skin lesions that have been observed (Chapter 9) are consistent with epizootics that might sweep through a population, affecting food assimilation, overall health status, immune function, or reproduction. Recent fecal studies have found both *Giardia* and *Cryptosporidium* spp.

(protozoan parasites) in a high percentage of right whales, although both the species of the protozoa and the origin of the infections remain unknown (Hughes-Hanks et al. 2005; Chapter 8). Diseases such as brucellosis and morbilliviruses are known to cause reproductive failure in domestic animals, and both have been found in free-ranging cetaceans (Miller et al. 1999; Van Bressem et al. 2001). Other infectious disease-causing agents of concern, such as herpesvirus, poxvirus, and calicivirus, have also been found in marine mammals (Van Bressem et al. 1999; House et al. 2002). Although none of these has yet been identified in right whales, they have caused significant morbidity and mortality in domestic and wild terrestrial mammals and some marine mammals.

The epidemiologic link between coastal-dwelling marine mammals and terrestrial-origin diseases has been well made for the southern sea otter. Meningoencephalitis caused by the protozoan *Toxoplasma gondii* is a significant cause of mortality in California sea otters, and it is transmitted only through the feces of cats (the definitive host for the parasite) in the form of oocysts (Miller et al. 2002). It appears that freshwater runoff led to the transmission of toxoplasmosis from a domesticated land animal population (cats) to a wild marine species (sea otters). Because these events are extremely challenging to tease apart, it is likely that similar modes of disease transmission are occurring in other near-shore marine habitats around both urban and agricultural areas and simply have not yet been detected.

Investigating the impacts of infectious diseases on right whales is extremely challenging. Necropsies have proven of little value because carcasses have been too decomposed to yield bacterial or viral organisms not related to decomposition. Current sampling options for diagnosing diseases in right whales include skin and blubber biopsies, fecal samples, and respiratory fluid. Blood collection is currently not an option in the field, although it may be in the future. Given the precarious status of this population, advances in diagnostic methods for diseases in free-swimming whales is an area in urgent need of research.

Marine Biotoxins

Biotoxins from blooms of certain algae (harmful algal blooms) have been increasing in the coastal zones of the Atlantic Ocean (and worldwide) over the past several decades (Hallegraeff 1993). This is believed to be caused by a combination of increasing sewage and fertilizer effluents, ballast water, and oceanic warming, which combine to create conditions favorable to development of algal blooms (Epstein et al. 1993; U.S. Commission on Ocean Policy 2004). The acute effects of the biotoxins of concern to right whales (saxitoxins, or paralytic shellfish poisoning, and domoic acid; Chapter 8) are usually neurological and could result in mortality if the exposure levels were high enough. The toxic effects of saxitoxin ingestion led to the deaths of seventeen humpback whales in Massachusetts waters in 1979 (Geraci et al. 1989). Exposure to domoic acid through the food web caused both mortality and spontaneous abortion in California sea lions (Gulland 2000; Scholin et al. 2000). Very little is known about the possibility of sublethal toxic effects of most biotoxins on mammals. Given these factors, it appears that the potential for marine biotoxins to impact right whale reproduction (either directly or indirectly) warrants serious study. Further, some harmful algal blooms are believed to have a human-related etiology, which may be manageable.

Marine Debris

Right whales feed in convergence zones and slicks where surface currents concentrate anything that floats, including not only prey items but also oil, contaminants associated with the surface microlayer, and floating trash. Plastic debris has been accumulating in the oceans for several decades, resulting in health risks to many marine organisms (Laist 1987). New England Aquarium researchers have found plastic bags, straps, rubber bands, and pieces of plastic tape in right whale fecal samples. The consequences of this plastic debris to right whales are not known.

Petroleum Product Discharges

Contrary to popular belief, most of the oil discharged into the oceans does not come from oil spills (NRC 2003). Around North America, sources of oil discharges into the ocean include natural seeps (61 percent), transportation of oil (including tanker spills) (3.5 percent), petroleum extraction (1.1 percent), and consumption (cars, boats, and aircraft) (>32 percent) (NRC 2003). Consumers are responsible for nearly 90 percent of the anthropogenic sources of oil in the marine environment. Worse yet, the coastal zone between Maine and Virginia is the recipient of more than 54 percent of the land-based oil inputs from North America, a whopping 29,000 metric tons annually. The biological impact of this high level of non-point-source pollution is unknown. However, long-term exposure to polyaromatic hydrocarbons is a likely consequence, as these compounds are robust to weathering and last a long time. Short-term exposure to petroleum hydrocarbons duplicating oil spills has been shown to cause minimal damage to pinnipeds and cetaceans (Geraci 1990), but chronic impacts are unknown. Angell et al. (2004) found elevated induction of cytochrome P450 1A1 enzymes in the integument of North Atlantic right whales compared to southern right whales, suggesting a measurable biological response to polyaromatic hydrocarbon exposure. Finally, although oil spills are rare, concerns have been voiced about the potential fouling of baleen plates if right whales were feeding near an oil spill site. Right whales may be able to avoid oil spills, and they may be able to clean their baleen, but their ability to do either remains unknown.

Acoustic Smog

The urbanization of right whale habitat may be most obvious in the increasing noise, or acoustic smog, that inundates the coastal waters of the western North Atlantic. Over the past century human activities have dramatically changed the right whale's acoustic habitat. The most significant and widespread contribution to ocean noise today is commercial shipping traffic, with the intense noise from seismic exploration presenting a second, more localized noise source (Chapter 10). Sonar, recreational boating, and military activities also make contributions in local areas. From a whale's perspective, the coastal zone of eastern North America is awash with the cumulative and constant noise from vessel traffic.

Parks and Clark (Chapter 10) provide an example of potential impacts. If historically right whales were able to hear each other at 16 km, modern underwater ambient noise levels have shrunk the communication area for a right whale in the coastal waters of the United States from an average of 813 km^2 to 80 km^2. Thus, the chance of two animals hearing each other today has been reduced to 10 percent of what it was one hundred years ago. Whether this rise in ambient noise has significantly reduced the probability of whales finding each other to mate or find food is unknown but seems highly likely.

It is possible that the acoustic trends in the ocean are reversible. Engineers seeking more efficient propulsion systems may develop quieter ships, and gradually, the worldwide din of shipping will decrease. However, there are increasing numbers of ships, fishing boats, and recreational boats, and this trend appears unlikely to change. If right whales rely heavily on sound for survival, then the rising tide of ocean ambient noise from human activities is a very serious threat to their survival. As Chapter 11 points out, the loss of the ability of right whales to communicate over long distances is comparable to the habitat fragmentation occurring on land. With urbanization of the right whale's world, every whale is listening to information from a much smaller piece of the ocean. The deleterious consequences of this fragmentation, well known on land, are unknown in the sea.

Habitat Loss and Degradation

If human activities in critical habitats exclude their use by right whales, the potential for population recovery could be reduced. Ship traffic, sea-floor mining, ocean dumping, and dredging could reduce the availability of habitat to right whales. Beyond the fact that right whales need to eat, habitat discussions tend to be vague about the features of an acceptable habitat. Researchers can guess that if underwater noise makes it impossible for whales to hear one another, it might eliminate that area as a suitable habitat. Studies on the habitat requirements of this species are needed for management of conflicts between humans and whales. At the moment, links between habitat quality and right whale health and population viability are speculative.

What Are the Cumulative Effects of Urbanization?

The obvious effects of urbanization are measured in terms of bodies on the beach. Deaths of right whales from shipping and fishing activities are easy to count, but they are also the easiest to prevent. Within ten years, it is conceivable that these sources of mortality in right whales could be nearly eliminated. One might imagine turning the busy shipping highway near shore into school zones (Fig. 17.2 and color plate 34).

However, the short-term dramatic drops in calf production and the decade-long slowing of calving, where females went from one calf every three years to one every five or more years, remains an enigma. The short-term declines appear to have been brief but catastrophic events, perhaps a short-lived, virulent disease, a dramatic climatic or oceanographic change, or exposure to toxins from a harmful algal bloom. But the longer increase in calving intervals continues to baffle scientists. It does not match well with North Atlantic Oscillation features, nor does the recovery in 2004 and 2005 match well with the overall *Calanus* abundance in the North Atlantic.

It is possible that researchers are witnessing the cumulative impacts of urban living (color plate 28). The only animal for which there is a large body of literature on the effects of urban living is *Homo sapiens*. In humans, constant urban living takes a measurable toll on health and survival. Increased air pollution in cities increases human mortalities (Dockery et al. 1993). Increased

Figure 17.2. Right whale breaching near a heavily developed coastal area. Florida Fish and Wildlife Conservation Commission.

noise has been associated with increased blood pressure in children (Evans and Lepore 1993). Drinking water contaminants have been implicated in spontaneous abortions and birth defects in some urban areas of the United States (Bove et al. 2002). There are many more examples in the literature.

The difficulties of determining a given cause of death or reproductive failure are made even more problematic because of interactions among multiple factors. For example, high contaminant loads can increase susceptibility to disease (Ross 2002). But so can low levels of genetic diversity in the Major Histocompatibility Complex region of the genome (Chapter 7), which codes for immunity. High levels of noise that masks communication abilities could also reduce the probabilities for mating encounters, which could limit reproduction. A harmful algal bloom could affect reproduction directly (domoic acid), or it could affect neurological function (paralytic shellfish poisoning) and indirectly affect communication, food-finding abilities, or memory.

Other Cetaceans Showing Signs of the Urban Whale Syndrome

There are many other cetacean species worldwide that utilize heavily developed coastal areas (or rivers) as habitats in all, or part, of their range. Several of these species are manifesting symptoms of the Urban Whale Syndrome, including decreased reproductive success, direct anthropogenic mortalities, habitat disturbance, and a high prevalence of cancer and infectious and para-

Figure 17.3. Southern resident killer whale from K-pod near the Seattle waterfront. John W. Durban / Center for Whale Research, WA.

sitic diseases. Three examples are briefly mentioned here, to illustrate that this is not a problem confined to the North Atlantic right whale.

Inland Killer Whales in the Pacific Northwest

A population of resident killer whales is found in the inland waters of Washington State and southern British Columbia (Fig. 17.3). This population is estimated to number approximately 300 and is divided into two subpopulations (northern and southern) according to their affiliations and range. This group of killer whales has similarities to the North Atlantic right whale, including small population size, having a single calf every three to five years, and living to about ninety years of age. However, unlike right whales, killer whales are organized into matriarchal communities, and they eat at a higher trophic level, feeding primarily on fish.

The southern resident killer whale population declined 20 percent between 1996 and 2002 (Krahn et al. 2002) and is considered in trouble. Three factors have been identified as potentially contributing to this decline. These killer whales have very high levels of PCBs (among the most contaminated cetaceans in the world) and are considered at high risk for toxic effects (Ross et al. 2000). Gaydos et al. (2004) have suggested that the population decline may be related to diseases that have impaired reproduction. In addition, Erbe (2002) has reported that extensive boat traffic associated with whale watching on the southern residents may interfere with communication, disrupt behavior, and possibly result in hearing damage.

St. Lawrence Beluga Whales

An isolated remnant population of approximately 600 to 700 beluga whales inhabits the St. Lawrence River estuary, an area heavily polluted by industrial effluents (Fig. 17.4). Despite protection from hunting for several decades, this population has failed to recover. Systematic necropsies of stranded belugas have found that the major causes of mortality are parasites (21.3 percent), cancer (18 percent), and infectious disease (16 percent; Martineau et al. 2003). The major cause of death in adult belugas is cancer, occurring in an astounding 23 percent of cases. Reports of neoplasia in terrestrial wildlife, and marine mammals in particular, are rare; the high cancer prevalence in belugas is comparable to that of humans and certain domestic animals (Martineau et al. 2003).

Toxicological studies have found high concentrations of organochlorines (PCBs, DDTs), benzo[a]pyrene, and other compounds (mirex, mercury, and lead) in the tissues of the St. Lawrence belugas, suggesting a link between the elevated prevalence of cancer and infectious diseases and chronic exposure to contaminants (De Guise et al. 1995). Ongoing research is examining the effects of exposure to these chemicals on immune system function in belugas and the failure of this population to thrive.

The Indo-Pacific Humpbacked Dolphin

The Indo-Pacific humpbacked dolphin is a near-shore cetacean found primarily near the mouths of large rivers throughout most of southeast Asia and the Indian Ocean (Fig. 17.5a). Although only limited studies of this species have been done, some subpopulations are currently living in extremely urban environments (Fig. 17.5b). The western Taiwan humpbacked dolphins are subjected to large quantities of untreated sewage effluents, industrial discharges, agricultural pesticides in freshwater runoff, depletion of prey fish by over-

Figure 17.4. Gulf of St. Lawrence belugas live in close proximity to the major shipping lanes serving eastern Canada and the Great Lakes. Robert Michaud / GREMM.

fishing, and directed mortality from fishing gear (Wang et al. 2004a). This species is also highly at risk from estuarine habitat loss, as the water use for agriculture and industry has significantly reduced (in some cases nearly eliminated) freshwater river outflows (Wang et al. 2004b).

Can Right Whales Adapt to an Urban Environment?

Adaptability is the key to survival for wildlife species where humans have altered their habitat. Because climate change is driven by human industrialization, wildlife habitat changes are now global in scale. Many animals have adapted successfully to urban environments (e.g., pigeons, squirrels, coyotes, peregrine falcons) and global warming (e.g., opossums, mosquitoes). However, others have not, as the declines in some North American songbirds have been linked to habitat fragmentation and regional climate change (Donovan and Flather 2002; Ballard et al. 2003). Further, losses of wildlife tend to be worst in specialists versus generalists, that is, animals that have a relatively narrow set of habitat requirements (Epstein 1997).

Figure 17.5. (a) Mother and calf Taiwanese humpbacked dolphins. John Y. Wang / Formosa-Cetus Research and Conservation Group. (b) The environment of the Taiwanese humpbacked dolphin is heavily affected by fishing and industry. Shih-Chu Yang / FormosaCetus Research and Conservation Group.

As noted in Chapter 5, right whales are specialists on small zooplankton, primarily copepods. Most right whale mothers calve in the coastal waters of the southeastern United States, regardless of where they go in the summer feeding period. In Chapter 16 the data suggest that the calving ground is an area where mothers go because of some combination of water temperature, calmer winter winds, depth, and perhaps turbidity, but certainly not because it is a good feeding area. Because calving location does not depend on a reliable food source, right whales may always be able to use this area, regardless of the level of contaminants and runoff in the area. Warming climatic trends may push the right whale calving ground farther northward, but it is possible they can adapt to such changes.

In northern feeding grounds, where right whales are dependent on dense aggregations of zooplankton to survive and reproduce, adaptability is more questionable. As Kenney points out in Chapter 15, the Gulf of Maine right whales are living near the southern boundary of the range of their primary prey item, *Calanus* copepods. This copepod species is dependent on oceanic temperatures, and global warming is probably going to induce a change in the *Calanus* distribution northward.

It is possible that right whales can find new feeding areas, as there are examples such as Porter (Eg #1133) of whales that have wandered across the North Atlantic Ocean, and a component of the population that lives in some as yet unidentified offshore summering ground. The fact that right whales specialize on copepods limits their options. On the other hand, they live a long time and can fast for prolonged periods, which means that they could have the opportunity for learning new habitat use patterns before they starve.

In sum, right whales appear to have some constraints on their patterns of habitat use that indicate that they will rely on areas heavily used by humans for years to come. This species almost certainly cannot adapt to the increasing levels of shipping and fishing gear found within their world. Therefore, those sources of directed mortality will have to be managed in a way to minimize these risks to right whales.

Effects of Population and Social Structure

It has been proposed by Whitehead et al. (2004) that culture needs to be a consideration in the conservation of some cetacean species. Culture is defined by these authors as information or behavior shared by a population, which is acquired from conspecifics through social learning. In the case of the western North Atlantic right whale, it has been suggested that maternally directed site fidelity, whereby mothers teach their calves to seasonally go to specific nursery grounds (i.e., Bay of Fundy or non-Fundy), is an example of vertical transmission of culture (i.e., from parents to offspring). This type of cultural transmission can result in subpopulations, as seems the case with the Fundy and non-Fundy right whales. These subpopulations most likely differ in terms of their exposure to anthropogenic threats, as the non-Fundy component of the population almost certainly uses offshore habitats that are farther from the reach of humans.

An example of loss of culture in right whales that has been cited is the apparent abandonment of historic feeding habitats in Labrador waters as a result of extensive Basque whaling in the area in the 1500s (Whitehead et al. 2004). The finding of a novel haplotype for the extant population in an old right whale bone recovered from this area would seem to support this hypothesis (Rastogi et al. 2004). However Rastogi et al. (2004) also found that very few right whales were taken by this fishery and that most of the catch consisted of bowhead whales, so the potential impact on right whale recovery may not be as significant as previously believed (Chapter 7). Additionally, a trip such as Porter's (Eg #1133) to an ancient right whale feeding ground on the other side of the Atlantic Ocean suggests that maybe not all historic knowledge has been lost.

Whereas vertical transmission of culture may impede adaptation to environmental changes, horizontally transmitted knowledge (within generations) can result in rapidly evolving adaptive behaviors (Whitehead et al. 2004), which could be favorable to survival. This type of learning has not been documented in right whales, but that may be the result of ignorance on the part of researchers. Clearly some right whales alter their behaviors based on experience. An example of this is "Slash" (Eg #1303), a female right whale that was first sighted in Massachusetts waters in 1979. Her name derived from the fact that she was missing a large section of a fluke blade from an encounter with a ship that had occurred before she was first seen by researchers. Slash is notorious among right whale biologists for her stealthy and evasive avoidance behaviors around boats. She is frequently photographed at a distance as she races away from the research vessel. She has outmaneuvered researchers trying to either photograph or biopsy dart her on many, many occasions. It seems likely that this vessel-avoidance behavior is based on her previous negative experience around boats. Whether she has transmitted this knowledge either to her calves or to conspecifics in the population is unknown and would be difficult to determine.

Can this concept of culture work in the right whale's favor in its struggle for survival? Could Porter's voyage to the precise area where eastern North Atlantic right whales had once been abundant be an example of right whale cultural memory? Could the non-Fundy whales "teach" the Fundy whales about safer offshore habitats with abundant food resources? Given that right whales have survived in the oceans for millennia, through varying climatic shifts, perhaps these behemoths are far more resourceful and adaptable than scientists realize. It would be ultimately ironic if they turn out to be more adaptable in the face of global environmental changes than humans are.

The Urban Whale: Survivor or Bellwether?

It is an open question whether reduced habitat availability, historic or newly introduced chemical pollutants, acoustic disturbance from vessel traffic, and other forms of habitat degradation are slowing the right whale population's recovery. There is no point in saving right whales from the direct kills of shipping and fishing if their habitats have been lost to the increasing urbanization of the ocean. Whales can tolerate a certain amount of habitat degradation, just as humans can. However, scientists don't know if these indirect factors are currently affecting reproduction, feeding, and survival of right whales.

Contemporary right whale problems will be much more difficult to control than hunting. For North Atlantic right whales, the seventy-year prohibition on hunting has been very effective, but accidental deaths from collisions with ships and entanglements in fixed fishing gear could very well push the species to extinction (Kraus et al. 2005). The responsibility for killing North Atlantic right whales has broadened from a small group of whalers to a much larger group, which includes all of us who eat seafood or purchase foreign autos, petroleum, appliances, and other products that arrive on ships. Northern right whales are perhaps the longest running example of humanity's failure to manage marine species, whether from directed hunting or losses from the urbanization of their habitat (Fig. 17.6).

However, the fact that North Atlantic right whales have survived at all is reason for optimism. Although this twenty-five-year study represents a large part of the professional career for the scientists involved, it is but a glimpse into the life history of the long-lived right whales. The long-term consequences of the relatively short-term trends that have been documented in this book remain to be seen. Only when there are several more decades of study of this whale will scientists be able to determine if the past two decades represented an unusually challenging period for this population.

There are too many unknowns to make any kind of accurate prediction about the future of this species. Genetic studies suggest that right whales have been at a relatively low population size for a long time, which means they may

Figure 17.6. As a young whale Shackleton (Eg #2440) wandered up the Delaware River to Philadelphia. Philip Hamilton / New England Aquarium.

be more stable at low numbers than scientists believe (Chapter 7). Furthermore, one-third of the population utilizes an unidentified habitat in the summer months, and the location of the winter breeding grounds remains unknown. Genetic studies also suggest that there may be additional "suburban or rural" right whales not yet included in the *North Atlantic Right Whale Catalog*. Perhaps it is this more elusive segment of the population that has carried the right whale population through tough times and will be a resource for the future. Satellite-tagging studies and the long-distance travels of individually identified right whales have shown they are capable of wide-ranging movements through the ocean and may not be as habitat restricted as has been believed. The recent rebounds in calf production are further cause for optimism.

Although the conflicts with humanity that are impeding right whale recovery are challenging, some of the most important problems are both well understood and potentially solvable. If adult right whale mortality from fishing and shipping can be managed, then perhaps the population can rebuild. Population models have shown that preventing the death of just two females per year would bring this population back into positive growth (Fujiwara and Caswell 2001), which seems like an achievable goal.

Humanity should take the story of the North Atlantic right whale seriously. Whether this whale species survives may or may not make a difference to the marine ecosystem. But if right whales go extinct, which other species will be next? When extinctions occur that are not understood, everyone should get very nervous. This is particularly true when those extinctions involve mammals with which humans share habitat, physiology, and life history vulnerabilities. It will always be difficult to prove that human activities are having direct effects on ocean systems and the animals in them. It is exactly those things that are difficult to prove that are so dangerous, because by the time the causes are fully understood, generations of wildlife and humans will have been affected. In the end, what Melville said about whaling applies to our modern treatment of right whales: "the moot point is, whether Leviathan can long endure so wide a chase, and so remorseless a havoc; whether he must not at last be exterminated from the waters, and the last whale, like the last man, smoke his last pipe, and then himself evaporate in the final puff" (Melville 1851).

5 September 1992
Bay of Fundy

For Calvin (Eg #2223), it was not a good day. At the tender age of eight months, she was still mostly dependent on her mother for sustenance, comfort, and learning. And on this day she had been orphaned by a large ship, her mother Delilah (Eg #1223) dying in front of an astonished fisherman who happened to be nearby. Researchers did not discover and identify her mother's carcass for three days, and the necropsy on Grand Manan Island took five days, casting a gloom over the right whale researchers and whale watchers on the island. Everyone was afraid that the calf would not survive because she had been seen frequently with her mother throughout the preceding month, and weaning does not usually take place until later in the year. We all prepared for the worst, anticipating that this small whale's death would follow the loss of its mother.

As a calf, she was insatiably curious, always leaving her mother to play with boats (color plate 33); hence, she was dubbed Calvin (for the mischievous boy of Bill Watterson's comic strip) before we knew her gender. Calvin was not seen again in 1992 after her mothers' death, leaving researchers wondering about her fate but without much hope.

Then in July 1993, photographs of a small whale were taken by Laurie Murison and Deb Tobin in the Bay of Fundy, shipped to the New England Aquarium, and matched to the little orphan Calvin! We were delighted to see that she had survived the premature loss of her mother as well as her first winter alone.

Figure 17.7. Calvin (Eg #2223) and her two month-old calf in the southeastern U.S. calving ground. Timothy Frasier / New England Aquarium.

For the next seven years, Calvin was seen in the Great South Channel and Cape Cod Bay in the spring and returned every summer to the Bay of Fundy. She was genetically sampled in 1994 (when we learned she was female!), tagged for a tracking study in 1998 in Cape Cod Bay, and touched by an ultrasound device to measure her blubber thickness three times, in 1997, 1998, and 1999. She was seen with mud on her head multiple times (indicative of deep diving), had a lamprey temporarily hitch a ride on her tail in 1993, and was seen interacting in her first surface-active group in 1995. On New Years Eve, 31 December 1999, she was seen for the first time in the coastal waters of Florida by an Aquarium survey team.

Then in August 2000, she was sighted in the Bay of Fundy entangled in fishing gear. Her next sighting was fortuitously in Cape Cod Bay, near the disentanglement team of the Provincetown Center for Coastal Studies. The Center's team made two attempts to disentangle Calvin, on 17 and 29 April, with partial success. The remaining ropes were loosely wrapped, and a National Marine Fisheries Service survey team sighted her in the Great South Channel on 8 June 2001, free of all remaining gear. Calvin did not visit the Bay of Fundy that year or for the next three years, spending her summers in areas unknown to researchers.

But, on 30 December 2004, she was observed in the coastal waters of North Carolina with a newborn calf (Fig. 17.7). And seven months later, Calvin brought her first calf to the Bay of Fundy, where her mother had first brought her. In the human communities around the Bay, there was a *quiet celebration: after twelve years, the famous orphaned right whale had returned with her own newborn! Calvin made the newspapers, caught the imagination of schoolchildren around the maritimes, and gave hope to researchers, whale watchers, fishermen, and ship captains in the area. She had survived against great odds, and with new shipping lanes, returned to a safer Bay than the one she was first brought to. She also had experienced enough of the urban ocean to know some of its dangers, and perhaps that knowledge will help her and all of her future calves to live safely in this new world.*

Scott D. Kraus

Angell, C. M., J. Y. Wilson, M. J. Moore, and J. J. Stegeman. 2004. Cytochrome P450 1A1 expression in cetacean integument: implications for detecting contaminant exposure and effects. *Marine Mammal Science* 20:554–566.

Ballard, G., G. R. Geupel, N. Nur, and T. Gardali. 2003. Long-term declines and decadal patterns in population trends of songbirds in western North America, 1979–1999. *The Condor* 105:737–755.

Bove, F., Y. Shim, and P. Zeitz. 2002. Drinking water contaminants and adverse pregnancy outcomes: a review. *Environmental Health Perspectives* 110:61–74.

Colborn, T., and M. Smolen. 1996. Epidemiological analysis of persistent organochlorine contaminants in cetaceans. *Reviews of Environmental Contamination and Toxicology* 146:91–171.

Colborn, T., and M. Smolen. 2003. Cetaceans and contaminants. Pages 292–332 *in* J. G. Vos, G. D. Bossart, M. Fournier, and T. J. O'Shea, eds. *Toxicology of Marine Mammals*. Taylor & Francis, London.

Colborn, T., F. vom Saal, and A. Soto. 1993. Developmental effects of endocrine-disrupting chemicals in wildlife and humans. *Environmental Health Perspectives* 101:378–384.

DeBoer, J., P. G. Wester, H. J. C. Klamer, W. E. Lewis, and J. P. Boon. 1998. Do flame retardants threaten ocean life? *Nature* 394:28–29.

DeGuise, S., D. Martineau, P. Beland, and M. Fournier. 1995. Possible mechanisms of action of environmental contaminants on St. Lawrence beluga whales (*Delphinapterus leucas*). *Environmental Health Perspectives* 103(Suppl 4):73–77.

Dockery, D.W., C. A. Pope, X. Xu, J. D. Spengler, J. H. Ware, M. E. Fay, B. G. Ferris, and F. E. Speizer. 1993. An association between air pollution and mortality in six U.S. cities. *New England Journal of Medicine* 329:1753–1759.

Donovan, T. M., and C. H. Flather. 2002. Relationships among North American songbird trends, habitat fragmentation, and landscape occupancy. *Ecological Applications* 12:364–374.

Epstein, P. R. 1997. Climate, ecology, and human health. *Consequences* 3:3–19.

Epstein, P. R., T. E. Ford, and R .R. Colwell. 1993. Health and climate change: marine ecosystems. *The Lancet* 342:1216–1219.

Erbe, C. 2002. Underwater noise of whale-watching boats and potential effects on killer whales (*Orcinus orca*), based on an acoustic impact model. *Marine Mammal Science* 18:394–418.

Evans, G. W., and S. J. Lepore. 1993. Non-auditory effects of noise on children: a critical review. *Children's Environments* 10:42–72.

Fujiwara, M., and H. Caswell. 2001. Demography of the endangered North Atlantic right whale. *Nature* 414:537–541.

Gaydos, J. K., K. C. Balcomb III, R. W. Osborne, and L. Dierauf. 2004. Evaluating potential infectious disease threats for the southern resident killer whales, *Orcinus orca:* a model for endangered species. *Biological Conservation* 117:253–262.

Geraci, J. R. 1990. Physiologic and toxic effects on cetaceans. Pages 167–197 *in* J. R. Geraci and D. J. St. Aubin, eds. *Sea Mammals and Oil: Confronting the Risks.* Academic Press, San Diego, CA.

Geraci, J. R., D. M. Anderson, R. J. Timperi, D. J. St. Aubin, G. A. Early, J. H. Prescott, and C. A. Mayo. 1989. Humpback whales (*Megaptera novaeangliae*) fatally poisoned by dinoflagellate toxin. *Canadian Journal of Fisheries and Aquatic Sciences* 46:1895–1898.

Gulland, F. 2000. Domoic acid toxicity in California sea lions (*Zalophus californianus*) stranded along the central California coast, May–October 1998. Report to the National Marine Fisheries Service Working Group on Unusual Marine Mammal Mortality Events. U.S. Department of Commerce, NOAA Technical Memorandum NMFS-OPR-17A, Washington, DC. 45 pp.

Hallegraeff, G. M. 1993. A review of harmful algal blooms and their apparent global increase. *Phycologia* 32:79–99.

House, C., A. A. Aguirre, and J. A. House. 2002. Emergence of infectious diseases in marine mammals. Pages 104–117 *in* A. A. Aguirre, R. S. Ostfeld, G. M. Tabor, C. House, and M. C. Pearl, eds. *Conservation Medicine, Ecological Health in Practice.* Oxford University Press, New York.

Hughes-Hanks, J. M., L. G. Rickard, C. Panuska, J. R. Saucier, T. M. O'Hara, L. Dehn, and R. M. Rolland. 2005. Prevalence of *Cryptosporidium* spp. and *Giardia* spp. in five marine mammal species. *Journal of Parasitology* 91(5): 1225–1228.

Krahn, M. M., P. R. Wade, S. T. Kalinowski, M. E. Dahlheim, B. L. Taylor, M. B. Hanson, G. M. Ylitalo, R. P. Angliss, J. E. Stein, and R. S. Waples. 2002. Status review of Southern resident killer whales (*Orcinus orca*) under the Endangered Species Act. NOAA Technical Memorandum NMFS-NWFSC-54, NOAA/ NMFS, Seattle, WA.

Kraus, S. D. 1990. Rates and potential causes of mortality in the North Atlantic right whale (*Eubalaena glacialis*). *Marine Mammal Science* 6:278–291.

Kraus, S. D., M. W. Brown, H. Caswell, C. W. Clark, M. Fujiwara, P. K. Hamilton, R. D. Kenney, A. R. Knowlton, S. Landry, C. A. Mayo, W. A. McLellan, M. J. Moore, D. P. Nowacek, D. A. Pabst, A. J. Read, and R. M. Rolland. 2005. North Atlantic right whales in crisis. *Science* 309:561–562.

Laist, D. W. 1987. Overview of the biological effects of lost and discarded plastic debris in the marine environment. *Marine Pollution Bulletin* 18:319–326.

Martineau, D., I. Mikaelian, J.-M. Lapointe, P. Labelle, and R. Higgins. 2003. Pathology of cetaceans. A case study: beluga from the St. Lawrence Estuary. Pages 333–380 *in* G. Vos, G. D. Bossart, M. Fournier, and T. J. O'Shea, eds. *Toxicology of Marine Mammals,* Taylor & Francis, London.

Melville, H. 1851. *Moby Dick.* Harper & Brothers, New York.

Miller, W. G., L. G. Adams, T. A. Ficht, N. F. Cheville, J. P. Payeur, D. R. Harley, C. House, and S. H. Ridgway. 1999. *Brucella*-induced abortions and infection in bottlenose dolphins (*Tursiops truncatus*). *Journal of Zoo and Wildlife Medicine* 30:100–110.

Miller, M. A., I. A. Gardner, C. Kreuder, D. M. Paradies, K. R. Worcester, D. A. Jessup, E. Dodd, M. D. Harris, J. A. Ames, A. E. Packham, and P. A. Conrad. 2002. Coastal freshwater runoff is a risk factor for *Toxoplasma gondii* infection of southern sea otters (*Enhydra lutris nereis*). *International Journal of Parasitology* 32:997–1006.

Monteiro L. R., and R. W. Furness. 1997. Accelerated increase in mercury contamination in North Atlantic mesopelagic food chains as indicated by time series of seabird feathers. *Environmental Toxicology and Chemistry* 16:2489–2493.

Monteiro, L. R., V. Costa, R. W. Furness, and R. S. Santos. 1996. Mercury concentrations in prey fish indicate enhanced bioaccumulation in mesopelagic environments. *Marine Ecology Progress Series* 141:21–25.

NRC. 2003. *Oil in the Sea III: Inputs, Fates, and Effects.* National Research Council Committee on Oil in the Sea. National Academy of Sciences, Washington DC.

O'Shea, T. J., and R. L. Brownell, Jr. 1994. Organochlorine and metal contaminants in baleen whales: a review and evaluation of conservation implications. *Science of the Total Environment* 154:179–200.

Rastogi, T., M. W. Brown, B. A. McLeod, T. R. Frasier, R. Grenier, S. L. Cumbaa, J. Nadarajah, and B. N. White. 2004. Genetic analysis of sixteenth-century whale bones prompts a revision of the impact of Basque whaling on right and bowhead whales in the western North Atlantic. *Canadian Journal of Zoology* 82:1647–1654.

Rolland, R., M. Gilbertson, and T. Colborn (eds.). 1995. Environmentally induced alterations in development: a focus on wildlife. *Environmental Health Perspectives* 103 (Supplement 4).

Ross, P. S. 2000. Marine mammals as sentinels in ecological risk assessment. *Humans and Ecological Risk Assessment* 6:29–46.

Ross, P. S. 2002. The role of immunotoxic environmental contaminants in facilitating the emergence of infectious diseases in marine mammals. *Humans and Ecological Risk Assessment* 8:277–292.

Ross, P. S., G. M. Ellis, M. G. Ikonomou, L. G. Barret-Lennard, and R. F. Addison. 2000. High PCB concentrations in free-ranging Pacific killer whales, *Orcinus orca:* effects of age, sex, and dietary preference. *Marine Pollution Bulletin* 40:504–515.

Scholin, C. A., F. Gulland, G. J. Doucette, S. Benson, M. Busman, F. P. Chavez, J. Cordaro, R. DeLong, A. De Vogelaere, J. Harvey, M. Haulena, K. Lefebvre, T. Lipscomb, S. Loscutoff, L. J. Lowenstine, R. Marine, P. E. Miller, W. A. McLellan, P. D. R. Moeller, C. L. Powell, T. Rowles, P. Silvagni, M. Silver, T. Spraker, V. Trainer, and F. M. Van Dolah. 2000. Mortality of sea lions along the central California coast linked to toxic diatom bloom. *Nature* 403:80–84.

U.S. Commission on Ocean Policy. 2004. An ocean blueprint for the twenty-first Century. Final Report. Washington, DC.

Van Bressem, M. F., K. Van Waerebeek, and J. A. Raga. 1999. A review of virus infections of cetaceans and the potential impact of morbilliviruses, poxviruses, and papillomaviruses on host population dynamics. *Diseases of Aquatic Organisms* 38:53–65.

Van Bressem, M. F., K. Van Waerebeek, P. D. Jepson, J. A. Raga, P. J. Duignan, O. Nielson, A. P. Di Beneditto, S. Siciliano, R. Ramos, W. Kant, V. Peddemors, R. Kinoshita, P. S. Ross, A. Lopes-Ferandez, K. Evans, E. Crespo, and T. Barrett. 2001. An insight into the epidemiology of dolphin morbillivirus worldwide. *Veterinary Microbiology* 81:287–304.

Wang, J. Y., S. K. Hung, and S. Yang. 2004a. Records of Indo-Pacific humpback dolphins, *Sousa chinensis* (Osbeck, 1765), from the waters of western Taiwan. *Aquatic Mammals* 39:189–196.

Wang, J. Y., S. Yang, and R. R. Reeves (eds.). 2004b. Report of the first workshop on conservation and research needs of Indo-Pacific humpback dolphins, *Sousa chinensis,* in the waters of Taiwan. The National Museum of Marine Biology and Aquarium, Cecheng, Taiwan. 43 pp.

Weisbrod, A. V., D. Shea, M. J. Moore, and J. J. Stegeman. 2000. Organochlorine exposure and bioaccumulation in the endangered Northwest Atlantic right whale

(*Eubalaena glacialis*) population. *Environmental Toxicology and Chemistry* 19: 654–666.

Whitehead, H., L. Rendell, R. W. Osborne, and B. Würsig. 2004. Culture and conservation of non-humans with reference to whales and dolphins: review and new directions. *Biological Conservation* 120:431–441.

Wolfe M. F., S. Swartzbach, and R. A. Sulaiman. 1998. Effects of mercury on wildlife: a comprehensive review. *Environmental Toxicology and Chemistry* 17:146–160.

Woodley, T. H., M. W. Brown, S. D. Kraus, and D. E. Gaskin. 1991. Organochlorine levels in North Atlantic right whale (*Eubalaena glacialis*) blubber. *Archives of Environmental Contamination and Toxicology* 21:141–145.

Appendix A: Permit Information

Research activities in this book have been supported by a variety of permits in the United States and Canada over the years. A listing of U.S. Scientific Research Permits to Take Marine Mammals used in these studies is given below as issued by the National Marine Fisheries Service. Canadian permits, issued by Fisheries and Oceans Canada since 1999, follow the list of U.S. permits. Photographs included in this book were taken under both the U.S. and Canadian permits. Permits were also obtained for the transport of right whale tissues across international boundaries from the Fish and Wildlife Service for the Convention on International Trade in Endangered Species. Details on Canadian permits before 1999 and International Trade permits can be obtained from the individual scientists.

U.S. Permits

Holder	Permit number	Dates
Howard Winn	501	July 1985–December 1989
Howard Winn	636	
Scott Kraus	716	October 1990–December 1995
Scott Kraus	1014	August 1996–December 2001
Charles Mayo	633-1483	June 1999–March 2005
Michael Sissenwine/Richard Merrick	775-1600	June 2001–March 2006
Teri Rowles	932-1489-05	February 2004–present
Scott Kraus	655-1652-00	March 2004–January 2009

Canadian Permits

Holder	Permit number	Dates
Scott Kraus	1999-026	
Moira Brown	1999-128/-130	
Scott Kraus	2000-045	
Moira Brown	2000-357	
Scott Kraus	2001-069	
Scott Kraus	2002-026/-589	
David Morin	2002-483	May 2002–December 2002
Douglas P. Nowacek	2002-568	–September 2002
Scott Kraus	2003-061/-062	
David Morin	2003-536	August 2003–December 2003
Scott Kraus	2003-537	August 2003–December 2003
Mark Baumgartner	2003-554	August 2003
Scott Kraus	2004-024/-025/-027	August 2004–December 2004
Douglas P. Nowacek	MAR-SA-2005-003	–December 2005
Scott Kraus	MAR-SA-2005-007	–December 2005

Appendix B: Opportunistic Contributors to the *Right Whale Catalog*

This appendix lists institutions and principal contacts responsible for major contributions (twenty sightings or more) of opportunistic photographed sightings of right whales.

Institution	Principal contact
Allied Whale/College of the Atlantic	Steven Katona, Judy Allen, Harriet Corbett, Timothy Cole, Stephanie Martin, Sean Todd
Associated Scientists at Woods Hole	James Hain
Atlantic Cetacean Research Center	Steven Frohock
Brier Island Ocean Study	Carl Haycock
Brier Island Whale and Seabird Cruises Limited	Shelley Barnaby
East Coast Ecosystems Research Organization	Deborah Tobin
Fisheries and Oceans Canada	Lei Harris, Kent Smedbol
Georgia Department of Natural Resouces	Michael Harris
Grand Manan Whale and Seabird Research	Laurie Murison
Groupe de recherche et d'education sur les mammiferes marin	Robert Michaud, Michel Moisan, Veronique de la Cheneliere
International Fund for Animal Welfare	Anna Moscrop, Carol Carlson
International Wildlife Coalition	Daniel Morast, Regina Asmutis-Silvia
Manomet Bird Observatory	Michael Payne
Marine Resources Council Volunteer Sighting Network	Harold Richter, Dianne Barille, Julie Albert
Mingan Island Cetacean Study	Richard Sears
New England Whale Watch	Scott Mercer
New Hampshire Seacoast Cruises	Leo Axtin, Jr.

Institution	Principal contact
NMFS Northeast Fisheries Science Center	Timothy Cole, Mark Baumgartner, Richard Merrick, Fredrick Wenzel, Richard Pace, Phillip Clapham
NMFS Northeast Regional Office	Patricia Gerrior, James Hain
NMFS Southwest Fisheries Science Center	Wayne Perryman
Observation Littoral Perce	Nathalie Cadet, Donald Cahill
Ocean Research and Education Society	George Nichols, Perran Ross
Oregon State University	Bruce Mate
Plymouth Marine Mammal Research Center	David Wiley, Fredrick Wenzel
Provincetown Center for Coastal Studies	Charles Mayo, Laurie Goldman, Philip Hamilton, Marilyn Marx, Jooke Robbins
Seafarers	Scott Kraus, Scott Marion
University of Guelph	David Gaskin, Jeffrey Goodyear
University of Rhode Island	Carol Price
Whale Center of New England/Cetacean Research Unit	Mason Weinrich
Woods Hole Oceanographic Institution	William Schevill, William Watkins, Karen Moore, Michael Moore, Carolyn Angell, Susan Parks, Douglas Nowacek

Appendix C: Other Resources

This appendix provides a brief listing of books, reports, and websites that contain general information about right whales and the ongoing research efforts of those dedicated to the conservation of this species.

Books and Reports

Anonymous. 2000. Canadian Right Whale Recovery Plan. A Canadian Recovery Plan for the North Atlantic Right Whale. World Wildlife Fund Toronto, Ontario, and Department of Fisheries and Oceans, Dartmouth, Nova Scotia, Canada.

Best, P. B., J. L. Bannister, R. L. Brownell, Jr., and G. P. Donovan (eds.). 2001. Right Whales: Worldwide Status. *Journal of Cetacean Research and Management* Special Issue 2. International Whaling Commission, Cambridge, U.K.

Brownell, R. L., Jr., P. B. Best, and J. H. Prescott (eds.). 1986. Right Whales: Past and Present Status. *Journal of Cetacean Research and Management* Special Issue 10. International Whaling Commission, Cambridge, U.K.

Clapham, P. 2004. *Right Whales.* Voyageur Press. Osceola, WI.

Feldhamer, G. A., B. C. Thompson, and J. A. Chapman (eds.). 2004. *Wild Mammals of North America: Biology, Management, and Conservation.* Second edition. Johns Hopkins University Press, Baltimore, MD.

Johnson, T. 2005. *Entanglements: The Intertwined Fates of Whales and Fishermen.* University Press of Florida. Gainesville, FL.

Kraus, S. D., and K. Mallory. 1993. *The Search for the Right Whale.* A New England Aquarium Book. Crown Publishers, New York.

Kraus, S. D., and K. Mallory. 2003. *Disappearing Giants: The North Atlantic Right Whale.* Bunker Hill Publishing, Charlestown, MA.

National Marine Fisheries Service. 2005. Recovery Plan for the North Atlantic Right Whale (*Eubalaena glacialis*). National Oceanic and Atmospheric Administration,

National Marine Fisheries Service. Silver Spring, MD. URL: http://www.nmfs. noaa.gov/pr/recovery/plans.htm.

Payne, R. 1995. *Among Whales.* Charles Scribner's Sons, New York.

Perrin, W. F., B. Wursig, and J. G. M. Thewissen (eds.). 2002. *Encyclopedia of Marine Mammals.* Academic Press. San Diego, CA.

Reynolds, J. E. III, and S. A. Rommel (eds.). 1999. *Biology of Marine Mammals.* Smithsonian Books. Washington, DC.

Twiss, J. R., Jr., and R. R. Reeves (eds.). 1999. *Conservation and Management of Marine Mammals.* Smithsonian Books. Washington DC.

Websites

Cornell University
        http://www.birds.cornell.edu/brp/ResWhale.html
Fisheries and Oceans Canada
      http://www.dfo-mpo.gc.ca/species-especes/species/species_rightWhale_e.asp
International Fund for Animal Welfare
      http://www.ifaw.org
New England Aquarium
      http://www.neaq.org/rwcatalog
NOAA National Marine Fisheries Service Northeast Fisheries Science Center
      http://www.nefsc.noaa.gov/
NOAA National Marine Fisheries Service Northeast Regional Office
      http://www.nero.noaa.gov/whaletrp/
      http://www.nero.noaa.gov/shipstrike
North Atlantic Right Whale Consortium
      http://rightwhaleweb.org
Provincetown Center for Coastal Studies
      http://www.coastalstudies.org
Trent University
      http://www.nrdpfc.ca/marinemammals.html
Wheelock College
      http://whale.wheelock.edu/rightwhale/
Woods Hole Oceanographic Institution
      http://www.whoi.edu/institutes/oli/currenttopics/ct_rightwhales.htm

Films

Dangerous Migration: Whale Crisis in Canada's Atlantic. 2000. Canadian Geographic Series. Copyright Summerhill Entertainment Inc. Distributed by Magic Lantern.

Right Whales. Champions of the Wild Series, Part 12. 1998. Directed by Chris Aikenhead. Produced by Christian Bruvere, Ian Herring and George Johnson. Copyright Omni Film Productions Ltd.

The Northern Right Whale: from Whaling to Watching. 1996. Second edition. Produced by NOAA National Marine Sanctuaries. Distributed by NOAA: Gray's Reef National Marine Sanctuary.

Whale Mission: Keepers of Memory. 2005. Directed by Jean Lemire and Caroline Underwood. Produced by Jean Lemire. Copyright Glacialis Productions Inc.

Acknowledgments

This book would not have been possible without the long-term contributions (and last minute assistance!) of the right whale research staff at the New England Aquarium: Amy Knowlton, Philip Hamilton, Marilyn Marx, Moira Brown, Lisa Conger, Elizabeth Pike, Lindsay Hall, Heather Pettis, and Monica Zani. The editors are grateful to Kerry Lagueux, Yan Guilbault, and Cynthia Browning for their extraordinary efforts on the graphics, organization, and completion of this book. Our special appreciation goes to Scott Landry for contributing his exceptional line-art drawings of right whales and to Laura Lane Cooke and Katie Koch for their assistance and patience throughout the process. Thanks goes to the North Atlantic Right Whale Consortium for permission to publish much of the data and many of the photographs in this book (collected by numerous individuals at many institutions) and to Bob Kenney, who maintains the Consortium database on which many analyses are based. The source data for the GIS maps were provided by the Environmental Systems Research Institute.

A special acknowledgment is due to Jerry Conway, Rob Stephenson, and Cathy Merriman for supporting right whale research and conservation in Canadian waters and to NMFS employees Diane Boreggaard, Phillip Clapham, Tim Cole, Mary Colligan, David Gouveia, Dana Hartley, John Higgins, Lindy Johnson, Richard Merrick, Richard Pace, Teri Rowles, Glenn Salvador, Greg Silber, Barb Zoodsma, and many other NMFS staff for supporting right whale research and conservation efforts in U.S. waters. Additional key state employees in this effort have included Billy Brooks (FL), Mike Harris (GA),

Laura Ludwig (ME), Dan McKiernan (MA), Jamison Smith (FL), Terry Stockwell (ME), and April Valliere (RI).

This book was greatly improved by thorough reviews of the draft manuscript by Malcolm L. Hunter, Jr., Joe Roman, Philip Hamilton, and Marilyn Marx. We are indebted to our editor at Harvard University Press, Ann Downer-Hazell, for seeing the potential of this book despite the difficulties of a multi-author publication. Our gratitude also goes to Alissa Anderson, David Foss, Tim Jones, and the other skilled staff at Harvard University Press who have worked hard to make this book a reality.

Supporters of specific projects described within this book are acknowledged at the end of the appropriate chapters. The agencies, foundations, and corporations that have provided the backbone of support for research on North Atlantic right whales over many years are acknowledged here. These include the National Marine Fisheries Service, Fisheries and Oceans Canada, Habitat Stewardship Program of Environment Canada, Marine Mammal Commission, National Science Foundation, Office of Naval Research, U.S. Navy, Minerals Management Service, National Ocean Service, U.S. Coast Guard, U.S. Army Corps of Engineers, Bureau of Land Management, National Fish and Wildlife Foundation, Massachusetts Environmental Trust, Northeast Consortium, Department of Marine Resources in Maine, Massachusetts Division of Marine Fisheries, Department of Natural Resources in Georgia, Florida Wildlife Research Institute (formerly the Florida Marine Resources Institute), Transport Canada, and the Icelandic Fisheries Research Institute. Nongovernmental support has been received from the Canadian Whale Institute, the Island Foundation, the Irving Oil Corporation, World Wildlife Fund-U.S., the Endangered Species Recovery Fund of World Wildlife Fund Canada, the Canadian Wildlife Service, the International Fund for Animal Welfare, the Oak Foundation, the Penzance Foundation, the Woods Hole Oceanographic Institution Right Whale Initiative, the Whale and Dolphin Conservation Society, the Arcadia Wildlife Preserve, Inc., the Davis Conservation Foundation, the Jackman Foundation, the McLean Foundation, and multiple contributors to the right whale adoption program. Additional recognition is due the Humane Society of the United States, International Wildlife Coalition, Wildlife Trust, Cetacean Society International, Public Employees for Environmental Responsibility, National Environmental Trust, Greenpeace, Greenworld, Sierra Club, the Center for Biological Diversity, and Defenders of Wildlife for their efforts on behalf of this species.

Information on all research permits covering this work can be found in Appendix A.

Finally, it is an honor to acknowledge the hundreds of colleagues who provided the photographs and reports of right whales from the North Atlantic Ocean. Researchers, fishermen, whale watchers, airplane pilots, tourists, dredge operators, ferry captains, and enforcement officers have provided images of right whales from places as far-flung as the Gulf of Mexico, the Gulf of St. Lawrence, Iceland, Norway, and the Azores. This book is the result of your efforts.

Contributors

CAROLYN M. ANGELL

Biology Department
Woods Hole Oceanographic Institution
Woods Hole, MA

MARK F. BAUMGARTNER

Biology Department
Woods Hole Oceanographic Institution
Woods Hole, MA

ROBERT K. BONDE

U. S. Geological Survey
Gainesville, FL

MOIRA W. BROWN

New England Aquarium
Edgerton Research Laboratory
Boston, MA

CHRISTOPHER W. CLARK

Bioacoustics Research Program
Cornell Lab of Ornithology
Cornell University
Ithaca, NY

PIERRE-YVES DAOUST

Atlantic Veterinary College
University of Prince Edward Island
Charlottetown, P.E.I., Canada

GREGORY J. DOUCETTE

Marine Biotoxins Program
NOAA/National Ocean Service
Charleston, SC

TIMOTHY R. FRASIER

Natural Resources DNA Profiling and Forensics Centre
Trent University
Peterborough, Ontario, Canada

LANCE P. GARRISON

National Marine Fisheries Service
Southeast Fisheries Science Center
Miami, FL

DOUGLAS GILLESPIE

Sea Mammal Research Unit
Gatty Marine Laboratory
University of St. Andrews
Fife, Scotland

ROXANNE M. GILLETT

Natural Resources DNA Profiling and Forensics Centre
Trent University
Peterborough, Ontario, Canada

PHILIP K. HAMILTON

New England Aquarium
Edgerton Research Laboratory
Boston, MA

KATHLEEN E. HUNT

Center for Conservation Biology
Department of Biology
University of Washington
Seattle, WA

AMANDA J. JOHNSON
National Marine Fisheries Service
Protected Resources Division
Gloucester, MA

ELIZABETH A. JOSEPHSON
National Marine Fisheries Service
Northeast Fisheries Science Center
Woods Hole, MA

JOHN F. KENNEY
National Marine Fisheries Service
Northeast Region
N. Kingston, RI

ROBERT D. KENNEY
University of Rhode Island
Graduate School of Oceanography
Narragansett, RI

AMY R. KNOWLTON
New England Aquarium
Edgerton Research Laboratory
Boston, MA

SCOTT D. KRAUS
New England Aquarium
Edgerton Research Laboratory
Boston, MA

MARILYN K. MARX
New England Aquarium
Edgerton Research Laboratory
Boston, MA

CHARLES A. MAYO
Provincetown Center for Coastal Studies
Provincetown, MA

BRENNA A. MCLEOD

Natural Resources DNA Profiling and Forensics Centre
Trent University
Peterborough, Ontario, Canada

WILLIAM A. MCLELLAN

University of North Carolina, Wilmington
Biological Sciences
Wilmington, NC

MICHAEL J. MOORE

Woods Hole Oceanographic Institution
Biology Department
Woods Hole, MA

DOUGLAS P. NOWACEK

Oceanography Department
Florida State University
Tallahassee, FL

RICHARD M. PACE III

National Marine Fisheries Service
Northeast Fisheries Science Center
Woods Hole, MA

SUSAN E. PARKS

Bioacoustics Research Program
Cornell Lab of Ornithology
Cornell University
Ithaca, NY

HEATHER M. PETTIS

New England Aquarium
Edgerton Research Laboratory
Boston, MA

RANDALL R. REEVES

Okapi Wildlife Associates
Hudson, Quebec, Canada

LORA G. RICKARD

College of Veterinary Medicine
Mississippi State University
Mississippi State, MS

ROSALIND M. ROLLAND

New England Aquarium
Global Marine Programs
Boston, MA

CHRISTOPHER K. SLAY

Coastwise Consulting, Inc.
Athens, GA

TIM D. SMITH

National Marine Fisheries Service
Northeast Fisheries Science Center
Woods Hole, MA

SAMUEL K. WASSER

Center for Conservation Biology
Department of Biology
University of Washington
Seattle, WA

BRADLEY N. WHITE

Natural Resources DNA Profiling and Forensics Centre
Trent University
Peterborough, Ontario, Canada

ART AND MAPS:

KERRY LAGUEUX

New England Aquarium
Edgerton Research Laboratory
Boston, MA

SCOTT LANDRY

Provincetown Center for Coastal Studies
Provincetown, MA

Index

Page numbers for entries occurring in figures are followed by an *f* and those for entries occurring in tables, by a *t*.